THE KOREAN POPULAR CULTURE READER

THE KOREAN POPULAR CULTURE READER

KYUNG HYUN KIM AND YOUNGMIN CHOE,

EDITORS

Duke University Press
Durham and London 2014

Typeset in Scala by Tseng Information Systems, Inc.

Library of Congress Cataloging-in-Publication Data
The Korean popular culture reader / Kyung Hyun Kim and
Youngmin Choe, editors.
pages cm
Includes bibliographical references and index.
ISBN 978-0-8223-5488-8 (cloth : alk. paper)
ISBN 978-0-8223-5501-4 (pbk. : alk. paper)

1. Popular culture—Korea (South)—History—20th century.
2. Korea (South)—Civilization—20th century. 3. Korea (South)—
Social life and customs—20th century. I. Kim, Kyung Hyun, 1969–
II. Choe, Youngmin.
DS916.27.K68 2014
306.09519—dc23   2013029329

This work was supported by the Academy of Korean Studies Grant
funded by the Korean Government (MEST) (AKS-2009-LA-3001).

To S I D D and I Z Z I

CONTENTS

Under the moniker of *hallyu* (Korean Wave), South Korean popular culture has come to be regarded by some as a source of national pride and by others, particularly in Asia, as neo-imperialist. Regardless of how one might characterize it, the rise of South Korean popular culture was difficult to foresee in the late 1990s, when the nation was roiling from the devastation of the 1997 financial International Monetary Fund (IMF) crisis. Because the IMF encouraged increased global competition, cultural liberalization policies (which had been postponed nearly half a century by postcolonial anxieties) were implemented starting in 1998. The impending legislation of satellite cable television also seemed to threaten further an unsupported cultural industry insecure after decades of political and cultural oppression. The spontaneity with which the Korean Wave gathered force thus caught the South Korean cultural industry by surprise, leaving critics of Korean cultural studies to make sense of *hallyu* and its legacy after the fact. In the contemporary context, it is fair to say that it is transnational consumption, as opposed to any self-reflexive and conscious national production, that initially defined and formed the parameters of Korean popular culture studies. As a result, the modes of understanding brought to bear thus far on the phenomenon have been necessarily situated in a broad regional, and perhaps even global, context. This formulation, however, establishes the field in such a way that Korean popular culture comes to be defined foremost as a pan-Asian phenomenon, a discrete entity morphing in transnational space that becomes increasingly detached from any specifically Korean past. Critics in the field of Korean Studies thus need to become concerned both with recontextualizing *hallyu* within a national context without eliding the undeniable significance of the transnational and with the question of what happens to Korean popular culture when it becomes a global commodity.

This volume is thus lodged between the discourses of cultural nationalism and transnationalism, which have come to bifurcate studies of Korean popular culture. The texts selected reinforce our aim to contextualize contemporary Korean popular culture within its local historical and sociocultural continuum, while historicizing its colonial and postcolonial legacies, in order to historically situate intraregional and interregional flows. The chapters collectively seek to understand the sociopolitical dynamics of Korean popular culture in the last century in order to reveal how contemporary Korean popular culture remains intimately connected to the history of colonial modernity; to the long process of postcolonialism; to nationally conceived postmilitarized and postindustrial identity formations; and to the current inclination toward neo-liberalist cultural flows. The stakes become all the more evident in this volume, with many of the pieces (regardless of period) converging on themes pertaining to the surface and affect and underscoring how the contemporary lens can effectively refocus our approaches to cultural historical analysis. Another aim is to consolidate the current, relatively dispersed state of Korean popular culture studies across the trans-Pacific in order to critically delineate the inherent problems and situate emerging and future directions for research. Aside from film and literature, the recent interest in a more largely defined Korean popular culture in U.S. academia is linked to the *hallyu* phenomenon. In contrast, the interest of cultural studies in South Korean academia can be traced back to the late 1980s, when the employment of cultural politics gained ground in the movement for social democracy, and to the early 1990s, when the cultural industries began to gain prominence. The initial reliance in the latter period on imported theories, especially on postmodernism and poststructuralism, subsequently gave rise to criticism regarding limitations in applicability to local conditions and to the call for a need to localize cultural knowledge production. In response, the selected pieces in this volume are written by scholars in the United States, Australia, New Zealand, the Netherlands, and South Korea, representing a wide range of locations, and it is our hope that the collection will facilitate dialogue across national and transnational paradigms. In terms of text selection, many of the chapters engage their subjects in such a way that considers cultural flows between Korea and its former occupiers, Japan and the United States. Within the limitations of space, we have tried to cover as many positions and attitudes as possible. The pieces were also chosen because they vary in terms of their approaches and reflect the growing diversity within the field. The volume is organized by popular cultural forms, which are understood as inherently intertextual, vertically and horizontally. Popular contemporary forms and practices are linked to related historical precedents, each part proceeding chronologically to allow readers to see the possible continuities and breaks. Though exclusions are inevitable, we have aspired to provide a substantial scope. The brief section introductions are meant to serve as only one of multiple possible points of entry into the various sections' content, and the summations as brief overviews.

The project in its entirety was made possible and supported by an Academy of Korean Studies Grant funded by the Korean government (MEST) (AKS-2009-LA-3001). It was guided by our editor at Duke University Press, Courtney Berger, her assistant Deborah Guterman, our art editor Christine Choi, as well as by the feedback from anonymous reviewers. A workshop preceding this volume to assess the state of Korean popular culture studies within Korean Studies at large in the United States and South Korea took place in June 2010 at the University of California, Irvine, and we give our thanks for the suggestions and feedback from Nancy Abelmann, Kyeong-Hee Choi, Ted Hughes, Kelly Jeong, Chang-Nam Kim, Suk-young Kim, Youna Kim, Boduerae Kwon, Donna Kwon, Dong-Yeun Lee, Jinkyung Lee, Namhee Lee, Hyung-il Pai, Jungsun Park, Hyun-Suk Seo, and Young-chae Seo. We also thank Jonathan Hall, Christopher Hanscom, Todd Henry, Kyung Moon Hwang, David James, Anne McKnight, Sunyoung Park, Michael Robinson, Serk-Bae Suh, and Timothy Tangherlini, who provided additional feedback in May 2011. We thank the following graduate students at UC–Irvine and the University of Southern California: Hyun Seon Park, Hyonhui Choe, Jessica Likens, Jessica Conte, and Wooseok Phil Kang. Also, we thank at UC–Irvine Mindy Han, the former department manager of East Asian Languages and Literatures, who handled everyday operations, the former dean of humanities Vicky Ruiz, and her associate dean Glen Mimura. Kyung Sin Park, law professor at Korea University, provided detailed professional opinions regarding the copyright laws pertaining to the photographs from the colonial era that are reprinted here. *Chosun Ilbo* additionally granted us permission to reprint several photographs from its archive. We also thank Jun Lee, Jay Oh, and Youngji Cho at the Management Planning & Strategy Department of *Chosun Ilbo* for making this book possible.

Indexing Korean Popular Culture

At a K-pop concert in the United States, thousands of young Americans scream as American pop performer will.i.am of the Black Eyed Peas joins the Korean act 2NE1 onstage to sing and dance to their Korean-language tune. Moments of cultural intersection such as this shed light on a new and often contradictory Korea. On the one hand, it is still a country—both North and South—that decries its lack of political legitimacy in the international community and dwells on the continuing aftereffects of its colonial occupation by Japan (1910–45), the Korean War (1950–53), and the ensuing partition. Because many Koreans on both sides of the border feel that Korea's postcolonial identity was neither completely nor coherently achieved, nationalism is still extolled in most social sectors. On the other hand, the South's remarkable economic development and democratization have enabled the country to produce and disseminate a cast of cultural output. Its music, dance choreography, television dramas, and films have appealed well beyond its borders and even to the U.S. market, a country from which it received "billions of dollars in aid" merely a few decades earlier.[1]

Korean popular culture has come a long way over the last decade and a half, especially considering that its most profitable export item even as late as the 1990s was the popular American sitcom *The Simpsons*, a show that relied on subcontracted Korean animators. However, the tide started to turn rapidly, and the Korean Wave (*hallyu*) began. The film *Shiri* was a smash success at the box office in Japan in 2000. Yon-sama (the nickname for melodrama male actor Bae Yong-jun) generated sky-high ratings for the television series *Winter Sonata* in Japan and other parts of Northeast Asia during the early part of the first decade of the twenty-first century. And idol groups such as TVXQ, Super Junior, Wonder Girls, and Girls' Generation have routinely claimed top spots in pop charts of Asia over the past five years. *Hallyu* accounts for an astonishing figure of US$4.8 billion in Korea's annual export revenue.[2] This "soft power" in entertainment—which also encompasses games, sports stars, and cartoons—churns out profits for South Korea as its "cool" image helps to brand the nation's many corporations, tour industry, food, and cultural commodities.

Culture can serve many purposes, but one function it has always served is ideological. Culture informs and helps to produce exchanges of power, autonomy/dependence, and hegemony. South Korea's prolific economy and regional cultural power do not necessarily remove it from the list of client states to the American popular culture hegemony. American films, television programs, sports stars, popular music, and musicals can easily be identified in the streets of Seoul today—as they have been since the U.S. military occupation that began immediately after Korea's liberation from Japan in 1945. Seoul's globalizing economy and glitzy urban landscape have made their presence even more widespread than before. Despite the appearance of Korean music acts such as Psy, Rain, and the Girls' Generation on American talk shows; the viral popularity of some of these idol acts' YouTube videos; the public respect that American celebrities—from septuagenarian Martin Scorsese to teenager Justin Bieber—show for Korean pop culture; and the Asian American communities' growing fascination with Korean dramas, the cultural exchange between the United States and Korea is nowhere near equal. It should therefore come as no surprise that many critics, commentators, and even fans marveling at the success of K-pop, K-drama, or Korean cinema over the past decade would feel it necessary to address questions about Korean popular culture's authenticity. On the Al Jazeera network, a thirty-minute special aired that was devoted to discussing the reasons behind the success of Psy's "Gangnam Style." The music video was extremely popular, attracting more than 100 million views on YouTube within a mere three months of its release. One of the questions posed to the panelists on the program was: "Is there something distinctive about K-pop?"[3] A cynic may argue that pop music, films, games, animation, television programs, and sports stars from Korea possess just as much authentic Korean flavor as, say, a Samsung mobile product, which was judged by a San Jose federal court to be an imitation of Apple's smartphones and tablet computers.

However, the task of understanding the attraction of K-pop and other cultural phenomena associated with Korea does not simply entail separating the good from the bad, the modern from the anachronistic, and the authentic from the mimicked. For this is the language of the culturally hegemonic and thus it simplifies a complicated part of the problem when dealing with a culture of a country that has undergone colonial and neocolonial experiences during the twentieth century. Culture, as Homi K. Bhabha once described it, must be "transnational and translational," not in order to thrive in mimicry but in order to simply survive.[4] This transnational and translational rule applies to cultural productions in a colonial and postcolonial setting such as Korea and also serves as a matrix for globally dominant postwar cultural industries. Hong Kong martial arts films and the French Nouvelle Vague (New Wave) cinema have reshaped Hollywood at various moments, and it would not be at all an exaggeration to say that American popular music would not have established its dominance had it not been for the major influx of Southern blacks from the 1920s to the present. As the essays collected here demonstrate, Korean popular culture is now on an international stage and can no longer be understood narrowly through a model of national identity. Critics in these following pages were encouraged to analyze a note, a frame, a taste, a run, a swing, a spin, a dribble, a scribble, a letter, or even a blog reply without necessarily identifying it as either Korean or foreign.

The Korean Popular Culture Reader, while not undermining the surprising success of *hallyu* and the fandom it was able to establish in many corners of the globe over the past decade, takes up a formal analysis and a historical discussion of Korean popular culture that departs from the "intra-Asian cultural flow" model that had been proposed by media studies scholars who tended to rely on primarily data-driven, audience- and fan-oriented research.[5] What joins these chapters together is the renewal of the importance of content analysis that expands the study of *hallyu* that previously has overused vacuous terms such as the "right chord of Asian sentiments."[6] While this turn toward form and production does not aim to dismiss all reception-oriented research, it reengages the political nuances of images and sounds that reveal Korean popular culture's capacity to deepen and widen popular cultural studies globally. Consequently this volume should be a first step toward a renewed commitment to diversify the interpretations of values set by the most obvious ideologies that determine image creation and is certainly a step beyond the superficial endorsement of the mass-media driven numbers game (that is, "How much did it sell in Japan?") and sensational headlines that dominate the Internet after a single K-pop concert in Europe.

To theorize the popular culture of an emergent nation outside the conventional framework of the traditional cultural capital is to disclose the way the discourses of the West construct the center-periphery divide and reassign the values of popular culture studies thus far affordable almost exclusively in the West. In this volume, chapters by Sohl Lee, Steven Chung, and Michelle Cho, for instance, deftly deploy Roland Barthes's concept of indexicality to argue against the danger of theory vanishing from the study of non-Western culture.[7] Lee's discussion of tour photographs taken in Pyongyang during Kim Dae-Jung's Sunshine Policy era, Chung's chapter on fashion photographs and women's magazine covers in 1950s Seoul, and Cho's focus on contemporary screen stars such as Won Bin and Kim Hye-ja all contend that the saturation of images in modern and contemporary culture requires an intellectual intervention that probes images' layered referentiality.[8] Indexicality, in the words of Tom Gunning, is "a physical relation between the object photographed and the image finally created."[9] An appropriate index of Korean culture suggests new ways of engaging referentiality, iconography, and signifying systems that extend far beyond the register of banality and political feebleness that sometimes undergird popular culture. When applied, for instance, to popular music, indexicality can yield a greater meaning for a song (the equivalent of a photograph) that is heard on the streets, on the radio or television, or on a YouTube channel. A familiar pop song draws from our own cultural reservoir (the equivalent of the original object photographed) via various psychic signals that are put to work (like light-sensitive celluloid emulsion reflecting off the photographed object). Like a classic *yuhaenga* (popular song) that is assigned to a young singer to be reinterpreted for a challenge in vogue Korean television programs such as *I Am a Singer* [*Na nŭn kasu ta*] or *Superstar K*[*shusŭk'e*], the notion of indexicality allows us to reinterpret and reexperience a sign that constantly renews itself by detaching itself from its original time and place.

The emergence of cultural studies in South Korea can be traced back to the late 1980s, when cultural politics gained ground in the movement for social democracy, and then to the early 1990s, when Korean cultural industries began to gain global prominence. However, it was during the early part of the Japanese colonial era (1910–45) that the first instantiation of the popular emerged. As Michelle Cho reminds us, the word *popular* has its etymological roots in Latin (*populus*, or *the people*); in Korean the translation is *minjok*, which since then has gone on to be synonymous with Korean nationhood or people. Of course, this description is not to suggest that popular culture or the people's art, as evidenced by *p'ansori* (mask dance) and the choreography of martial arts, was not present prior to the twentieth century in Korea. "Popular culture" is also an idiom that is just as impossible to translate into Korean. It is often translated as *taejung* (mass) *munhwa* (culture). But because *taejung* connotes "public" rather than "popular" or "entertainment," a more apt translation would be *inki* (popular) or *yuhaeng*

Figure I.1. Seoul streets and subways are plastered with images of young K-pop stars. Photo by Kyung Hyun Kim

(trendy) *munhwa*. Though this phrase sounds awkward and anachronistic in Korean, the word *inki* suggests a commercial aspiration that distinguishes it from *taejung*'s association with activism and a sociological notion of the people. Also, interestingly, while *taejung* (mass or public) signifies agendas and assumptions that are steeped in democracy, cosmopolitan ideals, and protests that reimagine resistant forms of political collectives, *inki* and *yuhaeng* stand for the very opposite: individualism, crass, market-driven merchandise, and star icons that sometimes belie the interests of the masses. Taking this distinction one step further, Jung Hwan Cheon in his chapter writes, "The concept of the 'popular' theoretically borders on schizophrenic, and even moves in the opposite, neurotic direction, that of *minjok*." But, as Cho observes, "the contemporary era no longer admits a clear distinction between the mass and the popular." Many of the essays gathered here locate the pulse of Korean popular culture between these two correlates, and the lexicons of *taejung/inki/yuhaeng* run parallel to the discourse of modernity. This is the reason Youngmin Choe, my coeditor, and I have decided to forego the discussions of almost all cultural phenomena predating the era of colonial modernity that took place during the early part of the twentieth century.

Though almost twenty years have elapsed since the inaugural issue of *positions: east asia cultures critique* selected "colonial modernity" as its central theme and the first conference held at UCLA on the subject of Korean colonial modernity by Gi-Wook Shin and Michael Robinson that later became a platform for their edited volume *Colonial Modernity in Korea*,[10] the complexities that seek partly to contest the rigidity of the binary relationship between the colonizer and the colonized through colonial modernity have not gained steam in Korean Studies in the United States. While no single-author monograph in the United States has fully taken on this topic, in Korea colonial modernity has become not only a hot intellectual item but a subject of broad public interest as well.[11] After the 1999 publication of Kim Chin-song's *Sŏul e ttansŭhol ŭl hŏhara* [Grant Dance Halls a Permit in Seoul], which was based on his research of popular culture and everyday life in colonial Korea, many books dealing with social life including dating and popular cultural consumption during that era have come into print. Boduerae Kwon's *Yŏnae ŭi sidae: 1920-yŏndae ch'oban ŭi munhwa wa yuhaeng* [Age of Dating: Culture and Trends of the Early 1920s], Jung Hwan Cheon's *Chosŏn ŭi sanai kŏdŭn p'utppol ŭl ch'ara* [If You Are a Man of Chosŏn, Kick a Soccer Ball], and Min-jung Son's *T'ŭrot'ŭ ŭi chŏngch'ihak* [Politics of T'ŭrot'ŭ] are some of the books that contributed to making the study of the colonial era less didactic and essentially nationalist.[12] Choe and I are extremely pleased to include essays from Kwon, Cheon, and Son, which are revised translations of their works originally published in these Korean monographs. These chapters survey literature (Kwon), sports (Cheon), and popular music (Son) and offer ways for the reader to think about the time and space of Korea simply divided between *minjok's* collective resistance against the Japanese colonial supremacy and the perpetuations of an automatic celebration of individual subjects at the dawn of modernization during the 1920s and the 1930s. Dwelling on modern emotions behind expressions of *yŏnae* (romance) in early epistolary novels, the fantasy of restored national manhood in the radio broadcast and the newspaper coverage that followed Sohn Ki-jung's victorious marathon run during the 1936 Berlin Olympics, and sorrowful yearning in 1930s *yuhaengga*, all of these chapters on colonial modernity reinscribe modernist aesthetics. It is within the regime of the sublime, either in the celebration of an athletic achievement or singing of a *yuhaengga*, where *minjok*, pure and uncontaminated, could fully denote the index of a fractured nation and where its past references were fully nullified and its subjecthood revoked.

The 1950s are often noted as a period in Korea most known for total war and destruction, political corruption, and the demise of indigenous culture. However, a closer inspection of the flow of popular music, film, and even clothing at the time belies what Steven Chung calls "the discourse of Americanization in 1950s South Korea." What is most striking about his essay and Kelly Jeong's essay on screen star Kim Sŭng-ho's iconic persona during the Golden Age of Korean cinema (roughly from 1955 to 1972) are the ways in which they pay attention to gender terms. Their nuanced readings of screen surfaces monumentalize still images from movies, fashion magazines, and photo exhibits as an ultimately productive terrain of indexicality. While Chung pays attention to the unsung heroes of the 1950s (stylists such as Ch'oe Kyŏng-ja and Nora No and various glossy covers from popular women's magazines), Jeong traces the threads of confluence between the United States and South Korea. The complicit patriarchic discourse—necessitated by the former's tender, liberal democratic ideology, after the devastating war, and Washington's sometimes mischievous and corrupt client, Seoul, *and* the discomforting ruptures attended by that government's insights—raises disturbing questions about South Korea's irresponsible cinematic treatment of women.

After the presidency of Kim Dae-jung in South Korea (1998–2003), whose legacy was partly established through his generous and liberal cultural policies, it is hard to imagine that culture was a low priority for other presidents before him. During Park Chung-Hee's presidency (1961–79), all segments of popular culture, as noted in various places in this volume (most notably in Hyunjoon Shin and Pil Ho Kim's "Birth, Death, and Resurrection of Group Sound Rock" and Kyu Hyun Kim's "Fisticuffs, High Kicks, and Colonial Histories: The Ambivalence of Modern Korean Identity in Narrative Comics"), were heavily censored for their failure to promote the ideas behind Park's rural revitalization campaign, anti-Communism, and export-driven economy. As Shin and Kim note in their chapter, the Park Chung-Hee regime took action against the new culture it deemed "vulgar" (*chŏsok*) and "decadent" (*t'oep'ye*). Popular culture during much of the 1970s was reduced to sanitary forms of entertainment that were sanctioned by the government.

It is probably not coincidental that the two chapters that cover the 1970s and 1980s are on the subjects of popular music on university campuses and in graphic novels. During this time of extreme political scrutiny, comics (*manhwa*) arguably emerged as one of the most significant cultural productions, providing both entertainment and social satire for the general public. One reason was at that time newspapers were spared from preproduction censorship, unlike the television and film industries. Ironically, adult *manhwa* thrived during the two decades of military dictatorship, as serialized entertainment in newspapers and sport and entertainment dailies made cartoonists such as Ko Woo-young and Hur Young-man celebrity *auteurs*. Kim Kyu Hyun's close reading of two 1970s texts by these two artists, Ko's *The Great Ambition* [*Taeyamang*] and Hur's *The Bridal Mask* [*Kaksit'al*], cuts across various historical blocs. Not only are they relevant during today's *hallyu* because the work of these two artists continue to serve as treasure troves for adaptations for television, movies, and musicals, but their dealings with Korea's experience with Japanese colonialism continually end up subverting their own nationalist agenda "by rendering the question of ethnic/national identity unresolved and ambivalent."

The landscape of Korean popular culture begins to change radically during the early 1990s, when censorship relaxes and the so-called college underground music and protest culture such as *madang gŭk* (open-space theater) are no longer required to impose countermemory against the ruling forces. At a time when the binarism between officially sanctioned television stars and programs and protest culture germinated largely within college campuses begins to erode, it is Seo Taiji and several other aspiring singer-dancers who form the group Seo Taiji & Boys and become the darlings of mainstream media and social and cultural activists. Seo would perfect dance routines, write his own songs, and choose hip-hop outfits that would later strike a deep chord with Korean teenagers in 1992. It is probably not an exaggeration to say that Seo would single-handedly create a template for the idol mania that soon began to define the *hallyu* era. Roald Maliangkay's chapter helps to locate Seo Taiji, arguably the most important pop icon in Korean history, by contextualizing him within Korea's socioeconomic terms of the time: the increased purchase power of the middle class, the popularity of postauthoritarian consumerist items in teenage fashion, the CD industry boom, and the proliferation of *norae* (Korean karaoke) and *norae-bang* (karaoke rooms/and clubs).

One of the most troubling areas in a volume that attempts to comprehensively cover all aspects of Korean popular culture is, unsurprisingly, North Korea. The reason is partly that, as discussed above, the term *popular* is netted within the axioms of individualism, commercialism, and the star system, which are utilized to market and sell capitalist merchandise. Scanning across the urban landscapes of Pyongyang, it is impossible to locate any faces that actually market products of any kind; neither does the country's single-channel television nor its newspaper feature advertisements or product placements. But it is not as if Pyongyang lacks a star. The late Kim Il-sung, its Great Leader, and his late son and successor, Kim Jong-il, the Dear Leader, are popular icons who register profound resonances with the people of North Korea. Travis Workman, in his chapter "The Partisan, the Worker, and the Hidden Hero: Popular Icons in North Korean Film," repudiates the widely accepted notion that the consumption of socialist realism rests on

Figure I.2. Pyongyang streets are plastered with images of dead Communist leaders such as Kim Il-sung.

a lack of viewing pleasure, and instead he urges us to rethink the bodily spectacle and emotional intimacy that North Korean cinema creates for its masses. Workman's main argument is that the "hidden hero" films from the North reverse Freud's famous dictum, "Where the id was, the ego must come into being," into "Where the superego was, the id must come into being," which then allows them to prefigure the Leader and his association with the hidden hero before even the ego is formed. This is an unusual way to think about the pleasure of viewing, which of course relies on the question posed above, "What is the indexicality of this image?" The prominence of either of the two Leaders presumably reduces any gap between the image and its referentiality. Why even bother figuring out the indexicality between the photograph and the actual object at which the camera is aiming when there is nothing deferred or subconsciously referenced?

This is precisely the question that is taken up by the South Korean photographer who spent several weeks in Pyongyang, Seung Woo Back, whose work, *Blow Up*, is the central concern in Sohl Lee's chapter. Her essay, as do the ones by Michelle Cho, Olga Fedorenko, and Stephen Epstein, continues to explore the complex exchange of the image's production and projected fantasy, which tend to overdetermine a cultural production's representational surface. What Lee notes in Back's work is how the photographer, who initially had thought that the censored images he had captured while traveling in North Korea in 2001 at the height of Kim Dae-Jung's Sunshine Policy era had no value (for they failed to solicit capitalist pleasure, which must impinge on the intriguing set of index photographs usually serve), found that the opposite was true when he enlarged the same "uninteresting" photos. Michelle Cho similarly argues that a gap must be created between the semiotic content of the screen celebrities, such as *minam* (good-looking boy) and *ŏmma* (mother), and the "true" characters that these stars sometimes depict before self-reflexive fun can take place. Cho's focus on director-screenwriter Bong Joon-ho's 2009 film *Mother*, which mounts South Korea's ceaseless projections of fetishistic properties and desires around stars' faces, bodies, and movements, extends the position raised elsewhere in this volume by Stephen Epstein. He, with the aid of James Turnbull, dissects not only the words and melodies of girl group songs but also their suggestive visual figurations in music videos and rejects the girl groups' empowerment argument (embraced by some local critics) and problematizes "a conscious manipulation of the male gaze, or narcissistic self-exploitation directed at same-sex peers that dismisses patriarchy only to career into the similarly problematic dictates of consumerist late capitalism." Complicating this debate between the subversion of austere gendered conventions and reaffirmation of pre-existing patriarchal (and even nationalist) discourse are the performative and grossly exaggerated nature of the girl group music videos, which tend to naturalize conflicting messages.

The confluence of mixed messages in gender and national identity continue to dominate other chapters on contemporary popular Korean culture as well. Rachael Miyung Joo, Olga Fedorenko, and Katarzyna J. Cwiertka all have contributed essays that each specify sports stars, advertisements, and food. Ironically these topics make up second-tier subjects of *hallyu*, while K-pop, K-drama, games, and cinema usually round up most academic rackets on the subject of recent Korean wave. However, no one can argue that sports, advertisement, and food are deeply rooted in the actual material conditions and routines of quotidian life in South Korea. Joo's "'She Became Our Strength': Female Athletes and (Trans)national Desires" brings together issues of mass culture representation, transnational border crossing, and sexual discrimination raised elsewhere in this volume in a more concentrated fashion. While acknowledging the meteoric rise of Korean female stars in golf and figure skating even in the mainstream U.S. media as "new women," Joo raises questions on the sustained racist, sexist, and ultimately parochial nationalist ideologies that undervalue the trajectories of their arcs of success across the globe. Fedorenko's chapter also compellingly draws on how advertisements make the alienation of work in a capitalist system not only natural but even worthwhile by encouraging enjoyment behind the consumption of commodities. Her astute ideological critiques against the seemingly benign advertisement campaigns that engage humor and humanism, while not completely abandoning new subversions that they potentially can realize, provoke the idea that all critiques of South Korea's recent economic success would now have to seriously consider a close analysis of mass culture. Cwiertka's chapter on *hansik* campaign examines culinary nationalism and the ways in which food intersects with Korea's economics, history, taste culture, and most importantly the desire to redefine national identity by repudiating its once-upon-a-time stereotype of pungent smell.

One of the most frequently used phrases to describe South Korea these days is "the most wired nation." Nearly every home in South Korea is connected to the Internet, and almost every living human being there owns a cell phone. But underexposed behind this high-tech–savvy image that provokes the envy of even the West is the unpropitious title Korea holds as the only country in the world where "Internet addiction" is a legitimate psychiatric disorder with a staggering number of 800,000 people or more at risk. If essays on earlier cultural productions (Shin/Kim or Chung) were concerned with readings that pegged textual matters either as ideological mimicry or aligned them as a resistant subculture that proposes an alternative to American cultural hegemony, the mimicry versus subversion debate vanished from almost all discussions on contemporary Internet culture. Both Inkyu Kang and Regina Yung Lee point to Internet sites for their research, and yet their articles diverge onto two completely different paths: Kang responds to the question of why game consoles have largely failed in a country where the game craze has caught on, while Lee attempts a Deleuzian interpretation of a unique U.S. fandom site that renarrates K-dramas through still recaps and commentaries. Kang attributes the immense unpopularity of game consoles and the popularity of the PC bangs in Korea to Confucianism. Youth culture, he suggests, can thrive only in a public space that is outside the remote reach of parental surveillance. The marketing of computers and Internet broadband in Korean homes as must-have learning devices rather than as gaming tools has also played a huge role in making South Korea an overwired nation. On this side of the Pacific, Lee probes the almost clandestine activities of cross-cultural translations on the web; from moving to still images, from aural sounds in Korean to English letters on monitor screen, and from Korean production to American reception, offering one final reminder that indexicality—and with it its photographic incarnation and modernist illumination—still matters in the age of the Internet.

John Whittier Treat explicitly wrote in the introduction to his edited volume of *Contemporary Japan and Popular Culture* that the "popular is the proprietary concern of nearly all the social sciences and the humanities, but is not the only object of study for any field."[13] In the Korean studies field, not unlike its Japanese counterpart, it is almost impossible to identify scholars who exclusively teach subjects on the popular. However, there is one fact that distinguishes Korean studies from Japanese studies: unlike Japanese Noh theater, Kurosawa films, and the literature of Yasunari Kawabata and Yukio Mishima during the postwar years that have become the anchoring points of Japanese studies in U.S. academia, Korean studies had a difficult time selling its tradition and modern aesthetics in course syllabuses until *hallyu* (Korean Wave) came along. Its churning out entertainment coveted by a huge number of young fans who happened to enroll in our classes in the universities has precipitated a demand-led research career change. While I hope this volume will find its way into many classrooms in the United States, I also admit to making the best of an awkward situation in which there is not yet a substantial branch of even a subfield called "Korean Popular Culture Studies."

This is actually one of the reasons we compartmentalized the sections the way we did: along field demarcations rather than along the lines of historical chronology. This way, each and every section forces a dialogue outside its own historical specificities and can easily point to the affective power, genre, and stylistic mutations of each of the popular discourses over time. Much of the material gathered in this volume came together when all of the scholars working in the different fields of literature, art history, history, ethnic studies, anthropology, film studies, musicology, and social sciences realized that we had a common theme at hand, but the seeds for it were sown when students walked into our classrooms in the United States, ready to talk about the latest cultural sensations in Korea. This book has given us the much-desired opportunity to intellectualize and extend those discussions.

NOTES

1. Bruce Cumings, *Korea's Place in the Sun* (New York: W. W. Norton, 2005), 306.
2. "Content Exports to Be Raised Up to $10 Bil. by 2017 . . . Gov't," *The Korean Economic Daily*, September 13, 2013. Accessed September 27, 2013. www.englishhankyung .com.
3. News segment from Al Jazeera network's *The Stream*, "K-pop diplomacy," published on September 3, 2012. Accessed May, 3, 2013, http://www.youtube.com/watch?v= rYt813fDWTw&feature=plcp.
4. Homi K. Bhabha, "The Postcolonial and the Postmodern," in *The Location of Culture* (London: Routledge, 1992), 172.

5. Some of the most representative research that explores Korean Wave as cultural contents that *flow and exchange* in the pan-Asian region are Chua Beng Huat and Koichi Iwabuchi, eds., *East Asian Pop Culture: Analyzing the Korean Wave* (Hong Kong: Hong Kong University Press, 2008) and Do Kyun Kim and Min-Sun Kim, eds., *Hallyu: Influence of Korean Popular Culture in Asia and Beyond* (Seoul: Seoul National University Press, 2011).

6. Eun-young Jung, "Transnational Korea: A Critical Assessment of the Korean Wave in Asia and the United States," *Southeast Review of Asian Studies* 31 (2002), 75.

7. It was Roland Barthes who continued to explore photography as a contingent determination of an index of a real object that is being photographed. See Roland Barthes, *Camera Lucida: Reflections on Photography*, trans. Richard Howard (New York: Hill and Wang, 1981).

8. During the Irvine conference in May 2011, where many of the essays featured in this volume were presented and discussed, Timothy Tangherlini, a discussant for the popular music panel, first foregrounded *indexicality*. Indexicality originates from *index*, which was used by American semiotician Charles Sanders Peirce during the latter half of the nineteenth century to underscore less than clear-cut signs that bear little resemblance to their original objects. His examples included a footprint, a weather vane, the word *this*, and a photograph. See Charles Sanders Peirce, *The Essential Peirce: Selected Philosophical Writings*, vol. 1, ed. Nathan Houser and Christian Kloesel (Bloomington: Indiana University Press, 1992).

9. Tom Gunning, "What's the Point of an Index? Or, Faking Photographs," in *Still Moving: Between Cinema and Photography*, ed. Karen Beckman and Jean Ma (Durham, NC: Duke University Press, 2008), 24.

10. Gi-Wook Shin and Michael Robinson, eds., *Colonial Modernity in Korea* (Cambridge, Mass: Harvard University Asia Center, 1999).

11. In response to popular demand for stories and historical accounts set during the colonial period, the South Korean film industry spewed out several high-profile films during the first decade of the twenty-first century such as Yun Chong-ch'an's *Blue Swallow* (*Ch'ŏngyŏn*, 2005), Jeong Ji-woo's big-budget *Modern Boy* (2008), and Kim Ji-woon's *The Good, the Bad, the Weird* (*Choŭn nom, nappŭn nom, isanghan nom*, 2008).

12. Bodurae Kwon's *Yŏnae ŭi sidae: 1920-yŏndae ch'oban ŭi munhwa wa yuhaeng* [Age of dating: Culture and trends of the early 1920s] (Seoul: Hyŏnsil munhwa yŏngu, 2003); Cheon Jung-hwan's *Chosŏn ŭi sanai kŏdŭn p'utppol ŭl ch'ara* [If you are a man of Chosŏn, kick a soccer ball] (Seoul: P'ŭrŭn yŏksa, 2010); and Son Min-jung's *Politics of T'ŭrot'ŭ* [T'ŭrot'ŭ ŭi chŏngch'ihak] (P'aju, Korea: 2009).

13. John Whittier Treat, "Introduction: Japanese Studies into Cultural Studies," *Contemporary Japan and Popular Culture* (Honolulu: University of Hawai'i Press, 1996), 3.

After having been so accustomed to mass media and the technical advancements (radio, television, movies, and the Internet) that have laid the foundation of modern popular culture, we often forget that writing is one of the oldest forms of mass culture. The postmodern era's diminishment of literature has not automatically triggered an end of writing. In this section, named "Click and Scroll," four chapters examine how the landscape of modern-day consumers is shaped by a quick fix with celebrity gossip, serialized *manhwa* (comics), computer games, and blog culture in both Korea and overseas. The world that inhabits the colonial space of Korea (discussed in Boduerae Kwon's "The World in a Love Letter" and Kyu Hyun Kim's "Fisticuffs, High Kicks, and Colonial Histories") and our contemporary lives, which are dominated by computers and cyber cultures (discussed in Inkyu Kang's "It All Started with a Bang" and Regina Yung Lee's "As Seen on the Internet"), seem worlds apart from each other. Yet the breakdown between domestic spaces and public cultures, and the mass fascination with foreign letters, vernacular scribbles, and personal notes that made this boundary between private and public worlds blurry, are common themes that bind the different periods represented in this section.

Another common link that binds three of the four chapters, from Kwon's account to Kyu Hyun Kim's essay on Ko Woo-young's graphic novels of the 1960s to Lee's "As Seen on the Internet," is the concern for the intimate form of writing that involves love letters (Kwon), autobiography (Kim), and recap blogs of popular television dramas (Lee). One of the pleasures derived from surfing the Internet is, of course, the pleasure of transgressing the boundary between privacy and public spheres — whether it be reading friends' walls on Facebook, users' replies to a *New York Times* book review or Netflix film reviews, or celebrities' rambles on Twitter. The very reason the values of social network media companies have skyrocketed over the past decade is because the Internet, unlike any other media, subscribes to the idea that many of the social norms and ethics around the traditional barriers between humans and machines or between private and public have imploded. The user-led innovation, amateur production, and participatory replies, blogs, and tweets continue to fulfill the enjoyment of "creative resistance" to a point where the discussions by French poststructuralists such as Michel Foucault and Michel de Certeau on the declining meaning of authorship and the renewed importance of everyday life sound almost as if they had presaged today's condition met by Internet-led life.[1] One of the French philosophers from the May '68 Generation who had witnessed the Internet and e-mail revolution was Jacques Derrida. In *Archive Fever: A Freudian Impression*, he speculates that "psychoanalysis would not have been what it was. . . . if e-mail, for example, had existed."[2] What Derrida claims is that postal communication and more particularly handwritten correspondence played a central role in shaping the archival landscape of psychoanalysis for Freud, his contemporaries, and many of his disciples. Privacy, personal intimacies, and the suspense of several days' delays involved in delivering handwritten letters were pivotal in constituting modern psychoanalysis in Europe a little more than a century ago.

Such traversing across past, present, and future by way of substituting quill and ink with keyboard and screen in Derrida's conjectures spills over to the concerns raised in this opening section. Kwon's account of the 1920s colonial space of Korea is through the questioning of how the private letters and the modern-day institutions of celebrity culture, postal services, and print technology had all amalgamated in order to produce bestselling books from the colonial era, such as *Flames of Love* (*Sarang ŭi pulkkot*), simply a collection of love letters — some of which were actually written by celebrity writers of the day. After closely reading both Kwon's fascinating account of the central role the postal service and letters by celebrities played in forming both the content and the conditions surrounding the origin of modern Korean literature and Lee's analysis of K-drama fandoms available in English-language websites, one must wonder whether or not popular writers like Yi Kwang-su, whose scandalous divorces and love affairs shook the nation still entrapped in Confucian values in the 1920s, would have tweeted his secrets on his blog or checked into fan sites that provide recaps of his serialized dramas had he been alive today. Would he, a notorious pro-Japanese collaborator during the latter part of Korea's colonial era, have posted pictures of himself with the Japanese governor-general? Would the legendary comic-book artist Ko Woo-young have published online his sketches of early childhood, a time when he was a conflicted Korean child living in Manchuria and his father was serving as a policeman in the Japanese imperial system? Would both Yi and Ko have done so had they lived to witness the era of sns-boom without the political backlashes celebrities still face if their roots are found to be pro-Japanese? In other words, would some of the early modern and late modern celebrities have "clicked and scrolled" and still thrived in a postmodern age when private lives of celebrities tend to shape the landscape of popular culture itself rather than the actual production and consumption of their creative outputs?

Though such questions are only hypothetical and cannot engineer any firm historical determinations, one is tempted to conclude—just as much as Freud ought to have been able to find enough number of patients suffering from mental ailments with or without the suspense of hand-written letter deliveries—that these modern celebrities born or raised during the colonial era would have been able to find their way to expose and dramatize their private lives and personal traumas on more than one social network platform, should they remain active today. No celebrity guest would have been more perfect than Yi Kwang-su for *The Healing Camp*: one of the most popular talk shows in Korea today. **KHK**

NOTES

1. See Michel Foucault, "What Is an Author?" in *Language, Counter-Memory, Practice: Selected Essays and Interviews,* ed. Donald F. Bouchard and trans. Donald F. Bouchard and Sherry Simon (Ithaca, NY: Cornell University Press, 1977), 113–38, and Michel de Certeau, *The Practice of Everyday Life* (Berkeley: University of California Press, 2002).

2. Jacques Derrida, *Archive Fever: A Freudian Impression,* trans. Eric Prenowitz (Chicago: University of Chicago Press, 1996), 17.

BODUERAE KWON

TRANSLATED BY YOUNGJU RYU

The World in a Love Letter

INTRODUCTION: DEFINING *YŎNAE*

According to literary critic Kim Ki-jin, the Korean word that refers exclusively to romance, *yŏnae*, was a twentieth-century invention. Writing in the mid-1920s, Kim noted that "the word *yŏnae* had begun to be used only recently," entering popular vocabulary seven or eight years before as the shortened form of the expression *chayuyŏnae* (free love).[1] Based on Kim's recollections, we can thus surmise that *yŏnae* became part of the common parlance in Korea at the end of the 1910s. Chinese and Japanese mediation was essential. In the classical world of Chinese letters, which had stretched over Korea, China, and Japan, the graph traditionally used to refer to the passion between the sexes had been *yŏn* (戀), but *ae* (愛) began to be used also as having a Western feel. *Yŏnae* emerged as the combination of the two graphs. The first observed use of the word *yŏnae* in East Asia occurred in the early nineteenth century, when Western missionaries in China chose the word as translation for *love*.

But it was in Japan of the late nineteenth century that the word *yŏnae* gained traction.[2] Behind *yŏnae* hovered words like *love*, *amour*, and *Liebe*, as well as the distinctly foreign sensibility that such words seemed to encode. "There is no Japanese equivalent to the English word *love*," lamented Kuriyagawa Hakuson, the author of an influential treatise called *The Modern View of Love* (1921, 1929). "When it comes to expressions like 'I love you,' and 'Je t'aime,' there simply isn't a way to render them adequately into Japanese. The linguistic sensibility that exists in English or French simply doesn't in Japanese."[3] *Yŏnae* was coined precisely in an attempt to translate this foreign linguistic sensibility. As a neologism born in the process of translation, *yŏnae* secured circulation by distinguishing itself from existing passions and stigmatizing them as vulgar and unclean. For this reason, *yŏnae* has sometimes been identified with its foreign origin and associated with the indignity and violence of foreign domination in the twentieth century.

In Korean, *yŏnae* translates the love between the sexes exclusively. The love of God, of humanity, of parents and friends all qualify as love, but not *yŏnae*.[4] This point of distinction was particularly important when the word began to be fashionable around 1920. Contained in the language itself was the notion that there was something special to be highlighted in the love between a man and a woman, that the connection between the sexes had to be singled out for attention among the myriad relationships that human beings forge over the course of their lives. In this regard, we can briefly examine the history of the word *sarang*, another Korean word that means love but has much broader usage today than *yŏnae*. *Sarang* initially meant to think about someone and was not used widely even after it took on the modern meaning of love. It was only after the spread of Protestantism that *sarang* came to be identified with God's love and gained wider circulation. In the turbulent 1900s, *sarang* was also pronounced in the realm of nation-state theory. "Of love [*sarang*], the highest, the most constant, and the most true and righteous is the love of country," insisted one editorial of *Tongnip sinmun* [The Independent].[5] "Is your love for His Majesty the Emperor greater than your love for your own life?" demanded another.[6] When another editorial exhorted its readers "to love your brothers and fellow countrymen . . . as you love God," the love in question was this *sarang* that was to be legitimated first and foremost in reference to God and the country.

Sarang, however, metamorphosed into the love between a man and a woman in Na To-hyang's novella of 1920, *Youth*. In one scene, a minister gives a sermon and concludes that "one who doesn't know love and doesn't practice love is one who is already dead" after waxing eloquently about the love of God and country. The protagonist reinterprets the minister's message in his own way: "I must love love. For loving love is loving God." This unbeliever who "bows his head before the illusion of a young woman, not before God," and who considers reason more absolute than God or the nation, is the protagonist of Korean literature in the early 1920s.[7] At a time when popular desire for education and culture was reaching a feverish height in the period immediately following the March First Movement of 1919, *yŏnae* emerged as the protagonist of its time. It enticed the men and women of the new generation who had just gained access to modern educational institutions. It brought about a revolt against the absolute authority that parents had held over marriage decisions and caused numerous scandals ultimately ending in an affair or even murder. *Yŏnae* was also the driving force behind the sudden popularization of unfamiliar expressions like "sweet home," the new emphasis on the couple-centered nuclear family over the traditional institution of multigenerational family, and the proposal for "men and women regardless of age to eat together in laughter and joy," overturning the age-old custom of mealtime separation by gender and age.[8] Not only did *yŏnae* lead to a myriad changes in everyday life at the micro-level, but it also transformed the very structure of feeling and form of communication that enabled these changes in the first place.

LOVE LETTERS AND THE IMMEDIACY OF TEXT

At the origin of modern Korean literature, we find love, the romantic kind. It was by leaning on the concept of romantic love that Korean literature tutored itself in the art of writing, nurtured the awakening of individual consciousness, and sharpened the powers of social critique. For Yi Kwang-su, the proverbial "father of modern Korean literature," romantic love was the point of entry for the project of modern literature as such (fig. 1.1). "To a Young Friend" (*Orinbŏsege*), his short fiction of 1917, traced the scattered tracks of wandering lovers by employing the form of love letters, giving rise to numerous imitators of its literary style in the process. Similarly the secret to the sensational success of Yi Kwang-su's famed novel, *The Heartless* (*Mujŏng*), rested with the structure of a love triangle at the heart of the plot. When modern literature fashioned itself as a confidential and immediate communication between a writer and a reader, it appealed both to the new sensibility of love and to the renewed medium of letters.[9]

A letter might seem a slow and cumbersome medium of communication today, but to the Korean public of the 1920s it represented speed. When the postal service was first launched in Korea in 1895, only 137 letters were collected in the first fifteen days and the small volume of mail almost guaranteed prompt delivery. Judging from postmarks, a typical letter mailed in Seoul in the 1900s took less than a day to reach another destination within the city. By 1925, the volume of mail had grown to nearly sixty million letters, but the post continued to represent the swiftest and the most direct means of communication. Literature also attests to the expeditiousness of postal communication.

The narrator of Yi Kwang-su's "To a Young Friend" receives a reply to his love letter in three days' time and imagines that "[Kim Illyŏn] must have mailed her response earlier that day after hesitating whether to send it or not." The very next day, he receives another letter from her in which she asks for his "forgiveness for the breach committed yesterday."[10] This experience

Figure 1.1. Yi Kwang-su was one of the pioneering figures of epistolary novels and writer of "To a Young Friend." By divorcing his first wife and marrying Hŏ Yŏng-suk, he created a nation-shocking scandal.

of the same-day delivery strengthened the illusion of immediacy attached to the letter. Though it may seem strange to us now, it was not unusual for the protagonist of early twentieth-century Korean fiction to send a letter home and expect a reply the very next day; "if the letter is sent on the night train, it'll get there by lunchtime tomorrow, and if they send a reply right away, I'll have it the day after."[11]

Such expeditiousness of mail added reality to references that ten letters were exchanged in a month and a thousand letters during eight years of romance.[12] Given the state of transportation at the time, when travel between the city and the country routinely took ten hours or more, the speed of letters as a means of communication must have struck the Korean public as all the more impressive. But no matter how immediate a letter may seem as a mode of communication, it is still a mediated communication. As the phony love letters in New Fiction works such as *It's Spring Again* (*Chaebongch'un*) and *The Cry of Wild Geese* (*Anǔisŏng*) show, there are few things in the world easier to forge than writing. In Hyŏn Chin-gŏn's *Fog Grows*

Thin (*Chisaenŭnangae*), the protagonist's friend intercepts a love letter and forges a reply himself, and in Yi Kiyŏng's "My Brother's Secret Letter" (*Oppa ŭi pimil p'yŏnji*), a playboy sends out ardent love letters to many different women at the same time. In short stories of Kim Tong-in and Yŏm Sang-sŏp, both entitled "The Will" (*Yusŏ*), even a document bearing life-changing consequences is not to be trusted. On the pretext of looking out for a younger friend's interest, the narrator of Kim Tong-in's story manipulates the friend's decadent wife and finally kills her after forcing her to change her will. In Yŏm Sang-sŏp's story as well, a character named D. writes a fake suicide note and is then overcome by puerile emotions at the sight of his distraught friends. At one end of the literary spectrum, there was already a clear sense of skepticism toward both the gesture of confession contained in a letter and its ornate rhetoric.

Such skepticism, however, could not unsettle the widespread view that the letter represented the most intimate and truthful form of communication. This belief, to be sure, could not have been possible without developments in the postal service that made letter-writing almost as quick and reliable a means of reaching another as a physical encounter. But also at work was the belief that the act of writing occasions an eruption of genuine emotions. In addition, the letter provided a physical token that allowed the distance from the loved one to be bridged. While early modern Korean literature contains ample instances of physical contact between the sexes—a good example is the problem an unwed mother posed in *Double Crystal Tears* (*Ssangoknu*), and sexual encounter is an important plot element in "To the Frail of Heart" (*Maŭm iyŏtŭn jayŏ*), "New Year's Eve" (*Jeya*), and "The Era of the Young" (*Chŏlmŭni ŭi sijŏl*) as well—the purity of *yŏnae* had already become a familiar ideology. People "believed in the sacredness of romantic love. They respected it."[13] In time, the argument that the spirit and the body are one would be articulated, but the dictum that *yŏnae* must be sacred and pure complicated the problem of direct physical experience. It was in this context that the letter emerged as a marvelous medium that promises the experience of love, albeit an indirect one.

"A crisp envelope" that seems to have been "doused with perfume" (*Fog Grows Thin*), a package containing a "pink Western-style envelope" and a "charming volume of Western poetry" ("That Night" [*Kŭnalpam*]), or "a letter written on jade-hued paper embroidered around the edges in red" ("A Blooming Maiden" [*Kkopinŭnch' ŏnyŏ*])—the materiality of a letter, not simply its message, had the power to move. The stationery, perfume, and little ornaments like dried flower petals enclosed with the letter were no less impor-

Figure 1.2. Published in 1923, *Flame of Love* was a smash hit in the market. It was a collection of love letters, including some by contemporary writers. Noh Jayŏng, its editor and main writer, created a model for the love letter and popularized a style of letter writing. His great success, however, was understood as evidence of the degeneration of literature rather than the enlargement of the literary field, and it led to his humiliation as a poet.

tant than the expression of one's inner self through language. Accordingly, detailed advice proliferated on the etiquette of correspondence. When writing to a gentle lady, for example, the writer was advised to use cream-rose or pink stationery and orchid perfume, and enclose forget-me-not petals; when writing to a student, silver-gray stationery, jasmine perfume, and two tickets to a music concert; and to a widow, white paper and black tulips. Once again, it was the woman question that drove these trends. As the sender, the woman had to find ways to express herself, and as the recipient she had to examine her image in being addressed a particular way. A letter's materiality emblematized the materiality of the woman's body; it was for this reason that the physical letter sometimes provided greater allure than the message it contained. The sight of a young man "gazing at the delicate, small letters written on an almost translucent paper," seeking greater satisfaction than what the text can give, became typical. Young men even prized a letter of rejection and would shower trembling kisses upon it, and the physicality of the letter sometimes drove them to utter ruin. In Kim Wŏn-ju's "To Avoid Lust" (*Aeyok ŭl piharyŏ*) a young man goes to the extreme of becoming a monk in order to keep himself from falling under a woman's spell, but is ultimately undone by a single letter—and the female body it delivers.[14]

THE ROLE OF INTERMEDIARIES AND THE INDIRECTNESS OF COMMUNICATION

The first attempt to institute a modern postal service in Korea dates back to 1884. The opening of the Bureau of Postal Services on December 4, however, became the famed scene of the Kapsin Coup.[15] It would take another decade for regular postal operations to begin, with the establishment of the Bureau at the capital and local offices in 1895 and Korea's admission into the Universal Postal Union in 1900. The service then continued to expand in scale even after 1905, when Korea became Japan's protectorate, so that by 1912 there were more than five hundred postal stations across the country. Postage ranged from 5 p'un to 5 chŏn in 1895, and a regular letter cost 3 chŏn to mail in 1920. At first, mail was collected and delivered once in the morning and once in the afternoon, but service was soon expanded to four times daily.

Although the basic system was thus in place for exchanging letters, the modern institution of postal service appears to have remained an unfamiliar curiosity to the Korean public at least for the first two decades of the twentieth century. In works of New Fiction (Sin so sŏl),[16] for example, characters exchange letters through messengers, relying on the institutional medium for international mail only. In Tears of Blood (Hyŏl ŭi nu), Ongnyŏn's mother writes her suicide note on the wall of her house but Ongnyŏn sends news through international mail; between the mother's act of writing, which is dated in the work as taking place in 1894, and the daughter's, which takes place in 1902, lies the founding of the Korean postal service.[17] This shift also coincides in the text with spatial expansion outward from Korea to the world as the heroine makes her way to Japan and from there to America. The very notion that the postal service could be used to send and receive personal letters and everyday tidings was not widespread at all until the 1910s. To be sure, there were such precocious exceptions as young Chŏngim and Yŏngch'ang from Autumn Moon Shades (Ch'uwŏlsaek), two twelve-year-olds who exchanged their newly established addresses, had their letters shuttled between Seoul and Ch'osan, and "waited for another [letter] though one had arrived only yesterday."[18] It was much more common to turn to the post in cases of emergency, when life hung in the balance, as Sublieutenant Pak did to reach Pingju in Microscope (Hyŏnmigyŏng).[19] On the last page of Tears of Blood, a postman "dressed in black, narrow-legged pants, wearing a cap that says 'Mail' on it, and carrying a leather pouch slung across his chest," peeking in through the front gate, was liable to be scolded for "sneaking a look at the inner courtyard of a genteel household." Put differently, a postman in Korea was a strange and curious creature who had not yet attained institutional transparency even in the first decade of the twentieth century.

The common mode of communication, especially between men and women, was to jot down a verse or a short message, "attach it to a broken piece of roof tile and throw it over the wall."[20] Even when characters were bold enough to attempt direct communication, letters represented a shady means of getting one's message across. "The Love Letter Case" reported in *Maeil Sinbo* (*Daily News*, Seoul) on June 29, 1911, furnishes an excellent example. A young assistant working in a local branch office of the military police develops amorous feelings toward a widowed gentlewoman next door. The episode ends tragically as the widow expresses her indignation by stabbing her suitor. The hapless young man is said to have made his feelings known by depositing a "love letter" via the alley outside Lady Kim's residence, requesting her to "leave her reply . . . under the stone bridge by the front gate." Newspapers report other similar happenings. A female neighbor one might come across by the well could serve as a go-between, but when no courier could be found, a lovesick young man would "toss five postcards over the wall into the house of the woman he had long admired" and hope for the best. A crack in the wall, a stone bridge outside the house, or narrow lanes through the grounds had to serve as communication paths at a time when lovers could not count on institutional anonymity of the messenger. This meant that the exchange of love letters required physical proximity and that, even though a letter was a means of creating presence-in-absence, its power to negate distance and overcome spatial divide was much too weak at this point in time.

What the writers of New Fiction used instead to bring their lovers together were intermediaries with clearly established identities. This convention was true not only in cases where the relationship was presented through a code of debauchery—as with Yi Sijong and the Kangnŭng Woman in *Mountains and Streams* (*Sanch'ŏnch'omok*)—but also in works containing early, disguised prototypes of *yŏnae* like Yi Haejo's *Red Peach Blossoms* (*Hŭisaenghwa*) and Ch'oe Ch'ansik's *Seashore* (*Haean*), *The Cry of Wild Geese*, and *Nŭngna Island* (*Nŭngna do*). In *Red Peach Blossoms*, Sangho cannot bring himself to start a conversation with T'aehŭi, a young woman student he sees on his way to school. In *Seashore*, Taesŏng reads about a student named Yi Kyŏngja and "admires her inwardly," having resolved to find himself a wife who could "converse suitably on academic subjects and accompany him to banquets to which he may be invited," but finds no way to approach her. In a similar way, Sanghyŏn and Chŏngae in *The Cry of Wild Geese* and Chŏngnin and Toyŏng in *Nŭngna Island* fail to arrange their trysts without relying on the help of a third.

Since lovers could not count on the neutral capacity of an anonymous institution to bring them together, they had no choice but to turn to intermediaries or even to coincidence. Sangho in *Red Peach Blossoms* seeks out Official Kim, T'aehŭi's uncle; Sanghyŏn, in *The Cry of Wild Geese* turns for help to the head of Map'o District, where Chŏngae lives. In *Seashore*, Taesŏng's trusted nurse turns out to be Kyŏngja's aunt, and in *Nŭngna Island*, Chŏngnin's savior from a perilous danger happens to be Toyŏng's older brother. It is through these intermediaries that the path of communication finally opened up between the hero and the heroine. Unable to say a word to each other for all the tender feelings that filled their eyes and hearts, these characters relied on the power of intermediaries. Unlike Kim Ongnyŏn and Ku Wansŏ in *Tears of Blood*, who engage in the shocking exception of "discussing marriage themselves," couples spoke to each other directly for the first time only after entering the bond of marriage.

SOCIAL CONDITIONS OF LOVE LETTERS

Before the onset of modernity, it was usually seduction by sound that jumpstarted amorous encounters between young men and women. The dashing youthful hero of traditional fiction or poetry often became mesmerized by a verse recited in a mellifluous voice or charmed by elegant music issuing from an expertly played flute or zither. He would then try to draw the heroine's notice by recitation or musical performance of his own. The reason for such priority accorded to sound may have been that lovers had to rely on auditory rather than visual sense at a time when free contact between the sexes was greatly hindered. In Korea of the 1900s, the convention of aural captivation as a means of attracting the opposite sex was very much in place still. In *Zither Among the Pines* (*Songroegŭm*), Kyeok, the daughter of a governor, and Kŭnam, a young businessman, begin their relationship by playing the flute in turns and exchanging verses in classical Chinese. In modern times, however, the bodily organ that would facilitate such enchantments became the eye rather than the ear. It could be said in fact that this shift in emphasis from sound to vision coincides with the very transition from the premodern to modern world. As already seen in *Red Peach Blossoms*, *Seashore*, *The Cry of Wild Geese*, and *Nŭngna Island*, young men and women began to perceive each other by locking eyes.

This exchange in looks was a newly heralded event. The figure of the female student that appeared in several works of New Fiction starting in the 1900s was rarely observed in reality, as there was no shared space where male and female students could meet. Elder Kim of *The Heartless* hires Hyŏngsik as a private tutor for his daughter only after first deciding to make him his son-in-law. For Sŏngsun in *The Pioneer* (*Kaech'ŏkja*) and Hyesuk in *Phantasmagoria* (*Hwanhŭi*), the only men they are able to meet are their brothers' friends. Despite the enlightenment discourse that exhorted women to recognize their duties as members of the nation on a par with men, women's sphere of activity was limited to the home. Female students were still rare, given the customs of the time when "a girl student ten years old . . . was considered old." As seen in the common narrative pattern of New Fiction—the heroine is forced to endure all manner of violence the moment she sets foot in the world outside—a woman who roams the streets was inevitably treated as a prostitute. That is to say, in an era when it was out of the question for a woman to be a flaneuse, a woman who ventured outside the home was caught up in the system of symbolic equivalences that posited a woman in the streets as always a streetwalker. Heroines of New Fiction who sought to bring about the implosion of this system found themselves seized by the power of the old symbolism. To escape it, one had to cast off traditional Korean costume and don Western clothes like Chŏngim in *Autumn Moon Shades* or like Chŏngsuk in *Peony Blossoms* (*Moktanhwa*), who became a cross-dresser and pretended to be a man.

The March First Movement of 1919 changed everything. The most significant milestone of the colonial period, it brought nearly ten percent of the entire Korean population out onto the streets over the course of several months. Over seven thousand Koreans were killed and forty thousand arrested. These numbers are all the more impressive when we consider the general lack of political organization and the poor state of nationwide communication channels at the time. The long-suppressed discontent over Japanese rule exploded into a demand for national independence, and though the political demand was immediately and violently squashed, the mobilization of the public, which included large numbers of women, transformed the social landscape thereafter. The year after the March First Movement, "it became impossible for schools to admit everyone because the desire to obtain modern education had grown to such a pitch among women in general"[21] and by 1923, the number of students in these new schools exceeded those in traditional village-style schools, drawing public attention to female students as objects of curiosity and envy. Public spaces in which men and women could meet began to open up as well. In *Autumn Moon Shades*, published in 1912, Kang Han-yŏng was still seen as a hoodlum for attending Sunday lectures meant strictly for female students, but by the 1920s, public events where male and female students could gather in one place were no longer so uncommon. The 1920s thus represented a clear break from earlier decades in its creation of spaces coinhabited by men and women.[22] Music concerts or public lectures were some of the more notable events that brought young men and women together. Men and women also brushed up against each other on trains, and unexpected encounters sometimes took place in a church. Seating was generally segregated but it could not stop romance from budding across the aisle, as women and men "saw each other and exchanged looks of love and sympathy."[23] (See plate 2's illustration of a young woman's clothing and hairstyle.)

A budding romance tends toward timidity. The fact that a social space could now be shared did not guarantee more than a simple exchange of looks, and means of making physical contact were only just being discovered. To be sure, it was far from the case that the twentieth century furnished the first opportunity in Korean history for young men and women to meet each other. But the concept of *yŏnae* brought with it far-reaching implications about social reform. *Yŏnae* was more likely to occur in urban settings and premised the institution of monogamy and reordering of family relations. It was even indirectly connected with a decline in the mortality rate and extension of biological longevity. Moreover, as a new import into the Korean language, *yŏnae* required a pose that suited the novelty of the word. Young men and women began to venture out into the streets, strolling together for the first time and risking the censure that they were dotting "the main thoroughfares of the city like gangsters and their molls."[24] They usually walked within a few paces of each other, not daring to hold hands: "The two of them shook hands firmly. Then they headed toward Sŭngdong Chapel, walking the streets of Seoul on a lonely winter night, maintaining a distance of three or four paces between them."[25] Or lovers would sometimes ride the same bus and get off through different doors, as though strangers, and exchange a few words while walking together: "Pretending not to notice the bus-girl's protestations, Yŏngsik got off by the back door. . . . He saw that Hŏ had already gotten off by the front door. . . . Hŏ walked up the path by the city walls and Yŏngsik followed like her guardian."[26] Even after occupying the same space and communicating their feelings through an exchange of glances, men and women remained hesitant about making direct physical contact.

A letter was a form of writing created by these times, by these circumstances. A missive conferred an illusion of immediacy and shattered this last bit of distance, the few paces that could not be overcome in reality after all that was said and done. The more timid and awkward one's actual contact with the object of desire, the more fervent became the confession of one's inner self in letters. The expansion of the postal service made it easier to approach the opposite sex in writing. In Yi Kwang-su's "Writing in Blood" (Hyŏlsŏ), letters were hand-delivered by acquaintances, and in Hyŏn Chin-gŏn's "Sacrificial Flower" and Na To-hyang's "The Time of the Young" younger siblings carry messages to and fro; but before long, such messengers became a thing of the past.

The view that each individual possesses a unique interiority, that the value of the individual's existence is amplified when this interiority is more delicately and passionately expressed, found perfect expression in the particular form of confession that the letter represented. The illusion of immediacy generated by letters gave Rapture's lovers the conviction to pledge themselves to each other, then betray that pledge, and ultimately commit suicide, even when there was nothing to bind them in real life but the memory of having exchanged a few phrases. For young men and women, letters provided an opportunity to carry on a meaningful conversation that could not be had in person and helped turn abstract passions and anguish burning in their hearts into concrete realities. "When the mere rumor of a single woman writing a letter to a man could make people revile her and call her horrid names, how could I possibly visit him at his boarding house? . . . So what else can I do but write letters?"[27] It was not uncommon for a romance to be carried on entirely through correspondence for three or four years between lovers who had never seen so much as a photograph of each other. A letter thus served as a substitute for meetings and conversations that could not be had in real life. Far from being a surplus byproduct of a physical romantic relationship, a love letter *was* the relationship, in and of itself.

CONCLUSION: MODERN KOREAN LITERATURE AND *YŎNAE*

Love is a topic that transcends time. As mammals that propagate through sexual reproduction, human beings are after all fated to mate, but the universality of love arises also from the unique human characteristic of "desiring the desire of the other." And love persists, even in a society that strictly limits direct contact between the sexes, and prescribes the rule of segregation by gender past the age of seven. Chosŏn, Korea, was such a society. Scholars agree that it may have been the most advanced of any society since the medieval age in terms of institutionalizing distinctions and hierarchy, but even in Chosŏn, cases of "love" resisted hierarchy as exemplified in major works of classical Korean fiction. Unyŏng does not retract her love toward the young literary licentiate even after suffering torture and death (Unyŏngjŏn); Simsaeng withdraws from the world after his lover dies from the despair of being unable to overcome status difference and ultimately dies of illness

himself *(Simsaengjŏn)*; and Ch'unhyang and Mongnyong achieve an unlikely happy ending to a romance that breaks the boundaries of hereditary
status *(Ch'unhyangjŏn)*. The passion that engulfed these heroes and heroines of fiction threatened the existing system of values and social hierarchy.

If the passionate love between the sexes posed a threat of subversion to
the social hierarchy, so did the literary form of the novel. Fiction's dangerous
power to "rob the reader of his wits" had relegated the genre to a low status
in the hierarchy of genres in traditional East Asian literature, and continuing the tenor of the traditional critique against fiction, some Korean literary
critics at the turn of the century expressed suspicion toward the novel for
its "falsity and unfoundedness" as well as "licentiousness."[28] Because it enticed the heart and filled it with ardor, and because it intrigued and dazed
the mind, one had to be on guard against the novel as against love.

It was Yi Kwang-su who played the pivotal role in making *yŏnae* and the
novel acceptable, even legitimate, by linking it to enlightenment. *The Heartless* broke new grounds precisely in pioneering a model both of an intellectual elite's relationship to his surrounding environment within the framework of enlightenment, and of the relationship between the sexes. In the
sequel to *The Heartless* entitled *The Pioneer*, Yi Kwang-su went even further
and conferred glory onto "a pioneer in *yŏnae* and sensibility," as exemplified by the character Sŏngsun, over "a pioneer in science and rationality,"
as represented by Sŏngjae. Yi Kwang-su's entire theory of enlightenment
hinged on *yŏnae*; the circuit leading ultimately to social reform and national
redemption wound through romantic love. Yi Kwang-su, the "father of modern Korean literature," was first and foremost a writer of *yŏnae* fiction.

The golden age of *yŏnae* in Korean literature, however, was short-lived.
After Yi Kwang-su, serious writers no longer put *yŏnae* front and center,
and created a grammar of fiction that displayed its capacity and purposive-
ness precisely by marginalizing the topic of *yŏnae*. Kim Tong-in and Yŏm
Sang-sŏp, the two representative writers of the early 1920s, remained reserved and skeptical about love, and by negating *yŏnae*, they strategically
distinguished their work from the "easy literature" consumed by the masses.
This bias was further inherited by writers of proletarian fiction, and modern Korean literature came to adopt "interiority" and "individual anguish"
on the one hand and "society" and "reality" on the other as the dual axes of
properly literary interest. After Yi Kwang-su, it was no longer possible to
profess complete faith in *yŏnae* without inviting the charge of writing sec-
ond- or third-rate literature.

What had changed? The popularity of the concept of *yŏnae* in Korea between the late 1910s and the early 1920s coincided with the retreat and

expansion in the so-called Cultural Rule era heralded by the March First Movement. *Yŏnae* bolstered the private realm, promoted the understanding of a person as a human being endowed with inner mind and feelings, changed the family system, and offered a new outlook on social reform. Becoming the subject of literature and art, generating new fashions, and introducing profound changes in minute details of everyday life, *yŏnae* seemed to provide the source of everlasting social reform after the political upheaval of 1919.

In the early 1920s, however, *yŏnae* rapidly lost its outward orientation and revolutionary character. Despite the lingering influence of foreign philosophers such as Peter A. Kropotkin, Bertrand Russell, Edward Carpenter, and Ellen Key, who declared that love was the basis of an outlook for world reform, the concept of *yŏnae* became divorced from the larger discourse of social reform. Losing its link to the ideology of enlightenment that had so animated Yi Kwang-su's early fiction, *yŏnae* came to focus more and more exclusively on the romantic relationship and was absorbed into the private goal of individual happiness. This is the connotation the word carries today.

Modern Korean literature emerged and matured in a century of colonial, semicolonial, and authoritarian rule. The collective imperatives that dominated the century conferred on the literary imagination a kind of intimacy with politics that defined *yŏnae* as its opposite. However, by locating *yŏnae* at the birth of modern Korean literature, before "interiority" and "individual anguish," before "social consciousness" and "realism," we can understand how the passion for the nation and for enlightenment, which ruled the novel form at its inception, was coupled with private passions inspired by romantic love. And it is this coupling that set the course for the history of modern literature.

NOTES

1. Kim Ki-jin, "Kwannŭng chŏk kwangye ŭi yulli jŏk ŭiŭi: yŏnae munje sogo" [The ethical meaning of sensual relations: A brief treatise on *yŏnae*], in *Chosŏn munsa ŭi yŏnaegwan* [Perspectives on Love of Chosŏn (Korean) Literary Persons] (Seoul: Sŏrhwasŏgwan, 1926), 16.

2. See the Japanese reading of the name in Yanabu Akira, *Ai* [Love] (Tokyo: Sanseido, 2001), 51–54. *Ai* also is the Japanese pronunciation of the character *ae* (愛). Comparing the history of *ai* in Japan and China, the author notes that while the character had a history of Confucian usage, there was no history in Japan.

3. Kuriyagawa Hakuson, *Kindai no renaikan* [The modern view of love], *Renaikanoyobizassan* [The view of love and other writings] (Tokyo: Kaizosha, 1929), 15.

4. In Europe, much confusion is said to have been introduced in the process of translation from Greek to Latin, as *agape* and *eros* were mixed up with words such as

amor, dilectio, and *caritas.* The inclusive nature of the word *love,* in other words, was another name for confusion.

5. Editorial, *Tongnip Sinmun* [The Independent], June 8, 1897.

6. Editorial, *Tongnip Sinmun* [The Independent], January 8, 1898.

7. Na Tohyang, "Chŏngchun" [Youth], *Natohyangchŏnjip,* vol. 1 (Seoul: Jipmundang, 1988).

8. *Tongailbo* [Tonga Daily], January 1, 1923.

9. "To a Young Friend" (*Orinbŏsege*): *Chŏngchun (Youth)* 1917, 7–11; *The Heartless* (*Mujŏng*) (Seoul: Hŏidongsŏgwan, 1918).

10. "To a Young Friend," 7, 118.

11. Kim Tong-in, "Chukŭmki" [Phonogragh], *KimTong-in chŏnjip,* vol. 1 (Seoul: Chosŏnilbosa, 1987), 176.

12. Hŏ Yŏng-suk, "Palnyŏnganeilchŏniba'kchang" [Twelve hundreds in eight years], *Samchŏlli,* October 1930, 63.

13. Moksŏng, *"Kŭnalpam"* [That Night], *Kaebyŏk,* December 1920, 127.

14. Kim Wŏnju, "To Avoid Lust" [*Aeyok ŭl piharyŏ*], *Samch'ŏlli* 1932, 4.

15. The Kapsin Coup (*Kapsin Chŏngbyŏn*) was a failed three-day coup d'état attempt by the Reformers Group in 1884.

16. New Fiction [*Sin so sŏl*] refers to a new trend of fiction that challenged the representation of contemporary life in the 1900s.

17. Yi Injik, *Tears of Blood* (*Hyŏl ŭi nu*) (Seoul: Kwanghaksŏpo, 1907).

18. Choi Chansik, *Autumn Moon Shades* (*Ch'uwŏlsaek*) (Seoul: Andongsŏgwan, 1912).

19. Kim Kyoje, *Microscope* (*Hyŏnmigyŏng*) (Seoul: Tongyangsŏwŏn, 1912).

20. Kim Si-sŭp, *Novella of Kŭmo* [*Kŭmoshinhwa*], trans. Yi Jae-ho (Seoul: Kwahaksa, 1980), 48–49. *Novella of Kŭmo,* which dates back to the fifteenth century, is generally regarded as the first fiction in Korean literature.

21. Cho Tongsik, "Sipnyŏnchŏn yŏhaksaengkwa chikŭyŏhaksaeng" [Girl Students, Ten Years Ago and Now], *Shinyŏsŏng,* January 1925, 15.

22. When Hyŏn Chin-gŏn in "The Sacrificial Flower" described men and women participating in a student association together and presented it as an "episode more than a decade old already," critics pointed out that such an episode could only be a very recent phenomenon.

23. Na Tohyang, "Phantasmagoria" ["Hwanhŭi"], *Natohyang chŏnjip* 2 (Seoul: Jipmundang, 1988).

24. Ch'oe Ch'ansik, *The Cry of Wild Geese* [*Anŭisŏng*], Seoul: Pakmunsŏkwan, 1914, 44.

25. Yi Kwang-su, "Kaechŏkja" [Precursor], in *Yikwangsuchŏnjip,* vol. 1 (Seoul: Samjungtang, 1963), 398.

26. Moksŏng, "Kŭnalpam" [That Night], *Kaebyŏk,* December 1920, 136.

27. Hŏ Yŏng-suk, "Palnyŏnganeilchŏniba'kchang," 63.

28. *Taehan maeil shinbo* [*Korea Daily,* Seoul], December 2, 1909.

Fisticuffs, High Kicks, and Colonial Histories
The Ambivalence of Modern Korean Identity
in Postwar Narrative Comics

This chapter was originally conceived as a brief history of Korean comic books between 1953 and today, focusing on how the comics reflect the changes in contemporary Korean experience and consequently how they appropriate modern Korean history. However, as I made progress on the research of the subject, I found that the scope would be too big and ill-defined. The questions of research design and intellectual scope as well as practical problems regarding available primary sources emerged. First, it became increasingly obvious that "reflection of Korean history" in the comics, if broadly interpreted, would have to encompass so many materials that such a topic would in necessity have to become a comprehensive history of Korean comic art. Yet focusing only on the so-called "current affairs" comics (*sisa manhwa*), which usually have satirical slant, was limiting; doing so would shut out some major innovative works of Korean comics. Second, primary sources turned out to be difficult to locate. Despite the seeming resurgence of interest in *manhwa* (comic arts or cartoons) in the last fifteen years or so, the state of archival preservation of the classic (and not-so-classic) comics of yesteryear remains far from satisfactory. There is no rhyme or reason as to why certain titles have been reprinted multiple times, while other equally popular works have disappeared even from the used-books circuit.

In the present chapter, I focus on how perceptions of modern Korean history, especially the colonial period (1910–45) as depicted in the acknowledged classics of narrative comics (the U.S. equivalent of "graphic novels") from the 1970s, challenge, subvert, and complicate the accepted ideological norms of anti-Japanese nationalism while superficially adhering to the latter.

The main texts taken up below are Ko Woo-young's *The Great Ambition* [*Tae-yamang*], and Hur Young-man's *The Bridal Mask* [*Kaksit'al*] and *The Iron Flute* [*Soet'ungso*].[1] These extremely popular works have been touted as models of "nationalist" narrative comics. However, contrary to popular perceptions, they illustrate complex and ambivalent interactions among the signifiers of ethnicity, nation, and social identities from the viewpoint of Koreans gazing back at their colonial experience. Instead of successfully suturing the wounds of the colonial domination by the Japanese, these texts problematize the very nature of these wounds, demonstrating the fundamental instability and fluidity of the "Korean" identity as constructed through nationalist discourse. This chapter explores the interstitial space between the increasingly sophisticated and multilayered efforts by students of Korean history and culture to analyze and understand the conditions of colonialism and postcolonialism on the one hand and the ever-urgent intellectual endeavors to make sense of the rapidly shifting grounds of political, social, and economic identities in the contemporary world, primarily characterized by the discourses of globalization and transnationalism, on the other.

As Khachig Tölöyan delineates in his prefatory essay to the inaugural issue of *Diaspora: A Journal of Transnational Studies*, the "transnational movement" was characterized by massive and instantaneous movement of capital, the introduction of "alien" cultures through the practice of "media imperialism," an increasingly "uncontrollable" influx of migrant workers, and plural affiliations of transnational corporations, affecting the manners in which the diaspora communities and nation-states interact with one another. The "nationalist" diasporic discourse, Tölöyan argues, has been characterized by its "silence" regarding "an endemic doubleness, or multiplicity of identities and loyalties" among the members of their communities, that was seen as necessary to maintenance of the integrity and preservation of the nation-state they ostensibly are "loyal" toward.[2] It is possible, however, that the new resources available since the last decades of the twentieth century are fundamentally challenging and shifting these deeply paradoxical relationships between the diaspora and the nation-state, as individuals become more open to the possibility of imagining personal identities decoupled from homogeneous (a very cherished myth in the case of both Koreans and Japanese) territorial communities.

If we add historical dimensions to the mix, this already convoluted picture is further complicated. "New" transnationalism certainly did not spring forth like Athena from the forehead of Zeus, fully formed and ready to claim her position as a new deity. It is a stage in the evolution of the transcommunal and transcultural relationships forged and dissolved throughout human history. The critical thing to remember is that imperialism and colonialism have been very important components, possibly *the* dominant forces, in creating these relationships in the modern world.

The Japanese empire and the colonized Korea in the first half of the twentieth century are not exceptions. The Japanese colonization of Korea has created a small number of diasporic communities devoted to "retrieval of the fatherland" and construction of a modern nation-state as well as the vast majority of Koreans who had to live, under a form of "double consciousness" or, as W. E. B. Du Bois so wrenchingly put it, "this sense of always looking at one's self through the eye of others, of measuring one's soul by the tape of a world that looks on in amused contempt and pity," even taking into account the relatively short duration of the Korean colonial experience compared with the experiences of many other colonized peoples.[3] To deny that the majority of Koreans had to grapple with "dual allegiance" and other problems of double consciousness under the Japanese colonial rule by claiming that Koreans, except for a few dastardly "collaborators," had always maintained their absolute fidelity to the fictive nation-state, the boundaries of which perfectly correspond to those of their ethnic and cultural identities, is to perpetuate the mythological hegemony of the ethnic nation over actual lived lives of Koreans.[4] This absolute dichotomy between "collaboration" and "resistance" in the Korean context is analogous to the postwar French myth of "total resistance" against the Nazi occupation and the Vichy regime, long since deconstructed by a significant output of scholarly research and, perhaps even more important, by artistic challenges from some of France's greatest filmmakers.[5]

Moreover, the Japanese empire by its nature was a multiethnic and multicultural entity that generated significant antinomies among its constituents, the "inland" (*naichi*) Japanese as well as the colonized Koreans. The reality of the multiethnic empire was far more important for Koreans than was ever properly acknowledged in postwar periods: it forced many of them to adjust to the conditions in which public and private, ethnic and national, and traditional and modern identities were often in conflict with one another in a single person. This reality was, for instance, acutely reflected in the self-perception and behavior of Korean settlers and migrants in Japan-created Manchukuo,[6] as we shall see in the case of Ko Woo-young below.

Few of these oscillations, bifurcations, negotiations, and reconfigurations of Korean identity were resolved to everybody's satisfaction following the defeat of the Japanese empire and reinstatement of "homogeneous" nation-states in the North and South. The colonial empire had already created a vast terrain of transnational relationships among Koreans, Japanese, Taiwanese,

Southeast Asians, Russians, and other ethnic/cultural groups in East Asia. To put it bluntly, it is a form of denial to pretend that these relationships and various forms of transnational culture constructed around them never existed and that any postcolonial reconfigurations of the identities could avoid dealing with these relationships, no matter how much nationalists and former imperialists wanted to "cleanse" (ch'ŏngsan) history of them.

Of course, even today there exist Japanese neoimperialists who attempt to exercise their hegemonic domination over Koreans and Korean-Japanese minorities (so-called zainichi) via extension of their colonial practices and ideologies. However, this fact does not obviate the need for students of Korean and Japanese history and culture to problematize the ways in which both Korean and Japanese national identities are reinforced by the "actually existing" transnationality of the relationships between Koreans and Japanese. One of the objectives of this chapter is to stress again that the exploration of postwar Korean popular culture cannot be adequately carried out without paying serious attention to how the legacy of colonial modernity of Korea[7] has suppressed this memory of "dual consciousness," with its implications of hybridity, malleability, and, ironically, strong individual agency. This type of absolutist nationalism, embraced by so many Koreans, negates their ability to negotiate whatever resources are available for them that they could use to construct their identities rather than succumb to some prefabricated and imposed-from-the-top-down notions of race, ethnicity, and cultural belonging. A fully integrated perspective is required, one that considers Koreans and Japanese first as complex human beings rather than representative units of the ethnic, national, or cultural entities they supposedly belong to. This redirection by no means automatically leads to "rehabilitation" of the colonial practices, as some critics and intellectuals seem to think; indeed, it is an essential step in diagnosing the true pathologies generated by colonialism and imperialism. As Gi-wook Shin rightly points out, while the Koreans certainly have had strong historically based causes to prioritize building of their own territorial nation-states in the early twentieth century, "the liberating potential of nationalism can be easily converted to the basis or rationale for domination and repression, intolerance and persecution, as seen in postcolonial Korea," both North and South.[8]

Thus, we must begin the analysis with the acknowledgment that despite Korea's "independence," the transnational conditions first occasioned by Japanese colonialism continued to inform ideologies, discourses, and practices in postwar Korea, no less so in the cultural realm than in the political and economic. The historical-theoretical reflections point to one of the reasons, other than their sheer popularity and superb skills as comic artists, this chapter focuses on Ko Woo-young (1938–2005) and Hur Young-man (1947-). Ko and Hur, despite their age differences, shared some intriguing commonalities relevant to the issues at hand. They had grown up within families positioned in the elite and/or administrative strata during the colonial period. In the postwar era, both men were objects of severe censure by the military dictatorship regimes yet kept a certain distance from direct political engagement. Both produced a stunning number of works that covered a wide range of genres and approaches, from martial arts, sports, romance, and period pieces to contemporary "business" comics, and at each phase of their careers they were able to renew their appeals to new demographic and new generations of readers. Both successfully adapted to or weathered maelstroms of industrial transformations and social changes in the 1970s, 1980s, and 1990s yet managed to train a significant number of protégés as well. In any conceivable way you want to define them, they are still representative comic artists of postwar South Korea. But it is their creative engagement with the troubling aspects of their own identities and modern Korean history that ultimately distinguish them as remarkable artists in the context of this essay.

The works by Ko and Hur must be placed in the larger context of the evolution of Korean comic arts in the postwar period. Already in the early 1950s there had been unmistakable signs of powerful emergence of *manhwa* as a medium of artistic and commercial expression, following genealogies of the Japan-imported modern visual art as well as those of traditional (precolonial) Korean popular culture. Magazines devoted to the comics were sprouting in the postliberation period of relative creative freedom, with the establishment of *Comics March (Manhwa haengjin)* in 1948, *Comics News (Manhwa nyus)* in 1949, and *Comics World (Manhwa segye)* in 1956. During this period, some pioneering works of postwar Korean *manhwa* were created and even enjoyed great popularity. Pak Ki-dang (1922–1979), who debuted as a cartoonist during the Korean War and also was a famous illustrator, produced a series of graphic narratives strongly reminiscent of popular colonial-period literature such as *ttakjibon* (colorful Korean equivalent of dime-store novels) but showcasing startling sophistication in character design and plotting. In his version of *The Journey to the West (Son O-gong,* 1957), an epic graphic novel by the 1950s standard (amounting to 250 pages when published as a hardcover from Sŏngmunsa), one can clearly see a stylistic transition (or merger, if you will) between illustrations for written text on the one hand and comic books on the other. There are relatively long stretches of text, a mixture of dialogues, and author's narrations and descriptions of events, yet the graphic portion is presented with a strong sense of dynamism, employing devices such as curved lines and puffs of smoke indicating fast movement and impact/explosion. This style further evolves into a division of labor between narrated text and characters' dialogue in "bubbles" for *The Chinese Fiddle of Tears* (*Nunmul ŭi hogung*, 1960) and *Gaus the Space Alien* (*Yusŏng'in Gausu*, 1961), a technique that yields a unique effect, akin to watching a film with subtitles in one's own language.[9]

Another artist, Kim San-ho (aka San Ho, 1939–), created what is undoubtedly Korea's first heroic science-fiction comic, *Raipai the Herald of Justice* (*Chŏng'ŭi ŭi saja raip'ai*), published between 1959 and 1962 as a four-part, thirty-two-volume series. Raipai was clearly modeled after American superheroes of the prewar era rather than a Japanese one: a hypermasculine, masked hero à la Zorro, decked with a cape and a Korean consonant *riŭl* emblazoned on his chest instead of the capital letter *S*.[10] Like Batman, he owns a custom-made airplane, *Swallow*, and operates inside a secret base dug into the Taebaek Mountains. *Raipai* introduced such stylistic innovations as diagonally drawn block-letter onomatopoeia (in the manner of American "Splat!" or "Pow!") to Korean comic arts. It makes sense that the next phase of Kim San-ho's career was to work as a comic artist in the United States, producing *Ghostly Tales* and *The Cheyenne Kid* for Charlton Comics and other American companies. What is remarkable in *Raipai* is that there is little in settings, characterizations, or designs that reminds us of Japanese manga, or animation; we cannot help but speculate what the status of sci-fi comics in Korea would be today had other talented artists been allowed to follow in the pioneering footsteps of Kim San-ho.[11]

It would be a gross simplification to assume that the rampant copying of Japanese manga by Korean comic producers between the late 1960s and 1980s—a matter of historical record—was the direct consequence of Japanese colonial domination of Korea. There is definitely a connection between the colonial modernity and its impact on Korean visual arts and media on the one hand and the powerful influence, both open and clandestine, of Japanese manga (animation) on Korean *manhwa* on the other, but such connection did not have to result in the glut of copycat manga that saturated the market up to the late 1980s. This phenomenon of mass-product copying involved, broadly speaking, what Koichi Iwabuchi describes as removal of "cultural odor": the imagery, signifiers, and tropes that reminded the Korean consumers of the Japanese culture. Yet in some cases, the products barely went through the process of "deodorization"—compared to, say, how Americans have "cleansed" Pokémon or other problematic Japanese products for consumption by the family audience. Consequently, Korean consumers were likely aware of the Japanese origins.[12] In any case, this situation is more properly understood as a consequence of the growth of the consumer market in South Korea, wherein mass production of comic arts has become an urgent necessity, accompanied by the ostensibly nationalistic practice of banning importation of the Japanese cultural goods in the name of protecting domestic production. Ironically but logically, once globalization really impacted the Korean market, copycat activities were no longer commercially urgent and died down to the extent that the mainstream media stopped deploying the issue as a fodder for ritualistic Japan-bashing campaigns.

There is no denying the fact that some of the biggest hits in the Korean comic scene in the 1970s and 1980s were pirated copies of the Japanese manga with barely an attempt to assign a Korean byname: Yokoyama Mitsuteru's *Babel the Second* (*Babiru Nisei*, 1971–73), Watanabe Masako's *The Glass Castle* (*Garasu no shiro*, 1969–70), and Igarashi Yumiko and Nagita Keiko's (aka Mizuki Kyōko) *Candy Candy* (*Kyandei Kyandei*, 1975–79), among many. Truthfully, few comic books by Korean authors from the 1970s to the early 1980s were able to define a generation's collective taste in popular culture the way these Japanese works had done. The earliest known example of the copying of the Japanese comic book is *Prince of the Jungle* (*Milim ŭi wangja*), a duplication of Yamakawa Sōji's *Kenya the Boy* (*Shōnen Kenia*, 1951–55), but with its Japanese background whitewashed (including a reference to the Pearl Harbor attack). Perhaps *Kenya the Boy* was chosen for its relative lack of the overt signs of "Japaneseness" and thus was less malodorous, as Iwabuchi's theory suggests, as were subsequent pirated versions that proved hits in the Korean market. According to the recollections of the comic artist Pak Ki-jun, Sŏ Pong-jae, who was responsible for "adapting" *Kenya the Boy*, quit the job because of the outrageously cut-rate payment; the publisher hired another comic artist but insisted that he use tracing paper to make an exact copy of the original, a practice that was unfortunately adopted and abused for nearly three decades in the Korean comic scene.[13]

With the liberalization of importation of Japanese cultural products in 1987, the Korean magazine *IQ Jump* serialized Toriyama Akira's *Dragon Ball* (*Doragon bōru*, 1984–95), signing a legitimate contract with Toriyama's BIRD Studio. This agreement opened up the path for Korean *manhwa* and Japanese manga to coexist in the domestic market. It was soon followed by the great success of Inoue Takehiko's *Slam Dunk* (*Suramu danku*, 1990–96). Although many opinion-makers in the late 1980s and early 1990s were exaggeratedly worried that the kind of sexually stimulating, high-energy Japanese manga would overwhelm the Korean market,[14] what happened in real life was that some Korean *manhwa* artists were able to adapt certain aspects of these manga into their own styles, while others went in countervailing directions, striving to find the alternative to the manga styles.

The conditions that drove many comic artists to copy Japanese manga for mass consumption were partly economic and partly political. In July 1967, a cartel of cartoon publishers named United Publishers (Haptong Ch'ulpansa) was created, monopolizing the distribution routes of comic books (the majority of which by then relied on rental outlets), distributing projects to the comic artists in the manner of sweatshop factories, and blackballing any artist who resisted this oppression and sought an alternative route of publication. The monopoly was briefly threatened when the Seoul daily newspaper *Hankook Ilbo* jumped into the *manhwa*-publishing bandwagon, but the latter's practice in the big picture was hardly different from that of United Publishers. This horrid situation forced many comic artists— including Ko Woo-young, who was making his mark by drawing one of the most distinctive children's comics to emerge in Korea, *Dr. Bighead* (*Jjanggu paksa*, that was actually the invention of his second-older brother, Ko Il-yŏng)—to abandon the rental market and seek out magazines and newspapers as alternative venues.

In addition, South Korean government censorship under President Park Chung-Hee found *manhwa* a convenient scapegoat for its campaign for social "cleansing." The Korean Books and Magazine Ethics Committee (Hanguk Tosŏ Chapchi Yulli Wiwŏnhoe), established in 1970 and adding newspapers to the objects of its surveillance in 1976, oversaw a semiannual pogrom against "licentious" comics "harmful to children." Mainstream media happily joined in the ritual persecution of *manhwa*, which reached its zenith (or nadir) in sensationalization of the February 1972 suicide of a young boy named Chŏng Pyŏng-sŏp, who allegedly had told his sister that he wanted to experiment and see if he could come back from life "like comic characters do," before hanging himself to death. But even before this incident, in 1971 the government impounded and destroyed 25,026 titles of "degenerate comics." Interestingly, of these the largest number, 4,936 titles, were war comics, suggesting the censorship on "excessive violence" might have been based on ulterior motives.[15] Censorship and media criticism dwelled on the perception that "licentious" and "promiscuous" Japanese popular culture was being absorbed into Korea via the pirated Japanese manga. Ironically, persecution and scapegoating of *manhwa* as a symptom of social ills often made such pathological dependence on the Japanese manga one of the few available options for survival that the Korean comic artists had at their disposal.

Despite the waves of persecution, new types of magazines for children, more expensive-looking with glossy covers and color illustrations, were opening up fresh venues for narrative comics. *The New Youth* (*Saesonyŏn*, 1964), *Shoulder to Shoulder with Friends* (*Ŏkkae tongmu*, 1967), and *The Chung'ang Youth* (*Sonyŏn Chung'ang*, 1969) quickly became essential companions for children growing up in the late 1960s and 1970s. Surprisingly, *Shoulder to Shoulder with Friends* was published and funded by the Yugyŏng Foundation, created by Park Chung-Hee's second wife, Yuk Yŏng-su, but was free of propagandistic hues and published many cutting-edge narrative comics by top artists of the times (including Hur Young-man's *Iron Flute*). Another trend was the resurgence of adult comics, following the movement of monthly adult magazines into a weekly format and resulting in the great success of *Sunday Seoul* (*Sŏndei sŏul*, 1968), one of the most popular tabloid weeklies of postwar Korea. Such well-known adult comic works as Pak Su-dong's *Dolmen* (*Koindol*, serialized from 1974) and Pang Hak-ki's *Baridegi* (serialized from 1977) first debuted in *Sunday Seoul*.[16]

Ko Woo-young, who had been eking out a life supplying pictures for other artists in the late 1960s, made a transition to children's magazines. His groundbreaking success came when Chang Ki-yŏng, president of Hankook Ilbo Media Group (which included *Hankook Ilbo*), decided that serialized narrative comic with fairly adult content could be published via newspaper. He wanted to try his idea in one of their other publications, *The Sports Daily* (*Ilgan sŭp'och'ŭ*); his decision was met with considerable objections from the staff, who did not believe cartoons with more than four panels could attract the attention of its readers. However, he silenced naysayers and gave Ko an opportunity to serialize *Im Kkŏk-jŏng*, the story of a legendary Chosŏn dynasty-era bandit, in *The Sports Daily*, beginning in 1972. The response was overwhelmingly positive: Ko's period piece epic, full of graphic scenes of violence (challenged from the get-go by government censors) and detailed, anatomically realistic depictions of human bodies, was said to have been a major contribution to the dramatic increase of *The Sports Daily*'s circulation numbers from 20,000 in 1972 to 300,000 in 1975.[17]

Ko's success with *Im Kkŏk-jŏng* saved him and his family from potential poverty and more or less defined the next phase of his comic artist career as an adult period-piece specialist. His realistic drawing style in that mode can trace its lineage to the Kyoto-born comic artist Kim Chong-rae (popular for *Red Earth* [*Bulgŭn ttang*, 1954], an exemplary anti-Communist propaganda piece, and *The Horizon of Tears* [*Nunmul ŭi supyŏngsŏn*, 1955], a sentimental tearjerker), Pak Kwang-hyŏn (*Shadowless Vengeance* [*Kŭrimja ŏpnŭn poksu*, 1958]), and the aforementioned Pak Ki-dang. However, Ko elevated Pak Ki-dang's graphic dynamism to a new level of sophistication, adding extremely realistic depictions of bloodletting, bodily impact, and fast-moving objects to the mix. I am almost tempted to claim that it was Ko who truly made the masculine bodies in comic arts *sexual*, effortlessly bridging the gap between the suppressed sensuality of his children's comics and the overt sexuality of his adult comics, in a manner perhaps analogous to the works of Tezuka Osamu.

Moreover, Ko has never given up on the author-narration/character-dialogue dichotomy discussed above in Pak's works; instead of shunning them as outmoded styles, he cleverly adapted them to enrich his narrative comics. Inserting himself as the author-narrator is one of his self-depricatingly humorous routines in his period pieces. For instance, Ko clearly models Liu Bei in the adult comic *Romance of the Three Kingdoms* (*Samgukchi*, 1978) after his self-portrait, while continuously intervening in the narrative to indicate his favoritism toward Guan Yu. Yet, in a deliberately contradictory move, Ko strips Liu Bei of the heroic qualities of loyalty and (Confucian) righteousness, a strategy that subtly shifts reader sympathy toward the antihero, Cao Cao.[18] Ko's refusal to capitulate to the accepted moral values and social attitudes tends toward creative frictions with objectives of the comics intended for children or young adults. This makes *The Great Ambition*, his transitory work between children's and adult comics serialized in *The New Youth* magazine from 1975 to 1977, especially interesting.

The Great Ambition is putatively a nationalist sports *manhwa*, in which a Korean tae kwon do master fights and subdues foreign opponents (sometimes depicted in a racist manner commensurate with the attitude toward foreigners in 1970s Korea). What is interesting is that its protagonist, Ōyama Masutatsu, whose Korean name is Ch'oe Yŏng-ŭi, in real life practiced karate, not tae kwon do; furthermore he served the cause of postwar Japanese nationalism (even of the right-wing, chauvinist type) by publicizing karate in the world, just as Rikidōzan, another Korean-Japanese sports figure, contributed to building postwar Japanese nationalism via his promotion of pro-wrestling in early 1960s.[19] In a trenchant case of transnational identity formation, rooted in the colonial period and since 1945 mobilized by the nation-states on both sides of the 38th parallel for their own ideological purposes, the Koreans living in Japan have often been used as a subject in Korean popular culture to promote anti-Communism, portraying the Korean-Japanese in the Chōsen Sōren (General Association of the Korean Residents in Japan) as Communist villains spying for North Korea, and ethnic nationalism, casting Koreans as a persecuted minority in Japanese society. In terms of narrative comics, Pak Ki-chŏng's *White Cloud, Black Cloud* (*Hŭin gurŭm, kŏmun gurŭm*, 1963), and *The Challenger* (*Tojŏnja*, 1964–

65) may be cited as classic examples. The latter is interesting as a precedent for *The Great Ambition* in that it also involves a young Korean armed with fierce nationalist ideology, struggling against Japanese influence in the realm of sports, in this case, pro boxing. Despite the protagonist Hun's excessive machismo and almost pathological attachment to his ethnic identity (at one point, he violently beats up an arrogant Japanese girl until she loses consciousness, announcing, "I can tolerate insulting me but I won't stand for you insulting my country!"), the author appears to be camouflaging Hun's strong class resentment and a sense of existential alienation by making Japan stand in for contemporary Korea. The "Japaneseness" of the background in *The Challenger*, therefore, is neither particularly detailed nor realistic. This is not the case with *The Great Ambition*, where Japanese characters and settings are illustrated with almost ethnographic detail.[20]

The Great Ambition is technically exacting and boldly experimental, with much of the drawing techniques used in ways to invoke cinematic experience. For instance, there is a magnificently rendered fight sequence between its hero, Ōyama, and the Chinese practitioners of tai chi chuan (tai chi). Here Ko deftly employs all manners of cinematic techniques—montage, time dilation, selective use of close-ups, and even "vibrating blurs," as if the camera observing the characters in a comic panel is violently shaking— to maximize the suspense and impact of their life-or-death struggles (see plate 1). Other pages showcase adaptations of such cinematic techniques as transition through parallel movement (from a stream of torn papers to a collection of national flags fluttering) and slow motion. One page even goes as far as to "slot" panels as if they are individual frames of film footage (see fig. 2.1).[21]

Ko's character depiction also strikes the delicate balance between portraiture and caricature, pushing cartoon conventions like sweat drops and double take toward more naturalistic but not entirely photo-realistic directions. The expressions of anger (often represented by slightly exaggerated gritting of teeth) and sorrow (Ko is a master of simulated lighting effects that keep a character's eyes in the shadows) as well as other complicated emotional states such as maintenance of a poker face or a low level of anxiety is superbly executed in *The Great Ambition*. In short, as an action comic eliciting the desired sense of excitement and awe from a viewer and in its character dynamism and restrained realism, Ko's *Great Ambition* can fully match or compare favorably with any Japanese *gekika* (more realistic adult manga, such as Chiba Tetsuya's *Joe of Tomorrow* [*Ashita no Jō*, 1968–73] or Saitō Takao's *Golgo 13* [*Gorugo Satīn*, 1968–present]) of similar genre and vintage.

Figure 2.1. Oyama/Ch'oe beats his opponent, a judo master, by landing a midair kick on the latter's jaw. "SLAMMMM!"

136

Now, one might contend that what Ko has done is substantially no different from the "cultural deodorization" by countless pirate *manhwa*, who had appropriated Japanese characters, plots, and ideas and simply switched them into Korean ones, say, turning a Japanese imperialist into a Korean nationalist with a quick redressing of costumes and makeup (sometimes literally). This criticism, however, is untenable in the case of *The Great Ambition*, and not merely because Ko's work is a complete original that does not originate from an existing Japanese comic, for there are unmistakable undercurrents of unease and ambivalence regarding the hero Ch'oe Paedal's (Ōyama's) "Korean" identity throughout the work. Despite the series' outward claim that Ch'oe/Ōyama is a pure-blooded Korean nationalist, there is no depiction of interaction between him and Koreans living in Korea, except during the colonial period, wherein Koreans are basically background dressing representing the generic "oppressed."

Moreover, in depicting his fight against Muay Thai boxers and Chinese kung fu artists, Ko slips in the painful history of Japanese wartime abuse of Southeast Asian and Chinese populations. Instead of simply disinfecting

닭고기 빛보다 더 붉은 하늘과 땅….

그야말로 온 천지가 저녁놀 속에서 빨간색으로 변하고 있었습니다.

지평선은 보이지도 않았습니다. 온통 불붙는 듯이 적황색으로 장관을 이루고 있어서… 오늘 이 순간까지 짙은 기억으로 남아 있습니다.

우리가 봉천역에 도착해서 널따란 플랫폼에 내려섰을 때는 이미 어두운 밤이 되어 있었습니다.

으리으리한 역 건물을 걸어 나올 때 여러 사람의 얘기 소리와 빨간 모자를 쓴 짐꾼들의 달구지 소리… 그리고 우리의 구두 소리가 천장에 메아리치던 것을 기억합니다.

그리고 처음 보는 봉천시…

눈부신 네온사인과 울긋불긋한 간판, 그리고 중국식의 상점 깃발들….

13

Figure 2.2. Oyama/Ch'oe recollects arriving at the Fengtian train station for the first time, to live at his father's ranch in Manchuria.

the narrative of any tinge of Japanese imperialist history, he makes the Thai people's anti-Japanese sentiments a misdirected anger and yet another obstacle for Ch'oe/Ōyama to overcome as a great martial artist. After triumphing over a Muay Thai boxer named King Cobra, Ch'oe/Ōyama tearfully entreats the angry and disappointed Thai audience not to blame him for the Japanese "evils" because he is a Korean. It is interesting that this episode is followed by a short passage in which he attempts to briefly explain to the readers, somewhat abashedly, why, if he loves Korean people so much, he is still living in Japan (and working as a Japanese karate expert[22]); this short insert raises more questions than answers and feels like a gesture of obligation.

Later in the story, Ko chronicles the early, privileged life of Ōyama/Ch'oe in Japan-occupied Manchuria of the late 1930s and early 1940s with heart-rending lyricism. "Moving out of the grandiose [Fengtian] station, I remember people's chatting voices, noises of the luggage carts pulled by red-capped workers and of our footsteps echoing in the sky-high ceiling," the latter recalls (see fig. 2.2). This is when we realize that the unstated affinity between

Ōyama/Ch'oe and Ko was their Manchurian childhoods, remembered with great nostalgia and which ultimately were responsible for their ambivalent identities as "Koreans." Ko's own autobiography details in beautifully evocative prose his childhood as the third son of a police officer who later settled in the Manchurian frontier as a ranch owner and a local notable and of a talented "modern woman" said to have passed the entrance examination for the Tokyo Imperial University Medical School. He recalls with little self-rationalization his experience of looking down on the Northeastern Chinese as an underclass unworthy of human contact and the utter alienation he felt from "fellow" Koreans (and the Korean language) as well as the thorough relief and sense of normalcy he felt in company of the Japanese, when he and his family had to escape into the northern part of the Korean peninsula and later across the 38th parallel following the defeat of the Japanese empire.[23] At this juncture, we cannot help but wonder if Ko, in trying to pass Ōyama/Ch'oe as an aggressive Korean nationalist, is overcompensating for his proximity to the Japanese as well as his "incomplete" Koreanness as a child growing up in the multicultural Manchukuo.

Yet *The Great Ambition* ultimately subverts its own nationalist agenda by rendering the question of ethnic/national identity unresolved and ambivalent. Like the Japanese sports manga Kajiwara Ikki's *Karate baka ichidai* (1971–77) dealing with Ōyama's life and his karate school (Kokushin Karate), a large chunk of *The Great Ambition* is devoted to Ōyama's disciple Ashiwara Hideyuki and his effort to establish the Kokushin Karate *dōjō* in Shikoku. Many fans of the comic series remember these episodes as the most moving portions of the whole, but here Ashiwara is clearly a Japanese, and a Korean nationalist rhetoric or anxiety about Korean ethnic identity has no place in his relationship with Ch'oe/Ōyama. In other words, he interacts only with the karate master as Ōyama Masutsu, his "Japanese" sensei. However, the latter also grapples with the tragic death of another disciple, Ariake Shōgo, presented as a shadow/anima figure (in the Jungian sense) to Ashiwara. When Ariake is first introduced, there is no indication that he is not a Japanese, but during the final chapter of the series, he is revealed as a Korean-Japanese struggling between his Japanese father's love for him and his devotion to tae kwon do, and by implication his own Korean ethnicity, ultimately resulting in an explosion of violence and James Dean–like death in a car crash.

Why did Ko bring to a close the entire enterprise, an epic narrative of a nationalist hero, on such a tragic note that reverberates with the sense of a failure? True, Ariake's story might have been a faithful rendition of what really happened, but in other portions of the comic (for instance, in Ashiwara's story), Ko shows no hesitation in adding fictional details and deleting certain inconvenient facts such as Ashiwara's real-life bitter breakup with his sensei to make the story more positive and moving. Would it be amiss to hypothesize that the melancholy and passivity afflicting the denouement of *The Great Ambition* signal an implosion of the nationalist project? Perhaps Ariake was destroyed not by Japanese intolerance for Koreans, as the surface reading of the plot might indicate, but by the unacknowledged understanding that the only true recognition as a person he (and by extension Ch'oe/Ōyama as well as the author, Ko) ever received was from the Japanese (represented by Ariake's adoptive father). The elder Ariake's love for his son is so movingly portrayed, the reader cannot but feel frustration or even anger toward the latter's refusal to accept it in the name of maintaining racial/ethnic differentiation between Koreans and Japanese. Ariake's single-minded devotion to tae kwon do almost begins to feel like a mirror image of the sense of superiority held by the colonial-period Japanese against other ethnic/national groups.

As an effort to suture the wound of Korean (and Manchurian) colonial experience by transfiguring the problematic body of a colonial hybrid character, who in social terms was Japanese *and* Korean, *The Great Ambition* is, I would argue, not successful at all. In its failure, nevertheless, Ko Woo-young maintained his integrity as an artist: in the end his own identity was too "hybrid" for him to maintain the charade of passing off Ōyama Masutatsu as Ch'oe Yŏng-ŭi, a pure-blooded Korean nationalist. Rather than merely copying Japanese manga to hypocritically and schizophrenically tell the narrative of anti-Japanese nationalism, Ko brings the Korean-Japanese (as well as "only Korean" and "only Japanese") characters and their dilemmas to the foreground, where it is acknowledged that their identities are not as stable as we presume them to be.

Just as Ko was emerging as a major star with a series of comic works based on Chinese literary classics, Hur Young-man famously debuted in 1974 with *Homebound Journey* (*Chibŭl ch'ajasŏ*). The comic work received great notice in a public contest, allegedly compelling one of the judges, the renowned cartoonist Sin Tong-u, to proclaim that "with a young genius like this coming around we oldsters should all retire."[24] In his apprenticeship days Hur first exclusively worked on the teen romance genre and, not unlike Ko, only gradually evolved his distinctive style, which maintains the right balance between the traditions of masculine realism (inherited from Pak Ki-dang, Ko Woo-young) and comic caricature (influenced by Kim Yong-hwan, Yi Hyang-wŏn). Hur then launched *The Bridal Mask* (*Kaksit'al*) in 1974, first serialized as bonus supplements to the monthly student magazine *Good*

Student (Udŭngsaeng) and later published in individual volumes, an immediate hit that put him in the constellation as a new star on the rise.

Interestingly, Hur has been accused of both extreme nationalism and overreliance on Japanese templates and character types. Critic Kim Yi-rang cites examples of *The Bridal Mask* and *The Asphalt Man (Asŭp'altŭ sanai,* 1991, adapted into TV drama in 1995) to discuss Hŏ's "self-reflective, defensive and open nationalism," which appears to be an almost subconscious compensation for having been "influenced too much" by the trendy Japanese manga.[25] This is an interesting observation, yet I still feel that Kim is not giving enough credit to the complexities of *The Bridal Mask* and its later variant, *The Iron Flute (Soet'ungso,* serialized in *Shoulder to Shoulder with Friends* in 1982).

The Bridal Mask does feature a typical nationalist heroic narrative, with the colonial-period Japanese police set up as villains, against whom a masked Korean superhero commits various acts of sabotage and mayhem barehandedly, employing his tae kwon do skills. Provocatively, *The Bridal Mask*'s hero, Yi Kang-t'o (a homonym for "This Land of Ours" in Korean, a recurring personage in some of Hur's narrative comics), starts out as a pro-Japanese collaborator working for the Japanese police in rooting out Korean "criminals" (independence movement activists). When he realizes that he shot his own brother in the course of his "job," Kim is devastated. He dons a traditional Korean mask owned by his brother to reinvent himself as a nationalist superhero: the Bridal Mask. *The Bridal Mask* unflinchingly shows the strains this secret identity imposes on the protagonist, and the profound sense of guilt that he carries throughout the series nearly overwhelms the kind of ethnocentric pleasure a reader might expect from a garden-variety anti-Japanese pop culture product. His secret identity isolates him from his Japanese friends as well as from a "normal" life as a middle-class citizen, and Hur does not gloss over these painful conditions with lip service to the glory of the Korean nation. Moreover, Hur refuses to portray the Japanese police or even military figures as congenitally evil villains to be knocked down like bowling pins. His depiction of the colonial Korea is not a row of shantytowns spotted by a few glittering houses owned by the Japanese. Many Koreans live comfortably, with or without explicit "collaborationist" ties to the colonial authorities.

Given *The Bridal Mask*'s reputation as an anti-Japanese comic narrative, its depiction of Korean-Japanese interaction is impressively thoughtful for a popular cultural work commercially produced in the 1970s, all the more so considering that it is entirely fictional, unlike *The Great Ambition*. Hur, despite the overlaid anti-Japanese and ethnocentric rhetoric that frequently invokes supremacy of the Korean ethnicity, tacitly admits through his characterizations and narrative turns that ethnic/national differences between Koreans and Japanese can be superseded by other concerns such as class consciousness, familial relations, and political beliefs. An episode in which a mysterious character called Motorcycle Man joins the Bridal Mask in acts of antimilitary sabotage illustrates this point. In a terrific mystery plot, the readers are led to think that the Motorcycle Man is another Korean nationalist, but his real persona is revealed to be a mild-mannered, bookish son of a high-ranking Japanese military-police officer. The Motorcycle Man is a closet leftist intellectual. The episode ends tragically, in a variant replay of the Bridal Mask's own life history. The military officer (who is also far from an ugly, buck-toothed caricature of an evil Japanese soldier) kills his own son, pleading to him to open his eyes to the larger truth of "sharing with those who are in greater needs"; then the father commits suicide (because of the guilt for having killed his son, it is made clear by the author, and not because of a sense of responsibility as a soldier in the Imperial Army). The episode ends with a middle-aged Korean woman mourning the death of the young Japanese man, remembering his (perhaps trivial) expression of kindness to her, amid the indifference of other Koreans, and joined by the saddened Bridal Mask in his "civilian" identity as Kangt'o.[26]

Indeed, as is the case with Pak Ki-jŏng's *Challenger* discussed above, there is a strong undercurrent of social and political criticism directed at the Korean society of the 1970s, underneath the anti-Japanese rhetoric. Hur himself hints at this in his new preface for the reprint edition of *The Bridal Mask* (which contains the first seven episodes of the series originally serialized in *Udŭngsaeng* [Honor student] magazine in 1976): "[The Bridal Mask] was a story of our people resisting the Japanese colonial domination, but also was a comic book that kicked butt, shouting 'eat this, you bastards,' of the ridiculous social structure of the times."[27] The Japanese militarists and the rich and powerful who collaborate with them are in important ways stand-ins for the Korean military dictatorship and the elite classes whose social success was marked by their capitulation to the former.

The Iron Flute expands on *The Bridal Mask*'s basic premise. Here the distance between Korean and Japanese identities has been brought even closer. As with *The Bridal Mask*, the protagonist Yi Kang-t'o (different figure from *The Bridal Mask*'s hero) starts out as an underling of the Japanese police, but his superpower of choice is Japanese kendo skills (he uses an iron flute instead of a bamboo sword to subdue his opponent) rather than Korean tae kwon do. This makes sense, since the original Iron Flute, whose mantle Yi inherits, turns out to be a Japanese friend of his, Uehara. The indescribable shock and trauma of this "reveal" is brilliantly depicted, almost surrealistically with melting faces and extreme distortions of comic panels, literally as a vision of Kang-t'o's mental universe collapsing unto itself. In *The Bridal Mask*, this moment of trauma that defines the protagonist's guilt is related to the readers in a flashback and therefore has much less visceral impact.

Iron Flute's ending is again in a way analogous to the dour (and terribly unsatisfying for the devoted readers who have remained faithful to the work's surface ideology) ending of *The Great Ambition*, almost absurdly tragic and ambivalent in meaning. Kang-t'o's Iron Flute essentially plays second fiddle to a fierce female character who trains wolves to kill a Japanese hunter responsible for the death of her husband, a hunting guide. But she takes her own life, unable to overcome the guilt of having drowned the wolves she herself trained. (The extremely frightening scene in which she is confronted by half-drowned wolves in her room is straight out of a horror film.) Kang-t'o witnesses all this but is utterly incapable of helping her or the wolves. As he stands in shock before the dead bodies, a young Japanese soldier, driven out of his wits by fear and confusion, shoots Kang-t'o dead. By the time this ending has rolled in, the righteousness of Korean nationalism and the evilness of Japanese colonialism have become secondary concerns, overwhelmed by a profound sense of despair, based on the suggestion that victims of oppression will in turn become victimizers, until it all ends in an apocalyptic destruction of everything.[28]

Despite his reputation as a nationalist, Hur's early hits attest to the patterns of complicated engagement with colonial history, imbued with a strong undercurrent of the skepticism directed at ideological certainties of nationalism and imperialism. He does not display the symptoms of having encountered the aporia of ethnic/national identity as do Ko Woo-young and his fictional stand-in, Ch'oe/Ōyama, in *The Great Ambition*, perhaps lacking their foundational experience of having lived in 1930s Manchuria, or more accurately Manchukuo, a space invented by the Japanese empire. But Hur shares with Ko the experience of having a father who was a police officer during the colonial period and also suffered through the trauma of the Yŏsu Incident (1948), during which Syngman Rhee's army, in the course of suppressing Communist rebel soldiers, persecuted and killed many civilians. This background, as critic Pak Sŏk-hwan points out, partly explains one striking characteristic of Hur's protagonists, their ambivalence toward their father(-figures).[29] But it also partly explains Hur's desire to promote masculine Korean nationalism on the outside as well as his propensity to destabilize this ostensible objective by questioning the basis of ethnic/national differentiation among the characters and implicitly showing that nationalism is just as ideological as Communism or Japanese imperialism. As Kang-t'o in *The Iron Flute* plaintively asks in confusion, "If Iron Flute who fought against the Japanese invaders was himself Japanese, what does that make me?"

As discussed above, Ko Woo-young and Hur Young-man's 1970s narrative comics dealing with the colonial experience and Korean nationalism are not quite what they have been known to be. These works problematize the ostensible ideological objectives of Korean nationalism by revealing how difficult (in truth, impossible) it is to whitewash the colonial hybridity of the modern "Korean" through attempts to artificially construct the morally clear-cut fantasy universe populated by "good" Japanese and "bad" Koreans. By complicating the identities and internal dispositions of the heroes themselves, the Bridal Mask and the Iron Flute emerge as pioneering figures in the annals of Korean superheroes, paralleling the evolution some American comic superheroes such as Batman had gone through during the 1960s and 1970s, from straightforward champions of American values and hegemony to psychologically tormented, morally flawed individuals unable to resolve real-life problems even with their superpowers. Ultimately they are unable (or unwilling) to suture the wounds of the colonial experience with the ideology of nationalism.

However, these failures constitute precisely one of the most important reasons these works continue to speak to us today. Even though they are products of the agonizing fissures and divisions in modern Korean identity, partaking of the colonial legacy as well as transnational exchange between postwar Korea and Japan in the realm of culture and arts, Ko Woo-young and Hur Young-man were able to utilize them as resources for their creative engagement with the very uncertainties and instabilities in that identity. It is this acknowledgment of and willingness to grapple with the psychological and cultural exigencies brought about by the modern history of Korea that mark Ko and Hur as brilliant artists, rather than their (surface) capitulation to the nationalist rhetoric that claims the superiority of the Korean race but paradoxically sees them (us) as eternal victims of history.

NOTES

1. I have followed the Anglicized spellings adopted by Ko and Hur (in the case of the former, when he was still alive) but kept the McCune-Reischauer system of alphabetization for other names throughout this essay.
2. Khachig Tölöyan, "The Nation-State and Its Others: In Lieu of a Preface," *Diaspora: A Journal of Transnational Studies* 1, no. 1 (1991): 3–7.
3. W. E. B. DuBois, "Of Our Spiritual Strivings," *The Souls of Black Folk* (Rockville, MD: Ace Minor, 2008), 12.

4. See Hildi Kang, *Under the Black Umbrella: Voices from Colonial Korea* (Ithaca, NY: Cornell University Press, 2005) for vivid and powerful first-person accounts of Koreans from a variety of socioeconomic backgrounds living under colonial conditions.

5. Compare Henry Rousso, *The Vichy Syndrome: History and Memory in France Since 1944* (Cambridge, MA: Harvard University Press, 1994) to the films *La chagrin et la pitié* [*The Sorrow and the Pity*] (directed by Marcel Ophuls, 1969), *Au revoir les enfants* [Good-bye, children) (directed by Louis Malle, 1987), *Une affaire de femmes* [*Story of Women*] (directed by Claude Chabrol, 1988), *L'oeil de Vichy* [*The Eye of Vichy*] (directed by Claude Chabrol, 1993), and more.

6. See Suk-Jung Han, "Those Who Imitated the Colonizers: The Legacy of the Disciplining State from Manchukuo to South Korea," in *Crossed Histories: Manchuria in the Age of Empire*, ed. Mariko Tamanoi (Honululu: University of Hawai'i Press, 2005).

7. On this point, see Shin Gi-wook and Michael Robinson, eds. *Colonial Modernity in Korea* (Cambridge, MA: Harvard Asia Center Publication, 2001).

8. Gi-wook Shin, *Ethnic Nationalism in Korea: Genealogy, Politics and Legacy* (Palo Alto, CA: Stanford University, 2006), 15.

9. Pak Ki-dang, "Son O-gong" and "Yusŏng'in Gausu," in *Pak Ki-dang sŏnjip: Hanguk Manhwa Gŏljaksŏn*, vol. 7 (Puch'ŏn: Puch'ŏn Manhwa Jŏngbo Sentŏ, 2008), 49–143, 247–293.

10. As for Raipai's strange-sounding name, the creator, Kim San-ho, explained in an interview that the comic is set in 2100 A.D., when it might not be unnatural for a Korean superhero to have a name other than the standard Chinese-derived, three-character one. Sŏ Ch'an-hwi, "Mangaji kkumŭl kkunŭn chakka Manmong Kim San-ho." Accessed May 12, 2013. http://navercast.naver.com/korean/cartoonist/86.

11. Son Sang-ik, *Hanguk manhwasa sanch'aek* (P'aju: Sallim Ch'ulp'ansa, 2005), 19–21.

12. See Koichi Iwabuchi, *Recentering Globalization: Popular Culture and Japanese Transnationalism* (Durham, NC: Duke University Press, 2002).

13. Pak Ki-jun, *Hanguk manhwa yasa* (Puch'ŏn: Puch'ŏn Manhwa Chŏngbo Sentŏ, 2008), 39–42. There is an interesting "gray area" between the almost mechanical copying of the Japanese products, in which their origins are hardly disguised, and the "creative adaptations" attempted by some quite talented Korean comic artists (Yi Tu-ho and Yi Wŏn-bok, for instance). Discussing this issue after all these years still remains taboo among Koreans.

14. See Yamanaka Chie, "Doragon bōru to deatta kankoku," in *Manga no naka no "tasha,"* ed. Itō Kimio (Tokyo: Rinsen Shoten, 2008).

15. Pak In-ha and Kim Nak-ho, *Hanguk hyŏndae manhwasa* (Seoul: Doobo, 2009), 96–97.

16. Pak In-ha and Kim Nak-ho, *Hanguk hyŏndae*, 20–27.

17. Pak Ki-jun, *Hanguk manhwa yasa*, 119–27.

18. Ko Woo-young, *Samgukchi*, 10 vols., restored edition (Seoul: Aenibuksŭ, 2007).

19. See Yoshikuni Igarashi, *Bodies of Memory: Narratives of War in Postwar Japanese Culture, 1945–1970* (Princeton, NJ: Princeton University Press, 2000), 47–72 for a discussion of Rikidōzan as a symbol of postwar Japanese nationalism.

20. Pak Ki-jŏng, *Tojŏnja*, 5 vols., restored edition (Seoul: Pada Ch'ulp'ansa, 2005). It is regrettable that the truly diverse responses of the older-generation comic artists active between the 1950s and 1970s toward the Japanese colonial experience and the Japanese in general cannot be explored in detail here. A surprisingly substantial number of them, including Ko Woo-young and Pak Ki-jŏng, grew up or were educated in Japan or Manchuria, and such personal experiences colored their depictions of their erstwhile dominators and enemies, negatively or positively.

21. Ko Woo-young, *Taeyamang*, vol. 2, 116–17, 136, and vol. 3, 66–69 (Puch'ŏn: Hanguk Yŏngsang Manhwa Chinhŭngwŏn, Ssi aen ssi rebolusyŏn, 2010). The five-part collection of *The Great Ambition* reprinted by the KOMACON (Korean Manhwa Contents Agency) in collaboration with Ko's son Ko Sŏng-ŏn is a landmark reissue in that the censored visuals, mostly scenes involving lethal weapons and bodily injuries, have been digitally restored, following painstaking restorations of the censored contents. However, the comic's dialogue still seems to be closer to the later revised version, which differs slightly from the dialogue originally published in the magazine.

22. Ko Woo-young, *Taeyamang*, vol. 2, 213–17.

23. Ko Woo-young, *Kurŭm sogŭi ai* (Seoul: Chaŭm Gwa Moŭm, 2007). This autobiography is a reprinted edition of *Ai nŭn ŏrunŭi abŏji*, originally published in 1978.

24. Pak Ki-jun, *Hanguk manhwa yasa*, 128.

25. Kim Yi-rang, "Minjok chuŭija ŭi kkum gwa hyŏnsil, Hŏ Yŏng-man," in *Hanguk manhwa ŭi mohŏmga-dŭl* (Seoul: Yŏlhwadang, 1996), 57–63, 67–70.

26. Hur Young-man, *Kaksit'al*, vol. 7 (Seoul: Ŏminsa, 1980). Unfortunately not all volumes of the *Kaksit'al* series are collected even in the Manhwa Gyujanggak edition. The episode featuring "Motorcycle Man" appears in volume 7, subtitled "Who Is the Traitor?" and can be accessed only in excerpts through web postings: http://blog.naver.com/PostView.nhn?blogId=rou&logNo=61602005.

27. Hur Young-man, *Kaksit'al*, reprint edition (Seoul: Hanguk Manhwa Chinhŭngwŏn, 2011), 7.

28. Hur Young-man, *Soet'ungso*, vol. 4 (Seoul: Seju Munhwa, 1988).

29. Pak Sŏk-hwan, "Asp'alt'ŭ kŭ sanai nŭn chigŭm ŏdi rŭl talligo itnŭnga," in *Hŏ Yŏng-man p'yo manhwa wa hwanho hanŭn kunjung-dŭl*, ed. Hanguk Manhwa Munhwa Yŏnguwŏn (Seoul: Kimyŏngsa, 2004), 114–17.

3   INKYU KANG

It All Started with a Bang
The Role of PC Bangs in South Korea's Cybercultures

Korea has been the graveyard of console gaming. Many game consoles were introduced there for decades, such as Game Boy, PlayStation, Xbox, and Wii, but they simply failed to take off. It must have come as a shock to many, because these gaming devices were tremendous successes around the world. One of the rare exceptions is the Nintendo DS handheld gaming system, which was accepted favorably in Korea. How can we explain the consistent failure of game consoles in one of the top tech capitals of the world that has embraced new technologies more passionately than others?[1] If game machines were destined for doom in Korea, how could the DS successfully crack open the Korean market?

This chapter explores how the PC instead of the console has become the dominant gaming platform in Korea.[2] By investigating the marginalization of game consoles, it attempts to critically examine the social forces contributing to Korea's unique gaming environment. A special emphasis is given to the enormous popularity of massive multiplayer online role-playing games (MMORPGS), nationally televised gaming leagues, and the peculiar space called "PC bangs," where online and offline experiences are readily mixed, with interesting results.[3] In so doing, this chapter investigates the cultural aspects many traditional approaches have failed to see.

This chapter suggests that there is no one-size-fits-all model to account for technology adoption. The challenge of the sociological approach to technological diffusion is not only that people do not respond to socioeconomic factors in a passive and predictable way but also that the factors influencing technological diffusion are full of random historical accidents and thus cannot be neatly quarantined for analysis. For example, analyzing how the inefficient QWERTY arrangement has dominated keyboards from the Remington typewriter to the Apple computer, Paul A. David concluded that "it is sometimes not possible to uncover the logic (or illogic) of the world around us except by understanding how it got that way" because a *"path-dependent sequence of economic changes is one* [in] *which important influences upon the eventual outcome can be exerted by temporally remote events, including happenings dominated by chance elements rather than systematic forces."*[4]

This case study seeks to show that computer and Internet use is determined neither by the inherent nature of technology nor by external sociological conditions. It explores not only sociocultural forces such as economy, residential geography, and government policy but also rarely discussed aspects of technological diffusion: how symbolic and ideological values of certain technology come to bear within society. More specifically, this chapter examines the relationship between technological diffusion and discourses of modernity and national identity in Korea. It focuses on the symbolic, discursive dimensions of the PC and the console, shedding light on their ongoing impacts on their adoption and use.

PC BANGS: THE BLURRED LINE BETWEEN ONLINE AND OFFLINE

During the late 1900s, when Korea was going through the financial crisis that swept Asia, the South Korean government tried to revive its economy by investing in the IT industry. The government promoted the use of the Internet in both the public and private sectors, believing that the high-tech industry would provide a solution to Korea's economic crisis by creating a new demand for hardware such as computers, modems, and servers as well as Internet services. The Korean government sped the privatization of Korea Telecom (KT), promoting competition in the IT sector. It also encouraged a widespread adoption of broadband through various policies.

> The South Korean government ensured competition by ending state-owned Korea Telecom's monopoly. The government spent billions of dollars building a fiber grid, reaching schools and government buildings, and offered another billion in financial incentives to phone companies that strung broadband links to homes. Tough competition drove prices down, demand surged and the country was on a roll.[5]

It is true that the Korean government has played an essential role in boosting broadband penetration by bringing strong competition and investing heavily in the IT field, but it was not necessarily its farsighted wisdom that made such policies possible. After all, the privatization of the public sector was part of the demand by the International Monetary Fund (IMF) and the World Bank in return for their bailout programs. Besides KT, several other state-held enterprises and financial institutions were sold into private hands, including Korea Ginseng & Tobacco, Korea Gas, Daehan Oil Pipeline, Korea District Heating, and Korea First Bank.

The South Korean government has always functioned as an industrial guiding hand, resulting not only in dramatic successes but also what Martin Fackler terms "spectacular failures," such as the "city phone" used strictly to make calls without receiving and the faked stem-cell scandal by Dr. Hwang Woo Suk.[6] The Korean government has hurriedly adopted new technologies, even when their actual applicability has not been fully tested. Sometimes the symbolic value of being the first to introduce a technology has been enough motivation for the unpromising investment. Luckily the government-led IT policy proved successful.

While the Kim Dae Jung administration (1998–2003) was making every effort to spread broadband technology, many Koreans were not fully convinced that the added speed would be worth the money. The PC bangs that started sprouting up around the country helped remove their suspicion by enabling people to test-drive the high-speed Internet. The PC bangs worked both as early adopters and as the showcases of broadband services. Korea's deepening economic crisis had left tens of thousands jobless. Many of them opened PC bangs. They already had a guaranteed number of customers: laid-off workers in need of cheap entertainment.

It is ironic that the success of the IT policy designed to boost the economy was indebted to the jobless. Although PC bangs successfully attracted price-sensitive patrons by offering a high-quality Internet connection, the PC bangs would not have been so successful if it had not been for Korea's unique *bang* (room) culture. Koreans had long been familiar with socializing for hours in small places like *da-bang* (tearoom), *manhwa-bang* (comics room), *norae-bang* (karaoke room), and *video-bang* (video room), to name a few settings, before PC bangs came along with a name with the friendly -*bang* suffix. Korea's *bang* culture has not only facilitated the absorption of the Internet but also influenced how the technology is used.

Online gaming is often seen as an antisocial experience. It is not, for many Korean gamers visit PC bangs as an important means for socializing. People "gather together to play games, video-chat, hang out, and hook up" there.[7] It is not unusual for Koreans to go to PC bangs in groups. Many patrons play games in teams late into the night after having dinner together. Although PC bang gamers spend hours staring at computer monitors, they often discuss strategies in a loud voice with neighboring friends. After completing missions, the fighters are likely to spend a few more hours at *soju-bang* (Korean-style bar) or *jjimjil-bang* (sauna). Many PC bangs have "love seat" stations with two computers and a bench for couples. Such considerations are appreciated not only by couples but also by single men and women.

> If you really watch the love seats, [. . .] it becomes apparent that they're not so much a porch swing as an Internet-mediated bar stool. Every so often a girl will saunter by one of the stations, eye the occupant, and then sit down—or not. As it turns out, singles are video-chatting in game rooms all over town. If they hit it off, the guy says something like "I'm sitting at love seat number 47 at this particular PC baang [*sic*], if you'd care to join me." If the girl is sufficiently intrigued, she hops on the subway or walks—nothing is more than 20 minutes away in central Seoul. She cruises by, checks him out, and if she likes the look of him in person she sits down, hoping the lighting and shading algorithms she used to enhance her features in the video chat don't make her seem unglamorous in person.[8]

Another element that has contributed to the popularity of PC bangs is the lack of private space for young adults at home. Many Koreans live with their parents until they get married, which reflects Korea's traditional Confucian extended family system. High housing expenses also block children from moving away from their parents. Korean youth are usually released from the surveillance of the watchful eye of their parents when they become college students or get a job, but the freedom does not resolve their lack of privacy, particularly when it comes to a romantic relationship.

The male-female dynamics in a Confucian society with conservative morals has heavily influenced the adoption and use of broadband. The positive implications of new technology have always given rich incentives to Korean early adopters, and it was especially true for computer and Internet users starting in the 1980s until the early 2000s. In Korea, owning and being able to use computers and the Internet was something to boast about. It was the symbolic value rather than the practical one that motivated young Koreans to learn to use the new technologies. What intrigued the early adopters was "not because they need[ed] information, but because they want[ed] to be seen as advanced."[9]

MEANING OF TECHNOLOGY

It is commonplace for Korean Internet users to end up in real-world meetings called *bungae-ting* (lightening meeting). Some have attributed Korea's unique cyberculture to the country's population density and residential environments, which no doubt have been an advantage, with more than 70 percent of the people living in crowded metropolitan areas. However, these two factors cannot fully explain the explosive popularity of PC bangs, where a unique mixture of online and offline experiences happens.

There are many similar-sized and equally populated countries, but few of them have witnessed the same phenomenon. The situation is similar in Japan, yet the young Japanese chose game consoles and Internet-enabled cell phones instead of public PCs in smoke-filled PC bangs. It may be true that Koreans' wide preference for residential towers has something to do with that. This explanation, however, raises a more fundamental question: Why do Koreans prefer living in high-rise apartment complexes in the downtown area to living in houses in suburbia?

A preference for tower blocks is never a natural and unavoidable result of a dense population and insufficient land.[10] The Netherlands and Belgium, for instance, have neither seen massive collective housing happen in spite of their scarcity of urban housing land nor developed such positive associations with the inhuman dwelling complexes as seen in Korea. A survey shows that well-to-do residents are more likely to live in tower blocks than their less wealthy counterparts in Korea. While 62 percent of the richest 10 percent of the population surveyed live in apartment blocks, only 16 percent live in apartments among the poorest 10 percent.[11] Three decades ago, however, the opposite was true. Collective housing was largely unpopular, especially among the rich, for over two decades after President Park Chung-Hee initiated urban development projects focusing on apartment construction starting in the early 1960s.

Urban apartment complexes have gradually gained popularity, ultimately becoming a symbol of status and wealth. In an analysis of the process by which the apartment has become the most desired residential space to South Koreans, Valérie Gelézeau notes the combined roles of the state, chaebol conglomerates, and the symbolic value of tall buildings in terms of progress and modernity.[12] The change in meaning of collective housing sheds light on the role of ideology in the diffusion of new technologies. The popularity of apartments grew as the building grew higher. Construction of tall buildings involved advanced skills and technology, associating high-rises with positive meanings.

The failure of console gaming is closely related to the reason computer technology has been absorbed quickly into the fabric of life in Korea. Korean parents have been won over both by computer manufacturers and telecommunication companies arguing that the computer and the Internet are a must for students. Buying consoles, however, seems to do nothing but add a source of distraction for their children, who should be busy studying. Unlike PCS, game consoles were explicitly "game machines." The contrasting attitudes toward game consoles and computers have led PCS to become the dominant game platform in Korea.

Korea's PC gaming emerged as the result of the negotiation between conflicting desires of parents and children. Although most children have their computers in their "study rooms" in Korea, many of them choose to play games in PC bangs on their way home after school. The PC bangs are similar to Internet cafés found in other countries, but they are "unique Korean institution[s]" in many ways.[13] First, most of the patrons spend time playing MMORPGS. All the popular games are preinstalled on PC bang computers, and people have to buy neither the software nor the high-speed Internet. At least 30,000 of these service centers blanketed Korea by 2000, up from just 100 in 1998, bringing high-speed access to the general public.[14] Although the broadband Internet has become cheap enough for most households, and smartphones have infiltrated Koreans' daily lives, the PC bangs still work as one of the most popular "third places" for young adults.

English has also had a sizable impact on the adoption of the PC, the Internet, and online gaming in Korea. Since the dominant language of computer operating systems and the Internet was English, having a good command of English was important. Gaming was no exception. Online gaming seemed to be a natural evolvement of Korea's broadband, shaped by PC bangs and young users. However, what turned it into a cultural phenomenon was StarCraft. Because it is an American game, all the menus and instructions are in English, which has helped avoid its being looked on as an unproductive pastime, unlike its Korean rival, Lineage. Even books such as *StarCraft English* were published to help gamers develop language skills while destroying enemies by teaching phrases like "Wanna turn up the heat?"

LEARNING ENGLISH: IT'S NO GAME?

Even before StarCraft came along, English was a major factor that accelerated the adoption of the computer and the Internet. Many parents bought their children computers to run educational software, and English was one of the most popular subjects. In the 1980s, learning the computer meant learning to use BASIC, one of the first programming languages in regular English. Plus, using the computer itself meant getting used to the language, because all the keyboards were in English. Daewoo and Sambo and other PC makers in Korea started manufacturing the machines mainly to export to English-speaking countries in the West. The computer was also perceived as a high-tech tool from the West, easily associated by Koreans with English.

Figure 3.1. In this Daewoo advertisement (1985), the computer promises children they will excel in English as they do in martial arts. The advertising copy says, "Your summer break is the perfect chance to pull ahead," proclaiming that the machine is "the shortcut to be a black belt English expert."

Most PC manufacturers used English as a marketing tool from the beginning (fig. 3.1).

Many Koreans believed that by using the Internet they could learn the English language. This trend was promoted by mainstream media and the government. Conservative newspapers like the *Chosun Ilbo* started a campaign called "KidNet" during the mid-1990s to encourage elementary schools to incorporate Internet education into curricular activities as a tool to learn English. Korean newspapers emphasized "the futuristic role of the Internet," and computers and the Internet itself provided users "a positive image of their identities," such as being intelligent, fashionable, and international.[15]

The language issue Koreans experienced has also had a significant influence on the shaping of computer and Internet technologies. In the past, the dominant PC users were young children who didn't have enough command of English. It took a long time until operating systems and software menus and instructions were translated into Korean, so many users got into the habit of pushing the "OK" button without giving much thought to what their choice would bring. As a result, Koreans have not only suffered from computer viruses but also eventually encountered computer interfaces with less strict security standards compared with other countries.

This early experience with the PC later influenced Koreans to shape a unique Internet environment. Thanks to the less picky users, Korean software developers took the liberty of experimenting with a wide range of interfaces, which may not have been possible in other countries. Instead of the SSL protocol that has become a global standard, for example, most Korean websites, including Internet banking, rely heavily on ActiveX controls. ActiveX is a powerful system developed by Microsoft that enables dynamic features on Web pages. In spite of such advantages, developers and users in most countries approach ActiveX cautiously since it can cause a security risk by letting malicious programs be downloaded and run on the computer. Korean websites tended to boast of having very strong audiovisual features, which were made possible by the leniency in the installation of plug-ins and the high-speed Internet fast enough to handle the increased amount of information.

Although video game players had not been generally respected in Korea, StarCraft brought a change to this trend and was perceived differently from other games. It was a completely new game in form and content. As a science fiction real-time strategy game, the game's futuristic image was accepted favorably by many Korean gamers. Playing the game involved understanding English menus and instructions, helping improve the image of gamers. As a result, StarCraft players may not be welcomed by girls' parents, but they can still make cool boyfriends.

At the center of the fast-growing popularity of online gaming, including StarCraft, have been female fans and gamers. Online gamers in Asia are predominantly male, making Korea a rare "exception where online gamers are almost equally represented by males (55.3 percent) and females (44.7 percent)."[16] The widespread interest in gaming among women has helped PC bangs to attract male patrons, making StarCraft the most popular game. It is not just a game; it is a "national sport" played by "five million people—equivalent to 30 million in the US."[17] There are professional gaming leagues and full-time cable channels that broadcast StarCraft tournaments. Pro players like Lim Yo-Hwan are national heroes. Lim's salary is over $300,000, and his official online fan club has more than 400,000 registered members.[18]

Frantic, piercing, the shrieks echoed down the corridors from one corner of the vast underground complex. There hundreds of young people, mostly women and girls, waved signs and sang slogans as they swirled in the glare of klieg lights. It was the kind of fan frenzy that anywhere else would be reserved for rockers or movie legends. Or sports stars. In fact the objects of the throng's adoration were a dozen of the nation's most famous athletes, South Korea's Derek Jeters and Peyton Mannings. But their sport is something almost unimaginable in the United States. These were professional video gamers, idolized for their mastery of the science-fiction strategy game StarCraft.[19]

The high proportion of female gamers is the combined result of positive discourses of online gaming among young people and the evolution of gaming into a spectator sport that can be enjoyed by nonplayers. Many of those not interested in StarCraft started playing the game while watching the televised tournaments. In a society still deeply influenced by conservative Confucian values, the Internet has provided the young with online and offline opportunities for casual encounters between the sexes.

CONFUCIANISM AT PLAY

Combined with the traditional mores, the cutthroat competition for college entrance has led parents and teachers to warn their teenagers off romantic relationships until they become college students. Before PC bangs appeared, cyberspace itself provided a welcome "escape from old-style mores that many find oppressive, especially the young" thanks to its anonymity.[20] PC bangs have thrived by giving young people the chance to translate online relationships into real-life ones.

Besides making cyberspace a romantic getaway from reality, Internet adoption has been facilitated by Confucian values in many ways. First, it helped by instilling a passion for education into Koreans. An emphasis on education and study is a hallmark of Confucius's thought, which has had a long-term impact on Korea's culture and social structure. In this philosophy, the only way to truly understand the world is through long and careful study, as opposed to intuition. Rulers must be enlightened like Plato's philosopher king, turning the state into the "embodiment of knowledge."[21]

Japan embraced computers earlier than Korea, but they were perceived mainly as "business machines." By 1991, 65.8 percent of computers sold were shipped to offices, and only 21.8 percent went to families in Japan.[22] The exact opposite was true in Korea; there, the computer was sold as an educational device from the beginning. Korean parents, who would do anything if their children have a better chance for success in school, did not hesitate to buy the expensive IQ 1000, the first MSX computer for the Korean

Figure 3.2. "IQ 1000, the choice of the best student in our class!" (1985).

market in 1983. Obviously they hoped that their children would be number one, as the little thumbs-up between the IQ and the 1000 in the logo promised (fig. 3.2). Every computer company in Korea during this period was busy advertising how PCs could help students do better at school, but some companies even had production lines exclusively for education. One of the model names was STUDY by Sam Bo Engineering.

The Korean state has virtually monopolized the country's education in both the public and private sectors through school entrance tests, civil service exams, certification programs, and education policies. The most elite universities are national and public ones like Seoul National University and KAIST, when the top students' usual dream is to become a high-ranking government official after passing the highly competitive civil-service exams.

It is very important to remember that it is the same bureaucratic governance by scholar-officials that has required computer education as part of the regular school curriculum and provided a guiding hand to the IT industry by dictating to the market and participating in the development of technologies.[23] The South Korean government has regularly announced "strategic industries," making computer gaming one of them. The government has actively played its part by subsidizing and reducing tax obligations for the digital industries and even recognizing or rewarding exemplary products and companies. Many technical colleges have established gaming-related departments or courses with support from the government. The government's intervention does not stop there; it also provides counseling and corrective programs to game addicts through the Korea Agency for Digital Opportunity and Promotion (KADO) and the Jump Up Internet Rescue School.[24]

Confucian values have also helped by readying gamers for the collective gaming experience of the MMORPG genre that has come to dominate Korea. This point is evinced by the explosive popularity of Lineage, a game that represents the Confucian hierarchy of Korean society and is suitable for those who are comfortable playing in teams—not only online but also offline.

> What makes Lineage a distinctively Korean experience is that when players assemble to take down a castle, they do so in person, commandeering a local PC baang [sic] for as long as it takes. In the middle of a battle, these people aren't text-chatting. They're yelling across the room. Platoons sit at adjacent computers, coordinating among themselves and taking orders from the Blood Pledge leader. Lineage has a fixed hierarchy, unlike American role-playing games, in which leadership structures emerge organically. At the outset, you choose to be either royalty or a commoner. If you're a prince or princess, your job is to put together an army and lead it. If you're a commoner, your job is to find a leader. You pledge loyalty and fight to take over castles, and no matter how great you are at it, you can never be in charge.[25]

Although NCsoft's Lineage was modeled after Western medieval fantasy role-playing games, it has some "cultural variations" such as "an emphasis on in-game quests that can only be completed by highly organized groups of players" whose characters observe "strict social hierarchies."[26] The epic game allows users to choose their avatars from the knight, wizard, elf, prince, or princess characters, but only the members of the royal class can recruit groups of followers to have control of the castles and levy feudal taxes. The "tightly defined clan structure" of the game has not appealed to American players, "who generally want to be the hero-king Lone Ranger."[27] As a result, the phenomenal success Lineage has enjoyed in Korea has not taken place in the United States in spite of the official launching of an English version. Eventually NCsoft permanently shut down all North American servers for Lineage on June 29, 2011.

The South Korean government has actively supported the game indus-try, but the negative perspective taken by Koreans toward gaming has not changed drastically. Some professional gamers have become national celeb-rities, helping youngsters to persuade their parents that gaming can be a serious profession. Most Koreans, however, maintained until recently that a game console is an "expensive toy," not a learning machine.[28] This wide-spread stereotype has made game console manufacturers like Nintendo, Sega, Sony, and Microsoft struggle in the Korean market for a long time. Korea remained a console graveyard even when the electronic dictionary and the MP3 player became must-buy products.

What turned Koreans away from the game console is not just the edu-cational overlap it lacks. The acrimonious relationship between Korea and Japan also discouraged Koreans from buying the game consoles, which were manufactured mostly in Japan during the 1980s and 1990s. There were a few owners of the Japanese-made machines, but most of them were illegally imported items. There was a strict ban on many Japanese imports in Korea, which was an effort by the military regimes (1963–87) to protect domestic products. Japanese-made consumer electronics "have traditionally been all but verboten, thanks to both trade policy and cultural resentment" for quite a long time.[29] The import ban was lifted in 1998, but the measure did not bring a dramatic change to the video game console market.

Korea's patriotic consumerism was largely a result of the government's effort to protect the domestic market, and chaebol companies have con-tinued to capitalize on such nationalist sentiments until today. For example, Samsung launched an advertising campaign in 2007 saying, "Samsung is now revising the skyline of the world. Korea's pride is being elevated at this very moment." It was about the Burj Tower Samsung was building in Dubai. Samsung had won the contract to build the world's tallest building, and it decided to run the ad when the building under construction reached the world's record 512 meters (1,680 feet).

The country's obsession with economic development was fully reflected in our education. We learned that it was our patriotic duty to report any-one seen smoking foreign cigarettes. The country needed to use every bit of the foreign exchange earned from its exports in order to import ma-chines and other inputs to develop better industries. Valuable foreign cur-rencies were really the blood and sweat of our "industrial soldiers" fight-ing the export war in the country's factories. Those squandering them on frivolous things, like illegal foreign cigarettes, were "traitors." I don't believe any of my friends actually went as far as reporting such "acts of treason." But it did feed the gossip mill when kids saw foreign cigarettes in a friend's house.[30]

Adding insult to injury, the small number of console owners preferred to buy pirated game titles on the black market. The piracy issue has solidified Korea's status as "a barren land for foreign video game makers," since software sales are the main income source for most console manufacturers.[31] Korea's widespread issue of software piracy has contributed to the monopoly of online gaming by making domestic game developers focus on online games that cannot be pirated, unlike PC or console game titles. As a result, even the giant Nintendo did not have an official branch in Korea until 2005. When Nintendo launched its new game console DS Lite, it attacked the Korean market not only with highly localized game titles but also with strong legal actions against software piracy.

Nintendo's key strategy was to launch two different kinds of unusual games. One translates Korean online games into console versions. Popular games such as Kart Rider and Maple Story were introduced to appeal to those who had already played them online. Nintendo's partnership with local game developers like Nexon helped alleviate grievances many Korean consumers had against Japanese companies. Nintendo announced that its strategy was "to increase the number of gamers by introducing light, easy, and fun games, which can be played by anyone regardless of their sex, age, and skill."[32] Kart Rider and Maple Story were perfect choices for Nintendo to appeal to female players, who took up a significant portion of Korea's gaming population while avoiding the nationalist protectionism still remaining after the government lifted the embargo on sales of Japanese console games.

Nintendo also put on the market game titles that did not look like games, including educational titles like Brain Age and English Training. Brain Age was advertised as helping its user to train his or her brain through various puzzles. English Training is a game that enables its players to practice English by reproducing sentences heard from the digital voice. When launching the portable console, Nintendo hired a top Korean movie star, Jang Dong-gun, because of his "nongaming person image" (fig. 3.3). Such a unique approach worked; the Japanese game company sold about 600,000 units of Nintendo DS in less than nine months after its launching as well as 1.2 million software titles during the same period.[33] The game console became an instant hit in Korea, something that had never happened before.

Figure 3.3. Nintendo's model for its portable console, movie star Jang Dong-gun.

The introduction of the game console as a learning tool helped win Korean customers' hearts.

When Nintendo Korea released its educational game titles, the company launched aggressive advertising campaigns including prime-time TV spots. The Brain Age commercial challenged the audience by asking, "How old is your brain?" It warned that even a teenager can have a fifty-year-old's brain age if his or her brain has not been properly exercised. The unconventional game software promised to "help stimulate your brain and give it the workout it needs." In its thirty-second spot, the smart-looking Jang Dong-gun checks his brain age on a sofa. He soon agonizes over the unexpected result: fifty-eight years old.

English Training chose to persuade the Korean audience in a more intense way. Nintendo Korea aired two different spots to promote the educational title, but both have the same embarrassing situation caused by the lack of English skills. One is about a family about to go through customs, where they are temporarily detained by a customs official pouring out questions in English. The family, consisting of parents and a child, stand frozen with blank smiles on their faces, completely at a loss. The camera zooms in on the father's face; he looks ashamed—almost terrified—of the situation he has put his family in owing to his inability. The close-up shot of the father's pale face effectively represents the face-losing experience Koreans,

Figure 3.4. TV commercial for *English Training*.

especially fathers, would want to avoid in the presence of their families. The commercial ends with suspenseful music.

There is another version: two young women at a fast-food restaurant (fig. 3.4). They want to place an order, but it seems that they do not understand what the worker behind the counter says. As the man keeps throwing questions aggressively, the scared-looking customers give him faint, polite smiles. One of the women repeats, "Yes," in an almost inaudible voice. The ad comes to an end with her terrified face gradually filling the screen with somber background music flowing.

The restaurant episode is very similar to the Japanese TV spot for the same game title, but there is a striking difference. The Japanese commercial features one young woman, instead of two, who faces the counter under-equipped. The Korean version depicts a more embarrassing situation in which the two friends have to reveal their poor English abilities to each other. The Japanese woman ends up receiving a giant hamburger as a result of her misunderstanding. The Korean ad, however, focuses on the fear of the ordering process itself. The Korean version does not have any comical elements, unlike its Japanese counterpart. It ends without showing what the Korean women end up with, but placing an order is enough motivation for many Korean viewers.

Korea remained virtually anticonsole until Nintendo's soft landing. Nintendo was lucky, however, to launch the portable game platform at the right time. The young customers Nintendo was targeting were already familiar

with carrying a similar-sized gadget: the electronic dictionary. English proficiency is required of all students who want to go to college or get a job, turning learning the language into a national obsession.

> The pressure begins before birth. Some parents play English nursery
> rhymes to children in the womb. One-year-olds can have private tutors,
> four- and five-year-olds are sent to English-only kindergartens that cost
> $1,000 a month. For older kids, there are special immersion schools
> where the Korean language is banned. . . . Thousands of families are split
> up for years, with the mother and child moving to an English-speaking
> country, leaving the father in Korea to pay the bills.[34]

Many Korean students believe that an electronic dictionary is a must-have
to learn English. Nintendo made effective use of this trend by establishing a
strong connection between their new product and education. Nintendo released Touch Dictionary, which turns the console into a fashionable double-
screened dictionary. About 32 percent of Korean students, from elementary
to college level, had been equipped with electronic dictionaries by 2006.[35]
The Nintendo DS console competed with old-fashioned electronic dictionaries that were as expensive as the DS but did not double as game consoles. In
this sense, Nintendo succeeded by selling their hand-held gaming device
as a learning tool, the same way computers were marketed during the early
1980s in Korea. The Nintendo DS could break out of the console graveyard
by tearing down the wall between gaming and learning. English learning
may not be a major motivation for some owners, but Nintendo has at least
provided them with a good excuse to buy a decent game player.

GAMING AS A SIGN OF DISTINCTION

Although the number of older users has increased gradually, computers and
the Internet were virtually monopolized by young people for roughly two
decades in Korea. Parents who bought computers for their children did not
know how to use them, and the machines found their way into the young
users' study rooms. Unlike many other countries, such as Japan and the
United States, where the PCs were commonly placed in the living room,
computers in Korea belonged completely to children, who spent hours at
them in their own rooms. Korean parents have unrivaled fame for their
watchful eyes on their children, but many of these youth have become heavy
users and even addicts behind the closed doors. Surveys show that Koreans
spend more time on the Internet than Japanese and Americans, which is
partly attributable to the location of the computers at home. On average, according to a 2007 survey, Korean Internet users spent 31.2 hours a month

online, significantly more time than Japanese users' 19.2 hours, due partly to the cultural difference in the perception of the machine, shaping its location and use.[36]

Still many children spend an unlimited amount of time in front of a computer monitor, putting up to 30 percent of South Koreans under 18 at the risk of Internet addiction.[37] The few students living with tech-savvy parents can enjoy the same freedom at PC bangs. There is still a clear generational gap in computer and Internet use in Korea in spite of the increasing number of older users. The computer and the Internet constitute youth culture in Korea—PC bangs, professional gaming, blogging, and social networking. The technologies not only define the culture enjoyed by the youth but also the space. As mentioned above, computers are routinely placed in children's rooms at home, and many parents borrow their computers when needed. PC bangs, however, are considered to belong to young people.

The generational division of space has a long history in Korea. Social space tends to be divided according to age, accepting specific age groups and rejecting others. Even places like barbershops and coffee shops are classified based on age. For example, coffeehouses are divided into tea rooms and coffee shops. What makes the difference between them is not so much what kinds of drinks are served as what types of customers frequent them. Tea rooms are for the old, while coffee shops are for the young. What separates barbershops (ibal-so) from beauty shops (miyong-sil) is not gender but age in Korea. A PC bang is classified as a place for the young along with a coffee shop and a beauty shop, reinforcing the meaning of the Internet and online games as youth culture.

Koreans have long been taught to pay respect to one's elders. Outside of personal and family relationships, however, older populations have been systematically marginalized and discriminated against in work and social situations. Age discrimination has been pointed out as one of the most serious human rights issues South Korea faces. Nobody would want to look old, as being and looking so could be a serious disadvantage for many Koreans. In this context, the Internet became a symbol for a generational distinction that draws a dividing line between the young and old. Computers had a similar function, which was succeeded by the Internet and then online gaming. Whether one can use the Internet became the litmus test to tell if he or she belonged to the "new generation."

At work, those who could not use computers and the Internet started being regarded as archaic, outdated, and incompetent. The widespread social pressure explains the computer learning boom in the 1990s among many middle managers who had never learned typing, not to mention handling computers. Computer skills started to be seen as a symbol of competence, knowledge, and professionalism. Only English had taken a similar position at work in Korea since the abacus was driven out of use. Just like English, the computer had strong symbolic, rather than practical, value among many Koreans.

In any society, gaming enthusiasts are mostly young people. Korea is no exception, but its gaming trend has distinctive elements. Most important, playing computer games has unique cultural meanings. Gaming is hardly perceived as a meaningful experience in the country known for its severely competitive education setting. Nintendo DS has brought about a dramatic change in the public's long-lasting resistance to gaming consoles, but it is not because Koreans have changed their attitudes but because the company has successfully marketed the player as an educational device. This point is supported by that fact that Nintendo's Wii has struggled since its launch without emulating its predecessor DS's spectacular achievement in Korea. Fewer than 40,000 units of the new game player were sold in its first month on sale, "far below the firm's expectation."[38]

TOWARD CULTURAL QWERTY-NOMICS

Although gaming is not considered particularly valuable in Korea, playing computer games has been seen a little differently from console gaming. What has made the PC the dominant gaming platform in Korea is its legitimate status at home. The discourse of the computer as a "study machine" has profoundly defined its use in Korea. Education PCs were naturally placed in children's rooms, where future StarCraft players spent unlimited time behind closed doors with PC games borrowed from friends. Other positive associations, such as English ability, new technology, and youth, have transferred to the Internet and online gaming.

David convincingly showed, in his QWERTY-nomics, that the impact of "historical accidents," which exert tremendous impacts on technological diffusion, "can neither be ignored nor neatly quarantined" for analysis.[39] For example, the financial crisis—a historical accident—turned out to be a blessing in disguise, at least in promoting broadband, by giving birth to PC bangs. They became test beds for the high-speed Internet, providing new business opportunities for struggling hardware and software manufacturers. PC bangs have also played a key role in introducing online gaming into Korea's popular culture.

If external social factors are too complicated to quarantine, cultural and ideological factors make matters even more complex. The emergence of the PC bang is often seen as a sudden, new phenomenon arising around the

1997 Asian financial crisis, fueled mainly by the economic motivations of the government, chaebol conglomerates, and laid-off workers looking for business opportunities. There are, no doubt, new elements to them, but PC bangs are also a continuation of the old: the popularity of commercial places with the familiar *bang* suffix and discourses of generational division ("If you don't play StarCraft, you are an old geezer").

South Korea's long-standing technonationalism and utopianism have been major driving forces for technological innovations. PC and broadband infiltration in Korea has been influenced by the symbolic and ideological aspects of the technologies. When the first personal computer was introduced in Korea in the early 1980s, the country's absorption of the technology was surprisingly fast considering the average annual household income at that time. Many Korean parents who would spare nothing for their children's education were willing to tighten their belts to buy the futuristic machine. Similarly the Internet seemed to embody the virtues Koreans highly valued: cutting-edge technology, knowledge, and globalization. The positive attitude toward computer and Internet technologies transferred to online gaming, making it the cultural icon of the new generation.

The role PC bangs have played in disseminating broadband vividly shows the constant influence of cultural and ideological vectors. Thus investigating how a technology is adopted and shaped cannot be reduced to a few determining factors to be used as a one-size-fits-all tool for prediction and generalization in different contexts. Society and culture are too subtle, multifarious, and changeable to neatly categorize. More important, people are never passive masses determined entirely by external conditions. That is probably what makes the subject so fascinating.

NOTES

1. Arjun Ramachandran, "Tech Capitals of the World." *Sydney Morning Herald*, September 13, 2007, www.smh.com.au/small-business/tech-capitals-of-the-world-20090619 -coot.html.

2. In Japan, the mobile phone has been the predominant platform used to go online since 2005. In sharp contrast to Japan and many other countries, most Koreans still rely on the wired Internet accessed on chunky PCs. According to a TGS survey in 2010, 72.9 percent of computer users in Korea replied that smartphones had not reduced PC usage.

3. A PC bang is a place that provides high-speed broadband Internet at inexpensive rates. What sets the PC bang apart from the Internet café in other countries is its hybridity; it is somewhere between an Internet café, a video game arcade, and a convenience store. PC bangs are used mostly for entertainment such as playing online games and video chatting rather than business purposes. PC bangs are usually

open for twenty-four hours a day, selling patrons a variety of items such as ramen noodles and cigarettes as well as hot and cold drinks. Most PC bangs are equipped with recliners so that commuters can take a nap while waiting for the first bus or subway in the morning.

4. Paul A. David, "Clio and the Economics of QWERTY," *American Economics Review* 75, no. 2 (1985): 332.

5. Birgitta Forsberg, "The Future Is South Korea," *San Francisco Chronicle*, March 13, 2005, B1.

6. Martin Fackler, "In Korea, Bureaucrats Lead the Technology Charge," *New York Times*, March 16, 2006, www.nytimes.com/2006/03/16/business/worldbusiness/16seoul.html.

7. J. C. Herz, "The Bandwidth Capital of the World." *Wired*, August 2002, http://www.wired.com/wired/archive/10.08/korea.html.

8. Herz, "Bandwidth Capital."

9. Sunny Yoon, "Internet Discourse and the *Habitus* of Korea's New Generation," in *Culture, Technology, Communication: Towards an Intercultural Global Village*, ed. Charles Ess (Albany: State University of New York Press, 2001), 254.

10. Valérie Gelézeau, *Séoul, Ville Géante, Cités Radieuses* (Paris: CNRS Editions, 2005).

11. Yongseok Ahn and Misuk Seo, "Wealthy Residents Tend to Live in Apartment Blocks" ["Don-jal-beol-su-rok-apart-san-da (돈 잘 벌수록 아파트 산다)"], *Midas*, November 2006. Accessed June 26, 2011. http://past.yonhapmidas.com/06_11/liv/04_001.html.

12. Gelézeau, *Séoul, Ville Géante, Cités Radieuses*.

13. Shameen Assif, "Starting with a Baang: Korea's Rooms Have a View on the Future," *Asia Week*, September 1, 2000. http://cgi.cnn.com/ASIANOW/asiaweek/technology/2000/0901/tech.net.html.

14. Mark Magnier, "'PC Bang' Helps Koreans Embrace Net," *Los Angeles Times*, July 21, 2000. http://articles.latimes.com/2000/jul/19/news/mn-55332.

15. Yoon, "Internet Discourse," 254–55.

16. Netvalue, "Who's Winning the Asian Online Gaming War?" *ZDNet*, April 23, 2001. Accessed August 25, 2011. http://www.zdnet.com/whos-winning-the-asian-online-gaming-war_p3-2021198772/.

17. Herz, "Bandwidth Capital."

18. Peter Lewis, "Broadband Wonderland," *Fortune*, September 20, 2004, 198.

19. Seth Schiesel, "The Land of the Video Geek," *New York Times*, October 8, 2006, http://www.nytimes.com/2006/10/08/arts/08schi.html.

20. Donald Macintyre, "Wired for Life," *Time*, December 4, 2000. Accessed April 1, 2011. http://www.time.com/time/world/article/0,8599,2040463-1,00.html.

21. Bruce Cumings, *Korea's Place in the Sun* (New York: W. W. Norton, 2005), 301.

22. Parker Smith, "Computing in Japan: From Cocoon to Competition," *Computer* 30, no. 3 (1997): 30.

23. Martin Fackler, "In Korea, Bureaucrats Lead the Technology Charge."

24. Martin Fackler, "In Korea, a Boot Camp Cure for Web Obsession," *New York Times*, November 18, 2007. http://nytimes.com/2007/11/18/technology/18rehab.html.

25. Herz, "Bandwidth Capital."

26. Dean Chan, "Negotiating Intra-Asian Games Networks: On Cultural Proximity, East Asian Games Design, and Chinese Farmers," *Fibreculture Journal*, March 16, 2006. http://eight.fibreculturejournal.org/fcj-049-negotiating-intra-asian-games -networks-on-cultural-proximity-east-asian-games-design-and-chinese-farmers.

27. Herz, "Bandwidth Capital."

28. Schiesel, "Land of the Video Geek."

29. Herz, "Bandwidth Capital."

30. Ha-Joon Chang, *Bad Samaritans: The Myth of Free Trade and the Secret History of Capitalism* (New York: Bloomsbury, 2008), xiv.

31. Jin-seo Cho, "Video Game Big 3 Geared for Battle," *Korea Times*, February 14, 2007. http://times.hankooki.com/lpage/200702/kt2007021317571210230.html.

32. Tae-jong Kim, "Can Nintendo Succeed in Online Heaven?" *Korea Times*, January 9, 2007. http://times.hankooki.com/lpage/200701/kt2007010918195853460.html.

33. Jin-seo Cho, "Nintendo Sells 580,000 Mini Game Players," *Korea Times*, October 28, 2007. http://www.koreatimes.co.kr/www/news/biz/2010/07/123_12656.html.

34. Mark Simkin, "Korean Education: An Unhealthy Obsession," transcript, Australian Broadcasting Company (ABC), Local Radio, "AM," March 29, 2005. http://www.abc .net.au/am/content/2005/s1333165.htm.

35. Jiseon Roh, "One Out of 2.5 Students Has an Electronic Dictionary," *Asia Economy*, July 20, 2006. http://www.asiaeconomy.co.kr/uhtml/read.php?idxno=20060 72014272044158.

36. comScore, "comScore Publishes the First Comprehensive Review of Asian-Pacific Usage," July 9, 2007. Accessed August 25, 2011. http://www.comscore.com/Press _Events/Press_Releases/2007/07/Asia-Pacific_Internet_Usage.

37. Fackler, "In Korea, a Boot Camp Cure for Web Obsession."

38. Jin-seo Cho, "Nintendo Sees Slow Wii Sales in Korea," *Korea Times*, June 2, 2008. http://www.koreatimes.co.kr/www/news/biz/2008/06/123_25183.html.

39. David, "Clio and the Economics of QWERTY," 332–33.

As Seen on the Internet
The Recap as Translation in English-Language K-drama Fandoms

The growth of online participatory cultures has produced vast arrays of digitized responses to popular media, the work of fans responding to the source texts and to each other, while facilitating recognition of and access to source texts across geopolitical and linguistic affiliations. Dramabeans.com is a website that posts daily content on a constantly updated set of Korean popular media, with a focus on episodic television. From its beginnings as site moderator javabeans's personal blog, the site has gained a comoderator, girlfriday, a rotating cast of recappers, and a fan base of its own.[1]

The site's primary post type is the episode recapitulation, or recap, a moment of reception that provides much more than mere episode summary. This documented excess focalizes examinations of the dynamics of transmission across media and language barriers in its online contexts. Fans remediate K-drama through the recap, engendering response through interactions in the comments, where fans often respond to the televisual broadcast, the fan-made subtitles, and the anglophone episode recaps as if they were a single unit. This chapter grew out of a desire to account for these phenomena, using Dramabeans.com as a case study, by considering the recap's situation in online cultures, and by analyzing the specifics of translation and mediation at the moment of reading.

In some ways, this chapter functions like a recap, an immersive echo of myriad experiences condensed onto the page, touching on sets of overlapping, sometimes conflicting discussions of representation, translation, fandom economies, subcultural societies, distributed online communities, and research methodologies before diving into close readings of its two exemplars. I have deviated somewhat from a strictly academic structure, in which a substantiated conclusion logically follows from a set of initial arguments. Instead, my discussions hold the appearance of linearity but not its substance, since linearity would require both a predictable route and no possibility of deviation. I have therefore assembled a primer to a few of the many issues surrounding online recaps and then performed a set of analyses on how the recap does its work, with particular focus on the details of intermedial transfer (how to keep the motion circulating through the stills) and affective encounter (strategies for maintaining mediated yet personal emotional responses).

THE RECAP AS CULTURAL ARTIFACT: DRAMABEANS.COM

Tracing the recap's long trajectories encapsulates a brief history of online response to popular media. From concise, individual "summary and indignant response" blog entries, the recap entered public forums, becoming the province of designated archivists, the recappers whose work would seed an entire community's reactive response. As a fan-based information-sharing method, the recap propagates the latest information on the fans' source material, providing these communities with increased impetus to regularly recreate the intensity of their relationship through discussions as much on the recapper's bias as on the source texts themselves. Each recapper's individual voice, opinions, wit, and consistency of presence are as privileged as the episodic information she or he presents; significantly the recapper lays no claim to any final interpretation. Instead, interpretation is a distributed collaborative process, changing with each response posted to the comments section. This form was popularized at the site Television Without Pity (TWOP), an aggregator that started out as a single-show blog and became an early example of centralized online fan-based responses to network television in North America. TWOP's primacy as a pan-fandom meeting place and archive was publicly acknowledged when it was acquired by Bravo in March 2007, throwing TWOP's "Spare the snark, spoil the networks" slogan somewhat in doubt.[2]

Discussion in the comments can range from nuances of interpretation to fan service counts, depending on the site's fan base.[3] Commenters responding to the initial recap can create shared points of agreement while simultaneously accelerating toward cheerful wrangling over detailed interpretations or fractious ad hominem disagreement, depending on the culture of the site. In this mode of interpretation, the text of any critical reading of the recap lies at its surface, within the fans' work and affiliations. Even leaving aside alternate forms of authorship or the complexities of online identity-play, a comprehensive survey of fandom demographics might provide information about fans' offline lives but would do little to interpret their labor. Beyond the formation of a singular fan, each fan community forms itself through its interactions, establishing social practices and shared terminologies, close-reading its source text to query facile conclusions and demand substantive answers, either from the source text or from one another. This cultural practice can be critical practice as well, an expression of enthusiasm that nonetheless addresses thorny problems or difficult concerns from within larger contexts of affective engagement.

The website Dramabeans.com provides valuable online space for this engagement. Currently one among several comoderated anglophone Korean pop culture sites, the site provides a centralized meeting place for anglophone fans as well as specific kinds of access to the K-drama and their associated cultural production. Korean drama is a form of episodic television occurring at the locus of hourlong drama and primetime soap opera, with attendant intricate romantic subplots. Dramatic contexts can range from historical epic to espionage thriller to romantic comedy, and while locations vary, the modern "trendy" series tend to take place in or near Seoul. In contrast to North American soap operas, K-drama usually air biweekly over a period of several months before reaching a definitive ending. For the most popular episodes, audience ratings can reach over 40 percent (for example, 2009's *Sons of Sol Pharmacy*, or 2012's *The Moon That Embraces the Sun*).[4] From 2005's *My Name Is Kim Sam-Soon* and 2007's *Coffee Prince* onward, growing K-drama awareness in online communities has led to specific needs for multilingual, frequently anglophone-centric forms of access.

The recap site Dramabeans.com is notable for its recap focus and strong writing, as well as its evident and unashamed K-drama partialities. Other comoderated sites tend to function as aggregators of information and less as aggregators of opinionated response, thus serving different purposes within fandom ecologies. Dramabeans.com seems to have begun as a result of site moderator javabeans's reentry into the world of K-drama through renewed appreciation as an adult; her website started life early in 2007 as a two-entry WordPress blog. The recaps themselves, starting with 2007's *Dal Ja's Spring*, seem to have initially been reposted from another very large K-drama and fandom centralization site, whose forums provide large networks of information and availabilities on current and historical K-drama. The first documented episode recap at Dramabeans.com opens with a discussion of javabeans's previous activity on K-drama forums:

> So I've been writing these episode summaries for Dal Ja's Spring on soompi—a site to which, if you are a kdrama fan and are yet unfamil-

iar, you must hie on over and acquaint yourselves immediately. Since I wrote up recaps for many (though not all) episodes, I figured I'd post them here as well. Why let hours of perfectly useful procrastination go to waste, right?[5]

The twelve comments on this first recap give no hints as to the site's eventual traffic. By the end of the *Dal Ja's Spring* recaps, in March of 2007, the number of posts per month rises from 2 to 32. That month also sees the emergence of two soon-to-be staples of Dramabeans.com: the Song of the Day (eventually tied to episode recaps) and the Random Friday post (eventually the Friday Open Thread). With 78 comments on javabeans' March 16 recap of *Dal Ja's Spring*'s finale and 133 comments on the March 11 analysis of *Hana Yori Dango 2*'s adaptation aesthetics, a readership emerged early in the site's life.[6] The quick rise in comment numbers suggests that javabeans was already known for the quality of her recaps in other forums and that a contingent of readers followed her to her own site.

Dramabeans.com gives often far-flung K-drama fans somewhere to congregate, where their interests and obsessions can be part of normal, non-niche, watercooler-level interactions, with all the possibilities of informed commentary and mutual exchange. Shared knowledge leading to wider discussions is the prerequisite for a conversation, or more accurately, for myriad linked conversations taking place simultaneously, which can become the germ or seed of a kind of online-specific cultural formation. That base of common knowledge is mediated in the burgeoning communities through Dramabeans.com's dedicated cadre of recappers. The site's accreted knowledge can constitute a nontrivial chunk of its participants' comprehension of K-drama itself, well beyond the specifics concerning the trendy drama of the week. The site's recaps do not stop at summary and analysis: javabeans and girlfriday also include various updates on the stars themselves, translating material as needed. For example, when Choi Jung-Won, lead actor of the drama *Wish Upon a Star*, wrote a photo essay of life on the set for the news publication *Ilgan Sports*, javabeans was there to bring it to her own readers as well.[7] By giving readers an echo of the relentless media saturation surrounding the trendy K-drama scene, the site also provides a brief submersive (but never quite *immersive*) cultural experience, a little dunk into the deep waters of specific cultural contexts.

What began as an individual effort by javabeans has spread into multiple simultaneous recaps by several recappers, the addition of comoderator girlfriday in June 2010, and multiple updates and posts per day. Dramabeans .com also provides translated interviews, a glossary, and a series of encyclopedic entries on the nuances of K-drama staples such as the piggyback ride, the word *oppa*, and the fraught transition from *jondaemal* (formal or polite speech) to *banmal* (informal speech).[8] Dramabeans.com documents site moderators javabeans's and girlfriday's fixations on specific actors, including Lee Seung-gi, Gong Yoo, and Kang Ji-hwan, which led to completed recaps of Kang's lower-rated 2010 drama *Coffee House*, as well as recaps of *One Night, Two Days (1N2D)*, a dual-commentary departure from K-drama into variety television propelled by Lee Seung-gi's popularity. However, javabeans's Kang Ji-hwan fixation was not enough to generate full recaps of early 2011's *Lie to Me*; lack of interest resulted in the intensely hybrid-form weecap, a capsule summary of the plot with an open thread for longer discussion beneath it; the weecap form is much less engaging, and thus demonstrates how much is present in a recap beyond mere plot summary. Dramabeans. com has also developed its own specific cultural practices, including the rotating headers that Dramabeans.com's graphically inclined commenters design gratis, and the ritualistic Friday Open Thread. But the recaps themselves, and the recappers' unapologetically idiosyncratic responses to their source texts, continue to hold a large piece of Dramabeans.com's online real estate. Even in the streamlined redesign, the newest recaps hold pride of place up top in the Featured section.

One component within this phenomenon is that the fansite actually has its own dedicated fans, readers who come specifically to the site and trust its work above others. Although *Coffee Prince* was perhaps not the most-watched K-drama of 2007, according to javabeans's final summation of her work, her 60,000-plus word recaps of the novel and scene-by-scene analyses of the drama garnered well over 2,000 comments, making it "nothing short of a phenomenon" on the site,[9] with an unofficial soundtrack that continues to generate a high number of page hits. These recap readers, by focusing on the site itself and not its putative primary sources, are exercising a privilege of readable texts: control over time, and reading in translation, viewing experiences not supported by the televised source. This behavior can also be interpreted as an outgrowth of instrumentalizing consumption: time, the most valuable commodity of urban modernity, must be conserved in order to allow either more consumption or more refamiliarization with the self, as mediated through participation in online collectives.

The specificities of transnational, bilingual online communication are heavily implicated in the seeming transparence of Dramabeans.com's mediations between source texts and fan recipients. But the recap implicates its readers into understandings mediated by the recapper's narrated response; that is, the recapper's involvement as recorded in the texts brings with it a wealth of information to which the reader gains access. This borrowed transparency ought to bring wariness: the relationship between anglophone fandoms and non-anglophone source texts can contain profound ideological difficulties. Online environments have sometimes been analyzed in terms of the ostensible flattening of offline *naturecultural*[10] groups into a single *netizenry* or online group affiliation, a seemingly analogous, very slippery term that bears only passing resemblance to national affiliations. While not propagating any rhetoric of national formation, Dramabeans.com still contains echoes of artificially induced offline cultural familiarity in the recapper's language capabilities, knowledge of common tropes, and awareness of media hype, which are thus partially preserved throughout the site. This information is present in the recapper's documents of episode reactions, and the reader's easy access to these borrowed competencies facilitates what seems like a transparent translational experience.

"FLEXIBLE NEGOTIATIONS": COMPLIANCE, CONSUMERISM, AND THE GIFT

There is no single account possible for the interplay of consumption and gifting within fandoms; market forces and social forces, and their cultural formations, precede and are not localizable within subcultural formations. Media theorist Matt Hills presents a compelling argument for the necessity of analyzing fandom accounts through a series of twisting reflexive inquiries. Hills's readings of fandom studies as an academic construct find closure or conclusion, and strict categorization of experiences, as the primary relations to fandom as taken up in its academic study. Hills suggests that this nonviable model of closure, narcissistic because falsely definitive, must be given up in favor of sets of self-reflexive inquiries into participatory cultures. He advocates these deliberate destabilizations as useful in laying out the stakes involved in their formation and maintenance, and to explore the specifics of fandom cultures, which are not univocal even within their own boundaries.[11] Fandoms are not often univocal, and writing about them either acknowledges their aggregate nature or falsifies their experiences, yet academic analysis seems to demand a kind of conclusive effort. Hills's methodology is therefore useful when delineating approaches to complex issues such as fandom funding or cultural appropriations within fandoms, since it allows an exploration of complexity with a concomitant acknowledgment of variance within a single culture, even on a single site.

Proposing online subcultures as an amorphous group, or considering their productive abilities only in revolutionary or reactive modes, would likely provide an incomplete account of Dramabeans.com's transnational and transactional mediations. Commodified consumption of its recaps is facilitated by the site's linguistically mediated translational power, which provides a translucent reading experience facilitated or mediated by the recapper's knowledgeable responses. Comparatist Shu-mei Shih views this kind of commodification as an expression of transnational access privilege on the part of the anglophone population, vectored through what she considers an unequal balance between powers of commodification within languages. That is, cultural production in other languages has the power to be translated, while anglophonicity compels translation. However, the dangers of this commodification, while real and expressed on the site in terms of value for time, are mediated through fandom itself, which uses its financial commodity presence (a seeming compliance with dominant cultural models) in order to fund and further the culture of the gift, in which the recappers maintain and curate the site, creating novel-length recap collections and posting content daily, actions which have only passing monetary justification. Shih's account of linguistically mediated unequal relations seems to condemn the work of the fans and recappers at Dramabeans.com to unending vacillation between consumption and production, with little chance to escape the flows of greater and lesser determinacy and power.

The localized control exerted by the site takes up an intermediary role of its own, placing the power of "decipherable localism," or the presentation of local national culture with the anticipation of ready decipherability, primarily with the fans behind Dramabeans.com. The positionality of a readily readable text in translation becomes very interesting when examined in light of Shu-mei Shih's insistence on mapping "*on whose terms* and *on what terms* that reach is made possible."[12]

The text in this case must be considered not only in terms of the specificities of K-drama and even the attendant media hype but also the K-drama cultural norms being presented as in need of explanation, as opposed to those that become transparent, the pellucid difference through which the online fan traverses with, at best, a faint intellectual twinge. This translucent reconstruction of cultural difference and its partial reclamation of offline local knowledge in the service of fandom could warrant Shih's pointed questions of representation and availability in online contexts. The anxiety underwriting this analysis lies in the projected subsumption of cultural production through loss of linguistic specificity—that is, translation can produce static, rendering the *K* in *K-drama* a letter and nothing more. As Shih acerbically puts it, "Through flexible negotiations between national and ethnic cultural codes, easy consumption and assimilation are guaranteed."[13] This ease of consumption at Dramabeans.com must then come under serious question as a viable circumvention of extant capitalist transaction models.

I have no wish to minimize this aspect of consumption practices as they occur at Dramabeans.com. However, Shih's reading is complicated by a set of simultaneously occurring practices at the site, whose interactions create a nonteleological exploration of ways to relate to the source texts. These questions emerge through the easy consumption of mass production, which Shih identified as part of a process of minoritization through the power of ready translatability. This ease of consumption, facilitated by its pop-cultural focus and smooth translations, has come under scrutiny, not least as a partial evasion of extant distribution and access models. What Benedict Anderson calls "a certain privacy to all languages"[14] is circumvented through immediate access to competencies and contextual information provided both within and around the recaps at the site. The reader slips into the cultural production of a social group through that mediated clarification of previously opaque cultural and linguistic barriers. This slippage creates problematic, productive excesses and multiple submersions into another popular culture, which belong to the reader during the recap through the recapper's mediation but degrade once outside that moment of shared affinity. By interpolating issues of cultural and linguistic specificity between and within the recaps themselves, Dramabeans.com creates an instability at the conjunction of linguistic exclusion and online translingual promiscuity, as well as a productive flow from the separation of offline affiliations, which can be used to read its interpolations into cultures of compliance and consumption.

Fandom conversations demonstrate wildly varying amounts of and desires for critical engagement, enthusiastic acclaim, or a sometimes volatile mixture of the two. An idiomatic indicator such as "Don't harsh my squee," in which *squee* is an all-encompassing term for uncritical enthusiasm, demonstrates this self-reflexive descriptor as a simultaneous imperative for acceptable interaction. While not a given, lack of overt contraindications in an original post usually indicates openness to critique while assuming affective sympathy for both source texts and fellow fans.[15] Of course, both modes exist at Dramabeans.com.

Of the two most common negative responses on the site, disagreements with the recap itself are encouraged by the structure of the recap and comments, as well as by the terms laid out in the site FAQs. The other, demands for faster or increased recaps, has drawn the ire of site moderators on several occasions. This fan base imperative to recap a specific drama joins the inevitable requests to post recaps faster (faster!) to create the kind of alienating experience that would render the recap in terms of functionality, making the site more responsive to readership input, but debarring the recappers from the precise affective engagements which render their recaps, with their lengthy analyses and real-time responses to the source texts, so attractive to begin with. The kind of affective labor present in the recaps at Dramabeans .com, where the recappers mediate their responses from the source texts to their readership, renders such a functional model of production in terms of ingratitude for the work being done.

Social response supposedly undergirds the gift-based economies of fan cultures, where the work one fan does is compensated by other fans' responses in the form of (positive) comments. This response constitutes one of the major forms of interaction between the fan and his or her fandom community, and as such, the responsive fan comment constitutes an important physical inscription of presence and engagement, both with the recapper's work and the fandom source, as well as the population of fans whose paths all cross at this particular site. The careful attention and affective engagement of fellow fans, as present in the comments, are supposedly the recapper's basic form of compensation, beyond the satisfaction and engagement of producing the recap in itself. While the gift exists in the recap itself, the unit of exchange is not only the comment but the thanks of the commenters too, their tangible gratitude for work done well.

The site remains committed to stringent analysis of its material, while unabashedly standing by the personal investment and enthusiasm of its recappers. However, as site moderator and originator, javabeans also sometimes receives derisive commentary, especially when there is a drama that some readers think she should be recapping.[16] Although the word *ungrateful* has been highlighted less in moderator responses than in the flood of other fans' defensive comments, the idea is certainly an underlying bolster of their indignant response. This idea of ingratitude suggests that the foundational gift-economy form of exchange within fandom must also contain a kind of affective taxation, requiring acknowledgment of work done, as well as the more familiar monetary compensation that increasingly characterizes even the supposedly gift-based fandom interaction. The site's production wanders between the readership's hopes and demands, the recappers' labor and desires, and all the fans' mixed affiliations, to produce destabilizations of both compliant and consumerist models of interaction.

Overviews of fandom can vacillate around questions of docility and compliance, especially in relation to the critical aspects of fandom production.[17] The impulse toward production in the spirit of communal fervor drives the participation of a fan within the community; as media theorist John Fiske puts it, "[The] moment of reception becomes the moment of production in fan culture."[18] This moment becomes crucial when dealing with the question of fan response as a kind of critical practice, since it includes complex overlapping phenomena. For Fiske, whose strict dichotomous structures of cultural and economic factors form his account of fandom interactions, this critical fandom-generated response is an excessive reactivity, differentiating a fan from a "normal" consumer of culture in degree of intensity but not in kind. I propose with Matt Hills that Fiske's approach, while attractively conclusive, risks obscuring some of the nuances of fandom's apparent cultures of compliance and gift, and offer instead a few readings of Dramabeans .com's consumer behaviors, ranging from the commodification of the recap through to a manifestation of gift culture through finance capital.[19]

We begin with the Althusserian interpellation of the fan at the moment of reception and with the recaps emerging from an intimately affective relationship with the source texts themselves as well the communities surrounding them.[20] Moving first to a more straightforward definition of compliance, simply assuming the recapper's immediately sympathetic stance to every aspect of the canonical text could, in the context of impassioned response, still be an mistake. The first answer on Dramabeans.com's FAQS[21] clearly demonstrates that, while unquestioning devotion is a legitimate and recognizable fandom form, it is not often in use at Dramabeans.com, a site whose headers include the phrase "blogging my K-drama obsession," while its founder observes on the About page that "just because it's pop culture doesn't mean discourse has to be shallow."[22] Any tensions between critical response and enthusiastic affection manifest as a rich archive of call-and-response, germinating instead of reiterating orthodoxies concerning source texts and community formation.

There is another nuance to the most compliant recap, moving from the attentive toward the devotional. Being in this kind of compliance with a source text requires fervent recapping, relaying details and nuances of intimate personal reactions as well as subtleties of characterization and narrative arc. This deeply felt sympathy moves the recapper from factual recountings toward speculations on future plot development, discussion of alternate possibilities, gripes with character inconsistencies or clumsy retconning,[23] and comparisons with other works in the same genre or by the same actors, as part of the recapping gesture. The devout recap thus shares characteristics with its apostate form, both relaying information dovetailed with attentive critical discussion. Fiske discusses the fan's devout productivity as a kind of epistemic intervention, saying that "it also participates in the construction of the original text and thus turns the commercial narrative or performance into popular culture," changing consumption in transformative ways.[24] This attractive claim is also deeply problematic, since it requires an unsustainable purification of capitalist structures from fandom action. As Matt Hills puts it, "Conventional logic, seeking to construct a sustainable opposition between the 'fan' and the 'consumer,' falsifies the fan's experience by positioning fan and consumer as separable cultural identities."[25] This continuing complication of fandom's devotional aspects complicates readings of gift and commodities in fandom contexts.

The gift economies, or exchanges based in social or affective response, become even more interesting and convoluted in these transnational and translational contexts. The gift culture funded through capitalist commodification dances at the edge of falling into market economies at all times and can be indecipherable from the market economy when considered in terms of moneymaking. However, the presence of the gift within the recappers' giving of themselves through their affective labor in making the recap keeps Dramabeans.com teetering between personal affiliative texts and what Fiske calls "industrially produced texts," which nonetheless provide opportunities for fans to "'excorporate' the products of the industry."[26]

However, discussion of revenue generation from fandom participation and production remains complex. One major concern within fandom communities is the exploitation of fan labor for others' financial gain, as well as host sites' attempts to edit and control information stored on their sites. These interacting issues have led to fan-based archive initiatives, notably the Organization for Transformative Works (otw) and its dedicated servers, purchased by fan donation.[27] Dramabeans.com's relationship to affective engagement and compensation, complicated by its generation of advertising revenue, falls between compliance (with capitalist/consumerist models of revenue generation) and opacity (since that compliance apparently occurs for reasons beyond pure remuneration). My own fandom interpolation suggests that these two considerations—the site's persistence and growth and the generation of ad revenue—are not only linked but sourced in a genuine desire to continue providing recaps and the concomitant fandom interaction in the comments.

After beginning as a personal nonrevenue-generating WordPress site and then moving through a brief Donations period, Dramabeans.com began running paid advertisements on the site's main page. The ads are in the sidebar and do not impinge heavily upon reader consciousness; sponsored posts are rare and well flagged as such. This restraint is a contrast from other blogs and fan sites, which may list sponsorships only at the very bottom of a post or allow ads to frame or be deliberately integrated within the reading material, thus capturing the reading eye and forcing reader participation. Posts at both Dramabeans.com and elsewhere demonstrate that javabeans considers generating revenue for the continuing maintenance of the site as contiguous with her commitment to the fan base.[28] Despite its engagement with capitalist modes of consumption and remuneration, the current schema of revenue generation at Dramabeans.com is also implicated in the maintenance of the gifting apparatus. The ads replace the Donations button, becoming the site moderator's method for decoupling content generation from direct donation in an effort to defray site maintenance costs while staying within accepted fandom mores. These questions of cost, upkeep, compensation, and deflection require reconsiderations of gift exchange and gift culture away from the decoys of technoecstatic models toward the infrastructural considerations governing representation and participation in larger online economies.

ON READING K-DRAMA: THE RECAP AS MEDIATING SOURCE TEXT

Moving the action of Korean drama from television screen to computer monitor contains two moments of translation, from moving drama to stills and text, and from Korean into English, as well as two moments of critical response in which the English-language text holds primacy of place. The fan tracks the recapper's movement across languages and media, remediating them as a unified virtual text from the dispersed textual amalgam encompassing not only the drama itself but its translation and reception as well. The persistent presence of the recap readers, whose primary experience of K-drama comes through the recaps, renders the recap a kind of mediated source text. For that source-rendering to occur, allowing these readers to participate in the larger fandom with something approaching commonality, the recap must bear significant resemblances to the K-drama it remediates, while simultaneously mediating between the source text and its fans. These multiple flows of meaning and affinity all pass through the recap itself, which mediates each in specific ways, while also becoming a strange version of source text as readers reweave its multiple mediations into a seemingly seamless cultural artifact. The structures creating and emergent from this remarkable mediation form the basis of the analysis of specific examples taken from Dramabeans.com.

Critical code theorist N. Katherine Hayles deploys medium-specific analysis in digital contexts to emphasize the underlying materiality of the medium under consideration, as well the intermedial reactions the medium enables, since media change with relation to each other. As she puts it, medium-specific analysis "attends both to the specificity of the form . . . and to citations and imitations of one medium in another."[29] For the purposes of Dramabeans.com, medium-specific analysis means discussing visual stills, the text of the recap, and the comments below the recap as simultaneously separate components that require consideration, as well as taking a multimedial cross section of an experiential moment gathered around the episode being recapped.[30] Materiality in this reading is not limited to the physical. As Hayles points out, "Materiality should be understood as existing in complex dynamic interplay with content, coming into focus or fading into the background, depending on what performances the work enacts."[31] Despite its online form, the recap has a material presence, combining textual, visual, and aural evidence to produce an echo or faint specter of the moving medium of the television drama. My analysis uses Deleuzean theory to discuss the ways in which that specter or echo can occur or emerge, through the pervasive emphasis on affective reaction within the recap, from its textual and visual aspects. Deleuze's focus on the affective work and subjective time of cinema provides a strong corollary for the consideration of the recap-reading experience, in which the disparate pieces of the recap texts (texts, images, songs) meld with the reader's physical hardware.

One of the recapper's most powerful tools is nonlinguistic: the screen captures, or screencaps, are still images taken from a moving source and inserted into the recap, bolstering the recapper's account through its visual record of affective engagement. This interplay deserves further consideration, since it is crucial to the recap's performative abilities. In Gilles Deleuze's contemplation of the philosophical fields opened up by the advent of cinema, he considers the dyad of movement (*Cinema 1*) and time (*Cinema 2*). Deleuze's insistence on the specificity of the nonlinguistic image—that it has a methodology of meaning different in kind from linguistic or text-based work—renders the screencap, the still image captured from the moving episode, an artifact in its own right. The intensity of the screencap retains the shock of movement in the context of the recap, serving to call the moment back from the reader's memory, or as a metonym for the movement arrested in the screencap itself. Extrapolating from this shock, the recap moves the screencap into motion, while the still image enables the creation of motion through its projection onto the brain-as-screen. Within the *movement-image*, which privileges movement across time, lies the *affection-image*, which Deleuze centers on the face: the "pulsion" or flows between admiration/wonder and desire/power are concentrated at this site of supreme meaning and ethical engagement.[32] In the Deleuzian analysis the close-up on the face has a well-documented affective role: as he puts it, "the pure affect, the pure expressed of the state of things in fact relates to a face which expresses it (or to several faces, or to equivalents, or to propositions)."[33] The close-up as screencap provides a "pure expressed" interpolated into the text of the recap, re-creating the shock of the brain through the break in the change of medium. Interpretation of screencaps occurs in terms of specifically sympathetic affective use. While the recap's textuality can streamline events or outright skip disliked storylines, the screencap functions as both break and involuntary affective engagement in the flow of the text.

In the context of K-drama recaps, the screencap as affection-image is therefore of critical importance. The screencaps at Dramabeans.com are heavily character-focused, concentrating on facial expressions or other affective weight as carried within each image. The initial interaction launches the affective mechanism unleashed within each episode; the longer-term relationship, built up between the screen character and the invested viewer, is an important characteristic of any successful form.[34] In the case of the recap reader, this link is strengthened not only through the textual renderings but the interpolation of the screencaps as well. Thus the screencap is a necessary innovation for translating an affective, moving visual medium like K-drama into the flat screen and still images of online engagement, allowing the recap to move, as Deleuze says, "from the stone to the scream"[35]—that is, from stillness into precipitate action, with immediate affective weight.

The screencap's power is in evidence throughout javabeans's recaps of Korean Broadcasting System's 2010 drama *Wish Upon a Star* (see fig. 4.1). In *Wish Upon a Star*, the two lead characters are faced with a set of contrived circumstances: lawyer meets spunky girl with many siblings; they must move in together with the lawyer's two brothers, and hijinks ensue. javabeans's recap of *Wish Upon a Star*'s eighth episode demonstrates the mechanics and specificities of Deleuze's image-based theory, as well as its larger implications for the transmission of affect as central to the recap's work. The recap of Episode 8 opens with a triptych of faces; in order to sustain viewer interest, the previous episode had ended in a vicious verbal exchange between the leads, with a small sibling caught in the middle.[36] Looking at the three faces from left to right re-creates the tense rhythm of the shot-reverse-shot, a technical convention for conveying a seamless conversation so familiar it has become nearly transparent. In this case, the screencaps pan from scowling lawyer to frowning heroine, with the crying child caught mid-sob, re-establishing the recap reader within the last episode's fraught affective landscape. The triptych of faces contains the entirety of this opening, and to look at each in turn is to engage the affective mechanism at work throughout the

Pal-gang slaps Kang-ha, angry that he would care about his house more than the safety of an injured child. I don't think he's actually that callous, but their tempers are running high and she is acting reflexively. They glare at each other.

Young Pa-rang understands the danger of angering Kang-ha and bursts into tears, begging him to forgive his sister. He cries that she didn't know what she was doing and didn't mean to slap him, and pleads not to be kicked out of the house.

There's a slight shift in Kang-ha's expression, and based on the next scene we can interpret this to mean that he feels bad. In his room, he replays the scene that just happened, but instead of focusing on the fire or his anger, his memory lingers on Pal-gang calling him a heartless bastrd.

Figure 4.1. Taken from *Wish Upon a Star*'s Episode 8 Recap, written by javabeans and posted January 29, 2010. Note the screencaps' integration into the larger recap. The text and screencaps in the figure are preceded by an introductory screencap, a brief note on javabeans's changing reception of the drama, and a link to a song by Dyne.

recap. The screencaps reveal the shot's own formulaic ubiquity, even as the close-ups of the faces elicit a measure of unwilled affective engagement, of a kind with the involuntary engagement required by film or televisual media.

The ubiquity of the close-up throughout the recaps of *Wish Upon a Star* is intensified by the placement of these screencaps in their shot-reverse-shot sequence, to have the characters facing each other even on the computer monitor. Together, the screencaps facilitate Deleuze's affection-image, in which the face in close-up "prepares a paroxysm,"[37] initiating a serial intensification of affect that passes between the faces in close-up until the scene "pass[es] from one quality to another, to emerge on to a new quality,"[38] which is then integrated into the reading fan's reactive, affectionate, enthusiastic participation. The screencaps are not chosen lightly: all on their own, they have a specific purpose, distinct from that of the written text. Instead of simply buttressing the words, the images participate in a primary concern of K-drama: not just narration, but incitement of affect. In this sense, the screencap is an integral part of the recap itself.

The affective power of K-drama, and the importance of its visceral immediacy to the reading as well as viewing publics, requires that the recap's still image and typed text convey that transformed and transformative weight from screen to reader. This is demonstrated in another example, the recapped emotional peaks in the 2007 drama *Coffee Prince*, a series which intensified K-drama awareness in anglophone online communities, not least because it brought new readers to Dramabeans.com. In *Coffee Prince*, a cross-dressing girl (Go Eun Chan) working odd jobs as "the man of the house," and a rich but disgraced chaebol heir (Choi Han Gyul), must work together to transform an ailing coffeehouse into a viable business venture. Their romantic relationship develops in fits and starts, alternately helped and hindered by Eun Chan's decision to continue passing as a young man. Han Gyul's subsequent crisis of sexual identity intensifies until it precipitates that critical drama turning point: his confession of love.

javabeans's recap of the series demonstrates the particular care with this moment, the crowning scene of Episode 10 (Tenth Cup), retaining precise descriptions and an abundance of screencaps. In a subsequent post, javabeans includes an excerpt from the actual shooting script with her own translation, including the production notes. javabeans prefaces the post by noting how it "is turning me into a starry-eyed fangirl," who would produce even more than the episode recap, before documenting translational practices before launching the entry:

> Yes, you may notice I've taken a few liberties with punctuation and such, which I've done because I find Korean and English have different cadences and speech patterns . . . I'd rather preserve the tone of a piece than transcribe to a perfectly literal but less-than-elegant effect.[39]

The ellipses, which dominate the notes, document an insertion of time into the translated transcription of this crucial scene. Consider their preponderance in the script javabeans translates in "Anatomy of a Scene: Tenth Cup," immediately after Han Gyul turns around for the last time and heads back to the cafe:

> HAN GYUL: [*aching heart, with warmth*] "Whether you're a man, or an alien . . . I don't care anymore."
> EUN CHAN, *heart hurting, overwhelmed*
> HAN GYUL: "I tried to get rid of my feelings and I couldn't . . . so let's go, as far as we can go." [*watching quietly, with a small smile*] "Let's try."

EUN CHAN, *heart aching . . . happy . . . lowering her head . . . soon overflowing with tears . . . worrying for the future.*

HAN GYUL, *looking at this Eun Chan . . . holding Eun Chan's lowered head carefully, protectively . . . his smile faltering . . . absorbed in his thoughts . . . happy but not purely so.*

EUN CHAN *carefully takes a step closer, wrapping her arms around Han Gyul's waist . . . wishing time could stop like this.*

The seeming excess of ellipses also signals an insertion of time into the script on the part of the mediator. The effect is to create an echo of the scene's real-time slowness, the spaces inserted in the service of affective response. The text of the recap enervates its screencaps with this same affective weight, cutting Han Gyul's sudden movement into a slow-motion diptych reminiscent of stop-motion chronophotography. Significantly, the recap switches to a near-transcription of the scene, emptying its prose to fill its images with power, while the script holds its ellipses to indicate interpolation into diegetic time. The entirety of the character, narrative, and emotional arc have built to this moment; in the recap, narration moves swiftly past Han Gyul's longing and indecision as everyone waits, breathless, for what Han Gyul will do as he walks in the door:

> *He runs in to face Eun Chan, staring intensely at her face . . .*
> *Startled, Eun Chan starts to explain that she's trying to fix some damage to Yu Ju's mural drawing.*
> *Still silent, Han Gyul swoops in purposefully—*

And it is the screencap that gives the recap readers the lovers' long-awaited kiss. In the delirium of the moment, the detailed narratives give way to a series of near-contiguous images linked to direct quotes, occurring in some slowed subjective time, heavily weighted with affective power, as Han Gyul finally confesses his attraction openly to Eun Chan: "Whether you're a man, or an alien . . . I don't care anymore."[40] This potent line encapsulates Han Gyul's character development, and its recording within the recap (as well as its afterlife on Dramabeans.com as the ultimate love confession) matches the visual record of Deleuze's metonymic affection-image as focused on Han Gyul. Into the stillness of his revelation comes a space, the ellipsis within Han Gyul's confession taken up by Eun Chan's stunned, silent face, passing to the reader through the proliferating screen captures. In this moment the faces meet, the text and image meld, and the screens superimpose their motion and stillness upon the brain.

This moment of crystallization bears comparison not to the movement-image in *Cinema 1* but the time-image of *Cinema 2*,[41] a moment heavy with the flicker of affective storms at play between the two leads and their view-ers—before the crystal-image shatters with Han Gyul's sudden movement, and the action continues. The crystal-image is Deleuze's term for a specific kind of sensory disruption in a film, which manifests as a dilation or split-ting of time, as sensory data fall out of synch with each other, and the past and present superimpose themselves on the viewer's perception: "Time has to split . . . in two dissymmetrical jets, one of which makes all the present pass on, while the other preserves all the past. Time consists of this split, and it is this, it is time, that we *see in the crystal*."[42] This crystallization marks the presence of the time-image, manifesting in the recap reader's melding of the screencaps, the ellipses, the narration, and the quoted script as she or he progresses through the devoted recaps of this crucial scene. In the mo-ment of reading, the fan experiences both affective echoes—his or her own, as recalled from watching the scene, and the recapper's deeply felt reaction, as captured in the recap.

CONCLUSION

The acts of translation involved in the recap, from distributed into partici-patory fan culture and from motion into stillness, reproduce the K-drama as multiple simultaneous texts, their affective weight tied to temporal flow. The deliberate deployment of text and image re-creates the flow and solidi-fication of time for the recap readers, almost against their stated desire to hurry through or linger less with the dramas. The recappers mediate these translations from within extant linguistic, economic, and affiliative infra-structures, negotiating within and online interchanges in something per-ilously reminiscent of good faith translation, even as their remediations open up critical and affective responses. In a similar spirit, I have attempted to open a series of ways into a larger inquiry, to consider the implications of this site's interactions both within and around online fandom cultures, by marking a series of approaches to relevant questions with overlapping sets of concerns. In the spirit of fandoms' profound engagements with and myriad responses to their texts, I request that my readers think of this chap-ter itself as a recap, and I hope it constitutes an opening move for many gen-erative conversations.[43]

NOTES

1. I am using the names the commenters, recappers, and moderators have chosen for themselves, a customary citational practice within online subcultures. In this case, the names "javabeans" and "girlfriday" do not appear capitalized when they are cred-

ited as authors on the site; I have rendered their names as given. I would add that these names are often deliberate pseudonyms, and within most online communities attempts to connect online and offline identities are considered not only deeply repugnant but also potentially dangerous. I have respected these fandom conventions to the best of my ability.

2. Television Without Pity, http://www.televisionwithoutpity.com/. Accessed May 30, 2010.

3. *Fan service* refers to gratuitous, often sexualized content within the episode, although the definition extends to include any fan-pandering detail, such as references to obscure characters or arcane plot points.

4. See javabeans, "Sol Pharmacy's finale makes it top-rated drama of the year," http://www.dramabeans.com/2009/10/sol-pharmacys-finale-makes-it-top-rated-drama-of-the-year/ and javabeans, "The Moon That Embraces the Sun: Episode 16," http://www.dramabeans.com/2012/02/the-moon-that-embraces-the-sun-episode-16/.

5. javabeans, "Summary: Dal Ju's Spring, Episode 1," February 25, 2007, http://www.dramabeans.com/2007/02/summary-dal-jas-spring-episode-1/.

6. Early entries on Japanese drama at Dramabeans.com do exist, but while Japanese and Korean drama remain closely linked through larger East Asian cultural flows and circulations (*Hana Yori Dango* is a prime example), the site's current focus is chiefly on K-drama, with sidelines in Korean music and film.

7. javabeans, "A Day on the Set with Choi Jung-won," March 6, 2010, http://www.dramabeans.com/2010/03/a-day-on-the-set-with-choi-jung-won/. The translations, though uncredited, are likely the site moderators' own work.

8. For example, the piggyback ride is explained through two other tropes: drinking and skinship, which culminate in the piggyback ride in K-drama convention. See girlfriday, "Pop Culture: Piggyback Rides," July 11, 2010, http://www.dramabeans.com/2010/07/pop-culture-piggyback-rides/.

9. javabeans, "Coffee Prince: Seventeenth Cup (Final)," August 27, 2007, http://www.dramabeans.com/2007/08/coffee-prince-seventeenth-cup-final/.

10. The term *natureculture* is a hallmark of the writings of both Bruno Latour and Donna Haraway, who use it to evade the question of whether causation or even correlation are the product of nature or nurture, especially when discussing formulation and dissemination of social praxes within specific groups. The use of the term in this context is meant to point out the artificiality of the designation *netizenry*, even as this grouping of recappers, readers, and commenters seems to beg a single name for their collective.

11. Hills pursues this self-reflexive trajectory by interrogating his own interpellations to account for the diversity of fandom practices. As he puts it, "the greatest difficulty with the label of acafandom is that it misleads us into thinking there's one referent to be championed, critiqued or defended." *Acafandom* is a portmanteau of "academic fandom," as derived from *acafan*, or a fan who is also an academic; the terms refer to the academic study perspective of a participant in that fandom who is using his or her academic training to analyze it. See Henry Jenkins's blog for more details on the terms and their development in academic contexts. Matt Hills, "Aca-Fandom and Beyond: Jonathan Gray, Matt Hills, and Alisa Perren (Part One)."

Accessed August 29, 2011. http://henryjenkins.org/2011/08/aca-fandom_and _behyond_jonathan.html.

12. Shu-mei Shih, *Visuality and Identity: Sinophone Articulations across the Pacific* (Berkeley: University of California, 2007), 60.

13. Shih, *Visuality and Identity*, 60.

14. Benedict Anderson, *Imagined Communities: Reflections on the Origin and Spread of Nationalism*, 2nd ed. (London: Verso, 1991), 148. Anderson's comment on linguistic exclusivity comes at the beginning of a longer meditation on the impossibility of acquiring all languages, as a preface to his discussion on the importance of perceived purity or continuity in the propagation of both nationalism and racism. See 148–49.

15. For further discussion of forcibly uncritical fan response, see Fanlore's entry at Squee: http://fanlore.org/wiki/Squee.

16. A sample of simultaneous commodification and analytic response can be found in the 352 comments on guest recapper thunderbolt's tongue-in-cheek mash-up recap of three different K-dramas, in response to javabeans' exasperated tweet concerning recent recap demands. Comments spanned the gamut from calls to recant (see the comment thread at 22, begun by Kate, and comment 93, from SprinkledPink), to heated justification (see comment 150, from amhrancas). thunderbolt, "Can You Hear My Boss Protect the New Gisaeng's Heart: Episode 1," Dramabeans .com, August 27, 2011. http://www.dramabeans.com/2011/08/can-you-hear-my -boss-protect-the-new-gisaengs-heart-episode-1/.

17. See Matt Hills's introduction and chapter 1 of *Fan Cultures* (London: Routledge, 2002), where he works out the value of maintaining a tense continuum across dispassion and affection, within gratification and consumption, when discussing fandom participation and production.

18. John Fiske, "The Cultural Economy of Fandom," in *The Adoring Audience: Fan Culture and Popular Media*, ed. Lisa A. Lewis (London: Routledge, 1992), 41.

19. Hills, *Fan Cultures*, 51–52. For a counter-example, see Hills's deliberate underminings of his own certitude and conclusiveness in his recommendations for auto-ethnographic self-reflexive research within fandom cultures, on page 81.

20. Louis Pierre Althusser's theory of interpellation into state-sponsored social relations considers the subject's emergence as simultaneous with the address by the state. I am not applying Althusser with an eye to the potentially hegemonic apparatus of (in)gratitude, but to the simultaneity of the emergence of subjective presence within fandom and the subject's address by a fandom text—in this case, the recap. A fan emerges at the moment of the reading as s/he responds in specific ways to the address of a fan recapper's texts, which elicits response through the affective engagements present in the recap.

21. "How come you're so sarcastic? Just tell us what happened in the episode/article, without your stupid opinions!" javabeans and girlfriday, "FAQ: Frequently Asked Questions," http://www.dramabeans.com/faq.

22. javabeans, "About," http://www.dramabeans.com/about/. This quotation has survived multiple reworkings of the page's contents.

23. *Retcon* is a portmanteau of *retroactive continuity*, a term which indicates the integra-

tion of a late-blooming plot revelation or character development into the series's extant world. A clumsy retcon is not well-integrated into this material, and is therefore clearly artificial to the audience: the plot or characterizations become nonsensical or contradictory, or else the worldbuilding no longer makes sense.

24. Fiske, "The Cultural Economy of Fandom," 40.
25. Hills, *Fan Cultures*, 29.
26. Fiske, "The Cultural Economy of Fandom," 47.
27. The Organization for Transformative Works's detailed mission statement can be found on its site, at http://www.transformativeworks.org/about/believe.
28. javabeans writes: "One of the questions I get asked the most on Dramabeans is how I manage to watch and recap so many dramas all the time . . . girlfriday and I both probably spend a lot more time on the site than could be considered healthy (it's all for you!), and on a few occasions I've made the conscious effort to scale back in order to balance out my life—but ultimately I always come crawling back like a junkie in need of her next kdrama fix. Which isn't even so much a metaphor as it is an accurate description of life." javabeans, "Intel giveaway," November 24, 2010, http://javabeans.wordpress.com/2010/11/24/intel-giveaway/.
29. N. Katherine Hayles, "Print Is Flat, Code Is Deep: The Importance of Medium-Specific Analysis," *Poetics Today* 25, no. 1 (2004): 69.
30. The songs linked on Dramabeans.com are important enough to warrant their own discussion, but since my analysis focuses on the text and image of the recap, I must reluctantly bracket the role of music as affective sink or holder, and move on.
31. Hayles, "Print Is Flat, Code Is Deep," 71.
32. Gilles Deleuze, *Cinema 1: The Movement-image*, trans. Hugh Tomlinson and Barbara Habberjam (Minneapolis: University of Minnesota Press, 2006), 87–91.
33. Deleuze, *Cinema 1*, 103.
34. The accelerated or "binge" watching pattern, where a 16-episode series is finished in a weekend, seems to alter the affective experience of the English-language K-drama fan. The links between speed, affect, access, and control suggest a larger set of interlocking phenomena, requiring a dedicated analysis, which unfortunately I cannot perform here.
35. Deleuze, *Cinema 1*, 89.
36. javabeans, "Wish Upon a Star: Episode 8," January 29, 2010, http://www.dramabeans.com/2010/01/wish-upon-a-star-episode-8/. This discussion focuses on the first triptych below the lead image.
37. Deleuze, *Cinema 1*, 87.
38. Deleuze, *Cinema 1*, 89.
39. javabeans, "Anatomy of a Scene: Tenth Cup," August 1, 2007, http://www.dramabeans.com/2007/08/anatomy-of-a-scene-tenth-cup/.
40. javabeans, "Coffee Prince: Tenth Cup," July 31, 2007, http://www.dramabeans.com/2007/07/coffee-prince-tenth-cup/. The line is repeated in "Anatomy of a Scene," posted the next day.
41. "Subjectivity is never ours—it is time." Gilles Deleuze, *Cinema 2: The Time-image* (Minneapolis: Athlone Press, 1989), 82–83. See especially chapter 4, "The Crystals

of Time," for elaboration of the time-image's dependence on affective weight for the moment of crystallization.

42. Deleuze, *Cinema 2*, 81.

43. Research for this chapter was partially funded by a doctoral fellowship from the Social Sciences and Humanities Research Council of Canada. Many thanks to Professors Margherita Long and Jonathan M. Hall, to the organizers and participants of the University of California–Irvine Korean Popular Culture Conference 2011, and to all the fans whose labor, response, and affection so deeply inform this work.

PART TWO   Lights, Camera, Action!

In theorizing the star system and the nature of iconicity in Korean cinema, the chapters in this section raise a number of ideological issues surrounding cultures of celebrity and fan consumption practices built around them, from questions about how images signify within this cultural economy to inquiries into the role of celebrity in the national imaginary. What role do stars play in mediating fantasy in any given historical period? What does one make of the preponderance of affective registers that circulate within these representations? How do gender and class shift the terms of analysis? The material in this section was chosen for their range within this focus. Chronologically they focus on South Korean cinema in the Americanized 1950s, the Golden Age (1955–72) leading into the politically and culturally austere 1970s, the first decade of the 2000s commonly referred to as the heyday of the South Korean film renaissance, and North Korean cinema from the late 1970s to the present. What they have in common is that all are lodged in either interim moments of transition or interstitial spaces between forms and genres and thus inherently bear the signs of historical contradictions, which the authors see as embodied by the stars that characterized them. Collectively the readings in this part are also self-consciously and critically aware of the tendencies that have been formative in the definition and function of Korean popular culture studies from and within a film studies perspective.

Steven Chung suggests that approaches to Korean popular culture have oversimplified periodization and thus produced blind spots. He points out that the

1950s, because of such ideological simplification, have remained among the least studied of the decades, when in fact precisely this period would appear to be critically most pressing in terms of understanding the peninsula's divided underpinnings. The immediate postwar period of the 1950s has been seen largely in derisive terms, as a culturally apathetic, vacuous, and impoverished time reflecting the nadir of national and cultural independence and strength. Following the reappraisal of films from this period in the late 1990s by feminist film theorists, Chung's project on the colorful and vibrant film and fashion regimes in South Korea's 1950s provides an anti-monolithic critique by focusing on the contradictions and ideological stakes inscribed into the superficial extravagance and pretensions in filmmaking, fashion, and fan culture. Chung reads the extravagance as radically symbolic; rather than seeing the films as erasing postwar destruction and destitution or representing that historical period, he reads them as attempts to imagine "a qualitatively different reality from the one promised by American liberalism and its South Korean adherents" through escapism and fantasy.

Kelly Jeong looks at the star system during the Golden Age of Korean cinema, focusing on South Korean actor Kim Sŭng-ho's iconic depictions of patriarchs and the meta-textual nature of his star image. What was astonishing about Kim Sŭng-ho's career was his ability to transition from the demise of the Syngman Rhee administration to the Park Chung-Hee dictatorship. Jeong suggests Kim Sŭng-ho's appeal to postwar audiences lay in the association of this on-screen persona with a more satisfying, idealized artificial reality that it represented while erasing the harsh quotidian reality on screen. Foregrounding the intertwined relationship between South Korea's postwar popular culture and the state's nation-building agenda, the star's relationship to the state is a codependent one in Jeong's account, whereby the political and cultural act in symbiosis with his stardom, helping to build it on one hand and exploiting it on the other. Jeong thus argues that Kim Sŭng-ho's charisma and stardom depend on a sense of humanity embodied by the actor but ironically function hegemonically by looking optimistically toward a better future while affirming particularly conservative emotional and cultural values.

In his study of North Korean socialist realism, Travis Workman draws on psychoanalytic theory to analyze the processes whereby melodramatic emotions are strategically utilized in order to induce sentimental identification, not just with the characters and stars but also with the political and moral ideas that they seem to represent. Workman's attention to the transformation between North Korean classic films on liberation and socialist reality and the "hidden hero" films (1977–present) reveals changes in national narratives and in modes of identification. His look at the North Korean star system suggests an intricate relationship between filmic and extra-filmic representation. North Korean film stars appear as a particular kind of character across various media creating cultural connections. Workman argues that the melodramatic and sentimental representations in these films, which are really ideological embodiments of political and moral ideas, function quite differently than in naturalist presentations. In particular, Workman foregrounds the variant techniques that these films employ to manufacture intimacy between the individual and the nation.

Michelle Cho focuses on the maternal figure signified by the actress Kim Hye-ja in Bong Joon-ho's *Mother* (2009) and its deployment of stars as figures of *generic individuality*, that is, a specific form of the individual-as-commodity that registers affectively with the national public that consumes them. Cho looks at stars' intertextuality, the complex processes through which celebrities come to signify abstract ideals or become associated with particular affective formulations, and as texts, stars carry their affective content from one film to another. Kim Hye-ja, for example, is known for her maternal roles, which is the reason it makes sense to think of them in terms of genre. *Mother*, for Cho, is a deft commentary on the implications of this particular construct; it is a film that self-consciously critiques the production and packaging of cultural icons and, in so doing, thinks critically about the generic parameters of film stars. YMC

5

STEVEN CHUNG

Regimes within Regimes
Film and Fashion Cultures in the Korean 1950s

The topos of Im Ŭng-sik's iconic 1956 photograph *Early Summer, Midopa* (fig. 5.1) is apparently clear: the weight of traditional Korean cultural practice is giving way to the lightness of Western lifestyle. The keenness of what Roland Barthes called the photo's *punctum*—that is, the deeply affective register of an image—is driven home by the seeming distress that passes on the face of the woman in the foreground: she is nearest to us, but in the burgeoning consumer culture epitomized in the scene's Western goods stores (Midopa was at the time Seoul's largest department store), she has already faded. The ascendant icon now is the almost ethereal figure of the lady of leisure, protected from the sun by her parasol, embedded in the newly scrubbed city streets (the way the patterned dresses echo the street's tiling). *Early Summer, Midopa* seems to present us with an emblem of "Americanization," a compressed rendering of the classic tropes, replete with gender and class antagonisms, of cultural imperialism. But in fact the image's semantic coordinates are far from obvious. The intrusion of Western clothing, so often embodied (but rarely so artfully) in precisely this juxtaposition of women's figures, is of course a ceaselessly deployed sign of cultural loss and transformation. As such, on those terms alone the scene is difficult to date—that is, until we look with some care at the clothes themselves and see not simply the generic *yangjang-hanbok* dichotomy but rather the bold floral prints and flared lines of the young women's dresses. To even an amateur student of fashion flows, these styles follow lines of adoption from American fashions of the 1950s and therein to the vast apparatus of postwar occupation and Cold War containment. The image's *studium*, Barthes' complementary term for the sociocultural import of pictures, is not defined

Figure 5.1. *Early Summer, Midopa* (Im Ŭng-sik, 1956).

without this sense of clothing's timeliness; in this respect the clothing's historicity is itself the photo's studium.

But this historicity is not the photograph's critical subject. Rather, it is the woman in the foreground, in particular her clothes, that begs a closer look. For, of course, her *hanbok* is not some timeless traditional vestiment but rather the subject of tremendous social, cultural, and political investment, regulation, and even caprice. One can think of course of the radical changes mandated in the 1894 Kabo Reforms, that frantic attempt to mark out a bulwark of Korean modernity, staked in part on a more enlightened system of dress. But more germane here is the way *hanbok* were charged with heterogeneous interest and meaning throughout the postwar era. The foregrounded woman's "early summer" dress is translucent and light, likely stitched of newly developed nylon, and the *chŏgori* short; its line is economic and its ornamentation almost nonexistent: an irreducible product of modern capital and its demand for efficiency. In the winter the outfit would appropriate another new material, velvet, to extravagant effect. The woman is therefore not as behind, and the young women not as far in the vanguard, as the photo at first blush might suggest. The image, characteristic of a core cultural discourse of the 1950s, Americanization, is thus rather more complex and points to the multiple "systems" at play in the period. And here it is fashion, in its traverse and ephemeral detail as much as its contingent materiality, that is the prompt for a more careful and flexible cultural history.

My aim in this chapter is to examine, through the dominant mass cultural forms of film and fashion, some of the layered ontologies and trajectories that belie the discourse of Americanization in 1950s South Korea. I am prompted here by the period's critical though often undertheorized position in conceptualizing political transformation in modern Korea. In the overt simplifications of thinking about culture in decades—in which, say, the 1930s immediately evoke urban modernism or the 1970s the sterility of the arts under authoritarian surveillance—the 1950s are particularly fraught with contradiction. The period is also one of the more ideologically staked. For both the liberal political scientists and economists writing with some despair in the latter part of the decade as well as for the ideologues rationalizing military intervention in the 1960s, the years following the Korean War were characterized by corruption, betrayal, and retrogression. The porosity of the nation's cultural borders and the seeming ubiquity of American commodities and everyday practices were projected as emblems of the era's problems. More recently, the 1950s have come to be revised within postcolonial and feminist criticism as a period of cultural and social radicalization, throwing into even greater relief the militarized order of the periods that sandwich it. But neither this opposition nor its consequences for historiography or social analysis present any real hermeneutic obstacle. Rather, it is the intellectual habit attached to periodization, abstract teleology, that threatens a clear vision of the cultural landscape of the 1950s. In many politicized accounts, the 1950s marks the nadir of national independence and strength, the point from which to draw a straight line of economic and cultural development.

I am prompted here also by the fraught role of visual surfaces, embodied most overtly in fashion and film, in reading Korea's cultural discourses and diagnosing its location within global cultural circulation. While the extant historiography of the period has pointed consistently to the close and revealing relationship between film and literature, film's nexus with fashion is equally illuminating. This is not only because the two forms were instrumental in shifting mass cultural sensibility palpably toward the visual but also because the incipient state of both industries in the 1950s meant that cooperation and cross-pollination were inevitable. Filmmaking and its extensive promotional apparatus became the best way to see the latest fashions, and fashion became a crucial means through which to emulate and embody the roles and fantasies films inspired. And it is precisely this mutual productivity that highlights the centrality of film and fashion to not only cultural but also political transformation. For, as many have noted, on the one hand clothing functions as a key site in contests for power in the way it can enforce discipline (think of school and military uniforms), mark social class, and sediment gender roles; and on the other hand, it can signal political opposition and symbolize social nonconformity. Watching films and consuming fashions in Korea, then, can be read as practices that exemplify apathy and enable hopeless social pretension but also facilitate modes of thinking and inhabiting social space differently. This is partly an effect of the psychic identifications central to both fashion and film: as Kaja Silverman reminds us, for Freud, "the ego is 'a mental projection of the surface of the body,' and that surface is largely defined through dress."[1] But perhaps more critically, it stems from the disavowing temporality that Roland Barthes persuasively argues is fashion's defining feature: "As soon as the signified *Fashion* encounters a signifier (such and such a garment), the sign becomes the year's Fashion, but thereby this Fashion dogmatically rejects the Fashion which preceded it, its own past; every new Fashion is a refusal to inherit, a subversion against the oppression of the preceding Fashion; Fashion experiences itself as a Right, the natural right of the present over the past."[2] This willed amnesia and ephemerality, as I will attempt to argue below, belies precisely the very historicity of the images of refinement and polish that dominate visual mass cultures of the 1950s.

There were certainly other spaces, media, and instruments that provoked or accommodated socially significant visual phenomena in the 1950s. The rapid transformation of cities, the influx of foreign capital and commodities, and the intensification of mass consumption patterns rendered myriad social spaces—from the intimate enclosures of stylish new cafés to the wide-open streets and public parks—as sites of spectacle and visual consumption. New modes of carriage and the new figures themselves (the modern or *après-guerre* boys and girls) became forms of spectacle and entertainment themselves, the subject of countless reports in the news media, both admonishing and celebratory, and engendered the popular pastime of people watching. Nevertheless, the cinema was by far the dominant medium of mass entertainment and consumption, carrying as it had the powerful investments of state-sponsored filmmaking from the colonial period as well as the "soft" dimension of the postwar American presence. Cinema dominated mass culture not only in unprecedented box-office attendance but also by radically reshaping the visual landscape in the diffuse networks through which its promotion and development operated. A number of slick film magazines appeared, which created a new language of faces and personas. Film celebrity, latent throughout the colonial and immediate postwar periods, advanced through its coupling with print and radio media and through the mobilization of film stars on behalf of commercial as well as governmental interests.[3] The cinema became a powerful social engine in the late 1950s in South Korea when the nation, in the early throes of reconstruction, became integrated with the apparatuses of the world capitalist economy. And while the bulk of this proliferation centered on Hollywood filmmaking, the machinery of production systemization, promotion and marketing, and stardom also found an important outlet in Korean cinema.

The film industry as a whole, however, was in the 1950s largely decentralized and fluid: most films were produced by one-off partnerships rather than through established studios. "Rational" and vertically integrated production systems would not appear until they were mandated by the mechanical policies that accompanied the advent of Park Chung-Hee's authoritarian developmentalist regime in the early 1960s.[4] The period's generic output was also relatively uneven (the only effective top-down controls worked to censor threats to Syngman Rhee's leadership and the promotion of communist sympathy), though the prevailing filmmaking idiom was represented by historical epics, family and women's melodramas, and urban petit-bourgeois comedies. If there was a dominant figure in the period, it was Han Hyŏng-mo, who made a string of box-office hits throughout the mid to late 1950s, including the sensational *Madame Freedom* [*Chayu puin*, 1956], which capitalized on the anxiety and excitement elicited by the period's radically shifting social values. Han's success, however, depended just as much on the polished stylization of his work, which often featured seemingly superfluous vignettes that highlighted in meticulous form the era's hottest stars and fashions. The long mambo performance in *Madame Freedom*'s dance-hall sequence, in which the eponymous protagonist's gaze is glued to a dancer's gyrations, is perhaps the most iconic instance of Han's characteristic spectacle. It is repeated, however, in small form in many of his lesser-known works, such as the striking wide-framing of the glamorous publishing office in *Female Boss* [*Yŏsajang*, 1959] (fig. 5.2) and, perhaps most conspicuously, in the montage sequence of *Pure Love Chronicle* [*Sunaebo*, 1957] in which the buxom lead changes into one voguish bathing suit after another in search of the man who saved her from drowning (figs. 5.3 and 5.4). Other filmmakers, most notably Sin Sang-ok in his late 1950s cycle of women's melodramas—*Confessions of a College Girl* [*Ŏnŭ yŏdaesaeng ŭi kobaek*], *Hellflower* [*Chiokhwa*], *A Sister's Garden* [*Chamae ŭi hwawŏn*], *It's Not Her Sin* [*Kŭ yŏja ŭi choe ga anida*], *Ch'un-hŭi*, and *Tongsimch'o*—produced work in a similar

Figure 5.2.
The publishing
office in *Female
Boss* (Han Hyŏng-
mo, 1959).

vein, setting films in contemporary, urban, and largely affluent settings, and maximizing the allure of the vast array of consumer commodities regularly paraded on-screen.

The social significance of these films lies of course in the way they manage the predicament of women in the aftermath of war and the sweeping transformations of capitalist modernity. And the bulk of scholarship has rightly concentrated on these themes.[5] But while these symptoms are undeniably compelling, the films possess another quality that is crucial to the cultural history being attempted here: their technical polish. On a basic level, the films demonstrate a quiet but obvious command over the basic apparatus of filmmaking. The lighting is consistent, rarely under- or overexposed, and is often used for dramatic effect. Editing is also relatively seamless, largely free of the jarring cuts and perplexing gaps that marred many contemporaneous films. And sound is efficiently controlled, with accurate postproduction dubbing and surreptitiously modulated music levels. In other words, everything in conventional filmmaking is in place. But the point of drawing attention to the technical competence of these films is not to project Han's or Sin's excellence as auteurs. Rather, it serves as a way of touching on the material history and significance of technical competence itself and also as a way of thinking through the conditions for the kind of visuality that is the theme of this chapter.

In an interview conducted in the late 1990s, Sin referred to the liberation and immediate postwar periods as "the point where whether you could see or whether you could hear was the real challenge in filmmaking."[6] The pertinence of his assertion is confirmed by even the most rudimentary scan of work from the late colonial period through to the mid-1950s. Whereas the "cooperation" films of the early 1940s are strikingly accomplished productions, the films made in the decade following the collapse of colonial power are crude and cheap by contrast.[7] It was only in the mid-1950s, with the merging of a number of factors, that the basic problem of "seeing and hearing" was solved in South Korean filmmaking. These factors included the

Figures 5.3 and 5.4.
Beach fashions in
Pure Love Chronicle
(Han Hyŏng-mo,
1957).

incipient circulation of private capital, the rapid resuscitation of filmgoing culture and markets, and the consolidation of regular, if somewhat disorganized, film production companies. Another critical part of this development was, of course, the training and experience many younger filmmakers received through the auspices of American information services. In fact, many of the leading directors of the next decades—Han and Sin, as well as Hong Sŏng-gi and Yi Hyŏng-pyo—either got their start as directors or first accessed the latest equipment and techniques through these agencies.[8] Additionally, many of the films produced in the immediate postwar years were captured using equipment borrowed, stolen, or otherwise procured through the American military. The latter half of the 1950s then is the moment that these young directors declared their independence; theirs was not solely or even primarily a political freedom, but rather a kind of artisanal autonomy, one they exercised by shooting refined—or, in the idiom of the day, *seryŏn-doen*—pictures.

The roots of this refinement and technical expertise are most easily found in the overwhelming influence of American cultural and technological imports—a situation perhaps best illustrated by the fact that until the restrictions mandated by the first Motion Picture Law in 1961, upward of three-quarters of the films being screened at any given time were Hollywood products. But the 1950s followed sufficiently closely on the heels of the long colonial period so that its vestiges, in concrete as well as abstract form, could not be effectively erased, despite the measures taken by successive governments to stanch the flow of Japanese popular culture into Korea. In fact it is precisely these measures—specifically the ban on Japanese films—that enabled a particularly robust form of cultural importation: plagiarism. As Jinsoo An and others have reminded us, 30 percent to 50 percent of the films produced as late as 1962 were thought to be copies or adaptations of Japanese films.[9] In a range of interviews conducted for the Korean Film Archive's oral history project, scores of filmmakers—from prominent directors such as Im Kwon-taek and Yi Hyŏng-pyo to lesser-known producers like Hwang Nam—testify to the keen interest in the workings of the Japanese film industry, facilitated through the smuggling of films, scripts, and film magazines (in particular the professional journal *Eiga Gijutsu* [Film Technology], later renamed *Eiga Terebi Gijutsu* [Film and Television Technology], the official organ of the Motion Picture and Television Engineering Society of Japan).[10] This close and covert study was driven in large part by the shock of witnessing what is popularly considered the golden age of Japanese cinema in the 1950s, jump-started as much by the international acclaim won by Akira Kurosawa's 1950 *Rashomon* and Yasujirō Ozu's 1953 *Tokyo Story* as by the sensational success of the so-called "sun tribe" cycle of the late 1950s. But it was also mediated by the living heritage of filmmakers—stitched closely together by the predominant master-apprentice training system of the postwar film industry—that stretched back into the heyday of filmmaking in the 1920s and 1930s. It must suffice here to note merely that Ch'oe In-gyu, whom Sin Sang-ok and others credited for doing the most to solve the "seeing and hearing" problems before the war in the late 1940s, advanced his craft under Japanese directors such as Imai Tadashi and in turn trained some of the next generation's leading filmmakers before his capture by the North during the war. The point here is not to question the originality of the early years of Korean film or the nationalist credentials of its practitioners—that argument is made earnestly elsewhere.[11] Rather, it is to call attention to the diffuse and often confused streams of influence, envy, memory and even nostalgia for Japan that existed alongside the novel stimulus exercised by American cultural power.

Similar cross-purposes and heritages obtain in the fledgling fashion industry of the 1950s. As noted above, the film and fashion industries were closely tied. The refinement and allure of films like Yi Yong-min's *Seoul Holiday* [*Sŏul ŭi hyuil*, 1956] or Sin's *A Sister's Garden* turn largely on their impeccable costuming. The men are invariably dressed in the crisp, fitted suits and narrow ties that echo the French more than the American vogue, lending them the air of the modern intellectual or playboy rather than the salary or family men that would dominate later filmmaking. But it is of course the women for whom clothing mattered most. They are graced in an often stunning series of the latest fashions: close-fitting suits with oversized buttons, flared skirts that float up with the subtlest movement, sleek black cocktail dresses with extravagant boas. Here, too, it is the French couture of Audrey Hepburn and Givenchy more than the glamour of Marilyn Monroe that is the informing principle. Much of the clothing was designed or pieced together by Nora No, an independent designer who had organized some of the earliest runway shows in Korea and who, according to Sin Sang-ok, "was really the only one then who could be called a designer."[12] The intimate linking of fashion and film is hinted at in *A Sister's Garden*, where the painter Tong-su (or rather, the actor Nam-Kung Wŏn) is captured, in striking footage of the public event, among photographers and other spectators watching models walking in a runway show (figs. 5.5 and 5.6). It is a striking scene that calls to mind the fact that the leading faces in fashion magazines and runway shows were not professional models but rather film actresses like Ch'oe Ŭn-hŭi, Kim Chi-mi, and Ŏm Aeng-nan.

In fact the mid-1950s marked the complex beginnings of a fashion industry that cannot be adequately understood through an Americanization framework. Clearly the massive U.S. military and cultural presence was crucial. American synthetics like the aforementioned nylon swept into the South following the war, augmenting production efficiency and undergirding both practical clothing (underwear and work uniforms that were durable and easy to clean) and more extravagant dress (scandalously transparent blouses that moved like silk). American capital and expertise also facilitated, as it did in so many sectors, the growth of the textile industry, subsidizing for instance the incorporation in 1954 of Cheil Mojik, the Republic of Korea's first textile company, which would anchor the light industrial sectors that spurred economic development throughout the late 1950s and 1960s.[13] During and shortly after the war, American charity organizations, bringing remnant and secondhand clothing in bulk from the United States, would

Figures 5.5 and 5.6. Tong-su takes in the runway show in *A Sister's Garden* (Sin Sang-ok, 1959).

function as the first contact point between many Koreans and Western fashions—a sort of Trojan horse for the import-substitution strategy that would dictate consumption patterns throughout the 1950s.[14] And more insidiously, the sex workers or "Western princesses" that thrived on the perimeters of U.S. military installations became vanguards of Western fashion, fostering a secondary industry of itinerant peddlers or *poddari jangsu* who would source American clothes to market at base camps.

But the lines of material importation and aesthetic circulation spilled beyond the borders of the U.S.-ROK dyad. Ch'oe Kyŏng-ja, who opened International Western Clothes [*Kukje yangjangsa*], one of the first and by far the most renowned Western clothing store in Myŏngdong in 1954, had started her career in Hamhŭng and then in Pyongyang, learning her craft from and making modern clothes for the considerable Japanese population there through the latter half of the colonial period.[15] After a brief stint in Taegu during the war, Ch'oe became, alongside Nora No, the premier clothier to celebrities and went on to found the Ch'oe Kyŏng-ja Fashion Research Institute, dedicated to training designers to meet flourishing demand. In June 1955, Ch'oe, Sŏ Su-yŏng, and other industry players founded the Korean Fashion Federation [Taehan poksik yŏnu hoe] (later, and to this day, the Korean Clothing Designers Federation), a comprehensive organization that included and regulated fields as diverse as flower arrangement, woodworking, and doll making. One of its key early measures was the regularization of fashion and textiles terminology, which to that point was saturated with Japanese. But rather than simply eliminating the so-called loan words altogether, the organization sought to standardize *han'gul* renderings for the vocabulary worth preserving and replace outdated terminology with English or Korean alternatives. Another core initiative was the concerted study of a Japanese fashion industry that, as in its film counterpart, alarmed watchers with the speed with which it expanded and diversified. Again, Federation members found routes around the import ban by smuggling, through third-party nations and international fashion events, Japanese magazines, patterns, and articles that could be used as models for the burgeoning domestic industry.[16]

So while American fashions were indeed the most visible and directly influential source of subsidy and inspiration, Western clothing (which could very well be American, European, Japanese, or some synthesis of all three) was being produced within a complex circulation of stolen gazes, appropriated technologies, and reappropriated styles. A better sense of this may be gleaned from a brief consideration of the fashion craze sparked in part by *Madame Freedom*. On the film's surface, especially from a distant observational vantage, the most radical and presumably alluring transformation is the protagonist Sŏn-yŏng's shift from *hanbok* to *yangjang*. And yet it was in fact the luxurious velvet *hanbok* Sŏn-yŏng and her high-society friends wear throughout the first half of the film that proved the greater social sensation. An older and traditionally very expensive fabric that became somewhat more accessible with the advent of more sophisticated looms in the middle part of the twentieth century, velvet was incorporated into the warp of *hanbok* precisely in the mid-1950s. Its popularity was such that a "velvet limitation" law [*pelbet otgam chehan ryŏng*] was passed in 1957 that allotted only one velvet outfit per person per year. This was partly precipitated by the perceived moral danger in the gap between the extravagance of velvet clothing and the devastating scarcity that characterized the immediate postwar years. But it was also a measure aimed against velvet's frequently contraband sources, chiefly Hong Kong for the lower-quality bolts, Kyoto for the more refined finishes.[17] This counterintuitive phenomenon prompts a series of reflections about fashion's historicity and function: that it was eminently possible to be modern through ostensibly traditional attire, that America was not the singular object of desire and fantasy, that the consumerist gaze, despite capital limitations and political restriction, could traverse borders in multiple directions.

I would now like to consider briefly some of the striking changes that took hold of the publishing industry in the 1950s. The liberation and immediate postwar periods witnessed on the one hand a remarkable expansion in periodical publishing, with upward of 174 new magazines launched between 1945 and 1954. Many of these folded within a few months, and many were either professional publications or monthly editions of newspapers or older periodicals.[18] But qualitatively new forms, with their own protocols and patterns of reading, appeared in these years as well. The most striking are the period's film and fashion magazines. While film reviews, gossip about film personalities, and advertisements for new releases had been published in major newspapers since the middle of the colonial period, it was not until the launch of two magazines, *Yŏnghwa segye* [Film World] and *Kukje yŏnghwa* [International Film], in 1955 that writing and representation of filmmaking and stardom found specialized and popular venues for circulation in the postwar period.[19] In many ways, they are fairly typical of the kinds of fan magazines in popular circulation in the same period in Europe, the United States, or other parts of the world. Film celebrities are clearly the primary attraction of the magazines—their faces are printed large on virtually every page, and they are the subject of regular "introduction," "interest," and "gossip" columns. Promotion of new releases is obviously another important component, both in the more straightforward full-page advertisements and in the reviews and reports, which are often nothing more than narrative summaries and cast introductions. Industry news from home and abroad, in particular about films currently under production or promised for import, and the occasional editorial reporting on trends or themes are regular, though clearly less essential, features. Often taking up the bulk of the pages, however, are full screenplays of recently released films—usually one but at times up to three to an issue—accompanied sparsely by stills from the films. There is some indication that this substantial textual presence may have been mandated or at least encouraged by censors[20]; this seems even more likely considering that the screenplays are almost exclusively for Korean films. But the more compelling and in some ways more obvious explanation is that these screenplays signal the very liminality of the film medium in this particular historical moment, poised somewhere between literate and visual, and highbrow and mass cultures. The weighty presence of the screenplays—drawn primarily, though not exclusively, from the literary [munye] genre of films—palpably anchors the cinema in the gravity of older, more serious art forms.[21] There was in these magazines clearly a tension with the promotion and indeed celebration of the newly revived medium, indicating that film had not yet marked out a sure position in the art-entertainment spectrum.

Another sign of that delicate balance is in the instructive and often hortatory tenor of the articles in these magazines. This is especially apparent in Yŏnghwa segye. Detailed explanations of film terms and techniques—ranging from simpler definitions of the long shot or the fadeout (replete with English renderings) to much more expansive clarifications of generic categories and cinematic styles—appeared regularly in the earlier issues. Each issue in the entire first volume of Yŏnghwa segye seems in fact to have prominently featured in the opening pages a kind of glossary of basic film terminology, starting in the first issue with brief definitions of the role of each member of a credited film company (producer, director, cinematographer, etc.) and progressing, by the sixth issue, to the more complex workings of a typical Hollywood studio. On another level, Yŏnghwa segye is peppered with shorter articles, letters, and single-panel comics that take on the task of creating proper filmgoing manners and ideas. In one letter in the inaugural issue, for instance, a writer complains about the "old-fashioned" [ku sik] habit of certain members of the audience of talking at the screen—

something that is identified with the "outdated" *pyŏnsa*-mediated cinema culture.[22]

Old-timers clearly had to adjust to the new theaters and learn the new conventions of filmgoing. And yet general, presumably younger audiences, too, at least in the eyes of the magazine's editors, needed to be told how a movie was made, what to look for, and how to appreciate what they were watching. All of this pressure on the way to watch films, and to substantiate their cultural position, is especially striking when we consider that films had already been screened in Korea for more than fifty years and that Seoul had seen an exuberant screen culture as early as the late 1920s. The most immediately obvious way to account for this seemingly excessive exhortation is to consider that nearly a generation—that is, between the nearly complete closure of the commercial film industry in the late 1930s through to the reconstruction of the (both local and import) industry in the latter stages of the war in 1953—had been deprived of anything like a filmgoing culture.[23] But while this is certainly a crucial factor, it is not the whole story. In order to get a better picture of what was going on in the magazine and film culture as a whole, we need to look more carefully at the images themselves.

A scan through the pages of these magazines quickly reveals a powerful tendency of filmmaking in the 1950s and the fashion and fan cultures that underwrote it. The eye, reflecting the magnifications of the big screen as well as the increasingly heavy traffic of the rapidly expanding cities perhaps, was being drawn much more consistently and analytically toward the face primarily and the body and its clothing secondarily. Film magazines like *Yŏnghwa segye* and *Kukje yŏnghwa* were by their very nature highly invested in the faces of actors—the production and promotion of stars, and hence of the films themselves, depended on it. The first ten or fifteen pages of every issue, therefore, were made up of full-page portraits of male and female actors, ready for clipping and pasting on walls or circulation among adoring fans. These were not, tellingly, stills taken from film sequences or even promotional shots for specific movies but rather were abstracted publicity shots, bereft of any context, serving only to highlight the actor's face and sometimes body—in other words, pinups. Detailed biographical profiles of individual actors in later pages are invariably accompanied by large, similarly abstracted portraits, and even the shorter blurbs sharing gossip about trysts and other significant tidbits are rarely published without smaller, cleanly framed (the standard oval shape) face shots. The abstract format of these portraits gives some indication of the cultural work of the film magazine: the culture of celebrity, and therein the orientation of the eye toward the face, in some ways exceeds or escapes the prosaic function of film promotion. And in this work the film magazine was clearly at the forefront. While the 1950s saw the establishment of a number of popular magazines, none of these, not even the highly popular and explicitly commercial month-lies such as *Sinch'ŏnji*, *Arirang*, or *Modŏn chosŏn* approached the pictorial saturation of the film magazine.

Tellingly, it was only *Yŏwŏn*, the leading women's fashion magazine launched in 1955, that could rival *Kukje yŏnghwa* or *Yŏnghwa segye* in this bald foregrounding of the image. In fact, that magazine was the first in Korea to feature offset pictorial printing and to feature advertising prominently.[24] By the April 1958 issue, the magazine featured full-page advertisements for OB Lager, which leveraged the image of leisured women in quiet repose to appeal to *Yŏwŏn*'s apparently aspirational readership. But the magazine had already staged a more signal departure in its inaugural issue with the advent of "Mode," a multipage special section that featured the era's most recognizable films stars wearing the latest fashions (fig. 5.7). The full-page images that constituted the spread were accompanied by captions indicating celebrity and designer names or providing tips on how or when to wear spe-cific styles. The first iteration showcased a young Ch'oe Ŭn-hŭi on the cusp of greater stardom, posing in the latest autumn fashions. The captions here draw attention to pertinent details of the outfits, transliterating their terms ("one-piece," "flare," etc.), highlighting the effects of specific cuts ("slim-ming for both thinner and thicker ladies"), pointing out construction de-tails (bias cut, offset buttons), and, perhaps most tellingly, trumpeting the local provenance of the garments—the caption on the spread's third image begins, "a smart domestic [*kuksan*] one-piece of black grebe that could stand up to any foreign design." By all indications the spread and the magazine as a whole marked a shift in the sensorial engagement with Korean publish-ing, instantiating not only a sharper focus on the image but also a keener processing of the social and material import of those images. *Yŏwŏn* therein actively participated in the intensification of what Christine Gledhill termed the "consumerist gaze" in popular media[25]; its stakes for women in light of the burgeoning culture of consumption was radically ambivalent—exposed and liberated, the subject and object of desire, exquisitely aware of fashion's ephemerality and social disparities.[26]

But like its film counterparts, *Yŏwŏn* throughout the period maintained a text-heavy profile, rich with short stories (leading female author Pak Kyŏng-ni was a regular contributor) and articles ranging in subject from the challenges of motherhood to the joys of Western classical music. Fashion was only one, albeit expanding, component of what was a comprehensive women's magazine, one that had few viable competitors and thus little rea-

Figure 5.7. Ch'oe Ŭn-hŭi's "Mode" spread in *Yŏwŏn*'s inaugural issue (1955).

son to specialize in a particular thematic or stylistic direction.[27] Later *Yŏwŏn* editions, especially toward the late 1960s, shed some of this textual weight in favor of more lavish photo spreads and celebrity profiles, just as the film magazines would eventually cut their multipage screenplay reprints. But it is important to stress here that the magazines' forms in the 1950s did not constitute a transitional stage en route to becoming bolder, less self-conscious visual media, but rather that they embodied the tensions central to early postwar cultural discourse. As a comprehensive magazine, *Yŏwŏn* suspended in its pages a high cultural sensibility (represented best perhaps by its regular full-color reprints of Impressionist paintings, or its multipage "etiquette" pictorials illustrating, for instance, the proper mechanics of Western-style fine dining [fig. 5.8]), and the burgeoning mass culture modes of reception and consumption. Structurally, magazines like *Yŏwŏn* and *Kukje Yŏnghwa*, despite their mass cultural foundations, resisted the full embrace of low cultural escapism, an index of which is the fact that nothing like the overt sexuality of contemporary American or Japanese women's magazines such as *Seventeen* or *Josei Jishin* [Ladies' own], or the invasive leering of fan

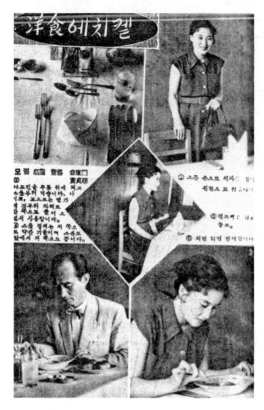

Figure 5.8. Dining etiquette in *Yŏwŏn*.

magazines like *Movie Story*, *Screen Romances*, or *Eiga Fan* [Film fan], ever made it into Korean publications. At the same time as they took the lead in training the eye to process static and moving images and in coaxing their readerships into taking greater initiative in assuming new social identities, the magazines maintained an affinity to older cultural sensibilities seemingly possessed of more gravitas. Therein they committed to paper the radical and at times comic contradictions—tips on applying eye makeup next to a report on the April 16 demonstrations, analysis of Italian Neorealism followed by giddy celebrity gossip—that came to characterize the decade's mass cultural production.

The film and fashion worlds of the 1950s, particularly in their refined and extravagant iterations, were largely derided by serious contemporary critics, and their status remained contested until the late 1990s. The bases for this negative assessment are numerous but generally converge on two central ideas: they were not Korean enough and they were not art. While praising their exceptional technical accomplishment, critics were especially tough on the appropriation of foreign material in the era's films. A review of Sin Sang-ok's *It's Not Her Sin* in the *Seoul Daily* [*Seoul sinmun*], targeting the work's French origins, argued for instance that the "unnaturalness" of the translation [*pŏn'an*] was only slightly mitigated by the appeal and acting skills of the two leads, Ch'oe Ŭn-hŭi and Chu Chŭng-nyŏ, and concluded that "while Sin seems to have gotten the hang of producing adaptations, taking up the fruits of other people's labor can never be art."[28] And a reviewer of *Ch'un-hŭi* (1959) in the *Korea Daily* claims that "with *Confessions of a College Girl*, *It's Not Her Sin*, and other translated works, Mr. Sin's films this year amount to nothing more than mannerisms."[29] This sort of appraisal continued in various ways throughout the following decades. While much more open to the fact of translation, leading film critic and historian Yi Yŏng-il complained in 1969 that many of the films of the late 1950s, including Sin's, were "ethically vacuous."[30] He also categorized the majority of the period's films as *sinp'a* derivatives, implying that they were marked by the emotional excess, narrative improbability, and social clichés that were the conventions of that form. Filmmakers themselves, reflecting on that phase in their careers, tended to dismiss or downplay the work of that period: Yu Hyŏn-mok, in his history of the Korean film industry, wrote that his 1950s work was largely "naïve" [*sobak han*] and "derivative," [*p'asaeng doen*][31] and Kim Su-yong "confessed" in his autobiography that he was not proud of his "juvenile" films.[32] In interviews and statements made throughout his career, Sin Sang-ok quietly directed attention away from his earlier work and toward the accomplishments of the 1960s. With the exception of *Evil Night* [*Ak'ya*, 1953], his first film, and *Hellflower*, celebrated as a neorealist masterpiece at home and abroad, Sin largely seemed to want to forget the "cheap" [*ssaguryŏ*] work of the 1950s.[33]

Critics in the 1990s, informed by feminist film theory and new sociological research, began to reappraise the period's films. Rather than engaging strictly with the films' expressions of cultural identity, they began looking more closely at the politics of spectatorship and reception as well as the social life of melodrama as a cinematic form. While skeptical about the patriarchal discourses in films such as *Madame Freedom* and *Hellflower*, they saw those films as potentially radical and empowering events for the lower-class, middle-aged women who made up the majority of audiences. "There must have been a special kind of pleasure," argued Yu Chi-na, "for those women in seeing the new, dangerous women on screen, no matter that they were always punished in the end."[34] The closed narrative structures and affective excess that defined melodrama and *sinp'a* were also seen as latent sites of unruly identification and solidarity. Following theorists like Linda Williams and Christine Gledhill, Chu Yu-sin called attention to the "emotional catharsis of seeing other women damaged, abused, repressed."[35] The melodrama and *sinp'a* of the 1950s were thus recast as "women's films" and read as venues of relief from the hardships of postwar reconstruction and patriarchal domination.

Both of these critical streams—rejection as foreign and/or crude, and sanction as affectively and/or politically affirmative—converge around two approaches to film: the notion of film and mass culture as distraction and the search for meaning underneath the surface of the image. Both, in different senses, disavow surfaces and attempt to uncover art or social significance in any place but the image—literary form, civic spirit, emotional surplus, psychological identification, and so on. These have informed an enormously productive approach to Korean film history, but they have also tended to veer around the significant shifts that have been suggested above. What distinguished the films of this period, especially those of Han and Sin, was precisely a capitalization on and play with surface. That this play covertly mimicked the contemporary images of the former colonizer and took unbridled pleasure in highlighting a new constellation of faces and fashions belied the radical symbolic work of the films—a point missed by both nationalist and feminist critics and elided in the stark high-low cultural tensions of the film and women's magazines. The period's films do not simply erase the physical destruction, ideological conflict, and overwhelming poverty that characterized early postwar Korea; but neither do they represent that history in any direct way. At the core of the undeniable escapism of the era's melodramas and romantic comedies was the push to imagine a qualitatively different reality from the one promised by American liberalism and its South Korean adherents. In the literary field, this dissatisfaction with the present took the form, in fits and starts, of an existentialism-tinged prose of despair.[36] In film, it took the form of an ambivalent critical engagement with Hollywood's offerings, typified in the faint praise for the 1955 *Seven Brides for Seven Brothers*, in which the reviewer noted its impressive cinemascope spectacle while acerbically applauding its "American-style odorless pleasures."[37] It also took the form of the mode proper to the medium: fantasy. But rather than otherworldly or psychic withdrawal, the fantasy time-space of Korean films was a just-out-of-reach bourgeois society of sexual intrigue, gender reversal, comic confusion, and lavish consumption. And, given the crude desolation of Seoul's postwar landscape, it is no coincidence that filmmakers turned to the quickly rehabilitated neighborhoods of Myŏngdong and Ch'ungmuro or even better to the easily controlled architecture of sets and, more crucially, to the faces of stars and the fashions of Europe, Japan, and America to mediate that critical fantasy.

Taking into view the palimpsest historicities and desires of the film and fashion worlds of the 1950s, it is possible to offer here a provisional conclusion: the escapist, apparently mimicked aesthetics of the period were not only the repressive effect of the American cultural machine or only a venue of distraction and pacification. Rather, the self-conscious identification with America also contained the radical fantasy of transformation and difference, the desire to realize a new sociocultural identity. Simultaneously the sophisticated luster of fashions and cinematic imagery in this period reached back implicitly to the refinement of the colonial period, when most of the filmmakers had apprenticed and enjoyed the material, if not moral, support of major, largely state-sponsored, Japanese studios. After a ten-year hiatus that saw the evacuation of Japanese capital and expertise as well as the full-scale destruction of the most active sites of film production, the young filmmakers of the late 1950s turned back nostalgically to the urbanity and style of their youth, projecting that memory onto the screen in the form of the slickest, most refined and technically accomplished images possible. The modern fantasy of 1950s Korean cinema was therein a palimpsest visualization of Japan and America—old and new, East and West—one which could condition the imagination of a different Korean modernity.

NOTES

1. Kaja Silverman, "Fragments of a Fashionable Discourse," in *On Fashion*, ed. Shari Benstock and Suzanne Ferriss (New Brunswick, NJ: Rutgers University Press, 1994), 183–96.

2. Roland Barthes, *The Fashion System*, trans. Matthew Ward and Richard Howard (New York: Hill and Wang, 1983), 273.

3. The use of performers in rallies and staged "public greetings" [*insa*] became standard practice in political campaigns and elections. See Kang Chun-man, *Han'guk hyŏndaesa sanch'aek: 1950 yŏndae p'yŏn* [A stroll through modern Korean history: The 1950s] (Seoul: Inmul kwa sasang, 2004), vol. 1, 109.

4. For an informative overview of motion picture laws in the 1960s and 1970s, see, Pak Chi-yŏn, *"Pak Chŏng-hŭi kŭndaehwa ch'eje ŭi yŏnghwa chŏngch'aek: yŏnghwa pŏp kaechŏng kwa kiŏphwa chŏngch'aek chungsimŭro"* [Modernization and film policy under Park Chung Hee: On the legislation of film Law and corporatization], in *Han'guk yŏnghwa wa kŭndaesŏng* [Korean cinema and modernity] (Seoul: Sodo, 2000), 171–221. The chapter also touches on regulations in the 1950s.

5. See the seminal collection of essays, Kim So-yŏn et al., eds., *Maehok kwa hondon ŭi sidae: 1950-nyŏndae han'guk yŏnghwa* [An age of allures and chaos: Korean cinema of the 1950s] (Seoul: Sodo, 2003).

6. Yi Yŏn-ho, "Sin Sang-ok: Tangsinŭn nugusimnikka?" [Sin Sang-ok: Who are you?], *Kino* (October 1997): 122.

7. Nine complete films from the colonial period have been uncovered and restored at the Korean Film Archive. One of these, *Mimong* [Sweet Dream] (1936), directed

by Yang Chu-nam, is considered a wholly native production—in fact, it was recently featured among a number of films as a national "cultural asset." The others were produced in cooperation with private Japanese film studios or later under the auspices of the imperial film corporation. Ch'oe In-gyu directed *Chip ŏmnŭn ch'ŏnsa* [Homeless Angels] (1941) and codirected *Sarang ŭi maengse* [A Statement of Love] (1945), which in different ways lionized the act of sacrifice for the imperial cause. See Kim Ryŏ-sil, *T'usa hanŭn cheguk t'uyŏng hanŭn sigminji* [Projected Empire, Reflected Colony] (Seoul: Samin, 2006) for a summary. The point that needs to be made here is that there is an undeniable disparity between Ch'oe's pre- and postliberation films in terms of their technical quality. With the generous financial backing of the imperial propaganda machine and the professional support of filmmakers at Toho and other private studios, *Homeless Angels* and *Statement of Love* are sprawling, impeccably produced films. By contrast, Ch'oe's liberation films, *Hurrah Freedom* [Chayu manse] (1946) and *The Night Before Liberation* [*Tongnip chŏnya*] (1948) are undeniably crude, bereft of the fundamentals of visual storytelling language and continuity—a contrast for which the lack of proper filmmaking equipment and the subsequent degradation of film prints can only partially account.

8. See Yi Yŏng-il's *Han'guk yŏnghwa chŏnsa* [The complete history of Korean film] (Seoul: Sodo, 2004) for a more detailed accounting of the period.

9. See Jinsoo An, "Figuring Masculinity at Historical Juncture: Manchurian Action Films," chapter 3 of his Ph.D. dissertation, "Popular Reasoning of South Korean Melodrama Films (1953–1972)" (UCLA, 2005), 162–65.

10. See, for instance, Yi Hyŏng-pyo's long interview in Cho Chun-hyŏng et al., *2008 Korean Film History: Oral History Records Series, Sin Films [2008-nyŏn han'guk yŏnghwasa kusul ch'aerok siriju <Chujesa> Sin p'illum]* (Seoul: Korean Film Archive, 2008), 163–215. Notably, these interviews do not circulate from the Korean Film Archive Library—a restriction imposed at the request of the interviewees, who were apparently concerned about the sensitive nature of some of their comments.

11. See Kang Sŏng-ryul, *Ch'inil yŏnghwa* [Pro-Japanese films] (Seoul: Rokŭ Media, 2006) and Kim Ryŏ-sil, *T'usa hanŭn cheguk t'uyŏng hanŭn sigminji* [Projected empire, reflected colony] (Seoul: Samin, 2006) for their vigorous critique of the filmmakers of the colonial period and the film historiography that has attempted to erase that past.

12. Interview with Sin Sang-ok, by Yi Ki-rim, *Han'guk yŏnghwa hoegorok: Sin Sang-ok 15* [Korean Cinema in Retrospect: Sin Sang-ok, 15], *Cine 21*, September 19, 2003.

13. Sunae Park et al., "The Process of Westernization: Adoption of Western-Style Dress by Korean Women, 1945–1962," *Clothing and Textiles Research* 11, no. 39 (1993): 43.

14. Ministry of Culture and Tourism, *Two-Thousand Years of Korean Fashion* [*Uri ot ichŏn nyŏn*] (Seoul: Misul Munhwa, 2001), 138.

15. Ministry of Culture and Tourism, *Two-Thousand Years*, 144.

16. Ministry of Culture and Tourism, *Two-Thousand Years*, 144.

17. Ministry of Culture and Tourism, *Two-Thousand Years*, 144.

18. Ch'oe Tŏk-gyo, *Han'guk chapji paeknyŏn* [100 years of Korean magazines] (Seoul: Hyŏnamsa, 2004), 549–61.

19. Strangely, while the authoritative *Han'guk chapji ch'ongnam* lists *Yŏnghwa segye* as

first having been registered in 1956 and then folding in 1964, the Korean Film Archive holds issues dating back to January 1955. See *Han'guk chapji ch'ongnam: Han'guk chapji 70-yŏn sa* [Korean magazine survey: 70 years of Korean magazines] (Seoul: Han'guk Chapji Hyŏphoe, 1972).

20. Private conversation with film historian Yi Sun-jin, Seoul, December 2008.

21. We may note here that an earlier, and in tenor more serious, film magazine, *Yŏnghwa yŏn'gŭk* [Film and theater], continued the marriage of the new medium to the old. See Ch'oe Tŏk-gyo. *Han'guk chapji paeknyŏn*, 554.

22. An Jinsoo examines the role of the *pyŏnsa* in Korean film history and the interesting persistence of its function following the advent of the sound picture in his study, "Fallen Women on Trial: Configuration of Popular Justice in Courtroom Drama Films," the fourth chapter of his Ph.D. dissertation, "Popular Reasoning of South Korean Melodrama Films (1953–1972)" (UCLA 2005).

23. This statement clearly needs qualification that would stray far beyond the bounds of this study. It will have to suffice here to note that following some foreshadowing and tacit action on the part of the governing authorities, the commercial film industry (which, of course, had never been free of strict government censorship) was shut down with the creation of the Chosŏn Film Production Company [Chosŏn yŏnghwa chaejak hoesa] in 1940. Many films continued to be produced in colonial Korea, but these were wholly created under the auspices of the Governor-General and were explicitly produced in support of the war effort. The exuberant film-fan cultures of the preceding decade were effectively killed off with the closing of virtually all private publishing houses. Commercial film production started again immediately following national liberation in 1945. Over the next five years, fifteen to sixteen Korean films were screened in theaters, including Ch'oe In-gyu's celebrated *Hurrah Freedom!* [*Chayu manse*] (1946). Nevertheless, under the tremendous pressure of the intense ideological split between groups on the right and left such as the Chosŏn Film and Theater Writers Association [Chosŏn yŏnghwa kŭkjak-ga hyŏphoe] and the KAPF spinoff Chosŏn Proletarian Film Federation [Chosŏn Proleta Film Federatio], as well as the repressive force of the The United States Army Military Government in Korea (USAMGIK) authorities, a commercial film industry was not viable. Finally, while feature films were indeed made during the war, venues and audiences were in near total disarray. See Yi Yŏng-il, *Han'guk yŏnghwa chŏnsa*, chapters 5, 6, and 7.

24. Cho, *100 Years*, 511.

25. Christine Gledhill, ed., *Stardom: Industry of Desire* (New York: Routledge, 1991), 23.

26. For a full study of *Yŏwŏn*'s social and ideological dimensions, see Kim Hyŏn-ju, "1950 nyŏn-dae yŏsŏng chabji <Yŏwŏn> kwa 'chedo rosŏ ŭi chubu ŭi t'ansaeng" [The women's magazine *Yŏwŏn* and the birth of the "housewife as institution"] in *Taejung Sŏsa Yŏn'gu* no. 18 (December 2007):387–416, and the essays in the collection *Yŏwŏn yŏn'gu: yŏsŏng, kyoyang, maech'e* [Yŏwŏn Studies: Women, Education, Media], ed. Han'guk yŏsŏng munhak hakhoe, "Yŏwŏn" yŏn'gu moim (Seoul: Kukhak char-yowŏn, 2008).

27. In this sense it is easy to draw a parallel between *Yŏwŏn* and the leading contemporary Japanese women's magazine, *Shufu no Tomo* [Housewife's friend], a compre-

hensive publication whose format and layout were unmistakably similar to *Yŏwŏn's*. Unfortunately little serious research on postwar women's publishing in Japan has been published in English.

28. *"Pŏn'an mul ŭi ko'ae"* [The Misery of Adaptation, *It's Not Her Sin*], *Seoul Sinmun*, January 18, 1959.

29. *"Saeryŏn doen sinp'a"* [Refined Sinp'a: Sin Sang-ok's Korean adaptation of *Ch'un-hŭi*]. *Han'guk sinmun*, May 22, 1959.

30. Yi Yŏng-il. *Han'guk yŏnghwa chŏnsa*, 266.

31. Yu Hyŏn-mok. *Han'guk yŏnghwa paldalsa* [The development of Korean film] (Seoul: Ch'aeknuri, 1997), 96.

32. Kim Su-yong, *Na ŭi sarang ssinema* [Cinema, my love] (Seoul: Cine 21, 2005), 51.

33. Kim So-hŭi and Yi Ki-rim, "Korean Cinema in Retrospect, Sin Sang-ok" ("Han'guk yŏnghwa hoegorok Sin Sang-ok"), *Cine 21* (July and August 2003).

34. Yu Chi-na, *"Han'guk mellodŭrama, wŏnhyŏng kwa ŭimi chakyong yŏn'gu"* [Korean melodrama: On meaning work and the classical form], in *Yŏnghwa yŏn'gu*, vol. 13 (Seoul: Seoul Sŭcopŭ, 1997), 16.

35. Chu Yu-sin, *"Mellodrama genre e taehan yŏsŏngjuŭi jŏk pip'yŏng: yŏsŏng kwan-gaek sŏng nonŭi rŭl chungsimŭro"* [Feminist critique of the melodrama genre: On the discourse of female spectatorship], in *Yŏnghwa yŏn'gu*, vol. 15 (Seoul: Kŭn Saram, 2000), 103.

36. See the excellent study by Theodore Hughes, *Literature and Film in Cold War South Korea: Freedom's Frontier* (New York: Columbia University Press, 2012), especially chapter 3, "Ambivalent Anticommunism: The Politics of Despair and the Erotics of Language."

37. *Tonga Ilbo* [Tonga Daily], October 23, 1955, 4, cited in Cho Yŏng-chŏng, *"Miguk yŏnghwa e taehan yang'ga chŏk t'aedo"* [Ambivalent attitudes toward American cinema], in *Maehok kwa hondon ŭi sidae*, ed. Kim So-yŏn et al., 99–127.

6

KELLY JEONG

The Quasi Patriarch

Kim Sŭng-ho and South Korean Postwar Movies

Cinematic representation [is] a kind of mapping social vision into subjectivity. In other words, cinema's binding of fantasy to significant images affects the spectator as a subjective production, and so the movement of the film actually inscribes and orients desire. In this manner cinema powerfully participates in the production of forms of subjectivity that are individually shaped yet unequivocally social.

TERESA DE LAURETIS, *ALICE DOESN'T: FEMINISM, SEMIOTICS, CINEMA*

In recent years the name of the late actor Kim Sŭng-ho (1918–1968) has enjoyed a posthumous comeback of sorts, as many of his films were introduced to wider audiences through film festival retrospectives and new DVD releases. One of South Korea's most familiar and prolific stars of the Golden Age of cinema (1955–72), his was already a household name for older generations of Korean audiences before this recent resurgence of his fame. It has been argued convincingly that, unlike just any other familiar movie actor, a star is a film legend whose private life is as well known as his or her on-screen personality. In this sense, Kim Sŭng-ho was a star.[1] In many of his 360 films, he portrayed a hardworking, good-hearted everyman who does his best to provide for his family and to keep his dignity and humanity, even under dire circumstances. Kim's most memorable roles, in films such as *Mr. Park* (*Pak sŏbang*, Kang Tae-jin, director, 1960) and *Coachman* (*Mabu*, Kang Tae-jin, director, 1961), featured him as a patriarch who struggles mightily against forces—both internal and external—that threaten his values, beliefs, and, most important, his family, which is his whole world (fig. 6.1). Kim became synonymous with the typical and/or ideal Korean father through such films of the Golden Age, the period that coincided with

Figure 6.1. Kim Sŭng-ho, who plays the patriarch in *Coachman*, is depicted as an anachronistic man—full of pathos and love for the horse.

the postwar, nation rebuilding phase of South Korean history. During this time, his films received several important national and international acting awards, including the Silver Bear Award at the 1961 Berlin Film Festival, and Kim became a beloved quasi father figure.[2]

It is significant that Kim Sŭng-ho's most prolific years as a film star correlated to the last years of the Syngman Rhee administration (Yi Sŭng-man, 1948–60) and the beginning years of the Park Chung-Hee administration (Pak Chŏng-hŭi, 1961–79).[3] Although the film industry hugely benefited from the change in the tax law that expanded and grew the industry during this period, it also had to contend with censorship and other government directives and policies that often undermined the integrity and autonomy of the art form and practice.[4] Against such a historical-social backdrop, as the most popular form of mass entertainment, the films of the Golden Age reflected the tremendous social chaos and sea change of culture in the years following the Korean War, a complex and dramatic narrative of South Korea's rise from the postcolonial, postwar devastation, and the top-down project of nation rebuilding, industrialization, modernization, and militarism.

This chapter is a consideration of Kim Sŭng-ho's depictions of patriarchs as cultural texts, which compose a meaningful facet of South Korean's postwar popular culture. First, it will examine how Kim achieved his on-screen persona and will investigate the textual and meta-textual characteristics and significance of this star image. It will also study his on-screen star persona as the face of an artificial reality that provided a more satisfying, idealized version of real life to the postwar Korean audiences, which paradoxically desired to erase the harsh extradiegetic reality (the reality of the world outside the film narrative) and yet enjoyed watching a close semblance of the quotidian on-screen. His portrayals of the father provide such pleasure, through the slippage between the depictions of the typical and the ideal. Further, this chapter will show how in the contours of his career Kim experienced, and even incorporated, the two tremendous politico-cultural events of his time—first the April 19 Revolution of 1960, which toppled the Syngman Rhee administration, and second, the military dictatorship of former president Park Chung-Hee, which began immediately after the revolution—to flesh out the ways in which the politico-cultural shifts both helped build but also used his stardom, a phenomenon that reveals the complex, intertwined relationship between South Korea's postwar popular culture and the state agenda of nation rebuilding.

Kim Sŭng-ho got his first film role as a bit player in 1939, but it was not until 1955 that he finally began garnering more attention as a solid supporting actor.[5] His first big role was in *The Wedding Day*, in which he famously stole the show and established himself as a reliable comic actor.[6] Kim is best known for playing two types of fathers during his career: one is typified by the tragic or dramatic role he plays in *Money* (*Ton*, Kim So-dong, director, 1958) and the other is a comic character in "home drama" or family melodrama genre such as *Romance Papa* (*Romaensŭ p'ap'a*, Sin Sang-ok, director, 1960).[7]

I have shown elsewhere that South Korea of the 1950s saw a rapid urbanization, development in mass communication, media, and means of transportation, and a huge rise in the number of students and rates of literacy (though some of these developments mostly happened around the city).[8] Although "liberal democracy" was the goal, this ideal had little to do with the national reality, even as people's expectation and anticipation of it grew rapidly.[9] Such developments no doubt prepared the ground for the massive revolution of April 19, which opened the next decade. According to the pioneering Korean film historian Lee Young Il (Yi Yŏng-il), the "new" cinema realism debate appeared in the mid-1950s. The rebuilding of the film industry needed a new ideological direction after the national division, and discourses about realism seemed to provide the answer. The first mention of "Korean realism" in print media appeared in the film magazine *Movie World* (*Yŏnghwa segye*) in 1957, around the time when Kim Sŭng-ho's career began in earnest.[10] Although he came from the stage tradition, his acting style was ultrarealistic rather than theatrical. The notion of realism in 1950s film is qualitatively different from that of the previous (that is, colonial) generation, and Kim's acting seems a perfect fit for this new kind of realism. Italian neorealism was named as the ideal model by leading critics such as Yu Tu-yŏn and Hŏ Paek-nyŏn that Korean cinema should emulate at this time, because of the two countries' similar political and cultural backgrounds, because of the population's experiences during World War II, and because this school of realism suggested a clear view of reality and led to the recovery of humanity.[11] Meanwhile, the concept of family increasingly changed from the Confucian notion of clan to a more survival-oriented nuclear family in the postwar years.[12]

It is crucial to understand the cultural atmosphere of the 1950s in order to discuss the star system during the Golden Age of Korean cinema. The 1950s was a remarkable decade of stars. The widespread popularity of the narratives about stars' private lives in magazines and even in "serious" monthly periodicals reinforced the growing importance of leading actors' private lives in public consciousness and popular imagination and thereby influence the lives of movie fans. Often the relationship between audience and star forms in the process of conflating the reality of the world inside and outside the film in people's popular discourses; for our discussion, this is the reason Kim's films are important, as they both shape and reflect the contemporary culture in this manner.[13] In Korea's postwar culture, which was quickly transforming itself in modern/Western ways, words such as *freedom, democracy*, and *individual* became keywords. But they do not necessarily always signify good things. On the one hand, the positive meanings associate the words with fairness and a progressive, Westernized mindset and lifestyle. On the other hand, the words also have negative connotations of sexual promiscuity, irresponsibility, and facile modernity or Westernization, as well as the idleness and boredom of the rich who had more access to the West through commodity consumption. In other words, these keywords sometimes function as popular descriptions emptied of meaning in the 1950s' cultural setting.[14]

The desire to be more Western was especially strong in the 1950s and manifested itself in some interesting ways. For instance, the melodrama films of the late 1950s often showed the characters living in Western-style houses (*yang'ok*), while those of the 1960s (such as Kim's family-drama–genre movies) typically featured the living space of a traditional Korean-style house (*hanok*).[15] Such cinematic depictions seem to indicate a neurotic emphasis on South Korea's being a part of the modern world that is understood only in terms of the West, symbolized in part by the house, a major backdrop of the 1950s film narratives. In this context, democracy is understood more as a kind of Western lifestyle rather than a political reality. And yet the private domain, culturally figured as the home, and the individuality of each family member, who makes up family and society, becomes a new focus of attention in cultural (and cinematic) discourses and representations. The American style democracy or individualism is far from the postwar Korean reality and only has a "psychological presence as reality" in people's consciousness; and yet it was partly such a training period of individualism in the 1950s that eventually was manifested as the April 19 Revolution.[16] In the long term, however, the decade's moral and cultural chaos and the people's inability to reign in the youthful energy of the April 19 Revolution to establish a permanent government in the Revolution's aftermath leads to the statist capitalist system of the decades that followed.

As it is true of other national historical moments of cultural chaos, postwar South Korean culture is full of remnants from the past. The most notable is the place of *sinp'a* (New Wave) tradition, which influences the genre of family drama much more than seems to be acknowledged today. A cultural import from Japan in the early twentieth century, *sinp'a* casts a long shadow on modern and contemporary Korean theater and film, despite its distorted content and form. It has been correctly surmised that Korea's ambivalent attitude toward modernity (pervasive even during the process of the country's modernization) is related to the place of *sinp'a*, or more precisely, *sinp'a* element, in Korean performance and theater traditions. One can think of a number of tragic patriarchal roles that Kim Sŭng-ho played, such as in *Coach Driver, Money,* and *Mr. Park,* in this vein.[17] His acting is mostly ultra-realistic in these roles, and yet he exhibits excessive emotional tone in climactic scenes, leaning on a *sinp'a*-style acting tradition (fig. 6.2).

Irrational and pathetic stories fill the *sinp'a* melodramas of the Golden Age cinema, and audiences eagerly welcomed them. What sociopsychological basis can we use to explain and understand this positive reception? Some argue, as we see in the next passage, that most spectators cannot sympathize with the happiness of others nor accept happy stories, and that *sinp'a* has made no positive contribution to Korean theater and cinema tradition: "It is sad to say, but audiences identified with the hapless characters and their tragic destiny; and, by crying for them, experienced a form of catharsis. [. . .] In a pre-modern society, happiness only comes by accepting misfortune, showing the ability of self-denial, and embracing the accompanying tears in the situation. Korean films deliberately exploited these ideals for commercial purposes and produced massive *sinp'a* melodramas. They did not

Figure 6.2. Kim often uses *sinp'a* facial expressions (greatly exaggerated, dramatic, or tragic) in his serious roles, such as the one he plays in the film *Money*.

contribute anything positive to the modernization of the Korean society."[18] However, such an attitude toward *sinp'a* may actually reflect the audience's own sense of confusion and discomfort in the face of modernity and modernization. The Manichean worldview and the formulaic reliability of *sinp'a* narrative most likely provided the contemporary audience some sense of the world as a morally stable place.

In mediating the relationship between the cinematic narrative and the audience, stars no doubt play a crucial role. But there is a further mediation, because, as Richard Dyer puts it, "Star images are constructed personages in media texts," and they "effect a 'magic' reconciliation of the apparently incompatible terms." Similarly, Kim Sŭng-ho is able to embody two very different kinds of patriarchs in his most successful films; one old-fashioned, poor, and ignorant and the other well educated and middle-class. Furthermore, his on-screen personae "embody social values that are to some degree in crisis," which "may be achieved not so much by reiterating dominant values as by concealing prevalent contradictions or problems."[19] Kim's acting is universally praised. Such critical appreciation of his acting seems to indicate a kind of multivalent capacity in his embodiment of characters, which encompasses both the tragic and the comic and everything in between, lending depth to even the most sketchy scenarios.

In this process of playing problematic patriarchs, Kim, the movie star, depoliticizes the audience's consciousness by individualizing it, making the social personal; more than anything else, many critics and contemporary audiences recall thinking of him as a "neighbor," a sŏmin (average person, with the connotation of being middle- or lower-middle class) just like "us." His portrayals dull whatever political edge his films had in the first place and "serve to defuse the political meanings that form the inescapable but potentially offensive or explosive point of departure of all media messages."[20] A good example is the sequence of the oldest daughter's death in Coach Driver. The father's Confucian stubbornness denies the last place of refuge for her and she kills herself, but because the film shows him weeping over her body and suffering greatly from her death, the disturbing questions raised about the part that he plays in her death are elided, and ultimately the audience feels sympathy for the grieving father.[21]

Laura Mulvey notes that the response of the Hollywood studio system in the 1950s, when it faced the massive crises of "the impact of the HUAC (House Un-American Activities Committee) investigation, indictment as a monopoly under the antitrust laws, and the coming of television," was the "particular resurgence of the family melodrama, the Hollywood genre associated with the dramas of domesticity, woman, love and sexuality" that depicted the "unease and contradiction within the very icon of American life, the home, and its sacred figure, the mother."[22] Similarly, a hugely popular genre in South Korean cinema in the turbulent years from 1957 to 1967 is a home (melo)drama, with its symbolic, unifying figure of the patriarch. Kim played many such roles in some of the most iconic films of the genre. The films of this period betray conservative views on family and marriage, and there is an obsessive move to (re)unite and (re)constitute the family, which reflects the contemporary social anxiety. Home drama genre movies such as A Sectional Chief of the Third Class typically feature a shot composition that visually unifies the entire family by containing its members in a single visual field, especially sitting around a table and happily sharing a meal (fig. 6.3).

In other words, Kim Sŭng-ho was popular precisely because he represented the nostalgic father—rather than the real father of the present, of the extradiegetic world. Through his roles he came to represent both the ideal and typical fathers, successfully creating an image of "the father" by repeatedly playing an archetypical role even while imbuing it with the reality of the quotidian details. Such a character appealed to audiences' sense of longing for the unspecified, pre-lapsarian golden past and a strong patriarch. This is a father-as-the-law figure, who is both capable and incorruptible. This was not the reality at this chaotic time, especially in the context of the April 19 Revolution, when "the father" was synonymous with corruption. In this way,

Figure 6.3. A family-unifying shot from *A Sectional Chief of the Third Class*.

the contemporary postwar audiences enjoyed both a semblance of the quotidian and an escape from it through massively popular films.

Along with the outward developments toward modernization, many observers point to internal changes as well, of people's mindset, imagination, and discourses. For instance, scholars such as Kwŏn Podŭrae and O Yŏngsuk have produced works that chronicle and examine the explosive growth of public discourses on the body, issues of individualism, and sexuality. Liberal democracy was of great public interest at this time, both as a kind of Westernized lifestyle and a cultural ideal in postwar Korea.[23] Private life, with its focus on individual experiences and desires, became the locus of intense and frequent articulation, along with the great opening up and growth of discourses on the body and sex.[24] And all of this is facilitated in large part by the magazine and print media market, enjoying a renewed life for the first time since the colonial period.[25] Hence it is not surprising that the dominant film genre shifted from the romantic melodrama in the 1950s to the home drama or family melodrama in the 1960s.[26] Now cinematic attention focused on a particular genre of melodrama that depicted the family as a microcosm of the nation. This is a popular cultural manifestation of how the South Korean nation was retrieved and reconstituted in the 1960s. The national culture, popular and otherwise, took on a different quality from the 1950s, and the change is visible even in historical films, the genre that provides more distance from social reality. By the 1960s, even historical genre dramas reflected the state-driven, authoritarian patriarchal modernization project of the decade, with its attendant ideological rigidity.[27]

The home drama genre movie had an episodic structure and generally opens as a comedy of the joys and sorrows of an average family. Suddenly toward the middle, a melodramatic turn of events takes over the narrative, but the film then returns to the earlier comic tone and ends happily with a neat resolution of conflicts, often with the final shot of the whole family happily gathered together in one place. The coexistence of the two emotional tones, comic and tragic/dramatic, is typical of these films. And although the varied emotional tones make some of them almost incoherent, they actually suit Kim Sŭng-ho as an actor well. As Lee Young Il and others point out, the actor brings out the pathos of the character or situation as the hero who is a *sŏmin*, even in comic roles.[28]

The extremely compressed nature of South Korea's state-driven, developmentalist journey into modernity is well documented by scholars of Korean history, politics, and economics. The films of this era show patriarchs burdened by the pressure to catch up with the rapidly changing mores and lifestyles that come with the nation's hurried modernization, urbanization, and Westernization in a rather negative light, and yet they seem to paradoxically defend and sympathize with such figures as well. Comedy genre films are especially noticeable in this trend.[29] These patriarchs are often helpless and inadequate, with a sense of injured pride. In many cases, their lack of authority is the result of financial difficulties; and it is no wonder, as poverty is a familiar trope of emasculation in various colonial and postcolonial national contexts. Kim Sŭng-ho played many such roles in the 1960–63 period.

The classic film *Romance Papa* is representative of the home drama genre and shows a new democratic patriarch who not only makes mistakes but also is humble enough to admit it to his children, who can debate and discuss their lives with him. The genre, in other words, humanizes the father. At the same time, such a father is most likely only an ideal. Another film, *A Sectional Chief of the Third Class* (*Samdŭng kwajang*, Yi Pong-rae, director, 1961) clearly expresses the zeitgeist of the post–April 19 Revolution era, which poses a challenge to the established generation. The father in this film is a rather powerless figure because of his relatively weak position at work and the implied lack of economic prowess. He is pushed and pulled in all directions by his children, his wife, and his boss and even endures the humiliation of being dressed down by his boss in front of his own daughter when she begins working at the same company.[30] Throughout the narrative, the father is not necessarily a pathetic figure, however, but a comic one. Indeed, the most telling of the changed times is perhaps the introduction of humor, a new narrative element, especially the patriarch as the comic relief. He is no longer a stern figure of absolute authority who demands unquestioning obedience and elicits fear from the rest of the family. The genre associates irreverence and whimsy with the once fearful authority figure of the father, and Kim Sŭng-ho's familiar and comforting on-screen persona plays a significant role in achieving this association for the audience.

As Kim Han-sang points out in his essay, which considers the actor in light of the Park Chung-Hee regime's politico-economic changes during the 1961–67 period, Kim Sŭng-ho experienced both the highs and the lows of his life and career during this era.[31] At the peak of his fame, Kim enjoyed his status as a three-time winner of the Asian-Pacific Film Festival's Best Actor award (the first such honor in Korean cinematic history), not to mention the numerous domestic awards he garnered; but this was also the period of biggest failure and decline and eventually ended with his death. During the previous administration, Syngman Rhee's "political thugs" (chŏngch'i kk'angp'ae) paid off by the regime, such as the notorious Im Hwa-su, used threats and physical violence to force actors and other entertainers to participate in anti-Communist films and pro-Rhee regime live shows and speeches. As a famous actor, Kim was also coerced to publicly endorse the regime and was later punished for it by the April 19 Revolutionaries. Then Kim made a comeback with the film *A Sectional Chief of the Third Class* only a few months later, which interestingly enough contains dialogue that directly criticizes social corruption and paints the Revolution in a positive light. Kim's portrayal of the character in this movie seems to be a reflection of his own unhappy past, as someone who in real life cannot fight against the violent coercion of the powerful and relents but in the end also repents. Instead of this personal history harming his star image, however, it actually adds a layer that makes him more sympathetic and human.[32]

The denial of the father as an ineffectual, corrupt authority figure is of great significance with respect to the April 19 Revolution, especially for its youthful leaders' generation. In addition, the family drama genre films often juxtapose the older generation's moral decay against the virtues of the sons' generation, creating the impression that the younger generation of patriarchs must take over their fathers' role in order to bring about family—and, by extension, national—harmony. There is no doubt as to the negation of the father. He is part of the old generation, a subject that could not be incorporated into the process given the rapid speed of urbanization and industrialization. But significantly his humanity redeems his character as someone with whom the audience can only sympathize rather than condemn.[33] In this way, men in real life who are powerless or absent would manifest themselves as sympathetic patriarchs in films. Further, it has been suggested that Kim's film personas as bankrupt, innocent men in *Money* and *A Dream of Fortune* (*Twejikk'um*, Han Hyŏng-mo, director, 1961) collapsed his real life with his star image, as newspapers reported his business failure and he was publicly humiliated through bankruptcy and a lawsuit.[34] Therefore "the nature of Kim Sŭng-ho's star quality in home drama is the result of an encounter between the particular role of the movie patriarch and Kim's acting abilities, the path of his personal life, and the contemporary social meaning of the father."[35]

Dyer argues, "With stars, the 'terms' [that is, constructive elements of persona-building] involved are essentially images. By 'image' here I do not understand an exclusively visual sign, but rather a complex configuration of visual, verbal, and aural signs. This configuration may constitute the general image of stardom or of a particular star. It is manifest not only in films but [also] in all kinds of media text."[36] Kim Sŭng-ho's star image is similarly constructed through media texts including publicity (for example, press interviews), films, criticism, and commentaries.[37] Kim builds his star persona in the 1950s as a man-next-door type of character, which enables him to play good-natured patriarchs in the home drama genre movies in the 1960s. These patriarchs are less than fully modern and experience some kind of crisis as a result of their unfinished subjectivity vis-à-vis modernity. They lack the latest (read: Western) knowledge and, despite their status as patriarchs, are depicted in such films as marginal members of the new society. For instance, one of the most interesting sequences in *Mr. Park* shows the titular character, who is invited to the home of his prospective in-law only to be humiliated because he does not know how to drink Western tea in a paper teabag (fig. 6.4). One can easily see why the contemporary audience would empathize with the character, because such episodes probably came from people's real-life experiences, the gestures of learning to master the new reality/modernity of the time, and the sense of being overwhelmed.[38]

South Korea was neither fully modern nor no longer pre-modern at this time, and the hybridity of the period is manifested in the film form itself. Movies of this time betray only a vague awareness of what we would call "film language," which is a Western notion. Often they are missing it altogether because the films come from, and still had elements of, older theatrical or performance traditions native to Korea. It is significant, for instance, that in Korean theatrical tradition attention is focused on the performer onstage rather than on plot or structure, following the most important elements in the classical Aristotelian theory of the theater. In this way, with a rare few exceptions, even the second generation of Korean directors active

Figure 6.4. Mr. Park fumbles with a teabag.

during the Golden Age focus more on the performers/actors than on other elements such as film language.[39]

As is true in a novel, a film character can be both a typical social type and an individual in the specific realization of that type in a particular character.[40] While Kim portrays a social type (a working-class father, for instance), he is still uniquely recognizable as the actor Kim Sŭng-ho. Often this enables the conflation of the actor with the roles he plays. And as Teresa de Lauretis's observation at the beginning of this chapter shows, the conflation of the social type and the individual is possible only with the audience's participation or emotional investment. This process, in turn, has much to do with that indefinable star quality that some performers seem to possess: charisma. In his book *Stars*, Dyer quotes E. A. Shils, who writes, "The charismatic quality of an individual [. . .] lies in [. . .] some *very central* feature of man's existence," and the appeal of such charisma is especially strong when "the social order is uncertain, unstable, and ambiguous and when the charismatic figure offers a value, order, or stability to counterpoise this."[41]

In the case of Kim Sŭng-ho this central feature of human existence is none other than "humanity," a universally recognizable yet amorphous quality. What is particularly compelling about Kim's depiction of patriarchs is their ambivalence. The *"very central* feature of man's existence" that Shils points out might be the fragility and uncertainty that Kim exhibits through ambivalence, even when he plays ideal (middle-class, culturally progressive, white-collar) fathers. It seems paradoxical at first glance that for the contemporary audiences experiencing a rapid modernization in the midst of the harsh postwar reality such depictions, paired with the familiar face of a middle-aged actor who seems so much like one's next-door neighbor, deliver precisely that illusion of order and stability. But actually it is the uncertainty of the father/Kim Sŭng-ho that convinces the audience, for it represents the audience's own experience and attitude toward their changing environment.

Such tension involving past, present, and future, represented by the culture clash between the old and new worlds, points to the contestation and instability of the cinema narrative when we examine Golden Age movies as popular cultural texts of the 1950s. They can be divided into genre flicks for the masses and artistic films that show the "true Korea," partially as products for film festivals. The Asian-Pacific Film Festival was especially important during the Golden Age, and award-winning films that could be exported to foreign countries became sort of an industry obsession.[42] But this is also the turbulent period that eventually exploded in student-led mass protests and proved a difficult time for the actor as well. One of Kim's comeback acts is *Mr. Park*, which led to *Coach Driver*, both of which garnered him multiple awards. When he wins the Best Actor award at the 1961 Asian-Pacific Film Festival, it seemed as if he could now be regarded not only as Korea's father but Asia's father as well.[43] The exaggerated media coverage and celebration of the actor's achievement at the national level confirm one's impression of the manifest culture in his films as a kind of nationally sanctioned and thus top-down expression of culture. Such culture can only be reactionary, however, as it is born out of a defense mechanism and a keen self-consciousness of a cultural and developmental time lag vis-à-vis the West.[44]

The desire for a strong ethnic nation, one that suppresses the chaos and instability of the times, surfaces in movies of this era as an attempt to reestablish the emasculated father, the figure who possesses the symbolic phallus. Patriarchy and discourses of nationalism thus align themselves with each other, and the father's lost power is recovered through the loyalty of the proxy patriarch, the son or the son-in-law, who builds his own patriarchy. From 1961 on, home drama genre films focus on erasing the national historical trauma embodied in the old father and recuperating his image in history in order to reestablish the modern national identity. Films such as *Coach Driver, Mr. Park, A Section Chief of the Third Class, Romance Papa*, and *A Salaryman* (*Wŏlgŭpjaeng'i*, Yi Pong-rae, director, 1962) tell the audience/Korean national subjects that the family must unite with the father at its center, in order for the nation to recover from the colonial past and build a modern ethnic nation. At the same time, the father in these films is a powerful signifier who paradoxically also has a temporary and unstable position, because he is a subject who cannot endure the speed of modernization, especially defined in economic terms. And perhaps because of this reason, he is the most human of all characters in these films. The notion of humanity embodied by a star such as Kim Sŭng-ho then takes on a hegemonic quality, in its affirmation of particularly conservative emotional and cultural values that engage in nostalgia even while the film narrative looks forward to a better future. But such a paradox embedded in the signifier of the patriarch in these films disappears with the rise of the state-sponsored official nationalism discourse in 1963, with the birth of the Third Republic under Park Chung-Hee.[45]

It is ironic that Kim, who was harshly criticized during the April 19 Revolution period for his pro–Syngman Rhee activities, reestablished himself as a male lead in films that criticized society and that these films greatly appealed to the audiences of the day. A good example is *Love Affair* (*Romaensŭ kŭrei*, Sin Sang-ok, director, 1963), which earned him his third Best Actor award at the Asian-Pacific Film Festival.[46] But after 1964, he was no longer able to play the kinds of fathers that had made him famous; rather, he played smaller, supporting paternal roles.[47] With the huge success of *Barefoot Youth* (*Manbal'ŭi ch'ŏngch'un*, Kim Ki-dŏk, director, 1964), the home drama genre waned as the youth romance genre became suddenly, explosively popular.[48] *Barefoot Youth* represents the new genre, in which young, handsome actors play the male leads and the older generation is depicted as corrupt and invested in maintaining the status quo to the point of irrationality. Also around this time, Kim was recycling his established image in films, playing similar roles again and again. By 1967, both the father and the actor who portrayed those fathers were pushed out to the margins of the modern, newly rebuilt nation/screen.[49]

In this light, it is symptomatic that a fascinating film appears at this time entitled *The Way of All Flesh* (*Yukch'eŭi kil*, Cho Kŭng-ha, director, 1967), in which Kim plays one of the most complex yet sentimental fathers of his film career. In the beginning of the narrative, Kim's character is a devoted father, husband, and a respected bank executive who enjoys playing classical music with his children at home. Then he makes a single misstep during a business trip and loses everything, including his job and his ideal family. In a poignant performance—and plot—reminiscent of the Professor in the German film *The Blue Angel*,[50] the former upper-middle-class family man becomes homeless and eventually dons a clown's nose and becomes a circus master, traveling the country with his much younger lover, who

Figure 6.5. Mr. Park watches and cries as his son and daughter-in-law fly away on an airplane.

led him to his current predicament. Kim's character in this film shows the limits of the postwar, post–April 19 Revolution fatherly dispossession and loss of authority stemming from his moral failure, which allows a young femme fatale to seduce him so easily. As a result, he ends up in the strange dream/nightmare world of a traveling circus, with its surreal mix of emotional highs and lows, fantasy and abject poverty.

A striking sequence in the film features a combination of tracking and close-up shots with a voice-over narration of Kim's character, now old and sick, and homeless once again. He happens to see the news of his children's musical concert and, through the kindness of his own daughter who takes pity on him (an old, homeless stranger), he is able to see them perform at a concert hall. The narration of his reflection is quite moving, as we see him walking away; it captures his loneliness, pride, and a kind of world-weary, humble acceptance of his place in life. What is more interesting is that there are other, similar sequences in his films, such as *Mr. Park* and *Coach Driver*, of Kim Sŭng-ho as an iconic father whose thoughts are revealed in a voice-over narration while the camera shows him walking away after some kind of profound realization about himself and his children. The sons' characters are never shown in this manner in the same films, as perhaps their generation represents action rather than self-reflection or regret. It is a meta-textual moment when the *real* intrudes on-screen, symptomatic of the changed sociocultural standing of the "father," a moment of reckoning manifesting on-screen that pays homage to the older generation even while confirming that generation's past mistakes and the new authority of the younger generation. In this vein, Jin-kyung Lee explains that the Park Chung-Hee administration "enhanced" the South Korean "collective masculinity" and that his "tactic of associating the prestige and status of the nation with [such] enhancement of collective masculinity was enormously effective in the context of a South Korean patriarchy that had suffered political, economic, and military subordination."[51]

Kim found his best fit in playing either a tragic, failed patriarch or a comic, bumbling father. He was anything but slick, urban, or modern, even when he played a modernized father who was a white-collar worker. He is forever the Other of the urban, younger, Westernized modern subject that his (movie) children's generation embodies. He is someone who struggles in vain against the larger socioeconomic forces "out there"—outside the home and also outside the film's diegesis. He is someone who belongs in the old world, who hence doesn't understand the terms of success in the changed world. Such portraits are pre-modern, or actually anti-modern. He invokes nostalgia, forgiveness, and sympathy for his human frailties even when he fails or, rather, especially because he fails. In the background of this patriarch's failure to take care of his family is not necessarily some contemptible personality flaw but the harsh external circumstances that work against him in combination with his own, entirely human shortcomings, such as ignorance or stubbornness. These films rarely criticize the reality of Korea's lack of true democracy or systemic corruption that make hardworking patriarchs stumble and fall into economic hardship and despair. Furthermore, the fathers that Kim Sŭng-ho plays in these films overcome their temporary tragic predicament by the end of the narrative, through a kind of deus ex machina measure that brings on a reversal of fate, and the films end happily. Today his films allow new audiences to think about the question of humanism as it relates to film stardom, as well as the ideological facet of popular culture, even while drawing pleasure from watching the films in ways probably not imagined by the filmmakers of the Golden Age Korean cinema. And if there is any intervention to be made through consumption and study of popular culture, all this is perhaps the reason we should take another look at Kim Sŭng-ho's films today.

NOTES

1. Richard Dyer, *Stars* (London: BFI, 1998), 178.
2. One cannot underestimate the degree to which the films of the Golden Age of South

Korean cinema influenced and affected contemporary audiences' lives. Although such an impact is difficult to measure, there is much anecdotal evidence that an actor like Kim Sŭng-ho was not only a household name but also virtually a neighbor in the minds of the audience. See, for instance, Nancy Abelmann and Kathleen McHugh, eds., *South Korean Golden Age Melodrama: Gender, Genre, and National Cinema* (Detroit: Wayne State University Press, 2005), 43–64.

3. The romanization of Korean words and names in this chapter follows the McCune-Reischauer romanization. But in cases where individuals are better known by their alternative romanized spellings of names, such as Syngman Rhee and Park Chung-Hee, I provided both.

4. The change in tax law that allowed an exemption on theater ticket revenue greatly affected the industry in the immediate postwar years, leading to a boost in investments in the film industry.

5. *Fooled by Love and Hurt by Money* (*Sarang'e sokko tone ulgo*, Yi Myŏng-u, director, 1939). Kim Sŭng-ho was an apprentice member of the famed Tongyang Theater troupe at this time. Like many other artists of the period, Kim also had a dramatic narrative of the Korean War. He and others apparently escaped while being abducted to North Korea by the People's Army Soldiers. Yi Kil-sŏng et al., *Kim Seung Ho: Face of Father, Portrait of Korean Cinema* (Seoul: Korean Film Archive, 2007), 14–17. With the exception of quotes from this book and film dialogues that have been subtitled into English, all Korean to English translation is mine.

6. *The Wedding Day* (*Sijip kanŭn'nal*, Yi Pyŏng-il, director, 1956).

7. It is beyond the scope of this chapter to study all of Kim Sŭng-ho's films. Instead, I will focus on some of his representative films in which he plays the two types mentioned here (dramatic and comic).

8. See Kelly Y. Jeong, *Crisis of Gender and the Nation in Korean Literature and Cinema: Modernity Arrives Again* (Lanham, MD: Lexington Books, 2011), especially chapter 4.

9. Pak Myŏng-rim, *Choices and Distortions of South and North Korea in the 1950s* (*1950 nyŏndae nambuk'haŭi sŏnt'aek'kwa kuljŏl*), ed. Yŏksa munje yŏn'guso (Seoul: Yŏksa pip'yŏngsa, 1998), 112–25. First quoted in Yi Kil-sŏng et al., *Kim Seung Ho*, 108.

10. Kim So-yŏn et al., *The Era of Attraction and Chaos: Korean Film of the 1950s* (*Maehok'kwa hondonŭi sidae: 1950nyŏndaeŭi han'gukyŏnghwa*) (Seoul: Sodo, 2003), 26–27.

11. Kim So-yŏn et al., *The Era of Attraction and Chaos*, 30–36.

12. Kim So-yŏn et al., *The Era of Attraction and Chaos*, 190.

13. O Yŏng-suk, *Korean Cinema and Cultural Discourse in the 1950s* (*1950 nyŏndae, han'gukyŏnghwawa munhwa tamnon* (Seoul: Somyŏng ch'ulp'an, 2007), 94–106.

14. Yi Kil-sŏng et al., *Kim Seung Ho*, 104–5.

15. Kim So-yŏn et al., *The Era of Attraction and Chaos*, 146.

16. Pyŏn Chae-ran, quoted in O Yŏng-suk, *Korean Cinema and Cultural Discourse in the 1950s*, 234–35.

17. The following are the most salient elements of *sinp'a*: (1) narratives repeatedly emphasize emotion (continued sadness and misfortune) and especially impose a particular emotion on the audience at the conclusion; (2) rather than following causality, narratives show frequent coincidences and reversals to create the emotions of happiness, crisis, or unhappiness; (3) the psychology of characters appears

to be similar to that of conventional Western drama in linear narrative teleology, but there is an excessive emphasis on the characters' emotional states. Im Chŏng-t'aek et al., *Modernity and Postcoloniality in East Asian Cinema (Tongasia yŏnghwaŭi kŭndaesŏng'gwa t'alsikminsŏng)* (Seoul: Yonsei taehak'kyo ch'ulp'anbu, 2007), 36–37.

18. Korean Motion Picture Promotion Corporation (KMPPC), *Scenario Collection, vol. 2: 1956–1960 (Han'guk sinario sŏnjip che 2kwŏn: 1956–1960)* (Seoul: Jimmundang, 1982), 426–27. First quoted by Yi Hyo-in in Korean Film Archives, *Traces of Korean Cinema from 1945–1959* (Seoul: Munhaksasangsa, 2004), 225.

19. Dyer, *Stars*, 97, 26–27.

20. Dyer, *Stars*, 25–27.

21. See Jeong, *Crisis of Gender*, for a more detailed analysis of the scene.

22. Laura Mulvey, *Visual and Other Pleasures* (Bloomington: Indiana University Press, 1989), 63–64.

23. See, for instance, Kwŏn Podŭrae, *Après-girl Reads Sasang'gye (Ap'ŭregŏl sasang'gyerŭl iltt'a)* (Seoul: Tong'guk taehak'kyo ch'ulp'anbu, 2009) and O Yŏng-suk, *Korean Cinema and Cultural Discourse*.

24. The discourses of the body, now newly made visible through institutions such as the Miss Korea Contest as well as prevalent images of popular actresses (not necessarily Korean), all but explode in the 1950s. For a related discussion on the mediated nature of the female subject to the partriarchal nation in the context of modern China, see Lydia Liu, "'The Female Body and Nationalist Discourse: Manchuria in Xiao Hong's 'Field of Life and Death,'" in *Body, Subject, and Power in China*, ed., Angela Zito and Tani Barlow (Chicago: University of Chicago Press, 1994), 199–213.

25. O Yŏng-suk, *Korean Cinema and Cultural Discourse*, 92–93.

26. This signals the end of the postwar "après-girl" depictions. This neologism, a combination of "après-guerre" and "girl," refers to a new cultural stereotype of a young, sexually liberated or even promiscuous woman in postwar Korea. Kwŏn Podŭrae, *Après-girl Reads Sasang'gye*, 79.

27. Kim So-yŏn et al., *The Era of Attraction and Chaos*, 178, 200.

28. Yi Yŏng-il, *History of Korean Cinema (Han'guk yŏnghwa chŏnsa)* (Seoul: Sodo, 2004), 349, 359.

29. Yi Hyo-in et al., *Study of Korean Film History 1960–1979 (Han'guk yŏnghwasa kongbu 1960–1979)* (Seoul: Korean Film Archive, 2004), 50.

30. Yi Hyo-in et al., *Study of Korean Film History*, 72.

31. Yi Kil-sŏng et al., *Kim Seung Ho*, 35.

32. Yi Kil-sŏng et al., *Kim Seung Ho*, 37–42.

33. Yi Kil-sŏng et al., *Kim Seung Ho*, 46–50.

34. Yi Kil-sŏng et al., *Kim Seung Ho*, 60–61.

35. Yi Kil-sŏng et al., *Kim Seung Ho*, 85.

36. Dyer, *Stars*, 34.

37. Kim Sŭng-ho's dedication is emphasized through anecdotes from the actor's life that show his commitment, sincerity, and devotion to his craft, his single-minded focus on being the best actor. This establishes two things: first, his humility and decency, proven through accounts of his hard work; and second, his professionalism. He is not just an entertainer—a lowly class indeed in the traditional Korean view

of social classes—but moreover someone distinguished from the rest of the crowd, worthy of respect and admiration owing to his professionalism. That is the reason Korean audiences responded (and still do) so positively to Kim Sŭng-ho, even beyond appreciating his acting skills. Yi Kil-sŏng et al., *Kim Seung Ho*, 60–63.

38. South Korea was heavily dependent on America for its postwar aid, so it is no accident that in the Korean context at that time the West is synonymous with America, especially American commodities. In *Mr. Park*, the future in-law is a Korean American from Hawaii, and her test of Mr. Park's refinement and culture is in the form of a Lipton teabag.

39. Im Chŏng-t'aek et al., *Modernity and Postcoloniality*, 28.

40. Dyer, *Stars*, 97.

41. E.A. Shils, "Charisma, Order and Status," *American Sociological Review* 30 (1965): 199–213. First quoted in Dyer, *Stars*, 30.

42. Yi Kil-sŏng et al., *Kim Seung Ho*, 18–19.

43. Yi Kil-sŏng et al., *Kim Seung Ho*, 24–26.

44. Borrowing from Amartya Sen's *Development As Freedom* (New York: Anchor Books, 1999), Jin-kyung Lee shows that the Park Chung-Hee era's push for anticommunist development was "reformulated . . . [as] freedom." *Service Economies: Militarism, Sex Work, and Migrant Labor in South Korea* (Minneapolis: University of Minnesota Press, 2010), 29.

45. Chu Yu-sin et al., *Korean Cinema and Modernity: From "Madame Freedom" to "Mist"* (*Han'gukyŏnghwawa kŭndaesŏng: "Chayu puin"esŏ "Angae"kka'ji*) (Seoul: Sodo, 2001), 53–59.

46. Yi Kil-sŏng et al., *Kim Seung Ho*, 27.

47. Yi Kil-sŏng et al., *Kim Seung Ho*, 28–30.

48. It would require the space of another essay to discuss all the reasons for the sudden arrival and extreme popularity of the youth romance film genre that eclipsed the popularity of the family drama genre. For the purpose of this chapter, I must state that the genre struck a chord with the audience, especially the dormant youthful audience, whose mores were expressed through the April Revolution but were quickly repressed with the establishment of the Park Chung-Hee administration. Unfortunately *Barefoot Youth* is not an original story but a copy of a Japanese original. However, it showcases the complex cultural histories and exchanges between Japan and Korea, which trace back to the colonial period and continue to the present.

49. See, for instance, Kim Sŏn-a's essay, which notes how the future patriarch (the son-in-law who, significantly, is a soldier) replaces the father (played by Kim), who leaves the family and is in turn abandoned and forgotten by them in *Confessions of the Flesh* (*Yukch'e'ŭi kobaek*, Cho Kŭng-ha, director, 1967). Chu Yu-sin et al., *Korean Cinema and Modernity*, 70.

50. *The Blue Angel* (1930).

51. Lee, *Service Economies*, 43.

7

TRAVIS WORKMAN

The Partisan, the Worker, and the Hidden Hero
Popular Icons in North Korean Film

"Like the lead article in the Party paper, cinema should have great appeal and move ahead of reality. Thus, it should play a mobilizing role in each stage in the revolutionary struggle."[1]
KIM IL-SUNG

"Here, the art of politics transforms itself into the politics of art—political imagination being assimilated to artistic imagination."[2]
BORIS GROYS

Discussing North Korean film in a volume on Korean popular culture may be met with some skepticism, because we normally do not use "popular culture" to refer to state media. The problems in translating popular culture into Korean, discussed in detail in the introduction, take on a different shape in North Korea. It is difficult to imagine anything like *yuhaeng* (popular fashion) in a place where all domestic media is produced by the one-party state. In North Korea, those who consume visual culture remain *taejung*, an older Marxist term for the popular masses, or *inmin*, a nationalist term for citizen. Although I am bending the definition of "popular culture" somewhat, I think it is useful to trace the popular within North Korea's seemingly anachronistic versions of it. The purpose is not simply to understand how North Korean film culture has been different from other national contexts, but to also see how its modes of identification, representation, and political narration have borrowed or been in conversation with commercial popular cultures, including that of South Korea. Tracing the North Korean popular culture by way of cinema's creation and reproduction of *taejung* and *inmin* has a general historical and theoretical significance for reading popular cultures, particularly as we look back at the late twentieth century and the Cold War.

This chapter focuses on North Korean socialist realism as popular cinematic spectacle. It defines how the spectacle of socialism and the nation functions, or is supposed to function, in North Korean film. Drawing on psychoanalysis, it analyzes the way that melodramatic emotion is used to provoke sentimental identification with characters and stars, and with the political and moral ideas to which these popular icons appear faithful. It also discusses transformations between classic films on liberation and socialist reality to the hidden-hero films (1977–present), in order to see how national narrative and modes of identification have changed in North Korean film over time.

TEARS IN THE SPECTACLE OF SOCIALISM AND THE PEOPLE

Considering that North Korea is the last Stalinist people's republic in the world, it is tempting to imagine that the interpretation of its cinema would require an altogether different set of concerns from popular cultural studies, which addresses itself to the cultural commodities of market capitalism. However, in order to recognize a minimal comparability between North Korean cinema and capitalist popular culture, and therefore some shared interests within the study of "actually existing" socialisms and popular cultural studies, we can recall that Soviet theories and practices of socialist realist filmmaking in the 1930s and 1940s, as well as the North Korean film industry they influenced during the Soviet occupation (1945–48), were greatly concerned with the popularization of cinema.[3] Although socialist realism was in many respects an elite discourse and artistic practice, it would be a mistake to disregard its popularity, the degree to which the program of popularization (taejunghwa) was truly effective at transforming art into mass culture.

In the 1930s, Soviet intellectuals began to theorize popularization and to judge the value of past and present works of art according to their level of progressive "popular spirit" (narodnost). They sought to "incarnate," through both historical and fictional biography, the positive heroes of socialism, to render intelligible to the people personalities that were transcendent in their humanity and their ideology.[4] The debates concerning popularization were some of the most significant among Communists in colonial Korea, and popularization was a key theme of theories of art, literature, and film leading up to and during the establishment of the Democratic People's Republic of Korea (DPRK).[5] Technically speaking, manufacturing the popularity of socialist realist cinema involved criticizing the formalism of avant-garde thinkers like early Eisenstein and Pudovkin and borrowing heavily from the mode of production and style of the classical Hollywood system, with its adherence to principles of temporal continuity, the primacy of narrative, and individual typology. It was popularized socialist realist films, including the later productions of the Stalin personality cult, that were the first influential imports to Soviet-occupied North Korea during the establishment of the DPRK (1948) and its film industry (1947).[6]

The three common terms used to describe North Korean films are: socialist realism, the Korean term *Juche* realism (*chuch'e sasiljuŭi*), and melodramatic realism.[7] The first term emphasizes the undeniable influence of Stalin-era Soviet cinema.[8] The second term emphasizes how the national narratives and other ideological content of North Korean films adhere to the discourses of *Juche* (the Subject), the official national ideology of the DPRK from the 1960s until Kim Il-sung's death in 1994. The final term emphasizes the fusion between melodramatic and realist aspects—depictions of excessive emotion, suffering, and victimization are situated within a Manichean moral and political universe with the intention of revealing the historical and political realities of the nation.[9] Each of these descriptions includes the term *realism*, but the meaning of realism has been left mostly unexamined in discussions of North Korean film. Realism does not refer solely to the conventions or style of a particular film but also includes a qualitative claim that these conventions and styles somehow constitute or reflect a real sociocultural formation. Understanding what realism might mean in these three categories is important for analyzing how North Korean cinema might function as popular culture; that is, how it contributes to the sense of a popularly shared reality.

Evgeny Dobrenko provides a number of significant insights into the status of reality in Soviet socialist realism, many of which pertain to the North Korean context.[10] The assertions in Dobrenko's argument that are pertinent to North Korean cinema are that the Stalinist political and cultural project was fundamentally representational, that the "transition to socialism" was accomplished, to a large extent, discursively, and that the realization of socialism through the aestheticization of society entailed a derealization of everyday life.[11] In the era of socialist realism, socialism itself "actually existed" only in representation, through its cinematic, literary, and discursive construction. Drawing from Jean Baudrillard, Dobrenko states that through the socialist realist system of representation socialism became hyperreal—that is, more real than the derealized everyday life—and, quoting Guy Debord, it became a spectacle, "not a collection of images, but a social relation among people, mediated by images."[12] The aestheticization of socialism in Stalinist culture glorified production, the ethic of labor, and political loyalty to the party's economic projects. However, these representations did not reflect the reality of productive relations in society, but themselves became society's primary product and commodity. Socialist realism boldly moved the political and economic basis of revolutionary socialism into the aesthetic, transforming socialism into an image and a story consumed by the popular masses.

In another discussion of the "total art of Stalinism," Boris Groys argues that the aesthetics of socialist realism, by both appropriating and criticizing the modernist avant-garde, actualized what the avant-garde could only dream of—the unification of art with life. However, historically speaking, if the total art of socialist realism permeated life nearly to the extent that its proponents hoped, this occurred through cinema as mass culture and mass spectacle rather than through older mediums.[13] It is no accident that both Stalin and Kim Il-sung recognized the power of film and considered it not only the most important art form but one of the primary means for creating a new art of living as well. Such a total permeation of life by art remains, of course, an incomplete process. In the case of cinema as popular mass culture, the aesthetic construction of socialism requires a constant effort to de-realize everyday life and subsume life and social relations into the spectacle.

A political economy of the sign similar to the one Dobrenko describes has always been an important aspect of the realism of North Korean cinema, and the idealism of this realism—the degree to which its romantic representations of history diverge from historical realities—has only increased along with the country's growing isolation and recent economic catastrophes.[14] In the case of juche realism, the spectacle is as much a spectacle of the national people (inmin) as it is of socialism. A perusal of On the Art of the Cinema (1973), a highly influential guidebook to film production attributed to Kim Jong-il, reveals the degree to which the Korean Workers' Party (KWP) has viewed cinema as the primary technique and medium for the construction of socialism and the creation of a national people.[15] The conflation of socialist reality and national belonging with cinematic spectacle comes through in passages of the text that prescribe a peculiar mode of method acting that almost completely erases the lines of distinction between dictator/director and between citizen/actor/character.[16] The text goes so far as to argue that one can determine whether or not an actress or actor is capable of pulling off the role of a heroine or hero by observing whether or not she or he embraces party ideology with full enthusiasm off screen.[17] North Korea's star system, in which the same prominent actors tend to take on the roles of heroes, is another example of this interpenetration of filmic and extra-filmic representation. The figure of the film star, who appears as a kind of character in other media (for example, journals and newspapers), creates cultural connections between film and other modes of representation. It is this interpenetration of cinema and the extra-cinematic, implied in the notion of spectacle, that has led Sunah Kim to describe the DPRK as a "cinema state."[18]

If socialist realism is real as a spectacle of socialism and *Juche* realism is real as a spectacle of the national people, then what about this third, rather awkward term, "melodramatic realism"? Jan Campbell offers an important critique of the formerly dominant view in film studies that melodrama, taking up the tradition of early cinema, plays out pre-Oedipal fantasies, whereas the turn to narrative realism is a turn to the Oedipal. She argues convincingly for a phenomenology of film that does away with such strict rationalist divisions between melodrama and realism.[19] However, in order to think through melodrama as realism, we need to reconsider how spectatorship and sentimental identification, particularly of embodied emotion, can create a sense of reality in tandem with, or even against, principles of spatiotemporal continuity, perspective, and structure.

Identification, however successfully or unsuccessfully provoked, is easily considered the primary mechanism of the real in socialist realism, because socialist realism never purported to represent or to index an extraspectacular social reality.[20] Because socialist realist cinema, in Kim Il-sung's words, "moves ahead of reality," theories of socialist realism have had to contend with a mutation in what Roland Barthes called the "referential illusion" of nineteenth-century literary realism.[21] According to Barthes, this realism circumvented the signified and established an illusion of direct accord between signifier and referent. Maxim Gorky and other early theorists argued that socialist realism would require an improvement upon this referential illusion of nineteenth-century realism, and their call for a new mythology and a new romanticism would be taken up and translated in North Korea, China, and other socialist countries.[22] The referent of socialist realism is not socialist reality as it is, but how it should be, and socialist realist filmmaking accordingly seeks the materialization of ideas and ideology. The referential illusion of socialist realism does not concern the indexing of physical objects or the exposition of underlying social structures, but rather follows Hegel's assertion that an artwork is beautiful and truthful when it is a "sensuous semblance of the Idea," when the aesthetic object contains traces of the Idea as referent.[23] In North Korean cinema and in melodrama more broadly, these semblances of the Idea are visualized primarily through embodied emotion.

How does one identify with an idea except through pleasure? As theories of spectatorship have pointed out, the mediation of consciousness by the spectacle is intimately related to the pleasure of spectating. Despite common claims that it is not possible for spectators to enjoy the consumption of socialist realism and its variants and that this lack of enjoyment differentiates socialist realist film from Hollywood film, this view falsely assumes that there could be no pleasure in watching highly idealized representations of revolution and the construction of socialism, in reaffirming one's faith in art's claim on social reality, or in identifying with common individuals who are situated narratively and emotively within this universe and this discourse.

For North Korean films, as for many of their South Korean counterparts, a sublime, or perhaps masochistic, pleasure can be gained from seeing the expression of extreme emotions on screen, emotions that are in obvious excess of those of daily life.[24] In those climactic moments that verify the ideological purity of a heroine or hero, emotional intensity guarantees truth and sincerity. When the party is impelled to intervene in order to redeem suffering, or the hero is spurred to political action, it is a visible spiritual or physical wound that is commonly the impetus. Suffering, ideology, and redemption are all incarnated literally on the surface of the body. Spectating the embodiments of ethical and political ideas—good and evil, oppression and freedom, correct and incorrect ideology, etc.—has undoubtedly been a source of pleasure for North Korean film audiences. Like Hegel's "sensuous semblance," this melodramatic embodiment of an emotional relation to ideas makes a very different claim on historical, political, and ideological reality from the naturalist presentation of facts or the exposition of underlying social structures in critical realism. The referential illusion of this cinema is that actions and expressions are always enactments and expressions of ideological truth or falsity.[25] Like films that were prominent under fascism and the aspects of Hollywood they appropriated, this referential illusion relies on the spectator's sentimental identification with embodied emotions that are a semblance of political and moral ideas.[26]

As Immanuel Kant pointed out in his aesthetic philosophy, an *idea* is only a rational concept with no relation to experience and requires an *ideal* (or "the presentation of an individual being as adequate to an idea") in order to be incarnated as a visual expression available to experience.[27] Much like the filmmakers of melodrama, Kant thought that the ideals of the moral and the beautiful could be sought solely in the human figure.[28] While the human figure of the popular icon is not the only possible object of identification in cinema, I argue that it is through the embodied emotions of what Sigmund Freud referred to more psychologically as the "ego ideal" that

North Korean melodramatic realism seeks to provoke identification with ideas of the moral, the beautiful, and the political. The pleasure through which the spectator of melodramatic realism identifies with ideas is often in excess of the film's narrative, which tends to code the negation or sublimation of pleasure as necessary for heroic action. At the same time, the pleasure of identification remains in tune with the excess through which the narrative is presented—the mise-en-scène, the dramatic acting, the music, and the cinematography.[29] In Freud's terms, the hero must choose the unpleasure of the reality principle over the immediate gratifications of the pleasure principle, but as theorists of melodrama have pointed out, spectating and identifying with this deferment of pleasure and the ideas that motivate it can also be pleasurable, particularly when this deferment of pleasure is conveyed through excess.[30]

Although embodied emotion remains the center of the referential illusion between the various genres of North Korean film, the techniques for manufacturing intimacy between the individual and the nation are not uniform. Variations in the representation of the temporality, political agency, and emotional sensibility of the national subject become apparent when comparing classical films—including those dealing with the revolutionary traditions and early films on socialist reality—with the later hidden-hero genre (1977–present). My comparison between classical and hidden-hero films in the next section focuses on a few key issues. The positive hero serves as an ego ideal within the moral universe of socialist realism, and the new individuality in the hidden-hero genre is a further attempt to purify the will of the hero of any external coercion.[31] At the same time, the role of the leader as group ideal changes from that of a teacher who educates the popular masses to a gaze that surveils and recognizes the independent, freely willed actions of the hero. Furthermore, identification with embodied emotion or the sentimental solidarity provoked by classic films is no longer directed toward the other members of the nation but rather toward the hero as object of the leader's recognition. In hidden-hero films, through what Stephanie Hemelryk Donald refers to as "the socialist-realist gaze," the leader as group ideal can easily replace the character of the hero as the primary object of identification.[32] Finally cinema, as a technology of government in a postrevolutionary society, contributes to the transformation of the nation's external borders into internal borders, so that the spectacle of socialism and the national people becomes more explicitly directed toward the regulation of the everyday life of the population.[33]

Like other national cinemas, North Korean cinema manufactures emotional intimacy between individual life stories and national history, an intimacy whose ideological effects are reinforced through the referential illusion of melodrama outlined above. This realism of emotion is not without its formal correlates. North Korean films are heavily narrative, and as in classical Hollywood and Soviet socialist realism, form is largely subordinated to the "*syuzhet*'s [plot's] presentation of the *fabula* [story]."[34] This centering of narrative is apparent in the first hundred pages of *On the Art of the Cinema*, which do not mention cinematography or editing at all and rather are dedicated to the discussion of literature as the foundation for scriptwriting, and as a humanics that creates a new life through narrative and the embodiment of ideology.[35] The text insists in particular on believable stories that tell of the gradual development of the protagonist's individual consciousness toward the embrace of party ideology and the fulfillment of the film's particular "ideological seed."[36]

The content of the ideological seed of a film differs according to genre. Setting aside the complex history of North Korean documentaries, North Korean texts categorize feature films in this way: films adapted from the immortal classics; films on the theme of the revolutionary traditions; films on the theme of the socialist reality; films on the theme of the Fatherland Liberation War (Korean War); films on the theme of intelligence and counterintelligence; films on the theme of national reunification.[37] These genre categories are by no means stable. For example, films that focus on the revolutionary traditions of the colonial period often move on to the Fatherland Liberation War and connect the resistance to Japanese imperialism seamlessly with the resistance to United States imperialism. In relation to heroism, a number of qualities of the partisan revolutionary are carried over into films on socialist reality, which deal more directly with the worker and the construction of socialism rather than with partisan struggle.

The two foundational moments of national history in classic films are the highly mythologized period of Kim Il-sung–led guerrilla resistance to Japanese colonial rule and the continuation of that partisan struggle during the Fatherland Liberation War against the United States and the South Korean "puppet state." Two of the most celebrated classics, *Sea of Blood* (1969) and *The Flower Girl* (1972), both depict a family's extreme suffering under Japanese colonial rule and the Korean landlord class that it historically propped up.[38] Imprisonment, blinding, and/or death are followed by the eventual coming-into-consciousness of the remaining family members through the intervention of national consciousness and the party. A quintessential Fatherland Liberation War film, *Wolmi Island* (1982) employs a similar narrative of victimization and redemption through the story of a small group of soldiers and civilians who for three days defend Wolmi Island against the United States's Inchon invasion.[39] These classic films on the revolutionary traditions and the war narrate the individual's emergence out of unconscious victimization into conscious activity, forging various analogies between this movement and the unfolding of national history. The climax redeems oppression by way of naturalized connections between the individual hero, the family, the nation, and the party.[40]

These films utilize a larger-than-life aesthetic; in the words of Kim Jong-il they "aim high," representing individual lives as bound to the collective mission to liberate the nation from colonial incursions. It is a shared experience of oppression and sympathy with others' suffering that gives rise to group identification and partisan struggle. Subjects gain political agency and correct political ideas by recognizing, more through shared emotion than political savvy, that their personal and familial suffering is enmeshed with the macropolitical conflicts of the colonized nation or the emergent nation-state. Such cinematic portrayals of colonial oppression, guerrilla revolution, and war are not realist in the sense that they reflect the complex historical reality of Japanese colonialism (1910–45), the establishment of the DPRK, or the Korean War (1950–53). However, as quasimythical texts, they shape the hyperreality of North Korean national history and situate the partisan hero within it through the depiction of emotion.[41] Toward the end of *The Flower Girl*, set in the 1930s, Kim Ch'ŏllyong escapes from a Japanese prison and leads peasant rebellions, in part to save his sisters (the captured flower girl, Kkotpun, and Sun-hŭi, who was blinded at an early age by collaborationist landlords). At the height of the narrative arc, when he argues that a larger revolt is necessary, a medium close-up shows Ch'ŏllyong embracing his sisters and crying as he explains the colonial class structure and the historical reasons for the plight of the Korean nation (fig. 7.1). This classical form of heroism was attributed to a non-Communist nationalist of the colonial period in *An Chung-gŭn Shoots Itō Hirobumi* (1975), which celebrates the historical person who resisted Japanese colonialism by shooting the Japanese resident-general in Harbin, China, in 1909.[42] It was rendered most sublimely in the three parts of *Five Guerrilla Brothers* (1968), set during the Japanese colonial period, in which dramatic long shots of the mountainous

Figure 7.1. The partisan hero of national liberation Kim Ch'ŏllyong, played by Merited Actor Kim Ryong-rin, sheds a tear and embraces his sister as he explains the colonial class structure and the reasons for the plight of the Korean nation. *The Flower Girl* (1972).

Korean landscape present a sublime object for contemplation and for political commitment to what Carl Schmitt refers to as the "telluric struggle" of the partisan in the colonial war.[43]

The innumerable films dealing with socialist reality made during or about the heyday of economic development in the 1960s tend not to deal with the epic sweep of national history but more locally with the worker's role in the construction of socialism. Although these films sometimes include elements of diachronic national narrative, they are more concerned with quotidian problems that emerge in factories or in agricultural collectives.[44] For example, in the quintessential Chollima work-team film *When We Pick Apples* (1971) the "ideological seed" is that agricultural workers should remain dedicated to increasing apple production.[45] The leader of the work-team thinks that fallen apples need not be harvested because of the abundance produced by the socialist economy, and a bride concentrates more on her upcoming wedding than on her work at the cooperative farm. The hero, a young woman named Chŏng-ok, intervenes to inspire the workers and the children of the village to respect food production, overcome their individualism, and maintain their ideological commitments to Chollima despite the country's economic successes (fig. 7.2). Like the film on the revolutionary traditions, classic films on socialist reality ask the viewer to identify with heroic characters by way of a shared sense of social mission articulated through an emotive language and imagery.

How do such emotive language and imagery change in the hidden-hero

Figure 7.2. After seeing the children harvesting apples in a wasteful manner, Chŏng-ok, played by Chŏng Yŏng-hŭi, explains the importance of producing and preserving crops for the village, the work team, and the nation. *When We Pick Apples* (1971).

genre, and how, therefore, has the aestheticization of politics transformed the North Korean cinema in the past few decades? Looking at Freud's discussion of identification in his work on group psychology is useful for understanding the pliability of the realism of emotion to a variety of political ends, whether between political systems or, in this case, between genres of political fiction. Using sympathy (the possibility or desire to put oneself in another's situation) as an example, Freud summarizes the characteristics of identification in this way: "First, identification is the original form of emotional tie with an object; second, in a regressive way it becomes a substitute for a libidinal object-tie, as it were by means of introjections of the object into the ego; and third, it may arise with any new perception of a common quality shared with some other person who is not an object of the sexual instinct."[46] This sort of identification between egos is an important factor in racial and national identification, and Freud goes on to state, "The mutual tie between members of a group is in the nature of an identification of this kind, based upon an important emotional common quality." Furthermore, he suggests, "This common quality lies in the nature of the tie with the leader."[47]

In Freud's reading of identification, the "common quality" is a rather loose empirical category, but it is a tool to compare distinct modes of provoking identification. In *The Flower Girl* and in many other films on the Revolutionary traditions, the visible suffering of the peasants is meant to provoke identification with their class position and an awareness of the injustice of colonial rule. The common emotional quality is a shared experience of victimization, however hyperreal or mediated by the cinematic apparatus this experience might be. By overlaying the discourse of party ideology with the expression of melodramatic emotion, the films attempt to transform the identification with visible suffering into identification with the redeemers of this suffering—the party, the hero, the leader, and the Revolution—but the emotional common quality remains tied to the collective and macropolitical experience of oppression. Likewise, in the Chollima film, the party, the hero, and the leader educate the masses, but the emotional common quality, while mediated by these agents, remains an attachment to the work-team's common goals and cooperative labor.

It would be an exaggeration to state that the leader is not present in these earlier films or that the personality cult has not been an important aspect of DPRK politics since its founding. Nonetheless, the hidden hero genre, by representing differently the temporality, political agency, and emotional sensibility of the ideal national subject, abstracts and isolates the hero as ego ideal from the social world that was constituted through previous manners of identification and renders spectacular an unmediated relation between individual and leader.[48] Further in his discussion of group psychology, Freud writes about the leader: "The primal father is the group ideal, which governs the ego in the place of the ego ideal."[49] In the hidden-hero film, the leader does not entirely *replace* the hero in precisely this way, but the genre does embolden the "socialist-realist gaze," so that the viewer is asked to identify with the perspective of the leader as much as the hero as object of recognition.[50] The viewer is also not meant to identify with the ego ideal because this hero understands more clearly or commiserates more authentically with a common emotion belonging to each member of a collectivity, nor because she or he has a better awareness of what will benefit all those who hold a common goal. The only common emotional quality between egos becomes the desire to be recognized by the leader, at the same time as this desire for recognition is disavowed through the genre's narrative trickery. The hero is shown throughout life to deflect the recognition of others, even when they openly misrecognize him or her, but eventual recognition by the leader and the party is guaranteed as a genre convention and as a contract with the viewer. This trickery, which could also be a source of pleasure, is supposed to purify the hero's will from the taint of narcissism, because it suggests that the leader is most likely to recognize those who self-effacingly disavow their desire for recognition.

In order to reorganize identification in this way, and to thereby transform the political content of the socialist reality film into something more patently totalitarian, the hidden-hero genre combines the temporality of the two most prominent classical genres. It takes the diachronic and mythical time of the Revolutionary film and combines it with an instrumental concern for mundane economic problems found in early films on socialist reality.[51] The hero has a single economic task—increasing rice production, reforesting the hillsides, manning the lighthouse—but the story is a long biography of the worker that revolves around personal travails with the events of national history and impediments internal to North Korean society.

Traces of Life (1989), purportedly Kim Il-sung's favorite hidden-hero film, uses romantic metaphors of the land and the landscape to establish such continuity between the epic time of the revolutionary film and the everyday tasks of postrevolutionary economic development.[52] The hidden heroine, Chin-ju, expresses discontent when her husband is called to duty during the Korean Demilitarized Zone Conflict (1966–69). The couple's idyllic newlywed life is suddenly torn apart, and on their final night together they fight about whether personal life or the nation should take priority. After her husband sacrifices himself sweeping ocean mines, the primary conflict in the film becomes whether or not, and how, Chin-ju will remain a faithful widow. His final letter to her, which she does not share with anyone before showing it to her children late in the film, says that an individual life is worthless without dedication to society. Reading the letter inspires her to fulfill her husband's wish to till the soil that Kim Il-sung "gifted" to him and his home village during the Revolution and its land reforms, but she "selflessly" refuses to tell any of the other characters this fact, even when they question her motivations and her devotion to her husband. At the end of the story, the party and the leader recognize Chin-ju for having remained faithful to her heroic husband in her chastity and her commitment to improving the soil and rice production in his home village. However, the plot moves between the narrative present of the National Heroes Convention, where Chin-ju is making a public speech to a large audience (fig. 7.3), and the flashbacks that make up her biography. The highly visible and official arena of the Heroes Convention is the only place where the old friends of her and her husband can discover, through the blurriness caused by their tearful reaction to her speech, why she moved away from the island after her husband's death.

The primary conflict of *Traces of Life* originates not in shared oppression

Figure 7.3. Sŏ Chin-ju, played by Merited Actress and star O Miran, addresses a large audience at the National Heroes Convention in *Traces of Life* (1989). "I keep two hero medals in my house. One is rewarded to my husband, who died in sacred battle for the defense of the country. Another is given to me for working twenty years to fulfill the party's agricultural policies."

or how to construct socialism collectively but in the Confucian ethical co-nundrum of how widows should behave and in other characters' misrecog-nition of the purity of Chin-ju's motivations. In contrast to the unified na-tion of classic films, Chin-ju has conflicts with lower-level party bureaucrats, disagrees with the scientific knowledge of misinformed and overly rational engineers, and seemingly transgresses the expectations of family, friends, and political authorities. In the place of the classic discourses of collective suffering, coming-into-consciousness, and redemption, or the education of individuality into collectivity, we have the inherent goodness of the ego ideal, conflicts with national history and the myopia of other North Koreans, an ethical dedication to an individual task, and eventual recognition as an ideal national subject. This temporality of the hidden-hero narrative resembles that of the Protestant ethic more than revolution or socialized production; the hero performs self-effacingly one task for the long duration of national history, because individual labor is inherently valuable; however, there is a generic contract that judgment and recognition will eventually come.

A *Forest Is Swaying* (1982) deals with the ecological problems of reforesta-tion and forest stewardship through a similarly expansive biography.[53] The protagonist of the film, Pak Sŏng-ryong, is a veteran of the Fatherland Liberation War who happens upon a small village on a hillside that has been deforested by United States bombing raids. He adopts an orphaned girl there and dedicates himself to replanting the hillside with pine-nut trees. Despite the skepticism of the local engineers, he uses his own botanical methods to finally get the pine-nut trees to grow. The nuts are sent to Pyongyang and the film ends with the adopted daughter delivering a message of thanks and an invitation to Pyongyang from the Great Leader (Kim Il-sung) (fig. 7.4). Again, the leader only belatedly recognizes Sŏng-ryong's lifelong labors, his noble patriotism, and the scientific truth of his humble but effective proletarian science. Visually speaking, the contract also asks the viewer to identify with the gaze of the leader as a constant presence in the unwitting hero's biography, even if the identity of the gaze is only revealed in the dramatic climax (supposedly the most pleasurable, or sublime, scene in the film) (fig. 7.5).

The national subject's work ethic and patriotism are shown to be under constant surveillance, but the hero's ignorance of this surveillance purifies his or her will from any hint of selfishness. Therefore, the hidden-hero film effectively fictionalizes M. Gus's maxim that "the Soviet hero wants what he must do and must act as he wants to."[54] The hero completely subordinates desire to the demands of the superego. The lack of any complex dynamic between desire and action makes the hero stereotypical. The ego can only briefly come into conflict with the traumas of the past or with the unconscious, long enough to hurtle the plot forward toward the fulfillment of the duty. Therefore, Chin-ju's mourning of her husband's death is highly melodramatic but leads quickly to her embrace of the economic mission that he has already laid out for her. Sŏng-ryong does not seem to remember the war, except as the event that created the possibility for him to fulfill his new mission as forester and surrogate father.

In this sense, the retrospective temporality of the hidden-hero film, in which the final recognition can be assumed from the beginning of the plot, conveys a vulgar ego psychology. It completely reverses Freud's (and Lacan's) dictum for examining the symptom and for releasing the superego's stranglehold on the id: "Where the id was, the ego must come into being [*Wo Es war, soll Ich werden*]."[55] The time of the hidden-hero film is "where the superego was, the id must come into being." Rather than unconscious desire preceding the formation of the ego, affecting how consciousness organizes itself around symptoms, what the hidden hero must do comes first, before any memory of trauma, any confrontation with death, or any other conflict between the ego and the unconscious. The excesses of desire are progres-

Figure 7.4. The visibly shocked Sŏng-ryong, played by 1970s and 1980s star Sŏ Kyŏng-sŏp, is congratulated by the villagers for being invited to Pyongyang by Kim Il-sung toward the conclusion of *A Forest Is Swaying* (1982).

Figure 7.5. A symbol for the subject-object of postrevolutionary dictatorship, Sŏng-ryong walks away from the villagers to weep; a crane shot creates a high angle, and then the camera zooms in quickly on his crouching body, as if to view the righteous and now faceless individual in isolation, entirely through the gaze of the Leader.

sively eliminated through narrative and are finally entirely displaced into the film's melodramatic elements, such as facial expressions and the melodramatic music. The historically authoritative voice-overs and the sublime quality of the leader's final recognition of the hero lend historical and ideological gravity to these melodramatic excesses, as well as a causal logic to the unfolding of the implausible narrative.

The daughter in *Miles Along the Railway* (1984) initially rejects her family and her inherited occupation of train engineer (performed by her father since the Japanese colonial period) and follows her romantic interest, an actor, to Pyongyang.[56] However, upon arrival there she immediately sees him with another woman. Though she is too ashamed to return to her family, her father discovers that she has committed the heroic act of saving her brother's train from derailment by moving a massive rock from the tracks; he finds her and she is welcomed back into the family and party. The film not only celebrates a kind of Stakhanovism, or individual dedication to exceeding production quotas, but also denies the possibility of any consistent conflict between this ethos and the unconscious. The hero's only acceptable desire is to want to be seen, to have one's personal struggle and suffering be recognized by the leader's gaze, which is thinly veiled throughout the film by the traditional techniques of realism.

Only through cinema or television could the construction of such panoptic vision reach the farthest borders of North Korean society. Following suit, hidden-hero films often celebrate loyalty in isolated rural, oceanic, or border locales. Labor performed at the distant edges of the country emerges into the view of the sovereign leader and becomes part of the spectacle of socialism. In *Lighthouse* (1977), one of the first hidden-hero films, the opening is a helicopter shot that zooms in on an isolated island, where the protagonist has manned the same lighthouse his whole life, enduring torture by the Japanese as a young man and helping ships find their way during the Fatherland Liberation War.[57] In *A Far-off Islet* (1998), a woman dedicates herself to teaching on a small island, where her two students inquire comically if their school is the smallest in the world.[58] Islands and other far-off rural settings allow these films to highlight the free will of the hidden hero, who performs his or her duties in places where recognition is least likely to be gained, but inevitably is.

Dobrenko points out that the violence that makes socialist realist heroism possible is hidden through all of these conventions of melodrama.[59] Such a "concealment of unportrayable violence" is apparent in the production, *Kites Flying in the Sky* (2008).[60] So-yŏn, who is training to be a marathon runner and has gained national fame, forgoes her career in order to adopt children who have been orphaned because of the famines of the 1990s (or what is called the Arduous March in North Korea). Her dedication to being a surrogate mother, which is discussed at various points as relieving the burden of the state and the Dear Leader (Kim Jong-il), masks the horrific historical violence of the famines. Although one of her adopted sons returns home without permission and discusses the difficulty of army life in a surprisingly candid fashion, a scene at a shop shows the way that heroism intervenes and conceals. When another customer in the store purchases the last bellyband, which So-yŏn wants to buy to help her son with his weakened stomach, her friend explains that she is the heroic woman who has adopted so many orphans of the Arduous March. The other customer gives the bellyband to So-yŏn, followed by others who give their wares to her once they realize she is a hero. The material purpose of the band and the reason her son needs it, what these facts mean for the people in the store as a community, all traces of the collective trauma that the film ostensibly addresses are concealed at that moment by So-yŏn's heroism and by the maudlin shoppers who cheer on her son's reaffirmed dedication to the army-first policy.[61]

The degree to which the politics of the hidden-hero film turn inward upon the domestic population is apparent in the spy-thriller *Our Lifeline* (2002).[62] This film follows the life of a grade-school teacher, infinitely loyal to Kim Il-sung for providing him with the opportunity to become literate at twenty years of age, as he "gives up the chalk" and "takes up the gun." He first becomes a security officer, again in a flashback sequence, when he finds out that a childhood acquaintance is a traitor who spied for the Japanese during the colonial period and is now spying for the CIA during the Fatherland Liberation War. The primary enemy of this hidden hero, however, is not the Japanese, Americans, or South Koreans but rather this North Korean traitor who functions as the protagonist's alter ego. Rather than belonging to a mythical nation combating imperialist forces, along with a few North Korean factionalists, the lifelong mission of the security worker is to examine and purify his own national identity by protecting the body of the sovereign from treasonous, internal enemies.

The contrasts between classic and hidden-hero films point to two primary ways that North Korean cinema has established the borders of national subjectivity. An external border, internalized into national identity, differentiates the nation from its enemies. A domestic border, externalized into society and the economic system, differentiates ideal national subjects from unethical opportunists. While a few iconic factionalists were sufficient to create this domestic border in classical films, the hidden-hero film elevates division and isolation to the degree that the leader mediates all social relations.[63] It provides a highly idealized representation of the possibilities for individual fulfillment within the North Korean political and economic system. It also seeks to incite a competition whose meager reward is to have one's self, humbly hidden from view for so long, revealed to the leader and to the camera in all of its truth.[64]

NOTES

1. This is a famous quotation attributed to Kim Il-sung that appears, among other places, on the title page of *Korean Film Art* (Pyongyang: Korean Film Export and Import, 1985). I have edited the translation for clarity.

2. Boris Groys, *The Total Art of Stalinism: Avant-Garde, Aesthetic, Dictatorship, and Beyond*, trans. Charles Rougle (London: Verso, 2011), 129.

3. Maya Turoskaya, "The 1930s and 1940s: Cinema in Context," in *Stalinism and Soviet Cinema*, ed. Richard Taylor and Derek Spring (London: Routledge, 1993), 34–53.

4. Groys, *The Total Art of Stalinism*, 48–63.

5. Kim Nam-ch'ŏn, "The Debates on Popularization and the Problem of Creative Practice" ["*Taejungt'ujaeng kwa ch'angjo-jŏk silch'ŏn ŭi munje*] (1946) in *Kim Nam-ch'ŏn Complete Works* [*Kim Nam-ch'ŏn Chŏnjip*], vol. 1 (Seoul: Pagijŏng, 2000), 840–51.

6. Charles Armstrong, *The North Korean Revolution (1945–1950)* (Ithaca, NY: Cornell University Press, 2004), 184–90.

7. Steven Chung, "The Split Screen: Sin Sang-ok in North Korea," in *North Korea: Toward a Better Understanding*, ed. Sonia Ryang (Lanham, Md.: Lexington Books, 2009), 85–107. Hyangjin Lee, *Contemporary Korean Cinema: Identity, Culture, Politics* (Manchester, U.K.: Manchester University Press, 2000). Kyung Hyun Kim, "The Fractured Cinema of North Korea: Discourses on the Nation in *Sea of Blood*," in *In Pursuit of Contemporary East Asian Culture*, ed. Xiaobing Tang and Stephen Snyder (Boulder, Colo.: Westview Press, 1996), 85–106.

8. Ham Ch'ung-pŏm, "A Study on the Process of Forming North Korean Cinema: Focusing on Relations with the Soviet Union" [*Pukhan yŏnghwa hyŏngsŏng kwajŏng yŏngu: Soryŏn kwa ŭi kwankye rŭl chungsim ŭro*]," in *Hyŏndae yŏnghwa yŏngu*, vol. 1: 115–49 (Seoul: Hanyang Taehakkyo Hyŏndae Yŏnghwa Yŏn'guso, 2005). Tina Mai Chen, "Internationalism and Cultural Experience: Soviet Films and Popular Chinese Understandings of the Future in the 1950s," *Cultural Critique* 58 (2004): 82–114.

9. Peter Brooks, *The Melodramatic Imagination* (New Haven, Conn.: Yale University Press, 1995).

10. Evgeny Dobrenko, *Political Economy of Socialist Realism*, trans. Jesse M. Savage (New Haven, Conn.: Yale University Press, 2007).

11. Dobrenko, *Political Economy*, 1–74.

12. Guy Debord, *The Society of the Spectacle*, trans. Donald Nicholson-Smith (New York: Zone Books, 1995), 7. Quoted in Dobrenko, *Political Economy*, 35.

13. Groys, *The Total Art of Stalinism*, 14–32.

14. Jean Baudrillard, *For a Critique of the Political Economy of the Sign*, trans. Charles Levin (St. Louis: Telos Press, 1981).

15. Kim Jong-il, *On the Art of the Cinema* (Pyongyang: Foreign Languages Publishing House, [1973] 1989).

16. Kim Yun-ji, "Kim Jong-il's *On the Art of Cinema* and North Korean Film: Focusing on North Korean Films from 1973 to 1980 [*Kim Jŏng-il ŭi 'Yonghwa yesullon' kwa pukhan yŏnghwa: 1973nyŏn put'ŏ 1980nyŏn kkaji chejak toen pukhan yŏnghwa rŭl chungsim ŭro*]," in *Sinema* 2 (2006): 31–65.

17. Kim Jong-il, "Actor and Character," in *On the Art of the Cinema*, 168–98.

18. Sunah Kim, Making the Cinema State: Observations on Socialist Film, through 'On the Art of the Cinema' [*"Yŏnghwa kukka mandŭlgi: 'yŏnghwa yesullon' ŭl t'ong hae pon sahoejuŭi yŏnghwa mihak e taehan koch'al"*], in *The Specter of Juche: A Critical Understanding of North Korean Theories of Art* [*Chuch'e ŭi hwanyŏng: pukhan munye iron e taehan pip'an-jŏk ihae*] (Seoul: Tosŏ Ch'ulp'an Kyŏngjin, 2011), 71–106.

19. Jan Campbell, *Film and Cinema Spectatorship: Melodrama and Mimesis* (Cambridge: Polity Press, 2005), 7–22.

20. Dobrenko gets at this aspect of socialist realism when he employs Slavoj Žižek's insight that ideology does not reflect, mask, or repress reality but rather constitutes it. *Political Economy of Socialist Realism*, 19. Slavoj Žižek, *The Sublime Object of Ideology* (London: Verso, 1989).

21. Roland Barthes, "The Reality Effect," in *The Rustle of Language*, trans. Richard Howard (Berkeley: University of California Press, 1989), 141–48.

22. Maxim Gorky, "Soviet Literature," in *Soviet Writers' Congress, 1934: The Debate on Socialist Realism and Modernism; Gorky, Radek, Bukharin, Zhdanov, and Others* (London: Lawrence and Wishart, 1977), 25–69.

23. G.W.F. Hegel, *Hegel's Aesthetics: Lectures on Fine Art*, vol. 1, trans. T.M. Knox (New York: Oxford University Press, 1998).

24. Pak Myŏng-jin makes similar connections between melodrama and realism and compares North Korean films to colonial Korean and South Korean *sinp'a* films. "The Possibility of Film Art Contributing to a Rapprochement Between North and South Korea" [*Nam bukhan chŏpkŭn e issŏsŏ yŏnghwa yesul ŭi kiyŏ kanŭngsŏng*], in *Tonga yŏngu* 19 (1989): 197–209.

25. Campbell, *Film and Cinema Spectatorship*.

26. Andrea Slane, *A Not So Foreign Affair: Fascism, Sexuality, and the Cultural Rhetoric* (Durham, NC: Duke University Press, 2001).

27. Immanuel Kant, *The Critique of Judgment*, trans. Werner S. Pluhar (Indianapolis: Hackett, 1987), 80.

28. Kant, *The Critique of Judgment*, 80–84.

29. This displacement of narrative excess is described by Thomas Elsaesser in "Tales of Sound and Fury: Observations on the Family Melodrama," in *Imitations of Life: A Reader on Film and Television Melodrama*, ed. Marcia Landy (Detroit: Wayne State University Press, 1991), 68–91.

30. Jason McGrath discusses the sublimation of the libido into politics and the party in Chinese revolutionary cinema in "Communists Have More Fun! The Dialectics of Fulfillment in Cinema of the People's Republic of China," *World Picture* 3 (2009), accessed August 20, 2011, http://www.worldpicturejournal.com/wP_3/McGrath .html.

31. The hidden hero is represented as a perfect, self-legislating Kantian subject. Kant also argued that morality could not be legislated by a heteronomous power, but that moral action must nonetheless actualize the universal. *The Critique of Practical Reason*, trans. Werner S. Pluhar (Indianapolis: Hackett, 2002).

32. Stephanie Hemelryk Donald, *Public Secrets, Public Spaces: Cinema and Civility in China* (Lanham, Md.: Rowman and Littlefield, 2000), 59–67. I will try to show that this gaze is not as uniform or omnipresent in socialist realist texts as Donald's analysis suggests.

33. My discussion of the internal border is based upon Etienne Balibar's reading of J. G. Fichte. "Fichte and the Internal Border: On Addresses to the German Nation," in *Classes, Masses, Ideas: Studies on Politics Before and After Marx*, trans. James Swenson (London: Routledge, 1994), 61–86.

34. David Bordwell, "Classical Hollywood Cinema: Narrational Principles and Procedures," in *Narrative, Apparatus, Ideology: A Film Theory Reader* (New York: Columbia University Press, 1986), 17–34.

35. In North Korea, scripts are called *yŏnghwa munhak*, or "film literature."

36. Kim Jong-il, *On the Art of Cinema*, 13–23.

37. *Korean Film Art* (Korean Film Export and Import, 1985).

38. *Sea of Blood* [*P'i pada*], directed by Ch'oe Ik-kyu (1969; Pyongyang: Korean Film Export and Import), DVD. *The Flower Girl* [*Kkot p'anŭn ch'ŏnyŏ*], directed by Ch'oe Ikkyu and Pak Hak (1972; Pyongyang: Korean Film Export and Import), DVD.

39. *Wolmi Island* [*Wolmido*], directed by Cho Kyŏng-sun (1982; Pyongyang: Korean Film Export and Import), DVD.

40. Kyung Hyun Kim, "The Fractured Cinema of North Korea"; Kim Sŏng-jin, "Reading the Narrative Structure in North Korean Art: Focusing on the Film, Revolutionary Opera, and Novel *The Flower Girl*" [*Pukhan yesul ŭi sŏsa kujo ilgo: Yŏnghwa, hyŏngmyŏng kagŭk, sosŏl 'Kkot p'anŭn ch'ŏnyŏ' rŭl chungsim ŭro*], *Hyŏndae munhak iron yŏngu* 25 (2005): 135–59.

41. Just as Joseph Stalin became a hero of the October Revolution through film and fiction, Kim Il-sung became a successful guerrilla revolutionary in the same way. Denise J. Youngblood, *Russian War Films: On the Cinema Front, 1914–2005* (Lawrence: University Press of Kansas, 2006), 82–106.

42. *An Chung-gŭn Shoots Ito Hirobumi* [*An Chung-gŭn Idŭngbangmun ŭl ssoda*], directed by Ŏm Kilsŏm (1979; Pyongyang: Korean Film Export and Import), DVD.

43. *Five Guerrilla Brothers* [*Yugyŏkdae ŭi ohyŏngje*], directed by Ch'oe Ikkyu (1968; Pyongyang: Korean Film Export and Import), DVD; Carl Schmitt, *Theory of the Partisan: Intermediate Commentary on the Concept of the Political*, trans. G. L. Ulmen (New York: Telos Press, 2007).

44. *When We Pick Apples* [*Sagwa ttal ttae*], directed by Kim Yŏngho (1970; Pyongyang: Korean Film Export and Import), DVD.

45. The Chollima movement was a collectivization and modernization program between 1960 and 1966 and corresponds with the most economically successful period in DPRK history. Hwang Chang-yŏp, who was one of the main architects of *Juche* thought and defected to South Korea in 1997, referred to the Chollima movement as the golden age of *Juche* thought. *National Life Is More Precious Than Indi-*

vidual Life: Peace in the Republic and the Unification of the Nation [*Kaein ŭi saengmyŏng poda kwijunghan minjok ŭi saengmyŏng: choguk p'yŏnghwa wa minjok ŭi t'ongil*] (Seoul: Tosŏ Ch'ulp'ansa Sidae Chŏngsin, 1999).

46. Sigmund Freud, *Group Psychology and the Analysis of the Ego*, ed. and trans. James Strachey (New York: W.W. Norton, 1990), 50.

47. Freud, *Group Psychology*, 50.

48. According to Hyangjin Lee and others, the hidden hero genre prospered in the 1980s because it fulfilled the instrumental need of the party to instill loyalty in a time of decreasing economic growth and political instability; unfortunately this explanation reduces all the meanings in these films to their political expediency. Hyangjin Lee, *Contemporary Korean Cinema: Culture, Identity, and Politics* (Manchester, U.K.: Manchester University Press, 2001), 43; Yu Kyŏng, "The Crisis of Socialism and North Korean Film: Concerning 1980s North Korean Film" [*Sahoejuŭi ŭi wigi wa pukhan yŏnghwa: 1980 nyŏndae pukhan yŏnghwa koch'al*], *Sinema* 2 (2006): 95–117.

49. Freud, *Group Psychology*, 76.

50. Donald, *Public Secrets, Public Spaces*, 59–67.

51. Sonia Ryang points out the noneconomic or nonutilitarian dimension of sovereignty in North Korea, but in hidden hero films the purely affective relationship between the leader and the individual is intertwined with instrumental concerns (which are thereby mystified). Sonia Ryang, "Biopolitics or the Logic of Sovereign Love—Love's Whereabouts in North Korea," in *North Korea: Toward a Better Understanding*, ed. Sonia Ryang (Lanham, MD: Lexington Books, 2009).

52. *Traces of Life* [*Saeng ŭi hŭnjŏk*], directed by Cho Kyŏngsun (1989; Pyongyang: Korean Film Export and Import), DVD. The information about Kim Il-sung's appreciation of the film is provided through a title image at the beginning of its sequel, *Genuine Life Goes On* [*Iŏganŭn ch'am toen sam*], directed by Kang Chung-mo (2002; Pyongyang: Korean Film Export and Import), DVD.

53. *A Forest Is Swaying* [*Sup'ŭn sŏlleinda*], directed by Chang Yŏng-bok (1982; Pyongyang: Korean Film Export and Import), DVD.

54. M. Gus, "Geroicheskii vek i iskusstvo," *Teatr*, no. 12 (1939): 15. Quoted in Dobrenko, *Political Economy*, 218.

55. Sigmund Freud, *New Introductory Lectures on Psychoanalysis*, ed. and trans. James Strachey (New York: W.W. Norton, 1990), 100; Jacques Lacan, "The Instance of the Letter in the Unconscious or Reason Since Freud," in *Ecrits: A Selection*, trans. Bruce Fink (New York: W.W. Norton, 2002), 162. I use Fink's translation, but replace *I* and *It* with *ego* and *id* for consistency.

56. *Miles Along the Railway* [*Ch'ŏlgil ŭl ttara ch'ŏn malli*], directed by Kim Kil-in (1984; Pyongyang: Korean Film Export and Import), DVD.

57. *Lighthouse* [*Tŭngdae*], directed by Kim Chun-sik (1977; Pyongyang: Korean Film Export and Import), DVD.

58. *A Far-off Islet* [*Mŏlli innŭn sŏm*], directed by Ch'oe Chuho (1998; Pyongyang: Korean Film Export and Import), DVD.

59. Dobrenko, *Political Economy*, 216–17.

60. *The Kites Flying in the Sky* [*Chŏ hanŭl ŭi yŏn*], directed by P'yo Kwang and Kim Hyŏnch'ŏl (2008; Pyongyang: Korean Film Export and Import), DVD.

61. Min Pyŏng-uk, "Research on North Korean Art Films of the Period of Kim Jong-il's Political System" [*Kim Jŏng-il ch'ejegi pukhan yesul yŏnghwa yŏngu*], *Kongyŏn munhwa yŏngu* 13 (2006): 153–90.

62. *Our Lifeline* [*Uri ŭi saengmyŏng*], directed by Kim Yu-sam (2002; Pyongyang: Korean Film Export and Import), DVD.

63. Hwang Chang-yŏp explained this fluctuation in visual representation in philosophical terms in his account of the debates over Juche thought in the 1960s, when three positions were taken on subjectivity: (1) the party is sovereign; (2) the popular masses are sovereign; (3) the leader is sovereign (*National Life Is More Precious*).

64. Following C.L.R. James's analysis of Stalinism as state capitalism, we can see this competition and this individualism as the cultural and semiotic correlates to the Stakhanovite notion of production. *State Capitalism and World Revolution* (Chicago: Charles H. Kerr, 1986), 45–49.

8 MICHELLE CHO

Face Value
The Star as Genre in Bong Joon-ho's *Mother*

Everyone recognizes [the film diva] with delight, since everyone has already seen the
original on the screen."
SIEGFRIED KRACAUER, *THE MASS ORNAMENT*

Every fashion stands in opposition to the organic. Every fashion couples the living
body to the inorganic world. To the living, fashion defends the rights of the corpse.
The fetishism that succumbs to the sex appeal of the inorganic is its vital nerve.
WALTER BENJAMIN, *THE ARCADES PROJECT*

FACE VALUE

In 2003, the South Korean National Commission on Human Rights organized several of the nation's most acclaimed directors to produce short
films about the forms of discrimination in South Korea that most concerned
them. The filmmakers—whose collected output ranges from entertainment
to independent cinema, from the films of the late 1980s and early 1990s
(subsequently designated the New Korean Cinema) to the millennial films
of the South Korean Film Renaissance, included Yim Soon-Rye (*Waikiki
Brothers*), Jeong Jae-eun (*Please Take Care of My Cat*), Park Kwangsu (*Chilsu
and Mansu, A Single Spark*), and Park Chan-wook (*JSA, Old Boy*). Though the
filmmakers were heterogeneous in their interests, aesthetics, and audience
appeal, the project expressed the commission's unified notion of cinema's
persuasive power in the public sphere, conferring upon cinema a privileged
rhetorical agency and concomitant civic responsibility. The resulting omni-
bus film, *If You Were Me* (*Yeoseotgae ui Siseon*),[1] addressed such topics as class
and gender discrimination manifested in the pressure to seek plastic sur-

gery (especially eyelid surgery to modify disparaged, racialized features), the social isolation of the disabled, the deployment of public shaming and guilt to maintain conformity to social norms, rampant sexism, the xenophobic mistreatment of migrant laborers, and upper-class anxieties over perceived anatomical barriers to proper English language pronunciation. While these topics have found coverage in South Korean news media, what is especially notable about *If You Were Me* is that each of the film's directors eschewed the conventional representational frame of documentary realism, using instead the popular genre form as the vehicle by which to deliver his or her antidiscrimination message, a choice that calls forth a consideration of the complex politics of pop culture's rhetorical force and communicative position.

Park Kwang-su's contribution to the project—a short entitled *Face Value* (*Ŏlgul kap*)—seems, at least superficially, to veer furthest from the social reflectionism in either neorealist or *film vérité* modes of cinema realism and their critical ethos of scrutiny or unveiling as a strategy of political intervention. A supernatural fable criticizing the prevalence of class and gender biases in South Korean social relations, the film presents the haunting of an entitled, upper-class male by a female ghost. The film derives much of its impact from the uncanny appearance of the supernatural in the most banal of spaces and commonly depressing interactions. Set mostly in the drab interior of a parking garage, the film introduces the male protagonist awakening in the gray, oppressive space, having fallen asleep in his car after a night of heavy drinking. At the exit booth, the man notices the attractive female cashier. Expecting a certain level of deference and perhaps a cheap sexual diversion, the man's demeanor rapidly devolves from desirous to abusive at the woman's dispassionate response. Throughout his tantrum, the man oscillates between invective and entreaty as he chastises the woman for thinking that her pretty face entitles her to uppity behavior, and then he attempts to flatter her by stating that her *ŏlgul kap* (face value)—the exchange value of her beauty—must be rather high. Despite the harassment, the woman refuses to be baited, and the man's frustration builds until he speeds out of the garage in a screech of tires, narrowly avoiding a collision with a group of mourners exiting a crematorium. The portrait of the deceased shows the image of the parking attendant with whom the man had just been arguing. The woman's visage and her attractiveness now signify an otherworldly vitality.

Embedded in this short film and in the Möbius strip of the phrase "face value" are questions concerning the meaning and function of celebrity culture in the South Korean context. In *Face Value*, the protagonist's histrionic misogyny gives shape to class discrimination and sexism, and the lack of subtlety in the film's depiction amplifies its pedagogical force. Despite the film's antipathy toward the protagonist, the lesson of the man's haunting is less clear: his position of privilege remains unchanged, and the moral education delivered by the ghost might be easily dismissed as a misperception or drunk hallucination. Moreover, the film's antidiscriminatory message about class falters on its unwitting confirmation of the exchange value of physical appearances; though beauty may confound traditional Confucian social hierarchies through its contrasting regime of value,[2] in its frictionless abstraction—its commodification and its symbolism of empty potentiality—beauty (in this case feminine beauty, which is also coded as a mute invitation to sexual predation) shores up capitalist values, such that physical beauty now signifies the plasticity of the body to capital and technology and an aesthetic of inorganicity and fashionability, rather than classical aesthetics' immutable ideal of the human body as a measure of nature and its perfection.[3] Furthermore, the haunting return of the face in the remainderless substitution of the portrait for the individual serves not so much as a cautionary tale but rather a dispassionate description of the ways in which face value, unlike other commodities, seems only to increase with its ubiquitous exchange, defying the inverse ratios of supply and demand. The insatiable hunger for self-transparency will always outpace supply, for what is demanded is by definition impossible. Though Park's film critiques the clichéd opposition between "inner" and "outer" beauty that animates the phrase ŏlgul kap (face value), equating class distinction and physical beauty as symmetrical types of false value, the film nevertheless interrupts its critique by demonstrating the continued force of appearances in their circulation.[4] Even in its superficiality, physical appearance, like class status, exerts a robust appeal, all the more powerful for its irrationality.

It is perhaps this tacit conclusion that speaks most directly to the social norms and conventions that condition the star system that structures South Korean popular culture today and that can begin to explain its simultaneous disavowal and celebration of the star's artifice. This chapter will discuss the film star as a figure of generic individuality, the ways in which this genre of exchangeable individuality is crucial to the circulation of the individual as commodity, and the deeply felt attachments to celebrity texts that correspond to the depthless substitution implied by the commodity's transmissibility. Thus, I focus here on the function of the star's intertextuality—the capacious yet structured ways in which celebrities come to signify abstract ideals in their absorption of particular affective intensities. A prime example is Bong Joon-Ho's *Mother* (2009), a film that masterfully deploys the signifying system of the star's generality in its casting of Kim Hye-Ja, an actress whose many earlier performances in benevolent maternal roles render her countenance both iconic (conveying generalized symbolic significance) and indexical (specifying her particular embodiment of these roles) as the film's eponymous *Mother*.

I also examine Won Bin's star text in comparison with Kim Hye-ja's generic, intertextual mother. His appearance in the role of *Mother*'s developmentally impaired yet beautiful son, Do-jun, was a career-redefining move after his return from mandatory military service (an interval during which his civic obligation to national defense ironically allowed him respite from the even more militant ranks of celebrity culture) and established a generic form of individuality that transformed his pretty-boy image into an ideal container for a posttraumatic model of subjectivity.[5] Won Bin's characterization is a deliberate engagement with the gender-bending discourse of the *minam* (beautiful man) figure and an intensification of the infantilized character of the younger brother, a type that Won Bin played with great success in earlier box-office hits such as *Tae Guk Gi: The Brotherhood of War* (*T'aekukki hŭinallimyŏ*, Kang Je-kyu, 2004). This production of a beautifully blank, inscrutably vacant character established Won Bin's star text as a site of maximum mutability and commercial appeal. Overall, this chapter seeks to describe the operations of the genre of the South Korean film star, in which the congealed signification of clichéd character types becomes an unexpected condition of the dismantling of sedimented national narratives, through the convergence of the audience's aspirational fantasies and these fantasies' deliberate disappointment.

Face Value concretizes the following observations that help outline the broader stakes of my reading of the genre of the film star in South Korean cinema today. First, the film, as well as the larger project in which it is engaged (*If You Were Me*), addresses its appeal to a unitary imagination of the national public, which it also constructs in its hailing. By addressing a group with an assumed temporal continuity, despite the fact that such an entity can be accessed only at sporadic points of concretion, precisely at the moment of its constitution in being addressed, *Face Value* also performs the role of film as social agent, as an apparatus that conditions the viewer's affiliation with a national public.[6] Such a co-constitutive relation between film culture and the national public continues to characterize South Korean popular film and media, both in production aims and audience reception, a complex exchange of projections and attachments that code and overdetermine these works' representational content. Complicating this relation is also the phenomenon of secondary interpellation in which this national public coheres around second-order reception, through reports of South Korean film and media's overseas popularity in regional markets and in the ostensibly global venues of international film festivals. Second, the film's title—*Ŏlgul Gap (Face Value)*—literalizes the notion of the celebrity or star as commodified visage. The individual and her social significance can be reduced to the image. The "face value" of the star is a sign engaged in a particularly public exercise of division and reintegration. As numerous studies of celebrity and fame have noted, the star persona has long activated the voyeuristic desire for the spectacle of split subjectivity—to uncover the "real person" behind the image.[7] On the other hand, the star text exhibits a remarkably effective unifying impetus, as the fantasy that the star simply *is* as she appears on-screen offers the viewer the promise of self-identity and plenitude as a magical antidote to the self-estrangement that characterizes the modern subject. Third, the film's genre as ghost story aptly illustrates the uncanny power of the screen celebrity or the individual *qua* image. The value attributed to the image/visage, as well as to the appearance of upper-class noblesse oblige that is belied by the main character's reprehensible behavior, persists despite the film's critique and attempted demystification of this value. Indeed, the value of the image is impervious to ideological correctives, since it is an effect of circulation rather than interpretation. The woman in Park's short film cannot be qualitatively differentiated from her image as funeral portrait, the value of which accrues in its substitutability. A related element of the star, in both *Ŏlgul Gap* and *Mother*, is the paradigm of visual rhetoric exemplified by the photograph, a visual sign that condenses face value as reified appearance and the ghostliness of the static image.[8] The photo-portrait is an effigy, though one that does not simply commemorate the late vitality of the deceased but constitutes this very vitality. The woman in the film is already an effigy in this relation, which lacks the gap between reality and representation that would be necessary to refuse the memorialization of face value and the spectral presence to which it refers.

FACE VALUE AND MASS CULTURE

At its core, this essay pursues a set of questions raised by studies of pop-cultural celebrity, more broadly, and those that concern the particular historical and cultural contexts of contemporary South Korea's culture industries: What are the generic parameters of the "star"? How does the vernacular expression of South Korean cinema lend insight into the conception of celebrity as global phenomenon instated by modernist cultural critique? How does the study of celebrity culture bring forth the divergent functions and forms of popular culture that mediate national and group identity?

In Siegfried Kracauer's examinations of German popular culture in *The*

Mass Ornament, from which I adopted this chapter's opening epigraph, the celebrity does not precede her image, but rather this image is the *original* manufacture of mass media—the public delights in encountering the film star because she repeats the semblance of her screen image. Thus, the star reverses the relationship between reality and representation. In a supporting vein, Benjamin's theses on fashion in the *Arcades Project* emphasize its inorganicity and dependence on the circuits of desire that determine the production and consumption of the commodity form. According to Benjamin, the fetishism of the inorganic, the representational, and the manufactured, that is to say, the fetishism of the media-produced entity, is the vital nerve of fashion, an elusive and fleeting force of desirability and status determined precisely by the irrationality of this desire to possess that which cannot be localized in the commodity alone. Benjamin's assessment reinforces the expectation that the star prioritizes semblance over reality and adds to the genre of the star the centrality of the opposition between nature and culture, organicity and inorganicity, whose tension reverberates throughout the experience of fandom and the construction of celebrity and star texts. Thus these earlier critiques of celebrity in the "age of mechanical reproducibility"[9] posit the following structural foundation of the star as genre: the reversal of reality and representation in the star's semiotic apparatus, from which follows the tension between natural or authentic behavior and affectation or inauthenticity, in other words, the expectation that the star's real self and her persona are opposed, alongside the intense desire for identification between the star's textual existence and her true character.

If, in the arena of mass culture, the "original" is just that ineffable, manufactured reality called "fashion," we are forced to recalibrate our conventional concepts of authenticity vis-à-vis mass-mediated signs. The *wished for* superficiality of the diva that Kracauer describes is a symptom of the reification of generic identity. Thus, the star is also a management apparatus, a product of what Deleuze and Guattari have called an "abstract machine of faciality,"[10] eradicating ambiguity and interpretation for an economy of signification without excess. My interpretation, though strongly influenced by these analyses of the imbrication of popular culture representation and capital's reification of value, does not quite hew to the narrative of the deleterious influence of popular culture on the masses subjected to its standardizing and sedating effects. The scholars of early twentieth-century European mass cultures, whose insights can be taken as points of departure,[11] have sometimes been interpreted as uniformly condemning popular culture, particularly as they expose the workings of the culture industries, which are said not to produce popular culture but instead to use culture as an apparatus of manipulation and control. As important as these criticisms of the culture industries are, especially at a moment when a resurgent interest in appropriating and administering cultural production seems indeed a global phenomenon attesting to neoliberal societies' insidious instrumentalization of creativity, this chapter seeks neither to defend nor attack popular culture; I instead attempt to place it in a *context* and describe how it works. In so doing, I assert the possibility of reading the operations of mass culture in a diagnostic manner, employing the star as a figure for negotiating the middle distance between celebration and condemnation of cultural commodities.

In the South Korean context, this debate centers on the universe of commerce and signification named by the discourse of *hallyu*, which takes on both a celebratory nationalist tone as well as an alarmist one, sounding the plaints of standardization, homogenization, and manipulation by state intervention in the production of televisual and film commodities. A third strain in the *hallyu* discourse emphasizes the agency of film art and auteurship against the alternately disparaging and congratulatory assessments of South Korean cultural commodities' growing regional and global marketability.[12] As a point of intervention in this discourse, I offer the case of Bong Joon-ho's *Mother*, a film that mounts a self-reflexive critique of the cinematic production of cultural icons/stars, packaged in the form of popular entertainment. In so doing, the film presents an incisive investigation of the star's generic parameters *through the activation* of the star genre's affective intensities.

In my reading of Bong Joon-ho's 2009 psychodrama, *Mother*, I primarily track the intertextual operations of stardom as *characterization*. Though Bong Joon-ho's *Mother* is a film that defies genre designations, broadly sketched it is a murder mystery with overtones of social commentary and a work firmly situated in a middle-brow cultural arena—neither high-art nor mass pulp.[13] Centered on the codependency of a mother-child unit and set in a small provincial town, *Mother* presents a sinister and moribund portrait of rural South Korea. A mentally challenged young man is accused and convicted of murdering a young female student, which unleashes his mother's fierce protective instincts. As she crusades to exculpate her son, the mother uncovers the seedy underside of the rural community, embodied in teenage prostitution, abject poverty, and a dysfunctional criminal justice system. However, the film crucially undercuts the characterization of the mother as avenging angel, as the relationship between mother and son is primarily characterized by boundary problems. In her zeal to prove her son's innocence, the mother becomes a criminal herself. When her investigation terminates in the confirmation of her son's guilt, she responds by killing the witness, securing her identity with her son by also becoming a murderer, and assuaging her conscience through a practice of ecstatic forgetting. The mother's excessiveness and the son's impassivity do not offset each other but rather produce a two-headed monster that wreaks further havoc on the community. As a perversion of familiar conventions, the film's detective figure—the mother—is shown to be the perpetrator of a crime that she cannot foresee, thus radically reorienting the ideological and epistemological valences of the detective genre.

The film deliberately presents types—overprotective mother, helpless, infantilized son, provincial townsfolk—which in their *generality* bring into relief the instability of social circumstances that betray these generic social roles, perverting the blood relation from a unit of social cohesion into a force of social disintegration. In other words, the film deliberately pushes its stars' public personae to their extremes in order to use their generic signification to indicate the shifting terrain of contemporary South Korean society, which subsequently reveals these generic roles as both a defense against and an instigator of the forces of chaos, destruction, and disintegration of social order.

As clichéd and reductive signifiers of generalized individuality, film and television stars present clues to the aspirations and fantasies of the contemporary South Korean viewership, while also affording access to the contradictions that maintain the status quo of a repressive relation to history. This star apparatus, however, also indicates a refusal of the sentimental and humanistic demand characteristic of a liberal model of subjectivity to resolve the past through an individualized recognition of culpability that produces a collective composed of properly repentant sovereign subjects (as opposed to one consisting of traumatized amnesiacs). In my reading of *Mother*, a film that relies as much on its stars for their prototypicality as their performances in their roles, I develop the implications of the film's dynamic and contradictory attitude toward the epistemology of trauma as well as the logics of remembrance, reparative justice, culpability, and individual conscience. These logics are embedded in the seemingly straightforward ideals of transparency and its naturalized value, whose contradictions emerge in the twisting and unraveling stakes of self-knowledge and individual accountability. Taking as a pivot the protean trope of face value, this chapter draws upon various analyses of the face, both as a cathected site of self-expression and, drawing from Deleuze and Guattari, as a *machine* of abstract signification and subjectivization. The face is also a common theme in the discourse of celebrity and a recurrent motif in *Mother*, a central preoccupation and visual key to the film's ingenious intertextual activation of the affective investments in both its protagonists and the stars who embody them. My aim is to articulate *Mother*'s reflexive critique of face value, which it pursues at both sociological and psychological levels but initiates through an appeal to the face value of its main actors and the effects their representative individuality exerts to forge a specific national and sentimental public around the celebration of the signifiers that these figures embody, an attachment that registers at the moment of these signifiers' uncanny violation.

Thus, this chapter moves among multiple registers of interpretation, exposition, and theoretical discourse to adumbrate the enigma of face value and its salience to the genre of the star in South Korean popular culture. Throughout I insist on the specificity of the contemporary South Korean context while also arguing for the transnational significance of Bong's film, to articulate *Mother*'s broader relevance as the relationship it demonstrates among history, cultural production, social relations, media, and political economies.

STARS, FACIALITY, DEAD METAPHORS

Despite the narrative explanation for the dread of the protagonist's encounter as the spectral presence of an actual ghost, Park Kwang-su's *Face Value* achieves an uncanny effect in large part because it gestures at the dominance of an economy of appearances that has come to reorient the values of South Korean society, appealing to a system of seemingly stable social relations and roles to compensate for the actual conditions of flux and instability. In the postauthoritarian period, this economy of surfaces comes not as a dictate of the militarized state but rather as a facet of the dynamism of the global economy, which is a constant force of repressive erasure of the magnitude of loss resulting from neoliberal policies of high-growth economics. Though ostensibly critical of gender discrimination, *Face Value*'s sexism emerges in its chain of associations between the supernatural, the feminine, and the duplicity of images, presenting the macho protagonist as a victim of a feminine agency headquartered in a supernatural realm inaccessible to masculine reason. Though the fixing of female identity established through the association of physical beauty and death is concretized in the photograph—the technical expression of face value—it bears the traces of a naturalized politics of gender with a much longer history in the patriarchal structures of Korean society.

Complicating the significance of face value as absent presence, as exemplified by the photographic image, the discourse of the face as a signifier of transparency has long been a common topos of theories of cognition, subjectivity, and experience. A general assumption of the face's inability to dissemble, that in the face, being and semblance are one, remains deeply rooted in the meaning and humanistic pathos imputed to the human face. In this conventional view, the face is understood to be transparent both because of its expressivity, "the preeminence of the face in emotional transactions,"[14] and also because it is understood to be nothing more than this expression itself; in the face, form and content are one. As an extension of the self, the face then serves as the *surface* or the meeting place of interior and exterior, private and social, modes of being. Moreover, this diplomat of the structuring division of interiority and sociality thus assumes the function of inaugurating private experience into social meaning. Tasked with this burden, the face becomes the condensation point of the desire for integration that it must maintain as the simultaneous barrier to and stage for the private self's public debut. The face abstracts these incommensurable longings while also maintaining the concreteness of self-presence. The significance of this duality, of the demand to read face value as both abstract and concrete while disavowing this fissure, is crucial to an analysis of the face value of celebrities, particularly in a contemporary political context in which a conception of interiority as possessive individualism is thoroughly implicated in the transformations of the public sphere, the limits of political action, and the constraints posed by the assumed dialectic between civil society and the state. The function of the star is to put a *face* on representative individuality—to naturalize it, assure it an integrated appearance, and render its value exploitable, even as its moral value remains uncontested. This function is what I would argue is generic about the figure of the celebrity, if we approach genre not simply as a set of formal rules and conventions of representation but instead, as Lauren Berlant has suggested, an "aesthetic structure of affective expectation."[15]

As such a structure, the movie star, Berlant writes, "come[s] to embody the fantasy form of iconic citizenship, of a large body moving through space unimpeded, as only a technologically protected person can do."[16] This description of the star as fantasy form has no relation to the embodied experience of personhood lived and felt by the individual star; rather, this fixing of the individual subject as sign as opposed to living being is the primary consequence of what Deleuze and Guattari have called "faciality." The semiotics of faciality are simultaneously precise and abstract in their conceptual rubric, since the face provides the template for the establishment of subjective interiority (the black hole, the void) and external surface of projection (the white screen) that together produce the binarized system of faciality. Against the view of the face as the expressive membrane of the subject and, as such, an access point to the subject's particularity, Deleuze and Guattari argue that faces "are not basically individual; they define zones of frequency or probability, delimit a field that neutralizes in advance any expressions or connections unamenable to the appropriate significations."[17] For Deleuze and Guattari, the face is not a system of the exteriorization of the individual's sentiment or affect; indeed, the face is not even related to the body. Instead, the face delimits the possibility of expression; like a genre, the face provides a set of parameters by which expression can be recognized.

In his essay on Deleuze and faces, Richard Rushton summarizes Deleuze and Guattari's criticism of the face: "that which reduces the face purely to its nominal register, that is, the tendency for the movements and deliberations of the face to be set in stone as meaningful or evidential, as an objective expression of that which lies beneath. . . . This is the teleological endpoint of the face-as-object: where every man, woman, and child becomes the equal of their face."[18] In Rushton's reading of faciality, the direst implications of the dominance of faciality as a regime of identification is its nurturing of "the desire for a perfectly transparent science of faces, in the manner of phrenology, perhaps, that will enable the classification and readability—and therefore a hierarchical ordering—of all the faces in the world."[19] The threat of this potential misrecognition of faciality for the human is also expressed in Deleuze and Guattari's text, which hinges on the face's overcoding of the corporeal. Deleuze and Guattari clarify that the "semiotic of the signifier and the subjective never operates through bodies. It is absurd to claim to relate the signifier to the body."[20] Face value, or the sign system of faciality, transforms a living being into a concept, in a manner that the star text exemplifies.[21] Indeed, when Deleuze and Guattari discuss the absurdity of relating the signifier to the body unless it is "a body that has already been entirely facialized," they are precisely naming the star text that has been condensed into dead metaphor, that is, face value.

PERVERSE SURFACES: KIM HYE-JA AS NATIONAL MOTHER AND WON BIN'S GENERIC INDIVIDUALITY

Kim Hye-ja presents one such example of a star, an actress whose public performance as a maternal figure, in the intimate context of televisual media, has reinforced her star sign as depthless and unitary, her face signifying an iconic, transmissible archetype of idealized maternity.[22] By the late 1990s, her role as good-humored, self-sacrificing mother had become cemented in the popular imaginary, especially in primetime weekend dramas like *Roses and Beansprouts* (*Jangmiwa K'ongnamul*, MBC, 1999). Kim's performance in *Mother* constitutes a bold violation of her identity as beloved national cliché; however, I would like to suggest that this violation occurs not because she is cast against type but rather because her maximal fulfillment of the maternal role exposes the perversion at the core of its fantasy form. A film that depicts maternal devotion, from its first frames, as a hysterical symptom stemming from the inability to distinguish between self and other that besets every mother-child relation, *Mother* pushes Kim's image as a caricature of maternal benevolence to its devastating limit.[23] As Bong shrewdly anticipated, the impact of her performance owes in large part to the public's intense investment in her celebrity image and its starring role in idealized scenarios of national character. In pushing the maternal fantasy to its monstrous extreme and furthermore suggesting that this monstrosity is not an aberration of saintly maternal nature but rather its logical end, Kim's performance reflexively indexes her star sign itself, pushing its idealized notion of maternal devotion to murderous extremes. Kim's role in *Mother* relies, to a large extent, on her celebrity, as explained by P. David Marshall's claim that "the celebrity element of the star is its transcendence of the text in whatever form."[24] In confirming this point, *Mother* brings forth the perversity that constitutes the desire for the figure of the maternal as force of nature, activating both a sympathetic attachment to this figure and a horrifying recognition of the implications of this attachment.

Mother's enigmatic opening scene has been praised for establishing a sense of uncanniness that activates the desire for revelation that then fuels the fascination of its murder mystery plot (fig. 8.1). Placing the film's eponymous character in a windswept field, the scene offsets its naturalistic tableau with the intrusion of drumbeats that swell into an extradiegetic guitar soundtrack and a slow zoom that follows the rhythm of the woman's trance-like state. Matching the swaying movement of the tall grass in which she stands, Kim Hye-ja's dance evokes the ritualistic mimicry of natural elements, transformed through repetition into the formalized bodily gestures of shamanistic rites. A smile momentarily alights upon Kim's face as her hand covers her eyes—replacing the visual organ as mirror of consciousness with the inscrutable expression of undefined hysterical affect (fig. 8.2).

In their extended review of *Mother* in *Film Quarterly*,[25] Nataŝa Ďurovičová and Garrett Stewart note the "visual pun" that links this estranging opening to the following scene, which introduces the mother's obsessive relationship to her son, cutting from "that vast expanse of wheat to the literal *slicing* of a single sheaf of dry stalks."[26] More than a matter of visual repetition, the opening sequence and the subsequent identification of the mother's vocation as herbalist and healer emphasizes her association with nature and corporeality, cementing the visual identification of maternity and nature as vital forces that resists the mediation of reason. At the same

Figure 8.1. *Mother*'s enigmatic opening.

time that the mother is figured as the embodiment of maternal instinct, to the extent that she feels no pain when she slices off the tip of her finger at the precise moment that a car collides with her son in a hit-and-run accident, her inscrutability and intense attachment to her son establish the ambiguity of her status as natural or perverse, devoted or demented, as the source of the film's uncanny force.[27] What is "natural" or "proper" as far as maternal responsibility, sacrifice, and devotion are concerned? Is the association of femininity, the maternal, and the natural world not also the source of enigma that has fostered the association of femininity with the occult as well as the perilous corporeality and unruly psychic energies manifested in hysteria? The naturalization of these associations makes Kim Hye-ja's role as madwoman *and* national mother (*kungmin ŏmoni*) co-extensive.[28] Further, the generic quality of the town and its residents, demonstrated by the insistence on identifying the mother of *Mother* only by her representative maternity—the townspeople, including the detective in charge of the case against Do-jun, never address her by a name other than *ŏmoni*—underscores the film's use of Kim Hye-ja as a fixed sign, removing indexical traces of historical events or live persons in the film's depiction of rural turpitude. *Mother*'s treatment of provincial life differs significantly from Bong's earlier *Memories of Murder* (*Sarinŭi Ch'uŏk*, 2003), which was based on the still-cold case of the nation's first serial killer. It also conspicuously lacks the typical emphasis on accented speech and regional dialects that contemporaneous depictions of rural towns emphasize, practically without exception. The use of *sat'uri*, or regional dialect, has become a powerfully recognizable signifier of the local and the particular against the cosmopolitanism of the capital city, Seoul. In recent works of film and television, provincial locales have signified either the sentimental values of home, tradition, and family, or—the flip side of this nostalgic construction—the unhomely/uncanny source of

Figure 8.2. Kim Hye-ja as the eponymous *Mother*.

terror.[29] *Mother* ingeniously taps into both associations, revealing them to be two sides of the same impulse to transform the countryside from a marker of authenticity to a site of myth and fantasy.

Ďurovičová and Stewart nevertheless read Bong's film as a response to "the troubled arc of Korean history," explaining *Mother*'s dismantling of the detective genre as "international genre formats [crossed] with the preoccupations of a national cinema" and assuming a national symptomology that anchors the film's "harrowing melodrama of violence and its generational backlash."[30] To complicate this reading, which posits the film as another in a series of cinematic calls to work through the lingering effects of traumatic national histories and thus blunts *Mother*'s impact by deeming it a return for Bong to the concerns of *Memories of Murder,* I would like to suggest that the film discursively engages the now established narrative of transgenerational trauma, using the sedimented significance of the stars as icons to critique the tendency to equate sign and subject. *Mother* primarily achieves this critique by bringing to the screen the largely unconscious processes of desire that motivate the apparatus of identification designated by Deleuze and Guattari's facial machine, that is, the retrenchment of tropes of transparency and reflexivity imputed to the face as the convergence of signification and subjectification.[31] Against its common perception as a melancholic response to the dissolution of family and community, the film seems instead to warn against overinvestment in an ideology of familism, which often slips into an ideology of nationalism as a defense against broader social maladies. Though Ďurovičová and Stewart read the film as an indictment of post-political conditions, writing, "as the price of no communism, there is little community left—society so atomized, and families so far from nuclear, that self-interest has become almost animal in its instincts,"[32] I would suggest, in contrast, that the belief in the preeminence of family is precisely what

Figure 8.3. A double image of mother and son alongside the corpse of the murdered student, Moon Ah-jung.

the film problematizes, since the blood tie serves as a socially sanctioned alibi for deranged identification. Thus, the social problem *Mother* tackles is not the decline of the ideology of kinship and an atomized population that cannot manage a collective history but rather the dangerous effects of the persistence this ideology. The film suggests this in an almost fifteen-second fade that creates a double image of the mother-son unit alongside the corpse of the murdered student, Moon Ah-Jung (fig. 8.3).

Mother skewers several familiar tropes of family, nurture, and community, beginning most obviously with maternal devotion. In the mother and Do-jun's family romance, the mother's preoccupation with her son stems not from an impulse of care but rather narcissistic identification. The film heightens this identification through symmetrical presentations of the mother-son relationship; mother and son often mirror each other's facial expressions, physical gestures, and speech—wheedling appeals to eat, drink, or go to sleep. The eye of the mother's detective persona, voyeuristically trained on her suspects, is echoed by the eye of the son in the moment when he reveals his recollection of his mother's long-ago attempt to kill him in a perverse love suicide. When, after a fit of desperate rage in which she kills the junkseller who confirms Do-jun's guilt, the mother realizes her crime, her plaintive cries of "*ŏmma*" (mother) suggest her identification with her son and her unconscious reinforcement of her earlier declaration to Do-jun, "You are me." Amplifying the conflation of mother and son, the murder of the junkseller is crosscut with Do-jun's accidental murder of the high-school prostitute, Moon Ah-Jung. Thus, *Mother* depicts a perverse relationship that is not oedipal but narcissistic and further heightens this identification in the instances of the mother's willed divestment of consciousness and subsequent disassociation, which Do-joon's mental vacancy mirrors.

Despite the repeated suggestion that mother and son are "one," however, what emerges in the film's climax, when the results of the mother's detective work lead to her crime of passion, is a reversal of the temporality of transgenerational trauma suggested by the model of repressed national history. We see the uncanny return of the son's crime, rather than the repetition of the mother's, because of the need to impose upon the son an identity that remains the mother's projective fantasy. In contrast, the mother's willful repression of her crime—her attempted double suicide—fails twice: first in Do-jun's accidental recollection of her transgressions and then in his refusal to accept her "cure" for memory: her purported knowledge of a special acupuncture treatment that will seal off bad memories. Moreover, the directionality of the transmission of repressed trauma does not conform to the usual patterns; rather than unconsciously absorbing and repeating the trauma, the older generation projects a traumatized subjectivity that doesn't stick, especially in light of the youths' embrace of technologies of mediation that distance reality and representation, most notably the digitized image subject to modification, correction, and erasure.

Other instances in which the film dismantles the clichéd appeal of family bonds include the recoding of the symbolic significance of rice (ssal), from nourishment to a means of exploitation. Moon Ah-jung's grandmother is an alcoholic who demands rice wine from her granddaughter. Ah-jung resorts to prostitution to earn money to satisfy her grandmother's addiction as well as to provide for herself; in her desperation, she occasionally accepts rice as payment for sex. Her abject condition erupts in her frequent nosebleeds, by which the motif of blood as a sign of corrupt kinship relations links her exploitation by her female relatives to the unsettling bond between Do-jun and his mother. Rice also figures as the substance that conceals Ah-jung's abuse; When the mother finally tracks down the cell phone that contains photographs of the men to whom Ah-jung has sold her body, Ah-jung's grandmother has hidden it deep in a bin of rice, which prevents it from revealing the extent of Ah-jung's suffering.

Despite its veneration of the sacred maternal embodied by Kim Hye-ja, Mother is concerned with revealing the victimization of younger generations by the mistakes and neglect of their elders. Before a brawl incited by the mother's appearance at Ah-jung's funeral, a woman in the late stages of pregnancy nonchalantly smokes a cigarette while Ah-jung's female relatives confront the mother. With her cigarette still dangling from her lips, the woman indecorously slaps the mother across the face as Ah-jung's grandmother curses and douses the combatants with rice wine. Later, when the mother questions neighborhood hoodlums who were also Ah-jung's cus-

Figure 8.4. A close-up of the mother holding a cell phone photograph of the junkseller witness.

Figure 8.5. Shallow focus alternating between the mother's and the junkseller's faces.

tomers, she lights a cigarette as she completes her transformation into flinty-eyed interrogator, an allusion to the earlier figure of bad motherhood. Moreover, Moon Ah-jung's exploitation indicts a wide swath of irresponsible adults, from her neglectful aunts and malevolently senile grandmother to the array of middle-aged men who solicit her for sex. The only adult who escapes censure is the friend of the mother who joins her in her campaign to exonerate Do-jun. This friend, however, has not been able to conceive a child and thus remains untainted by the biological fact of reproduction.

In contrast to biological reproduction, the film presents the system of mechanical reproduction via the digital image. Ah-Jung's cell phone, which contains surreptitiously captured photographs of her customers, becomes a key to the mother's investigation. In an exchange at the jail where Do-jun is confined, close-ups of the mother, son, and the junkseller who witnessed the crime link the face value of the digital image to the sign function of the mother's face (figs. 8.4 and 8.5).

Digital manipulation of photographs take precedence over both memory and reality in two other instances: first, when the mother asks her friend,

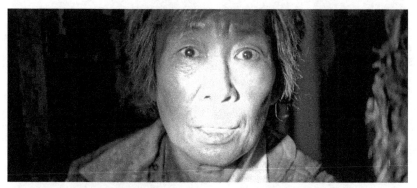

Figure 8.6. Moon Ah-jung's grandmother—a character defined by madness.

Figure 8.7. A similar madness signified by the exaggerated affect of Kim Hye-ja's performance.

who owns a photo lab, to retouch a photograph of Do-jun as a young child, to restore it to the state of the mother's idealized memory image; second, when Ah-jung's friend comes to the lab to have her school portrait fixed, to remove the scar that disfigures her cheek. In both cases, the retouching satisfactorily "corrects" the faces, emphasizing the priority of surfaces.

The film's alternation between long shots that convey the landscape and rural setting and close-ups of the faces of its protagonists suggests a preoccupation with faces that highlights the films' prioritization of the face value of its stars. Several scenes emphasize the marvelous expressivity of Kim Hye-ja's face, often fixed in a mask of motherly concern. A scene that juxtaposes Ah-jung's grandmother and the mother explicitly spotlights the face of each character, associating the two in their unsettling intensity (figs. 8.6 and 8.7).

In contrast to the exaggerated intensity of these faces, close-ups of Won Bin's face emphasize its blankness (fig. 8.8), particularly in instances when people comment upon his appearance. The flashback image of Do-jun as a child (fig. 8.9) presents the same quality of impassive acceptance, indicating its availability to the mother's and, by extension, the audience's projections.

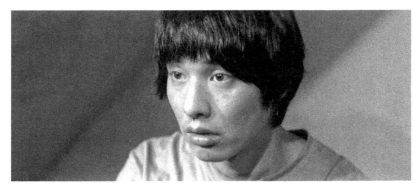

Figure 8.8. Do-jun's impassive face.

Figure 8.9. A flashback image of Do-jun as a child.

Digital images manage memory through revision, as digital memory can be unproblematically overwritten. The images, which lack interiority, present a model for change that produces a fantasy of one-dimensional subjectivity that would not suffer the challenges of either alienation or reflexivity. This generic subject is a fantasy presented by Do-jun and Won Bin's star text, disrupting the association of surface and depth and resolving via dissociation the contradictions of face value.

Though Won Bin's performance in the role of the son, Do-jun (which incidentally happens to be Won Bin's given name), is overshadowed by Kim Hye-Ja's mother, it merits closer attention. Won Bin's portrayal of Do-jun leaves the character's inner life an open question. Do-jun's mind is an ambiguous container, storing memories and mental images of the past but lacking a reliable cognitive filter. A blank repository without the faculty of judgment, Do-jun's memory leads to the mother's undoing, as it mercilessly retains the mother's transgressions, which she seeks to repress through willed amnesia. Because of his capacity to accommodate both historical memory and his mother's projective fantasies without the interference of conscious judgment, Do-jun presents a figure of doll-like appeal, which is also a function of his appearance. Several times in the film, characters comment on Do-jun's attractiveness, attributing to him the significance of his face value. In conversation with her friend, the mother proudly calls Do-jun a *minam* (beautiful boy), and her faith in Do-jun's innocence arises from her inability to recognize Do-jun as other than he appears. While Do-jun's one-dimensionality seems imposed upon him by others, his very existence owes to this imposition, as he lacks the self-reflexivity to determine his own identity. As a holding space for memory whose identity is afforded the meaning attributed to his physical appearance, Do-jun manifests an important dimension of Won Bin's star text and offers a key to Won Bin's face value.[33]

Yet the film at points hints at the possibility of Do-jun's self-awareness, raising the question of whether his ignorance, like his mother's, might be a volitional act of self-erasure aimed at protecting himself from acknowledging his role in the breakdown of social order. The film shows the catastrophic effects of the deliberate refusal of memory as a tactic for muting the voice of conscience. At the same time, however, it presents a scenario in which the relief afforded by amnesia may be a survival strategy and necessary defense. Do-jun manifests the type of subject produced by such a context, and Won Bin's portrayal supplies this subject a material substrate. Do-jun is a subject as cipher; his unfathomable interiority, or lack thereof, discourages viewer identification, as well as troubling the conventions of moral and legal culpability. The question that *Mother* thus brings to light is how to sustain a mode of shared sociality when, according to a neoliberal logic of possessive individualism, even ignorance and amnesia have become the prerogative of the individual.

Won Bin's return to cinema screens in *Mother*, in his second round of life as an actor,[34] draws the veil from the construction of the star as container for affective attachments, as well as the illusion of interiority as a realm of experience exclusive of social structures. Appearing in a role that revisits his earlier portrayals of young, vulnerable male characters, Won Bin's lack of interiority in *Mother* estranges the sentimentality of his earlier characterizations, particularly his performance of Jin-Seok, a sensitive young man engulfed by the overwhelming tide of national tragedy, in the blockbuster Korean War epic *T'aegukgi* (2004), in which Won Bin gives face to the traumatized subject of modern Korean history. Do-jun abstracts the historical subject by emphasizing the inability of interior states to account for either actions or historical events, thus refusing the logic suggested by Kim Hye-ja's portrayal of traumatized subjectivity of a return of the repressed. Discounting the privatization of social responsibility, Won Bin's star text throws into relief the intractable dilemma of historical and national trauma as a function of the inability of fixed identities to manage the inconsistent conditions of rapidly shifting social conditions.

CONCLUSION: POPULAR SUBJECTS AND THE STAR AS GENRE

In his next film appearance after the start of his "second life" in Mother, Won Bin chose a project that would cleave his star image, interrupting the series of younger brothers or sons he had played in his earlier films. As the antisocial former special agent who goes after a gang of drug dealers and organ harvesters to save an orphaned child in Man from Nowhere (Ajŏssi, 2010), Won Bin remains nameless and mostly silent, delivering most of his acting through action and fight scenes. As an explicitly generic character, an ajŏssi or Mister, Won Bin presents an idiosyncratic form of individuality constituted by the refusal of identity. A generic chameleon, Won Bin appears both instantly recognizable and transformed in this role.

Won Bin's star text, like Kim Hye-ja's, presents a unified bodily image, an ideal imago of personality, subjectivity, and identity in the public sphere. What differentiates the two stars, however, is the mode in which this integrated image signifies. Kim Hye-ja's star text activates a fantasy of idealized maternity that shores up a melancholy attachment to fixed identities. Won Bin's star text, in contrast, functions as a sign of reinvention—a depthless sign that reroutes affect away from historical memory toward a generic present. This holistic image is what conditions the star's potent attractiveness and fans' passionate and irrational attachments. I would like to suggest that the desire for these images of integration correlates to the tacit recognition of the lack of substance in these images. Though the tendency is to fill in this space with the form of national past as spectral force, this move interrupts itself by contradicting the assertion of the positive value of interiority on which a surface-depth binary is premised. Analyzing the star as genre allows us to examine this negotiation with the failure of the promises of images to help constitute a positively articulated national subjectivity, a seamless integration of national, public selves, and private experience. The star as genre also helps us to interpret the intense affective attachments to idealized yet insubstantial images: the more the presumption of unitary identity is insisted upon, the more passionate the investment in idealized images.

In his introduction to the volume High Theory/Low Culture, Colin McCabe posits a definition of popular culture that primarily derives its contours from a Euro-American articulation of the modernist opposition between high and low cultures.[35] McCabe reminds us that popular has its root in populus (the people, defined as subjects of Roman law), highlighting an important tension in the term: "*popular*, emanating from the people; *popular*, applied to the people."[36] This opposition also inhabits the discourses of popular culture in South Korea, especially in the contrast between *minjok* (variously translated as people, race, ethnicity, nation) and *taejung* (public or popular). One might think of *minjok* and *minjung* (the people, the masses) as corresponding to the popular defined as the spontaneous expression of popular sentiment emanating from the people and *taejung* to the notion of the popular that is imposed, either by the state or the market (as in *taejung munhwa* or pop culture). However, the contemporary era no longer admits a clear distinction between the masses and the popular. It may seem that the branding and marketing of national and regional cultures and state sponsorship in the sectors of design and entertainment (including urban planning, film, music, television, animation, and postproduction), now highlighted as strategies of cultural programming, require a liberal model of bourgeois individualism to retain the compensatory rewards of the discourse of the popular as either folk/tradition or mass media. However, this view excludes the possibility of mass-mediated culture operating in any other manner than as a vehicle of manipulation, establishing the dominant narrative in the South Korean context as the succession or supersession of *minjung* (people's culture) by mass culture rather than their continuing dialectical relation. Works such as *Mother* challenge this interpretation and demonstrate the capacity of cultural artifacts to critique their own conditions of possibility.

In light of the opposition, in the context of modern South Korean history, between the concepts of the popular and the masses, the intricacies of the development of *daejung munhwa* (popular culture) in accordance with a notion of consumer nationalism as well as state support of culture industries in the last decade must factor into a reconsideration of how the popular bears on the question of *minjok*, beyond a fixation on the content of mass media representation. The relationship between people's culture (*minjung*) and pop culture (*daejung*) cannot be encapsulated by the syncretism of high and mass culture that characterized the period of "high postmodernism," or what Laura Kipnis has called the postmodern's "dominant episteme."[37] "Popular culture" sometimes becomes a celebratory euphemism for "highly capitalized mass media"[38] in an attempt to disguise its complicity in maintaining the fundamental asymmetry of mass culture, that is, the fact that those with capital and power generally determine its content, while those without have difficulty being heard when they attempt to respond in the arena of so-called free civil discourse. A key question we must ask is how both senses of popular culture (*daejung munhwa*) as highly capitalized mass media deploy irrationality for their processes of rationalization, if irrationality is a known and powerful dimension of pop-culture consumption, celebrity culture, and fandom. Fandom exemplifies the paradoxes of material consumer practices of affiliation with a nebulous, imagined community.[39] How does the star catalyze such an imagined community, and what relation does the individual fan have with the collective? Though the notion of fandom as collectivized individuality (in the mode of imagined community) questions conventional concepts of individual agency, the star genre provides a generic form of individuality from which a larger group can be extrapolated. As an impersonal form of individuality in which psychological interiority can be projected yet evacuated, the star functions as a container for individualized manifestations of group feeling, in a shifting field of differential relation between concepts of national, ethnic, and popular identity.

NOTES

1. *If You Were Me (Yeoseotgae ui Siseon)*, directed by Jeong Jae-Eun, Park Chan-wook, Park Jin-pyo, Park Kwang-su, Yeo Kyun-dong, and Yim Soon rye (2003; Seoul, South Korea: Chungeorahm, 2003), DVD.

2. My thanks to Jane Chi-Hyun Park for pointing out the relatively recent valorization of feminine beauty in South Korea, noting its association with the denigrated figures of the courtesan or *kisaeng* and the *mudang* (female shaman).

3. See Mary Anne Doane's essay "Scale and the Negotiation of 'Real' and 'Unreal' Space in the Cinema," in *Realism and the Audiovisual Media*, ed. Lúcia Nagib and Cecília Mello (New York: Palgrave MacMillan, 2009), 66–77, for a genealogy of the discourse of the human form as universal measure, consolidated in the European Renaissance and exemplified by Leonardo da Vinci's *Vitruvian Man*.

4. Exposure and publicity are the very preconditions of value, according to P. David Marshall, in his explanation of the etymology of celebrity, from the French *célèbre*: "Celebrity acknowledges a new sense of the public sphere . . ." since such *celebrity* or publicity has become a central metaphor for value, "a type of value that can be articulated through an individual and celebrated publicly as important and significant." *Celebrity and Power: Fame in Contemporary Culture* (Minneapolis: University of Minnesota Press, 1997), 6.

5. In *Man from Nowhere (Ajŏssi)*, directed by Lee Jeong-Bum (2010), a bona fide star vehicle, Won Bin's persistent visibility as a cultivated figure of plasticity lends him the ability to maintain a consistency of *blankness*, signifying a depthless, hypermasculine action star, which the film's title already designates as a generic body.

6. I refer here to Michael Warner's description of the autotelic constitution of publics in *Publics and Counterpublics* (New York: Zone Books, 2005).

7. A rich body of literature, mostly focused on the construction of Hollywood stars and celebrity culture, discusses the dialectic of exposure and concealment, public and private, embodied in stars as discursive sites. See Richard Dyer, *Stars* (London: British Film Institute, 1979) and *Heavenly Bodies: Film Stars and Society* (New York:

Macmillan, 1986); P. David Marshall, *Celebrity and Power*. For a large-scale study of fame in Western culture, from classical to contemporary epochs, see Leo Braudy, *The Frenzy of Renown: Fame and Its History* (New York: Oxford University Press, 1986). For discussions of celebrity culture and female spectatorship, see Jackie Stacey's *Star-gazing: Hollywood Cinema and Female Spectatorship* (New York: Routledge, 1994).

8. Roland Barthes discusses at length the association between photography, death, and memory in *Camera Lucida: Reflections on Photography* (New York: Hill and Wang, 1981) as does Eduardo Cadava in *Words of Light: Theses on the Photography of History* (Princeton, NJ: Princeton University Press, 1997).

9. Walter Benjamin, "The Work of Art in the Age of Its Technological Reproducibility," in *Selected Writings*, vol. 4, *1938–1940*, ed. Howard Eiland and Michael W. Jennings, trans. Edmund Jephcott (Cambridge, Mass.: Harvard University Press, 2003), 251–83.

10. Gilles Deleuze and Félix Guattari, *A Thousand Plateaus: Capitalism and Schizophrenia*, trans. Brian Massumi (Minneapolis: University of Minnesota Press, 1987), 168.

11. These critics include Siegfried Kracauer, Walter Benjamin, Theodor Adorno, Max Horkheimer, and others associated with the Frankfurt School. See especially Adorno and Horkheimer's *Dialectic of Enlightenment* and Adorno's *The Stars Down to Earth*.

12. For contrapuntal analyses of *hallyu* discourse, see Kyung Hyun Kim's *Virtual Hallyu: Korean Cinema of the Global Era* (Durham, NC: Duke University Press, 2011) and Chua Beng Huat and Koichi Iwabuchi, eds., *East Asian Pop Culture: Analysing the Korean Wave* (Hong Kong: Hong Kong University Press, 2008). *Hallyu* is also a term frequently discussed in newspapers and popular publications that report on the increasing popularity of Korean cultural exports in foreign markets.

13. As Jinhee Choi and others have noted, Bong's films have helped engender the discourse of the "quality" commercial film—works that provide the stimulation of art film complexity in popular entertainment packaging—in South Korean film criticism.

14. See Rei Terada's discussion of the face in her study of poststructuralist theories of emotion, *Feeling in Theory: Emotion After the "Death of the Subject"* (Cambridge, MA: Harvard University Press, 2003). She writes, "The face is to visibility what the voice is to audibility: of all physical surfaces, it has the greatest reputation for expressivity, an alleged ability to externalize invisible emotions in a virtually unmediated way" (53).

15. Lauren Berlant, *The Female Complaint: The Unfinished Business of Sentimentality in American Culture* (Durham, NC: Duke University Press, 2008), 4.

16. Lauren Berlant, *The Queen of America Goes to Washington City: Essays on Sex and Citizenship* (Durham, NC: Duke University Press: 1997), 104.

17. Deleuze and Guattari, *A Thousand Plateaus*, 167.

18. Richard Rushton, "What Can a Face Do?: On Deleuze and Faces," *Cultural Critique* 51 (Spring 2003): 223.

19. Rushton, "What Can a Face Do?" 223.

20. Deleuze and Guattari, *A Thousand Plateaus*, 181.

21. Deleuze and Guattari explicitly denote the face of the star as a site of this transfor-

mation: "When does the abstract machine of faciality enter into play? When is it triggered? [. . .] the political power operating through the face of the leader (streamers, icons, and photographs), even in mass actions; the power of film operating through the face of the star and the close-up; the power of television. It is not the individuality of the face that counts but the efficacy of the ciphering it makes possible, and in what cases it makes it possible. This is not an affair of ideology but of economy and the organization of power (*pouvoir*)" (*A Thousand Plateaus*, 175).

22. See Marshall's analysis of television as an ancillary system of celebrity in his chapter "Television's Construction of the Celebrity" in *Celebrity and Power*, 119–49, and Laura Kipnis's work on television's familiarizing and *feminizing* force, "Towards a Left Popular Culture," *High Theory/Low Culture*, ed. Colin McCabe (Manchester, U.K.: Manchester University Press, 1986), 21.

23. See Kim's appearance in the modern-day fairytale *The Princess Hours* (*Goong*, MBC, 2006).

24. Marshall, *Celebrity and Power*, 14.

25. Nataša Ďurovičová and Garrett Stewart, "Amnesias of Murder: *Mother*," *Film Quarterly* 64, no. 2 (winter 2010): 64–68.

26. Ďurovičová and Stewart, "Amnesias of Murder," 63.

27. Feminist readings of the relation between monstrosity and the maternal in literature, film, and psychoanalysis include Julia Kristeva's *Powers of Horror: An Essay on Abjection*, trans. Leon S. Roudiez (New York: Columbia University Press, 1982); and Barbara Creed's *The Monstrous-Feminine: Film, Feminism, Psychoanalysis* (New York: Routledge, 1993).

28. Not in spite of but, I would argue, *because* of Kim Hye-ja's complete territorialization as *kungmin ŏmma* (국민엄마), her performance in *Mother* has only reinforced her marketability as a quintessential maternal archetype. She was the top-voted Korean actress as "national mother" in April 2011 by a KBS 2TV poll, and her star image continues to be used to sell prepared foods under the "Mom (김혜자의맘)" brand. See blog http://tothen01.egloos.com/3457784 (accessed August 12, 2011) for packaging images of these products, in a post on the "convenience store lunchbox wars," about different celebrity product endorsements in 2011. "Mom" here is a play on words, referring also to *maŭm* (마음) or feeling/heart, the implication being that Kim Hye-ja's *maŭm* has gone into the food that will feed the masses.

29. Recent films that mythologize rural communities as sites of uncanny horror include *Moss* (*Ikki*, Dir. Kang Woo-suk, 2010) and *Bedevilled* (*Kim Bok-nam sarinsakŏnŭi jŏnmal*, Dir. Jang Chul-soo, 2010).

30. Ďurovičová and Stewart, "Amnesias of Murder," 64, 65.

31. Gilles Deleuze and Felix Guattari, "Year Zero: Faciality," in *A Thousand Plateaus*, 167.

32. Ďurovičová and Stewart, "Amnesias of Murder," 64.

33. The figure of the *minam* has been discussed in relation to a pan-Asian aesthetic developed out of the gender-redefining images of Japanese *shojo* manga and girls' comics popular elsewhere in Asia, as translated into live "idol" groups. Sun Jung argues that *minam* or what she terms "soft masculinity" has cultural precedent in Confucian ideals in which proper masculinity is defined by nonphysical traits like

cultivated intellect and fidelity to moral and spiritual codes of conduct. See Sun Jung, *Korean Masculinities and Transcultural Consumption: Yonsama, Rain, Oldboy, K-pop Idols* (Hong Kong: Hong Kong University Press, 2010). While I find this argument insightful in certain cases, I am skeptical of the value of linking the transformations of gender performance in the *minam* character to a historical tradition of Confucianism, though considerations of class are undoubtedly an important factor. Won Bin's place in the *minam* discourse suggests that the signifying apparatus of the *minam* relies to a large extent upon its value as pure semblance. This, however, is not simply a claim that the *minam* is analogous to the objectified female body, as the beautiful man still maintains the undeniable privileges afforded by patriarchy.

34. Won Bin is quoted in "Won Bin's 'Second Life' with *Mother*" published in the *Korea Times*, May 18, 2009: "If it was round one until now, then 'Mother' signals the start of round two in my life as an actor." http://www.koreatimes.co.kr/www/news/art/2010/10/141_45090.html.

35. Colin McCabe, "Defining Popular Culture," *High Theory/Low Culture: Analyzing Popular Television and Film,* ed. Colin McCabe (Manchester, U.K.: Manchester University Press, 1986), 1–10.

36. McCabe, "Defining Popular Culture," 5.

37. Laura Kipnis, "Towards a Left Popular Culture," 21.

38. This is Michael Warner's phrase in *Publics and Counterpublics,* 50. His concern is that "highly capitalized mass media" would be naively celebrated as "popular," as though it presents the experiences and concerns of the people.

39. Benedict Anderson's discussion of nation as "imagined community" influences Warner's conception of a public as similarly both concrete and immaterial. Benedict Anderson, *Imagined Communities: Reflections on the Origin and Spread of Nationalism,* 2nd ed. (London: Verso, 1991).

PART THREE Gold, Silver, and Bronze

Figure Part 3.1. Leni Riefenstahl *(right)* and Sohn Kee-chung, one of her subjects in the documentary *Olympia* (1936), reunited after twenty years. Courtesy of Sohn Kee-chung Memorial Foundation.

There are two fundamental reasons an intelligent article on athletic events and sport stars is difficult to spot in academic journals. First, opportunistic snobbery can mislead anyone to think that writing about sports is somehow less challenging than doing a piece on revered subjects such as literature and the arts. Second, because of the connection between team sports, choreography, and orgasmic nationalist pleasures, most intellectuals tend to find athletic events such as the Olympics and the Super Bowl to be no less distasteful than a gusto coalesced from forces of masculinist perversion and rekindling of latent fascist spirits, dividing the world neatly into physically superior beings and inferior ones. Modern sports, admittedly, more so than perhaps any other medium of popular culture analyzed in this volume, is tightly associated with nationalism. Despite these stereotypes against sports, there are many instances in history, because of the value of fairness and antiracism that every sports competition putatively has to uphold, where the division between the colonizer and the colonized or between whites and people of color has become contested, offering hope and redemption to many subalterns. In the film *Mississippi Burning* (directed by Alan Parker, 1988) actor Gene Hackman, playing the role of the lead FBI agent investigating the 1964 murder of three young black men who had been promoting black voter registration in the South, remarks that baseball is the "only time when a black man can wave a stick at a white man and not start a riot." Sports—whether it be Jackie Robinson in baseball, who broke the color barrier well before the Civil Rights Movement began in the United States, or C. L. R. James in cricket, a black Trinidadian Marxist intellectual who recognized the importance of the game in facing the race and class divisions on his home island and throughout the British empire in the early twentieth century—has often helped society to critically recognize the contradictions that the racial barriers and prejudice have produced.

Korea has had reasons to wave not only sticks at the *man* but also laurel wreaths in front of the Japanese attending the 1936 summer Olympic games in Berlin during the colonial marathon. Gold medalist Sohn Kee-chung accepted his medal wearing a shirt with wreaths pinned to it to cover the shame of having to wear the Japanese flag's rising sun. As captured by Jung Hwan Cheon's detailed coverage of Sohn Kee-chung's victory race via the NHK live radio broadcast, Korean pride was unprecedented at his winning an Olympic gold medal, the first for a Korean. His accomplishment created what Cheon called a "syndrome" that culminated in mass euphoria—one that translated into transgressions of psychic and social boundaries that normally police the borders between the colonizer and the colonized. At the same Olympics, where African American sprinter Jesse Owens, winner of the gold medal in his event, was famously snubbed by Adolf Hitler, Sohn rose to the top of the marathon world and even became one of the stars of Leni Riefenstahl's film documentary *Olympia*.

Sports—quite possibly more than any other segment of popular culture—are capable of creating overnight sensations. Unlike movies, pop songs, and television, where the rise to stardom almost always has to be well charted, scripted, and rehearsed, drama in sports is sometimes unscripted, unexpected, and unpredictable and leads to euphoric eruptions.

The term *syndrome* comes up often in Cheon's chapter. This psychic term, derived from the Greek term *sundromē*, which means "concurrence of symptoms,"[1] is useful because Sohn's victory at a time of Koreans' political and even ethnic uncertainty would begin mobilizing not just one particular form of schizophrenia and anxiety that Koreans faced but several. The symptoms were projected by several fears: it was the fear of war draft, the fear of evisceration of Korean language, names, and identity that would soon be mandated by the *naisen ittai* policy inaugurated in 1939, the fear of not having enough cash during the period of intense modernization and capital accumulation, the fear of Korea divided into radical Communists and moderate nationalists, and the fear of an even stronger Japan globally when Tokyo bid to host the 1940s Olympics.[2] The distinction between Japanese and Korean could neither be ignored nor openly embraced by the colonized Koreans because Japan attempted to not exterminate them (unlike the policy regarding Jews in Nazi Germany), but pursued assimilation policies in its colonies to make subjugated people, in Leo T. S. Ching's term, "become Japanese."[3] So when Sohn beat runners from not only Japan but also the rest of the world, these symptoms, which had already clogged the psychological drain system of Korean intellectuals like Yi Sang, who intently listened to the live broadcast of the Olympic marathon in the colonial capital,[4] erupted in a form of euphoria that would crescendo into "hooray" chants for independent Korea by many people gathered at town centers. Sohn united Koreans and momentarily erased the confusion created by colonial modernity that is neither celebratory nor absolutely derogatory about Korea's colonial experience.

The complicated condition of Koreans' standing in the world could not immediately clear up after Korea's liberation in 1945. The bloody war between North and South, the subsequent military occupation by the United States, the vestiges of colonialism, national division, mass immigration to the U.S.A., and the economic uncertainties in the globalized, neoliberal era have all contributed to reinscribe nationalism as a default sentiment for Koreans to overcome postliberation anxieties and traumas. Sports, of course, has comprehensively and deeply been embedded in Korea's nationalist discourse well after 1945.

Instead of "syndrome," Rachael Miyung Joo, borrowing from Lauren Berlant, employs the phrase *aesthetic structure of affective expectation* to describe the phenomenon of Korean female athletes in Korean and the United States as "translocal symbols of Koreanness that travel both physically as athletes on professional touring circuits and digitally through transnational media networks."[5] While many chapters in this book deal with the interlocking relationship between the star and the mass media (Kwon, Jeong, Workman, Cho, Maliangkay, Epstein, and Federenko), Joo's is perhaps the only chapter that focuses solely on the interplay between celebrity culture and textual analysis. Since Korea shows no sign of retreat from a culture saturated by celebrity images and stories that construct popular ideologies that end up interpellating an individual to his or her community, this is a welcomed intervention. One generally anticipates that celebrities born out of sports may be different from those from movies, popular music, and Internet platforms, because it is not necessarily looks that cultivate a sports hero; rather it is purely performance on the field or in the arena that defines stardom. However, Joo argues that the stars she examines are no less free from the hegemonic ideological formation. She focuses on both Korean and Korean American female stars such figure skater Kim Yuna and golfer Michelle Wie, and critiques how they continue to be characterized with notions of traditional femininity, middle-class conformity, and nationalism when selling products and endorsing patriarchal ideologies in both Korea and the United States. The ambiguities that began with Sohn Ki-Jung (who sold Asahi Beers and Kikkoman Soy Sauce immediately after the Olympics even after expressing his public and private displeasure at being represented as a Japanese and not a Korean immediately after his victory in Berlin) continue to thrive in the contemporary era when female stars both battle and submit to Confucian ideals.[6] KHK

NOTES

1. See http://www.thefreedictionary.com/syndrome (accessed on May 20, 2012).
2. Because of World War II, the 1940 Tokyo Olympics was cancelled. It would not be until twenty-eight years later that Tokyo would host the Olympics.
3. Leo T. S. Ching, *Becoming "Japanese": Colonial Taiwan and the Politics of Identity Formation* (Berkeley: University of California Press, 2001).
4. Jung Hwan Cheon, "Bend It Like a Man of Chosun," this volume.
5. Rachael Miyung Joo, "She Became Our Strength," this volume.
6. Cheon, "Bend It Like a Man of Chosun."

9 JUNG HWAN CHEON

TRANSLATED BY JESSICA LIKENS

Bend It Like a Man of Chosun

Sports Nationalism and Colonial Modernity of 1936

FOREWORD

This text was originally written not in thesis form but in a storytelling method of writing and is a part of a larger book published in Korea in 2005, which employs the method of reconstituting events and their temporal and spacial context. I am uncertain whether or not this text, pieced together using excerpts from my book, adequately fleshes out what I set out to explore in that book, namely performative aspects of Korean nationalism and the explorations into the structures of colonial modernity.

I have written this piece with the intention of focusing on the capacity that sports have for a powerful kind of cultural politics and to consider the correlation between the growth of modern nationalism and the development of sports. In dealing with this subject, I must also refer to the shared ability that both nationalism and modern sports have for being able to simultaneously embrace the general public and the growth of mass media. Therefore, this chapter focuses on the three topics of nationalism, sports, and the masses, dealing with these subjects using the archive of Son Ki-jŏng's Olympic victory.

In August 1936, a syndrome appeared that heated up the Chosŏn peninsula, with Sohn Kee-chung (Son Ki-jŏng)'s triumph as its source. The colonized people of the time were fully trained and prepared to be nationalist spectators. It was journalism that kindled this fever and capitalism that fanned the flames. This popular boom or syndrome was not fundamentally different from the nationalist excitement that one can become an active agent of or simply observe today. Inside the people living during Korea's colonized period, the people of the Republic of Korea or those of the Democratic People's Republic of Korea already lay dormant. Syngman Rhee and Kim Il-sung, and to an even greater extent Park Chung-Hee and Chun Doo-hwan, all clearly understood the role of sports nationalism as it pertains to the nation and could not help themselves from working toward amplifying that role.

The syndrome in the summer of 1936 was possible owing to a more than sufficiently developed commercial media, institutionalized trend phenomena, and the existence of individuals who followed these trends diligently, as well as an explosion of nationalist and mass psychology. In the mess of ultrarational and antilogical superiority complexes and inferiority complexes that appear in popular syndromes, the most rational and insidious reason of state and exceedingly levelheaded capitalist reasoning lie underneath. The work of reading these popular phenomena and their underlying dialectic concerns every cultural and social scholar as well as politician and social activist. If we give a name to this kind of society, it can be called a "nationalistic mass society."

THE EVENING OF JUNE 18, 2002

I was sitting in front of the TV in a restaurant in Pongch'ŏndong in Seoul with friends and schoolmates in order to watch the live broadcast of the Round of 16 soccer match, which pitted South Korea against Italy in the 2002 Korea/Japan World Cup. That evening, the people that I was with were not "the guys" who generally liked soccer, nor were they those heavy drinkers who are gripped by finding any excuse to drink with others; rather, with me were those who, prior to June of that year, had never watched a live soccer game from start to finish in their lives and who couldn't understand why there are throw-ins or has to be an offside rule. (In fact, as far as I know, they didn't have any particular *need* to understand.) In other words, this included those women who were more versed and had a deeper interest in dissecting and evaluating the physical appearance of good-looking Korean players like An Chŏng-hwan or Kim Nam-il than in enjoying the flow of the soccer match. For my friends and me as well, it was a new experience—it was the first time in our lives we had watched a soccer game with that many other women. What exactly was going on that particular June?

In the forty-third minute of the second half, when Korea's defeat seemed certain, Sŏl Ki-hyŏn scored a goal to tie up the game. Everyone in the restaurant was literally on his feet, jumping around, stamping, and hugging one another happily. Screams and cheers of joy echoed from the neighborhood around the restaurant as well. Having become quite tipsy, I merely observed the scene of people hopping about and did not move from my spot on the

Figure 9.1. The mass fan rally during the 2002 World Cup for the Korean national soccer team was both a nationalist event and a nonpolitical festival. Courtesy of *Chosun Ilbo*.

floor. Before extra time began, I furtively slipped out of the restaurant in order to organize my thoughts, which by now had become confused. As far as I was concerned, I would have felt more at ease had the game just ended with Korea losing 1–0. That June, I was suffering from a kind of schizophrenia.

June 10 was Korea's match against the United States. It poured in Seoul. Until that day, I hadn't experienced any real internal conflict. All I needed to do was simply activate the mentality of my inner "Korean soccer fan," which was pretty much on autopilot. When Hwang Sŏn-hong scored the first goal during Korea's opening game against Poland, I nearly cried. How much heartache Hwang had suffered since the 1994 U.S. World Cup![1] And the day that South Korea tied the United States (the tension was particularly high for this game, as the short lives of middle-school students Mi-sŏn and Hyo-sun from Ŭijŏngbu had been ended by a U.S. army armored car three days earlier), it was a game we could have won, we *should* have won, but Ch'oe Yong-su, who was the son of a fruit vendor in the neighborhood next to my hometown, unfortunately just had too many thoughts running through his head and wound up fumbling a clear chance in front of the goal. That night, in bars, people even got into fights.

I am a Korean soccer fan. Of course, I had regularly woken up in the wee hours of the morning and watched the Korean team's away games: the 1983 U-20 World Cup games and the 1986 World Cup games in Mexico, all the World Cup games in Italy in 1990, those in the United States in 1994 and in France in 1998. What I call a "Korean" soccer fan refers to those unhappy individuals (among whom ninety percent are men) who, because of karma from their past life and having been born on the Korean peninsula, whether they like it or not, arrive on this earth bearing the destiny of having to root for the Korean national team for their entire lives. This is inevitable, be they socialists who espouse proletarian internationalism or natives of Chŏllado, which was once an internal colony of the Republic of Korea.

Of course, I have attempted to be the kind of fan who doesn't watch only the games of his own national team but becomes a citizen of the greater "soccer world," which extends beyond simple nationality. I watched some of the satellite broadcast Primera and Serie A matches, and during that problem month of June 2002 bought a ticket that cost more than one hundred dollars and went to Suwŏn Stadium. I was determined to watch the Brazilian national team play, as they were difficult to see in person more than once in a lifetime. Nevertheless, I am a "national" soccer fan. My becoming a Korean soccer fan was half decided by my nationality, which was determined by birth and beyond my choosing, and half as the result of my growing up with the national team.

My internal conflict began in earnest as Korea's entrance into the Round of 16 became certain and World Cup fever became a full-fledged national syndrome. The zeal that ignited at Kwanghwa Gate started to overcome my pure happiness,[2] although it wasn't our victory per se that I was unhappy about. That June such zeal had truly become a syndrome, and this syndrome undoubtedly carried with it a terrible kind of nationalism. Yun To-hyŏn's song[3] from this time and Korean flags as big as buildings intensified my feelings of intellectual discomfort. In no time at all, even the country's name was changing to Tae~hanminguk (Republic of Korea). Previously, this formal appellation had not been used with such positive connotations. In fact, it was a term that had generally been used only by right-wingers or when the tone was a kind of negative self-satire.

That June, there was really no place for simple Korean soccer fans like me. Beginning with the match against Italy, whenever the Red Devils' pregame rituals of unfurling colossal Korean flags were broadcast during the singing of the national anthem, I wanted to change the channel.

In contrast to the general enthusiasm, critical intellectuals and conscientious groups such as Ingwŏn undong sarangbang (Group for Human Rights) consistently wrote pieces that warned about this kind of seemingly old-fashioned, nationalistic syndrome. Pak No-ja,[4] a scholar of Korean history in Norway and a columnist for Korean-language dailies, even wrote that the Korean people's "Red Devil Syndrome" served as a reminder of the Nazi's Nuremberg torch marches.[5] It was a scathing critique.

However, even while suspecting the legitimacy of such claims, my first reaction was defiance. "Oh, so you're saying we're Nazis?" surged up in my mind. I didn't like the antinationalist, elitist attitude among people in the humanities, which is dispersed throughout this criticism, and it was unpleasant to realize that others couldn't seem to understand the complicated nature of Korean people's emotions, which have been entangled with sports for such a long time.

I couldn't make up my mind; my inner schism ran deep. The perceived viewpoint of the non-Korean made my schizophrenia more severe. Namely: "Are we really skillful enough to go into the semifinals? Even if it is our home turf, isn't that a bit much to hope for? What will European soccer fans think? Why do Korean people act so ridiculously happy when a member of the opposing team gets thrown out of the game? Was it really a fair call when Totti got thrown out in the match against South Korea?" And so on and so forth. So, I reckoned that Korea's entrance into the semifinals was similar to a kind of gluttony—"Are you sure that we deserve to be in that spot?" A kind of inferiority complex that had been building within me for a long time worked in conjunction with the prejudice I bore as a citizen of the world of soccer about soccerlike correctness. My timid inferiority complex questioned, "The truth is we're third-rate; should we really be permitted to have such good fortune?" Therein lay the internalized inferiority complex of the colonized.

At that time, my position was halfway between the kind of reasoning arguing for the harmlessness of June 2002's "voluntary mobilization" and Pak No-ja–style logic. Now, I can adequately reflect on the fact that the basis of my mental discomfort was not so much related to the chants of *"Taeˇhanminguk"* (Republic of Korea) and *"O, p'ilsŭng k'oria"* (O, Korea is determined to win at any cost) but more to the fact that I didn't want my love for soccer, lumped together with my long-trained, complicated inferiority complex, to be monopolized by capital and nationality, and that June I didn't want to join the quickly formed blind following comprised by many other soccer fans.

That June's innocuousness would later be proven. Although it wasn't exactly an accurate characterization, as critics pointed out, this kind of nationalistic soccer mania was a voluntary mobilization and a sort of festival. In it, there was hardly any of the serious and sacred determination that totalitarianism seeks. In fact, the hollowness of that June attested to its harmlessness, although at the time we shouted slogans like "From the semifinals in the World Cup to the top four among global economies!" and believed that the president of the Korea Football Association (KFA) was a strong candidate for president of South Korea.[6]

Syndromes are necessarily hollow. And this is precisely the essential ground upon which the syndrome could thrive. In other words, it is fortunate that not the authentic love of Korean soccer that cried out, "We must unconditionally go into the Round of 16 this time," nor the insidious "political monopoly" of the politicians who appeared at the soccer stadium for the first time in their lives, wearing red T-shirts that didn't look right on them and waving their hands awkwardly, nor, as in my case, the homegrown "lifelong resentment of the soccer fan," nor any such characteristics of poor merit were able to truly infect soccer.

On a fundamental level, modern sports have played a role in reproducing nationalism and androcentrism, and among all sports soccer is probably the biggest culprit. As a result, it is fortunate that I was able to watch it together with, for example, those middle-aged and young women who don't know simple rules such as throw-ins and who quibble over whether Kim Nam-il or An Chŏng-hwan is better looking, or the young women who wore miniskirts made out of the sacred Korean flag. While of course for a moment they became "the people" and cheered for the Republic of Korea because of soccer, thanks to these individuals who were not really insiders in regard to "national and political soccer," the syndrome I describe was ameliorated somewhat. This syndrome was able to flourish because it was a phenomenon that broke free from the tyranny associated with modernism and was not completely territorialized by power and capital. That June was also a carnival for family and couples, removing it a step from the natural inclinations of modern soccer, which is written on indelibly by the history of war and nation. It is even rumored that a lot of infants were conceived that June.

SPORTS AND MODERNITY DURING THE COLONIAL PERIOD

Interest in the deep reflection and symbols of ideology naturally led to the scrutiny of sports at the beginning of the twentieth century. Sports are one form of an expression of modernity. They are an important undertaking of all modern nation-states. The highly rational logic of games and the merciless and strict lawlike political customs between modern states illustrate that games have been designed and developed for the intervals between wars.

Furthermore, if I were to speak in a manner similar to that of Western philosophers,[7] sports constitute the connecting thread to that which is social and are a mark of negotiation between body and nature, which is etched onto the ego. We remember the ball games and running that we did when we were in elementary school—no, perhaps even before that, in alleys or on the ridges between rice paddies or in the parking lots of apartment complexes. We recall the relationships that we began to form with friends our own age at that time, and the rules that we learned as well as successes and failures that we experienced together. These relationships have already taught us the joy but also the despair and shame that can come from competition and cooperation. Through these experiences, we have learned all about being conscious of that which originates from our bodies or of the bodies of those drawing near to us. Our school gym classes were a process during which we verified and reverified these feelings.

On the athletic field, our bodies were either stronger or weaker than the bodies of others when it came to breaking through the air's resistance and bearing up against the earth's gravity. Like our faces, which were always bared for everyone to see, our bodies, too, became objects for comparison: more or less beautiful than those of others, larger or smaller, longer or shorter, slower or faster, softer or denser. Furthermore, during competitions on field day, "I" became subjugated to the totalizing force of "we." Such memories of the self as well as the establishment of "us" formed the essence of sports. Unfortunately we, like our impoverished ancestors before us, have not had much experience in interacting with those beyond "our people." In the face of the ethnic group, citizenry and social class have been powerless.

Having started taking shape in the 1890s but shifting through a variety of identities, it was not until the 1920s that Korea's sports nationalism began to assume more of a complete form. In the days of the *Taehan cheguk* (1897–1910), there had been an emperor, and though it was nothing more than a joke, it was called an "empire." It was during this short period that modern sports first appeared in Korea. Of course, at that time as well there was frequently a conflation of sports and nation, but rather than an inferiority complex, what was important was pure loyalty to militarism and nation (and to the emperor). As of yet, there was not much of an inferiority complex—this would be founded on the people's group unconscious and sports, which united after the loss of national sovereignty through the active officiating of bourgeois nationalism and cultivation ideology or self-strengthening.[8]

"If You Are a Man of Chosŏn, Kick a Soccer Ball" was the title of an article that appeared in the magazine *Kaebyŏk* (開闢, *Creation*) in November 1920. This article, the title of which was so full of implications, stated that since Koreans of the Chosŏn era were carried on the backs of their relatives in childhood and had a custom of kneeling, their legs were short, and even if they were to put on Western-style suits, they did not have the right posture.

Therefore, although baseball, which was at the height of its popularity, and tennis were beneficial, soccer was recommended. When one plays soccer, the legs grow longer and stronger, so ethnic physical defects could be corrected. The ultimate reason that such ethnic physical defects had to be fixed was to grow as large and as strong as Westerners; that is, to be as "loyal to repay the 'nation.'" In 1920, since there was no nation left for Koreans, it was not revealed which country "the nation" referred to, but it goes without saying the term certainly did not mean the Japanese Empire.

The aforementioned inferiority complex among Koreans would develop and be perfected in the 1930s, penetrating into the twentieth century and continuing without interruption. Within this endless flow, Sohn Kee-chung's (Son Ki-jŏng) victory in the marathon at the 1936 Berlin Olympics was an epoch-making event that would form the highest peak. This win led to the dramatic completion of cultural nationalism, which had been nurtured for nearly forty years. In addition, it was the moment in which a dramatic switch took place from an inferiority complex to a superiority complex. Sohn Kee-chung was a perfect emblem for a strong Korean people, who perceived themselves to be racially superior to the Japanese and certainly just as good as Westerners.

For these reasons, Sohn's victory caused a fervent syndrome to rise up, which heated up the peninsula of Chosŏn in the summer of 1936. At this time, the people of the colony had received more than adequate training and preparation to become nationalist spectators. Journalism kindled a fire, and capitalism augmented the accompanying fever. This popular boom or syndrome is not fundamentally different from today's nationalistic sports fever, of which we can either become agents or passive observers. The syndrome has not yet been cured.

WHAT HISTORY CAN'T SAY WITH WORDS

In comparison with the vast whole of what actually takes place, the "memory" of history is extremely one-track. How one will recount history is an eternal problem for historians and writers. This book's storyline, that is, history, has been a kind of narrative experiment. While in fact this kind of experiment is not unfamiliar, in this chapter I have attempted to narrate the linkage between the macroscopic and the microscopic. For example, the Sohn Kee-chung syndrome was not the only thing that happened in August 1936. That summer, the rainy season was disastrous. The people who lived in many of the areas in the south were suffering from flood damage, and the day laborers who had done cargo work in Map'o, Sŏgang, and Yong'gang were out of work and starving. The governor-general of Chosŏn, Ugaki Kazushige, left his post and returned to Tokyo. Although he did so because he saw an opportunity to become prime minister, ultimately Ugaki's dream would not come true; he succumbed to the strength of military authorities who were more unyielding than himself. As a militant nation, Japan was stretching out more aggressively. Meanwhile, a poor bachelor who lived in Map'o caught a sexually transmitted disease in the red-light district. Frail and depressed, he threw himself into the swollen Han River and killed himself. Twenty-seven-year-old Yi Sang had contributed his short story "*Nalgae*" (Wings) to the *Cho'gwang* and was waiting for it to come out in the September issue. It was the eve of critics Kim Ki-rim and Ch'oe Chae-sŏ turning this story into an enduring masterpiece. Between the starting and stopping of the rain, on August 6 it was sunny and hot in Seoul. A Christian thinker and Yangjŏng High School teacher named Kim Kyo-sin that lived in Chŏngnŭng went to bathe in mineral water at a grotto in the Pukhan Mountains and hurt his foot. In the summer of 1936, there was an incident over the erasure of the Japanese national flag in the *Tong-a Daily* in a picture topping off the zenith of the "syndrome" surrounding the Olympic victory.

THE SLEEPLESS KWANGHWA GATE
Sunday night — August 9, 1936

In Seoul, rain was streaming down. It was the long uninterrupted rain of the monsoon season. On Sunday nights, there was little foot or car traffic even at the road at Kwanghwa Gate.

However, that night, the scene was very different — and not only because of the rain. Drenched, the road at Kwanghwa Gate was in a state of fever. Small groups of people carrying umbrellas congregated, and the lights in the windows of the big buildings on the street shone brightly.

On this night, Kwanghwa Gate was determined to stay up all night. For 500 years, the gate, a symbol of the Chosŏn Dynasty, had been the main gate to Chosŏn's royal palace, Kyŏngbokgung. Through that door, the king and his family, as well as every civil and military official of the court, who ruled the Korean peninsula, had entered and exited. The street in front of the palace, known as "the road at Kwanghwa Gate," was like history itself, covered with a veil of both the honors and the humiliations of the dynasty. But now, the Great Japanese Empire's granite colonial government building was completely obstructing the gate. From the street, Kwanghwa Gate could not be seen.[9]

At number 139 on the road at Kwanghwa Gate as well, where the office building for the *Tonga Daily* was located, the lights burned bright. It was at the foot of this building that the most people were gathered to listen to the live, play by play radio broadcast of the Olympics, which was streaming from the speaker which had been brought out to the second story window of the *Tonga Daily* offices. Beginning at 11 o'clock that night, JODK[10] (Seoul's radio station) was scheduled to do a live broadcast of the marathon competition from the Eleventh Summer Olympic Games in Berlin. An announcer from NHK (a Japanese station) conducted an on-the-scene broadcast from Berlin in Japanese.

On this night, Sohn Kee-chung (a.k.a. Sohn Ki-tae, 1912–2002) and Nam Sŭng-nyong (1912–2001), competing in the Berlin Olympics (August 1–16, 1936) as members of the Japanese national team, finally stepped forth into the fray of a kind of "holy war."[11] Even before leaving the country, these two as one had been the beneficiaries of the hopes of all the Korean people. This was especially the case for Sohn Kee-chung.[12]

Sohn Kee-chung won the October 1933 Chosŏn Sin'gung (shrine) Games Championship marathon, and appeared on the scene like a comet. At that time, his record was 2 hours, 29 minutes, and 34 seconds. Although it was "unofficial," this was a groundbreaking new world record. After that, Sohn Kee-chung began to sweep all of the marathon competitions that were held in Chosŏn and Japan. In particular, he was strong in big events. He made a clean sweep of the November 1934 Chosŏn-wide General Track and Field Championship, the March 1935 Japan-wide Marathon competition, and the November 1935 Eighth Meiji New Style Competition. Consequently, before leaving for the Olympics, Sohn was already a big star.

It was not only the Chosŏn people who had high expectations for him. Even before Sohn Kee-chung appeared on the scene, Japan was strong in the marathon event and had presented several good runners. The Japanese dreamt of winning the marathon, which they called the "Flower of the Olympics." However, in reality, Yamada Kanematsu had ended up only taking fourth place in the 1928 Olympics at Amsterdam, and Tsuda Seiichiro fifth in the 1932 Los Angeles Olympics. Winning the marathon was the earnest wish of the Japanese sports world.[13]

The Berlin Olympics were the perfect opportunity. The best world record for the marathon had lingered around 2 hours and 30 minutes for a long time; the Japanese competitor Kusunoki Kozo held the best official record of 2 hours, 31 minutes and 10 seconds. What's more, in 1935, the first to break through this wall of the nearly indestructible record of two hours and 30 minutes were Sohn Kee-chung and Japanese competitors.

Western journalists were also paying attention to Sohn Kee-chung. The German publication *Olympia Zeitung* predicted a four-way competition between Argentina's Juan Carlos Zabala, the South African Republic's

Johannes Coleman, and the United States' Johnny Kelley, along with Sohn Kee-chung. American sports expert Maxwell Stiles foresaw a three-way rivalry between Zabala, Sohn Kee-chung, and Ernie Harper (Great Britain).

On August 1, 1936, the Eleventh Summer Olympic Games at Berlin opened at last. This event, which was attended by 49 countries and 4,069 athletes, was the largest and most elaborate that the Nazis, whose influence had been spreading for quite a while, had organized up to that point. Yet, the Berlin Olympics were also the worst Olympics, as they most clearly illustrated the ways in which sports can be misused by nationalism and racism, and were a "celebration of the people"[14] which demonstrated without a doubt the way in which sports can truly imitate war.[15]

THE "EXTRA" ERA: THE GROWTH AND COMPETITION OF NEWSPAPERS

In 1936, even if one were to take the whole country into consideration, there were still no more than forty thousand Chosŏn households with a radio. It was the age of the newspaper. Roughly, the *Chosŏn Chung'ang Daily* was printing about thirty-two thousand copies and the *Tonga Daily* thirty-one thousand. Officially, the number of subscribers to Chosŏn-language newspapers was not even one hundred thousand in total, but if we take into consideration the number of people who "passed on and read" newspapers with their family members or local communities, then the influence of newspapers was far greater than this one hundred thousand.

A novelist of that period, Ch'oe Sŏ-hae, said it was the "era of the extra." The fastest way to deliver information was not the radio, but extra editions of the newspaper. These one-sheet extras, with print the size of someone's fist and filled with exclamation points, would cover the ground once or twice a week as people made their way to and from work, providing information about the military situation in Manchuria, the coup d'etat in Tokyo, or the Han River flood.

That year at the Olympics, the power of the newspaper was tremendous. The newspapers that were read in Seoul did all of the work they could possibly do, as though they were born and existed solely for the sake of 1936. To use the language of the time, they "dedicatedly offered up body and life."

Because no less than seven Chosŏn athletes took part in the Olympics, even before the start of the games the interest of the Chosŏn people naturally burned red hot. Newspapers fed that heat, pouring fuel on the fire until it had become a blaze. Using the breaking news system, companies mobilized all of their abilities. As one might guess, the competition was extremely fierce between the different papers.

Behind the competition between newspaper companies, the instigating force was, of course, capital. In other words, through bourgeois journalism, or in more negative terms, through sensationalism and commercialism, the modernity of the newspaper was able to be completely realized. After the 1930s, the "principles" that Chosŏn's newspapers championed were not so much the end goal as they stood in for each newspaper's "brand." With a nationalistic tone for the *Tonga Daily* and a socialist inclination in the case of the *Chosŏn chung'ang Daily*, these papers attempted to catch readers' attention.

After goldmine plutocrat Pang Ŭng-mo took over the *Chosŏn Daily* in 1933, the press's commercial competition became fiercer. Pang Ŭng-mo employed what would previously have been unprecedentedly aggressive management tactics with the intention of making the *Chosŏn Daily* the "number one newspaper." From its initial stages, Pang Ŭng-mo's *Chosŏn Daily* lured away prominent writers like Yi Kwang-su and Ham Sang-hun from the *Tonga Daily*, and beginning in 1935, made increasingly aggressive investments. They even made a purchase of an airplane for collecting news, they built a huge, ultramodern-style company building, and increased the number of pages in their papers from ten to twelve.

Finally, in 1935, the emotional antagonism between the *Tonga Daily* and the *Chosŏn Daily* reached a new limit, and a "war" broke out between the two. Just as the *Tonga Daily* owner Kim Sŏng-su was reprimanded by the governor-general's office regarding the Posŏng Vocational School admission quotas,[16] the *Chosŏn Daily* wrote an editorial that rubbed salt into the wound. The incident that resulted in the heightening of emotions which ultimately caused the real fight was the editor-in-chief of the *Chosŏn Daily*, Sŏ Ch'un, coercing Kim Sŏng-su into publishing an advertisement congratulating the *Chosŏn Daily* on the completion of its new company building. Posŏng Vocational alumni and students came forth and an extensive anti–*Chosŏn Daily* campaign erupted.[17] The two newspaper corporations' endless competition jolted the colony's intellectual society. Journalist Kim Kyŏng-jae accurately grasped the true nature of this opposition, criticizing the argument by saying that since Chosŏn's newspapers were now privately owned companies and commercial organizations, not public institutions, there was no justification for the conflict, which was really only commercial competition.[18]

The *Chosŏn chung'ang Daily*, which had previously been relatively weak, also attracted conglomerate capital beginning in 1935 and plunged into the competition headfirst. Sŏng Nak-hŏn, Kim Sŏng-gwŏn, and so forth, or what was known as the "Sŏng family conglomerate," invested two hundred thousand *wŏn*, actualizing "economies of scale." Consequently, the competition between the medium's capital became a tense, three-party war.

As a new form of entertainment and a detour for nationalism, sports provided the perfect material to correspond to the competition between newspapers. The *Tonga Daily*, which was the most devoted to Olympic coverage, appointed former marathon runner Kwŏn T'ae-ha, who had gone to Germany to watch the competition, the Track and Field Athletic Meet's honorary secretary Chŏng Sang-hŭi, and Germany-based international student Yu Chae-ch'ang as temporary correspondents. They also commissioned Pae Unsŏng, an artist who had been working in Berlin, to do their illustrations.[19] Furthermore, they sent personal messages of encouragement to Sohn Kee-chung and Nam Sŭng-nyong from time to time. On the day of the opening (August 1), the *Tonga Daily* wrote an editorial entitled, "The Olympic Games" and encouraged these athletes, saying, "go out and fight, win, and return to us."

That summer, even the *Chosŏn chung'ang Daily*, which generally decorated its front page with a top news story about the civil war in Spain, was not significantly different. CEO Yŏ Un-hyŏng personally wrote encouraging letters, sent the participants gifts, and published articles about the Olympics every day. On the day of the opening, the paper printed a good-sized article entitled, "With the Ultimate Goal of Glory, the Seven Men Who Have Been through Intense Training Run Bravely to the Front Lines" ("최후의 영광을 목표로 百鍊鋼의 七 선수 陳頭에 勇躍").

Literally, the Chinese characters in the title meant that these seven competitors at last went out into the battlefield bravely as though they had been polished in the fire 100 times. These were the seven competitors from Chosŏn who were shoved in with the Japanese team. Besides Sohn Kee-chung and Nam Sŭng-nyong, the seven included soccer player Kim Yong-sik, basketball players Yi Sŏng-gu, Yŏm Ŭn-hyŏn, and Chang Yi-jin, and boxer Yi Kyu-hwan.

The *Chosŏn Daily*, which had a relatively small number of readers, also strove not to lose out in this competition. (In 1930, the *Tonga Daily*'s contemporary official circulation was 37,802 copies, with 23,486 copies in the case of the *Chosŏn Daily*.) Two months before the opening of the Olympics, Sohn Kee-chung was about to depart from Kyŏngsŏng Station for Berlin (June 3, 1936), but had to visit the *Chosŏn Daily* right before leaving. That day, the CEO, Pang Ŭng-mo, and the executive board of the paper mobilized in front of the station, asking Sohn to have his picture taken holding the *Chosŏn Daily* banner.[20]

Had the conditions allowed, Chosŏn's private media companies would have simply put together a (non-Japanese) independent press team for the Berlin Olympics. But that was impossible. For the Chosŏn press, there was a wall that could not be scaled, known as the governor-general's office. No matter what they did, they were still only the press of the colony. And sadly, they had yet another rival that would prove difficult to beat.

The radio, which could transmit live broadcasts or the news only at restricted times, was in reality not yet a viable opponent. The real adversary of the Chosŏn press was rather Japanese newspaper companies, which were able to dispatch their press agents to Berlin in person on a large scale and had a more developed breaking news system. The *Osaka Daily* and the *Osaka Asahi* had a lot of domestic readers. Realistically, even had they combined all of Chosŏn's power, the *Tonga*, *Chosŏn chung'ang*, and *Chosŏn* would not have been able to catch up in terms of their breaking news systems, skill in covering stories live at the scene, the accuracy of their stories, and most of all in terms of their pictures. The pictures printed in the Japanese newspapers were taken by Japanese reporters themselves and were sent from Berlin via wireless transmission.[21]

The *Osaka Daily* and the *Osaka Asahi* were both publishing extra issues every day, spreading news of the Olympics throughout Chosŏn. They scattered extras with the intention of conveying news of the opening on August 2 and about Murata placing fourth in the track and field 5,000 meter race on August 3, not to mention Tajima Naoto's winning the gold medal in the triple jump on August 5.

KIM KYO-SIN AND YI SANG LISTEN TO THE RADIO BROADCASTS

On the night of August 2, 1936, JODK began broadcasting live to all of Chosŏn from the Berlin Olympics. That year, NHK did play-by-play broadcasts from the Olympics for the first time in history; hence it was also the first time for JODK.

On the night of August 2, Kim Kyo-sin (1901–1945), an instructor at Yangjŏng High School who lived in Seoul's Chŏngnŭng, turned on his radio to listen to the live broadcast. Kim Kyo-sin, who was also the coach of the basketball team, was built solidly and had been an all-around athlete since his days at Hamhŭng Agricultural School. A tall man, he was especially good at basketball and tennis, and he had always played as a representative for his schools or places of work. During his school days, he had been a marathon runner; thus, after becoming a teacher at Yangjŏng High School, he and Sohn Kee-chung formed a special relationship.[22]

While a student at Tokyo Teaching High School, Kim Kyo-sin was taught by Japan's great thinker Uchimura Kanzo (1861–1930). Uchimura had originally been a Methodist, but later became a prominent advocate of the Non-church Movement.[23] Kim Kyo-sin likewise decided to shape his life in accordance with the Nonchurch Movement, one of the most progressive forms of Protestant thought. His classmates from Tokyo Normal High School, Ham Sŏk-hŏn and Yanaihara Tadao, the latter of whom would become the president of the University of Tokyo, would be his lifelong allies. He also enjoyed friendly intellectual relations with Ryu Yŏng-mo and Yi Kwang-su; Yi Ch'an-gap, Yu Tal-yŏng, and Yun Sŏk-jung were taught by him.

After returning to Chosŏn, Kim Kyo-sin began teaching and put much of his energy into spreading the Nonchurch Movement. Starting in 1927, through what were almost exclusively his own efforts he designed, edited, and began to publish the monthly magazine, *Sŏngsŏ Chosŏn* (*Bible Chosŏn*). At Yangjŏng High School, Kim Kyo-sin's nickname was the "double-edged sword." With the exception of God, he feared nothing, and he was a man who refused to compromise.

When twenty-three-year-old Yangjŏng High School student Sohn Kee-chung took part in the second Olympic competitor qualifier cum Meiji Shrine Competition (1935) that was held in Tokyo, Kim Kyo-sin was right there beside him, acting as the coach of the Yangjŏng High School basketball team, which was also present.[24] The members of the basketball team, too, were taking part in the competition as "representatives of Chosŏn." On November 3, the day of the marathon event, Kim Kyo-sin and Kim Yŏn-ch'ang, another instructor from the same school, hired a taxi together so that they could circle the marathon course with Sohn Kee-chung and cheer him on.[25]

Kim Yŏn-ch'ang stuffed the taxi full of bananas, lemon-lime soda, pineapples and biscuits. The taxi drove a little ahead of Sohn Kee-chung with the windows open, as Sohn had requested so he could see his teacher's face. Although Kim Yŏn-ch'ang yelled to Sohn repeatedly, "Aren't you thirsty? Aren't you hungry?" while tapping his feet nervously, Sohn Kee-chung just shook his head slightly and continued to run wordlessly. It was Sohn's style not to eat or drink much while running.

Kim Kyo-sin set his jaw and didn't speak a word. Kim Yŏn-ch'ang's mouth was dry and he wanted to scream with nervous anticipation, but Kim Kyo-sin, like a stone Buddha, simply followed with his eyes the image of Sohn Kee-chung, wearing the number 623 on his back and the Chinese character for the "Yang" in "Yangjŏng" embroidered on the front of his athletic wear.

On this day, too, Sohn Kee-chung fully illustrated his strength in large competitions. In the first half, he simply followed the leader, but upon starting the second half he began to put out a fearsome amount of speed. His getting ahead of Nakamura, who had been running at the front, would take place after he had turned the halfway point. After that, Sohn left everyone in the dust. Even though there was nearly a five-minute gap between himself and the second-place runner, Nakamura, Sohn still refused to slow down.

Finally, Sohn Kee-chung crossed the finish line at two hours, twenty-six minutes, and forty-two seconds. He had reduced his personal best record by approximately three minutes, setting a new world record. Kim Yŏn-ch'ang, extremely excited, turned to look at Kim Kyo-sin sitting beside him. Though his mouth was still tightly closed, there were beads of sweat standing out on Kim Kyo-sin's forehead, and tears welled up in his eyes and rolled down his cheeks.

That afternoon, Sohn Kee-chung stood not on the ordinary victory stand with those who took second and third place, but alone on a special victory stand. In order to congratulate him for setting a new world record, a special awards ceremony was arranged. Since the 1932 Los Angeles Olympics, when Yoshioka Takayoshi had been the first Asian to advance to the finals in the 100-meter sprint event and later set a new world record, no one had ever received such treatment. Because this was such an important event, the *Kimigayo* was performed. Forty thousand spectators joined together and sang along to the national anthem:

May the reign of the Japanese emperor continue for myriad years!
Until sand becomes boulders and moss forms on those boulders.

Listening to the song, Sohn Kee-chung clenched his jaw tightly. Lowering his head deeply, he shed large tears.[26] This image of Sohn Kee-chung would be deeply engraved in the minds of the Japanese.

Seoul—the night of the opening of the Berlin Olympics. Another Chosŏn man who considered himself to be a "twentieth-century athlete" was at a bar, listening to the live broadcast while drinking all night long. He was none other than the poet and novelist Yi Sang (1910–1937). Having graduated from Kyŏngsŏng Technical High School and working for the governor-general's office as a registered architect, in 1934 Yi Sang released the most bizarre poem in the history of Korean poetry, the serial poem *Ogamdo* (Crow's-Eye View). Although he had also written several novels, he was not yet a well-known figure. However, almost all of the works that would make him a prodigy within the world of Korean literature would be written in that year, 1936: *Bongbyŏlgi, Tonghae, Kwŏnt'ae,* and *Chongsaeng'gi*; in the August that the Olympics took place he had contributed "Wings," the short story that would forever make him a part of literary history, to the *Morning Light*.

In a period of just seven years, from Yi Sang at age twenty until he was twenty-seven, Yi Sang wrote in both Korean and Japanese, using his writing to penetrate the contradictions of modernity and the colonies. Moreover, he *physically* experienced the modernity of the colony. He was not an artist who was incorporated into democracy or any other kind of structure. Rather, Yi Sang was characterized by poverty, unkempt hair, heavy drinking, tuberculosis, and hemoptysis, all of which were a good match for his love of paradoxes and cynicism. Yi Sang was born fated to die young.

On August 2, 1936, Yi Sang's younger sister, Ok-hŭi, tricked her brother and ran away to Manchuria with an untrustworthy fellow named K-. It was a case of *kakeochi*—eloping for the sake of love—which was fashionable at the time. The sister appeased her brother with fine words, saying that since K- was going to Manchuria alone, her brother had nothing to worry about, and suggested going out to Kyŏngsŏng Station to bid K- farewell. Trusting his sister, Yi Sang went to Kyŏngsŏng Station. Realizing too late that he had been tricked, Yi could do nothing but return home alone. The next day, his younger sister left for Manchuria, and Yi Sang, caught between a rock and a hard place, waited for news of his sister and idly met up with his friends who had come from Tokyo, drinking from the early evening on into the night.

On the radio in the bar, the Olympic broadcast began at eleven o'clock. Yi Sang, who had been listening, shook his head from side to side, his mind made fuzzy from the influence of the alcohol. Suddenly his life and that of his runaway sister seemed unremittingly senseless, and he began to feel contemptible. As soon as that feeling had been imprinted in his mind, self-pity also began to arise in a steady stream.

The world in the radio was different. In that place, there was no crazy Seoul—depressed and desperately poor yet simultaneously excited by groundless desires. There, the real world was spread out before one, and there were bodies that were firm with potency performing energetic acts. Athletes always stimulated Yi Sang's thinking about a sense of time and the "modern." Yi Sang's comment, made when he was suffering from late-stage tuberculosis, that he considered himself to be a "twentieth-century athlete" was venomous satire directed toward himself and the world.

THAT DAY, IT WAS EXTREMELY HOT IN BERLIN
Destiny's Start Time

It was drawing close to the start time of the marathon at the Eleventh Summer Olympic Games in Berlin. From the radio speaker at the front of the *Tonga Daily* building, the words of the NHK announcer Yamamoto began to stream out like rapid gunfire. Among the Chosŏn people who tuned in were many who were not very good at Japanese and could not understand what he was saying very well. Moreover, the live broadcast also included unfamiliar sports terminology and German place names. Those who couldn't understand had to interrupt, asking those next to them mid-broadcast about what was being said.

Meanwhile, at Sohn Kee-chung's home in Sinŭiju, Sohn's relatives and reporters were gathered. Even their neighbors had come to join in and listen to the radio together. That was not all. Besides those at the road at Kanghwa Gate, there were also a good number of people gathered in front of Chongno's Taech'ang Shoe Store and in the whole area of Chunghakdong, as there were also stations with breaking news at these locations. The students below Sohn Kee-chung in school who were on the Yangjŏng High School track-and-field team were staying together at the Songdo Inn in Hwang'gŭmjŏng (now Ch'ungjŏngno), and had the radio switched on.[27]

In the *Tonga Daily* VIP room as well, the men who had been invited sat around in a circle and listened carefully to the live broadcast. Present were Yangjŏng High School's principal, An Chong-wŏn, the chief of school affairs, Sŏ Pong-hun, the director of the Koryŏ Athletic Games Competition, Ch'oe Chae-hwan, and the chief of the YMCA department of athletics, Chŏng Kwŏn—leading figures of the athletic world, alumni of Yangjŏng High School, and 1932 Los Angeles Olympics marathon runner Kim Ŭn-bae, who had won sixth place. Sohn Kee-chung and Nam Sŭng-nyong were not the first people from Chosŏn to enter the Olympics as Japanese marathon runners; Kim Ŭn-bae and Kwŏn T'ae-ha had participated in the Los Angeles Olympics, taking sixth and ninth place respectively.

The guests in the VIP room were a news item in themselves. Depending on the outcome for Sohn Kee-chung and Nam Sŭng-nyong, every move these guests made would soon become the subject of editorials in the morning paper. Until the live broadcast started, these individuals mentally surveyed the site of the Olympics in Berlin, listening to the description of the marathon course from An Ch'ŏl-yŏng, who had returned from there, and soothing their agitated nerves.

Finally it was destiny's start time—11:02 P.M. on August 9, 1936, or 3:02 in the afternoon in Berlin. That day, the weather in Berlin was extremely hot, with the high temperature exceeding eighty-five degrees.

From the radio speaker, the bang of the starter's gun was audible. The roar of the hundred thousand spectators who had gathered at the stadium could be heard together as a dull rumble. The Chosŏn people at Kwanghwa Gate likewise began to shout out cheers, lift up their arms, or shake their umbrellas up and down crying, "Sohn—Kee—chung!" "Nam—Sŭng—nyong!"

Among the fifty-six competitors, Sohn Kee-chung departed from the main stadium in twenty-second place. Beginning from the six-kilometer point, he began to race with the leading group. In the first half, the leader was Argentina's Zabala, who had won at the Los Angeles Olympics. At the fifteen-kilometer point, Zabala clocked a phenomenal lap time of forty-nine minutes and forty-five seconds, and Sohn Kee-chung along with British competitor Harper passed the point exactly one minute after him, at fifty minutes and forty-five seconds. In terms of place, Sohn was now fourth.[28]

Midnight on August 10, 1936. The competitors were passing the seventeen-kilometer mark. It was still the first half of the race. Sohn Kee-chung was still in the lead group, trying to catch up to Zabala, when the live JODK broadcast was suddenly halted. It was not due to a technical problem with the broadcasting. That year at the Olympics, NHK was allowed to broadcast play-by-plays only twice per day, at eleven o'clock at night and at six thirty in the morning. The live broadcast would not resume until six-thirty the next morning. Although the people had been aware of the fact that the broadcast would be cut short, as soon as it was actually stopped they exploded in anger.[29]

That night at his home in Chŏngnŭng, Kim Kyo-sin also had his radio on. Kim kneeled and clasped his hands together, and he prayed for Yangjŏng High School's fifth-year student Sohn Kee-chung. As the live radio broadcast was halted, Kim Kyo-sin at last stretched out the legs he had been kneeling on and lied down to go to sleep. The exhilaration in his chest didn't subside easily.

"CHOSŎN HAS BEATEN THE WORLD": "NOW I CAN DIE WITH NO REGRETS"

As the clock struck one in the morning on August 10, Kwanghwa Gate started to buzz with activity once more.

The winner at the Los Angeles games, Argentina's Zabala passed the halfway point with the outstanding record of one hour, eleven minutes, and twenty-nine seconds. Up to the twenty-kilometer mark, Zabala was in first place. But that was because of his excessively quick pace, brought on by the drive to win for the second time in a row. Beginning with the twenty-five-kilometer mark, Zabala's form began to lose its precision. Sohn Kee-chung, on the other hand, maintained a steady pace and left Harper behind, tailing Zabala. At last, around the time that Zabala was reaching the thirty-kilometer mark, he crouched to the ground. Now number 382 (Sohn Kee-chung) had no one in front of him. It was at around 12:40 a.m. in Chosŏn, beginning with the thirty-one-kilometer point. After one in the morning, this news was conveyed even to Chosŏn.

As soon as the reports flew in that Sohn Kee-chung was running in first place, the people began to applaud and get worked up. Nam Sŭng-nyong, too, had picked up his pace and was now close to the leading group. As it neared one in the morning, it seemed as though there were even more people gathered than before as a result of the spreading of the news that Sohn Kee-chung actually had a chance of winning. The excitement grew.

Before anyone realized it, it was past 1:30, about the time that someone ought to be reaching the finish line. Either Sohn Kee-chung or Nam Sŭng-nyong must have crossed it, but there was no news. The people, standing in the rain, grew more anxious in anticipation.

"Oh, this is vexing!"

The time continued to go by, and two o'clock was imminent.

At that moment, a female announcer appeared at a second-floor window of the *Tonga Daily* company building.[30] "Sohn Kee-chung was the first to reach the finish line—he won!"

Thus the first piece of news was very short and simple. In the first instant that the people heard what she said, they stared at one another in bewilderment. It was exactly the news that one had hoped to hear, and yet they still couldn't really believe it. Yet after a moment, the people realized the import of what they had just heard.

They threw aside their umbrellas and hugging one another, jumped up and down rapidly.

"Hooray, hooray, long live Sohn Kee-chung!"

"Hooray, hooray, long live Sohn Kee-chung!"

Kwanghwa Gate seemed to shake with the roar.

Eventually, before three full minutes had passed, the announcer appeared at the second-floor window once more. Covering the mouths of their neighbors, the people gazed at the announcer's mouth. The second piece of news was far more detailed.

"Again, we have news from Berlin. Sohn Kee-chung came in at two hours, twenty-nine minutes, and twelve seconds, creating a new Olympic record, and Nam Sŭng-nyong has also come in in third place."

Warm tears began to form in the eyes of the people. Whether because of the rain or their tears, the faces of some of the people were completely wet.

Now the cheers that could be heard were not only "Long live Sohn Kee-chung!" and "Long live Nam Sŭng-nyong!" but suddenly "Long live Chosŏn!" popped out of someone's mouth too. For a moment, the people stared at one another. "Long live Chosŏn" was a dangerous and symbolic phrase—it immediately raised associations with "Long live Chosŏn independence." This phrase, "Long live Chosŏn independence" (*Chosŏn tongnip manse*), had become the most popular and simultaneously the most political slogan since 1910. The working-class liberation struggle, the National Unification Party Movement (*Minjŏk yuildang undong*), and the women's liberation movement all ultimately were vested in these six Korean syllables. After the March First Movement, the next time that "Long live Chosŏn independence" would be shouted by a large group of people in the center of Seoul would be in June 1926, at the time of the funeral of the emperor Sun-jong. In 1929 as well, when the student protests for independence that began in Kwangju spread up to Seoul, the students chanted this slogan. Even in these cases, newspapers could only write that the crowd of people demonstrating cried out, "Long live Chosŏn oooo!"

From in front of the Taech'ang Shoe Store in Chongno and the breaking-news station in Chunghakdong where people had gathered, as well, the cheers resounded in the night sky. At the Songdo Inn in Hwang'gŭmjŏng, where the Yangjŏng High School track-and-field team had gathered, the entire building shook amid the dancing and screams of "hurray!" The Yangjŏng High School principal, An Chong-wŏn, said, choking up, "Now I can die with no regrets."[31]

SYNDROME, SYNDROME

Sad!!?

On August 10, Kim Kyo-sin woke up at five o'clock just as on any other day. The rain had not slowed overnight. Mixed with the sound of the rain, every once in a while a clap of thunder was interspersed. After doing some free gymnastics to quickly stretch out his body, Kim sat upright at his low desk and took out the sheaf of paper that was the manuscript for *Bible Chosŏn*. He had left the proofs out the previous night while listening to the live broadcast of the marathon.[32] Before he knew it, it was six o'clock and gradually, though it was still raining, the sky started to brighten. Kim Kyo-sin said a quick prayer and then turned on the radio.

That morning, NHK and JODK informed their audiences about the final stages of Sohn Kee-chung's win as soon as the program started. Those who had woken up early or hadn't been able to hear the final results and fell into a fitful sleep pricked up their ears to hear the radio broadcast.

At 6:30, news broadcaster Yamamoto came on again. Relatively calmly, Yamamoto quickly summarized the race's circumstances, from the start just up to Sohn Kee-chung's powerful win at two hours and approximately twenty minutes, in about a minute. After that, the tone of his voice began to suddenly rise to a peak: "Will the honor really be handed to Sohn? Although the ladies are currently preparing for group gymnastics in the field, approximately 10,000 people from the German Young Men's Association are waiting for our Sohn, craning their necks to look. At last, applause breaks out from the entire crowd."[33]

A fanfare rang through the air, informing the audience that the first-place competitor had arrived at the main stadium. As expected, the very first runner to come through the door for the marathon at the main stadium was Sohn Kee-chung. "Sohn, as expected, is first! Sohn is first. Right now he's coming into the main stadium. It looks as though he will break the finish-line tape. Sohn! He's in the lead, with the finish line right before him."

The crowd gave him a standing ovation. The distance between Sohn Kee-chung and Harper, in second place, was a staggering two minutes. The commentator Yamamoto's voice rose to a climax: "Sohn is the first to arrive! Sohn is first! He will break the tape in just fifty meters. Forty meters, thirty meters, twenty meters, ten meters! At last he's broken the tape. Japan has won the marathon magnificently. Japan is magnificently the winner of the marathon."[34]

For the many people of Chosŏn who hadn't been able to hear the breaking news, it was only now, for the first time, that they became aware of the win. It was five hours after Sohn Kee-chung had reached the finish line. Belatedly, the people wept and cheered.

At some point, Kim Kyo-sin, who had been kneeling in front of the radio, suddenly couldn't hold back the hot tears that were welling up. "Lord, thank you." The cry did not escape his lips. However, the insides of his large fists were saturated with perspiration.[35]

Before long, at two minutes past seven, the details from an interview with Sohn Kee-chung and Nam Sŭng-nyong conducted right after the win by a staff person from the Japanese network were broadcast. In this interview, Sohn Kee-chung calmly stated in Japanese, "I beat Zabala. We competed fair and square, and in the end I'm happy that I am able to bring the laurel wreath of victory back to my fatherland. All of you from the homeland that have supported me, I know that you are my strength—it's simple, but please take this as my message of thanks to you."[36]

But at 6:50 in Chosŏn on this day, Sohn's mood was quite different in a phone interview conducted by the *Chosŏn Daily*'s Tokyo branch manager, Kim Tong-jin.[37] When Kim said, "I don't know how to congratulate you on this honorable triumph. How happy are you?" Sohn Kee-chung couldn't say a word in response. For a long time he said nothing at all, but then the sound of Sohn crying could be heard coming through the receiver. Throughout this whole phone interview, Sohn continued to speak haltingly, unable to hold back the tears that were rushing forth.

> (Pause) It's great that Nam and I won. I'm happy, but the truth is for some reason after winning I kept feeling overwhelmed and I can't stop crying. Nam is in the same state as I am. (Pause) The more I hear people greeting or congratulating me saying I won, the more the tears take over.

Why should Sohn Kee-chung have been so sad? As soon as he won, he sent a postcard to a friend living in Naju in South Chŏllado, a certain Mr. or Ms. Lee. The story of this postcard, postmarked August 11, is told in three simple Korean syllables: "sŭl-p'ŭ-da" (sad), after which Sohn added "!!?"

Indeed, the comment, "For some reason he just wants to cry," reflected the state of mind of the Chosŏn people, who felt the necessity of hiding their emotions. The Chosŏn people had internalized the oppression of the colonial authorities, but now they did not have to hide their feelings and fully exposed their state of mind, crossing the line of regulation and self-censorship.

THE SYMBOL CALLED SOHN KEE-CHUNG

It was true. Chosŏn had defeated the rest of the world. For a period of about a month, the entire Chosŏn peninsula was seized with ardent fever. That summer it rained far more than usual. Yet even in the midst of flood damage, the Chosŏn people, from the elderly to little kids, all walked around with the name "Sohn Kee-chung" on their lips.

The image of Sohn Kee-chung standing on the victory stand with the laurel wreath on his bowed head, silently listening to the Japanese national anthem, became a symbol of the people of Chosŏn in the 1930s. This symbol fit perfectly with the early modern period Chosŏn people's self-image, which has been referred to as that of the "suffering king (queen)," Ham Sŏk-hŏn. The syndrome set off by Sohn Kee-chung was actually a way of venting resentment.

With the exception of a small number of nationalists who inaugurated an uncompromising "national liberation struggle" that was partly socialist, Chosŏn's nationalism while under the control of the Japanese Empire had already gone abroad and was not physically present or was the practical "postpone independence theory" (tongnip yubo ron), which had combined with "cultivation" ideology. In the peninsula, it was impossible to match against the Japanese Empire, that is, the enemy, politically or militarily. The national revisionists only advocated cultivating the roundabout and fantastic "skill" of culture and education. Therefore, it was none other than sports that was discovered by cultural nationalism as the means for developing the best national skills. Furthermore, Sohn Kee-chung was the long-prepared, pure essence of cultural nationalism, which used sports as a vehicle.

There is no such thing as an emotion that is not learned or trained. Ideology is not simply a reflective surface for systemized thoughts and concerns. Ideology is learned through the experience of reality; when needed, it expresses an emotional reaction and overpowers reason. Moreover, there is no such thing as ideology that is not both a symbol of and a vehicle for ritual. For all ideologies, a noble hero and a flag flapping high in the air, beautiful and solemn music and ceremony are necessities. Mass culture is the best means for providing these symbols and rituals. Films and plays, in fact all of mass media, decisively contributed to the proliferation of the birth of the hero called Sohn Kee-chung and the subsequent syndrome.

THE SYNDROME MIXES WITH MONEY

As the Olympics and Sohn Kee-chung became new mass symbols, capital came forth in order to use them as a means of making money. Hyŏn Chun-ho, who had been the president of Honam Bank, decided to take responsibility for Sohn Kee-chung and Nam Sŭng-nyong's school expenses, and the Han'gyŏngsŏn Shoe Store in Chongno chose to provide shoes to Sohn Kee-chung for life.[38] Details such as these were reported in large type day after day in the newspapers.

Japanese big businesses also used the Sohn Kee-chung syndrome for marketing purposes. The famous beer company, Asahi Beer, chose as their main catchphrase, "The Japanese flag is raised on the [flagpole], the national anthem rings out," and added, "In every home, make a toast with top-ranking Asahi!" putting pictures of the Japanese flag and the Olympic stadium in the background.[39] Thanks to Japan's winning streak, including the Sohn Kee-chung's gold medal, beer sales increased. As for Kikkoman soy sauce, they used the famous pictures of Sohn Kee-chung breaking the tape at the finish line as the background in their advertisements.

The phrase "Congratulations on conquering the world" began to be inserted into every large ad, and advertisers used the mark or illustrations of the Olympic rings to catch people's eye. The representative record brand Okeh Records, for example, advertised September's new albums using the Olympic rings symbol.[40] The competition was especially hot between the primary advertisers in newspapers of the day, the "healthy body" and directly related pharmaceutical industries. These pharmaceutical companies went beyond using ads and illustrations that incorporated associations with the Olympic win and utilized somewhat more actively the general syndrome. Hihumi, a "household medicine for external use on skin diseases," took out a full-page ad in the *Tonga Daily* on August 25, using an illustration of a running track-and-field athlete, and the "external medicine Myohu" took out a full-page ad on page six the following day, hammering out "Let's Congratulate Sohn, Nam for Having Conquered the World" in type the size of a fist.[41]

On August 14, the Pyŏnghwadang Stock Company advertised their product Paekbohwan, known for being a health-aid food, by printing the four syllables "World's Number One" (*segye cheil*) at the top in large letters along with an Olympic medal and below that wrote: "Long Live Sohn Kee-chung." This was followed by: "Paekbohwan, loved by the multitude, is already being used by Olympic competitors," and it was advertised: "The athletes from the most recent Olympics in Germany use it." There was even "proof" that this advertisement was not false or overstated by claiming that the president of the *Chosŏn chung'ang Daily,* Yŏ Un-hyŏng, had distributed eleven containers to the Chosŏn athletes who took part in the Olympics via the newspaper's athletic club.[42] Then, "Illip Tonic. Neos A. Arusu Pharmaceutical Company, Located in Japan" was advertised, using the Olympics in a relatively subtle manner.

Just as autumn was beginning, on August 25, the commercialism of Sohn Kee-chung reached its peak in a Paekbohwan advertisement in the *Tonga Daily.* On this day, the advertisement featured the words: "The tonic that this year's German Berlin Olympics competitors use is actually only Paekbohwan, and Paekbohwan is indeed the number one blood restorative in the world." The warning, "Those who do not yet know of or doubt Paekbohwan's effectiveness and don't take it lack the fortune of being healthy," was also included.

The Yuhan Corporation, which had a reputation for choosing not to engage much in false advertising, judged that it would be more beneficial to the company's image to step back from this intense mud-wrestling contest of sorts and act as though they were stepping away from the fight. They subtly criticized Pyŏnghwadang, saying that unlike what tabloid advertisements had claimed, the benefits experienced by Sohn Kee-chung and Nam Sŭng-nyong were not gained from taking any restorative, not even their own company's "Neoton" Tonic. The winning of the two competitors came not from the power of medicine but only from "their vigorous physical talent, their inexhaustible willpower, and their unyielding passion for their greatest goal, to conquer the world, from which their ardent and absolutely pure brilliant determination stemmed." However, "Upon our discovery of the unity with our Yuhan Corporation's spirit, ideals and truth, we cannot help but loyally extend our heartfelt admiration for both of these young men's conquest of the world."[43]

The syndrome, which appeared as a result of Sohn Kee-chung, was created, amplified, and maintained by nationalism and capitalism. Even after the syndrome was ended by the strength of the Japanese Empire, it continued to have considerable aftermath and must have created broad common "memories." Furthermore, the syndrome was not simply sucked in by contemporary capitalism and ethnicity but in addition created new value and symbolism concerning the Olympics and sports. Thus, via the "capital/ethnicity (nationality)/media" triangular system, sports nationalism was maintained, reproduced, and cast in a new, Korean-style mold.

NOTES

1. Hwang was given a hard time by Korean soccer fans after missing a number of important goals in the 1994 World Cup.
2. Many had gathered around Kwanghwa Gate to watch the matches on the big outdoor screen.
3. O! P'ilsŭng k'orea [Oh, Korea is determined to win at any cost!].
4. The Korean name of Vladimir Tikhonov, an associate professor of Korean Studies at the University of Oslo, born in the former U.S.S.R. (what is now modern-day Russia).
5. Pak made this comment in the weekly newsmagazine Hangyŏre 21 in a conversation between him and Hong Se-hwa. Pak No-ja and Hong Se-hwa, "Purgŭn akma ka kyegŭp ŭisik hŭrinda" [It's the Red Devils That's Diluting Class Consciousness], Hangyŏre 21, no. 414 (June 19, 2002), accessed on March 5, 2010, http://h21.hani.co.kr/arti/world/world_general/5422.html.
6. The KFA president at the time and the controlling shareholder in Hyundai Heavy Industries Group, Chŏng Mong-jun, ran for president in 2002.
7. In particular, Deleuze comes to mind.
8. Another apt translation could be "cultivation of one's skills or ability." Sillyŏk yangsŏng ron was an often-used phrase during the nation-building phase that began during the colonial era.
9. During the Chosŏn period, the Ŭijŏngbu and the Six Ministries were located on the road in front of Kwanghwa Gate, so it was called Six Ministry Road (Yukjo kŏri). Six Ministry Road was so wide that even the Japanese Empire admired it. As part of the Japanese Empire's 1912 and 1936 city planning, when the roads were repaired the Government General's Office set the width at 30 kan (53 meters), resulting in its becoming narrower than during the Chosŏn era. In 1914 it was named the Road at Kanghwa Gate, and after liberation it became Sejong Road.
10. JODK is the call sign for the international broadcast. This call sign was another way that the people of the time referred to the Kyŏngsŏng Broadcasting Station.

11. On and after August 10, 1936, the newspapers used the expression "holy war" (sŏng-jŏn) in talking about Sohn Kee-chung's marathon win.

12. See for instance, *"Marason paengnimdaehoe-ŭi yesang sunjoroŭmyŏn son-gun il ich'ak"* [Predicted that Sohn will arrive first in the Berlin Marathon if things go smoothly], in *Chosŏn chungang Daily*, June 10, 1936; *"Son-kun chep'ae-nŭn hwakjŏngjŏk nam-kun-to yŏksi t'uji-ka ch'ungch'ŏn"* [Sohn's conquest is certain, Nam's fighting spirit also soars], in *Chosŏn chungang Daily*," July 28, 1936.

13. Tadayoshi Kamata, *Nisshōki to Marason: Berurin Orinpikku no Son Gijyon* [The flag of the rising sun and marathon: Berlin Olympics and Sohn Kee-chung] (Tokyo: Ushio Shuppansha, 1984).

14. *The Festival of the People (Fest der Völker)* is also the title of the film made as the official record of the 1936 Berlin Olympics, made by Germany's female director Leni Riefenstahl.

15. Simultaneously, in southern Europe (Spain) international war was truly breaking out. In July, Francisco Franco's Fascist military started a rebellion, and before long the subsequent civil war between them and the people's front government forces had diffused throughout all of Europe. Seeing that France and the U.S.S.R. were going to support Spain's government forces, Nazi Germany raised tensions by supporting Franco, all the while holding aloft the banner of world peace by means of their hosting of the Olympics. On the third day after the opening of the Olympics, on August 3, Germany made it clear that it intended to interfere, dispatching its navy's capital ship to Spain. Ultimately war broke out, with the Fascists and the Royalists on one side and the socialists and the liberals on the other; more than 500,000 people would die in this war, which the Fascists won. Both George Orwell (b. 1903) and Earnest Hemingway (b. 1899), who were in the heyday of their youth when the blood ceased to flow, saw this tragic defeat with their own eyes and created some of their greatest work.

16. Kim ran the school, which was found to be accepting more students into certain departments than was permitted by the quotas in order to earn supplementary tuition.

17. See Kim Tong-hwan, *"Chosŏnilbo tae tongailbo sangjaeng sakŏn chinsang kŭp pip'an"* [The conflict between the *Chosŏn Daily* and the *Tonga Daily*: Truth-level criticism]," *Samch'ŏll* (July 1935), 27–38. Unlike the current Tonga and Chosŏn newspapers, until the 1990s the two were always in a state of competition. Since then, with Tonga's loss of influence and fall to a being a second-rate paper, the relationship between the two papers has actually become quite close.

18. Kyŏng-jae Kim, *"Yangdae chaebŏl-ŭi chep'aejŏn chŏnmo"* [The whole story of the struggle for supremacy between the two corporations], *Samch'ŏlli* (July 1935).

19. The artist Pae Un-sŏng was the first Chosŏn international student to study art in Europe. Under Nazi rule, he was one of the few foreign artists whose work was secure, and he was even famous enough to rent an exhibit hall on Paris's Super-express and open a private exhibition. Hitler's preferential treatment toward Pae Un-sŏng, in spite of his being an artist who was a person of color, is regarded as being on the level of political consideration.

20. See *"Perŭllin kanŭn Son Ki-jŏng "chosŏnilbo-wa hamkke"* [Sohn Kee-chung going to

Berlin—together with the *Chosŏn Daily*], *Chosŏn Daily*, July 28, 2004; *Kim Kyo-sin chŏnjip (The Complete Works of Kim Kyo-sin)*, ed. No P'yŏng-gu. Vol. 6. Puk'i, 2001.

21. In Japan as well, 1936 was the first time that photographs were transmitted via wireless transmission. See http://www.c20.jp/20c/1936.html. Accessed on May 21, 2013.

22. Regarding the life of Kim Kyo-sin and his relationship with Sohn Kee-chung, I generally consulted *Kim Kyo-sin chŏnjip*, ed. No P'yŏng-gu (Seoul: Puk'i, 2001–2).

23. Uchimura, who was an instructor at Tokyo Cheil High School, where the highest elites were taught, committed lèse majesté against the emperor in 1980 at Tokyo Cheil during the commemoration of the proclamation of the Imperial Edict on Education. He refused to show his respect for what was a nationalist education proclamation and the emperor's edict (the Emperor's Word). He followed his conviction to obey his conscience as an educator and a follower of God. He argued that one had to be free from government authority, capitalists, nobility, and even educators in order to be qualified to love one's fatherland and that doing so could be a way of loving God. Oonuki Emiko and Yi Hyang-ch'ŏl, *Sak'uraka chita, chŏlmŭmto chita* [The cherry blossoms wilt, youth wilts] (Seoul: Moment'o, 2004), 181.

24. In this competition, Chosŏn's representative basketball team from Yangjŏng High School lost 24 to 29 in the third round to Kwandong Institute and was eliminated.

25. The general content found in these passages comes from Kim Yŏn-ch'ang's "Sŏn-saengŭi imochŏmo" [The thoroughness of a teacher], in Kim Kyo-sin, *Kim Kyo-sin's chŏnjip*, vol. 6 P'yŏng-gu (Seoul: Puk'i, 2001–2), 345–5; *Kim Kyo-sin chŏnjip 5-ilgi 1*, 413. Several records report that after this awards ceremony Sohn Kee-chung ran up to Kim Yŏn'ch'ang and, on the verge of tears, asked, "Why don't we have a nation?"

26. According to the November 4, 1935, edition of Tokyo's *Hochi Newspaper*. See the aforementioned book by Kamata, *Nisshōki to Marason*, 41.

27. The surrounding contents are derived from the August 11, 1936, edition of the *Tonga Daily*.

28. Kang Hyŏng-gu, *Son Ki-jŏng-i talryŏon kil* [The path run by Sohn Kee-chung] (Seoul: Selreksyŏn, 2004), 8.

29. As this broadcast was the same in Korea and Japan, the live broadcast was interrupted in Japan as well.

30. This content has been reconstructed using the August 8, 1936, edition of the *Tonga Daily* as its foundation.

31. *Tonga Daily*, August 10, 1936, and August 11, 1936.

32. Reconstructed using Kim Kyo-sin, *Kim Kyo-sin chŏnjip 6: ilgi 2*, ed. No P'yŏng-gu (Seoul: Puk'i, 2001–2) as the foundation.

33. Kamata, *Nisshōki to Marason*, reads: "Throwing in his body, taking first place in the marathon race. We are waiting to welcome our Sohn. Applause is rising out in the stadium."

34. The content of this broadcast is described in Kamata, *Nisshōki to Marason*, 331. I have used recollections of the announcer at that time, Yamamoto, as the background.

35. I have used *Kim Kyo-sin chŏnjip—ilgi 2* as the background to reconstruct this section.

36. *Tonga Daily*, August 10, 1936.

37. *Chosŏn Daily*, August 11, 1936.

38. *Maeil sinbo*, August 26, 1936, 2.

39. *Maeil sinbo*, August 17, 1936, 3.

40. *Maeil sinbo*, August 23, 1936.

41. See *Tonga Daily*, August 25 and 26, 1936.

42. *Tonga Daily*, August 14, 1936, 7.

43. "Congratulations Messrs Sohn and Nam," This appeared as an advertisement line in *Samch'ŏlli*, November 1936, 137.

"She Became Our Strength"
Female Athletes and (Trans)national Desires

Wearing a skating costume of royal blue with a cascade of rhinestones falling down her back, Kim Yu-na stood on the Olympic winner's platform watching the South Korean flag, the *taegŭkki*, raised above the national flags of Japan and Canada. She had won the gold medal in women's figure skating at the 2010 Winter Olympics with a set of record-breaking performances. For two programs, she skated without an obvious flaw, executing technically difficult elements while demonstrating beautiful musicality. Kim Yu-na captured the crowning achievement in her sport and solidified her status as the *yŏwang*, or queen, of figure skating and sport in South Korea and its diasporas.

Throughout the Olympics, the nationalist fervor around her performances achieved a level of global recognition.[1] In English-language media, articles on Kim Yu-na were often accompanied by a discussion of the immense pressure that she had to bear, given that Koreans intensely followed not just her competitions but her every move and mention too. These accounts pointed to her national popularity but rarely detailed the conditions of possibility— the commercial, media, and sporting contexts—for the emergence of Kim as a transnational icon. Instead the media coverage took for granted that Kim deserved this national status of assuming the transcendent importance of global sport. Furthermore, given the hyperfemininity and sexualization that characterizes women's figure skating, the relationship between Kim's accomplishment of a rarefied femininity and her national significance was seldom, if ever, analyzed in mainstream media accounts.

Korean female athletes like Kim Yu-na demonstrate how contemporary discourses of national identity are shaped through the gendered, classed, racialized, and sexualized narratives of transnational media.[2] Transnational mediations of athletes produce gendered ideologies of nation in professional media sport that proliferate through the media-saturated and celebrity-centered worlds of South Korean and Korean American public cultures. In this chapter, I detail discourses of nation and gender that inform media coverage around Korean female athletes and argue that media representations of these athletes convey ideas of Korean womanhood and nation that inform processes of national and transnational meaning-making in South Korea and the United States.

While the rising visibility of Korean female athletes offers many interpretive possibilities, these female athletes represent hegemonic ideas of gender, nation, and race. The chapter begins with a discussion of the significance of the golfer Se Ri Pak as catalyzing the growth of a media genre focused on the Korean female athlete and, by genre, draws from the definition offered by Lauren Berlant, who refers to genre as an "aesthetic structure of affective expectation."[3] Korean female athletes within this genre function as translocal symbols of Koreanness that travel both physically as athletes on professional touring circuits and digitally through transnational media networks.

Focusing primarily on representations of Korean athletes in the Ladies Professional Golf Association (LPGA), the following section details how the rise of Korean women in the sport has caused essentialist discourses about the physical abilities of Korean females to proliferate. These discourses assume a shared national biology, which functions to explain the success of Korean females in golf. Myths about Korean athletes' biology resonate with stereotypes about the physical capacities of Korean (and other Asian) women in the global workforce as robotic, indefatigable, and unskilled labor. Associated with these biological ideologies are arguments that female athletes need strict guidance and require the patriarchal protection of their parents and the nation. The next section details patriarchal discourses attributed to Korean cultural traditions, which are not only used to help explain the unique rise of Korean female athletes but also work to maintain relationships of inequality of gender and generation.

In transnational mass media, the sexuality of Korean athletes is presented in contradictory ways as daughters to be protected within the Korean family and as hypersexualized Asian women to be marketed in transnational commercial contexts. The final two sections of the chapter focus primarily on how Korean female golfers are represented within the contexts of U.S. corporate multiculturalism. The successes of Korean athletes come to represent a fulfillment of an American Dream narrative that offers the Korean athlete as evidence of the continuing promise of opportunity in the

United States. Although Korean female athletes have been subject to broad stereotyping and media racism, they have opened new sporting and media markets in Korea and Asia. Furthermore, as women's media sport comes to be dominated by representations of female sexuality, sexualized representations of Korean players shape a kind of ideal feminine subject that contributes to heteronormative representations of female athletes.

By covering how the female athlete is situated within both Korean nationalist and U.S. nationalist discourses, this chapter offers a critical reading of the contradictory and competing discourses of gender and nation that these athletes have come to represent. Korean female athletes, through their mediations, generate and circulate the affects of nation(s) within transnational contexts. Sara Ahmed argues, "In affective economies, emotions do things, and they align individuals with communities—or bodily space with social space—through the very intensity of their attachments."[4] The circulation of athletes in media sport produces some of the most intensely affective frames for shaping and producing national emotions. These affective dimensions highlight the critical political importance of paying close attention to the national ideologies embedded in global sport.

A REASON TO SMILE

The Ladies Professional Golf Association is a highly visible context for the transmission of media images of Korean female athletes. The organization constitutes an important part of the media landscapes that connect South Korea and Korean America and is one significant example of a truly transnational sporting phenomenon. An important reason to focus on the LPGA lies in the fact that the intensely affective attachment with female athletes began with the remarkable success of the golfer Se Ri Pak. As the first successful South Korean national in the LPGA, Pak won two of the four major tournaments on the tour in her rookie year of 1998. Her performances saturated Korean and Korean American media coverage, and by the end of the golf season she was declared a national hero by then president Kim Dae Jung. Her initial successes occurred while the nation was reeling from the trauma of the Asian financial crisis, and clearly her importance was intensified during this period of immense social anxiety.[5] She came to symbolize how South Korea might pull itself out of the crisis through global competitiveness, individual drive, and private capital.

Her wins in the U.S. Open and the McDonald's championship were particularly significant as they occurred on a U.S., some might say international, stage. She became a figure of national triumph, like a phoenix rising from the ashes of a collapsed financial system. Her dramatic win in the U.S. Open induced a burst of national emotion, and this feeling of victory became a commodified national obsession circulated through commercial media and advertising. In an ad for Samsung's Anycall cellular phone, action video of Se Ri Pak playing golf and photographic images from the 1998 U.S. Open Championship are superimposed with the following text:

Uri ka ŏryŏul ttae, kŭnyŏ nŭn uri ŭi him i toeŏtda./ Uri ka chich'yŏ issŭlt-tae, kŭnyŏ nŭn uri ŭi miso ka toeŏssŭmnida./ Tasi, kŭnyŏ ŭi miso rŭl pogo-sip'sŭmnida. Chigŭm aenik'ol ŭl hasaeyo. (In our difficulty, she became our strength. In our weariness, she gave us a reason to smile. We want to see her smile again. Please use Anycall now.)

At the end of the commercial, a series of evocative black-and-white photographs flash before the viewer, recounting the suspenseful play-off ending in the 1998 U.S. Open win and evoking subjective memories as the viewer fills in the time-space between the photographs. A female voice whispers, "Tangsin ŭi han madi ka him i toebnida. Pak Se Ri hwa-i-t'ing! (One word [of your encouragement] can make a difference. Se Ri Pak Fighting!)." The ad ends with a photo of Pak in tears of joy accompanied by a floating image of two cellular phones and the text, "Ŏnje ŏdisŏna hangugin ŭn aenik'ol. (Whenever or wherever, Koreans use Anycall)."

Samsung's commercials connect their communications devices with Se Ri Pak's wins as a way to fuse its commercial desires for global competitiveness with national aims. These feelings of national emotion are eagerly sought by mass media and state interests, reflected in the investment in and anticipation of success in global sporting competitions such as the World Cup and the Olympics. A decade after Pak's debut, the number of Korean-identified women in LPGA golf soared, and Korean-identified females comprised more than one-tenth of the active players in the U.S.-based tour.[6]

WORKING WOMEN

According to the Ladies Professional Golf Association, 43 of 123 international players were South Korean as of July 2011.[7] The list of international players did not include Korean-born players who were naturalized U.S. citizens or Korean Americans born in the United States, including Michelle Wie.[8] While the increasing participation of Korean players may now seem commonplace, the considerable growth of Korean golfers began with the entrance of Se Ri Pak in 1998.[9] In 2004, Thomas Bonk of the Los Angeles Times reported, "Pak is credited with almost single-handedly changing the face of women's golf."[10] She has been followed by a great number who have now established a significant Korean presence in international golf tournaments and have indeed reshaped the cultural landscapes of the LPGA.

As national icons, successful female golfers demonstrate how Koreans should adjust to the neoliberal contexts of a globalizing Korea. Rather than the products of state-funded elite sports directed toward international competitions like the Olympics, Korean female golfers achieve their training through private capital and individual initiative. They demonstrate how free-market rewards can be appealing incentives for private investments and personal efforts. Se Ri Pak was perhaps the first athlete to be described as a *sup'och'ŭ chaebol* (sports conglomerate), a transnational meta-commodity who endorsed a number of U.S. and Korean-based companies including Adidas, the CJ Group, Samsung, Maxfli, TaylorMade Golf, and Upper Deck.[11] While these players may depend on private wealth and capital, the entrepreneurial success of Korean and Korean American players remains a victory for the nation. The golfers and their private wealth are represented as the pride of the nation, and possibly, its future potential for success.

With the rapid growth of Korean golfers in the LPGA, many raised questions about how such a large number of Korean female golfers could be so successful in such a short period of time. Generally, it was stated that the sheer number of Korean golfers had to do with a Korean cultural propensity toward hard work and competition. In mass media accounts, the individual success of players was often attributed to natural Korean tendencies, such as a strong work ethic, self-discipline, mental strength, and steady family support. Rather than simply repeating these uncritical and problematic iterations about "Korean nature," it is important to understand how cultural ideologies produce particular narratives of possibility (while limiting others) for Korean women. These essentialist ideas have a constitutive power and have played a large role in promoting the practice of particular sports, including golf, for young Korean women.

In South Korea, the dominant discussion of golfers assumes that their success is due to their talent, hard work, and the sacrifice of their families. Eui Hang Shin and Edward Adam Nam believe that the intense training of Korean female golfers is based in the testing and examination culture of South Korean society. They state, "This relentless cycle of mental preparation for a single examination on which students are given only one chance per year translates well into the single-mindedness and never ending practice sessions seen in the Korean golfers."[12] Their statement highlights a socially sanctioned attitude toward extreme forms of mental and bodily discipline for children and youth. While educational practices certainly play a large role in producing subjects that are able to engage in high stakes competition, examination culture does not enforce competition for its own sake. Examination culture is situated within broader social and economic contexts that produce particular kinds of workers.

Revealing an essentialist pose, Shin and Nam perpetuate the stereotype prevalent in South Korean and Korean American contexts that Korean women are naturally well suited to forms of sport that require extreme precision and concentration, such as archery, billiards, figure skating, and golf. For example, there is a general societal expectation that Korean women will win medals in the archery competitions of the Olympics. From the 1984 Olympics until the 2004 Olympics, Korean women won all available gold medals in the archery competition.[13] National mythologies about the biology of Korean females have resulted in targeted financial investments and educational opportunities in particular fields that require precision, mental acuity, and dexterity. These myths are materialized in the bodies of Korean female athletes through their high rates of success in these particular fields during international competitions. These nationalist narratives also motivate and mobilize private capitalist investments in the potential athletic achievements of Korean girls and women.

One theme that often appears in non-Korean media is that Korean golfers display a robotic quality—the idea that they lack emotion, creativity, and individuality. Shin and Nam remark, "Korean golfers are entirely focused and devoted to the game of golf and their training."[14] They quote extensively from a feature written by Michael Bamberger for *Sports Illustrated* that describes Pak's golf swing as "hypnotically robotic, thoroughly repeatable and extremely beautiful." Bamberger continues to state that Pak was the "closest thing yet to a human version of Iron Byron, the ball-testing machine . . . a golfing machine—no brain, no emotion, automated excellence."[15] Rather than critiquing the implicit stereotypes embedded in the statement, Shin and Nam confirm these orientalist descriptions following enthusiastically, "Yet this cool single-mindedness displayed by Korean golfers may be the secret to their success."[16]

The language used in U.S. media sport (and, in some cases, academic analyses) to describe Asian golfers often perpetuates orientalist stereotypes of the Asian female as robotic, unemotional, and single-minded and follows depictions of Asian American female workers in transnational capitalism.[17] The language used to describe women's work devalues their labor as "unskilled," which requires mindless repetition rather than complex thinking. Ong points out that "unskilled" work has been discussed as "biologically suited to the 'oriental girl' due to her feminine traits."[18] Laura Hyun Yi Kang notes that the Asian/American female body within the transnational capital-ist contexts is "often described with the inherent characteristics as childlike innocence and docility, digital nimbleness, physical stamina, keen eyesight, sexual largess, and muscular flexibility."[19]

Transnational sport operates as an arena for the reproduction of national stereotypes framed within political, social, and economic contexts. During the Cold War, athletes from socialist countries were often stereotyped as collectivistic, militaristic, and emotionless. In contemporary contexts of globalization, Korean athletes are valorized as national heroes for disciplin-ing their bodies, garnering global media attention, and demonstrating eco-nomic results. The female golfer strengthens the economic ideologies of segmented labor markets that treat tasks as gender-specific and age-specific and that constrain definitions of what is possible for men and women. These narratives of female labor question whether golfers raise new opportunities and possibilities for women as they are so easily appropriated into the patri-archal capitalist narratives of subordinate female labor.

PATRIARCHAL NATIONALISM

As Aihwa Ong has noted in her study of Chinese capitalists, *Flexible Citizen-ship*, the mechanisms of transnational capitalism are facilitated by kin rela-tions structured through gender inequalities.[20] The narratives of LPGA golf reproduce ideas of patriarchal family relations in transnational contexts. Korean nationalist discourses of the LPGA represent the golfer as daugh-ter subjugated to her father, family, and nation. Within the ideology of the successful Korean golfer, the work habits of female golfers are inculcated under the authoritarian watch of dedicated parents who push their daugh-ters to practice excruciatingly long hours and encourage them to compete to win. In some cases, it is reported that Korean parents invest everything they have—their money, resources, and personal lives—into their daugh-ters. Often, they move from South Korea to the United States or Australia to raise their daughters in golf-centered environments, to send their children to golf academies, and to live in areas where golf can be played year-round. While on tour, many South Korean golfers reportedly travel with their fami-lies, who operate as support staff taking care of details not related to the actual play and professional obligations.

While family support explains the success of many, if not most, profes-sional female athletes competing in elite individual sports like figure skat-ing, tennis, and golf, family support has been noted as a particularly salient cultural advantage for the Korean female golfer. Beginning with the visi-bility of Se Ri Pak's father, Pak Joon-cheol, U.S.-based media focused its attention on the idea of a Korean family model headed by a father.[21] In this family narrative, the father is perceived as the primary motivating force behind his daughter's education and training. Many top Korean players, including Se Ri Pak, Mi Hyun Kim, and Grace Park, have acknowledged their fathers as the strongest influence in their careers.

In this Korean father-daughter LPGA narrative, successful daughters act as the conduits through which their fathers' efforts and dreams are realized. Obviously this narrative impacted Ty Votaw, LPGA commissioner from 1999 to 2005, who apparently believed that Se Ri Pak "gave the entire country of Korea the motivation and inspiration for fathers and daughters to say, 'Hey, if she can do it, we can do it.'"[22] While the actions of the father are the basis for the daughter's success, the mother's labor is peripheral or entirely erased. The mother remains an invisible woman relegated to the domestic labor of nurturing and cooking. Shin and Nam perpetuate the myth of the female golfer by stating:

> Their fathers are their caddies, coaches, and confidantes. Their mothers are bulwarks of support and familiarity, sacrificing their marriages and family lives to pick up and move to the states [sic] to care for their daughter's needs. It is this never ending devotion of parents to their children's needs that plays a heightened role in these players' victories.[23]

While individual cases differ, in golf it is generally assumed that the athletic training of the child rests on the shoulders of the father as the initial expert, who accompanies his daughter and redirects his own interests to discipline and perfect her performance.

The father's obsession with his daughter enables him to assert his masculinity within a transnational context. Within women's golf, patriarchal family relations appear to grow stronger as they are conveyed as essential to the success of a female golfer. In this media narrative, father and daughter must bond to fight competitors in a foreign land. This interest of Korean fathers in their golfing daughters is often described as a borderline pathology, as Korean fathers are often seen as aggressive and overzealous. Se Ri Pak's father reportedly forced her from a young age to repeatedly walk up and down fifteen flights of stairs day and night and to sleep in graveyards to overcome her fears. Fathers have been charged with violating rules such as coaching from the gallery and encouraging cheating, as with the father who was accused of kicking his daughter's ball out from behind a tree to give her a better lie.[24]

The contradiction between the celebration of the individual as competitor in golf and the Korean female as member of a family is often explained away as a cultural difference—as an essentially different approach to the world by Korean people.[25] In this orientalist discourse, Korean female golfers are not adult subjects who can, of their own accord, enter into social relations, labor relations, and sexual relations. They remain children in a patriarchal family context. The golfer is sexualized as nubile yet virginal and out of the reach of young foreign admirers. She remains in her father's "house," protected by his watchful presence. Grace Park, often discussed as one of the most attractive and stylish Korean players, was appointed in 2004 to be an international representative of the LPGA as a nonvoting board member. She stated that she would live with her parents until she was married because she is Korean.[26] Shin and Nam state, "Se Ri Pak *enjoys* the guidance of her father, who keeps her focused on her dream [emphasis added]. In regard to movies and boyfriends, Pak's father once said to her, 'Ten years from now. Golf now, that later.'"[27] While Shin and Nam are convinced that such discipline fosters the success of Korean female players, they fail to critique the system of gender inequality that enables such patriarchal control.

Nationalist narratives operate through this patriarchal dominance over daughters. The father comes to stand in for the national interest as he protects the progeny of the Korean nation in foreign contexts and ensures its enduring success. The national interests that ride on the success of female golfers depend on the investment of the father who ties the nation and its daughters. The connection between patriarchal nationalism and this father-daughter narrative in golf is exemplified by a television advertisement for Samsung's Anycall cell phone titled, *Him ŭl chunŭn sori* [The sound that offers strength]. This title draws on the closeness of Pak's name to the word *sori*, or sound. Playing off the idea that Pak gave strength to the nation, the commercial itself suggests that her father is the source of her strength (fig. 10.1).

The commercial begins by showing several video clips of Pak playing golf alone on a course. Then she narrates, "*Kodog i na ege k'ŭn kot'ong ŭro tagaŭlttaemada na rŭl irŭk'yŏ chunŭn sori ga itda* [Whenever I am struggling with isolation, there is a sound that picks me up again]." A cell phone rings, and a man's voice on the line states, "*Seri ya, hŭndŭllimyŏn andwae* [Seri, you must not be shaken]." Back in narration, Pak states, "*Na ege him ŭl chunŭn sori ga itda* [There is a sound that gives me strength]." Then an announcer's voice states, "Anycall."

This ad works through the assumption that the Korean national public understands the role of Pak's father in her golf career. It is clear that the man's voice is supposed to be her father and that it is his authority that gives her strength. While her isolation may be from the fact that she is far away

Figure 10.1. Se Ri Pak speaking to her father in Samsung Anycall television advertisement.

in a foreign country and competing in an isolating sport, she maintains her connection to her family, national public, and homeland through her cell phone. The ad suggests that while Pak might give the nation strength, her strength relies on her father.

In the case of transnational movement and migration, this patriarchal narrative is not an innocuous one but rather has tangible consequences as to how Koreans imagine the nation and their place in relation to it. The dominant narratives of patriarchal nationalism in sport have enduring consequences, as they produce an acceptable space for the iteration of gendered hierarchies that might otherwise be rejected. As Purnima Mankekar has argued, the nation in diaspora often remains a domain where patriarchy and male dominance remain free from criticism.[28] The national family as represented by the golfer's family becomes the symbol of the nation in an era of globalization and highlights the significance of maintaining the ties of blood kinship despite interactions with diverse groups and movement across borders. The narratives of Koreanness in these transnational contexts often reinforce ideologies of nation, gender, and class that reproduce social relations of inequality in both South Korea and Korean America.

THE PROMISE OF AMERICA

Until the late 1990s, the LPGA remained largely a sporting context for white women from the United States, the United Kingdom, Northern Europe, and Australia,[29] with a few notable exceptions such as Althea Gibson and

Nancy Lopez.[30] In the last decade, however, there has been a fundamental shift in the racial makeup and arguably the cultural tenor of the professional women's game because of the rapid entry of competitive tour players from Asia, particularly South Korea. Korean female players have been accompanied by journalists, spectators, fans, as well as commercial sponsorships and endorsements from companies like Korea Telecom and the CJ Group that hail from their places of origin. The clothing of Korean female golfers is often punctuated by logos from Korean companies that have little or no recognition in U.S. consumer markets.

In an effort to capitalize on the popularity that has followed the entry of Korean golfers, the LPGA revamped its marketing strategies to promote itself as an exciting, contemporary, international, and sexy sporting organization. While there have been detractors who have decried the loss of the white bourgeois traditions of golf, the LPGA website proudly displays its efforts to embrace multiculturalism through a "celebration" of international non-U.S. players who hail from places such as Australia, Mexico, Scotland, Japan, and Sweden. Koreans and other non-Anglo players are now playing a central role in globalizing the golf market by generating interest in golf and its related media and merchandise in places where golf exists as a relatively new or newly popular phenomenon. Furthermore, these dramatic changes are connected to the entry of Korean players and the growth of a consumer middle class in both South Korea and Korean America.

The growth of Koreans in LPGA golf has not been without detractors, who exhibit protectionist and racist attitudes decrying the loss of the "essence of golf" and its traditions. In the November 2003 issue of *Golf Magazine*, Australian LPGA player Jan Stephenson remarked, "The Asians are killing our tour—absolutely killing it. Their lack of emotion, their refusal to speak English when they can speak English. They rarely speak." Stephenson's now well-known and oft-cited remarks were promptly and summarily dismissed by the LPGA, as her statements were in direct conflict with LPGA policies on diversity and interests in global expansion.[31] The professional golf establishment in the United States, spurred by the popularity of Korean and other international golfers, shifted its commercial strategies to accommodate and promote international and racial diversity. While golf has been slow to incorporate the tenets of multiculturalism, it has followed a familiar narrative of racial incorporation as it took a successful minority player to open the sport to prove the worth of the minority to the majority.

To global corporations, Korean golfers offer a high level of marketing potential owing to the connections between golf and nation. While there was no active recruitment scheme on the part of the LPGA for foreign players as of 1999, Korean players became part of a new expansionist business plan of the LPGA and its sponsors. In 2003, Nike's global sports marketing director Kel Devlin stated that South Korea, where thirty percent of its 2.5 million golfers were women, presented more potential for growth than the United States.[32] In a high-profile investment in Korean markets, Nike offered a lucrative multimillion-dollar sponsorship to Grace Park in 2003, the first athlete to represent the newly formed LPGA division. Michelle Wie, another Nike acquisition, has been highly touted as a "marketer's dream."[33]

The position of Korean female golfers as national media stars has changed the entire marketing strategy of the LPGA itself, which has been plagued with low ratings since its debut on television.[34] In an attempt to shore up profits, the LPGA attempted to institutionalize what it perceived as the essential components of profitable practices through the Fans First initiatives. In 2004, Commissioner Votaw acknowledged the primary impact that Asian players have had in increasing the profitability of the LPGA.[35] "We're thriving," he stated. "Competitions have been enhanced by the presence of Asian players."[36]

The Korean players work well within the corporate multicultural contexts of the LPGA as they demonstrate how foreignness operates to prove the continuing economic promise of U.S.-based corporations and, by extension, the United States. Essential to reproducing the idea that the United States remains a place of opportunity is the immigrant myth that relies on the idea that immigrants attain economic success entirely through their own hard work and self-sustained efforts. Bonnie Honig writes: "In the capitalist version of the myth the immigrant functions to reassure workers of the possibility of upward mobility in an economy that rarely delivers on that promise, while also disciplining the native-born poor, domestic minorities, and unsuccessful foreign laborers into believing that the economy fairly rewards dedication and hard work."[37] Korean golfers are celebrated for demonstrating appropriate foreigner behavior as they help U.S. corporations make profits by expanding markets abroad while relying on their own private funds. Furthermore, Korean golfers are hailed for offering praise for the United States that American citizens so easily forget. Golfer Grace Park is quoted as saying, "This country offers so much more than anywhere else. That's why we come here. This is where the best courses are, the best teachers, the best competition. I think that I will stay for a long time."[38]

LPGA golfer Christina Kim, who was born in the United States to Korean immigrant parents, is often represented as both Korean and American. She has stated that she is "damned proud of being an American." Yet, she is often targeted to be a representative of Korean golfers by the U.S. media. She asserts, "I can understand both sides because I'm of both cultures."[39] She has used her own Korean expertise to make overarching statements that the discipline of Korean golfers is "an instinct that's bred into the Korean people and passed down from one generation to the next."[40] In this case, her position as a Korean American allowed her to speak with authority on matters of Koreanness, and her comments work to perpetuate essentializing myths about Korean homogeneity.

A 2006 advertisement for Sony Cybershot digital cameras featuring Michelle Wie suggests that Korean and Korean American players do not necessarily choose their own representations and that within a U.S. context Korean players continue to be racialized as Asian. The print advertisement features the teenager sitting legs crossed in the lotus position with a golf ball in one open palm and a digital camera in the other. She is dressed in velour yoga pants and an orange jersey camisole decorated with an Asian bird motif. She is seated on a lotus-leaf–styled golf green framed by a mandala made of 7-iron clubs. This embellished photograph approximates Buddhist iconography (with an admixture of Hindu elements) in a tongue-and-cheek way through its colors, symbolism, and the positioning of the central figure. Beyond its mockery of religion, the image erases her national distinctiveness and strategically evokes orientalism in an attempt to shape her into an icon that represents a generalized Asianness. While athletic skills are hinted at through the golf motif, she is not wearing golf gear but rather is barefoot and dressed in yoga garb. The image belittles Wie's success at golf by focusing on her race and sexuality as an "oriental girl," rather than her athleticism.

In the American media, Korean players operate as agents through whom national and racial differences are understood. Clearly, the decision to announce the English-only policy at a mandatory South Korean player meeting on August 20, 2008, demonstrated that the LPGA saw the rise in the number of South Korean players as a threat to its future.[41] The policy stated that players who had been on tour for two years had to pass an oral evaluation of their English or they would be suspended from tour play. By announcing this tour-wide policy to a group of South Korean players prior to announcing it publicly, the organization sent a message to players that they would be evaluating their "cultural" capacity to remain on the tour. It was clear that the sudden announcement of the policy was a desperate attempt to reduce the number of Korean players on the circuit. After a few days in the sports news media spotlight, the controversial policy was dropped as the legality of the policy and its implementation were in question.

In the changeover in leadership from Ty Votaw to Carolyn Bivens, there emerged an attempt to create a bifurcated tour: one that appealed to the Anglo heritage of golf by featuring young, new, sexy talent as representing a glamorous and primarily white tour and another that maintained the pace of international growth for the LPGA. In the attempt to present both images, the LPGA praised and targeted Korean players. The treatment of Korean players in the LPGA demonstrates how the institution remains tethered to a U.S. nationalist multiculturalism that welcomes foreigners as sources of capital but remains dedicated to maintaining a dominant tradition based in race and class exclusivity.

THE ANTI-BUTCH CAMPAIGN

As a way to further promote its newfound popularity, the LPGA in 2002 created a five-year plan for financial growth that featured the Fans First initiatives, which pushed all athletes to be mindful of the Five Points of Celebrity. The Five Points were performance, approachability, passion and joy, appearance, and relevance.[42] These items were understood as placing greater emphasis on the appearance and personalities of the players than their performance as athletes. In response to the announcement of the Five Points of Celebrity, there was criticism from feminist critics of sport and Title IX advocates, who protested against the implied sexualization of female athletes. The opponents of the Five Points argued that these guidelines reflected the crass corporate interests of the LPGA. The representatives of the sporting industry, however, argued that these changes were made on behalf of the interests and desires of the fans, given that it was essentially an entertainment industry where the viewer-spectator-fan was placed first in all decisions.[43] According to the new LPGA initiative, players were encouraged to increase their media savvy through bold athleticism, public personas, and appearance (read: sex appeal).

In 2004, Votaw was quoted as stating, "Asian players embody the Five Points of Celebrity perhaps better than some do here."[44] It was clear that the LPGA believed that Korean golfers were national celebrities in South Korea, and some might venture to argue that the Five Points were inspired by the celebrity Korean golfers were already enjoying. These guidelines, however, have operated as a double-edged sword for Korean players. There have been criticisms that Korean players lack proper golf etiquette and care only about their own success while ignoring other professional duties, such as pro-am tournaments and sponsor receptions. In response to these accusations, Votaw reminded Korean golfers that "performance is only part of the package."[45] Essentially, the Five Points of Celebrity are used as a way to tell all players that they aren't doing as much as possible to make money for the association and its sponsors, as there is always some part of the package for any one player to improve upon.

This emphasis on femininity has been interpreted as a not-so-subtle attempt to enforce compulsory heterosexuality in the LPGA. This is particularly significant in the LPGA, which represents a women's sport that has had a long-standing presence of lesbian players and fans.[46] Abigail Feder-Kane, in her study of women's figure skating, argues that absolute gender differences between women and men are reproduced less through physical differences than the stylistic emphasis on the appearance of the players. She states, "When physical capabilities no longer distinguish men and women, femininity is overdetermined to keep female athletes from being labeled as masculine or lesbian." In the case of figure skating, femininity is produced "by 'hiding' all signs of labor such as sweat, muscles, and grunting."[47]

The hyperfemininity of the Korean players serves to emphasize gender difference by erasing sexual ambiguity. The form-fitting tailored clothes of Grace Park, the dangling chandelier earrings and wide belts of Michelle Wie, and the pixie girlishness of Kim Mi Hyun provide a primary focus of media attention. In contrast to the idea of the asexual robotic worker, the sexualization of the Korean body appeals to the target market of the LPGA, which continues to privilege heterosexual male viewers. The celebration of heterosexual femininity in the LPGA also marginalizes the significant lesbian community of players and fans who have defined a particular LPGA aesthetic sensibility over the last thirty years.[48] This shift can be read in the changes to the public appearance of Se Ri Pak. She was transformed from a dowdy twenty-something golfer at her debut to the tidy player of today through a national makeover. The masculinity of Pak—her broad shoulders, strong legs, dark tan, oversized polo, baggy shorts, and flat, short hair covered with ill-fitting baseball caps—did not detract from her initial national fame. Pak was, by far, the most popular athlete in South Korea at the end of the twentieth century. Over the years, her public image has been transformed through a wardrobe revamp and the use of heavy makeup. She is often featured in women's magazines in tailored designer sportswear with highly stylized hair. In photos, she strikes poses that emphasize her "feminine side"—taking a stroll in the woods, relaxing on a couch, playing with her dogs, and cooking in her kitchen. The transformation of the tomboyish national icon to the womanly figure of today demonstrates that while femininity was not a requisite for her national importance, she was normalized into public femininity through the transnational circuit of images of professional golf.

The hyperfemininity of Korean female golfers promote a hegemonic heterosexuality in women's professional sport as their "look" caters to the imagined gaze of heterosexual men. The emphasis on the sexualized straight female body operates to assuage corporate anxieties over perceived lesbianism and lesbian aesthetics in golf and, more broadly, organized women's sport.[49] This is not to say that the hyperfemininity of female golfers then precludes other kinds of sexual desires. Clearly, their sexualization also attracts female consumers, both lesbian and straight, yet the marketing strategies continue to privilege heterosexual men while marginalizing other sexualities even while these marginalized perspectives function as profitable niche markets.[50] Furthermore, as the strategies for emphasizing Asian female sexuality against Euro-American lesbian aesthetics demonstrates, heteronormativity is produced in and through transnational contexts.

LIBERATED LADIES?

To conclude, the figure of the Korean female golfer demonstrates how national discourses of gender and sexuality operate in powerful ways through representations of athletes that move across national contexts. The ability of some Korean female athletes to thrive as individuals within transnational capitalist contexts results in their projection as ideal cosmopolitan subjects of the nation. The argument might be made that Korean women can, in fact, better adjust to speedy transformations in the global economy than Korean men since they are not burdened by traditions and hierarchies, such as homosocial networks, military obligations, and duties to family legacies, that might prevent men from adapting as readily to economic change. The female golfer symbolizes the opening of possibilities for Korean women in the transnational workforce in the two last decades and the ability of women to take advantage of the opportunities presented in a globalizing context.

Contemporary myths about "new women" in South Korean society conjure the image of a global subject who is capable of traveling, learning languages, adjusting to new contexts, and pursuing her own interests. Such a "new woman" might be exemplified by skater Kim Yu-na, who has far surpassed any other Korean athlete in acquisition of wealth and global recognition while remaining a national icon. Her 2010 Olympic success elicited comparisons to the amazing year when Se Ri Pak won two majors, and her figure skating win was also said to offer hope in a time of economic struggle. Unlike Pak of 1998, Kim was already wealthy and well known by the time she won the gold medal; today she represents a complete convergence of celebrity and sport as a performative and feminine figure who easily moves between athletic competition and commercial media. She has grown up within the context of national fame and has blossomed within the global contexts of *hallyu* and Internet-based fan communities.

Kim Yu-na also represents a different kind of relationship to parental and national authority. Accounts around the 2010 Olympics seemed to valorize her Canadian coach, Brian Orser, as a proxy father figure who was living out his unfulfilled Olympic dreams through his student. After the termination of their relationship, Orser blamed Kim Yu-na's mother for overreaching in her daughter's career. While Kim retorted that she was no longer a child, it was well known that her mother played a significant role in her career as an overall manager, business partner, and advisor.[51] Clearly, she has presented a different kind of relationship between female athletes and parental authority than the golfers mentioned above, yet the emphasis on parental and family control remains.

In the first half of 2011, Kim Yu-na participated as part of the South Korean delegation that successfully won the bid for the 2018 Pyeongchang Olympics. She was among other committee members, including then-president of South Korea Lee Myung Bak, Lee Kun-hee, chairman of the Samsung Group, Park Yong-sung, chairman of Doosan Industries, and freestyle skier Toby Dawson. She was presented as the pride of the nation and as proof that South Korea had the ability to host the Winter Olympics. In a Korea Gallup poll, more people felt that Kim Yu-na was the key to winning the bid than any other member of the committee.[52] Most in their twenties felt that Kim Yu-na was the main reason for the win, while those over sixty gave more emphasis to Lee Myung Bak and Lee Kun-hee. This poll highlighted changing attitudes toward traditional patriarchal corporate and political power with an emphasis on global commercial celebrity in the digital age. While some might read Kim Yu-na as highlighting a shift in gender power in South Korea, the Olympic Committee reflected continued male patriarchal dominance in corporate and political sectors. During the Durban announcement, where South Korea successfully won its bid to host the 2018 Winter Olympics, the image of Kim Yu-na ensconced among these men of corporate and political power seemed to suggest that she remained a young woman to be presented and protected by the men of the nation.

This analysis of sport demonstrates that myths about the new Korean woman continue to be overlaid with discourses of patriarchy and male dominance. Female athletes are still characterized with notions of diligence and docility within patriarchal contexts of work and family. Korean female athletes are rarely presented as individual adults outside the contexts of their families and their fellow nationals. Furthermore, in the United States, Korean female athletes are subject to prevailing myths around racial difference, especially through exotic Asian sexuality. They are positioned within an athletic media sport complex that subjects them to forms of sexualization that highlight their ultrafemininity and desirability to heterosexual male consumers. The athletic skills of world-class female athletes are often diminished, as the women are expected to present themselves as desirable and sexy marketers for sports and their sponsors. As Feder-Kane has pointed out, athletes in these feminine sporting contexts are presented as ladies who do not sweat.[53]

These icons produce powerful national affects that explain a great deal about their continuing popularity and relevance. Their symbolic significance lies in their ability to evoke powerful national narratives in the contemporary contexts of transnational media and capital flows. While a Korean or Korean American individual might not be a fan of sport per se, the media coverage of these sporting icons has produced regular representations of Koreanness and Americanness in both South Korea and the United States. As long as these athletes continue to be marked by national differences, they will continue to produce and circulate ideologies that define how the relationship between nation and gender is understood in both national and transnational public culture.

NOTES

An earlier version of Rachael Miyung Joo's "'She Became Our Strength': Female Athletes and (Trans)national Desires" was published in Rachael Miyung Joo's *Transnational Sport: Gender, Media, and Global Korea* (Durham, NC: Duke University Press, 2012).

1. Jeré Longman, "Balanced on a Skater's Blades, the Expectations of a Nation," *New York Times*, February 22, 2010, http://www.nytimes.com (accessed July 12, 2011).
2. See Grewal 2005; Mankekar 1999.
3. Berlant 2008, 4.
4. Sara Ahmed (2004, 119).
5. See Song 2009.
6. All Korean-heritage players are referred to as Korean except when discussing national citizenship. The notion of Korean-born is problematic, as several South Korean citizen players were born outside the Republic of Korea, including Aree and Naree Song, identical twins who were born in Thailand to a Thai mother and Korean father. They changed their Thai surname, Wonglukiet, to a Korean one in 2003. Also Angela Park, who entered the LPGA in 2007, is of Korean ethnicity but was born in Brazil. Furthermore, some South Korean golfers have become naturalized U.S. citizens after entering the tour, and some have claimed dual citizenship.
7. See "2011 International Players," http://www.lpga.com. (accessed July 13, 2011). The number of South Korean players entering their rookie years grew from one in 1998 to thirteen in 2007. The number of Korean American players entering their rookie years rose from two in 2007 to seven in 2011.

8. While I recognize that significant differences exist between South Korean and Korean American golfers, particularly in relation to Korean and U.S. nationalist discourses, I do not focus on this important issue in this chapter.

9. South Korean player Ok-Hee Ku won one LPGA tournament in 1988 and subsequently played on the Japanese tour. Michael Arkush, "Asian Golfers at home in L.P.G.A.," *New York Times*, September 1, 2003, Sports, 6. Also, Pearl Sinn-Bonanni entered the LPGA in 1991 as the first Korean American on the tour.

10. Bonk added, "In a relatively short time, South Korean golfers have become a force on the LPGA Tour." "Pak Mentality," *Los Angeles Times*, June 10, 2004, Sports, D.

11. See Arjun Appadurai, *Modernity at Large: Cultural Dimensions of Globalization* (Minneapolis: University of Minnesota Press, 1996).

12. Eui Hang Shin and Edward Adam Nam, "Culture, Gender Roles, and Sport: The Case of Korean Players on the LPGA Tour," *Journal of Sport and Social Issues* 28, no. 3 (2004): 223–44; quotation at 231.

13. In the 2008 Olympics, the Korean team won gold, but in the women's individual competition the Chinese archer, Zhang Juan Juan, beat three South Korean competitors including the silver medalist, Sung-Hyun Park, ending this streak.

14. Shin and Nam, "Culture, Gender Roles, and Sport," 231.

15. Quoted in Shin and Nam, 231.

16. Shin and Nam, "Culture, Gender Roles, and Sport," 232.

17. Aihwa Ong, *Spirits of Resistance and Capitalist Discipline: Factory Women in Malaysia*. (Albany: State University of New York Press, 1987); Chun-man Kang, *Han'guk hyŏndaesa sanch'aek: 1950 yŏndae p'yŏn* [A stroll through modern Korean history: The 1950s], vol. 1 (Seoul: Inmul kwa sasang, 2004), 109.

18. Ong, *Spirits of Resistance*, 152.

19. Laura Hyun Yi Kang, *Compositional Subjects: Enfiguring Asian/American Women*. (Durham, NC: Duke University Press, 2002), 165.

20. Aihwa Ong, *Flexible Citizenship: The Cultural Logics of Transnationality* (Durham, NC: Duke University Press, 1999).

21. Graig Dolch, "Foreign Relations," *Palm Beach Post*, November 19, 2003, Sports, 1C.

22. Bonk, "Pak Mentality."

23. Shin and Nam, "Culture, Gender Roles, and Sport," 233.

24. This incident is often cited in feature articles on controversies surrounding Korean players. Following the incident, commissioner Ty Votaw called a meeting of all Korean and Korean American players, caddies, and coaches to discuss the rules. "Players Meeting to Discuss Claims of Cheating Korean Dads," Associated Press, August 5, 2003, Sports.

25. Todd Crosset emphasizes the individual nature of playing golf in the LPGA with its focus on individual achievement and individual play. *Outsiders in the Clubhouse: The World of Women's Professional Golf* (Albany: State University of New York Press, 1995).

26. Park is quoted as saying, "Koreans are more traditional, very conservative. Children stay with their parents until they get married. Until then, they are in their own shell." In Joel Boyd, "Seoul Train: Controversy Hasn't Derailed Korean Influx on LPGA Tour," *Chicago Sun Times*, May 30, 2004, 94.

27. Shin and Nam, "Culture, Gender Roles, and Sport," quotations at 234. Some have pointed to the role of Tiger Woods's late father, Earl Woods, in his career as a comparative figure. There are similarities that might be drawn from a militaristic training standpoint. The predominance of this father-son narrative in the case of Woods operates within a U.S. national context that pathologizes the "black" family. See Henry Yu, "How Tiger Woods Lost His Stripes: Post-Nationalist American Studies as a History of Race, Migration, and the Commodification of Culture," in *Post-Nationalist American Studies*, ed. John Carlos Rowe (Berkeley: University of California, 2000), 223–48.

28. Mankekar, Purnima, "Brides Who Travel: Gender, Transnationalism, and Nationalism in Hindi Film," *Positions* 7 (1999): 731–61.

29. The game of golf was introduced in the United States at the turn of the twentieth century and functioned as an arena of leisure and social reproduction for elite Anglo men and women (Crosset, *Outsiders in the Clubhouse*, 12). Professional women's golf began in the 1940s, and the U.S.-based LPGA was officially established in 1950. The use of the term *Ladies* in LPGA evokes a past of white patriarchal exclusivity, and its continued use projects a nostalgic sense of genteel domesticity and class privilege. Women continue to be excluded from private clubs, such as Augusta National Golf Club in Augusta, Georgia, where the PGA Master's Tournament is held annually.

30. Katherine M. Jamieson, "Reading Nancy Lopez: Decoding Representations of Race, Class, and Sexuality," in *Reading Sport: Critical Essays on Power and Representation*, ed. Susan Birrell and Mary G. McDonald (Boston: Northeastern University Press, 2000), 144–65.

31. For the commentary on Jan Stephenson's remarks, see Eric Adelson, "Stephensons' Comments Grossly Unchallenged," ESPN *The Magazine*, online edition, October 15, 2003, http://sports.espn.go.com/golf/news/story?id=1637830 (accessed May 21, 2013). See also Ron Sirak, "View from the Bunker: On Asians and Racism," *Golf Digest*, online edition, August 25, 2005, http://www.golfdigest.com (accessed February 1, 2006).

32. In Michael Buteau, "Nike Signs Park As It Hopes to Make Inroads in LPGA," *Milwaukee Journal Sentinel*, March 2, 2003, 12S.

33. In Louise Story, "A Teenage Golfer May Also Be a Marketer's Dream," *New York Times*, online edition, July 18, 2005, http://www.nytimes.com (accessed July 22, 2005).

34. Crosset, *Outsiders in the Clubhouse*.

35. In Lindsey Willhite, "LPGA Happy Pak Got Things Rolling," *Chicago Daily Herald*, June 4, 2004, Sports, 1.

36. Cecilia Kang, "Cultural Conflicts Arise on Women's Golf Tour Attempts to Charge Asian Pros Criticized," *San Jose Mercury News*, November 1, 2003, http://www.mercurynews.com (accessed August 12, 2004).

37. Bonnie Honig, "Immigrant America? How Foreignness 'Solves' Democracy's Problems," *Social Text* 56, no. 16 (1998): 1–27; quotation at 1.

38. Bob Harig, "Women's Golf. Korean Infusion," *St. Petersburg Times*, June 29, 2004, 1C.

39. Kang, "Cultural Conflicts Arise."

40. Quoted in Vic Dorr, Jr., "Country Clubbin'. Korean Golfers Credit Success to a Cultural Propensity for Discipline," *Richmond Times Dispatch*, May 5, 2004, Sports, E-1.

41. Beth Ann Baldry, "LPGA to Demand English Proficiency," in *Golf Week*, http://www.golfweek.com (accessed August 29, 2008).

42. Kang, "Cultural Conflicts Arise."

43. ABC Television, "Game, Sex, Match," *Nightline*, August, 26, 2002.

44. Dolch, "Foreign Relations."

45. Kang, "Cultural Conflicts Arise."

46. Crosset, *Outsiders in the Clubhouse*, 93–95.

47. Abigail Feder-Kane, "'A Radiant Smile from the Lovely Lady': Overdetermined Femininity in 'Ladies' Figure Skating," in *Reading Sport: Critical Essays on Power and Representation*, ed. Susan Birrell and Mary G. McDonald, 206–33 (Boston: Northeastern University Press, 2000), quotations at 208.

48. This is not to say that hyperfemininity and lesbianism are mutually exclusive, but elsewhere I discuss the significance of the LPGA to a particular lesbian consumer culture, symbolized by the lesbian spring break, "The Dinah." See Crosset, *Outsiders in the Clubhouse*, 127–29.

49. Crosset, *Outsiders in the Clubhouse*.

50. Toby Miller, *Sportsex* (Philadelphia: Temple University Press, 2002).

51. Nancy Armour, "Kim Yu-na Leaves Coach Brian Orser," *USA Today*, August 25, 2010, http://www.usatoday.com (accessed July 11, 2011).

52. "Kim Yu-na Most Valuable to Pyeongchang's Winning Bid: Survey," *Yonhap News*, July 11, 2011, http://english.yonhapnews.co.kr., accessed July 18, 2011.

53. Feder-Kane, "'A Radiant Smile.'"

PART FOUR   Strut, Move, and Shake

Upon visiting YouTube sites that have uploaded K-pop videos, one is bound to be surprised by the sheer number of hits some of the Korean girl idol groups have generated. As Stephen Epstein and James Turnbull report in this Part, Girls Generation's "Gee" and Wonder Girls' "Nobody" each have well surpassed 50 million views on YouTube.[1] Though this is a league or two below Psy's record-setting "Gangnam Style," which as of October 2013 had displayed a counter with more than 1.78 billion views, the heavy rotation of the K-pop girl group videos by fans or curious users place them in the category of global superstars such as Lady Gaga, Beyoncé, and AKB48, at least on YouTube. Most of the Korean pop acts feature the same hit songs in Korean, English, and Japanese, which would combine to more than 100 million views. Love it or hate it, the K-pop phenomenon has spread not only to Southeast Asia but also to Europe, the Middle East, and Central and South America. Though K-pop, beyond Psy, remains obscure to many Americans, this is largely because most of us who live outside the big metropolitan centers like New York and Los Angeles can be parochial.

Fantastic mass-driven numbers of these popular songs in user content sites such as YouTube, however, do not automatically translate into a text worthy of artistic merit or scholarly attention. If that were the case, then we would all be studying nothing but the latest sensations wearing skimpy clothes and singing bubble-gum pop or showing off stupid pet tricks. And yet. And yet. The viral popularity of these

K-pop videos, which also generate users' own appropriations and reappropriations on YouTube, begs the question as to why the user-generated contents websites have emerged as the ideal platform for these Korean musical acts to create dialogue with the outside world. K-pop acts, or more specifically female K-pop singers, as Epstein and Turnbull argue in this volume, are visual stars who epitomize the "stoking of male fantasy"[2] and just as seductive identification from young females. While the thrust of feline sexuality and its erotic appeal to viewers around the world are one of the obvious reasons behind the YouTube sensation created by K-pop, these four articles assembled in part 4 offer more than just ostensible explanations for the popularity of K-pop; it is the deft forms of *parody* Korean musicians have had to master throughout the twentieth century, marked by Japanese colonialism and U.S. military occupation, that have paved Korean music's path toward its hybrid characteristics, which register loud and clear on contemporary K-pop. One obviously needs to look no further than Psy's viral video on the affluent district known as Gangnam, south of the river Han in Seoul, in order to grasp the importance of satirical humor in the tradition of Korean popular culture.

Literary critic Richard Poirier's essay "Learning from the Beatles," written immediately after the release of *Sgt. Pepper's Lonely Hearts Club Band* in 1967, proclaims that the Beatles' popularity was dependent on not only the ballads and lyrics of Lennon and McCartney but also the band's theatricality. In what has become a pioneering essay on performance studies, Poirier writes, "One of the Beatles' most appealing qualities is, again, their tendency more to self-parody than to parody of others."[3] Throughout the Beatles' career, their fickleness can be found in their flamboyant costumes and immature gestures in both their films (both short and feature-length), which featured classic songs such as "I Am the Walrus," "Yellow Submarine," and "Lucy in the Sky with Diamonds." It wasn't just the enriching, nuanced, and allusive songs that made the Beatles famous but also their silliness and perhaps idiocy—enhanced by their drug use—that were so pleasurably sweet to the hundreds of millions of fans who tuned in to listen to them.

Parodies, especially when accompanied by humor, almost always necessitate a subversive maneuver that cuts across the boundary between egomania (colonizer) and servitude (colonized) because of their capability to inauthenticate or erase the original source and thereby the actual divide between subject and its mimicked object. Stupidity or naïveté is not exactly a quality that is appreciated in academia or in politics, but it is certainly well received on YouTube.[4] The capriciousness in musical acts so critical to parodies is also a popular element in K-pop music videos. For instance, Wonder Girls' "Tell Me" depicts one of its member reenacting a famous scene from *Wonder Woman* when she stops a speeding school bus with her bare hands (fig. Part 4.1). This video and many others such as Girls' Generation's "Gee"

Figure Part 4.1. Wonder Girls' So Hee parodies the famous bus-stopping scene based on an episode of the American television action drama *Wonder Woman*.

actually parody American high school locker rooms and football fields, which make America more real than the videos produced in America themselves. This amazing ability to mimic and parody the dominant cultural practices by a cavalcade of Korean acts is embedded in Korean history, which stretches much further than the history of YouTube and Psy's sensational one-hit wonder. As Min-Jung Son notes in her chapter, "Young Musical Love of the 1930s," in this volume, modern pop music was "an inspirational source to free themselves from the established Confucian traditional customs."

Differences, however, are glaring when comparing the self-parodies of the Beatles and the parodies of Korean pop acts. As Poirier points out, the Beatles were exceptional at self-parodies. At the height of their creative career, the Beatles, feeling no need to parody American superstars, would turn to the childlike realm of fantasy that included toys (trains and a yellow submarine), animals (blackbirds, ponies, and walruses), and circuses (trampolines, tricks, and hoops) in order to advance their music. With Koreans, it is a different story. Inflicted by their colonial and neocolonial experiences, Korean musical acts almost always turned to their dominant counterparts to find inspirations. The Korean pop stars, in other words, would constantly have to tune into hegemonic cultural references (Japanese and then later American) in order to produce styles and gestures that were self-deprecating and funny but nevertheless fell far short of satires that satiated sophisticated taste around the globe. For the Beatles, the need to fantasize about becoming, for instance, Elvis Presley was unnecessary; for Korean girl idols—past and present—their fantasies of becoming either the Supremes or Beyoncé were and still are prerequisites to their success. Also, needless to say, it might not even require an erudite, perceptive mind to point out that without global recognition of the iconographies of the Western, a penultimate American genre, Psy's horse-dance probably could not have reached the kind of audience that it did. These insufficiencies then, in my mind, signify the Korean singer's inability to strip his or her voice from the political predicament that represents a minor culture and naturalize what Jacques Lacan calls the *"objet petit a"* in which the voice, not unlike an infant gazing into the mirror who recognizes no form or necessary existence, becomes detached from the body to be a harrowing object of nomadic and homeless identity. This discordant and ironic representation is the reason that, even as girl groups and boy idols parade in the same military uniforms and engage in collective salutations, they could never reach the point of a fascist choreography or Nazi art that is, in Susan Sontag's words, "prurient and idealizing."[5]

What Kyu Hyun Kim has elsewhere argued as Korean *manhwa*'s "deodorization" of Japanese *manga* during the 1960s and the 1970s is just as relevant here in this section.[6] From Son's chapter on colonial-era music in the 1930s to Hyun-joon Shin and Pil Ho Kim's chapter on 1970s and 1980s "group sound rock" and Roald Maliangkay's "The Popularity of Individualism: The Seo Taiji Phenomenon in the 1990s," Korean musicians' haunting struggle with the burdensome colonial past and present is more than whispered. More than perhaps any other popular medium—such as popular fiction that must be translated into Korean vernacular language even when it is shamelessly copying passages from the latest foreign genre or films that must be reenacted by Korea's own actors and directors even when they are making copycat films—music can never truly be free from criticisms of plagiarism because it is technologically simple to replace or rip off any dominant culture's melodies, beats, and genres, and the temptation to copy the latest musical trends is irrepressible wherever popular music is produced. As discussed in the opening introduction on "indexicality,"[7] every song, to achieve mass popularity, has to be identified in the listener's ears as a hybrid set of several dominant musical tropes. For instance, even one of the most innovative songs by legendary guitarist-composer Shin Joong Hyun, the 1974 "Miin" (Beauty), inspired by *changt'aryŏng* (traditional beggar's song), Shin and Kim argue, has been blended with Jimi Hendrix's "'Voodoo Chile,' that together make up the song's famous opening guitar riff."[8] This hybrid of Western rock and traditional Korean music has set off a new surge of energy among many imitators like Jang Ki-ha and the Faces, while, in a satirical innovation, its now familiar guitar riff has become an emblematic soundtrack that punctuates many situations of satirical parodies in television sitcoms and movies. Hence, well before the nine members of Girls' Generation donned their bright-colored American-style cheerleading outfits and grabbed pompoms and football helmets that seem out of cultural context in Korea, where no high school engages in cheerleading or football activities, and well before Seo Taiji had popularized "the snowboard look," as Roald Maliangkay observes in this volume, and certainly before Psy picked out the Western props such as cowboy hats, boots, and whip for his music video,[9] Koreans had humbly to negotiate with the dominant melodies and icons from Japan and America.

The Beatles would not have been more than just a footnote in twentieth-century history if the only songs from their catalog had been giddy bubblegum tunes and children's songs and the group remembered mostly for their boyish looks and sea mammal suits that still inspire YouTube imitations. Their name is permanently printed on every wall of fame because of their mature melody, discordant unity, and melancholic poetry displayed in many more songs that rival even the work of some of the best classical composers Western civilization has ever known. Thus far, Korean popular music has yet to produce one single progression of chords that has created a ripple effect of global critical response without the aid of inane music videos and excessive use of hair gels. Whether this pattern will rapidly change in the twenty-first century is a question that plagues the hybrid Korean culture and the scholarship around it even as all of us try to gasp for a fresh breath of air after the euphoric sensation created by "Gangnam Style." Idiocy, as conservative presidents George W. Bush and Lee Myung-bak have taught us, may be hilarious and useful to sell bad policies or products, but it cannot innovate societies, let alone pop culture. KHK

NOTES

1. Stephen Epstein with James Turnbull, "Girls' Generation? Gender, (Dis)Empowerment, and K-pop," this volume.

2. Epstein with Turnbull, "Girls' Generation?," chapter 14 this volume.

3. Richard Poirier, "Learning from the Beatles," in *The Performing Self: Compositions and Decompositions in the Languages of Contemporary Life* (New York: Oxford University Press, 1971), 127.

4. After all, one of the most popular video ever to play on YouTube is "Charlie bit my finger—again!" which is a fifty-six-second clip of a toddler biting the finger of his three-year-old brother.

5. Susan Sontag, "Fascinating Fascism," in *Movies and Methods*, ed. Bill Nichols (Berkeley: University of California Press), 41.

6. Kyu Hyun Kim, "Fisticuffs, High Kicks, and Colonial Histories," chapter 2 this volume, 40.

7. Kyung Hyun Kim, "Introduction: Indexing Korean Popular Culture," 9.

8. Pil Ho Kim and Hyunjoon Shin, "Birth, Death, and the Resurrection of Group Sound Rock," chapter 12 this volume, 285.

9. Roald Maliangkay, "The Popularity of Individualism: The Seo Taiji Phenomenon in the 1990s," this volume.

Young Musical Love of the 1930s

As Korea adopted a Western modern lifestyle and social values during the colonial period, Koreans began to develop a unique form of urban art and culture. Among others, popular music, called *yuhaengga* (music in fashion), was a crucial cultural production in which young urban bourgeoisies were enthusiastically involved. Unlike rhythm-oriented Korean folk music, *yuhaengga* absorbed Western orchestration and melody-centered musical idioms. Young urbanites were fascinated with the newly imported sound, while other people interpreted it differently especially according to their gender and social status. Female performers tended to preserve traditional singing styles, such as heavy vocal inflections and nasal sounds, whereas male singers utilized operatic vocalization to emulate Western art singing performance practices. Though *yuhaengga* was a newly invented cultural production by modern Koreans, it also provided a cultural space in which Koreans re-articulated their traditional cultural identity while reflecting on modern values.

This chapter focuses on several key issues. First, I focus on how Koreans appropriated foreign musical idioms for their local demands. As Xiaomei Chen offers the term "anti-official Occidentalism" in her analysis of Chinese modern culture, Koreans also made use of modern culture to liberate their traditionally constrained selves.[1] Modern pop music was not only the most up-to-date urban culture but also an inspirational source for Koreans to free themselves from established Confucian traditional customs. This chapter will deal with the question of how this particular modern music became a national expression, where Korean aesthetics, emotions, and ethos were embodied through the analysis of several hit songs of those times, including Ko

Poksu's 1934 hit song *"T'ahyang"* (Living Away) and Lee Nanyŏng's 1935 hit *"Mokp'oŭi Nunmul"* (Tears of Mokp'o).

This chapter will also examine the business system of major recording companies in the 1930s that signed exclusive and hierarchical contracts with lyricists, composers, and star singers. Several interesting issues arise when examining the social backgrounds of those who were involved in this industry. Each recording company had a booking manager (*munye pujang*), who was usually a famous lyricist. Lyricists were mostly intellectuals who received higher education in the cities, while singers, particularly females, did not. The gender difference in terms of their social status will be examined in connection with their sonic characteristics and performance practices.

In doing so, this chapter will also problematize political debates over the national identity of *yuhaengga*, which asserted that it originated from Japanese *enka*. *Enka*, however, was not even coined as a term up until about 1973, when Nippon Columbia, a major *enka*-producing company, categorized what are now considered *enka* as *ryūkōka* (syn. *yuhaengga*).[2] Strictly speaking, *yuhaengga* might have been closely related to *ryūkōka*, not *enka*, a strategically invented national music genre. Furthermore, the relationship between *yuhaengga* and *ryūkōka* were not unilateral: Koga Masao (1904–1978), the father of *ryūkōka*, spent his early life in Korea and was deeply influenced by traditional Korean music. In addition, Korean *ch'angga* (choral song), an early version of *yuhaengga*, originated from the Japanese *shōka* (syn. *ch'angga*). In other words, each region produced its own locally negotiated music, expressing locals' words, emotions, ethos, and performance practices, even though they featured substantially similar sonic elements.

THE FIRST KOREAN POPULAR SONG

Pyŏlgŏn'gon (different world), a top best-selling monthly pop magazine of the modern period, was devoted to informal short stories, travel essays, novels, and poems.[3] An article titled *"Kŭkchang mandam"* (Theater critic) in the March 1927 issue, focusing on the atmosphere of a silent-movie theater, complained about the hackneyed repertories of the orchestra's performance during a ten-minute interlude, the outdated, wordy speeches of the film's narrator, *pyŏnsa* (talker), and the theater's fully packed ladies' seats.[4] The essay gives us a partial idea of what Korean urban life in the late 1920s looked like. Women began to enjoy popular culture in the public space, Western music became familiar cultural territory for urban moviegoers, and Western music and films were showcased together in the same cultural space.

The strong tie between modern song and film is revealed in several cases. For instance, "Nakhwayusu" (Fallen blossoms on running water) known as the first Korean popular song (1927), was the theme song for a film with the same title. "Nakhwayusu" (originally "Lakhwaryusu") was written by a famous film narrator, Kim Sŏjŏng, and sung by Lee Chŏngsuk, the younger sister of the film director, Lee Kuyŏng. The narrator, Kim, was also the screenwriter and kept his real name, Kim Yŏnghwan, in the film business. Presumably Kim, like several other musicians, preferred to use a stage name in the popular music industry. Well known as a children's singer, Lee performed this simple song to a waltz rhythm, her warm and bright timbre set in a quite traditional vocal style. She frequently adopted slurs between separate notes, especially leaping notes. Additionally she employed practices that had been widely praised in female performances of traditional Korean music, such as adding grace notes, utilizing a nasal voice, and vibrating the fifth note.[5]

The idiomatic word *nakhwayusu* refers to longing for lost love. Both fallen blossoms (*nakhwa*) and running water (*yusu*) are personified as heartbroken lovers who wish to stay together but at the same time also wish for the other's happiness. Their love cannot be fulfilled unless they forsake being blossoms or running water. Blossoms must fall out to encounter flowing water, whereas running water must stop flowing to stay with the blossoms. The film *Nakhwayusu* undoubtedly depicts the unfulfilled love between an artist and a female entertainer (*kisaeng*). Artists customarily belonged to a lower class of the traditional social stratification; however, they became one of the most eligible grooms as the urban bourgeois emerged as a leading power of the contemporary culture. *Kisaengs*, a crucial subgroup of chic ladies called *modern girls*, rapidly perceived this social transformation. In addition, stories of *kisaeng* weren't unfamiliar to songwriter Kim, a *kisaeng*'s son. The lyrics run:

> *Kangnamtari palgŏsŏ Nimŭi Nodŭn Kot*
> *Kurŭmsok e Kŭ ŭi Ŏlgol Kariwŏjŏnne*
> *Mulmangchop'in Ŏndŏge werohi sŏsŏ*
> *Murettŭn I hanpamŭl hollo saeune*

> The land under the bright moon, where my love used to play
> His face is hidden behind the cloud
> Standing lonely on the hill filled with full-blown forget-me-nots
> Spending a night alone, floating on the running water.

The skeletonic melody in C major is basically pentatonic (1–2–3–5–6), which is easily heard in Korean folk songs as well as in many other children's songs all over the world. However, its lyrics are obviously trendy, singing about a forbidden, yet prevalent relationship during the modernization period in Korea. Love was an absolutely alluring, especially to the young Kŏrean minds of the transitional era in which arranged marriage was still rigorously implemented. Korean youngsters articulated their frustration about the traditional marriage custom, singing the most modern song of the time.

In addition, *kisaeng*-related love stories, among others, were *à la mode* not only because people liked them, but also because *kisaengs* were major consumers of them. The fact that the unprecedented 1937 hit of a melodramatic play, or *shinp'a* (new wave),[6] was a tragic story of a *kisaeng* was not accidental. There was even a rumor that the most popular theater in the 1930s, Tongyang kŭkchang (oriental theater), could not survive without the regular visits of *kisaengs* and their companions, middle-class men.[7]

Kisaeng stories were also prevalent in the themes of musical theater called *akkŭk* (music theater) in the late 1940s, as *shinp'a* was recycled for their plots. The theater programs were composed of two or three plays and a variety show, and in the 1930s began to include a short comical musical theater piece. Thereafter, the comical musical theater pieces became an independent melodramatic genre that the majority of leading commercial theatrical companies developed to electrify audiences. Examples include the 1936 megahit *shinp'a* performance "*Sarange sokko tone 'ulgo*" (Deceived by love, crying over money) and another favorite piece in 1938, "*Hangguŭi ilya*" (A night in port). Both pieces were tragic stories about *kisaeng* who devoted their lives to unconditional yet unrequited love. Love, especially tragic love, truly became a popular subject shared among young people of the modern era.

ABSORPTION OF WESTERN SONGS

Musical change began with *ch'angga*, which distinguished itself from traditional Korean songs. Korean texts set to Euro-American melodies were mostly used as the curriculum of the modern education. Music historian Park Ch'anho has argued that it originated from the Japanese *shōka*, Japanese songs that had been used for musical education in elementary schools and junior high schools since the beginning of the Meiji Era.[8] As shown in the early Chinese school song collections such as *change ji* (*shōka* songbooks), popular composers in China and Korea were diligent in applying Japanese school songs domestically. Their musical settings implied a strong influence of missionary hymns and military bands, the two most powerful institutions to educate people during the modernization period.[9]

Set to different lyrics, the functions of *ch'angga* extended to the independence movement and simple diversion. In these forms, they were called *aeguk ch'angga* (patriotic choral songs) and *yuhaeng ch'angga* (popular version of *ch'angga*), respectively. Music critic Lee Yŏngmi noted that *ch'angga* branched into various forms as the Japanese colonial government's censorship came down hard on *aeguk ch'angga*. Exposed to various Western contemporary musical styles through Japan, such as tango, canzone, chanson, and jazz, Koreans subsequently turned their attention to musical elements other than lyrics. The word *jazz* was arbitrarily used for those different Western genres until it was differentiated from others under the heavy influence of the swing era since the late 1930s.

The triple meter of "*Nakhwayusu*" reflects a contemporary waltz beat that was widely loved as a ballroom dance in the early twentieth century, whereas some music critics believe that it was derived from a traditional Korean triple rhythm.[10] After independence from Japanese colonial rule, Korean traditional music scholars and nationalists took an essentialist view of music and analyzed what aspects determined the identity of Korean music. Once they began to search for the core elements of Korean music, the triple meter, among others, became recognized as a fundamentally Korean musical element. A somewhat similar interpretation can be applied to the singer's vocal practice of using heavy vibration and nasal voice. *Yuhaeng ch'angga* thus evolved to a localized style through an interplay between popular and traditional musical idioms.

Meanwhile, an intermediate genre for the public through the synthesis of high and lower traditional music was internally formed. Ethnomusicologist Peter Manuel points out that new cultural product initiated by urban bourgeoisie in the early modern era would be the "intermediate" that emulates high culture in a simpler way.[11] In this regard, Korea produced cultural products as *p'ansori* (a dramatic narrative form for solo voice and drum), Chinese literature written by members of the commoner class, and subjective representation in paintings.[12] *Chapka* (a mixture of different songs) is one of the most popular intermediate musical genres. It originated from *sijo* (poem song), a traditional three-verse song exclusively pertaining to the upper class. As modernization brought social mobility to the strictly hierarchical Korean society, *sijo* began to change to a longer and freer song called *sasŏl sijo*. *Chapka* adopted this longer poem/song as a crucial element to be blended.[13]

Chapka was well received by a wider audience and was included in the first commercially recorded Korean song repertories. The song was titled "*Chŏkpŏkka*" (Song of Red Cliffs) and was a dramatic song for the Battle of

Red Cliffs, also known as the Battle of Chibi, which occurred during the Three Kingdom Period at the end of the second century. Columbia released the record on March 19, 1907.[14] Besides recordings, the popularity of *chapka* is apparent by the fact that it was chosen as a competition piece for the special event, *Kisaeng Norae Kyŏngyŏn Taehoe* (three-day song contest of *kisaengs*), held on March 19, 1937.

Given this coexistence of Western music and intermediate songs generated from traditional music, the Korean public's musical taste during the modern era was threefold, consisting of *yesul kayo* (art popular song), *shinminyo* (new folksong), and *taejung kayo* (mass popular song), as analyzed by music scholar Ch'oe Ch'angho.[15] *Yesul kayo* was Western style semiclassic music that reflected the taste of a relatively higher class; *shinminyo* was a standardized version of traditional Korean folksongs called *minyo*; *taejung kayo* was a Koreanized style of Western popular music, generally named *yuhaengga* by record labels. As Korean public tastes grew more individualized, *yesul kayo* was categorized as art songs called *kagok* (also referring to classical art song); *shinminyo* became recognized, especially by the media, as a form of traditional folk song, no different from the original *minyo*; and *yuhaengga* became the mainstream of Korean popular music until the early 1970s.

In this circumstance, musicians in the earlier period never limited their works to one genre. For instance, Hong Nanp'a (1898–1941), known as "the Korean Schubert," worked for Victor Records during 1934–37 and wrote thirteen pieces of *yuhaengga* under his stage name, Na Sowun. He was to be remembered for *"Samakŭi Yŏhan"* (Sorrow of Desert) and *"Pangrangga"* (Song of the vagabond). Meanwhile, Mun Howŏl (1905–1949), the composer of the first known *shinminyo "Nodŭl Kangbyŏn"* (*Nodŭl* riverside), wrote diverse *yuhaenggas* such as *"Sewŏra Kajimara"* (Please stop, time) and *"Chongno Chujega"* (Theme song for *Chongno*). More interestingly, most singers performed at least two of the three categories. Former baritone Cha'e Kyuyŏp (1906–1949), who had been trained as a classical singer in Japan, reached the number one spot on the 1935 top popular male singers chart tabulated by *Maeil Sinbo*, a national newspaper. The top female popular singer on the same chart, Wang Subok (1917–2003), was a traditional *kisaeng* in Pyŏngyang. Their recordings obviously reflected their musical backgrounds, made up of more than two genres.

FORMATION OF *YUHAENGGA*

Even though almost all opinions remain disputable regarding which was the first genre of Korean popular music, it is apparent that in many other areas *t'ŭrot'ŭ* (trot) has undoubtedly been regarded as the oldest genre in the

Plate 1. Oyama/Ch'oe is attacked by a student of tai chi at a hot springs resort.
"Rɪɪɪɪɪɪɪɪᴘ!! ᴀɪʏᴀ!
Just as his opponent loses his balance, Ch'oe rams into his side, making use out
of the man's accelerated speed of fall. ᴜɢʜ!"

Plate 2. Cover of *New Woman*. Drawing of a student in the 1920s—her hair is Victorian style. Her *jogori* (traditional jacket) is markedly long and the skirt shorter. She is also wearing stockings and Western-style shoes.

Plate 3. "Sohn is the first to arrive! Sohn is first! He will break the tape in just fifty meters. Forty meters, thirty meters, twenty meters, ten meters! At last, he's broken the tape. Japan has won the marathon magnificently. Japan is magnificently the winner of the marathon." Courtesy of *Chosun Ilbo*.

Plate 4. World Cup: Red Devils on the Streets of Seoul. Courtesy of *Chosun Ilbo*.

Plate 5. Inexperienced in love, Yoona and other Girls' Generation members are rendered weak and foolish by their desire for a handsome male employee in "Gee."

Plate 6. In "Bad Girl, Good Girl," Miss-A lash out at hypocritical men who are initially attracted by their sexual appeal but ultimately judge and reject them for it.

Plate 7. Seung Woo Back: Installation view of *Blow Up* (2005–7) composed of 40 digital prints in 20-by-24-inch frames. Courtesy of the artist.

Plate 8. Seung Woo Back: Installation view of *Blow Up (detail)*. Courtesy of the artist.

Plate 9. At the sold-out sm Entertainment World Tour Concert at the Honda Center, Anaheim, Calif., on May 20, 2012.

Korean popular music scene. *T'ŭrot'ŭ* was called *yuhaengga* until it was differentiated from American pop genres introduced to Koreans much later, during the Korean War. Mass media has recently recoined it with the respectful title of *chŏnt'ong kayo* (traditional popular song), giving serious consideration to its deep-rooted influences on the formation of Korean pop culture. Tracing the early history of this specific genre will lead us to understand how Koreans appropriated foreign musical idioms for local demands, developing their own styles and repertories.

The following is the first verse of "*Hwangsŏng ŭi chŏk*" (Space of yellow castle), renamed later as "*Hwansŏng yett'ŏ*" (Ruins of old yellow castle). This song, known as the first hit *yuhaengga*, was written by one of the greatest songwriting duos, Wang P'yŏng (1908–1940, stage name of Lee Ŭngho) and Chŏn Surin (1907–1984); performed by an eighteen-year-old actress, Lee Aerisu (stage name of Lee Ŭmjŏn, 1910–2009) around 1928; and recorded by Polydor Records in 1932.

HWANGSŎNGŬI CHŎK
Hwangsŏng Yett'ŏ-e Pamidoeni Wŏlsaengman Koyohae
P'yehŏ-e Sŏrin Hoep'orŭl Marhayŏ Chunora
A—Kayŏpta Inae Momŭn Kŭ-Muŏt Ch'ajŭryŏgo
Kkŭdŏmnŭn Kkumŭi Kyŏrirŭl Hemeŏ Wannora

Space of Yellow Castle
As night came to the ruin of a yellow castle, moonlight gets serene.
I will tell you my sad memory about the ruin.
Ah—how pitiful I am!
I am wandering on this road of an endless dream,
looking for something.

This song has sold approximately fifty thousand copies in the 1930s, which would mean around five million copies today.[16] The songwriting duo's inspiration for this song was their personal experience with the old yellow castle, Manwŏldae; located in Kaesŏng, the former capital of the Koryŏ dynasty, it was built in 919 and demolished around 1362 owing to the invasion of Red Turban rebels from the north. Whether the duo wrote this song on the spot is questionable. However, they were truly trying to express people's sorrowful emotions of the colonial experience by reflecting on this forgotten ruin of an old yellow castle.

The fairy tale of Lee Aerisu has long been forgotten since her first and last big hit, "*Hwangsŏng ŭi chŏk*." She began her career as an actress and singer with a musical theater troupe at the age of nine. When she performed this song one night during the intermission of a play, her rendition was an unprecedented success and gave her the opportunity to sign with a major record label. Despite her fame, she left the entertainment business forever because her in-laws exhorted her not to continue performing professionally. Marriage and a career in entertainment, especially for women, did not make for a great combination in those times. Though people welcomed female entertainers onstage, they did not accept them proudly as members of their family.

Another anecdote regarding the female entertainer Kim Yŏnsil (1911–1997) shows the social stigma attached to female entertainers. Similar to the case of Lee Aerisu, Kim was also an actress and singer though she was better known as an actress. Kim naturally started her acting career, as her brother was a film narrator of Tansŏngsa, a popular movie theater in Seoul. However, she suffered from a failed marriage and sang film songs in a dark corner of the theater during the playing of domestic movies such as *Arirang*, *Nakhwayusu*, and *Sedongmu* (Three friends). The newspaper *Chungwoe Ilbo* commented that she would probably have become a *kisaeng* or someone's mistress if she hadn't been able to sing.[17]

Returning to lyrics, sorrow was the absolute favorite subject for early Korean popular songs. Another sorrowful text set to a slow waltz rhythm was *"T'ahyang"* (Leaving away) in 1934 by Ko Poksu (1911–1972), one of the most popular male singers in the 1930s, who debuted as the third-place winner of a Columbia Records singing contest. As reflected in his repertoir, which included songs such as *"Huip'aram"* (Whistle, 1934) and *"Samak gŭi han"* (Remorse of desert, 1935), his vocal timbre was generally characterized as a sigh. The lyrics run:

> *T'ahyangsari Myŏt'aedŏn'ga*
> *Sonkkoba Heŏboni*
> *Kohyang Ttŏnan Sibyŏnyŏne*
> *Ch'ŏngch'unman Nŭlgŏ*

> How many years have I lived away,
> I am counting them on my fingers.
> Ten years of living away from my hometown
> has taken my youth away.

Another memorable hit song of the 1930s was *"Mokp'oŭi Sŏrum"* (1935), also known as *"Mokp'oŭi Nunmul"* (Tears of *Mokp'o*) by Lee Nanyŏng (stage name of Lee Ongne, 1916–1965), a female superstar of Okeh Records. The song depicts a young bride's heartbreak from watching her husband leaving home for a better job (or presumably military service). Another hit of the time, "*Aesuŭi Soyagok*" (Serenade of Sorrow, 1937) by another superstar from Okeh Records, Nam Insu (stage name of Kang Munsu, 1921–1962), was also an elegy. He sang about a man's longing for his loved one. The lyrics run:

Wundago Yetsarangi Oriomanŭn
Nunmullo Tallaebonŭn Kusŭlp'ŭn I-pam
Koyohi Ch'angŭl Yŏlgo Pyŏlbichŭl Pomyŏn
Kŭnuga Pullyŏjuna Hwip'aramsori

Even though I know crying won't bring back love
Tears soothe my heart tonight
Looking upon the stars through the open window
I wonder who would whisper to me

Yuhaengga is, according to Park Ch'anho, mostly about sorrowful longing for one's loved ones and hometown.[18] Research conducted by Korean literature scholar Cho Kyuil supports Park's argument. Cho analyzed the lyrics of 437 songs produced between the 1930s and the early 1940s and categorized them according to their themes. The result shows that 148 songs were about love, especially heartbreak; 71 songs were about nostalgia; and 21 songs were about sadness, hopelessness, and agony.[19] Symbolizing colonized Korean modern individualities, singers provided people with an emotional exit from their cruel reality.

POLITICIZED MUSICAL IDENTITY

The essential differences of *yuhaengga* from previous songs such as "*Nakhwayusu*" include a specific modal structure called *yonanuki*: mi-fa-la-ti-do (in minor *yonanuki*) and do-re-mi-sol-la (in major *yonanuki*). This aspect of *yuhaengga* has been a disputable issue among nationalist elites and popular musicians since it has been considered a traditional Japanese musical idiom. Hwang Pyŏnggi, a well-known traditional Korean musician, brought up the delicate issue in a 1984 publication of a national newspaper, *Han'guk Ilbo*, questioning the origin of *yuhaengga*.[20] Hwang impugned the integrity of *yuhaengga*, saying that it was a Korean imitation of Japanese *enka*. According to him, musical elements adopted in *yuhaengga* such as modal structure, duple rhythm, and 7–5 syllabic stanza lyrics came from the Japanese tradition.

The debate regarding the nationality of *yuhaengga* initiated by Hwang was called *ppongtchak nonjaeng* (debate over *ppongtchak*, a derogatory term for *yuhaengga*) and frequently became an arguable issue. The assertion has currently been seconded by another musicologist, Shin Hyesŭng. Shin analyzed that most *yuhaenggas* released between 1920 and 1945 were composed on this pentatonic scale and their melody contained a trichord motive of descending notes, do-ti-la.[21]

Meanwhile, popular musicians, postcolonial scholars, and contextualists have pointed out that an essentialist viewpoint cannot fully explain the dynamic phenomenon of art and culture. Some of them, on the other hand, have even tried to connect the elements of *yuhaengga* to traditional Korean music. Musicologist Sŏ Wusŏk said that the 7–5 syllabic stanza of *yuhaengga* was drawn from *koryŏ kayo* (a prose form of *Koryŏ* period between 918 and 1392), and music columnist Kim Chip'yŏng argued that the duple rhythm of *yuhaengga* could be easily found in traditional Korean folksongs, such as farmers' songs from the southern regions. Both responses to Hwang's article were published in the same newspaper, *Han'guk Ilbo*, a few weeks later. Another interesting response in the journal *Ŭmakhak* was presented by musicologist Min Kyŏngch'an, as seen in the following passage:

> All the songs in the first [Korean] textbook were written in Japanese language. More than 90 percent of the songs were composed in major keys. As to the scale, more than 90 percent of the songs were made in *yonanuki* modes. Most of the songs were written in the Western art music forms, such as strophic forms.[22]

Min differentiated *yonanuki* from traditional Japanese modes such as *miyakobushi*, asserting that they are a Japanese interpretation of Western scales. Min even went further to say that Japanese colonial education was geared toward the Westernization of the traditional Far Eastern musical culture, and *yonanuki* was a byproduct of these efforts.

Japanese *enka*, a word derived from the speech song during the Meiji period, was coined around 1973, whereas Korean *yuhaengga* became labeled as *t'ŭrot'ŭ*, a word of English origin, around the 1980s when the debates broke out on whether to keep this genre or not. The national identity of *t'ŭrot'ŭ* was obviously a politically sensitive issue even after Korean independence. However, the musical production process during the modernization period was more complicated than it looked. Korean singers visited Tokyo and Osaka to record their songs with the Western-style Japanese orchestra because there was no recording studio in Korea, while Koga Masao moved to Inchŏn, Korea, in 1912 (at the age of seven) and lived mostly in Inchŏn and Seoul before returning to Japan in 1923. He studied at Sŏllin Commercial High School in Seoul.[23] According to a 2010 interview with JPNews, a Korean Internet newspaper that specializes in Japanese news, Takari Ichiro, the chairman of Enka Association, said that Koga was heavily influenced by traditional Korean music and that *enka* melodies he created originated from Korean tradition.[24]

Yuhaengga was by all means a cultural embodiment of the colonized Koreans' experience of losing their loved ones, hometowns, and country. The music appeased Koreans' deeply devastated hearts and souls. There is an anecdote that can prove this: the songwriting duo Wang Pyŏng and Chŏn Surin were even arrested because of the Japanese colonial government's concern about the huge impact of their songs on Koreans.

RECORDS

Six major recording companies, including Columbia, Victor, Polydor, Okeh, Chieron (often called *Sieron*), and Taihei (also known as *T'aipyŏng*), got ahead in the Korean music industry in the 1930s when *yuhaengga* was formed as the first modern song style for the public. Each company hired well-educated executive directors, called *munye pujang* (literature director), who took charge of writing lyrics, selecting new albums to be promoted, recruiting singers, booking events, and formulating strategies to lead musical trends of the time. As Manuel points out, newly emerged middle-class men were perfectly qualified for the position, since major listeners of the song style identified with young urban bourgeoisies who readily absorbed foreign popular culture.[25] The urban bourgeoisies were key agents who led the rise of the world popular music.

The *munye pujang* of the major records in 1933 were Lee Kise (1888–1945), An Ikcho (1903–1950), Wang Pyŏng (1908–1941), Lee Sŏgu (1899–1981), Kim Nŭngin (1911–1937), stage name of Sŭng Ŭngsun, and Min Hyosik. They worked for Victor, Columbia, Polydor, Chieron, Okeh, and Taihei Records, respectively. A close examination of their educational profiles might give us an idea of the modern urbanites in Seoul. Lee Kise as a forerunner of *shinp'a* theater was the editor and publisher of *Maeil Sinbo*, a major national newspaper. An Ikcho, the older brother of the composer of the Korean national anthem, An Ikt'ae, released his own classical record and later became a physician. Wang Pyŏng was already a nationwide famous singer-songwriter and actor for trendy theaters. Lee Sŏgu was an influential journalist and playwright. Kim Nŭngin, the songwriter of the 1933 hit *"Tahyangsari,"* was also a journalist. In the case of Min Hyosik, he was described as quite talented and passionate even though he was not involved in literature.[26]

Samch'ŏlli (the entire land of Korea), another pop magazine in the modern period, delivered an article titled *"Yuktae hoesa lekodŭ chŏn"* (A battle of six major record labels) on October 1, 1933. According to this column, each label released around 50 items each month, and easily sold 1,000–~2,000 copies of each record. The six record companies signed any entertainer who was good at singing and acting to an exclusive contract, as seen below. In the earlier years of Korean pop culture, singing, acting, and dancing were cross-fertilized, and often presented together on the same stage. For this reason, a number of singers in those times performed in plays or films, and vice versa.

Labels	Singers
Chieron	Kim Yŏnsil, Na Sŏn'gyo,[27] Kim Yŏnghwan, Ch'oe Hwanghwa, Namgung Sŏn[28]
Columbia	Ch'ae Kyup'il, Kim Sŏnch'o,[29] Im Hŏnik, Kim Sŏnyŏng
Okeh	Sin Pulch'ul,[30] Chŏn Ch'unu, Sin Ŭnbong,[31] Sŏ Sangsŏk, Paek Hwasŏng
Polydor	Wang Subok, Wang P'yŏng,[32] Kim Yonghwan,[33] Sin Ilsŏn[34]
Taihei	Lee Nanyŏng[35]
Victor	Lee Aerisu,[36] Kang Sŏgyŏn,[37] Ch'oe Namyong, Chŏn Ok,[38] Kang Hongsik

The multinational record industry came to Korea by way of Japanese agents to sell phonographs and records. The record companies were ambitious to open up new markets, establish agencies, and garner a catalogue of native records to attract attention from the local public.[39] The record companies did not only record the major East Asian musical traditions but also produced acculturated songs with European instruments for the primarily urban record buyers.[40] This explains how Korean *yuhaengga* was recorded.

Singers and their management crew still had to travel to Japan, mostly Tokyo and Osaka, to record their albums, since that was where recording studios were located. A column commented that extra expenditure for the recording also entailed the overheated competition among the labels.[41] They had to sell at least 2,000 copies of each item to make ends meet. The recording expenses were as follows:

1. Price of a record: 1–1.50 won[42]
2. Singer's guarantee per record: 40–100 won
3. Travel expense: 100–150 won
4. Each exclusive contract per year: 80–90 won
5. Songwriter's fee per piece: 10 won[43]

An article in the October/November 1933 issue of *Pyŏlgŏn'gŏn*, "*Lekodŭ ŭi yŏlgwangside*" (The craze over records), deals with major record companies' intense talent searches. Okeh and Taihei Records, for instance, secretly

Table 11.1. Top ten singers (Samch'ŏlli, November 1935)

RANK	MALE SINGERS	RANK	FEMALE SINGERS
1	Chae Kyuyŏp (Columbia)	1	Wang Subok (Polydor)
2	Kim Yonghwan (Polydor)	2	Sŏnwu Ilsŏn (Polydor)
3	Ko Poksu (Okeh)	3	Lee Nanyŏng (Okeh)
4	Kang Hongsik (Columbia)	4	Chŏn Ok (Polydor)
5	Choe Nanyong (Paihei)	5	Kim Pokhŭi (Victor)

visited the parents' home of a promising sixteen-year-old singer, Lee Nan-yŏng, to gain permission to sign her. As a result, Okeh received consent from Lee's mother and a legal note from Taihei to give her up. Lee eventually reached the number three spot in a poll by *Samch'ŏlli* in 1935 for the most popular female singer.

SEOULITES OF THE MODERNIZATION ERA

There were diverse social and economic determinants affecting the forma-tion of Korean urban middle class, such as Westernization and the rise of capitalism. The social and economic transformation that began in the seven-teenth century was accelerated, and the consequences of this were revealed in a census of Seoul. In the early Chosun era, the population of Seoul was approximately 200,000: 10 percent aristocrats, 15 percent freeman com-moners (called *sangmin*), 3.8 percent officers, and 50 percent slaves; whereas the population of Seoul in 1895 consisted of 34.2 percent aristocrats, 2.3 percent middle-class people (called *chungin*), and 55.5 percent freeman com-moners.[44] Slaves, the majority of the population in the early Chosun, dis-appeared, and 27 percent of all Seoulites were involved in commerce. The economically influential Seoulites grew to 400,000 in 1935, when the total population of Korea was estimated at around 21 million.[45]

An article from the November 1935 issue of *Samch'ŏlli*, "*Kŏriŭi Kkoek-korirŭl Naebonaen Chakkok Chaksajaŭi Kosimgi*" (Interviews with songwrit-ers who produced top ten singers, singing-birds on the street), reports that record sales reached 400,000, and that one-third of these sales were for songs in Korean. The top ten singers are listed in table 11.1.

Urban aesthetics of the modernization period, meanwhile, were devel-oped upon the basis of gender politics. The singers' sociocultural back-grounds were quite different and influenced their musical aesthetics. The class backgrounds of the top female singers, Wang Subok, Sŏnwu Ilsŏn, and Kim Pokhŭi, were *kisaeng*, while Lee Nanyŏng and Chŏn Ok were from musical theaters. They were still heavily exposed to traditional Korean art but were readily receptive to modern lifestyles. In the meantime, male singers were more aggressively engaged in Western modern performance practice, even emulating the vocal timbre of Western classical music: Ch'ae Kyuyŏp received higher musical education in Japan and Kang Hongsik was trained in opera troupes in Japan. The other male singers in the top ten roster also received higher education in urban areas. The aesthetics of male singers were consequently less Korean, which eventually gave female performance practice the opportunity to play a key role in expressing an essential attribute of this specific music genre, even today.

RADIO

Korean music lovers had another media source, the radio, to follow contemporary songs. The first Korean broadcasting system, Kyŏngsŏng Pangsong (Seoul Broadcasting; also known as JODK), a Japanese state-run broadcaster, was constructed in November 1926 and its first transmission took place on February 16, 1927. It provided programs in both Japanese and Korean with a ratio of three to one. Its listening ratings were, however, quite disappointing, since most Koreans could not understand Japanese. Only 7.81 percent of Koreans could understand Japanese in 1933, according to a Korean broadcasting statistical yearbook.[46]

Under the rule of Japan, this newly constructed form of commercial mass media struggled to satisfy the state and at the same time sustain itself. The system, once nicknamed *tanan pangsongguk* (broadcasting station in need), eventually founded a Korean-speaking channel in 1933. In this regard, historian Michael Robinson points out the Korean people's endeavor to build their own modern cultural identity:

> This study ["Broadcasting in Korea, 1924–1937"] focuses on the creation of Korean radio insofar as it illuminates the problems and difficulties inherent within the Japanese effort to "assimilate" their colony. The central problem for the Japanese was to create and spread the new medium of radio in order to use it as a tool for acculturating Koreans to Japanese values. Ultimately, they inadvertently created a space for Korean cultural construction that undermined their original intent.[47]

A radio set was found in every one hundred households in 1937, which implied that JODK had finally became a nationwide radio station in the late 1930s. Table 11.2 shows when radio became a popular form of mass media in Korea.[48]

An article in the national newspaper *Donga Ilbo* on November 2, 1933,

Table 11.2. Record of registered radio sets in Korea from 1926 until 1944

YEAR	KOREANS		JAPANESE IN KOREA	
	NUMBER OF REGISTERED RADIOS	PERCENTAGE OF RADIO USERS	NUMBER OF REGISTERED RADIOS	PERCENTAGE OF RADIO USERS
1926	336	0.01	1,481	1.27
1927	949	0.03	4,161	3.50
1928	1,353	0.04	7,102	5.79
1929	1,573	0.05	8,558	6.72
1930	1,448	0.04	9,410	7.45
1931	1,754	0.05	12,493	9.58
1932	2,738	0.07	17,641	13.58
1933	6,401	0.17	25,444	18.75
1934	9,584	0.25	30,660	21.68
1935	14,537	0.37	37,958	26.21
1936	22,777	0.56	49,349	32.28
1937	40,107	0.99	71,168	44.93
1938	48,966	1.19	78,433	49.38
1939	75,909	1.84	90,425	56.23
1940	116,935	2.76	109,694	66.28
1941	144,912	3.31	125,882	73.35
1942	149,653	3.26	126,047	70.28
1944	168,884	3.70	131,348	71.80

said that the radio introduced new songs to the public first, even before records, and led contemporary music trends. The hypothesis that approximately 1 percent of Koreans could change a national cultural trend is not easily imaginable from today's perspective; however, urban music lovers were definitely the front-runners in the trendy pop culture during the modernization age.

LIVE PERFORMANCE

Korean listeners had different opportunities to be exposed to pop culture as performers began to make their regional tours. The recording industry, in other words, developed creative ways to bring in revenue by organizing musical troupes known as *akkŭktan*[49] (musical theater troupes). As *akkŭk*, once a repertory of plays, became an independent show style promoted by

Table 11.3. First Performance of Major Musical Theater Troupes

DATES	MUSICAL THEATER TROUPES
December 19, 1938	*Okeh Grand Show*
February 2~4, 1941	*Victor Kagŭktan*
March 13~15, 1941	*Columbia Akkŭktan*

major record companies, its focal point shifted from drama to music. Okeh Records initiated its own troupe called Okeh Grand Show in 1938; Victor and Columbia subsequently formed Victor Kagŭktan (also called Pando Akkŭktan, literally Peninsular singing theater troupe) and Columbia Akkŭktan (also called Lamira Kagŭktan) in 1940.[50] Victor and Columbia, two leading recording companies in the 1920s, were now emulating later starter Okeh's strategy.

The places where they performed were mostly modern theaters contemporarily constructed in the mid-1930s. For instance, Pumin'gwan (also known as Keijo Public Hall) in Seoul served as one of the major venues for entertainment, most commonly modern performing arts while remaining the Seoul metropolitan council hall. The newly constructed three-story hall that accommodated an audience of 1,800 was chosen as the first stage by all of the three major *akkŭktans*, as shown in table 11.3.[51]

Among others, Okeh's robust devotion to the tour was fired up, as the founding chairman of Okeh, Lee Ch'ŏl, was demoted to *munye pujang*, chief manager. Lee, a risk-taker who had once led a revolutionary price cut for records a decade before, bringing the price per record to one won, now focused on live performance tours of musical theater troupes. Music theater troupes expanded their visits to neighboring countries to attract a wider range of consumers and even made a visit to the last prince of the Chosŏn Dynasty, Yŏngch'inwang (1897–1970), who had been exiled to Japan. The prince had a special fondness for the music theater troupes. The tours became more prosperous in the 1940s as the Asia-Pacific War progressed, beginning with the Sino-Japan War in December 1941. Record companies could not survive without Western investment. According to native music columnist Hwang Munp'yŏng, the numbers of musical theater troupes came to 59 in December 1945.[52]

Since their performances consisted of play and comedy, and not just music, musical theater troupes included performers such as dancers, actors/actresses, comedians, singers, and band members. Earlier forms of their shows were fundamentally similar to those in vaudeville, an American theatrical genre of variety entertainment that was widely popular in urban areas from the early 1880s until the early 1930s. Each performing crew was made up of diverse entertainers such as popular and classical musicians, dancers, comedians, and even acrobats.

Lee Chŏl made earlier efforts to develop his show in the late 1930s, transforming a plain recital into a systematic variety show. On December 19, 1938, he organized an ambitious show titled "Okeh Grand Show" (originally Oke Kŭrandŭ Shodan). The program included various types of music and short plays, performed by superstars such as Ko Poksu, Lee Nanyŏng, Nam Insu, and Kim Chŏnggu. Well-known musicians and writers such as Son Mogin, Park Sich'un, Mun Howŏl, and Kim Haesong (also known as singer Kim Songgyu) wrote and arranged their repertories of contemporary popular songs, instrumentals, and plays.

In an interview I conducted, former actress and singer Wŏn Hŭiok (b. 1933) remembered that each program of *akkŭk* was generally divided into two parts in the late 1940s, when she started her entertainment career as a member of one of the most preeminent troupes, Paekcho Kagŭktan.[53] The first part was a tragic musical theater piece; the second part was a variety show. She said that their mission for the performance was to make the audience cry by immersing them in drama during the first part, and then to make them laugh until they washed away their pain and sorrow during the second part. She further compared it to traditional Korean exorcism, *p'udak-kŏri*, a Korean shaman ceremony ending in agony. This two-part program— a sorrowful musical theater piece and a variety show—was, for whatever reasons, standardized until it disappeared in the early 1960s.

CONCLUDING REMARKS

There have been diverse popular songs expressing sorrowful love. However, this chapter has interrogated what made *yuhaengga*, just another sad ballad, different in the minds of modern Koreans in the 1930s. The newly imported yet accessible cultural product was apparently attractive to those who aspired to possess modern personas. This project might give us an answer to how modern Koreans, particularly modern urbanites, embodied their emotions and stories in popular music to prompt the audience to identify with them. For sure, pop music production is not simply based on music-makers' intentions but is also influenced by politico-economic circumstances. The melancholic melodies and themes of *yuhaengga* truly conveyed the Korean colonial experience.

In addition, *yuhaengga* production was deeply related to such variables as recording business, theatrical landscape, and gender politics during the era commonly known as colonial modernity. For instance, elite executive directors of recording companies, called *munye pujang*, played a key role in maneuvering popular music production. These well-educated urban middle-class men were in charge of almost every part of the producing process, including writing of the lyrics. However, performing practices were different because female singers were still heavily involved in the traditional Korean art and culture. Ironically, such gender politics made the popular music scene more diverse and appealing to a wider audience.

NOTES

1. Xiaomei Chen, *Occidentalism: A Theory of Counter-Discourse in Post-Mao China* (Lanham, Md.: Rowman and Littlefield, 2002), 123.
2. Christine Yano, *Tears of Longing: Nostalgia and the Nation in Japanese Popular Song* (Cambridge, Mass.: Harvard University Press, 2002), 210.
3. *Pyŏlgŏn'gŏn* was founded in Seoul in 1926 and ceased publication in March, 1934.
4. *"Kŭkchang Mandam"* (Theatre Critic), *Pyŏlgŏn'gŏn*, March 1927, 95.
5. Cho Sunja, interview in *Nanŭn Sesangŭl Noraehaetta* (I sang about world), Masan MBC, February 2, 2003.
6. In the early twentieth century, two types of modern drama were introduced to Korea: *shinp'a*, an imitation of Western sentimental melodrama, and *shingŭk*, influenced by Western realistic drama. Cho Oh-Kon, "Korea," in *The Cambridge Guide to Asian Theatre*, ed. James R. Brandon (Cambridge: Cambridge University Press, 1997), 184.
7. *"Yewŏn Chŏngbosil"* (Information Chamber of Entertainment), *Samch'olli*, March 1, 1941.
8. Park Ch'anho, *Han'guk Kayosa* (History of Korean popular song) (Seoul: Hyŏnamsa, 1992), 25.
9. Andrew F. Jones, *Yellow Music: Media Culture and Colonial Modernity in the Chinese Jazz Age* (Durham, NC: Duke University Press, 2001), 33.
10. Lee Yŏngmi, *Han'guk Taejung Kayosa* (History of Korean popular songs) (Seoul: Sigonsa, 1999), 60.
11. Peter Manuel, "Popular Music, II. World Popular Music," in *The Grove Dictionary of Music and Musicians*, 2nd ed. (New York: Macmillan, 2001).
12. Lew Young Ick, "Chapter 12. Dynastic Disarray and National Peril," in *Korea Old and New: A History* (Seoul: Ilchokak, 1990), 191.
13. Park Aekyŭng, *"Chosŏnhugi Sijowa Chapkaŭi Kyosŏpyangsanggwa Kŭ Yŏnhaengjŏk Kiban"* (The relation of Sijo-Chapka and its basis of performance in the late Chosŏn dynasty), *Han'gukŏmunhak* 41 (2003): 271.
14. Pae Yŏnhyŏng, *"K'olumbia Lekodŭŭi Han'gukŭmban Yŏn'gu"* (A study of Korean Columbia Records, 1), *Han'gukŭmbanhak* 5 (1995): 39.
15. Ch'oe Ch'angho, *Minjok Sunan'giŭi Taejung Kayosa* (Korean popular music during the colonial period) (Seoul: Ilwol Sŏgak, 2000), iii.
16. See *"8onyŏn'gan Kwagyŏ Sumgigo San Chŏnsŏrŭi Yŏgasu"* (A legendary female singer without revealing her past as a singer for 80 years), *Han'guk Ilbo*, October 28, 2008. Also found at Wikipedia, *"Hwangsŏng Yettŏ,"* accessed March 13, 2011, http://

ko.wikipedia.org/wiki/%ED%99%A9%EC%84%B1_%EC%98%9B%ED%84
%B0.

17. *"Saenghwallo Pon Kŭdŭrŭi Naemak"* (Private life of them—actresses, revue girls, dancers, and so forth), *Chungwoe ilbo*, November 14, 1929.

18. Park, *Han'guk Kayosa*, 65.

19. Cho Kyuil, *"1930nyŏndae Yuhaengga Kasa Koch'al"* (A study of popular music lyrics of the 1930s), *Inmun'gwahak* (Journal of the Humanities) 31 (2000): 271.

20. Hwang Pyŏnggi addressed this issue in detail on November 6, 1984, in the newspaper *Han'guk Ilbo* (Seoul); Kim Chi-P'yŏng and Sŏ Wusŏk responded on November 22; Hwang Pyŏnggi and music critic Park Yonggu re-responded on November 29; Kim Chip'yŏng and pop musician Park Ch'unsŏk on December 6; four subscribers responded on December 20; two social scientists finalized the debates on December 27.

21. Shin Hyesŭng, *"1945nyŏn Ijŏn T'ŭrot'ŭ Kayoŭi Sŏnyulyuhyŏng"* (The melody types of Korean popular songs before 1945), *Inmun'gwahak* (Journal of the Humanities) 31 (2001): 299.

22. Min Kyŏngch'an, *"Sŏyangŭmakŭi Suyonggwa Ŭmakkyoyuk"* (Consumption and Education of the Western Music), *Ŭmakhak* 9 (2002): 17.

23. *"Sŏninsang ch'ulsin Ilchakkokka Kohassi Kamgaeŏrin Naehan"* (Sŏninsang graduate Japanese composer Koga visiting Korea), *Kyŏnghyang Sinmun*, April 18, 1969, 3. Also see Koga Masao Music Museum, accessed April 25, 2011, http://www.koga .or.jp/about/index.html.

24. *"Chigŭm Ilbone P'iryohan gŏn Toni Anin Chŏng"* (What Japanese people now need is not money but sympathy), jpNews, December 30, 2010. http://www.jpnews.kr /sub_read.html?uid=8082.

25. Manuel, "Popular Music, II," 157–58.

26. *"Yuktae Hoesa Lekodŭ Chŏn"* (A battle of six major record labels), *Samch'ŏlli*, October 1, 1933.

27. Na Sŏn'gyo was trained at Takarazuka in Japan and became a founder of a girls' akkŭktan, *Nangnangjwa*.

28. Kang Hongsik appeared in a couple of 1920s films and played in Ch'wisŏngjwa and Chosŏn Yŏn'gŭksa.

29. Kim Sŏnch'o played in Shinmudae and Ch'ŏngch'unchwa, leading commercial theater troupes.

30. Sin Pulch'ul was a famous for his legendary satirical comedy.

31. Sin Ŭnbong was a heroine with Chosŏn Yŏn'gŭksa and Yŏn'gŭksijang.

32. Wang P'yŏng played in Chosŏn Yŏn'gŭksa and appeared in several films.

33. Kim Yonghwan started his career in a local theater troupe, Tongbang Yesuldan.

34. Sin Ilsŏn was famous for her first film, *Arirang* (1926).

35. Lee Nanyŏng played in Teyang Kŭkchang, a commercial theater company.

36. Lee Aerisu stated her career as an actress in such theater companies as Sin'gŭkchwa, Minjung Kŭktan, Ch'wisŏngjwa, Chosŏn Yŏn'gŭksa, and Yŏn'gŭksijang.

37. Kang Sŏgyŏn, with her older sister, was an actress in T'oyŏrhoe, a leading troupe in the modern realism theater.

38. Chŏn Ok was an actress with Na Yunkyu Productions, a leading film production

company in the 1920s, and played for T'oyŏrhoe. She became the founder of *Baek-cho Kagŭktan*, a leading *akkŭktan* (song theater troupes) in the 1940s to 1950s.

39. Frederick William Gaisberg, *The Music Goes Round* (New York: Macmillan, 1942), 48.

40. Pekka Gronow, "The Record Industry Comes to the Orient," *Ethnomusicology* 25 (1981): 274.

41. *"Yuktae Hoesa Lekodŭ Chŏn,"* October 1, 1933.

42. During the Japanese colonial period, 1 won was worth 1 yen. U.S. dollar/yen was approx. 3.50/1 in the mid 1930s, according to one measuring system, accessed March 28, 2011, http://www.measuringworth.com/datasets/exchangeglobal/result .php?year_source=1930&year_result=1940&countryE%5B%5D=Japan.

43. Donga Ilbo, *"Naŭi Kyoyurok"* (My personal memoir), July 18, 1981.

44. Chŏng Chaejŏng, *"Kŭndaeŭi Sŏulsariwa Taejungmunhwa"* (Seoul life and popular culture in the modern period) in *Popular Art of the Modern Age*, ed. Kwŏn O-Do (Seoul: Seoul Museum of History, 2003), 144.

45. Seoul City, "Seoul Population Census," accessed March 28, 2011, http://www.seoul .go.kr/v2007/publicinfo/statistics/data/4_04_05.html.

46. Korean Broadcasters Association, *Han'guk Pangsong 70nyŏnsa* (Seventy-Year History of Korean Broadcasting) (Seoul: Korean Broadcasters Association, 1997), 95.

47. Michael Robinson, "Broadcasting in Korea, 1924–1937: Colonial Modernity and Cultural Hegemony," in *Japan's Competing Modernities*, ed. Sharon A. Minichiello (Honolulu: University of Hawai'i Press, 1998), 360.

48. Kim Yŏnghui, *"Ilchaesidae Ladioŭi Ch'ulhyŏngwa Ch'ŏngch'uija"* (Radio and radio listeners during the Japanese colony), *Han'gukŏnronhakbo* 46, no. 2 (2002): 165.

49. "Ka" of *kagŭktan* (song theater troupes) refers to song, while "ak" of *akkŭktan* refers to music, strictly speaking. However, both terms arbitrarily signified various kinds of musical theaters, from a European-style opera to a blend of all. Victor and Columbia records also whimsically applied these terms to their posters.

50. *Lamira* implies *la* and *mi* of Solmization. "La" and "mi" have been regarded as the key notes in traditional Korean folk music.

51. Kim Hoyŏn, *"Han'guk kŭndae Akkŭk Yŏn'gu"* (A study of modern Korean musical theater), unpublished dissertation at Dankook University, 2003, 61–75.

52. Hwang Munp'yŏng, *"Episodŭro Pon Han'guk Kayosa"* (Reading Korean popular song history through episodes), *Ŭmaktonga* 14 (1985): 263.

53. Wŏn Hŭiok, interview by Min-Jung Son, June 30, 2010.

Birth, Death, and Resurrection of Group Sound Rock

INTRO: "THE LADY IN THE RAIN"

The song begins with a guitar playing a pentatonic melody line. Another guitar follows with a slight pitch-bend, a brand-new trick at the time of recording. Then the lead singer steps in, crooning mellifluously as the background vocals repeat after him at each measure. During the bridge, the lead guitar slides into a surf-rock–inspired solo to accentuate the gorgeous soundscape of *"Pisogŭi Yŏin"* (The Lady in the Rain). The polished form belies the fact that it was the one of the very first rock 'n' roll songs written and recorded in Korean. The major credit is due to composer and guitarist Shin Joong Hyun (Sin Chung-hyŏn), better known as "Jacky" or "Hicky" Shin among the American GIs garrisoned in South Korea (henceforth Korea) during the 1950s and 1960s.

Born in 1938, Shin belongs to the generation of Koreans hard-bitten by the Korean War at a young age. His generation was also the first to experience American popular culture up close, mainly through the broadcasts of American Forces Korea Network (AFKN). "The AFKN quenched my thirst for music," Shin has recalled. "I was instantly fascinated by jazz and rock 'n' roll, which brought me to my true passion and inner self."[1] Before long, he found himself performing in front of American servicemen the music he had learned from the AFKN. Like many of his contemporaries, Shin cut his teeth as a professional musician on the stages of the U.S. military clubs.

In 1964, when Shin's newly minted band, the Add Four (fig. 12.1), came out with *"Pisogŭi Yŏin,"* the entertainment business for the U.S. military was at the height of its boom. However, the escalation of the Vietnam War and the subsequent shift of American military focus away from Korea portended a downhill road ahead. As if anticipating the eventual passing of the good

Figure 12.1. Shin Joong Hyun *(far left)* and the other members of Add Four. Courtesy of Shin Joong Hyun.

times, *"Pisogŭi Yŏin"* is steeped in a somewhat premature nostalgia. "The unforgettable lady in the rain," whose exotic "yellow raincoat" and familiar "dark eyes" make an interesting contrast, creates a visual metaphor of Korean musician yearning for "foreign" music.

The young Shin Joong Hyun was the perfect poster child for the American cultural onslaught on not only Korea but the entire U.S. zone of influence in East Asia as well. Immediately after the end of the Pacific War, musicians in American-occupied Japan and Korea learned to make their living playing the music of the occupiers. By nurturing numerous musicians who would later become major players in the domestic music industry, the U.S. military club scene left an indelible mark on Korean music culture.

Most notably, Shin Joong Hyun and other like-minded musicians shared with the Korean youth the style and ethos of the 1960s psychedelic rock they had assimilated from the scene. Thus the U.S. military base, a powerful symbol of American hegemony, turned into an improbable incubator of a fledgling Korean counterculture movement. Despite the accusation of "alien culture" from the conservative elite, this counterculture movement boldly staked a claim in nationalism, challenging the authorities on their own ideological turf. Since then, Korean rock has been on an odyssey where the global encounters the local and the national, power blends with resistance, and mimesis turns into creation. In particular, the Group Sound era we focus on in this chapter shows not only the deep historical roots but also the complex geographic routes Korean rock came from.

THE CRADLE OF ROCK: U.S. MILITARY CAMP SHOWS

The main source of American popular music in the years before the Korean War was the clubs of the U.S. Army Twenty-Fourth Division, which had entered the country soon after the Japanese surrender in August 1945. Business really took off after the Korean War as the Twenty-fourth Army Division expanded to the Eighth Army Corps. Although the United Service Organizations (USO) camp show tours brought in some of the best American entertainers, such as Nat King Cole and Elvis Presley, they could not satisfy the huge demand coming from the more than 150 camps and bases all around the country. The U.S. Army thus hired Korean musicians to fill the void, and amid the destitution of postwar Korea many hungry musicians flocked to bases for the precious jobs.

The growth of camp show entertainment increased professionalism in business. The hiring procedure became formalized, with the U.S. military hiring show troupes organized and managed by entertainment agencies. Usually it began with a pre-audition at an agency. If musicians or bands were deemed worthy, they were allowed to join the show troupe, which then went on to the real audition in front of the U.S. military authorities, who would make the final decision as to whether the troupe was qualified. According to various witness accounts, music and entertainment industry experts dispatched by the Pentagon presided over the auditions. Each troupe that passed the audition was also given a grade of AA, A, B, or C, and assigned to either the high-end floor show or the mid-level package show

The camp show act was not a simple music concert. It was also an entertainment variety show performed by the entire show troupe, or *ssyodan* in Korean. A typical *ssyodan* consisted of a big band orchestra, singers, comedians, dancers, and other performers. The band was the centerpiece of the *ssyodan*, as the title of the show on the bill was usually accompanied by the bandmaster's name. The *ssyodan* bands catered to the diverse musical tastes of the American military personnel—"the Beatles or the Beach Boys for the white GIS, country music for the old white NCOS, and soul music of the Temptations or James Brown at the black clubs."[2] Consequently musical versatility was crucial to the survival of a band playing U.S. military clubs. Rather than sticking to one particular style or genre, most musicians tried to master as many as they could.

The level of competition among the musicians to enter and stay on the camp show circuit was very high. This competitive pressure intensified

Figure 12.2. Percussionist Kim Tae-hwan on the camp show stage with *ssyodan* dancers. Courtesy of Kim Tae-hwan.

musical training in general and increased cramming to learn the latest hits on the American pop chart in particular. Having gone through rigorous formal training in all kinds of Western musical genres, floor show musicians like Shin Joong Hyun "had to be able to play any sheet music at first glance, no matter how difficult it was, to stay on the job."[3] Without sheet music and formal training available, the only way for the package show musicians to hone their skills was to record the AFKN broadcast on tape, transcribe each instrumental part, and then practice day and night in the management company warehouse. In this way, the U.S. military camp shows and clubs became a training ground for the Korean musicians playing American pop. By the late 1950s, music from the U.S. camp show scene began spreading out and finding its way to various entertainment venues for Korean audiences. First, Tin Pan Alley–style pop singers crooned their way to stardom, and more beat-oriented music, including rock 'n' roll, soon followed.

The typical *ssyodan* band at the floor show was made up of the four rhythms—guitar, bass, drums, and piano—joined by string and brass sections, similar to the American big band, only slightly smaller in size. The package show was put on by a six- or seven-piece band of four rhythms plus one or two horns. Following the jazz tradition, musicians called it the "combo band." The standard Korean combo band was still purely instrumental. Vocals were performed by a singer or singers from outside the band. The typical rock-band formation à la the Beatles or the Rolling Stones came later and was at first called the "vocal group" (*pok'ŏl kŭrup*), since the band took care of vocal parts without the aid of a guest singer.

ROCK MUSIC AND "FATHERLAND MODERNIZATION"

Two distinguished vocal groups made an early transition to the rock band format. One was the Add Four, led by Shin Joong Hyun, and the other was the Key Boys, featuring guitarist Kim Hong-t'ak and then-drummer Yun Hang-gi, who later became one of the premier singers of his generation. The crucial moment of Korean rock came along when the Add Four made their debut with the album *Pisogŭi Yŏin*.[4] Coincidentally the Key Boys' debut record was released about the same time, making 1964 Year One of Korean rock. As true pioneers, both bands took a daring first step into the uncharted territory of the domestic market. Somewhat predictably, their ambitious recording projects turned out to be a commercial bust. As Shin Joong Hyun recalls, record stores "were returning the unsold copies en masse no later than a week after release."[5] The groups' solid career at the U.S. military camp shows did not do much to win Korean audiences. Although the music style was still a novelty among the Korean masses, the use of the traditional pentatonic minor scale must have made *"Pisogŭi Yŏin"* sound less alien to them. In fact, it was only a few years later that this song was made popular by other musicians.

When the two seminal vocal groups began to play for the Korean masses, they had only a small niche that would be receptive to their music. Time was on their side, however, as Korean society at large was opening up to American popular culture during the state-led modernization period of the 1960s and 1970s. Since General Park Chung-Hee's military coup in 1961, the state's high-speed industrialization policy, Fatherland Modernization (*Choguk Kŭndaehwa*), had entailed rapid urbanization and harsh oppression of dissenting voices. The major socioeconomic impact of modernization on the popular music culture was the mass consumption of Western-style pop music among ordinary Koreans. Until the mid-1960s, record players were rarely seen in Korean households, save in a handful of those who were relatively well-off. Foreign pop records were hard to come by even if one could afford them. Prior to the economic takeoff of the 1960s, only two major sources of Western pop were available to the few people curious enough to reach for them. One was the AFKN that the young Shin Joong Hyun loved so much. The other was *ŭmak kamsangsil*, a kind of music café in downtown

Seoul that attracted aficionados of Western music. Not only did these cafés have such cool, exotic names as C'est Si Bon, Die Schöne, and the Renaissance; they were also equipped with high-fidelity audio systems and a lot of Western classical and pop records. They also featured live disk jockeys, many of whom later took important gatekeeper positions in the music and entertainment industries.

The economically ascending 1960s saw new sources of Western culture channeled to a wider mass audience. Between 1961 and 1964 three new private broadcasting companies joined the AFKN and the state-controlled Korean Broadcasting System (KBS). Competition among the broadcasters created more consumer choices, a greater demand for talent, and a shift of focus from live performances to recorded music. Meanwhile, the introduction of twelve-inch vinyl LPs in 1962 gave Korean recording companies an opportunity to break the mold of the cottage industry and tap into the emerging mass market.

THE BIRTH OF GROUP SOUND ROCK

More and more Korean vocal groups came into being in the wake of the Add Four and the Key Boys. According to a reportage article, approximately thirty well-known bands and at least fifty or more lesser-known ones were active by 1969.[6] Their renewed repertoire was filled with songs by the Beatles and the Rolling Stones, in addition to those by the Ventures and the Beach Boys. By the late 1960s, the U.S. military club scene began to sag, and the vocal groups playing there had to find a way to make it into the domestic market. This proved to be an uphill battle. While it was relatively easy for a *ssyodan* big band to transform itself into a broadcast orchestra, neither major music venues or broadcasters welcomed the vocal groups with open arms. There was little room for a vocal group to make it on its own.

What these bands needed was the proverbial new bottle for new wine. They discovered it in small and midsized venues located in downtown Seoul. Music cafés (*ŭmak kamsangsil*) had been setting up small stages for Sunday live shows since the early 1960s. Soon thereafter, newer and bigger venues, called live-music salons (*saengŭmak ssarong*), mushroomed in the same area, hosting live shows daily. Now some bands could do double shifts playing at salons in Myŏngdong by day and GI clubs in It'aewŏn by night.[7] While rock was steadily gaining its ground as an underground club culture, Shin Joong Hyun was preparing for another shot at the mainstream audience from a different angle.

In the waning months of 1969, a fresh-faced female duo stunned the nation by winning the prestigious Annual King of Singers award from one

Figure 12.3. The Questions at the Go Go Gala Party. *From left to right*: Pak In-su *(vocal)*, Shin Joong Hyun *(guitar)*, and Kim Tae-hwan *(drums)*. Courtesy of Shin Joong Hyun.

of the major television networks. The Pearl Sisters, Pae In-suk and In-sun, were the brainchild of Shin Joong Hyun, who took on the dual role of composer and music director. Having been active barely a year, the Pearl Sisters quickly climbed to the top by making the most of their sex appeal. These two charming real-life sisters in their early twenties shook their bodies in such a way that shattered the Confucian ideal image of "wise mother, good wife." Beside the Pearl Sisters, Shin continued to score hit after hit with other charismatic female singers, such as Kim Ch'u-ja, Kim Chŏng-mi, and Yi Chŏng-hwa.

However, Shin Joong Hyun was not entirely satisfied with his newfound fame, partly because his desire for rock music remained strong despite the embittered Add Four record. Since then he had gone through at least three different bands—the Donkeys, the Questions, and the Men—and too many lineup changes to count. By this time, he had immersed himself in Anglo-American psychedelic rock. With the bands, he routinely covered Jimi Hendrix and other such acts on stage and recorded his own psychedelic compositions in the studio. Figure 12.3 is a rare photograph of Shin Joong Hyun's psychedelic rock performance at the legendary Seoul Civic Center circa 1970.

With the new sound and repertoire came a new term for bands like Shin's. What had been called vocal groups turned into "group sounds" (GS) as the electric guitar became as important as the human voice in their music.[8] The

Korean group sound era began with music festivals and contests that show-cased both old U.S. camp show veterans and up-and-coming bands. One of the most prominent festivals was the annual Playboy Cup Vocal Group Contest. The grand prize of the 1970 contest went to Kim Hong-t'ak's He Six, the band he formed after splitting with the Key Boys. As a male vocal group, He Six was best known for the luscious vocal harmonies in the *Ch'owŏn* (Prairie) series, mid- or slow-tempo ballads about romance on a prairie. As a GS, on the other hand, He Six was playing psychedelic rock with an audacity and intensity second only to Shin Joong Hyun's. If Shin Joong Hyun's sound evokes Jimi Hendrix, Kim Hong-t'ak's nimble and sophisticated guitar work bears resemblance to Carlos Santana's. Another rising star was Cho Yong Pil (Cho Yong-p'il) who won the best vocalist award at the last Playboy Cup in 1971. Nobody at the time, however, would have anticipated Cho's megastardom a decade later.

The same year the Playboy Cup folded, an outdoor concert festival took place in a riverside resort area near Seoul. During a three-day period the Ch'ŏngp'yŏng Festival drew crowds of thousands, whose communal experiences were similar to Woodstock and the Summer of Love in the U.S. The global youth counterculture had arrived in Korea: long hair, bell-bottoms, recreational drug use, and antiauthority attitudes. GS rock, along with the fledgling modern folk movement, provided a soundtrack for this new cultural drama. The liberal proponents called it the youth culture (*ch'ŏngnyŏn munhwa*), whereas the conservative opponents had much more sinister names for it.

CRACKDOWN ON "DECADENT CULTURE" AND THE GO-GO MIDNIGHT REVOLT

Once the authoritarian Park Chung-Hee regime decided to take action against the new culture it deemed "vulgar" (*chŏsok*) and "decadent" (*t'oep'ye*), the Korean Summer of Love was all but done for. In August 1970, the police began stopping young people on the street for a snap inspection known as *changbal tansok* (long-hair crackdown). Men got a free haircut on the spot if their hair was deemed too long. Women's skirts had to be long enough to cover their knees. The streets of Seoul turned into a theater of the absurd, where police officers, armed with measuring sticks, were imposing "the discipline of the body" on the hapless passersby.

Many GS musicians reluctantly had their long hair trimmed in order to avoid trouble, but the situation was bound to get uglier as the political climate continued to worsen. After barely beating his archrival Kim Dae Jung in the 1971 presidential election, Park was determined to tighten his grip on the populace and secure dictatorial power. In October 1972, Park declared martial law, dismissed the National Assembly, crushed the opposition, rounded up dissidents, and rewrote the constitution to make himself a de facto permanent president. So began the era of hard authoritarianism known as Yushin. In the meantime, the crackdown expanded its scope from fashion and hairstyle to "decadent culture" in general (*t'oep'ye munhwa tansok*). Any deviation from the "wholesome national culture" was not tolerated. The GS musicians feared that they had a bull's-eye on their backs since their music was widely perceived as the centerpiece of the youth culture. Sadly, they were not mistaken.

The crackdown put the existing apparatus of control and censorship into a high gear. Concerts and festivals involving GS were cancelled owing to police harassment. By 1972, loud and noisy rock shows had all but disappeared from the downtown live music salons where He Six had been king until just a year earlier. However, the group sounds were not so neatly purged; if anything, they were becoming "sleazier," retreating from daytime leisure to the hedonistic nightlife of go-go dancing.

The go-go club (*kogojang*) was a nightclub that replaced live music salons as the main venue for GS. The biggest difference between the salon and the go-go club was dance. People went to the club to dance, not simply listen to the music. The first batch of go-go clubs was run as a part of hotel operations in downtown Seoul. Soon ordinary nightclubs jumped on the bandwagon by switching to go-go clubs. The go-go craze sprawled out from downtown Seoul to the suburban centers and other major cities. GS flourished on the stage. Shin Joong Hyun showcased his new band, the Men; Yun Hang-gi, one of the original Key Boys, made a comeback with the Key Brothers. Tommy Shim (*Sim Hyŏng-sŏp*) came out of the U.S. military clubs and formed the legendary hard rock band Phoenix. Young Sound, Tempest, Pioneers, the Last Chance, the Devils, the Dragons, and many more were also big names on the go-go scene.

Even though the go-go scene helped GS musicians keep on performing and earning their living, its contribution to the creative aesthetics of Korean rock was limited at best. Except for the famous few who could afford to squeeze in their original work or experiment with new tunes from Anglo-American rock, the majority of the bands stuck to the standard go-go fare. The crowd pleaser was always something simple, familiar, and danceable. Over and over again through the night, such all-time go-go favorites as Creedence Clearwater Revival's "Proud Mary" and Santana's "Evil Ways" were played at a plain eight-beat rhythm known as the go-go beat. The lack of originality or creativity in music was beside the point, for the go-go culture was, first and foremost, about dance. All-night go-go parties were bonding rituals among young dance lovers. They were also an act of defiance, breaking the midnight curfew that had symbolized the culture of fear and restriction for several decades.[9] In the aftermath of the aborted Korean Summer of Love, the midnight revolt at the go-go club created another kind of communal experience among regular participants. As Tommy Shim recalls:

> Clubs were popular hangouts for young hipster boys and girls in Seoul. Every morning [at 4 A.M.], when the curfew was over and the club closed, the band members and the partygoers went out together to grab a bite or have a cup of coffee. We were like a family. It'aewŏn at that time was a paradise for hippies. I don't know what it's like now, but there used to be small clubs on both hillsides playing live music every night, competing with one another.[10]

Therefore, "decadence" not only survived; it actually thrived under the radar of the authorities, who appeared hell-bent on clamping it down. In retrospect, the whole decadent culture propaganda created a self-fulfilling prophecy; it was, above all, the crackdown and the negative media campaign that drove the youth culture out of the broad daylight into the dark of the night, where it grew even more audacious in undermining traditional sexual mores and work ethic. In that sense, the go-go revolt was a warning sign that the heavy-handed cultural oppression would eventually backfire.

THE RISE AND FALL OF THE FIRST WAVE OF GROUP SOUND ROCK

The go-go craze was greeted with sensationalist media coverage, which framed the phenomenon as something of a moral panic.[11] There was also an air of condescension, especially from the conservative elite commentators who accused the young people of blindly following Western lowbrow culture. A neutral visitor to a go-go club, after watching the GS onstage mindlessly repeating "Proud Mary" or "Beautiful Sunday" might concede that these critics had a point. The originality deficit was not confined to the go-go scene; it had been a chronic problem since the U.S. military camp show years.

What the detractors either did not see or chose to ignore was the intense efforts of the leading GS to find their own voice and achieve authenticity, the elusive goal of rock music ideology. Needless to say, the GS musicians had a desire for originality and creative expression just as any other self-respecting musicians did. Besides, they were also keenly aware that as long as they simply covered Anglo-American rock, they would win little respect from avid fans of this genre who found Korean GS rock inauthentic and derivative.

It was about time for these GS musicians to shoot for mainstream respectability. Their music had become better attuned to the Korean taste since the Add Four and the Key Boys years. Recordings, live performances in a variety of small and large venues, and occasional media exposure had made them better recognized by the public. Shin Joong Hyun, again the leading figure in this effort, was joined by others of the same mind. Old rivals from He Six and the Men—Shin's former outfit—joined forces to form Kŏmŭn Nabi (Black Butterfly). Shin also organized a new band, Yŏptchŏndŭl, which released its eponymous debut album in 1974.[12] When Yŏptchŏndŭl's song "Miin" (The Belle) topped the chart the following spring, Kŏmŭn Nabi's "Tangsinŭn Mola" (You Don't Know) was not far behind.

Aside from its commercial success, "Miin" had a monumental cultural impact. Ordinary people, especially young schoolchildren on the streets, were humming along with the folksy melody and rhyme loosely based on *changt'aryŏng*, the traditional beggar's song for food. Shin blended this with an apparent homage to Jimi Hendrix, borrowing a motif from "Voodoo Chile" to create the famous opening guitar riff in "Miin." In addition, Shin gave it a touch of vibrato akin to *nonghyŏn*, a technique widely used with traditional Korean stringed instruments. As a result, the lead guitar in "Miin" sounds like the *kayagŭm* (a twelve-stringed zither), generating a hybrid of Western rock and traditional Korean music. Even one of the most conservative mainstream newspapers praised Shin's feat: "Shin Joong Hyun's 'Miin' is said to create the Yŏpchŏn style by adding the Western rock beat to our *karak* (traditional Korean melody). . . . It is perceived as a desirable trend against the blind following of Western pop music."[13]

Riding high on the success of "Miin," Shin held a big concert entitled "Shin Joong Hyun Jam in the Pacific" in October 1975. This event signaled that GS rock had finally reached the peak of mainstream popularity. The first act of the show was none other than the rival Kŏmŭn Nabi, who came out to show solidarity among GS. The next was a tribute to Shin the composer, featuring the female singers who had become major stars thanks to his songwriting prowess. In the finale, Shin Joong Hyun and Yŏptchŏndŭl performed a twenty-minute heavy jam that "literally shook the ground."[14]

"Miin" was not heard at the concert, however, having been banned from performance or broadcast and pulled from store shelves three months earlier. Government censorship finally zeroed in on Shin Joong Hyun and other GS musicians. Between 1965 and 1975, a total of 223 Korean songs and 261 Western pop songs were blacklisted by the censors. Shin had nineteen songs on the list, the most among the living songwriters. The lyrics of his banned songs contained nothing really controversial: no political message, no social critique, and no sexually explicit language. In fact, only a handful of Korean songs were banned for such reasons. The censors gave only terse and vague explanations for their decisions, charging the songs with, for instance, vulgar lyrics (*kasa chŏsok*), immature singing style (*ch'angbŏp misuk*), or aggravating mistrust and cynicism (*pulsin p'ungt'o chojang*). Like the crackdown on decadent culture that set the stage for the proclamation of the Yushin dictatorship, the surge of cultural oppression was concomitant with a repressive political agenda. Between January 1974 and May 1975, President Park Chung-Hee issued nine emergency decrees that criminalized any kind of antigovernment activities, including speeches and writings critical of the regime. Once again, the crackdown on political dissidence (*puron*) spilled over into cultural decadence (*t'oep'ye*). This time, the regime was determined to root out cultural decadence, even if this required extraordinary measures.

On December 4, 1975, newspaper headlines broke the story that Shin Joong Hyun and four other GS musicians were under arrest and being investigated for marijuana use. The marijuana scandal (*taemach'o p'adong*) finally undid the counterculture movement of the 1960 and 1970s. Despite huge publicity, the investigation ended with just seven people in custody. According to some personal communications, however, the majority of GS musicians were investigated, and rumors circulated that they would be transferred to a psychiatric hospital to check their degree of "chemical dependency." One newspaper went overboard, predicting that nearly eighty people would be indicted.

The obviously trumped-up marijuana charge made a mockery of the rule of law, since there was no clear legal ground for the prosecution of marijuana use. The Law on Hemp Control was enacted on April 7, 1976, nearly five months after the marijuana scandal had broken out. Only then was marijuana possession made a felony punishable by up to ten years in prison. As legal prohibition and punishment still remain on the books, it is hard to imagine today that once upon a time marijuana smoking was openly discussed in public. In a magazine article published well before the scandal, Shin Joong Hyun talked freely about "happy smoke"—a slang term for marijuana—and even alluded to LSD experiences.[15] The criminalization of marijuana changed this atmosphere by attaching to offenders the strong social stigma against drug addicts. Shin and other arrested musicians were fortunate in the sense that the government did not punish them to the fullest extent of the law. However, another kind of punishment was awaiting them. Shin was released after four months in jail, only to find out that he was banned from any kind of public performance. With its brightest star in eclipse, the first moment of GS glory was quickly fading away.

WHEN THE HAPPY SMOKE BLEW AWAY:
THE EMERGENCE OF CAMPUS GROUP SOUNDS

It goes without saying that the marijuana scandal dealt a devastating blow to GS rock. Many of the musicians were banned, criminalized, and stigmatized as druggies. Censorship severely curtailed their creative expression as well. To add insult to injury, live music performed by GS began losing ground to the worldwide popularity of disco music, which swept across the Korean nightclub scene. In the meantime, the recording industry and audio equipment manufacturers were thriving thanks to the fast-growing Korean economy in the late 1970s. Listening to records became more important than attending live shows, especially for the young dedicated music fans who increasingly valued Anglo-American pop and rock records over the stricken local music scene.

In this grim situation, those GS members who managed to avoid the crackdown sought for their survival in "trot go-go," a hybrid between the go-go rhythm and the trot-style melody. Trot go-go was fairly popular among the mainstream audience but did not sit well at all with the rock fandom that considered it a sellout. Except maybe for Saranggwa P'yŏnghwa (Love and Peace), who played the cutting-edge style of disco/funk-tinged rock, the ardent rock fans largely looked down on GS during the post-marijuana scandal interregnum. At the same time, because of their U.S. military camp show origin, GS remained vulnerable to the cultural conservatives' accusation of peddling "decadent alien culture."

Subsequent generations of Korean rock musicians came from more innocuous places, starting from the institutions of higher education. College rock bands, known as "campus group sounds" from the late 1970s through the 1980s, certainly learned from the original GS saga. Whereas the professional GS musicians from the U.S. camp shows were often called *ttanttara* (lowly entertainers), college students back then enjoyed a privileged status in the Confucian social hierarchy, giving the music they created an instant respectability. Quite a few of them sought to instill Korean-ness in their music. Some wrote their lyrics in an old Korean poetry format, while others sang about patriotic themes that must have appealed to the cultural conservatives as well.

The first time campus GS made a splash among the general public was in 1977, when the Sand Pebbles from the College of Agriculture at Seoul National University won the Grand Prix of the very first Campus Song Festival (Taehak Kayoje). MBC, one of the "Big Three" TV broadcasters at the time, hosted this broadly popular contest show for amateur college singers and bands. In fact, the Sand Pebbles had been in existence since 1971 with the status of a student club—or *haksaeng ssŏk'ŭl* (student circle) in Korean parlance—officially sanctioned by the school. Another campus rock band/student music club boasting even longer history was the Runway, from Korea Aerospace University (Hanggongdae). They came into being in 1967, merely three years after the Add Four and the Key Boys debut albums. In terms of time period, there is a significant overlap between the U.S. camp show veterans and the new wave of college amateurs. Just like their professional brethren, campus GS had held their own battle-of-the-bands style contests since the late 1960s. While most of these contests were too small to notice, the National College Vocal Group Contest hosted by TBC, another one of the Big Three TV channels, drew considerable media attention four years before the Sand Pebbles' breakthrough at the MBC Campus Song Festival.

In many ways, the early campus GS constituted a minor league to the major league professional GS. Some of these supposed amateurs stepped outside school campuses to play covers of Anglo-American rock in various small venues frequented by college crowds, such as coffeehouses, dive bars, beer halls, and impromptu go-go parties. The minor league also disappeared as the marijuana scandal and the disco boom engulfed the GS live music scene. However, this particular crisis turned out to be a real opportunity for the college boys to grow up to be their own men, starting with the Sand Pebbles' Grand Prix–winning song, "Na Ŏttŏkhae" (What about Me).

BAND OF BROTHERS AND CAMPUS SUPERGROUP: SANULLIM AND SONGOLMAE

The MBC Campus Song Festival was an instant success with the national audience, developing into an annual fixture and cultural institution that turned no-name amateur college musicians into overnight media celebrities. Not all contestants were rock bands, but as the Sand Pebbles proved in the first year, there was little doubt that GS delivered the biggest impact and energy to the show.[16]

It has been noted that the Sand Pebbles is a student club, and as such, the band lineup changes as old members graduate and new members enter for each school year, not unlike a collegiate sport team. In addition, the school band tradition and the Korean-style junior-senior relationship (*sŏnhubae kwan'gye*) play an important role in the modus operandi of school-sanctioned campus GS. The 1977 lineup that won the Grand Prix benefited from the tradition since "Na Ŏttŏkhae" had been written by their senior and original founding member of the club, Kim Ch'ang-hun. He and his two brothers, elder Ch'ang-wan and younger Ch'ang-ik, had already formed a trio named

Sanullim (mountain echo) by the time the Sand Pebbles went up on the Campus Song Festival stage.

True to the form of Korean family, the first-born Ch'ang-wan was firmly in charge of Sanullim. He was not involved directly in the Sand Pebbles unlike his younger brother Chang-hun, even though both of them attended the same college. But this previously unknown trio of brothers was able to secure a recording contract on the coattails of the Sand Pebbles' overnight fame, and the rest was history. In December 1977, the *Sanullim First Album* arrived to awaken the Korean rock scene from its hibernation since the marijuana scandal. Within just two years, Sanullim released a total of five albums before the two younger brothers departed temporarily to fulfill the military service obligation. These recordings were stuff of a legend—so much so that they have become highly sought-after items among international record collectors and music connoisseurs since the 1990s.

Sanullim's lo-fi sound of fuzz tones and psychedelic drones, along with a remarkable knack for catchy melodies, solidified the mystique of the band that has increased with the passage of time. Their lyrics were "wholesome" enough to pass the censorship board with flying colors. For instance, the chorus of their early hit "Ani Pŏlssŏ" (Is It Already?) goes, "Our heart is full of hope for a bright daylight / The street is full of friendly faces passing by here and there." But Kim Ch'ang-wan alleges, in a rather cryptic manner, that the lyrics were meant to be ironic in the face of censorship:

> Without censorship, they would have been very "decadent." The [original] lyrics we wrote at the time were explicit. Our songs are largely misunderstood as being wholesome and more conciliatory than others, because the censorship worries forced more lyrical revisions. Does anyone really think we didn't know any better than singing those kinds of songs under the [political] circumstances of the times?[17]

Whether his accounts are ex post rationalization or not is beside the point. If anything is clear, it is the impact of censorship on the creative process of an artist and how to possibly get around it relatively unscathed.

By the next year, 1978, campus GS collectively became a force to be reckoned with. The other two of the Big Three broadcasters hastily joined the college song contest hoopla to catch up with rival MBC. Campus GS shined brightly in particular at TBC's Beach Song Festival (Haebyŏn kayoje), where the Runway, the Black Tetra, the Fevers, the Blue Dragon, and Pŏnnimdŭl (Friends) stormed the stage as main contestants. The runner-up award went to the Black Tetra, which featured the handsome and charismatic Ku Ch'ang-mo singing "Kurŭmgwa Na" (The Cloud and Me). The Runway's

Figure 12.4. The two wings of the band Songolmae (Peregrine falcon), Ku Ch'ang-mo *(left)* and Pae Ch'ŏl-su *(right)*. From the inner sleeves of the third album, *Songolmae III* (Jigu: JLS-1201788, 1983).

"Sesang Morŭgo Sarannora" (Living without a Worry in the World), with a tinge of traditional Korean poetry rhyming, was voted the fan favorite thanks largely to the mustache-wearing dynamo Pae Ch'ŏl-su. Three years later, these two central figures of campus GS would eventually join forces in the post-campus supergroup Songolmae (*Song'golmae*; peregrine falcon). Songolmae was indeed super, especially until Ku Ch'ang-mo quit the band to launch a solo career in 1985. In one fell swoop, Songolmae captured the hearts and minds of the young Korean teenagers with their funky "Ŏtchŏda Majuch'in Kŭdae" (A Chance Encounter with You) and backed the initial success with hard rock and power ballads. As captured in figure 12.4, the two wings of Songolmae, Ku and Pae, projected different, sometime opposite images—a pretty boy and a tough guy—tailor-made for the new era of color TV broadcasting.

Technically speaking, both Songolmae and Sanullim could have been disqualified as campus GS because some, if not all, of them were no longer students at the time of their respective debuts. Still, these two bands represented the best campus GS had to offer in the transitional period between the 1970s and 1980s. Sanullim was more daring, complex, and experimental, but Songolmae sounded more polished and accessible. The Korean "indie rock" movement from the late 1990s has affirmed their long-lasting influence by releasing tribute albums to both bands.

CONTINUITY AND DISCONTINUITY: ARE CAMPUS GROUP SOUNDS KOREAN PROTO-PUNK?

The mass fervor for the Campus Song Festival and other similar college popular music contests continued until about 1981, during which time the recording industry made quick cash by selling compilations of award-winning songs. Some of those awardees took a quick route to stardom with the support from the hosting TV channels and the recording industry: "The compilation records of young, fresh song contest winners proved to be a boon to the depressed music business. Thus recording companies wooed these singers with huge sums of advance payment, and the broadcasters also tried to take advantage by featuring them on the company PR campaigns."[18]

A few of them had distinguished music careers like Sanullim and Songolmae, or became familiar TV personalities, while others faded away from the public view rather quickly. Regardless of their staying power in the media spotlight, there is little doubt that their ascendance gave a much needed jolt to the media entertainment industry as a whole, which was still reeling from the aftereffect of the marijuana scandal. From the marketing point of view, the "fresh-faced amateur" on the college campus was a much better sell than the disgraced "decadent professional" on the nightclub stage. In the eyes of the mass media and the public, the former represented a clean break from the latter. For example, one of the major newspapers made a list of four "charming" characteristics of campus GS:

1. The amateur freshness and wholesome messages.
2. All songs are written by the band members themselves.
3. Conspicuous individuality that does not care for commercial viability.
4. The effort to incorporate the traditional Korean melody and lyrics.[19]

How much did the new campus GS actually break with the old-school professional GS? The biggest difference is obviously the socioeconomic background, a veritable class distinction between the two groups of musicians. Musically, however, they were closer to each other than most people thought. As Sanullim has admitted only recently, their psychedelic sound was in part inspired by Shin Joong Hyun, whose name they could not even mention in the late Yushin period. The Runway—Songolmae's previous campus GS incarnation—did cover Shin's tune along with the Anglo-American rock

Figure 12.5. The three brothers of Sanullim: *(from left)* Ch'ang-wan, Ch'ang-ik, and Ch'ang-hun don the same stage outfit. From the back cover of the third album, *Sanulim che samjip* (SRB: SR-0130, 1978).

canon. Even though some commentators retrospectively hailed Sanullim as "the forefather of Korean punk rock" in light of the Sanullim renaissance in the indie and punk scene since the 1990s, the music style, the band itself, and the culture surrounding it bore little resemblance to Anglo-American punk rock except for historical timing and amateurism. Other campus GS were often downright tame in their relationship with the media entertainment industry that exploited their naiveté with regard to business matters.

The blue jeans-and-T-shirt–wearing campus GS made a stylistic break from the old-school professionals who preferred formal stage attire, often including suit and tie. There might have been a "meaning of style" in this, to borrow from the subtitle of the celebrated work on subculture, but again it was not quite the same as that of the British punk.[20] Besides, Sanullim went against the predominant campus GS fashion code by sticking to old-school formality, as shown in figure 12.5.

Originality and wholesomeness are another set of issues between the old and the new wave of GS. Save for Shin Joong Hyun and a few others, the stereotype of old GS was those who played "foreign music" in a seedy go-go club. By contrast, campus GS appeared in the sanitized environment of national TV. Their songs were of their own writing, sometimes with a strong Korean flavor. But when they turned pro, the situation was not much better than the U.S. military show veterans before them: foreign pop music in a nightclub. Sanullim refused to follow this path and practically had to abandon their career in the mid-1980s "because of hunger," as the middle brother, Kim Ch'ang-hun, put it bluntly.[21] Exhausted of playing the nightclub circuit almost every night, Songolmae was grounded by the late 1980s. Both these bands were still quite popular in the media, not to mention with their dedicated fans, but no alternative system for sustainability was available for campus GS and their professional offshoots.

Finally, a few words on the complexity and contentiousness of the relationship campus GS had with the college crowds, in which they belonged themselves. The college campus in the late 1970s to early 1980s was a contested terrain under the heavy cloud of political oppression. Student activists were unfriendly or even outright hostile to campus GS and especially to those officially sanctioned. Some of these bands/student clubs received special treatment from the school authorities, who regarded winning an award at the college song contests as a public-relations bonanza. The political tension blew up in a spectacular way at Seoul National University in November 1981, when a group of student activists armed with wooden sticks and rocks crashed the on-campus concert of the Oxen, the official GS of Kŏn'guk University. The dispute over campus GS, however, did not deter their enormous impact on high schools. Largely shielded from the contentious politics of the adult world, many high school students found in the music a perfect antidote to their daily lives of discipline and punishment, and an easier way to learn skills than covering Anglo-American rock from the get-go. Soon high school bands mushroomed all over the country, and yet another wave of Korean rock bands would follow.[22]

OUTRO: FROM HISTORIOGRAPHY TO GEOGRAPHY

GS rock spans the early 1960s through the mid-1980s, the period of military rule by Park Chung-Hee and Chun Doo Hwan. Although the legacy of GS rock is a complex and contested one that has reverberated through Korean popular culture as a whole, here we will limit our discussion to its lasting impact on popular music in the 1980s and thereafter.

Censorship and control over popular music continued well into the 1980s, but Park's assassination in 1979 gave freedom to those who had been banned since the marijuana scandal. Chun's redoubled oppression of political dissidence did not extend to cultural "decadence." If anything, popular culture and music became more "liberalized" than the previous decade. In this atmosphere, some of the former GS rock musicians blossomed into superstars of the 1980s. From the old school U.S. camp show professionals came Cho Yong Pil, who, along with his band Widaehan T'ansaeng (Great Birth), boasted of an enormous crossover appeal to Koreans of all ages, including rock fans.[23] As mentioned previously, Sanullim and Songolmae built the long, prosperous career on their campus GS origin. Even Shin Joong Hyun made a comeback with the new band Music Power, although he was never able to reach the pinnacle prior to the marijuana scandal. Instead, it was his eldest son, Sin Tae-ch'ŏl, who would break a new path with the heavy metal band Sinawe (Sinawi) only a few years later. Besides these big-name rockers, there were plenty of GS musicians who came to occupy key positions in the music industry, taking on the roles of songwriters, arrangers, session players, producers, and so forth. Still, by and large, rock music in the pure sense remained at the fringe of mainstream Korean pop. In such a twisted fashion, the worldwide hegemony of rock music in the 1960–70s had its presence felt throughout Korean music business.

It is clear that Korean rock history cannot be reduced to a single, linear narrative centered on the Anglo-American hegemony; rather, there are multiple, discontinuous narratives filled with contradictions, contestations, and ruptures. The pop musicologist Keith Negus probably did not have Korean rock in mind when he stated, "the geographic routes are more important than the historical roots."[24] Nevertheless, his remark rings true when we consider the historical roots and the geographic routes of GS rock. Representing an imagined America, the U.S. camp show scene was the historical roots of Korean rock. But from there it took multiple geographic routes that ran the gamut of various places, such as downtown music cafés, hotel nightclubs, recording and TV studios, elite college campuses, high school band rooms, and the government committee offices where censorship decisions were made.

The routes of GS rock crisscrossed the relatively narrow cultural terrain of Korea, in which the national repertoire was selected inconsistently through mediation, regulation, and discursive modulation. Korean rock was neither a mimesis of the Anglo-American music genre nor was it fully embraced as national popular music by the public at large. It was born in the alien territory of the U.S. military bases, faced death at the jailhouse of the police state, and then resurrected in college campuses and high school playgrounds. This kind of complicated history/geography of Korean rock still continues today, to the delight of some and to the dismay of others.

NOTES

"Birth, Death, and Resurrection of Group Sound Rock," by Pil Ho Kim and Hyunjoon Shin, is reprinted from *positions: east asia cultures critique* 18, no. 1 (2010): 199–230. Reprinted by permission of the publisher.

1. Shin Joong Hyun, *Shin Joong Hyun Rock* (Seoul: Tana Kihoek, 1999), 79.
2. Tommy Shim, e-mail interview by Hyunjoon Shin, September 2, 2002.
3. Shin Joong Hyun, in-person interview by Hyunjoon Shin, August 17, 2012.
4. *Pisogŭi Yŏin: The Add Four First Album* (LKL Records: LKL 1014, 1964).
5. Shin Joong Hyun, in-person interview by Hyunjoon Shin, August 13, 2002.
6. *Sunday Seoul*, May 4, 1969.
7. It'aewŏn is the famous nightlife quarter for U.S. military personnel and other Western foreigners. Myŏngdong is the fashion district of downtown Seoul.
8. The term "group sound" originated in Japan and referred to the specific style influenced by the Ventures, the Beatles, the Animals, etc., whereas in Korea it was a synonym for rock band. For the Japanese GS, see Shuhei Hosokawa, Hiroshi Matsumura, and Hiroshi Ogawa eds., *A Guide to Popular Music in Japan* (Tokyo: IASPM-Japan, 1991), 15.
9. The curfew was first imposed by the U.S. Army Military Government in 1945. This Cold War relic was not lifted until 1982.
10. Tommy Shim, e-mail interview by Hyunjoon Shin, September 2, 2002.
11. *Chugan Kyŏnghyang*, May 5, 1971.
12. *Sin Chung-hyŏn-gwa Yŏptchŏndŭl* (Jigu: JLS-120891, 1974). A literal translation of *yŏptchŏndŭl* would be "coins." It was an old ethnic slur that designated colonized Koreans during Korea's colonial period (1910–45), later turned into an expression of self-loathing among Koreans. Shin Joong Hyun used it as an ironic rhetorical device to express his national pride.
13. *Chosŏn Ilbo* (Seoul), April 25, 1975.
14. *Ilgan Sŭp'och'ŭ* (Seoul), October 19, 1975.
15. "Sin Chunghyŏnŭi 'Haep'i Sŭmok'ŭ' T'ambanggi" (Reportage: Shin Joong Hyun's "happy smoke"), *Sunday Seoul*, February 28, 1971.
16. Since the late 1990s, the Korean film industry has intermittently produced movies based on the nostalgia for the campus GS period. See Eva Tsai and Hyunjoon Shin, "Strumming a Place of One's Own: Gender, Independence, and the East Asian Pop/rock Screen," *Popular Music* 32, Special Issue 1 (2013): 7–22.
17. Kim Ch'ang-wan, in-person interview by Hyunjoon Shin, February 11, 2003.
18. *Seoul Sinmun*, August 8, 1978.
19. *Chung-ang Ilbo* (Seoul), June 12, 1979.
20. Dick Hebdige, *Subculture: The Meaning of Style* (London: Routledge, 1979).
21. Kim Ch'ang-hun interview, *Weiv* 5, no. 2 (September 1, 2003) http://www.weiv.co.kr/view_detail.html?code=interview&num=2227 (last accessed on September 5, 2011).
22. The latest wave of GS-inspired rock is represented by Jang Gi Ha (Chang Ki-ha). See Hyunjoon Shin, "The Success of Hopelessness: the Evolution of Korean Indie Music," *Perfect Beat* 12, no. 2 (2011): 129–46.
23. Cho also found success in Japan and became a pan-Asian star by the mid-1980s.
24. Keith Negus, *Popular Music in Theory: An Introduction* (Cambridge: Polity Press, 1996), 163.

13 ROALD MALIANGKAY

The Popularity of Individualism
The Seo Taiji Phenomenon in the 1990s

From the early 1960s until the late 1990s pop acts had to approach the South Korean (hereafter Korean) market carefully in order to avoid being censored or banned by the various ethics committees. Although the first steps toward democratic elections were made in 1987, the committees would take more than a decade to release their grip on recorded and live popular entertainment.[1] They continued to scan the music for references to Japan, North Korea, or Communism as well as unacceptably crude expressions, though they no longer banned per se those lyrics that called for freedom of expression, a change of government, or pacifism.[2] From the mid 1990s onward the committees further relaxed their stance on popular entertainment, which led to a marked growth in the number of live pop concerts. The change in policy was possibly underpinned by the increasing difficulty of maintaining control over popular entertainment, which was one of the drivers behind the fast increase in Internet use among Koreans, and the reassurance that the public had come to embrace a significant degree of conformity and self-censorship. An added factor may have been that the success many new acts were having abroad encouraged policymakers not to interfere with their momentum and risk damaging Korean business interests, using the triumphs to boost feelings of nationalist pride instead. But the most influential pop act of the new era had posed a serious challenge that was still reverberating. Whereas its fan base had not directly opposed the authorities, the act had questioned the intentions of policymakers in light of the fast changing sociopolitical climate.

In the early 1990s, when media corporations were beginning to create and manage increasing numbers of so-called talents (*t'aellŏnt'ŭ*) — pop idols who rely heavily on their work for the visual media—a number of mainstream acts emerged that included a mixture of rap, hip-hop, and R&B elements. In the West rap was commonly associated with social criticism,[3] and it is likely that the Korean performers who incorporated the style were thus considered to be self-managed and to write and compose at least some of their music themselves. One of a few mainstream acts in Korea that indeed fit that description was the band created by Seo Taiji in 1991. Although Seo's groundbreaking music and presentation found instant appeal, he continued to innovate and set many popular trends in music, dance, and personal styling throughout the 1990s. Borrowing sounds and dance routines from a wide range of musical styles, including rap, hip-hop, and metal, his act became a major inspiration for the new generation of students as well as other successful boy bands such as H.O.T. and Sechs Kies, which did not innovate much and relied considerably on their teenage idol status in their repertoires and performances.

One major difference these bands had with previous acts was that their success came at a time when the record industries were able to target consumers directly through various media,[4] as well as through numerous spin-off products without too much interference from the authorities. The early 1990s were also a time when most families had color televisions, private cars were filling up Seoul's streets, the first pop magazines emerged for teenagers, and most dance music acts began to lip-synch their music "live" on TV. Another change was that many students now had a considerable amount of disposable income,[5] which enabled them to keep up with the latest trends. Information on foreign fads, including those from Japan, was now coming to Korea at a rapid pace. Foreign travel restrictions had been eased, and a fast-growing number of Koreans were traveling abroad for sightseeing and educational purposes, while many Korean Americans were coming back to Korea for travel, study, and employment.[6] The Internet did not become widely available in South Korea until the mid-1990s, but various other new technologies, including personal stereos and *noraebang* (private karaoke room), helped disseminate bands' music, lyrics, and image among students.

This chapter discusses the years in which Seo Taiji's main act, Seo Taiji & Boys, came onto the music scene and analyzes what aspects of the band's music and performing style played a role in its fast rise to stardom in the early to mid-1990s. It examines what distinguished the band from others and deliberates its role in the nation's burgeoning democracy. I argue that Seo's relative social reclusiveness, his increasing association with Los Angeles's music scene, and the fact that he continued to challenge the ethics committees with his music, lyrics, and performing style allowed him to incorporate elements from foreign subcultures, of which he became both an advocate and symbol despite his mainstream success. Even so, the students that formed his fan base were driving the fast expansion of the realm of popular culture, which made a degree of ownership of Seo's advocacy of freedom and individualism a requirement rather than an option. The expression of social criticism, so it seems, sometimes entails little more than keeping up with the latest trends.

THE PRODIGY ARRIVES

Seo Taiji (original name Chŏng Hyŏnch'ŏl, b. 1972) began his professional music career playing the bass guitar for the fourth album of hard-rock band Sinawe *(shinawi)*. When in 1991 the group disbanded, approximately one year after he joined it, he dropped out of school and began writing music on his computer, hoping to eventually start his own band.[7] He recruited dancers Yi Chuno and Yang Hyŏnsŏk and formed his own act, Seo Taiji & Boys (fig. 13.1), which focused heavily on dance and had Seo doing most of the singing and the other two members regularly carrying out five- to ten-second dance solos. The band's debut album, *SeoTaiji and Boys*, was released on March 23, 1992. It comprised ten songs, including the hits *"Nan arayo"* (I Know), *"Ijae-nŭn"* (Now), *"Hwansangsog-ŭi kŭdae"* (Girl of My Dreams), and *"I pam-i kip'ŏgajiman"* (Although It's Getting Late). The music video for *"Nan arayo,"* which appears to have been inspired by the videos for Technotronic's "Pump up the Jam" (1989) and Snap's "The Power" (1990), was an instant phenomenon. More than 1.5 million copies of the debut album were sold within a month from the date of its release and at the end of the year the band had taken all the music awards.[8] The band produced three more albums (1993, 1994, 1995)[9] that together reached a sales volume of 3.5 million.[10]

The most innovative aspect of Seo's music was his use of rap and sampling to create what are perhaps best described as fast dance or rock ballads.[11] The rap was usually added to the melodic line of the main solo voice, following the same or double the tempo over up to four measures. It did not commonly use crotchet triplet patterns, but often included appoggiatura-type grace notes, with a small number of tuplets. The result sometimes makes the rap sound hurried, as if the fact that the words fit the beat poorly is unintentional. Having a broad taste in music, Seo mixed in riffs and phrases from all kinds of Western popular music. Yi Tongyŏn, who wrote one of the main books on the phenomenon of Seo Taiji, pointed out to me that the song *"Nŏ-wa hamkke han shigan sog-esŏ"* (In the Hour I Spent with You) is very similar to the 1989 song "Girl I'm Gonna Miss You" by Milli Vanilli, a band

Figure 13.1. Seo Taiji and Boys sporting their signature snowboard look. Courtesy of *Kyŏnghyang shinmun* (Capital and country News), October 21, 1995, 25.

Seo said he liked at the time.[12] But inspiration did not come merely from Western pop. On *"Hayŏga"* (In Any Case Song), one of the hit songs of his band's second album, Seo famously included traditional Korean folk music, both in the song's melodic structure and in the final chorus, which includes a solo played on a *t'aep'yŏngso* (funneled double-reed wind instrument). The amount of sampling was now reduced, from approximately 90 percent to 40 percent, with musicians playing most of the band instruments used in the recording.[13] Hard rock and metal influences became much more prominent on the third and fourth albums, but the songs remained upbeat overall and many continued to suit hip-hop dance.[14] On the fourth album the influence of North American gangsta rap groups House of Pain and Cypress Hill is evident. Eun-Young Jung finds that the sound of Seo's "Come Back Home" is similar to Cypress Hill's song "I Ain't Going Out Like That" (1993).[15] The dissonant whistle found on *"P'ilsŭng"* (Victory), meanwhile, is first featured on House of Pain's "Jump Around" (1992) and Cypress Hill's "Insane in the Brain" (1993), while Seo's high-pitched nasal voice on "Come Back Home" is strongly reminiscent of that used by Cypress Hill's lead rapper, B-Real.

Owing to the prominence of distorted guitar sounds, however, most of the songs on the album are best described as fast rock ballads.

Dance remained a distinctive feature of the band. Other boy bands would also incorporate slick dance routines into their performances, but Seo Taiji & Boys were the first to turn them into a dominant feature. Their performances often began with a very tightly choreographed b-boy dance routine during which Seo's first lines were sometimes inaudible because of the screaming (and not infrequently hyperventilating) fans. The styling of the three band members would commonly show the influence of rap and hip-hop genres, but the clothes were on many occasions cross-matched to add to the effectiveness of the dance routines. Kim Chip'yŏng argues that rather than the music and dance, it was the band's fashion that really broke with convention.[16] It started off with a combination of tailored jackets, neatly buttoned-up oversized dress shirts—sometimes two on top of each other—and loose, tapered black pants over black leather shoes. As the style of the group became more "street," shirts were often left unbuttoned on top of oversized T-shirts, while the trousers were replaced with gardening overalls, phat or harem pants. Clothing items associated with a wide range of styles were combined, including formal Western dress suits, Korean folk costumes, and the Scottish kilt. Although the group changed styles many times over the years, items were often reused, including the dress shirts, which they continued to wear neatly buttoned up. Over the course of its four albums (1992–95), the band would popularize various styles. One of these, which Koreans referred to as the "snowboard look," saw the members wearing ski hats, oversized parkers, mouth covers, and dark sunglasses with colorful rims.[17] They often wore caps, hats, and bandannas but during the first half of the decade maintained conservatively gel-spiked hairstyles. This style changed in 1993, when Yi Chuno and Yang Hyŏnsŏk grew semi-long dreadlocks, an act that eventually led to a ban by the national channel, KBS-TV.[18] The censorship was supported by many journalists who applauded the band members' return to a conformist hairstyle soon after[19]; ironically two years later the band members all grew their hair semi-long and died it various bright colors, but no ban was imposed.

Many of the U.S.-based bands, including House of Pain and Cypress Hill, that appear to have influenced Seo's music and style of performance, at least at some stage, promoted nonconformity and varying degrees of anarchy. Nevertheless, as Eun-Young Jung points out, even though some of Seo Taiji's songs strongly criticized aspects of contemporary Korean society, they never advocated or romanticized violence or social discord.[20] When the dreadlocks of Seo's band members led to a ban by KBS-TV, newspapers explained the move by referring to the gang culture it was associated with. However, Kim Hyŏnsŏp argues that it wasn't so much the gang culture itself that led to the ban but rather the association of reggae music with resistance.[21] Since Seo's music did not, however, contain many reggae elements at all, Kim's comment was probably motivated by the image of dreadlocks only. Indeed, it wasn't merely Seo's choice of words or nonverbal symbolism but also the unfamiliar sound and presentation of his music that represented a rejection of social norms.[22] Since Seo took the various elements out of context and mixed them with others, most Koreans would have judged Seo's act on what it represented in Korea, as opposed to what the specific elements connoted in their country of origin.[23] The sounds, clothing accessories, and hairstyles Seo popularized may have been associated with Los Angeles's gang culture in the United States, but it was the fact that the look was generally associated with a strong nonconformism in Korea that led to the partial censorship of Seo's act.

Despite the group's enormous success and its bold introduction of new styles of music, dance, and fashion, it remained conformist in its conduct and presentation in between acts. Seo spoke softly during interviews, and when addressing his audiences expressed modesty and gratitude. There was no profanity, no sexism, no use of any substance, no piercings, and no tattoos. Eun-Young Jung says that whereas the lyrics of American gangsta rap often embraced "violence, misogyny, drugs, rape, and gun culture," such elements were "less prevalent in Korean inner-city communities."[24] In fact, none of these elements can be found in Seo's lyrics even though they were very specific in their criticism of the older generation's arrogance. Keith Howard finds that the lyrics on the first albums were harmless,[25] but on the third album the songs *"Kyoshil idea"* (Classroom idea), *"Chek'il-paksa-wa haidŭ"* (Dr. Jekyll and Mr. Hyde), and *"Nae maŭmiya"* (That's How I Feel) strongly criticized the older generation and the education system. The first song was banned from TV and radio, and although the lyrics were fairly strong, they were given a pass by the ethics committees.[26] The first stanza is as follows:

> Enough. Enough. Stop that kind of teaching. No more, it's more than enough now.
> Every morning you lead us into a tiny classroom by 7:30, forcing the same things into the 7 million heads of children around the country.
> These dark, closed classrooms are swallowing us up.
> My life is too precious to be wasted here.[27]

On the band's fourth album, however, the criticism of the older generation in the song "*Shidae yugam*" (Regret of the Times) was more poignant. The censorship committees demanded that three particular verses be removed or rewritten (here marked using bold font):

> What are you waiting for? It's here, the sound of the forsaking of all life.
>   Something is going to turn this world upside down. Ooooh . . .
> You make so much noise, but you have nothing but pride.
> Your hypocrisy makes the skin on your face wriggle.
> Educated elders are walking down the street holding pretty dolls.
> It seems that the day everyone has been secretly hoping for is coming
>   today.
> Lips stained black. **Gone is the era of honest people.**
> [. . . .]
> How far do you think you can fly with those broken wings of yours?
>   **I wish for a new world that'll overturn everything.**
> [. . . .]
> **I hope I can avenge the grudge in my heart.**
> Tonight![28]

Although the revision was a condition for the song's inclusion on the album, Seo initially refused to comply with the demand. When fans heard about the controversy, many staged public protests, the ensuing debate even spurring the government to organize an independent inquiry.[29] In the end, Seo chose to record an instrumental version of the song,[30] though of course because of all the public commotion over the banned phrases the censorship had become pointless.

Seo's consistently modest attitude and responsible public conduct did not change parents' minds about rap music and lyrics in general. They disapproved of that type of music, and so they disapproved of Seo's music too. Heejoon Chung argues that many parents, in particular those with a middle- or upper-class background, actually hated Seo because he was a high-school dropout who questioned social norms,[31] but Chung provides no evidence to support his claim. Some parents will have undoubtedly questioned the appropriateness of Seo as a role model for their children, and yet it appears that, much as in the United States, in Korea many parents and music critics did indeed disapprove of rap culture in general,[32] but did not harbor strong antipathy toward the artist himself. Seo's clean, teenage appearance and romantic lyrics, especially in the first years of the music genre's introduction to Korea, showed that he ought not be tied to the violence with which the genre was associated in the United States. Perhaps more important, whereas

"노래도 아니다"

신세계

Figure 13.2. An ad for the Shinsegye department store made use of Seo Taiji's disappearance. The text box underneath the caption, "'They're not even songs,' a common complaint among the older generations," explains that Seo Taiji not only wrote new songs; he created a new world too. Courtesy of *Tonga ilbo* (East Asia daily), May 1, 1996, 37.

many fans took on the style fads Seo created, they generally conformed to Korean social standards in terms of their ideals and public behavior. Especially when Chung elaborates on the reasons for parents' dislike of Seo, it appears it is merely his own very prejudiced views that he is expressing:

> First of all, there is his noise-like music and hard-to-hear lyrics. His style and appearance [were] another problem. His ambiguous appearance in terms of sex delivered a unisex fashion mode to the teens. In addition, he was spreading not only Afro-American music, but also their dance, fashion and hairstyles. His dance was not pretty for parents, and he subverted every conventional dress code, appearing on TV wearing a hat with the price tag still hanging on it. Dreadlocked hair, which banned him from TV appearance for some time, was that of Jamaican gangsters. He introduced Korean youth to the intimidating street life of Afro-Americans.[33]

At the beginning of 1996, Seo shocked many of his fans when he suddenly disbanded the group and went to Los Angeles (fig. 13.2).[34] Following a two-year hiatus, in July 1998 he returned with a solo album called simply

Seo Taiji. Although Seo did not engage in any public marketing activities to support the sale of his album and was absent from his music videos, the punk-rock and metal-infused album sold more than a million copies. With the dance aspect removed from both the music and the presentation, Seo's music was now too rough for the palates of teenagers.[35] Young people had begun to tune into other, far more romantic and lighthearted major acts instead, such as H.O.T. and Sechs Kies, and the girl groups S.E.S. and Fin.K.L. These groups also incorporated some hip-hop elements and continued to make use of random English phrases, but they did not voice any strong social discontent and sang mostly ballads and dance tunes, making very good use of the prevalence of music videos.

TURNING OVER SUBCULTURES

Seo Taiji & Boys had a great impact on young people's preferences in music, dance, and fashion. When in August 1997 the Samsung Economic Research Institute carried out a survey to find out what Koreans considered their most important cultural product, the band came out on top, ranked even higher than Arae-a han'gŭl, Korea's own word-processing software and one of the very few programs that allowed PC users to withstand the omnipresence of Microsoft's Word.[36] Seo Taiji became a protagonist of the culture of the New Generation (*shinsedae*) that comprised so many of his fans, a generation that had grown up consuming a wide range of cultural items from the United States and was associated with individual choice, considerable spending money, and overseas travel.[37] Despite having a much more international view of sociocultural issues and considerable buying power, however, middle- and high-school students continued to be faced with enormous pressure to be successful at the national university entrance exams. As they spent most of their seven-day study weeks at schools or after-hours cram schools, they were keen consumers not only of the various new foreign fast-food outlets but also of the new technologies that allowed for live and recorded music enjoyment on the go, such as personal stereos and *noraebang* enterprises, which according to Mi Park replaced eating and drinking venues as the primary locus for public singing.[38]

In part because, in contrast to middle- and high-school teachers, Korean university lecturers rarely failed underperforming students as long as they were enrolled in class, most college students were living fairly hedonistic lives, spending considerable amounts of time and money on food, entertainment, and fashion. But college life offered only temporary respite. Since many young people dreamed of breaking free from the turgid mold that saw teenagers and college graduates subjected to unequal and unnecessary pressure in education and in the job market, respectively, the "individualism" they were accused of was, in fact, a shared longing for structural social change. When they spoke of individualism and the pursuit of Western products and values, critics took this as a sign of faltering respect for the traditional social values and pointed at their overall affluence and the fact that unlike their predecessors of the so-called 386 Generation they comprised the century's first generation not to have directly experienced any of the hardships so many had suffered during and prior to the violent democracy movement of the 1980s.[39] Figures from the Korean National Statistics Office show not only that the percentage of urban household income spent on leisure increased dramatically between 1970 and 1997 but also that that of rural households barely changed, which can be explained by the significant migration of young people to the cities for work and education.[40] Some therefore blamed the New Generation and the university students in particular for the rise in consumerism in the 1990s. Their criticism was exacerbated by the fact that the number of university students had grown considerably in the 1970s and 1980s and that a fair number of them were able to add to their already substantial spending money by teaching middle- and high-school students privately.[41] Young people from Seoul's rich Apkujŏng area were targeted especially and sometimes referred to as "orange folk" (orenjijok), because they commuted using the subway line marked in orange on the map and were soft, like oranges.

Seo strongly repudiated the notion of belonging to this social group, pointing out that he was a worker (nodongja) who knew very well from experience what it was like not to have money to eat.[42] For those who took the criticism from the older generations to heart, which may have included a fair number of teenagers from the Apkujŏng area, Seo's lyrics offered support. His words responded to the scrutiny by pointing (back) at the poor quality of education and the enormous pressure the students were under. College students may have been more reserved in their appreciation of Seo's music and the fads and message of social criticism it incorporated, but many appreciated his music nevertheless and were excited about the many musical and stylistic innovations it helped usher in. Meanwhile, Seo's status as an advocate of the New Generation was not only confirmed by his music, lyrics, and presentation but also by his seeming disinterest in marketing activities. Unlike most of his peers, Seo maintained the image of a true artist by minimizing his involvement in all too blatantly commercial activities. He did not fully capitalize on his fame by appearing in all kinds of shows and advertising and effectively turned into a social recluse in 1996. This attitude toward the business aspect of his music added to his appeal as a true musician and thus to his mystique, which also served to sell albums.

Throughout the 1960s, 1970s, and 1980s, pop acts were not given much freedom to challenge social conventions. Heavy metal and experimental instrumental music and rock were played, but only by bands relegated to the urban underground scenes.[43] The New Generation, on the other hand, became associated with new genres of music that, unlike previous pop songs, could not find much, if any, appeal among the older generations. Lee Kee-hyeung cites a report in the newspaper *Segye Ilbo* (World daily) of January 14, 1993, which argued that because the majority of people over thirty could not appreciate the music popular with teenagers and college students, a gap had been created between them and the New Generation.[44] Of greater impact on this gap was, however, the fast expanding realm of popular entertainment. Lee comments:

> Nowhere was the power of youth more visible than [in] the popular entertainment sector, especially popular music, literature, film, and advertising. To them cultural consumption was a form of production and an expression of their identities. [. . .] Through their richly textured cultural activities and consumption, youth created their own norm: [the] right to be different and [to] demonstrate different cultural tastes.[45]

Despite the increasingly public display of wealth among many students, being a Seo Taiji fan did not require excessive spending per se. Whereas this may explain why in studies of local subcultures in the 1990s the divide between classes was considered secondary in importance to that between generations, as also argued more generally by Sarah Thornton,[46] the hierarchies of the dominant culture always reverberate within the realms of subcultures. By being actively involved in creating and consuming the ideas and symbols related to popular culture, the young were able to break free from the past and look both inside and outside Korea for inspiration and innovation. Dick Hebdige's conceptualization of subculture as "a form of resistance in which experienced contradictions and objections to this ruling ideology are obliquely represented in style" is useful in that it prioritizes the form of resistance to the dominant social norm.[47] Because Seo's fans were mostly middle class and the first to benefit from the burgeoning democracy, they were unlikely to turn their rejection of the ruling ideology into a strong visual, public statement. Following popular trends like Seo Taiji's music, which associated more expressive forms of resistance, allowed students to play with dissonance while conforming to the expectations set by their social environment. In regard to the minority of fans who made their dislike of the hegemony more public, Theodor Adorno would have us explore the nature of the collaboration between them and the superstructure, arguing that negotiating with the dominant culture ought not to satisfy those seeking to express their true challenge to it. His concept of pseudo-individualism fits into the dominant culture's grand scheme in that it uses a degree of freedom of expression to support the notion that the status quo, the hegemony, is natural—that, in other words, it has popular support.[48] If one considers that in Korea the pressure to meet previously existing standards of education and financial success did not ease throughout the 1990s, then Adorno's hypothesis may indeed have applied. It is nevertheless possible to term the New Generation, with whom Seo's music was strongly associated, a subculture because it sought to express its ideas in environments where it had a dominating presence, such as the Internet and specific urban areas,[49] even though it generally conformed to popular norms outside those realms.

Arguing that they "never seriously pursued overtly political analysis of the subculture and its many acts of 'insurrection' beyond the domain of style and signification,"[50] Kee-hyeung Lee accuses Korean analysts of too readily assuming that the incorporation of the New Generation's subculture in the dominant culture was inevitable. It would indeed be wrong to assume that the superstructure will always have the edge and that in this case the possible impact of the new generation and its various subcultures was negligible from the outset. Since the superstructure comprises major industries, they have to ensure commercial success. Seo's decision not to commit to long-term marketing strategies, for example, in some ways added to his power, because his record company (Bando Records) would have wanted to secure its investments and optimize its sales.[51] But whereas the incorporation and subsequent diffusion of the elements of subculture in Seo's music through capitalist commoditization[52] was somewhat slowed down by the artist's refusal to maximize profits, it could not stop it. The relatively small company would make great profits off the sales of Seo's albums, although it went bankrupt sometime during the economic crisis in 1998 when a share of its operations was subsequently taken over by Samsung Music.[53]

Seo Taiji was able to make good use of the media for many years and was able to virtually disappear from them by moving abroad. His fans may have liked only one or two aspects of his work, but by purchasing a copy of his albums they supported his standpoints even though they may not have truly believed in them much themselves and may not have followed through in their own personal lives. For them being "in the know" and thus associating with the peer group that Seo represented was of foremost importance.[54] Indeed, in popular culture ownership, in the form of knowledge or experience or wealth, plays a key role. It may be gained through wit, special encounters, or daredevil accomplishments but also by rather passively following popular fads and trends. The consumption and selection of popular culture by individuals is rarely as deliberate as the enormous marketing budgets might suggest. To pursue only that which suits one's own needs and interests best is virtually impossible, and so one is often led toward products and ideas by the sources of information one has come to rely on. In large social structures, complacency is a time-effective and relatively risk-free way of securing one's place in society and thus one's position of power. For many students, having purchased a copy of or at least heard the latest Seo Taiji album, which associated many forms of nonconformism, became a requirement for acceptance by the peer group.

CONCLUSION

In the 1990s the star of Seo Taiji shone brighter in Korea than any other star to date. Although one could argue that part of his talent lay in mixing other people's creations, he nevertheless innovated Korean music, dance, and fashion. Seo came to represent a generation that wanted to break with the past and expand its horizon both culturally and spatially. He was able to ride a wave of new technological developments in popular culture that allowed for his music to be played and shared anywhere at any moment of the day. The era of teenage idol stardom had arrived, and the realm of popular culture of which it was part was expanding fast. Because many aspects of the band's music and performing style continued to raise issues with the ethics committees, the band remained both an advocate and symbol of various subcultures, despite its mainstream success, a situation that was exacerbated by Seo's refusal to commit himself to long-term marketing strategies. As part of the prodemocratic *minjung* (populist) movement of the 1970s and 1980s, singer-songwriters such as Kim Min'gi had preceded Seo in addressing social wrongs, but they had focused more on political violence and injustice in society in general and they had to tread carefully in order to avoid the censors. Unlike their very personal, introverted performing style, Seo's music was extravert and his lyrics more direct. But the changing sociopolitical climate allowed him to be more nonconformist and gave greater priority to the integrity of his work.

By buying and supporting Seo's music and singing along to his lyrics at a *noraebang*, often after many hours of uninterrupted study, his fans could express their support for his interests and his ideas, but of course many did so only in their limited spare time, in between heavy study schedules. Seo provided them with a voice of discontent in a package that eschewed convention and set new standards, but the settings in which it was consumed remained largely conformist. In order to be successful and accepted by their social environment, the average student continued to work hard and behave according to the norm. The students and their parents may have had very different ideas about people's individual rights and duties and about what happiness entailed, but it appears that their ideals did not differ too much and that they shared the opinion that education at an established institution and the financial security it promised would broaden their horizon. The realm of popular culture to which the students dedicated much of their spare time afforded them a louder voice in society, but it also compounded peer pressure. Whereas the requirement to keep up with a popular trend such as that represented by Seo's latest album may have served to provide them with some instant relief because of its symbolic importance, it ironically also added a criterion for acceptance by their peer group.

Since the 1990s few acts have earned the admiration of both teenage and college students, male and female alike. Whereas Seo's music may have created a temporary gap between generations, he managed to form a bridge between two social groups that the university entrance exams and the involvement of major entertainment industries would soon divide again. Possibly because teenage students were growing somewhat wary of complex or negative lyrics and even the arguably unromantic styling, from the mid-1990s onward acts emerged that were not only more positive and more uniform[55] but also focused more on the performers' physical appeal. Record companies would create many acts that were less musically innovative, but combined deeply romantic ballads with upbeat dance tracks and good looks. With the use of elaborate, often narrative music videos that highlighted the latter, the industry was able to compete with the many foreign acts that now appeared on music TV stations and on the large screens of the popular rock cafés. They were the first ripples of the Korean Wave.

NOTES

1. See Mun Okpae, *Han'guk kŭmjigog-ŭi sahoe sa* [A social history of censored Korean music] (Seoul: Yesol, 2004), 158–59. On October 4 and 31, 1996, respectively, the Korean Constitutional Court ruled that the strict Movie Law and the Law on Discs and Videos that had formed the basis of many cases of censorship were in contradiction with the constitutional guarantees for freedom of expression. Im Sanghyŏk, "Yŏnghwa-wa p'yohyŏn-ŭi chayu: Han'guk yŏnghwa shimŭi chedo-ŭi pyŏnch'ŏn" [Cinema and the freedom of speech: Korea's changing film censorship], in *Han'guk yŏnghwa sa: kaehwagi-esŏ kaehwagi-kkaji* [A history of Korean movies: From the enlightenment period to the enlightenment period], ed. Kim Mihyŏn (Seoul: Com-

munication Books, 2006), 101; "Court Decides Record Censorship Is Unconstitutional," from online news site Digital Chosun (www.chosun.com), October 31, 1996.

2. For an overview of the criteria on the basis of which the committees scrutinized entertainment in the 1970s and 1980s, see Roald Maliangkay, "Pop for Progress: South Korea's Propaganda Songs," in *Korean Pop Music: Riding the Korean Wave*, ed. Keith Howard (Folkestone, U.K.: Global Oriental, 2006), 51.

3. Jeanita W. Richardson and Kim A. Scott, "Rap Music and Its Violent Progeny: America's Culture of Violence in Context," *The Journal of Negro Education* 71, no. 3 (Summer 2002): 175–76.

4. Yi Tongyŏn, *Sŏ T'aeji-nŭn uri-ege muŏshiŏnna* [What might Seo Taiji have meant to us?] (Seoul: Munhwa kwahaksa, 1999), 43.

5. Kee-hyeung Lee, "Looking Back at the Cultural Politics of Youth Culture in South Korea in the 1990s: On the 'New Generation' Phenomenon and the Emergence of Cultural Studies," *Korean Journal of Communication Studies* 15, no. 4 (November 2007): 61.

6. See Keith Howard, "Coming of Age: Korean Pop in the 1990s," *Korean Pop Music: Riding the Korean Wave*, ed. Keith Howard (Folkestone, U.K.: Global Oriental, 2006), 88; Jin-Kyu Park, "'English Fever' in South Korea: Its History and Symptoms," *English Today* 97 25, no. 1 (March 2009): 52; Seung-Kuk Kim, "Changing Lifestyles and Consumption Patterns of the South Korean Middle Class and New Generations," in *Consumption in Asia: Lifestyles and Identities*, ed. Chua Beng Huat (New York: Routledge, 2000), 69.

7. Yi Tongyŏn, *Sŏ T'aeji-nŭn uri-ege muŏshiŏnna*, 166; Pak Chunhŭm, *I ttang-esŏ ŭmag-ŭl handanŭn kŏs-ŭn* [Saying you play music in this world] (Seoul: Kyobo mun'go, 1999), 303.

8. Keith Howard, "Coming of Age: Korean Pop in the 1990s," 87; Kee-hyeung Lee, "Looking Back at the Cultural Politics of Youth Culture in South Korea in the 1990s," 59.

9. Starting with *Seo Taiji & Boys #2*, and following common Korean practice, the group's second, third, and fourth albums were named after the order in which they were released.

10. Kim Chip'yŏng, *Han'guk kayo chŏngshinsa* [A spiritual history of Korean songs] (Seoul: Arŭm ch'ulp'ansa, 2000), 245. It is important to note that many bootleg copies of the album were sold on the streets on cassette tape.

11. Although he was not the first to perform rap in Korea, it was Seo who introduced rap to the public. Sŏn Sŏngwŏn, *Taejung ŭmag-ŭi ppuri* [The roots of Korean popular music] (Seoul: Tosŏ ch'ulp'an kkun, 1996), 210.

12. Yi Tongyŏn, e-mail correspondence, July 8, 2011. Seo admitted that for some time he considered setting up an act like that of Milli Vanilli with Yi Chuno and Yang Hyŏnsŏk. Yi Tongyŏn, *Sŏ T'aeji-nŭn uri-ege muŏshiŏnna*, 167.

13. Yi Tongyŏn, *Sŏ T'aeji-nŭn uri-ege muŏshiŏnna*, 172.

14. Eun-Young Jung defines the song "*Kyoshil idea*" [Classroom idea] on the third album as "rap-metal." Eun-Young Jung, "Articulating Korean Youth Culture through Global

Popular Music Styles: Seo Taiji's Use of Rap and Metal," in *Korean Pop Music: Riding the Korean Wave*, ed. Keith Howard (Folkestone, U.K.: Global Oriental, 2006), 114.

15. Eun-Young Jung, "Articulating Korean Youth Culture through Global Popular Music Styles," 114.

16. Kim Chip'yŏng, *Han'guk kayo chŏngshinsa*, 245.

17. Yi Tongyŏn, *Sŏ T'aeji-nŭn uri-ege muŏshiŏnna*, 225; Sŏn Sŏngwŏn, *Rog-esŏ indiŭmagŭro* [From rock to indie music] (Koyang: Arŭm ch'ulp'ansa, 1999), 207; Kee-hyeung Lee, "Looking Back at the Cultural Politics of Youth Culture in South Korea in the 1990s," 60–61.

18. In 1993 and 1994 various Korean mainstream acts showed the influence of reggae. Sŏn Sŏngwŏn, *Taejung ŭmag-ŭi ppuri*, 219. Seo Taiji would grow long dreadlocks toward the end of the 1990s.

19. Kim Hyŏnsŏp, *Sŏ T'aeji tamnon* [Discourses on Seo Taiji]: *Seotaiji Syndrome* (Seoul: Ch'aeg-i innŭn maŭl, 2001), 129.

20. Eun-Young Jung, "Articulating Korean Youth Culture through Global Popular Music Styles," 112.

21. Kim Hyŏnsŏp, *Sŏ T'aeji tamnon*, 129–30.

22. Yi Hyesuk and Son Usŏk, *Han'guk taejung ŭmak sa* [A history of Korean popular music] (Seoul: Ries and Book, 2003), 316.

23. Laura Miller points out that this mixing of styles has also occurred in Japanese youth fashion, a phenomenon sometimes explained as having a "country-neutral quality" (*mukokuseki*). Laura Miller, "Youth Fashion and Changing Beautification Practices," in *Modern Japanese Culture*, vol. 2, ed. D. P. Martinez (London: Routledge, 2007), 89–90; Kōichi Iwabuchi, *Recentering globalization: Popular culture and Japanese transnationalism* (Durham, NC: Duke University Press, 2002), 78.

24. Eun-Young Jung, "Articulating Korean Youth Culture through Global Popular Music Styles," 118.

25. Keith Howard, "Coming of Age: Korean Pop in the 1990s," 87.

26. Eun-Young Jung, "Articulating Korean Youth Culture through Global Popular Music Styles," 113.

27. See Kim Hyŏnsŏp, *Sŏ T'aeji tamnon*, 82–83, 210; Eun-Young Jung, "Articulating Korean Youth Culture through Global Popular Music Styles," 113.

28. Mun Okpae, *Han'guk kŭmjigog-ŭi sahoe sa*, 157–58.

29. Mun Okpae, *Han'guk kŭmjigog-ŭi sahoe sa*, 157–58.

30. Heejoon Chung, "Sport Star vs. Rock Star in Globalizing Popular Culture: Similarities, Difference and Paradox in Discussion of Celebrities," *International Review for the Sociology of Sport* 38 (2003): 104.

31. Heejoon Chung, "Sport Star vs. Rock Star in Globalizing Popular Culture," 104.

32. Rachel E. Sullivan, "Rap and Race: It's Got a Nice Beat, but What about the Message?" *Journal of Black Studies* 33, no. 5 (May 2003): 607–8; Eun-Young Jung, "Articulating Korean Youth Culture through Global Popular Music Styles," 112, 122n7; see also Ha Chaebong, "*Nuga Sŏ T'aeji-rŭl turyŏwŏ hanŭn'ga (TV pogi)*" [Who would be scared of Seo Taiji? (TV monitoring)], *Chosŏn ilbo* [Korea daily], November 18, 1995, 16.

33. Heejoon Chung, "Sport Star vs. Rock Star in Globalizing Popular Culture," 104.

34. Sŏn Sŏngwŏn, *Rog-esŏ indiŭmag-ŭro*, 209.

35. Yi Yŏngmi, *Han'guk taejung kayosa* [A history of Korean popular songs] (Seoul: Shigongsa, 2000), 297.

36. "Han'guk yŏktae ch'oego hit'ŭ sangp'um: 'Sŏ T'aeji-wa aidŭl ŭmban'" [Korea's biggest product for several generations: "The albums of Seo Taiji & Boys"], *K'oria wik'ŭlli* [Korea weekly, New Malden, U.K.], August 8, 1997, 7.

37. Kim Chip'yŏng, *Han'guk kayo chŏngshinsa*, 245; Kim Hyŏnsŏp, *Sŏ T'aeji tamnon*, 107; Kee-hyeung Lee, "Looking Back at the Cultural Politics of Youth Culture in South Korea in the 1990s," 50.

38. Mi Park, *Democracy and Social Change: A History of South Korean Student Movements, 1980–2000* (Bern: Peter Lang, 2008), 206. The initially unlicensed *noraebang* ventures began to emerge in 1991. Kim Hyegyŏng, "Noraebang-ŭi shilt'ae-wa yŏga sŏnyong-e kwanhan yŏn'gu" [A study of the state of noraebang and the use of people's spare time], *Ŭmak-kwa minjok* [Music and the people] 10 (1995): 286, 289. Another important new development was that of the so-called rock café that usually differed from regular bars by showing music videos on large screens in a Western setting. Kee-hyeung Lee, "Looking Back at the Cultural Politics of Youth Culture in South Korea in the 1990s," 49.

39. Kee-hyeung Lee, "Looking Back at the Cultural Politics of Youth Culture in South Korea in the 1990s," 57–58. The term "386 generation" was coined in the 1990s. It was inspired by the 386 processors Koreans used in the 1990s and referred to those in their thirties who had attended university in the 1980s and had been born in the 1960s. Ko Kilsŏp, "386 sedae-ŭi 'kŭnal': chuch'e hyŏngsŏng, sedae chŏngshin, kŭrigo sam-gwa chŏngch'i" [The days of the 386 generation: the formation of autonomy, the spirit of the generation as well as its lives and politics], *Munhwa kwahak* [Culture science] 62 (June 2010): 117.

40. Seung-Kuk Kim, "Changing Lifestyles and Consumption Patterns of the South Korean Middle Class and New Generations," 69.

41. Seung-Kuk Kim, "Changing Lifestyles and Consumption Patterns of the South Korean Middle Class and New Generations," 64.

42. Kim Hyŏnsŏp, *Sŏ T'aeji tamnon*, 100, 108; see also Eun-Young Jung, "Articulating Korean Youth Culture through Global Popular Music Styles," 111.

43. Keith Howard, "Coming of Age: Korean Pop in the 1990s," 88.

44. Kee-hyeung Lee, "Looking Back at the Cultural Politics of Youth Culture in South Korea in the 1990s," 60.

45. Kee-hyeung Lee, "Looking Back at the Cultural Politics of Youth Culture in South Korea in the 1990s," 68.

46. Sarah Thornton, *Club Cultures: Music, Media and Subcultural Capital* (Cambridge: Polity Press, 1995), 11–2; Kee-hyeung Lee, "Looking Back at the Cultural Politics of Youth Culture in South Korea in the 1990s," 66.

47. Dick Hebdige, *Subculture: The Meaning of Style* (London: Methuen, 1979), 133; Kee-hyeung Lee, "Looking Back at the Cultural Politics of Youth Culture in South Korea in the 1990s," 65.

48. Theodor W. Adorno, "On Popular Music" (1992), chapter reprinted in *Cultural*

Theory and Popular Culture: A Reader, ed. John Storey (Dorchester, U.K.: Prentice Hall, 1998), 203–4; see also Dick Hebdige, *Subculture: The Meaning of Style*, 16.

49. Kee-hyeung Lee, "Looking Back at the Cultural Politics of Youth Culture in South Korea in the 1990s," 50.

50. Kee-hyeung Lee, "Looking Back at the Cultural Politics of Youth Culture in South Korea in the 1990s," 65.

51. John Fiske points out that buying is an empowering activity, as it entails choice and thus the possible rejection of the superstructure's control. John Fiske, *Reading the Popular* (London: Routledge, 1989), 26.

52. See Dick Hebdige, *Subculture: The Meaning of Style*, 94–96.

53. In the mid 1990s, when the number of Internet users began to grow rapidly, CD copying and rewriting technology brought about a steep increase in the unlicensed sale and exchange of copyrighted media. This in turn led to a significant drop in record sales in Korea, starting in the late 1990s. Record Industry Association of Korea (RIAK), *Ŭmban shijang kyumo* [Record market size] *1995–2002*. Online report, 2003.

54. Zillmann and Bhatia have shown that an individual's preference toward a particular kind of music affects the degree of their attractiveness to others. Dolf Zillmann and Azra Bhatia, "Effects of Associating with Musical Genres on Heterosexual Attraction," *Communication Research* 16 (1989): 263–88.

55. Yi Yŏngmi, *Han'guk taejung kayosa*, 319.

14

STEPHEN EPSTEIN with JAMES TURNBULL

Girls' Generation? Gender, (Dis)Empowerment, and K-pop

The hottest phrase in Korea nowadays is undeniably "girl group." But girl group fever is more than just a trend: it's symbolic of a cultural era that is embracing the expulsion of authoritarian ideology.

So begins the table of contents blurb for a story on the rise of girl groups (*kŏl kŭrup*) in the March 2010 issue of *Korea*, a public-relations magazine published under the auspices of the Korean Culture and Information Service. Beginning in 2007, with the success of the Wonder Girls, ensembles composed of from three to nine females in their teens or early twenties have dominated South Korean popular music.[1] Certainly the explosion of the term *kŏl kŭrup* in recent public discourse is undeniable: a search of the KBS news archive, for example, turns up the first use only in 2008 with but three citations for the entire year.[2] By 2009, however, this number had increased to 39, and in 2010 KBS-News ran 174 items employing the term *kŏl kŭrup*. Interest continues to expand: in 2011, 356 stories on KBS featured the term.

Equally notably, governmental forces are taking advantage of this trend. In May 2010, one girl group's song—"Huh" by 4Minute—was championed as "extolling freedom of choice" and used as part of a radio propaganda broadcast to North Korea[3]; the following month, the Defense Ministry discussed broadcasting girl group music videos on screens along the DMZ as part of psychological warfare operations.[4] In contrasting but related fashion, the recent success of Korea's girl groups in Japan has become central to promoting a second surge of the Korean Wave and has been heralded by the media in sometimes strident fashion: "Korean Idols 'Occupy Japanese Archipelago,' Lay Waste to Japan" (*Han aidol 'ilyŏldo chŏmryŏng,' ilbon chot'ohwashikida*) reads the title of one particularly egregious article.[5] Strikingly, a number of reports on the high-profile dispute of girl group KARA with its management focused not on the suit itself or the controversial labor structure of the entertainment system but rather on the effect the dispute might have on Korean assertions of brand nationalism.[6]

These examples illustrate the extent to which girl groups have become both a newsworthy topic for media authorities and a tool to be wielded by official interests. As "Korea, Inc." deploys its cultural industries in a bid for global market share, the genre's success has led to a hyperbolic discourse seeking to transcend the narrower realm of pop music. The *Korea* article continues:

> No matter our age or gender, these girls allow us to dream once again, moving us with their cheerfulness and a feeling of fresh radiance. The vibrancy of their songs, dances, clothes, and performances is so irresistible that every move is picked up by the world's radar. They render the term "singer" insufficient. They are at the edge of the frontier of popular culture, but they are not just pioneers—they are the culture.[7]

Nonetheless, despite top-down promotion and accompanying breathless celebrations, the liberating nature of the phenomenon remains debatable. Of course, whenever the market drives musical creation and groups are manufactured rather than arising organically, "authenticity" becomes suspect, and the organization of Korea's music industry allows idol groups minimal artistic autonomy. Furthermore, within a context of changing social mores and reduced profits from Korea's notoriously high levels of illegal downloading, the need for entertainment companies to attract attention for their own performers amid the current glut of groups has led to an increased sexualization of music videos, performances, and commercial endorsements.[8]

Particularly questionable is the correlation of a preponderance of successful young female ensembles in Korean pop music with an expulsion of authoritarian ideology. In this chapter, we engage in a reading of the lyrical and visual codes of the music videos of Korean girl groups from 2007 to early 2011 in order to challenge the notion that the phenomenon signals escape from patriarchy or embedded power structures. As we will argue, although elements of current packaging may be novel, the gender ideologies propagated by such groups as Girls' Generation, KARA, T-ara, Wonder Girls, Miss-A, 2NE1, 4Minute, and similar ensembles have offered society, and young women in particular, at best a highly ambivalent empowerment.

While a substantial body of work exists on gender and Western popular music generally and music videos specifically,[9] and scholars have addressed Korean gender ideologies in film and drama,[10] thus far surprisingly little work has been done on gender and contemporary Korean popular music, despite the salience of gender as a key issue driving its production and consumption and pop music's prominence as a site for the transmission of, and contestation over, gender roles.[11] The considerable evolution in representations of gender and sexuality in Korea since the turn of the millennium renders this lacuna all the more noteworthy. One might cite, for example, the rise of Korean soft masculinity via the *kkonminam* (lit. "flower-handsome man"); sympathetic portrayals of homosexuality (for example, the 2005 hit film *The King and the Clown* and the 2010 drama *Beautiful Life*); and increasing public awareness of transgenderism, as witnessed in the popularity of entertainer Harisu.[12] Popular representations of the feminine have also diversified: in film, the confrontational but nonetheless desirable protagonists of *My Sassy Girl* (2001) and *My Wife Is a Gangster* (2001) exemplify a blurring of gender roles; *The Art of Seduction* (2005) and *Bewitching Attraction* (2006) treat the commodification of provocative femininity within consumer society; and 2008's *My Wife Got Married* and *Live Together* each take female sexual desire and subjectivity as central themes.[13] In comparison, representations of gender roles from girl groups have shown rather less variation.

We treat girl group music videos as a crucial component in the contemporary dissemination of ideologies of gender and sexuality for a few significant reasons. First, although more traditional consumption of Korean pop music exists, albeit with cassettes and CDs having yielded to digital media playback, Korean popular music is driven by the visual, not only via live performance on television but in music videos (regularly referred to as M/V in Korea) too. As Hoon-Soon Kim notes, "The music video has captivated the younger generation . . . and has changed the notion of music from that of something primarily auditory to something to watch as well."[14] Music videos are now consumed in large numbers on the Internet. As of March 2012, the two most watched videos of all time on the Korean YouTube channel were both from girl groups: the official video for the song "Gee" by Girls' Generation, which had been viewed 67 million times, and "Nobody" by competitors Wonder Girls, seen over 56 million times. The savvy use of YouTube, literally and figuratively a key "site" for the experience and distribution of music at a mass level, has now become a core component of Korean entertainment companies' promotion strategies, especially at the international level.[15] Memorable images from music videos and signature dances for songs become touchstones in Korean popular culture and circulate widely.

A second consideration is that, with few exceptions, performers do not compose their own music but become part of the stable of conglomerates, at the moment headed by the triumvirate of SM Entertainment, YG Entertainment, and JYP Entertainment, who together manage most of the groups discussed below. Indeed, one may well regard Korean popular music artists as general entertainers (and thus see unintended irony in the earlier Deok-hyeon Jeong characterization of the term *singer* as "insufficient"), for with the collapse of recorded music sales success has come to depend not so much on vocal talent as dancing ability, physical attractiveness, and the projection of image through appearance in live performances, television programs, advertisements, and so on. In this environment, music videos become not an autonomous expression of performer sensibility but a marketing tactic concocted by managers to sell a cultural product. In order to be effective, a music video (M/V) must resonate with the zeitgeist in the way it conforms to, or in some cases challenges, normative expectations; in this sense it becomes part of a discourse "that is socially constructed by the interplay among mainstream mores and values, consumption practices, and subjective interpretation of its meanings by its audiences."[16]

Concentrating on a reading of lyrics and music videos therefore requires caveats. While the reception of any text is open to contestation, the rapid crosscutting between shots and decontextualizations of music videos do far less to foreclose particular interpretations than the generally more coherent narratives of film or fiction, and the medium's succession of fragmented, spectacular images set to musical accompaniment allows individuals enormous range in the construction of meaning. In a study of audience reaction to Madonna's music videos, J. Brown and L. Schulze also demonstrate wide differences by race, gender, and fandom levels in how viewers perceived a given piece[17]; likewise, within Korea itself age and gender, among other considerations, will have an impact on audience interpretation of videos. Furthermore, pop music now plays a crucial role in Korea's increasing dialogue with the outside world. K-pop's enthusiastic global fan base means that domestic interpretations cannot be accorded exclusive validity any more than one can privilege American understandings of an Eminem or Lady Gaga video as more "correct" than others.

Consequently we stress that our own readings of Korean girl group music videos, while hopefully illuminating, are meant to stimulate discussion rather than be authoritative; our aim is to infiltrate the triumphant discourse of the cultural industries and their champions with a critical appraisal in light of a germane question: are the postmodern expressions of Korean music videos "just another representational strategy that sustains gender discrimination by reinforcing the cultural logic of consumer capitalism," or do "they form a resistant style of expression that can break away from the binarism of the existing patriarchal system"?[18]

Recurrent tropes in the studied presentation of girl groups undercut claims to a progressive ethos. Instead of nuanced views of gendered social identities, Korean girl group music videos and lyrics, albeit with key exceptions, reinforce a dichotomization of male and female. As Ch'a U-jin argues, in one of the few academic analyses of the girl group phenomenon to have appeared thus far, management companies have targeted varying audiences through product differentiation, with Girls' Generation and KARA at one pole, epitomizing the stoking of male fantasy, and at the other 4Minute and 2NE1, who strive for identification from young females.[19] Nonetheless, regardless of where videos fall in relation to this continuum, not only do the roughly 100 girl group videos from 2007–11 surveyed for this chapter almost without exception focus on the female image as visual spectacle; they can also be subsumed within a limited set of categories.[20] Most notably, while girl group singers often express desire openly, the viewer in such videos is regularly constructed as male, and the potential assertion of subjectivity is accompanied by a coy passivity that returns initiative to men. Another set of songs suggests women's exertion of control, but influence is wielded through recourse to the force of a feminine sexuality that renders males helpless and thus transmits a message that narcissistic desirability is the route to redress power imbalance. Even two additional categories of songs, ostensibly directed toward young females through referencing solidarity in acting according to one's own wishes or wreaking revenge on unfaithful boyfriends, nevertheless remain committed to a self-objectifying preoccupation with an external gaze or continue to define women in relation to men. While this typology is not exhaustive and we consider the exceptional case of the group f(x), the prevalence of songs from these categories challenges more benign interpretations of the current dominance of girl groups in Korean pop culture.

OH, OPPA!

Let us consider, then, examples of the first set of girl group videos, those in which desire, often unrequited, for a male is expressed. While it is difficult to assess the impact of a given song, sales, chart listings, and Internet video hit counts offer a reasonable gauge of significance, and accordingly we begin with an analysis of one of the most iconic and ubiquitous Korean hits of the last few years, "Oh!" released in January 2010 by Girls' Generation, currently the reigning princesses of K-pop.

A stylistic tic of Korean girl group videos is a brief introductory sequence that sets up the song proper and provides a frame of reference in which to read it. "Oh!" begins with the nine members of the group relaxing playfully in an apparent communal living situation. After eight seconds of music that resembles a calliope and reinforces a carnivallike atmosphere, the viewer sees a computer displaying an image of the nine members of the band wearing football cheerleader outfits and each holding a placard to spell out in English "GIRLS' ♥ YOU." The group members thus announce collective affection for a second person addressee, ambiguously treated as singular or plural, in a strongly gendered image that renders this "you," and the viewer, male. The video then launches into the song itself, the visuals cutting between the band at home and in ensemble dance performances at a football stadium:

> *Oppa*, look at me, take a good look at me
> (This is the first time I've talked like this, ha!)
> I fixed my hair and put on makeup
> (How come you're the only one who's so oblivious?)

Several points deserve comment: first of all, the term of address applied here for the male, as in most girl group songs, is *oppa*. Literally this means "elder brother of a female" and can be used by young women to address a slightly older male, often with a connotation of amatory interest. In Korea's age-based hierarchy, the term by definition subordinates the female, and its use thus becomes part of the repertoire of *aegyo*, a calculated performance of cuteness that infantilizes those (most frequently female) who engage in it in the hope of gaining the favor of a superior or attracting romantic attention.

One should also consider the decision to present Girls' Generation as cheerleaders for American football, which is far from a major sport in Korea. Invocation of a fantasy America is not uncommon in Korean music videos, presumably not only to facilitate international appeal, eye-catching images, and the free flow of imagination that characterizes the genre but also to obviate a need to conform closely to Korean reality. Here, the pairing of football players with cheerleaders emphasizes gender differentiation as well: the men's pads and helmets, which obscure their faces throughout, accentuate power and virility; in comparison, the women appear fragile and delicate, an impression enhanced by close-ups of affected *aegyo* poses. Elements of hero worship are also evident, as members of Girls' Generation are seen holding, embracing, or kissing the helmet, which comes to embody a rugged, desirable, hard masculinity (see, for example, 0:35–0:39 in the M/V).

The lyrics apologize for the girls' forwardness and desire for attention as they announce that never before have they spoken so daringly:

Thump thump, my heart is beating . . .
Oh! Oh! Oh! I love you *oppa*
Ah! Ah! Ah! So, so much
Please don't laugh! I'm shy
I really mean it, please don't tease me
But there go my silly words again . . .

The overwhelming attractiveness of *oppa* has impelled a sexual maturation. He is presented as the first object of affection, yet nonetheless remains impassive. Homosocial harmony offsets intimations of rivalry, and the video's images and lyrics present an incongruity between claims of shy innocence and flirtatious overtures, revealing dress and eroticized dance moves. In other words, there coexist fantasy-fueling projections of both virginal demeanor and eager collective anticipation of defloration. This tension is pervasive in this category of girl group videos, serving as a quasi-master trope.

In Girls' Generation's 2009 megahit "Gee," enough similar elements are present as to suggest conscious formula. The video opens with the members of the group configured as mannequins in a clothing store, and the treatment of the group as figurines, void of personality, further effaces an individuality already weakened by ensemble performance and apparel designed to create a visual effect of overall likeness.[21] Here the mannequins are seemingly inspired to life by their communal desire for the attractive male employee, and the song becomes an ode to romantic awakening, beginning in English: "Uh-huh. Listen, boy, my first love story." As in "Oh!" the lyrics point to shyness in falling in love (*sarange ppajyŏsŏ sujubŭn gŏl*), a heart thumping with excitement, and self-deprecating references to being made a fool (*pabo*) by desire (see plate 5). Close-ups of the women's hands brought to upper body and face in childlike fashion, intended to be endearing, again feature throughout (note especially the successive cuts at 0:38–0:40 and 0:59–1:04), and professions of shyness are interspersed with dance shots of the members in their signature hot pants.

This motif of dolls brought to life as fantasy figures becomes even more sexually charged in the video to Girls' Generation 2009 follow-up single "*Sowŏnŭl malhaebwa*" (Tell me your wish), which employs, unusually, two brief introductory sequences before the song proper. In the first (0:00–0:16), the members of the group materialize around an oversized genie lamp to the accompaniment of sitar and tabla (see fig. 14.1), setting the mood for lyrics that relate the girls' submissive willingness to serve as fan-

Figure 14.1. Opening sequence of "Tell Me Your Wish" by Girls' Generation.

tasy objects and effectively convert them into ciphers whose existence depends on flattering male desires:

Tell me your wish
Tell me the little dreams in your heart
Try to draw the ideal woman in your head
Then look at me
I'm your genie, your dream, your genie.

The second introductory sequence (0:17–0:28) employs a disco-inflected soundtrack that begins with a sleek (or unctuous, depending on one's perspective) masculine voice saying, "Hey," and goes further in establishing the video as an erotic daydream. The gendering of the camera's gaze becomes explicit: in three successive point of view shots, a male, hands visible in front, comes upon a trio of welcoming band members. In the first shot the subject opens a door and discovers girls fighting with pillows on a pink bed that remains suggestively visible at various points throughout the m/v; it is almost as if the camera has intruded upon a harem, or more to the point, a pornographic video set, and thus renders the viewer a voyeuristic accomplice as the girls' initial surprise yields to delight. In the second shot, the male is welcomed into a club scene and is drawn toward soft drinks stacked on a table. Eager anticipation of a male presence becomes particularly striking in the third shot as—reminiscent of a stag party—a group member jumps out of a cake in welcome. A recapitulated three-shot sequence (2:27–2:37) adds hints of erotic progression from coy refusal to acquiescence and satisfaction: in the first, by the bed, one member wags a finger at the subject as if to say "naughty boy" but is preempted by another who gives a come-hither gesture; in the second, the subject snaps a photo of the girls' posing, and the third involves the provocative smearing of white frosting from a cake that says "I ♥ U." The video, unsurprisingly, is otherwise composed of seductive dance sequences with eroticized shots and ample attention to the group's bare legs.

Girls' Generation is, of course, hardly the only girl group whose videos hold out the fantasy that the viewer is a male addressee desired by eagerly awaiting females who will not act until he makes the first move. The visuals of "Mister" by KARA, for instance, feature the ŏngdŏngi ch'um, a dance that became notorious for its titillating swaying of the buttocks, and the lyrics detail growing interest in the song's addressee and include hopeful invitations: "I like you and my heart is getting bolder (come closer, closer). My heart keeps thumping . . . Hey, mister. Look over here, mister." Nevertheless, ultimate initiative remains with the male, who again is placed in a superior position with the English title address and flattered into imagining his uniqueness ("I've never felt like this before").

The trope of simultaneous innocence and anticipation persists even when lyrics and images come into conflict with each other: the protagonist of T-ara's video for "Like the First Time," for instance, is presented as a naïf whose girlfriends tell her she needs to meet a man, and they then provide advice on slimming, style, and comportment. The song's lyrics, however, specifically invoke experience ("This isn't my first love/I'm not innocent"), and the rap break, both lyrically and visually, transforms the protagonist from ingénue to wizened aggressor, as she claims that she will refuse a man who constrains her, and the choreography progresses to overtly sexual gestures. Nonetheless, the video returns to the image of the protagonist shyly awaiting her crush's approval: they meet at a café for a first date and when he invites her onward to continue their rendezvous, she is congratulated by her girlfriends, who are watching expectantly in the background, and then dashes after him giddily. The video thus presents a striking example of Korean popular culture's current attempts to accommodate contradictory imperatives, not always with great logic, and with consequences for a reading of the empowering nature of the recent surge in girl groups.

I'M SO HOT . . .

In her study of Korean music videos shortly after the turn of the millennium, Kim notes that "women are presented in polarized images . . . as either an innocent and sweet girl or a provocative and sexy femme fatale" but also that many images fall between the two extremes, such as a "sexy yet inno-

Figure 14.2. So Hee gives a knowing look in the Wonder Girls' "So Hot," acknowledging the power she wields over the male gaze.

cent girl" and focus on "her body dancing sexily."[22] By the latter part of the decade, this third option had become almost exclusive in girl group videos: lyrical and visual strategies steer away from "either/or" toward "both/and," urging, in varying proportions, a melding of the two poles as a goal to strive for: claim to virtue remains, but sexiness trumps it as de rigueur quality.[23]

Patriarchal continuity remains obvious in the songs analyzed above, which depict an essential harmony between the sexes, governed by projections of availability and an encouragement of pursuit that returns power to the male. In contrast, a further set of songs suggests that the sexes are engaged in an antagonistic, zero-sum struggle for control. Although such songs, in encouraging action for women beyond flattering male fantasy, less patently submit to traditional norms, they too undercut their own movement toward a more hopeful world.

Consider "Irony," the first single from the Wonder Girls, whose success launched the current surge of girl groups. The song's introductory sequence contains a shot of the Wonder Girls' logo, followed by a wolf whistle. Although the English term "wolf whistle" does not translate literally into Korean, it is a useful phrase here, for in the ideological universe of girl group videos, men are regularly *nŭktae* (wolves) and women, not infrequently, *yŏu* (foxes). These traditional animal metaphors continue to resonate in contemporary Korean popular discourse and envisage men as dangerous predators and women as sly creatures, the latter figured specifically in the *kumiho,* a nine-tailed fox of folklore that would transform into a beautiful woman and seduce men in order to eat their liver.

In songs that reflect such a worldview, women rely on physical attraction to gain an advantage; rather than simply performing to the dictates of the male gaze, such videos demonstrate its knowing exploitation. The Wonder Girls' 2008 hit "So Hot" flirts, almost literally, with narcissism as a desirable goal and deserves analysis for its simultaneous satire and nurturing of such an attitude. The video opens as the front of a giant gift-wrapped box drops away to reveal the group members strutting within. Each wears a piece of clothing with leopard print that conveys a knowing feline sexuality. The video then intersperses shots of them dancing provocatively within the box and being fawned over in turn by male admirers, to the accompaniment of an infectious hip-hop beat and over the top lyrics:

Why do you keep looking at me?
Am I that pretty?
Well, even if I am, if you stare at me like that
I get a little embarrassed

Humor is undeniably present here: one group member turns up her nose at the gifts her suitors present her with and then gazes longingly at a huge diamond in a store window, only to have the men scatter in fright. Group leader Sun Ye accepts a bouquet from a man who jumps for joy, at which she immediately flings the flowers over her shoulder. Nor is the group afraid to poke fun at itself: member So Hee stumbles while walking on a red carpet and pulls herself up as if nothing happened.

But what message does the video convey ultimately? The humor present might allow one to dismiss it all simply as a joke, but for the fact that at the song's release the Wonder Girls were arguably the top pop stars in the land and constructed in popular discourse as iconically "hot." Consequently, for them to claim to be so as they dance seductively only engages the irony that titled their first single in confused fashion. The *naesung* (that is, a coy disavowal of inner intention) of the group's members within the video in claiming to be embarrassed by stares is thus matched by the song's meta-strategy.

Engagement with, and manipulation of, the male gaze, moreover, could hardly be more self-conscious: So Hee plays to admiring cameras beneath a theater marquee, and paparazzi lurk in the bushes snapping shots of the group's rapper Yu Bin lounging at a pool. Yu Bin, however, coolly reverses the dynamic. When a man is so smitten by her that he falls off balance and belly flops into the water, she rates his dive like an Olympic judge: zero. In other words, the video shows the Wonder Girls arousing interest in themselves and reveling in controlling access. That So Hee's shirt in the dance sequences reads "Stop" is surely no coincidence. Thus, the glamorous world they inhabit encourages jealousy for the attention they receive and power they wield, despite their (mock) protestations that celebrity is tiresome. As the rap climax relates: "All the boys be lovin' me/girls be hatin' me/they will never stop/'cause they know I'm so hot, hot." Nonetheless, even as the video sanctifies obsession with appearance, it impels a reminder that attention is a scarce commodity: Sun Mi, dressed in a cheerleader costume and surrounded by football players, has another woman twirl by and her fickle admirers immediately turn to the newcomer. The video holds out empowerment and insecurity as its dual rewards, because at any moment somebody "so hotter" than thou may come along.

Controlling the male gaze also figures in "Bang!" by After School, which frames the purpose of abandon in dancing as "making the fellows go crazy." A more concerted treatment appears in their song "Ah!" which adds the tease of a relationship between teacher and student and is set in a fantasylike girls' high school (a couch is clearly visible in the classroom). The song has the group members in eroticized school uniforms, presenting themselves to an attractive male teacher for appraisal, certain of their seductive power:

> You've fallen in love with my slender legs and the way I look,
> If I give you a wink you'll fall further
> You think you're special, but how's my body?
> You're going to crumble before me.

As with "So Hot," the potential for empowerment within the song calls itself into question as it derives from unabashed manipulation of desirability, given additional impact by the video's school setting.

2010's "Bad Girl, Good Girl" by Miss-A, one of the most intriguing and successful recent girl group videos, addresses the duality of its title head-on and in doing so inverts the framework of control and conflict found in "So Hot." Here the members proclaim that when they dance, they are "bad girls," but in love they are "good girls," and criticize the hypocrisy of males who are mesmerized by their sexual appeal but then reject them for the negative stereotypes their provocative style calls forth. The video also opens in a high school as one member aggressively knocks a student aside; another grinds her heel into the book he has dropped. In addressing the male gaze explicitly, the lyrics insist on a distinction between the external and the internal ("you don't know me/so shut up, boy") and lash out at male assertions of patriarchal privilege, portraying them as cowardly:

> You couldn't say anything in front of me
> But you trash talk me behind my back . . .
> Why do you judge me?
> Are you afraid of me?
> You look at me as if I'm pathetic
> But your own staring is ridiculous. . . .
> You lose it when you watch me dance
> But the hypocritical way you point afterward
> Is really ridiculous

The song therefore stands the *naesung* of "So Hot" on its head: instead of dissembling ulterior motives, this song claims that the truer essence lies within. Nonetheless, despite the song's confrontational lyrics, the video renders problematic the appropriation of dancing like a "bad girl" as pure self-expression, as it acquires much of its force from the eroticism of its choreography, noteworthy even by the standards of K-pop, and one cannot escape the fact that the video is a product designed as spectacle to arrest attention. Though explicitly addressed to males and perhaps evoking empathy on the part of women who might be tempted to join in singing "shut up, boy," the song justifies commitment to the increasing demands of the public gaze in Korea's intensely mediated consumer culture: blithe self-commoditization and positive sense of self go hand in hand, even if prejudices need to be addressed. In this light, it is not difficult to see the song as a cynically brilliant strategy on the part of impresario Jin Young Park. What is more difficult, however, is to see the song as genuinely empowering self-expression on the part of a band that includes among its four members two Chinese women who are not native speakers of Korean and then-sixteen-year-old member Suzi (see plate 6).

4Minute, cited above as offering a song professing freedom of choice and addressing females as their primary audience, hold out similarly ambivalent freedoms. Their first single, for example, declares their intention to become a "Hot Issue:"

> From head to toe, hot issue
> Every single thing about me, hot issue
> Take control of everything
> I'm always a hot it hot it hot it hot it i-i-i-i-i-i issue . . .

Are you jealous of everything about my style
But you can't copy me so carelessly
If you want, try to follow, try to follow my style

With brash claims to be in control of their destiny, they urge other young women to follow them, but do so within the context of competition that relegates their fans to wannabe status and additionally sees their appeal in terms of contemporary Korean standards of beauty: "my waist is slenderer than yours/I've got long, slim legs."

Their follow-up single "Huh" follows a similar lyrical pattern and speaks of a desire to be famous and determination to ignore naysayers who don't believe they can appear on TV or in magazines or can become better looking: they will, again, act the way they want (*nae mamdaero*). Similarly, "I Me My Mine," whose title could scarcely be more self-centered, also speaks of acting *nae namdaero*. Just as motifs recur in the first set of videos examined above (shyness, thumping heart, for example), so a studied formula emerges in 4Minute's stance (acting to one's desires, being in control, declaration of hotness, encouraging followers). But acting as one wishes for 4Minute means recognizing the tenets of consumer and celebrity culture, and thus their lyrical assertions of control suggest a pseudo-individualization that Adorno would likely have pounced upon.

4Minute's recent video "Heart to Heart" exemplifies a final further category of recurrent videos that deserve consideration here. In this song the group gleefully engages in cruel pranks on the boyfriend of a member who has been caught chatting up girls at a club. In its use of a revenge motif, it resembles both the Wonder Girls' "Irony," which depicts how one member, egged on by the rest, uses a voodoo doll to torment an unfaithful boyfriend, and "I Don't Care" by 2NE1, in which the group triumphantly humiliate cheating boyfriends in front of other women through magical entry into a time-stop world (fig. 14.3). In all three videos "girl power" solidarity draws on a wellspring of wish fulfillment. "I Don't Care" has been described by 2NE1's lead singer CL as providing a warning message to men and advice for women.[24] The song thus exemplifies a change that YG Entertainment executive Jinu Kim describes in recent years: "Lyrically, it used to be: 'Oh, you hurt me so bad, I'm going to curl up in a dark corner and cry my eyes out.' Now, it's like: 'I don't care anymore about you, don't be messing with my heart.'"[25] Nevertheless, it remains worth noting that selfhood is still defined in relation to a validating—albeit rejected—male, that revenge is collectively rather than individually exerted, and that elements of fantasy undercut the possibility of revenge in reality.

Figure 14.3. 2NE1 humiliates cheating boyfriends in front of other women in "I Don't Care," using revenge as a mode of empowerment.

Among girl groups 2NE1 in particular has gained a reputation for feisty independence, and Kim estimates that as much as 70 percent of their fan base is female. This distinctiveness is evident in "Can't Nobody," an ode to partying in which, like Miss-A, they describe themselves as "bad but good." Declaring themselves equipped with an immature charm and fearless youth (*ch'ŏrŏpsŏ kŭge maeryŏgin gŏl, kŏbŏpsŏ nae ch'ŏlmŭmin gŏl*), they are determined to raise the volume and wake up the world because right now they "don't give a fuck." However, among the roughly 100 songs surveyed for this chapter one of only two songs about not recovering well from a breakup comes in fact from 2NE1. Their 2010 hit "Go Away" has a visual narrative of grief after losing a boyfriend, which ends with the race car that CL is driving winding up in a fiery crash. Nonetheless, our invocation of Adorno above does not mean that consumers cannot apply resistant readings to Korean music videos in a manner more reminiscent of Stuart Hall's approach to audience reception: YouTube user comments show that a significant number of fans choose to interpret the narrative in such a way that the crash allows CL to gain revenge upon the boyfriend who has deserted her, because not to do so would conflict with their own internalization of an empowering meaning that the group holds out for them. As the top comment on the English-subbed version of the video read: "Broken heart with ATTITUDE! Like it!"[26]

As we move to the conclusion, it is crucial to underline K-pop's rapid evolution: during the period between when this chapter was composed and it went to press, the restrictive song categories we have sketched were being increasingly challenged and stretched. The group f(x) also deserves particular consideration in this regard, for their lyrics and videos suggest that SM Entertainment, perhaps surprisingly given the overpowering heteronormativity of their presentation of stable mates Girls' Generation, has left spaces of indeterminacy that allow a queer reading of the former group's material. Moreover, YouTube statistics indicate that f(x) finds resonance above all with young women, virtually without exception, in contrast to other groups discussed, including 2NE1; each of their videos' largest audience has been females in the 13–17, 18–24, and 25–34 age range, respectively.

This ambiguity relies in great part on group member Amber, who has become a beloved figure among K-pop followers precisely for her strikingly androgynous look. It is surely no accident that in a fan video of "Surprise Party" at 1:26–1:36, where the lyrics state, "I want to congratulate you, boy," Amber and fellow band member Sulli have their arms around each other,[27] with Amber looking so boyish as to prompt a double take. Unlike Girls' Generation, who regularly direct their songs to an *oppa*, f(x)'s hit "Nu Abo" begins with an address to an *ŏnni* (the term of address used by a female to an older sister) and has lyrics that may be read as expressing uncertain adolescent sexuality:

> What should I do, *ŏnni*,
> Listen to me for a second
> *ŏnni*, I don't know people
> I'm really eccentric
> People tease me . . .
> Listen to me for a second, *ŏnni*.
> *I'm in the trance*
> What's this feeling now?
> This is the first time for me . . .

It must be love.

Amber's Michael Jacksonesque crotch grab at 2:40, decidedly rare from females in K-pop, as the group sings, "This is how we do it, our love f(x)," along with the video for "Chu," in which the band members give a communal thumbs-down to a male and female couple kissing on television, otherwise unexplained, all reinforce potential for subversive readings.

The unusual territory that f(x) has staked out for itself becomes especially clear when one contrasts their video for the song "Chocolate Love" with the mirrored version by Girls' Generation, as the two impel comparative viewing (each video, itself an advertisement for a Samsung phone, is bookended with excerpts of its counterpart). Whereas the Girls' Generation version variously has the members solo, in trios, or as an ensemble, playing to the camera in lacy white garb that conveys the formulaic sexy innocence analyzed above, the f(x) video displays the band members in dark, tight-fitting leather. The choreography too is far edgier, with the group frequently intertwined in pairs, their faces close enough to imply coupled intimacy. Adding to this homoerotic tension are more overtly sexual elements than in the Girls' Generation version, including frequent close-ups of the members' erotically swaying hips, the raising and spreading of their legs in quasi-burlesque fashion at 3:15, and, not least, the shot of group member Sulli reclining against Luna, hand draped across Luna's thigh as Luna places her hand on Sulli's shoulder, from 3:27–3:31. The song's lyrics that speak of a hidden, shocking love, in conjunction with the visuals, encourage a Sapphic interpretation if one is prepared to accept its possibility.

CONCLUSION

How ultimately does one then assess the collective effect of a pop phenomenon? In this chapter we have attempted to demonstrate that, despite an official discourse promoting the meteoric rise of girl groups as emblematic of an empowering shift toward an egalitarian society, an analysis of the lyrical and visual codes of girl groups suggests overall a more ambivalent situation. Furthermore, the significantly increased dependence on the female form as a mainstay of popular culture demands a critical reading, even if it alternately suggests such differing strategies as catering to male fantasies of innocent yet willing throngs of young females, a conscious manipulation of the male gaze, or narcissistic self-exploitation directed at same-sex peers that dismisses patriarchy only to careen into the similarly problematic dictates of consumerist late capitalism. Indeed, given the hegemonic social structures of today, it is difficult to see how cultural products can truly empower young women, although glimmers of hope may lie on the horizon.

While the conundrum has appeared at times almost irresolvable, context does play an enormous role: it is important to acknowledge here the, to many, surprising reception of Girls' Generation in Japan, where fans have been overwhelmingly young females. Although we have argued, hopefully cogently, for ways in which Girls' Generation videos treat them as fantasy figures for male consumption within Korea, young Japanese women, as widely reported, have found identification with Korean girl groups empowering, as they see them as role models and evincing a more adult sexuality than homegrown J-pop idols.

Within Korea analysis of the overall effect of the rise of girl groups also requires considering public reaction to the phenomenon as it emerged in

2007, particularly the young age of some performers. While Girls' Generation and the Wonder Girls were hardly the first groups to have members in their mid-teens, an increasingly sexualized presentation, driven by industry pressures, distinguished them from counterparts from a decade previous such as FINKL, Baby VOX, and SES. Kim Soo-ah notes that despite initial feminist objections, over time the newfound adult male fandom of this recent surge came to be framed popularly as an avuncular concern for the welfare of the girls, with sexual elements ignored.[28] Indeed, as Kim argues, despite a heated online debate between noted cultural critics Kang Myeong-sok and Yi Gyu-Hyeong, eventually Korean media and society generally found it difficult to acknowledge the possibility of more prurient interests in the sexy presentation of girl groups as a factor in their popularity.[29]

Arguably, this discursive triumph, fostered by the enormous success of the Wonder Girls in 2007, opened a window for sexualization to increase, and, given the logic of the globalized market and contemporary Korean media determination of appropriate roles for women, this objectification has enabled lyrical stances of either innocent passivity or more self-assured declarations of control, but each conjoined with increasingly provocative visual display. Girl groups and their current prominence in Korean popular culture thus intersect here with real life in more serious ways: a 2010 Ministry of Gender Equality and Family investigation found that 60 percent of girl group members admitted to pressure from managers to wear revealing clothing and/or perform dance moves with which they were uncomfortable.[30] In considering the larger effect of their videos within the Korean context, moreover, one should recall the country's score on the United Nations Development Program's 2008 calculation of the "Gender Empowerment Measure," the lowest in the Organization for Economic Cooperation and Development (OECD) and well behind that of many developing nations.[31] Not only has the participation rate of women in the workforce, also consistently among the lowest in the OECD, stagnated at 50 percent or below since the International Monetary Fund (IMF) crisis and decreased in the latest global downturn[32]; Korea also stands out as being one of only two OECD countries where employers can legally demand photographs on resumes.[33] In such circumstances, the message that concentration on sexual attractiveness allows a measure of control within a highly competitive society has the effect of co-opting consumers into feeling that they are exercising rational choice in accommodating, rather than challenging, this state of affairs.

Though presented in carefree fashion, girl group videos then are far from apolitical cultural products. The prominent placement in Girls' Generation's "Tell Me Your Wish" video of the drink Meiro Beauty N, which they were endorsing at the time, underscores the increasing confluence of media and capitalism, with the potential for vested interests in encouraging unhealthy body ideals. In this light, a particularly disturbing aspect of T-ara's video for "Like the First Time" is the intensive weight-losing regimen forced upon the protagonist, Hyomin, in order to prepare for her date. She is seen riding a stationary bicycle frantically, and then she and another of the member of the group cheer when a measuring tape confirms the reduction of her waist size. The video normalizes female complicity in society's surveillance by presenting it as the responsibility of friends to ensure that a peer adapts to the demands of the beauty industry.

The media further exacerbate such effects: a March 2011 episode of *Ranking Show High 5* castigated various girl group members for having sturdy, muscled legs that arose from dancing instead of the slimmer ideal.[34] It then becomes not a far step from the world of music videos and celebrity shows to real life, as performers focus on perceived imperfections with consequent loss of self-esteem and the possibility for serious physical health issues: not only was Hyomin already slim by any standards but also concerns have emerged that she genuinely suffered from anorexia nervosa.[35] Her situation is not unique: the women in Girls' Generation are said to be kept on a diet of 1,200 calories a day by their trainers, and member Seohyun was reportedly 9kg (20 pounds) underweight in February 2011.[36]

The pervasive media determination of ideal body image readily percolates down to the public, and statistics demonstrate a significant acceleration in body dysphoria in this millennium,[37] with increased percentages of women (and, significantly, men as well)[38] seeking plastic surgery as a tool for advancement in a competitive job market; as early as 2002 a study found that fully half of high-school girls in Korea were unable to donate blood because of anemia and malnutrition caused by dieting.[39] Nor it is merely academics who take note; an offhand comment from a YouTube user, on a now-deleted clip of a Girls' Generation song promoting a product, testifies to awareness and resentful acknowledgment of disempowering consumption messages propagated by Korean girl groups:

> "So I just ate a bag of chips. Like, those large bags. Then I came and watched this CF [commercial film] . . . I feel so fat. ;~; excuse me while I go burn all the junk food in my house and go exercise for 10 hours. Soshi [that is, *Sonyŏ shidae*], why must you have such an effect on me? I WANT TO EAT MY FOOD IN PEACE."

And finally, to return once more to the celebratory discourse from *Korea* magazine that initially prompted our investigation of this topic, reason remains to question precisely what form of empowerment is offered by the rise of girl groups in contemporary Korea:

"Some are so surprised by the elder generation's enthusiasm for girl groups that they cannot help but mention the Lolita complex. Nevertheless, that would be an example of an exaggerated principle that remains from the past authoritarian era. In the course of shifting from a masculine-dominated era to one of feminine equality, the imposing frames of age and gender are being slowly torn down. The time has come in pop culture where a man in his 40s can cheer for teenage girl groups without being looked at suspiciously."[40]

A cynical conclusion is difficult to avoid, as the logic here reaches almost comical proportions: the empowerment present in the rise of girl groups as a phenomenon is not that it brings young women to a heightened sense of their own possibilities in the world, which is mentioned nowhere in the chapter, but rather that Korea's pop culture commodification of sexuality has reached the point that for middle-aged men to focus their gaze on underage performers becomes cause for rejoicing rather than embarrassment. One might reasonably wonder in whose interests a discourse of empowerment is being disseminated.

NOTES

1. For an account of the structural factors that led to the explosion in idol groups in recent years, see Kim Soo-ah, "Sonyŏ imiji ŭi pulgŏrihwa wa sobi pangshik ŭi kusŏng: sonyŏ kŭrup ŭi samch'on p'aen tamnon kusŏng," Midiŏ, jendŏ wa munhwa 15 (2010): 79–119; and Shin Hyun-joon, "K-pop ŭi munhwajŏngch'ihak," ŏllon kwa sahoe 13, no. 3 (2005): 7–36.

2. The term yŏsŏng kŭrup (female group) has been in circulation longer than kŏl kŭrup but never achieved widespread currency.

3. Bomi Lim, "S. Korea Renews Propaganda with Pop Song, Eating Advice," Bloomberg News, May 24, 2010, accessed March 27, 2011, http://www.bloomberg.com /news/2010-05-24/south-korean-song-blasted-into-north-as-propaganda-war -revived-on-sinking.html.

4. "Girl Bands to Assist in 'Psychological Warfare,'" The Chosunilbo, June 11, 2010, accessed March 27, 2011, http://english.chosun.com/site/data/html_dir/2010/06 /11/2010061100432.html.

5. Kang Kyŏng-nok, "Han aidol 'Ilyŏldo chŏmryŏng,' ilbon chot'ohwashikida," Ashia Kyŏngje, August 26, 2010, accessed March 27, 2011, http://www.asiae.co.kr/news /view.htm?idxno=2010082608205252860&sp=EC.

6. See, for example, Daum Yŏnye, "Kara sat'ae hallyu kwoench'anhna ajik chikchŏpchŏgin t'agyŏk ŏpta," February 22, 2011, accessed March 27, 2011, http://media.daum.net /entertain/enews/view?newsid=20110222072404743.

7. Jeong, "Swept Up," 48.

8. Nam Chi-ŭn, "*Mommaeman poinŭn kŏl kŭrup 'kwayŏl' shidae*," *The Hankyoreh*, August 30, 2010, accessed March 27, 2011, http://www.hani.co.kr/arti/culture/entertainment /437420.html; Kim Pong-hyŏn, "'*Sekshihan' sonyŏ shidae choahanŭn ke choeingayo?*" *Pressian*, February 4, 2010, accessed March 27, 2011, http://www.pressian.com /article/article.asp?article_num=60100203164550&section=04.

9. See, for example, Lisa A. Lewis, *Gender Politics and MTV: Voicing the Difference*, (Philadelphia: Temple University Press, 1990); and Julie Andsager and Kimberly Roe, "'What's Your Definition of Dirty, Baby?' Sex in Music Video," *Sexuality & Culture* 7, no. 3 (2003): 79–97.

10. For example, Kyung Hyun Kim, *The Remasculinization of Korean Cinema* (Durham, NC: Duke University Press, 2004); and Soyoung Kim, "Do Not Include Me in Your 'Us': Peppermint Candy and the Politics of Difference." *Korea Journal* 46, no. 1 (2006): 60–83.

11. English language exceptions include Hoon-Soon Kim, "Korean Music Videos, Post-modernism, and Gender Politics," in *Feminist Cultural Politics in Korea*, ed. Jung-hwa Oh (Seoul: Prunsasang Publishing, 2005), 195–227; Heather Willoughby, "Image Is Everything: The Marketing of Femininity in Korean Pop Music," in *Korean Pop Music: Riding the Wave*, ed. Keith Howard (Folkestone, U.K.: Global Oriental, 2006), 99–108; and Eun-Young Jung, "Playing the Race and Sexuality Cards in the Trans-national Pop Game: Korean Music Videos for the U.S. Market," *Journal of Popular Music Studies* 22, no. 2 (2010): 219–36. For Korean work specifically on girl groups in addition to Kim, "*Sonyŏ imiji*," see Ch'a U-jin, "*Kŏl kŭrup chŏnsŏnggi*," *Munhwa pipyŏng* 59 (2009): 270–83. Lee Dong-yeon's edited collection *Aidol: H.O.T.esŏ sonyŏshidaekkaji, aidol munhwa pogosŏ* (Seoul: Imaejin, 2011) appeared too late for the authors to take into close consideration.

12. On the *kkonminam*, see especially Sun Jung, *Korean Masculinities and Transcultural Consumption: Yonsama, Rain, Oldboy, K-pop Idols* (Hong Kong: Hong Kong University Press, 2011). On Harisu, see Gloria Davies, M. E. Davies, and Young-A Cho, "Hallyu Ballyhoo and Harisu: Marketing and Representing the Transgendered in South Korea," in *Complicated Currents: Media Flows, Soft Power, and East Asia*, ed. D. Black, S. Epstein, and A. Tokita (Monash University ePress, 2010), 09.1–09.12.

13. On blurred gender roles, see Myoung Hye Kim, "Woman to Be Seen but Not to Be Heard: Representation of Woman in the Contemporary Korean Movie *My Wife Is a Gangster*" (paper presented at the Twenty-Third Conference of IAMCR, Gender and Communication Section, Barcelona, Spain, July 21–26, 2002); and Stephen Epstein, "The Masculinization of (Women in) Korean Cinema?" (paper presented at the annual meeting of the Association for Asian Studies, San Francisco, California, April 2006). For an account of female sexual subjectivity in 1990s film, see So-hee Lee, "The Concept of Female Sexuality in Korean Popular Culture," in *Under Construction: The Gendering of Modernity, Class, and Consumption in the Republic of Korea*, ed. Laurel Kendall (Honolulu: University of Hawai'i Press, 2002), 141–64.

14. Kim, "Korean Music Videos," 195.

15. Evan Ramsted, "YouTube Helps South Korean Band Branch Out," *The Wall Street Journal*, January 14, 2011, accessed March 27, 2011, http://online.wsj.com/article

/SB10001424052748704458204576073663148914264.html; Ja-young Yoon, "You-Tube Taking Hallyu on International Ride," *Korea Times*, February 8, 2011, accessed March 27, 2011, http://www.koreatimes.co.kr/www/news/biz/2011/02/123_81039 .html.

16. Phillip Vannini and Scott M. Myers, "Crazy About You: Reflections on the Meanings of Contemporary Teen Pop Music," *Electronic Journal of Sociology* (2002), accessed March 27, 2011, http://www.sociology.org/content/vo1006.002/vannini_myers .html.

17. J. Brown and L. Schultz, "The Effect of Race, Gender, and Fandom on Audience Interpretations of Madonna's Music Videos," *Journal of Communication* 40 (1990): 88–102. An anecdote reveals a variety of interpretation in the Korean context: one coauthor conducted a blind survey of his contemporary Asian society class, asking whether students found the Wonder Girls' "So Hot" video primarily empowering, degrading, funny, obnoxious, ironic, or none of the above. All six answers generated multiple responses.

18. Kim, "Korean Music Videos," 195–96.

19. Ch'a, *Kŏl kŭrup chŏnsŏng shidae*, 273.

20. For a YouTube playlist that incorporates the videos referred to in this chapter in order, see http://www.youtube.com/view_play_list?p=B1C588AD8DCCB5D6.

21. One might also consider how the notion of "living dolls" structures the depiction of Girls' Generation; 2011 witnessed the debut of the unsubtly named girl group 5Dolls. Compare Aljosa Puzar, "Asian Dolls and the Western Gaze: Notes on the Female Dollification in South Korea," *Asian Women* 27, no. 2 (2011): 81–111.

22. Kim, "Korean Music Videos," 222.

23. For more on the rise of such a cultural turn within Korean society, see Joanna Elfving-Hwang, *Representations of Femininity in Contemporary South Korean Literature* (Folkestone, U.K.: Global Oriental, 2009), 140–41.

24. Yoon Hee-Seong and Wee Geun-woo, "[Interview] 2NE1," *Ashia Kyŏngje*, September 9, 2009, accessed March 27, 2011, http://www.asiae.co.kr/news/view.htm?sec =ent9&idxno=2009090316583528776.

25. "Hip Korea," Discovery Channel, March 2010, accessed March 27, 2011, available at http://www.youtube.com/watch?v=Hr2sOwBGwG8.

26. User Xiu91 on http://www.youtube.com/watch?v=iABwt-B111E. Accessed March 27, 2011.

27. http://www.youtube.com/watch?v=SGoo c7PvWrM. Accessed March 27, 2011.

28. Kim, "*Sonyŏ imiji.*"

29. Kim, "'*Sekshihan' sonyŏ shidae.*"

30. "*Haksupkwŏn poho mihup tung ch'ŏngsonyŏn yŏnyein kibongwŏn ch'imhae shimgak,*" Ministry of Gender Equality and Family, accessed March 27, 2011, http://enews .moge.go.kr/view/board/bbs/view.jsp?topMenuId=NEWS&topMenuName=%B4 %BA%BD%BA%B8%B6%B4%E7&subMenuId=1&subMenuName=%C1%A4% C3%A5%B.C.%D3%BA%B8&boardMngNo=1&boardNo=1545.

31. "S. Korea Drops to 68th in Women's Rights," *The Hankyoreh*, March 10, 2009, accessed March 27, 2011, http://english.hani.co.kr/arti/english_edition/e_international /343215.html.

32. Yoo-Sun Kim, *Working Korea 2007* (Seoul: Korea Labor and Society Institute, 2008), 19; Hyo-sik Lee, "Downturn Takes Toll on Women Workers," *Korea Times*, July 6, 2009, accessed March 27, 2011, http://www.koreatimes.co.kr/www/news/biz/2009/07/123_48021.html.

33. Chŏng Chae-sŏk, *"Iryŏksŏ e 'sajin' toech'ukdoelkka,"* *Focus Busan*, June 9, 2010, 6.

34. Available at http://ystar.cu-media.co.kr/news/news_view.php?no=43773, accessed March 27, 2011.

35. "T-ara's Hyomin Has a Terrible Body?" *allkpop*, May 26, 2010, accessed March 27, 2011, http://www.allkpop.com/2010/05/t-aras-hyomin-has-a-terrible-body; "T-ara Fans Worried about Hyomin's Weight Loss," *hellokpop*, January 6, 2011, accessed March 27, 2011, http://www.hellokpop.com/2011/01/06/t-ara-fans-worried-about-hyomins-weight-loss.

36. "SNSD's Trainers Clear Up Their Diet," *allkpop*, December 20, 2009, accessed March 27, 2011, http://www.allkpop.com/2009/12/snsds_trainers_clear_up_their_diet; "Seohyeon's Health Report Reveals She Is 9kg Underweight," *koreaboo*, February 6, 2011, accessed March 27, 2011, http://www.koreaboo.com/index.html/_/general/seohyuns-health-report-reveals-she-is-9kg-r3326.

37. Y. H. Khang and S. C. Yun, "Trends in General and Abdominal Obesity among Korean Adults: Findings from 1998, 2001, 2005, and 2007," *Journal of Korean Medical Science* 25, no. 11 (2010): 1587.

38. See http://www.youtube.com/watch?v=QovjzfdDx7c, accessed March 27, 2011.

39. Minjeong Kim and Sharron Lennon, "Content Analysis of Diet Advertisements: A Cross-National Comparison of Korean and U.S. Women's Magazines," *Clothing and Textiles Research Journal* 24, no. 4 (2006): 357.

40. Jeong, "Swept Up," 48.

PART FIVE   Food and Travel

In his famous book, *The Society of the Spectacle*, Guy Debord describes the spectacle in terms that resonate with many of the chapters that appear in this section. "The spectacle is the existing order's uninterrupted discourse about itself, its laudatory monologue. It is the self-portrait of power in the epoch of its totalitarian management of the conditions of existence."[1] In this account, the modern state's investment in the spectacular is fundamentally driven by a kind of narcissism, a desire to represent in some kind of less abstract, external form nothing less than its own power. The essays gathered under the rubric of "Food and Travel" have this concern at their heart, the extent to which the state is capable of projecting its fantasies about itself into the public sphere.

In relation to the oppressive authoritarian regimes of Park Chung-Hee to Chun Doo-hwan, popular culture of the period could function as a potential platform for resistance against the dominance of the postwar South Korean nation state. Although the contemporary period's relative artistic and ideological freedoms could be said to be the legacy of the postwar democratic movements characterized by struggle against the status quo, it can also be argued that much of these hard-won progressive and emancipatory liberties are now being exercised within the parameters of what might be termed "state-sanctioned arts." The clarity of distinction is no longer as evident. Since the late 1990s, the popular arts, both mainstream and countercultural, have benefited tremendously from government-supported infra-structures specially designed to sustain and promote the appreciation of Korean culture abroad by facilitating cultural production.

Although the role of the state is more muted than in Debord's account, one wonders if the fantasies that underlie its efforts are the same. Given this new complicity between the state and the cultural producers that might otherwise serve as its critics, new approaches become necessary to interpret the vagaries of resistance against power in Korean popular culture in the contemporary neoliberal context, especially in a context in which the cultural sphere replaced the socioeconomic sphere as the site of struggle and ideological fervor. Coinciding with the shift from pre- to post-democratic governments, this transformation was also accompanied by a shift from class-based politics to one based in identity politics as well as a radical proliferation of representational media.[2]

The material in Part 5 focuses exclusively on the contemporary period and attempts to conceptualize approaches to state-sanctioned art in neoliberal South Korea, such as advertising, national food campaigns, and North Korean tourism photography. These categories certainly overlap. Advertising, for example, has played a crucial role in promoting Korean food as well as tourism to Korea. The interest of these chapters in these state-sanctioned arts is fundamentally in what they can tell us about the sociological, economic, and historical forces that underlie them. Rising interest in culinary culture and tourism indicates not only the presence of a strong, leisurely middle class in South Korea but also the social production of the feeling of cultural confidence through the marketization and promotion of Korean food and travel to Korea. What is also interesting about the pieces in this section is that Japan continues to be a critical factor: both the food and tourism industries remain shrouded in colonial legacies, which they continue to combat while proudly advancing in cultural developments dependent on these very foundations. As Katarzyna J. Cwiertka's chapter suggests, the rise in standardized, commercial production and global export of food is a direct result of changes in Japanese consumption patterns of Korean cuisine since the 1980s.

Olga Fedorenko proposes to see advertising not just as entertainment but also as a subaltern culture. She illustrates South Korean advertising's tendency to "interpellate consumers with sentimental, humanist campaigns" and the ways in which the advertising industry negotiates capitalism under neoliberalism to articulate itself as a platform for popular sentiments and critical sites of contestation, social values, and representational politics in public discourse while remaining within the constraints of commercial imperatives. Rather than the efficacy of advertising, Fedorenko argues for an awareness of advertising in Korean culture as an integral part of public life and as a "cross-media space of discourse." She argues for a treatment of advertising as a social phenomenon that must be historically, socially, and culturally contextualized.

Cwiertka looks at the "Global Promotion of Korean Cuisine" campaign, a government-led initiative that aims to popularize Korean food globally. She looks at the commodification and consumption of Korea's culinary heritage, the influence of *hallyu* marketing strategies on its own, and the carefully manufactured nature of the product geared toward distinction rather than proximity to the original. She argues that in the post-1997 era, which is defined by a dramatic increase in transnational consumerism, consumption and patriotism overlap and the propagation of Korean cuisine abroad becomes an assertion of national heritage. Cwiertka also draws our attention to Japan and the specific politics of food in this specific postcolonial context, in which Japan's changing attitudes toward Korean cuisine has significant consequences.

Sohl Lee's chapter looks at the cultural phenomenon of touring North Korea in the late 1990s through the photography of Seung Woo Back, which necessarily operates within while subverting the strict guidelines established by the North Korean government. Lee argues for photography as a privileged medium of representation in facilitating "a new inter-Korean narrative forged from the bottom by South Korean masses." For Lee, Back's images, taken in the tourist zones in North Korea, exemplify a new touristic fantasy of South Korean citizens, which can now transcend the North Korean border, and represents a new attempt to re-examine the ideological division of the Korean peninsula, despite the attempts of North Korean authorities to control the content of the photographs. She argues for a consideration of such photographic representations of North Korea by South Koreans as democratic. YMC

NOTES

1. Guy Debord, *The Society of the Spectacle* (Detroit: Black and Red, 1983), section 24.
2. See Soyoung Kim, "'Cine-Mania' or Cinephilia: Film Festivals and the Identity Question," in *New Korean Cinema*, ed. Chi-Yun Shin and Julian Stringer (Edinburgh: Edinburgh University Press, 2005).

15

OLGA FEDORENKO

South Korean Advertising as Popular Culture

ADVERTISING AS POPULAR CULTURE?

"When you leave home, it's dog's suffering" (*chip nagamyŏn kae kosaeng ida*) was a popular way to humorously express pessimism in the wake of the 2008 financial crisis in South Korea. The expression originated in a slogan from a 2009 advertising campaign for Korea Telecom (KT). The ads showed situations of homelessness, indebtedness, and unemployment, which were real fears for many Koreans at the time, when it was unclear how soon the crisis would bottom out and how badly Korea would be hit—and promised KT's home entertainment package as an escape from this "dog's suffering." The complex intertextuality won the campaign a broad cultural resonance: an opinion poll found it the most memorable campaign of 2009.[1] The slogan itself was a play on an old saying, "When you depart from home, it's suffering" (*chip ttŏnamyŏn kosaeng ida*), which was jazzed up with a controversial colloquialism "dog's suffering,"[2] thus introduced into active daily language despite protests from language purists and concerned parents. Moreover, the campaign referred to a recent TV series,[3] casting the lead actor to play the same role in the ad as he did in the TV show, as a middle-aged man who had lost his job, was abandoned by his family, and ended up homeless wandering the streets on a snowy day. The campaign's engagement with socioeconomic realities, its intertextuality, and spillover of "dog's suffering" into everyday vernacular illustrate the popular-cultural life of advertising, the theme of this essay.

In South Korea as well as in other capitalist societies, commercial advertising, while created as a sales tool, in its everyday circulation is distinguishable from other cultural products primarily by its form. Advertising draws on the same pool of cultural references, relies on the same mass media, casts the same celebrities, and engages the same audiences as other media. Advertising slogans find their way into public discourse, unusual advertising is discussed with acquaintances and blogged about, and advertising images animate fantasies and ambitions, whereas some ads address social issues, resonating beyond advertising's commercial purpose. Discussing how people twist and turn advertising messages to fit everyday situations, communication scholar Neil Alperstein compared advertising to improvisational jazz. He illustrated this point by tracing the multiple uses of the "Where's the beef?" slogan of a 1984 commercial for Wendy's hamburgers, which was appropriated in everyday vernacular to make jokes and to show cultural competency, by journalists in social commentary, and even in the presidential election campaign of Walter Mondale.[4]

If North Americans rhetorically ask, "Where's the beef?" to question the substance, South Koreans might emphasize someone's cluelessness by saying, "Do you even know the taste of crab?" (*ni dŭr i ke mas ŭl' ara*), referring to the 2002 "Old Man and the Sea" campaign for Lotteria Crab Burger, which showed an old fisherman hauling home a giant crab hardly fitting in his shoddy boat and grinning victoriously at young fishermen. Or, to jokingly deflect a question, they could note, "Even my daughter-in-law doesn't know" (*myŏnŭri do molla*), quoting a mid-1990s ad for hot pepper paste, where an owner of a legendary restaurant says that no one knows the secret of her hot sauce. Ads are among shared cultural references that reproduce the imagined community of the nation,[5] and popular campaigns are often described as "only a spy wouldn't know" (*morŭmyŏn kanch'ŏp*), the expression itself echoing public service ads that urged vigilance against spies. The cultural significance of advertising in South Korea is celebrated by the Advertising Museum in Seoul, which opened in 2008 to educate children about advertising and its benefits.

If audiences bracket out advertising's sales pitch and appropriate advertising content to enrich their cultural repertoire, the advertising industry produces advertising as if it were cultural content. Just as the above-mentioned KT ad illustrated, advertising plunders cultural, social, and political stock to capture the attention of consumers who, constantly bombarded by advertising blitzes, are skilled at avoiding unwanted messages. Some ads attempt to break through the information clutter by mongering fears, cultivating insecurities, or titillating with sexual innuendos. Other ads latch onto popular sentiments, not shying away from challenging customs and hierarchies. Such were the popular 2002 ads for the telecommunication company KTF (Korea Telecom Freetel), which challenged the traditional respect for seniority, claiming, "Age is just a number," and showing young people taking leadership in business and older people taking classes at university.

South Korean advertising does not recoil from political controversy either. After Kim Dae-jung initiated the Sunshine Policy toward North Korea, many ads played with North Korean themes, often highlighting the humanity of North Koreans. A 2000 TV commercial for the Internet portal Daum, for example, illustrated the power of the Internet to break walls: it showed a frog crossing the border between the North and the South, provoking a faint smile in a North Korean soldier on duty. Even the difficult issue of comfort women became fodder for advertising, as the 1994 ads for the sports shoemaker Pro-Specs deployed images of a young model dressed up as a comfort woman, accompanied by the copy: "Are we to be conquered? Will we conquer? History can be repeated." Whereas some Korean critics disapprovingly compared the Pro-Specs campaign to the sensationalism of Benetton's ads of the time, in general the campaign was warmly accepted. Advertising professor Kim Kyu-Cheul, for example, credited it for forcing the painful issue into public consciousness,[6] and the print version of the ad appears in the Advertising Museum in Seoul, in the exhibit that celebrates the liberalization of media content in the 1990s.

Despite being driven by commercial purposes, advertising often seeks to engage target consumers in meaningful, thought-provoking ways, stirring aspirations that go beyond the acquisition of commodities and addressing societal issues and even historical traumas. Ads provide comic relief mocking problematic practices—or appeal to nationalism and indulge in nostalgia, generating pathos and offering cathartic pleasures, similar to those of melodrama. Advertising's omnivorousness and readiness to incorporate the new and recast the old makes advertising—both its expressive content as a public text and diverse ways of its consumption—a dynamic space where changing social and historical milieus are creatively engaged, where social norms are asserted and negotiated.

My essay sketches projects attempted through, with, and against advertising in contemporary South Korea. I use advertising in a nonspecific way because my concern is with advertising as a cross-media space of discourse; I am interested, not in the effects of particular advertising campaigns, but in advertising as a part of public life. Overall, I make a case for South Korean advertising being a vibrant part of popular culture and show how ads not only rehearse popular sentiments but also themselves become sites of contestations over social values and representational politics, despite being constrained by commercial imperatives. After theorizing advertising as popular culture in the next section, I trace a trajectory of an advertising campaign to illustrate the popular-cultural life of advertising. The central sections outline the common tropes of South Korean advertising—humor, humanism, sex appeal—and relate them to local struggles. Last, I explore how advertising blends with entertainment and offer a critique of advertising as a subaltern culture.

POPULAR CULTURE, IDEOLOGY, "MOMENTS OF FREEDOM"

If, following Stuart Hall's thinking, popular culture is defined through its rootedness in actual material conditions and lived experiences,[7] advertising campaigns are part of popular culture because, as a discourse, advertising talks about people and socially praised aspirations. Advertising content resonates with lived realities, making them communicable and thus empowering those experiencing them. As Hall argues, popular culture is assembled from whatever is available—including commercially produced cultural products—and the outcome is not a coherent popular culture that opposes the dominant one but rather a jumble of fragmented, contradictory impulses for containment and resistance.[8] Advertising is one of those commercially produced cultural products that comprise popular culture because of their relevance for making sense of everyday experience.

What makes advertising's popular-cultural appropriations rife with contradictions is that advertising's content, no matter how emancipatory, is subordinated to selling commodities. As Marxist theorist Wolfgang Haug explains, to help the seller realize a commodity's exchange value, advertising systematically enhances the sensuous appearance of the commodity and exaggerates the use value that a buyer is to obtain from the commodity's consumption. By aestheticizing commodities, advertising privileges the valorization needs of capital over human needs of buyers.[9]

To apply Slavoj Žižek's analysis of ideology,[10] advertising also invests subjects in the economy of enjoyment, which supports this exploitative structure. Advertising advances an ideological fantasy that explains the lack in a subject, and in society in general, by the lack of consumption and asserts consuming, and by extension participating in the capitalist economy, as a way to recover the impossible enjoyment (Lacanian *jouissance*). Articulating an ideological fantasy, advertising endows commodities with disproportionate significance and disavows that consumption of commodities can satisfy only a limited number of human needs. Advertising is ideological also because it disavows the fact that even if completeness through consumption were possible, what drives capitalist economies is not fuller satisfaction of human needs but pursuit of surplus value. Nevertheless, the fantasy articulated by advertising makes alienations of work and everyday life in a capitalist society appear worthwhile, while consumption of commodities provides enough enjoyment to bind subjects to this ideological formation.[11]

This picture of advertising as a sophisticated instrument of capitalist reproduction may appear totalizing, but approaching advertising as popular culture exposes cracks in this structure. Tracing the popular-cultural life of advertising highlights, to borrow from anthropologist Johannes Fabian, "moments of freedom," which unsettle existing relations of power.[12] Namely, I argue, the power relation between buyers and sellers is unsettled when advertising is consumed as a popular-cultural product and its message about the joys of consumption is bracketed out: In the process, buyers make advertising relevant for everyday life beyond their consumption practices and appropriate advertising as a cultural resource, whereas sellers cater to these "unauthorized uses" and sponsor advertising that increasingly eclipses the commodity itself, blending with entertainment. Linking the commodity with complex needs for social success and self-fulfillment, advertising ends up being a discourse about lifestyles and values, in which the commodity is no longer the protagonist but only an excuse for its emergence. Where advertising succeeds in capturing imaginations, it also potentially fails, as advertising consumers escape its commercial and ideological interpellation.

Treating advertising as a dynamic site of contestations, where ideological fantasies are staged and where their inconsistencies are exposed and exploited, differs from manipulation critiques of advertising, which assume omnipotence of advertisers and ignore the messy realities of advertising production and consumption. It also differs from enthusiastic celebrations of any unintended uses of advertising as subversive and resistant.[13] Further, it resists simplistic culturalist explanations and instead emphasizes power relations within which advertising is consumed and produced, to highlight contradictions and contestations, "moments of freedom" as well as moments of complicity and incorporation into dominant discourses. In other words, thinking of advertising as popular culture restores the complexity of this phenomenon, which, owing to its ubiquity in capitalist societies, tends to be assumed obvious and unworthy of rigorous engagement. An important implication of approaching advertising as popular culture is a recognition that even though advertising is found in all contemporary capitalist societies, it cannot be presumed to play the identical role in different places, just as popular culture is deployed to fight diverse struggles in various locales. In other words, attention to popular-cultural aspects of advertising demands that advertising be treated as a complex phenomenon embedded in social life and its diffuse effects be traced in concrete conjunctures and analyzed against social and cultural contexts.[14]

To illustrate how advertising becomes a site of contestations in South Korea, I outline a trajectory of a 2009 advertising campaign by telecom giant KT. Seeking to bury its image of a clunky government-associated corporation, KT ran a series of animated ads for TV and the Internet. Each of the nine ads followed the same comical plot: a protagonist encounters a positive event and exclaims, "Wow!" only to encounter an even more positive event and then shout, *"Olleh!"* (pronounced like the sports chant *olé*), after which the KT logo is displayed. In one ad, for example, a lumberjack throws an iron ax into a pond, and an old wizard appears, extending three shiny golden axes, and the lumberjack says, "Wow!" in amazement; then he throws the same plain ax in the pond again, and three young women appear, showing off shapely legs and each holding a golden ax, to which the lumberjack ecstatically shouts, *"Olleh!"* (fig. 15.1). Other episodes included a young couple seeing off their son to a summer camp (*wow*) and then the father seeing off both his child and wife (*olleh*); a sexy blonde kissing a young attractive man (*wow*) and then kissing an old wrinkly "millionaire" with a posh car (*olleh*) (fig. 15.2).

The "Olleh" campaign enjoyed explosive popularity, voted the second most memorable campaign of 2009.[15] The mass media covered the campaign as if it were news. The progressive newspaper *Hankyoreh*, for example, published a favorable article under the title, "Having Shed the Dinosaur Image, Young and Joyful '*Olleh*.'"[16] Bloggers reposted the articles, together with the ads themselves and additional commentaries. Many netizens collected "Olleh" ads on their webpages, and soon parodies and imitations appeared. One of them, for example, showed a man who jumped from a boat to save an attractive drowning damsel in distress (*wow*) and then found himself surrounded by a flock of voluptuous mermaids (*olleh*). During the campaign, KT employees wore T-shirts with "*wow*" and "*olleh*" scenes from the ads, and soon instructions on how to make your own "*olleh*" T-shirt appeared online. The exclamation "*olleh*" made it to TV programs and everyday conversations.

The ad also provoked a debate about representations of women in the media. Some netizens criticized the "Golden Ax" and "Summer Camp" episodes for belittling women and eroding family values. Eventually media division of the feminist organization Womenlink (*Yŏsŏng minuhoe*) requested that KT pull the campaign. The ads, Womenlink argued, cast women in supporting roles only, thus reproducing the stereotypes of gender roles; Womenlink's analysis showed that only one of the nine ads had a woman as a protagonist having an "*olleh*" moment. KT responded that pulling the ads

Figure 15.1. A screenshot from the "Golden Ax" commercial from KT's *"Olleh"* advertising campaign. Produced by Cheil Worldwide (2009).

Figure 15.2. A screenshot from the "Millionaire" commercial from KT's *"Olleh"* advertising campaign. Produced by Cheil Worldwide (2009).

was impossible but promised to consider Womenlink's points in the future. Womenlink posted its criticisms online and went on the national TV channel MBC to announce a boycott of KT until the company stopped the campaign. Many newspapers covered the story, and numerous bloggers commented on Womenlink's report, some approvingly, some criticizing those offended by the ads for lacking sense of humor. A week from the boycott announcement, KT withdrew the ads.

The feminists' victory was confirmed when in about six months KT picked challenging outdated norms as the theme of its next campaign. New ads ran under the slogan, "Flip the usual way" (*ta kŭrae rŭl twijibŏra*), and its episodes mocked the "usual ways," such as all middle-aged women having the same perms and office workers ordering the same cheap dish when bosses treat. Significant in the light of the earlier controversy, one of the ads directly promoted women's equality by ridiculing patriarchal norms: The ad mocked the "usual way" when only women cook for the Lunar New Year festivities, pronouncing, "Those who don't work, won't eat." Similar to the earlier campaign, KT ads assumed a fun, entertaining tone, but the critical message and a call to change discriminatory traditions acknowledged Womenlink's and netizens' demands.

The trajectory of the *"Olleh"* campaign exemplifies the popular-cultural life of advertising. The ads were consumed not as information about available services but as cultural products, while KT's commercial interestedness was discarded as irrelevant. Mass media and netizens praised the ads' value as a cultural resource and ignored the usefulness of the information the ads provided to potential consumers. The commodity itself remained in the background—if one were to guess from the ads, KT could have been a seller of anything from hardware to luxury cars. Further, the ads were not merely a source of entertainment; they were read in relation to *lived realities* and *social issues*, and they were expected to affirm the desirable ideals that might be lacking in life. Advertising consumers demanded that the advertiser guide the conduct of South Koreans in a progressive way—and the advertiser honored this vision of advertising as an influential public text, not just a commercial announcement. In the end, KT decision-makers were receptive to the popular input, and the subsequent KT campaign attacked what many saw as actual problems of South Korean society. The advertiser served the advertising audience, which exceeded potential subscribers of KT services to include all TV-watching and Internet-surfing South Koreans, with an entertaining critique of the parochial usual ways.

The *"Olleh"* campaign achieved a particularly high profile, but this dynamic unfolds with other ads as well, and approaching advertising as popular culture brings these contestations to the forefront. Advertising producers strive to reflect the vision of target consumers, but importantly advertising's audience does *not* coincide with the target consumer niche, and the *target* consumers are not necessarily the most vocal among *advertising* consumers. Thus advertisers are forced to accommodate the visions of those who wish to enlist ads to promote particular social agendas, making advertising relevant for articulating their experiences and aspirations. In such ads, the commodity hovers as an unobtrusive ghostly presence, easily ignored by those uninterested, and the ads themselves blur with other cultural products, no longer a discourse about the joys of consumption but about contested values and socially controversial topics. The following sections take a broader look at South Korean advertising to examine this tendency and the diverse contestations it accommodates.

"CAPITALIST REALISM" AND HUMOR

The first commercial ads that appeared in Korea in the late nineteenth century were textual announcements about available commodities.[17] Even though the usage of images increased throughout the first half of the twentieth century, advertising had remained what communication scholar Jib Fowles calls "simple" advertising, "where all the content pertains to the commodity being sold."[18] Bleeding into popular culture truly occurs with "compound" advertising, which praises the commodity indirectly by having attractive models and desirable lifestyles connote it in ads.[19] This departure from the commodity creates space for advertising to tell complex stories, comment on everyday situations, and speak to immaterial desires, placing ads in the realm of public texts. In South Korea, compound advertising became noticeable from the 1970s, when the increasing numbers of consumer commodities became available, television spread, and the advertising industry grew to account for 0.7 percent of GDP.[20]

As Korea scholars argue, during the times of military dictatorships popular consent to the regime that privileged big business and sacrificed the masses was maintained with promises of future prosperity for the entire nation.[21] Advertising was one of the venues for articulating the fantasy of an affluent, equitable future—and for framing entrepreneurship as a patriotic activity. Ads for South Korean conglomerates (*chaebŏl*)—produced by their in-house agencies[22]—borrowed from the developmentalist and nationalist discourses, and corporate advertising ventriloquized the government propaganda, reflecting the notorious business-government collusion. The historical exhibit in the Advertising Museum indexes the "Miracle on the Han River" (1968–80) with a 1978 Samsung ad featuring the turtle warship, which signified Korea's naval victories over Japan in the sixteenth century and, in context, read as Samsung's pledge to outdo Japan in the economic competition. A 1977 LG ad in the same exhibit urged, "Your family's child might become president of this country in the future; raise him well," hinting at the foreseeable achievement of popular democracy. South Korean advertising well illustrates the argument by communication scholar Michael Schudson, who highlighted aesthetic similarities between national consumer advertising and socialist-realist art to suggest that advertising functions as "capitalist realism," the "official art" of capitalist societies.[23]

The solemnity and ideological pathos of corporate advertising contrasts with humorous advertising, which has been the staple for campaigns targeting a broad national market. Casting comedians or comic actors to express exaggerated appreciation for the advertised product, humorous ads often mocked alienations of everyday life, sometimes to offer the advertised product as a solution but more often than not just to draw the viewers in. One of the early favorites was a 1977 ad that launched the now-famous brand Nongshim Ramen. In the ad, two well-known comedians of the time have a politeness contest over a cup of instant noodles. The younger man insists that the older should eat it because "elder brother first" (in accordance with the traditional respect for seniority). The elder man tells the younger to have it, saying, "Younger brother first." Eventually the younger brother yields and grabs the bowl, but then the elder brother is shown changing his mind and reaching for the bowl too. Arguably the secret of the ad's appeal has been not only a good laugh but also the humorous challenge to the custom of privileging seniority, rigid hierarchies posing a perennial quandary in Korea. Over the years, Nongshim, Lotte, Yakult, and other advertisers have produced an array of slapstick gems, which are fondly mentioned in the sociocultural histories of Korea and are reposted by nostalgic bloggers.

Regarding such slapstick ads, creative director and advertising critic Kim Hong-tack laments, "The single focus of these ads is to create laughter irrespective of their relevance to the product, to the extent that they could be thought of as 'nonsense ads.' The fact that these types of ads, which aim only to be funny without any attention to the context, are still being produced in large numbers is both regrettable and surprising. These ads exist because they still elicit a good response from consumers."[24]

What is a target of critique for an adman testifies to the pressure on the advertising industry to produce ads that are enjoyable for advertising consumers—the ads that blend with popular culture and subordinate sales promotion to entertainment. Laughter and humor have long been understood as vehicles for challenging hierarchies and expressing social protest, and

Korea boasts a rich tradition of satire in the arts and literature. Humorous advertising, too, can offer liberating openings either for comic relief and a quick escape from the alienation of the everyday or occasionally for mocking oppressive practices.

The escapist pleasures that humorous advertising offers are lauded by advertising critic Pak Hye-ran, who links humorous advertising to humanism. Drawing examples from recent campaigns, Pak muses, "I think that genuine humorous advertising is not advertising that makes one's mouth smile but the advertising that makes one's heart naturally smile, so that an advertising message . . . within fifteen short seconds disarms the heart of a cautious and defensive consumer. As life becomes more complicated, as economic conditions become more difficult, humorous advertising and humanist advertising are said to exude light. Because humorous or humanist advertising oozes a good mood that relieves all worries and stress for even a moment and disarms one's heart."[25] Pak concludes her piece by evoking an Aesop's fable (which inspired Kim Dae-jung's Sunshine Policy) about the Sun succeeding in removing a traveler's coat with warm rays, whereas the Wind failed with violent gusts. This metaphor aptly captures the ethos of South Korean advertising, which prefers to interpellate consumers with sentimental, humanist campaigns.

"ADS THAT SPREAD HUMANISM"

Humanism has been the dominant trope of South Korean advertising, and sentimental, feel-good messages saturate corporate image advertising. Among the long-celebrated campaigns is the 1984 "Lunch Box" (*tosirak*) ad for the Ssangyong Group, which appeared in newspapers on national Teachers Day and told a sentimental story about a teacher giving away his lunch to impoverished students under the guise of his stomach being unwell. As advertising critic Mha Joung-Mee wrote, "This ad has shown that one ad can move people's hearts more than a poem or a novel," and advertising historian Shin In Sup compared the popular appeal of "Lunch Box" with the famous poem "Azaleas" by Kim So-wol.[26]

The lavishly praised "Toward People" (*saram ŭl hyang'hamnida*) campaign by SK Telecom is an exemplar of the sentimental intensity contemporary Korean advertising strives for. Started in 2005, the first seasons of the campaign featured slideshows of black-and-white photographs that celebrated regular people in the midst of everyday life, to the accompaniment of an instrumental rendition of the Beatles' "Let It Be." The award-winning "Hero" edition of "Toward People," for example, extolled mundane heroism: a black-and-white photograph of a smiling man on whose arms two young children

Figure 15.3. "Wonder Woman." A screenshot from the "Hero" commercial from the "Toward People" advertising campaign for SK Telecom. Produced by TBWA Korea (2005).

are hanging is captioned "Superman"; a mother holding a newborn is "Wonder Woman" (fig. 15.3); a boy helping a girl cross a busy street is "Captain Atom." In the last photograph, people on a subway platform push up against the outside of one side of the train, in reference to a real accident when someone fell on the subway tracks and was saved by other passengers who lifted the subway car. "We all are a hero for someone," stated the last caption.

Rather than read these ads cynically, as some observers might be inclined, media consumers in South Korea celebrate such advertising. As a blogger wrote about SK Telecom's "Hero" ad, "Of course I like funny ads, but because I think that advertising is *one of the methods to move* people's hearts, I tremendously like ads that touch me emotionally" (emphasis in original).[27] A published collection of letters from consumers about their favorite ads featured pieces that praised advertising for inspiring contributors to love or to connect with others, or for humanizing technology. The editors summed it up, "For advertising that they like, consumers chose ads that spread humanism."[28] This ideal for advertising to strive for public interest and a positive social impact is frequently articulated by advertising regulators, advertising professionals, and regular people.

Appreciation for so-called humanist advertising makes sense if its relatedness to melodrama is examined. The popularity of melodrama in Korea has been extensively commented on by scholars, and melodrama's appeal is commonly attributed to the experience of the "compressed modernity," a dizzying pace of social and economic transformations Koreans lived through in the twentieth century.[29] As the argument goes, the imposed terms and conflicting forms of the transformation—the experience of the Japanese colonization, civil war, a succession of authoritarian military dictatorships, and neocolonial relations with the United States—have left ambivalence in their wake, which manifested in the pervasiveness of melodramatic sensibility.

According to melodrama theorist Peter Brooks, melodramatic excesses are vehicles for dealing with anxieties about moral order and ultimately about the meaning of life, which modern subjects had to work out on their own in the absence of the sacred, which would guarantee the stability of the ethical universe. Melodrama particularly resonates in rapidly changing societies. On the one hand, melodramatic excesses provide outlets for repressed emotions and desires, which otherwise are impossible to resolve compatibly with dominant social structures. On the other hand, melodrama articulates the "moral occult," a domain of invisible forces and ethical imperatives that see to the evil being punished and the innocent rewarded. Melodrama is animated by the moral occult, Brooks argues, because melodrama "proves" the invisible moral laws in modern societies when conflicts are resolved in a way that affirms those invisible moral laws. As a result, melodrama absolves the viewers from anxieties over lack of meaning and ethical collapse.[30]

Advertising seeks to attract the same audience as the mainstream media and consequently draws on the same ideological and aesthetic conventions. In advertising as well, the melodramatic mode is employed to draw attention, to encourage identification and empathy, to accommodate emotional excesses. Humanist advertising generates emotional excess and pathos by evoking Brooks's moral occult: such ads articulate the hidden humanist laws and side with those laws against business rationality. Because humanist ads deal in the moral occult and prove that humanism is still operative, they can "move one's heart." In a sense, to watch a corporation testify to the principles of public good in an ad is as satisfying as to watch a villain commend to the forces of good in a regular melodrama. In South Korea, capitalist profit-seeking has had shaky moral grounds historically, and as in many other places big business is often perceived as corrupt and inhumane.[31] To have corporations speak for public interest and humanism through advertising, a marketing instrument employed to bring commercial profits, is to buttress the universality, permanence, and stability of humanist values. This longing for moral values in advertising is a longing for moral virtues to override the contradictions of capitalist modernity.

Humanist advertising is driven by a utopian imaginary of humanist capitalism practiced by responsible, socially conscious companies with sound humanist values. Such an ideological fantasy covers up the exploitative nature of capitalism, which has been experienced by many Koreans, both at the times of the developmental state and more recently, when Korea's remarkable economic successes failed to translate into prosperity for all. Especially after the 1997 crisis, in the face of growing unemployment, precarization of labor, and increasing income gap, humanist advertising was an easy way for businesses to divert popular criticisms: sponsoring feel-good ads, like the "Toward People" campaign, demonstrated ethical integrity of corporations and also nurtured the fantasy of humanist society to strive for in the face of difficulties, contributing to orchestrating popular consent for neoliberal restructuring. Advertising thus articulated an appealing fantasy that the goal of affluent, equitable society is still achievable within capitalism, as long as Koreans adopt humanist worldviews and buy from humanist corporations.

SEX APPEAL IN ADVERTISING: COMMODITY AESTHETICS HIJACKED

Promoting humanist values might be advertising's adaptation to Korea's realities of "compressed modernity" and lacking hegemony of capitalist profit-seeking, but more traditional advertising, which seeks to enhance commodity appearance, has been common as well, and it lends itself to popular-cultural appropriations differently. Advertising's explorations of sexual appeal not only sensualize and sexualize commodities with various degrees of subtlety, but they also make it a resource to work on sexuality-mediated identity aspects and to rewrite gender scripts, as testified by the "*Olleh*" and "Flip the Usual Way" campaigns—and also to buttress freedom of expression.

Images of attractive models were deployed in Korean advertising since at least the late 1950s, but tight censorship and prudish public sentiments had prevented advertisers from using direct sexual appeal till the 1990s, when overall media liberalization created a more permissive climate for media expression.[32] The year 1994 witnessed the first Korean ad with a nude—a lathered naked model turned her or his (in different editions) back toward the viewer, to promote body-care products in mainstream newspapers; the female version of the ad is featured in the Advertising Museum in Seoul as a testimony to liberalization of creative expression. Also in 1994, some Korean women's magazines ran explicit Calvin Klein ads, provoking a discussion of whether they symbolized cultural imperialism or desirable liberalization,[33] and 1995 saw an upsurge in ads using nudity and sex appeal.[34] A new level of leniency toward bodily exposure and expressions of female

Figure 15.4. A screenshot from the "Am I your first?" commercial from the "Think Casual" advertising campaign for Cool soju brand of the Lotte Chilsung Beverage Co. Produced by Daehong Communications (2009).

sexuality was brought by the 2002 Soccer World Cup, when mass media showed scantily clad Korean female fans publicly discussing the sexual attractiveness of soccer players.[35] Advertisers were quick to exploit the new frontiers of public decency, and ads for clothing, snacks, and particularly alcoholic drinks took up sex-appeal aesthetics.

It might be tempting to condemn such advertising as commodifying sexuality and objectifying women (and occasionally men), but if it is approached as a site of popular culture it also reveals contestations of gender roles and social norms about sexuality. Particularly bold in using sex appeal have been ads for soju, a traditional Korean liquor, whose cheapness and relative strength have secured it 40 percent of alcohol consumption in Korea.[36] With primary soju consumers being middle-aged men, advertisers entice them with titillating images of top female celebrities in revealing outfits. In the fall of 2009, one such campaign, "Think Casual" for Cool soju, achieved notoriety not so much because of the visuals—typical for all soju ads of the time, it featured a minimally dressed young model, singer Uee, performing a sexually suggestive dance (fig. 15.4)—but because of the advertising copy. The most controversial ad of the campaign featured Uee saying to her date, "I'm cool" (*nan k'ul' hae*) . . . Am I really your first?" in response to which the guy stumbles and other men around are shown all unable to come up with a coherent answer. Uee laughs and tells them, "Think casual" (in English), and then performs what became known as the "cool shot dance," consisting of energetic squats and pelvic thrusts.

In response to the campaign, many netizens praised Uee's attractiveness and admired her dancing; the "cool shot dance" achieved a viral popularity, young women recording their own versions and posting them online. Many others, however, were offended by what they saw as encouragement of promiscuity, noting that Uee looked "too easy," that her coolness about sexual matters was inappropriate for her young age and "innocent face." As I investigated the campaign, I was surprised to learn that the advertising team behind it included a few young and well-educated women who saw the ad as empowering and were hoping that young people, whom the ad targeted to broaden the traditional demographics of soju consumption, would perceive it in the same way. In other words, fulfilling the humanist ethos of South Korean advertising, they pushed for individual sexual freedom against oppressive norms, and the "Think Casual" campaign became a site for negotiating parameters of female sexuality. The advertising agency took a leading role in challenging patriarchal mores—reflecting the worldview of advertising workers, who saw themselves representing the worldviews of the target consumers.

In addition to revisiting appropriate gender roles, "sex appeal" advertising questioned what it meant to be Korean in the twenty-first century. (Hyper) sexuality has been viewed as a feature of foreigners, whereas Koreans, particularly Korean women, have been expected to be virginal and straitlaced. In accordance with such stereotypes, few Korean models appeared in lingerie advertising until recently.[37] Consequently reliance on sex appeal in advertising is often seen as a result of Westernization, with contradictory connotations, welcomed by some as emancipating and lamented by others as corrupting. On the one hand, the above-mentioned "Think Casual" campaign was critiqued by some netizens as "too Western" and thus inappropriate for Korea. On the other hand, many advertising producers and some cultural critics frame sex-appeal ads in terms of liberalization and freedom of expression and often lament the conservatism of Korea's regulation and public sensibilities, which is said to prevent Korean advertising from creatively using erotic images. Similarly the Advertising Museum in Seoul equates possibilities to use nudity in advertising with possibilities to talk openly about North Korea and comfort women, the ads illustrating these trends exhibited in the same display.

Sex-appeal advertising in South Korea thus refuses to be categorized into simplistic categories of "sexist," "conservative," or "progressive" and instead offers a complicated node, where meanings of freedom are contested, gender roles are disturbed, and even proper Koreanness is negotiated. Though "sex appeal" is a classic strategy of sensualizing commodities, commodity aesthetics becomes subordinated to other projects of advertising producers and consumers, who both seek to use advertising as a vehicle to promote their worldviews to dominance, taking advantage of the resources advertisers invest in producing persuasive messages.

MORPHING INTO ENTERTAINMENT

In addition to articulating popular aspirations, what draws Korean advertising in the orbit of popular culture is how heavily it relies on celebrities. Casting a celebrity has been a proven way to attract audiences' attention since the dawn of modern advertising, and in the first decade of this century, 70–75 percent of Korean ads featured celebrities,[38] many of them endorsing several products simultaneously. As celebrity endorsers usually perform the same roles in the ads and in the popular-cultural products for which they are known, advertising blends with celebrity-driven entertainment, becoming another venue for consuming information about celebrities.[39] In such ads, celebrities' presence often overwhelms the advertised commodity. With the "Think Casual" campaign, for example, netizens debated whether the message of sexual freedom was too controversial for Uee and for Korean society—mentioning the soju itself only in passing.

The rise of consumer-centered (as opposed to product-centered) marketing after the 1997 IMF crisis further propelled advertising's merger with entertainment. The path for the transformation was paved by the exposure to provocative creative work of international advertising agencies during the 1988 Seoul Olympics and by the postdemocratization relaxation of censorship requirements. In the late 1990s, as businesses adapted to neoliberal restructuring and flexible accumulation, marketing shifted from selling specific products to building brands and promoting lifestyles, whereas advertising has since grown postmodern, progressively relying on nonverbal communication and cultivating ambiguity of meaning.[40] Some ads experimented with surreal aesthetic and nostalgic kitsch, the former represented by SK Telecom's TTL series in 1999, which showed a young woman wandering in a creepy underwater space, and the latter by 1998 "Touch touch 002" ad, where an archetypical *ajumma* hopped across roofs, accompanied by a kangaroo, to get better reception for an international phone call.[41] Other ads transgressed out of the advertising genre, taking advantage of the Internet to show ads that exceeded the 15 seconds maximally allowed on broadcast television. "Love is always thirsty" campaign for the "2%" Lotte beverage mimicked TV melodramas, showing intense fights between a young couple played by popular actors, the short TV ads marginally comprehensible without having seen longer online versions. Cell phone ads blurred genres by copying music videos.[42] Korean advertising has been driven toward entertainment by its humanist ethos as well: as discussed above, humanistic ads forgo the sales message and indulge the public in pathos and melodrama.

Advertising thus has grown less advertising-like. Ads employ ambiguous imagery; they talk less about commodities and more about everything else, from sex to humanism. Reading such ads as sales messages requires knowledge of advertisers' lines of business, whereas to consume them as cultural products, neither subversion nor selective reading nor any other additional effort is necessary. By taking commodity aesthetics to the limit, postmodern advertising paradoxically deranges advertising as a capitalist institution, pushing it further away from selling commodities to the realm of creative expression. As a CNN observer lamented, commenting on the global advertising developments, "advertising is increasingly morphing into another form of entertainment," which he diagnosed as "a disturbing trend for many large corporations, who [sic] may find that instead of boosting sales, they are wasting millions of dollars on advertising campaigns that simply boost the egos of marketing executives and ad agency types who dream of being the next Martin Scorsese or Woody Allen."[43]

Examining the popular-cultural life of advertising in postdemocratization South Korea reveals how advertising mutates as a social institution in late capitalism, a trend noticeable in other locales as well. Regulators traditionally police the boundary between advertising and nonadvertising in the mainstream media, limiting advertising spatially and temporally. With the spread of the Internet, however, advertising producers can experiment with formats and challenge genre conventions. Moreover, the Internet has eroded the traditional benefit (or alibi, depending on the point of view) supplied by advertising, that it delivers useful information about available commodities. Nowadays online search engines will fetch on demand more complete and reliable information than any 15-second commercial or a full-page ad could convey. To remain relevant, advertising has to reinvent itself, and it adapts by increasingly blurring with popular culture—understood not simply as popular entertainment but as an arena in which to articulate lived experiences and propagate worldviews.

However, it is uncertain whether permeating advertising with socially engaged messages truly disrupts its sales function. Campaigns that are appropriated into popular culture are often followed by sales increases for the advertiser. Advertising still serves the needs of capital first, and this is the limit of creative appropriations of advertising by consumers—or even by producers who strive to promote the public good, taking advantage of advertisers' generous marketing budgets. Moreover, no matter how socially engaged advertising content is, it does not interfere with how dependence on advertising revenues structures commercial media industries, gagging radical critiques and thus minimizing challenges to existing power relations.[44]

Contesting representations in advertising might challenge certain oppressions, but advertising is never their primary cause, only a symptom, and social changes triggered by advertising are usually trivial and do little to touch structural inequalities. Buying from corporations that produce humanist advertising will not make capitalism any less antihumanist and in fact might work as a safety valve that allows for ineffectual resistance, thus reincorporating rebellious subjects. This contradictory mixture of resistance and containment impulses that advertising harbors likens it to Gramscian subaltern culture, which gives an outlet for discontent but is incapable of articulating a coherent worldview that would effectively challenge domination.[45] Advertising occasionally critiques actual hierarchies and oppressions, but to remedy them it explicitly or implicitly prescribes consumption—of the right products bought from the right corporations—thus reproducing the ideological fantasy that invests desires into consumption and binds subjects to capitalist relations of production, synchronizing individual pursuits of fulfillment with the capital's drive for ever-increasing production of commodities. Still, it is in the midst of popular culture where "moments of freedom" germinate, critical openings well up, and alternative worldviews emerge, from which something new might arise. Thus it is worth exploring new opportunities that popular-cultural appropriations and subversions of advertising enable, while being aware of their limitations.

NOTES

1. Korea Broadcast Advertising Corporation (KOBACO). KOBACO Newsletter #72, January 21, 2010, http://www.kobaco.co.kr/kor/newsletter/20100121/02_KOBACO.html (accessed January 21, 2010).
2. "Dog" (kae) is a common element in Korean swear words.
3. "Anae ŭi Yuhok" (SBS, 2008–2009).
4. Neil M. Alperstein, Advertising in Everyday Life (Cresskill, NJ: Hampton Press, 2001), 103–7.
5. Benedict R. Anderson, Imagined Communities: Reflections on the Origin and Spread of Nationalism, 2nd ed. (London: Verso, 1991).
6. Kim Kyu-Cheul, Saenggak Innŭn Kwanggo Iyagi (Seoul: Epublic Korea, 2006).

7. Stuart Hall, "Notes on Deconstructing 'the Popular,'" in *Cultural Theory and Popular Culture: A Reader,* ed. John Storey (Upper Saddle River, NJ: Pearson/Prentice Hall, 1998), 453. Hall's vision draws on Antonio Gramsci's argument that inequality and subordination are reproduced because the dominated are unable to initiate a transformation by formulating a coherent worldview to challenge the hegemonic accounts of the world, which keep them subordinated. See Kate A. F. Crehan, *Gramsci, Culture, and Anthropology: Reading Gramsci* (London: Pluto, 2002), 104–13.

8. Hall, "Notes on Deconstructing 'the Popular,'" 443.

9. Wolfgang Fritz Haug, *Critique of Commodity Aesthetics: Appearance, Sexuality, and Advertising in Capitalist Society* (Cambridge: Polity Press, 1986).

10. Slavoj Žižek, "Fantasy as a Political Category: A Lacanian Approach," in *The Žižek Reader,* ed. Slavoj Žižek, Elizabeth Wright, and Edmond Leo Wright (Oxford: Blackwell, 1999), 87–102.

11. For a Žižekian/Lacanian discussion of advertising, see Yannis Stavrakakis, "Objects of Consumption, Causes of Desire: Consumerism and Advertising in Societies of Commanded Enjoyment," *Gamma* 14 (2006): 83–106.

12. Johannes Fabian, *Moments of Freedom: Anthropology and Popular Culture* (Charlottesville: University Press of Virginia, 1998), 133.

13. For an overview of various positions on advertising, see William Leiss, Stephen Kline, Sut Jhally, and Jacqueline Botterill, *Social Communication in Advertising: Consumption in the Mediated Marketplace,* 3rd ed. (New York: Routledge, 2005).

14. The concept of "popular culture" has been critiqued for the implicit dichotomies it contains in Arjun Appadurai and Carol A. Breckenridge, "Why Public Culture?" *Public Culture Bulletin* 1, no. 1 (1998): 5–9. The authors propose to frame related phenomena as "public culture," defining it as an arena where cosmopolitan and local cultural forms shape each other. It is possible to think about advertising in such terms; however, focusing solely on cultural debates conducted through advertising naturalizes advertising as a social institution and ignores how advertising mediates the bottlenecks of capitalist organization of production.

15. KOBACO Newsletter #72.

16. "Kubonkwon Kongryong Imiji Pŏtko, Chŏl'ko Chŭlgŏpke 'Olle,'" *Hankyŏre,* July 28, 2009, http://www.hani.co.kr/arti/economy/marketing/368295.html (accessed October 6, 2009).

17. For a detailed history of Korean advertising, see Shin In Sup and Sŏ Pŏm-sŏk, *Han'guk Kwanggo sa,* 3rd ed. (Seoul: Nanam, 2011).

18. Jib Fowles, *Advertising and Popular Culture,* Foundations of Popular Culture, vol. 5 (Thousand Oaks, Calif.: Sage, 1996), 11.

19. Fowles, *Advertising and Popular Culture.*

20. The advertising industry hit 0.7 percent of GDP in 1978, accounting for 169,941 million won, according to *Kwanggo Yŏngam 2008* (Seoul: Cheil kihwek, 2008), 1064.

21. Laura C. Nelson, *Measured Excess: Status, Gender, and Consumer Nationalism in South Korea* (New York: Columbia University Press, 2000).

22. The predominance of in-house advertising agencies has been a defining feature of South Korea's advertising industry. For details, see Kwangmi Ko Kim, "Advertising

in Korea: International Challenges and Politics," in *Advertising in Asia: Communication, Culture, and Consumption*, ed. Katherine Toland Frith (Ames: Iowa State University Press, 1996), 125–53.

23. Michael Schudson, *Advertising, the Uneasy Persuasion: Its Dubious Impact on American Society* (New York: Basic Books, 1984), 218.

24. Hong-tack Kim, "Characteristics, History, and Forecasts of Creativity in Korea," in *Korean Advertising: Facts and Insights* (Seoul: KOBACO, 2007), 257.

25. Pak Hye-ran, "Maŭm ŭl' Mujang haeje sik'i nŭn Kibun Choŭm," *Kwanggo Chŏngbo*, no. 11 (2005): 13.

26. Mha Joung-Mee (Ma Chŏng-mi), *Kwanggo ro Ing'nŭn Han'guk Sahoe munhwa sa* (Seoul: Kaema kowon, 2004), 142; Shin In Sup, "Kwanggo ŭi Ponjil ŭi Taehan Pip'ŏn Pang'ŏ," *Daehong po* 100, no. 9 (1992): 40–43. The poem itself can be found in Kim Sowol, "Azaleas," in *The Columbia Anthology of Modern Korean Poetry*, trans. David R. McCann (New York: Columbia University Press, 2004), 19.

27. *Honja Ttŏnanŭn Yŏhaeng* blog, September 29, 2007, http://dus11984.blog.me /60042665579 (accessed January 9, 2011).

28. Korea Advertisers Association, *Naega Choahanŭn Kwanggo: Sobija ga Ppopŭn Pesŭt'ŭ Kwang'go* (Seoul: Sodam, 1992).

29. Nancy Abelmann, *The Melodrama of Mobility: Women, Talk, and Class in Contemporary South Korea* (Honolulu: University of Hawai'i Press, 2003); Keehyung Lee, "Speak Memory! Morae Sigye and the Politics of Social Melodrama in Contemporary South Korea," *Cultural Studies—Critical Methodologies* 4, no. 4 (2004): 526–39.

30. Peter Brooks, "The Melodramatic Imagination," in *Imitations of Life: A Reader on Film and Television Melodrama*, ed. Marcia Landy (Detroit: Wayne State University Press, 1991).

31. See Carter J. Eckert, "The South Korean Bourgeoisie: A Class in Search of Hegemony," in *State and Society in Contemporary Korea*, ed. Hagen Koo (Ithaca, NY: Cornell University Press, 1993); Roger L. Janelli and Dawnhee Yim Janelli, *Making Capitalism: The Social and Cultural Construction of a South Korean Conglomerate* (Stanford, Calif.: Stanford University Press, 1993).

32. Mha, *Kwanggo ro Ing'nŭn Han'guk Sahoe munhwa sa*, 250; Shin In Sup, "Kwangpok ihu," in *Hanguk Kwanggo 100-nŏn* (Seoul: Korea Federation of Advertising Associations, 1996), 51.

33. Shin, "Kwangpok ihu"; also personal correspondence with Shin (March 30, 2011).

34. "Nudŭ Model Kwanggo Sŏnjŏngsŏng Nollan," *Yonhap News*, February 24, 1995, http://news.naver.com/main/read.nhn?mode=LSD&mid=sec&sid1=101&oid=001& aid=0003907062# (accessed March 20, 2011).

35. Hyun Mee Kim, "Feminization of the 2002 World Cup and Women's Fandom," in *The Inter-Asia Cultural Studies Reader*, ed. Kuan-Hsing Chen and Huat Chua Beng (London: Routledge, 2007), 539–49.

36. An Mi-hyŏn, "Soju '0.1 do Chŏnjaeng," *Seoul Sinmun*, August 26, 2009, www .seoul.co.kr/news/newsView.php?id=20090826015007# (accessed October 13, 2010).

37. See James Turnbull, "Korean Sociological Image #52: Are Celebrities Removing the Stigma of Lingerie Modelling?" The Grand Narrative blog, November 4, 2010,

http://thegrandnarrative.com/2010/11/04/korea-lingerie-advertisements/ (accessed March 17, 2011).

38. Precise statistics are hard to find and most authors quote their estimates without providing sources. Hong-tack Kim quotes 70 percent in "Characteristics," 273.

39. Analyzing a similar trend in 1990s Japan, anthropologist Gabriella Lukács in *Scripted Affects, Branded Selves: Television, Subjectivity, and Capitalism in 1990s Japan* (Durham, NC: Duke University Press, 2010) argues that the cross-genre circulation of celebrities was the strategy of Japanese television networks to reach increasingly fragmented audiences under a post-Fordist regime. Her analysis helps situate the obsession with celebrities in contemporary South Korea by analogy, though Korea-specific research is needed for a more nuanced understanding of the local celebrity culture.

40. Martin Morris, "Interpretability and Social Power, or Why Postmodern Advertising Works," *Media, Culture & Society* 27, no. 5 (2005): 697–718.

41. Kim, "Characteristics," 221.

42. Kim discusses in detail the advertising campaigns that imitated music videos, blockbuster movies, or TV series, "Characteristics," 271–72.

43. Paul R. La Monica, "The Problem with TV Ads," CNNmoney.com, http://money.cnn.com/2007/03/21/commentary/mediabiz/index.htm?postversion=2007032111 (accessed March 26, 2007).

44. James Curran and Jean Seaton, *Power without Responsibility: The Press, Broadcasting, and New Media in Britain*, 7th ed. (New York: Routledge, 2009).

45. Crehan, *Gramsci, Culture and Anthropology*.

The Global *Hansik* Campaign and the Commodification of Korean Cuisine

DEMARCATING *HANSIK*

At the 2008 Korea Food Expo, the South Korean Minister of Food, Agriculture, Forestry, and Fisheries, Chang Tae-pyong, announced the Global Promotion of Korean Cuisine (*hansik segyehwa ch'ujin*) Campaign, a government-led initiative with the goal of turning Korean food (*hansik*) into one of the five most popular ethnic cuisines in the world by 2017. The campaign took off slowly in 2009, coordinated by the Korean Cuisine Global Promotion Team (*hansik segyehwa ch'ujindan*), with the wife of South Korean President Lee Myung-bak as its honorary chairperson. Although not a government body per se, the promotion team included many high-ranking South Koreans who had frequently issued public statements concerning the introduction of concrete initiatives to achieve this ambitious goal.[1]

For example, in spring 2009 the Ministry of Food, Agriculture, Forestry, and Fisheries(*nongsin susanbu*) identified the chief strategies for overhauling Korean cuisine to attract overseas consumers, clearly positioning restaurants as cultural centers and cooks as diplomats promoting the "Korean brand." According to the *Korea Times*, minister Chang announced the need to make every effort to "recommend the virtues of *hansik*, to let the world know how valuable and enjoyable Korean foods are." Why? Because *hansik* is "the face of our country," explained Chang.[2] In an interview with the newspaper six months later, Chang revealed that 2009 was merely a preparatory year and that the campaign would reach full speed in 2010.[3] "Developing more *hansik* brands" would be one of the top priorities, which was to be achieved through expanding the number of Korean restaurants abroad, coupled with plans to standardize the names, descriptions, and recipes of representative Korean dishes. Promotional activities through traditional channels such as the Korean embassies and the Korea Tourism Organization (*Han'guk kwan'gwang kongsa*) were to be intensified, and new ones, such as dispatching Korean chefs to hold cooking classes at globally renowned culinary schools, were initiated.[4]

On March 17, 2010, the task of spearheading the efforts to globalize Korean cuisine was entrusted to the Korean Food Foundation (KFF, *hansik chaedan*), set up especially for this purpose. The foundation is funded by donations of 700 million wŏn (about $620,000) from the above-mentioned Korea Tourism Organization, the Korea Agro-Fisheries Trade Corporation (*nongsu sanmul yudong kongsa*), the Korea Foundation (*Han'guk kukche kyoryu chaedan*), the National Federation of Fisheries Cooperatives (*susanŏp hyŏptong chohap*), the National Agricultural Cooperative Federation (*nongŏp hyŏptong chohap*), the Korean Food Research Institute (*Hanguk sikp'um yŏn'guwŏn*), and the Korean Racing Authority (*Hanguk masahoe*), which is a generous sponsor of activities relating to horse racing and breeding.[5] Chung Woon-chun, the former Minister of Food, Agriculture, Forestry, and Fisheries, serves as the chair of the KFF.

An issue that assumed a central position in the promotion of Korean food abroad from the beginning was delineating the *hansik* territory. In contrast to Japanese cuisine, for which *sushi* is clearly the international key player,[6] there is no clear consensus on which dishes should enter the pantheon of Korean cuisine. For example, the website Food in Korea, launched in 2008 by the Korea Agro-Fisheries Trade Corporation, identifies a "Korean Food Top 10," providing detailed descriptions of the historical origins and recipes of Korean food.[7] The list includes—in this order—*kimch'i* (a spicy vegetable pickle), *pulgogi* (thinly sliced grilled beef), *pibimpap* (rice mixed with vegetables and beef), *naengmyŏn* (chilled buckwheat noodle soup), *samgyet'ang* (chicken ginseng soup), *chapch'ae* (clear noodles stir-fried with vegetables), *sinsŏllo* (a seafood, meat, and vegetable stew), *ttŏk* and *hankwa* (two types of Korean confectionery), and ends with two broader categories of drinks. A slightly different top-ten selection was introduced on a promotional website of the Korea Tourism Organization: *kimch'i, pibimpap* ("a traditional Korean dish eaten by royalty"), *kalbi* (grilled beef ribs), *pulgogi, samgyŏpsal* (grilled strips of pork belly), *samgyet'ang, naengmyŏn*, seafood dishes, and *ttŏk*.[8] The official website of the Korean Food Foundation offers a more comprehensive overview of Korean cuisine than the top-ten lists on the above-mentioned websites and includes *kimpap* (rice rolled in laver), *pudae tchigae* (a spicy stew of sausage, luncheon meat, macaroni, and vegetables), and *ttŏkpokki* (rice cake in chili sauce).

In the case of all of these selections, it is not entirely clear who has made them and on what grounds. The problem is not so much *who* has the authority to demarcate the *hansik* territory but rather where to draw the line in the selection and reinvention of Korean cuisine to meet the demands and expectations of foreign consumers. Sidney Mintz's argument that national cuisines worldwide are being transformed into "tourist artifacts"[9] is particularly true of Korea's culinary heritage, which is being commodified for display and consumption abroad. Strongly influenced by the marketing strategies of *hallyu* (Korean Wave), the version of *hansik* that is being propagated through the current campaign is a carefully manufactured product, designed to sell culinary distinction in a highly competitive global arena. How far removed will the final product become from the original?

KOREAN CULINARY NATIONALISM

The growing international appreciation of Korean culinary heritage is fostering national pride, especially in view of the fact that its pungent taste and strong smell have in the past been largely disapproved of by non-Koreans and have not infrequently served as a source of stigma.[10] The application of food as a badge of national identity is also a long-standing tradition, as is providing common offensive names for certain nationalities and ethnic groups.[11] As cultural geographers have argued for years, "Foods do not simply come from places, organically growing out of them, but also make places as symbolic constructs, being deployed in the discursive construction of various imaginative geographies."[12] The attractiveness of food as a bearer of culture perhaps lies in the fact that the representations of other societies seem "more immediate and concrete when they treat the common experiences of hunger and eating, inevitably invoking personal memories, sentimental association with familiar foods, and a shock of delight or revulsion at descriptions of strange foods. . . . This universality of food gives it enormous potential as an indicator of cultural difference."[13]

Yet culinary nationalism today is of a very different nature, actively promoting national interests rather than merely reflecting national culture.[14] The strategists behind the Global *Hansik* Campaign have consciously inculcated the image of Korean cuisine as the food of yesteryear, unaffected by industrialization and other evils of the modern world. This image fits the nostalgic view of Korean cuisine currently prevalent among South Koreans themselves. The Global *Hansik* Campaign is the culmination of a growing nostalgia for and appreciation of domestic cuisine, a phenomenon that has been on the rise in South Korea since the late 1990s. This development is described by Korean experts as an "emphasis upon the positive quality of the national food and a renaissance of national culinary culture."[15] In parallel with similar developments elsewhere,[16] this rediscovery of Korea's own culinary heritage has followed a period of rapid economic growth and an increasing familiarity, even infatuation, with foreign food. As Raymond Grew pointedly observed, it is greater freedom of choice that causes the issues of identity to arise, and it is the consciousness of change that stimulates the inventive use of tradition.[17]

This widespread transformation in South Korean consumption practices, which took place at the end of the twentieth century, manifested itself most profoundly in the culture of dining out.[18] The eating-out expenditure of South Korean households as percentage of total food expenditure increased from 6 percent in 1982 to 47 percent in 2007.[19] Moreover, abundance and variety became the key attributes of South Korean gastronomy, allowing the majority of its population not only to enjoy a diet that had previously only been affordable for the elite but also to indulge in foreign culinary trends.

Generally speaking, until the 1980s the main place in which ordinary South Koreans could encounter foreign food was the Chinese restaurant.[20] This situation began to change with the encroachment of American fast food. Curiously, the very first fast-food store that opened in South Korea was Lotteria—a Japanese imitation of McDonald's. The brand had been operating in Japan since 1972 and was part of Lotte Group, a large food-processing conglomerate founded in Japan in 1948 by a Korean immigrant, Shin Kyŏk-ho.[21] The company had actively invested in the South Korean food-processing industry soon after the liberalization of South Korean–Japanese relations in 1965. In 1979 it opened the first American fast-food outlet on the Korean peninsula, followed in the ensuing years by Burger King, KFC, McDonald's, and Pizza Hut, which all arrived largely in preparation for the 1988 Seoul Olympic Games.[22]

Many Koreans became concerned that the South Korean economy would be adversely affected if they patronized foreign restaurants. At the time a preference for foreign food was commonly perceived as a sign of conspicuous consumption and vanity, and it was accompanied by a fear that, through the consumption of foreign products, Korean culture would fall victim to Japanese or Western infiltration.[23] The rising standard of living and rapidly transforming consumption patterns also created a major dilemma for those who desired to appear, simultaneously, nationalistic and international. The growing ambivalence toward achieving a globalized lifestyle while losing one's Korean identity was largely generated by government campaigns against *kwasobi* (literally "excessive consumption")—the term applied to the phenomenon of consuming beyond what was considered appropriate.[24]

These campaigns, conducted during the late 1980s and early 1990s, focused on patriotic frugality, warning South Koreans against the dangers inherent in extravagance.

The idea of the South Korean government acting as an advocate of frugality and restraint in consumption was by no means new. The first such government campaigns date back to the Korean War and were successively reused in the following decades with the blessing of Park Chung-Hee, who was inspired by similar discourses in Japan.[25] What made the 1990s campaign different, however, was the approaching expiration date for the image of a prosperous future, which was the central component of South Korean nationalism. The generation of Koreans who had endured decades of hardship with the promise of affluence in mind were, by the late 1980s, ready to reap the rewards of their sacrifices. Ironically, after 1997, when the Asian financial crisis hit the export-oriented South Korean economy, domestic consumption began to be reconsidered by policymakers as the vanguard of the country's economic revitalization. In the post-1997 era consumer patriotism is no longer defined primarily in terms of frugality; rather, consumption itself has been elevated to a "nation-saving act."[26] Foreign culinary trends have been further embraced and diversified, as demonstrated by the skyrocketing popularity of Italian, Indian, Thai, and other ethnic restaurants, as well as the phenomenal success of Starbucks coffee shops and their imitators.[27] However, this persistent encroachment of foreign culinary trends and transnational consumerism has engendered the reassertion of Korea's own culinary heritage. To eat Korean food has increasingly become a matter of conscious decision rather than a taken-for-granted habit. In fact, while the number of restaurants serving foreign food in South Korea remained relatively stable between 1993 and 2006, in exactly the same period restaurants serving Korean food experienced spectacular growth—from 151,438 to 261,395 establishments.[28] Thus, South Korean consumers brought their sense of identification with the nation to the increasingly complex dining-out market, setting themselves the task of making consumer choices that were in the best interests of the nation.[29]

PROPAGATING KOREAN CUISINE ABROAD

The idea of utilizing cuisine as a means of propagating Korean culture began to surface in South Korea at the time of the 1988 Seoul Olympics. One of the first venues for disseminating information on Korean food abroad was the quarterly *Koreana*, published from 1987 with the goal of "increasing awareness about Korea's cultural heritage overseas." Since 1991 the journal has been the mouthpiece of the Korea Foundation, an institution established in affiliation with the Korean Ministry of Foreign Affairs, to "promote a better understanding of Korea in the international community and to foster global friendship by conducting exchange activities between the Republic of Korea and foreign countries around the world."[30] Published in eight languages (English, German, Spanish, French, Arabic, Russian, Chinese, and Japanese), *Koreana* is distributed free of charge to universities, libraries, museums, research centers, and other cultural institutions in over one hundred countries. While food appeared only sporadically in the journal during the first decade of its existence, information on "the culinary culture of Korea" has now become a regular feature of every issue, in the form of a "Cuisine" column.

Conforming to the general character of the journal, food-related articles featured in *Koreana* tend to emphasize the unique characteristics of Korean cuisine, highlighting the time-honored traditions surrounding the production, preparation, and consumption of food in Korea. This tendency is also strongly pronounced in the publicity surrounding the Global *Hansik* Campaign—Korea's treasured culinary legacy that the world has yet to discover. Moreover, the strategists behind the Global *Hansik* Campaign have consciously communicated the image of Korean cuisine as healthy food. This health factor was symbolically confirmed by the "sperm-count experiment," one of the very first projects launched by the Korean Food Foundation after its inception in March 2010. The experiment was undertaken with the objective of demonstrating the health benefits of Korean food and involved counting the sperm collected from two groups of men—one group ate only Korean food, the other only foreign food, for a little over one month. "The sperm count of a man in his twenties who lives in the city eating a predominantly meat-based Western diet was comparable to that of a country dweller in his fifties whose diet is mainly composed of Korean food," explained the chairman of the foundation, Chung Woon-chun, in a cover story for *Korea IT Times*. He concluded by observing that these results demonstrate the excellent health benefits of Korean food.[31]

In the early 1990s, the healthy qualities of Korean food abroad were featured prominently. For example, *kimch'i* was embraced in Japan as a wonderfood with the ability to increase stamina, prevent cancer, and even generate weight loss.[32] The emphasis on the connection between health and Korean food was extended from dishes to ingredients during the *shint'o puri* campaign of 1992. This campaign aimed to convince urban citizens to eat domestic produce to protect the livelihoods of their producer-compatriots in the countryside following the introduction of free-trade agreements for agricultural products. The slogan *shint'o puri* (literally "body and earth are one"), popularized through the joint efforts of the Agricultural Cooperative Federation (*nonghyŏp chung'anhoe*) and the Ministry of Food, Agriculture, Forestry, and Fisheries, is derived from the Buddhist concept of the inseparability of the karma of an individual from that of his or her surroundings. Yet, in its popular usage, *shint'o puri* came to imply that food from Korean soil was best for Korean bodies.[33] The publicity that surrounded the various activities of the Agricultural Cooperative Federation in propagating this idea succeeded in inculcating a common belief among South Korean consumers that food produced in Korea was better tasting and healthier than imported produce.

Ironically, as a result of the rising standard of living and the proliferation of dining out since the late 1980s, meat eating has assumed a central place in the Korean diet, making South Koreans increasingly dependent on meat imports. The rise in demand could not be met by domestic production alone; by 2006 Korea ranked globally as the sixth largest importer of chicken and the seventh largest importer of beef.[34]

Yet the seeds of public mistrust in imported food caused by the *shint'o puri* movement resurfaced in 2006, when a variety of organizations, including trade unions, farmers' groups, and NGOs (nongovernmental organizations) formed the Korean Alliance against the Korea-U.S. Free Trade Agreement (KORUS-FTA). Hundreds of thousands of Korean citizens took to the streets to condemn the "beef deal" signed on April 17, 2008, which lifted restrictions on the import of U.S. beef to Korea.[35] Imports had been banned in December 2003, after the detection of a positive case of BSE, and resumed in 2006 on the condition that only deboned, skeletal-muscle meat would be allowed. During the following year, however, the importation of U.S. beef to Korea was suspended eight times due to the detection of bones in the meat.[36]

The beef trade issue of the KORUS-FTA became a national crisis, with the new Korean government reorganizing its entire cabinet to appease public discontent. The Global *Hansik* Campaign, as a serious commitment from the South Korean political establishment to invest in cuisine as a global ambassador for Korean culture, offered a useful channel for the re-alliance of the government with Korean culinary nationalism. Regardless of whether the projected ambition of Korean cuisine rising to global prominence will indeed be realized by 2017, the *hansik* project offers the potential for the government to improve its public image, which was bruised by the 2008 food-safety crisis. On the other hand, its involvement in assuming control over the global flow of Korean food is not without risk for the government. For example, the Korean Food Foundation is establishing an accreditation program for existing Korean restaurants abroad. Sixty out of more than 180 Korean restaurants in Tokyo have already been selected for inclusion in a pilot promotional booklet. This program is planned to be expanded to a number of other cities around the world, including Los Angeles, New York, Beijing, Shanghai, London, and Paris.[37]

The plans of the Korean Food Foundation to certify Korean restaurants abroad may meet with criticism similar to that exacted upon the infamous Japanese "sushi police." This "police force" was part of an initiative undertaken in 2006 by the Japanese Ministry of Agriculture, Forestry, and Fisheries to issue official seals of approval to overseas eateries serving Japanese food. It was widely ridiculed and criticized by the global media. "The discourse of intervention," argue Sakamoto and Allen, "mobilises an essentialist and nationalist rhetoric that rejects the value of non-Japanese restaurants (often owned and run by Asian 'others') that 'pretend' to be 'real' Japanese. It assumes a nonproblematic notion of ownership and authenticity regarding what is considered to be Japanese national cuisine and attempts to exert control over it."[38] Precisely the same issues are at stake with South Korean initiatives to watch over the quality of Korean food served in overseas restaurants. The similarities derive from the greater context of increasing investment by Asian governments in the promotion of their cuisines. The concept of "soft power," coined by Joseph Nye to discuss the reputational and ideological power of nation states,[39] has increasingly been linked with cuisine. Asian governments have become particularly conscious of the potential of national "culinary soft power," defined by Farrer as "the acknowledged attractiveness and appeal of food culture that adheres to a nation, region, or locality."[40]

The South Korean government is following in the footsteps of earlier Thai and Japanese initiatives, and the government of Malaysia has also recently launched projects aimed at promoting the status of its national cuisine abroad. The Thai government launched its "Kitchen of the World" project in 2001, with the aim of increasing the number of Thai restaurants overseas to 20,000 by 2008. It focused on two strategies: standardization and an emphasis on quality. In order to achieve the former, the Thai government encouraged Thai restaurants overseas to restrict the number of dishes to those most popular with foreigners. To control the standard of Thai restaurants, the government awarded the "Thai Select" label to qualifying restaurants.[41]

The Japanese government began to conceive ideas that utilized popular culture to create a Japan Brand in 2004, and the state strategy for the dissemination of Japanese food abroad was approved a year later. The idea for the certification schemes launched in 2006 was modeled on the existing

Italian and Thai models but met with severe criticism within and outside Japan and even raised accusations of racism and xenophobia.[42]

While the misguided efforts made toward protecting Japanese cuisine were chiefly directed at non-Japanese entrepreneurs operating Japanese restaurants, the majority of Korean restaurants worldwide are run by Korean nationals. Thus, the South Korean certification system deals with Korean restaurateurs who have remained outside the sphere of influence of the Korean state. Plans announced by the Ministry of Food, Agriculture, Forestry, and Fisheries to streamline the promotion of Korean food have thus far included the intention to standardize the translation and transliteration of Korean dishes (announced in November 2009) and to make uniform the recipes of dishes served in Korean restaurants worldwide. However, voices have been raised regarding the interference of the state in the affairs of independent restaurateurs.[43] Business owners have been far from eager to abandon their freedom and are distrustful of state coordination of their menus, measures which fit with the long "tradition" of the South Korean government controlling the consumption practices of its citizens.

There are further complications in the South Korean government's ambition to elevate Korean cuisine to global supremacy and to function as a watchdog for the authenticity of Korean culinary tradition—its northern brother. The inclusion of *naengmyŏn* (chilled noodles), the North's most famous dish, in the pantheon of Korean food to be promoted worldwide has already invited a polemic on who owns the rights to North Korean food.

JAPAN: FROM *KIMCH'I* TO *MAKGŎLLI*

Japan deserves particularly close treatment in this study, not only because of the contested nature of the relationship between the two countries but also because of to the strong influence of changing Japanese attitudes toward Korean food on Korea's perception of its own culinary culture. Japan is an important market for Korean products, but at the same time a fierce competitor in the quest for global culinary recognition. The colonial legacy does not make the relationship any easier but, despite the antagonisms, the popularity of Korean food and drink in Japan since the 1980s has played an essential role in the rising consciousness among Koreans that their native fare may be attractive to foreigners.

Older generations of Japanese encountered Korean food in the form of *yakiniku* (grilled meat). Before the economic boom of the 1980s, Korean-style barbecued meat was the prevalent form of meat consumption among the Japanese, and *yakiniku* remains one of the most popular meat dishes in Japan. Until the 1990s, the popularity of *kimch'i* fell far behind that of grilled meat, as its pungent taste did not agree with most Japanese palates and the strong, garlicky odor of the pickle was not socially acceptable, especially on the breath of diners. The mid-1990s marked a watershed in the Japanese attitude toward *kimch'i*: its production in Japan increased nearly fourfold, while its importation from Korea increased by nearly tenfold, from 3,432 to 30,000 tons. By 2000 *kimch'i* ranked as number one among all the pickled vegetables produced (and consumed) in Japan, far ahead of traditional Japanese-style pickles.[44]

The skyrocketing popularity of *kimch'i* in Japan had a critical impact on the South Korean *kimch'i* market. First of all, the Japanese interest stimulated a growth in the commercial production of *kimch'i* in South Korea—previously *kimch'i* pickling (*kimjang*) had been primarily conducted for individual consumption in each household. South Korean soldiers deployed to Vietnam during the late 1960s were the first consumers of factory-made (canned) *kimch'i*, followed during the 1970s by Korean construction workers in the Middle East. However, the *kimch'i* processing industry only truly began to thrive after the Korean pickle was embraced by Japanese consumers in the 1990s. Today most restaurants and catering services in South Korea rely on industrially processed *kimch'i*, as do the majority of urban consumers. Although per capita consumption declined from 35.1 kg in 1991 to 32.4 kg in 2004, the industry continues to thrive owing to a steady decline in the *kimjang* ritual.[45]

Like the manufacture of soy sauce (*kanjang*), soybean paste (*toenjang*), and red chili pepper paste (*koch'ujang*), for centuries *kimjang* was strictly a homemade affair. Preparation methods and flavor varied considerably by region, and each family had its own recipes handed down from generation to generation. Producing and consuming homemade condiments created a bond among family members. The gradual shift from homemade to factory-made *kanjang* has powerfully affected the taste of Korean food: the distinctive flavors of household soy sauce have become uniform, while industrial methods result in products that differ in taste and aroma from traditional *kanjang*.[46] Similarly, the commercialization of *kimch'i* production resulted in the standardization of its flavor. At the beginning of the industrialization process, most *kimch'i* factories were located in the vicinity of Seoul, and since then the flavor produced in this area has become the commercial "national" *kimch'i* standard. Han goes so far as to argue that the commercialization of *kimch'i* production has reinforced the "consciousness of Koreans that they comprise a single ethnic group."[47]

Thus, the successful reception of *kimch'i* in Japan aided its rapid transformation into Korea's "officially sanctioned" national symbol. Moreover, it was Japanese attempts to capitalize on the manufacture of *kimch'i* that inflamed Korean claims to its "ownership." This dispute, commonly known as the Kimchi War (*kimch'i chŏnjaeng*), began in 1996, when Japan proposed to designate *kimuchi* (Japanese pronunciation of *kimch'i*) an official Japanese food at the Atlanta Olympics. At this point Japanese-Korean trade relations were already under stress because Japan was exporting a Japanese "instant" version of *kimch'i* that lacked the distinctive flavor derived from the fermentation process. In response, South Korea filed a case with the Codex Alimentarius Commission (CODAC), part of the United Nations Food and Agriculture Organization, arguing for the need to establish an international *kimch'i* standard.[48] In September 2000 the Twentieth Session of the Codex Committee on Processed Fruits and Vegetables advanced the Draft Standard for Kimchi for final adoption, which took place on July 5, 2001. The decision was interpreted by the Korean press as a failure on the part of Japan to challenge Korea with its poor *kimch'i* imitation. However, as Han explains, the accepted standard was not exactly a Korean victory but rather the product of lengthy negotiations between Korean and Japanese officials that began in 1997.[49]

Kimch'i is not an isolated example. Success on the Japanese market seems to have set the stage for national recognition, followed by efforts toward global promotion, for a number of Korean products. One of the most contemporary examples is *makgŏlli*, as demonstrated by Theodore Jun Yoo's recent study.[50] Long regarded as a poor man's alcohol, this unrefined, milky, fermented rice drink is enjoying a renaissance. In 2009 *makgŏlli* topped *soju* and wine as the most popular alcoholic beverage in South Korea, and it is now served in high-end *makgŏlli*-themed bars and *hansik* restaurants.

What makes the *makgŏlli* revival particularly interesting is the fact that it was the Japanese, not the Koreans, who rediscovered the drink. The enormous popularity of *makgŏlli* in Japan in 2009—exports of *makgŏlli* to Japan increased by 26 percent that year—received wide coverage in the South Korean media, sparking the interest of Korean consumers.[51] As was the case with *kimch'i*, a healthy image played a critical role in igniting Japanese interest in *makgŏlli*. Its alleged ability to increase longevity, lower cholesterol, reduce blood pressure, and boost the immune system began to be emphasized in Korea as well, aided by nostalgia for an earlier Korean lifestyle that had been lost on the way to economic affluence. These two themes were central to the advertising strategies of *makgŏlli* manufacturers on home ground.

The South Korean government also became actively involved in supporting the revival of the *makgŏlli* industry. As Yoo explains,

Much like the industry, which received major subsidies from the government after the crisis in 1997, *makgŏlli* breweries started receiving similar preferential treatment and in 2009 were promised $106.7 million in subsidies and tax breaks for the next five years.[52] In addition, government agencies like the South Korean Ministry of Food, Agriculture, Forestry, and Fisheries (MIFAFF) have sponsored a variety of events such as the "Makgeolli Transformer Exhibition" on September 3, 2009, featuring "locally brewed" *makgŏlli*, from all seven provinces to educate local consumers and prospective foreign importers.[53]

Ironically microbreweries that manufacture *makgŏlli* rely heavily on yeast imported from Japan,[54] much like the Korean cattle that rely on imported feed. Moreover, as happened in the "Kimchi War," the Japanese have now acquired patents to the malts necessary for the production of *makgŏlli*, depriving the Koreans from ever accessing them. Yoo provides the telling example of Pocheon *makgŏlli*, a famous rice wine brewed in Kyŏnggi province that was registered as a trademark in 2008. Because the name was registered at the Japan Patents Office in Tokyo, local breweries in Korea are no longer able to export Pocheon *makgŏlli* to Japan.

HANSIK AND HALLYU

An important development that has helped to set the stage for the Global *Hansik* Campaign is the Korean Wave, or *hallyu*, a remarkable rise in the popularity of Korean music, film, and television throughout Asia during the 1990s and early 2000s. The historical drama *Taejanggŭm* (*Jewel in the Palace*) offers a symbolic connection between *hansik* and *hallyu*. Airing on Korean television in the autumn and winter of 2003/2004 with phenomenal success, the drama met with an equally triumphant reception in Japan, Taiwan, and other parts of Asia, evidently igniting the popularity of Korean food in the region. The series depicted the life of a sixteenth-century woman who combined a career as a royal chef with that of the king's private physician. Cooking scenes featured prominently throughout the story, with intrigues and the power struggles in the highly stratified, all-female royal kitchen constituting the core of the plot. From Tokyo to Hanoi, Korean restaurants thrived and the demand for chefs trained specifically in royal cuisine (*kungjung ŭmsik*) skyrocketed as a result of the popularity of the series.

As the cuisine of the royal court was much more refined than the daily diet of most Koreans and than the standard menus of most Korean restaurants at home and abroad, the series sparked a transformation in the image of Korean food. Instead of being regarded as red and spicy fare, prepared with the abundant use of meat and fat, perceptions shifted and Korean food was thought of as a sophisticated and balanced cuisine, worthy of appreciation from the cosmopolitan and health-conscious global consumer. This shift is particularly reflected in the growing promotional emphasis on the aesthetics of Korean dishes. For example, the cover story of the March 2010 edition of *Korea* magazine—the mouthpiece of the Korea Culture and Information Service (KOCIS), part of the Ministry of Culture, Sports, and Tourism[55]—begins with the following paragraph:

> Around the world, Korean food is no longer seen as just "hot and spicy dishes from an East Asian country." After discovering a range of healthy and delicious dishes in Korean restaurants the world over, people have come to realize the diversity of Korean fare. While some ingredients and preparation techniques are similar to those found elsewhere, Korean cuisine truly embodies the nation's culture. Furthermore, the many fermented dishes that are part of meals have recently gained prominence as part of the "slow food" movement, leaving little doubt that Korean flavors are making waves overseas.[56]

Korean television miniseries have contributed considerably to the growing number of tourists visiting Korea, as both the South Korean government and these miniseries utilize place marketing to attract tourists to the country and specifically to filming locations.[57] This also holds true for the network's series *Taejanggŭm*. The show's set, located in MBC's Yangjoo Culture Valley, has been restored to how it looked during filming and has reopened as a theme park. It remains a popular tourist destination for visiting fans, spanning over 2,400 square yards. The park offers 23 separate sets to visit, including the king and queen's residence, the palace, and the royal kitchen, with detailed descriptions of all the artifacts on display.[58] A range of activities are regularly organized to entertain the visitors. For example, tourists can experience a ride in a Korean palanquin, try on traditional Korean costumes, play games, and sample Korean food.[59]

Following the success of *Taejanggŭm*, more television series focusing on food have appeared on South Korean television, of which the most important is *Sikkaek* (*Guest Who Comes to Eat*). The screenplay was based on Hur Young Man's (Heo Yeong Man) cartoon series of the same name published weekly in *Dong-a Ilbo* newspaper. Twenty-four episodes were aired in 2008.[60] The series was preceded by a movie called *Sikkaek: Le Grand Chef* (2007), and followed by a film sequel, *Sikkaek: Kimchi Battle* (2009). The series is important because, in contrast to *Taejanggŭm*, where food formed merely a background for the main storyline, the focus of *Sikkaek* is on the

Figure 16.1. Rain, the first ambassador of Korean cuisine.

food itself and, more important, on Korean food. Each episode focuses on a particular food item that requires much preparation before it can finally be consumed.

The synergy between *hallyu* and Korean food is represented by a growing number of films and television dramas with a focus on food. The spin doctors of the Global *Hansik* Campaign have employed pop-singers as *"hansik* ambassadors." In 2009, the artist and actor Rain (b. June 25, 1982, as Jung Ji-Hoon), the first Korean to win an MTV Award, was appointed as an ambassador (fig. 16.1). Two promotional clips featuring Rain praising *pibimpap* and *kalbi* have been produced, consistently projecting the message of healthy Korean cuisine prepared with fresh, seasonal ingredients.

Pibimpap Clip
Don't you just crave for a bowl of *pibimpap* on a day like this? Lightly stir-fry or boil seasonal vegetables and healthy ingredients. Place them in a bowl of rice with *koch'ujang*.
Simply beautiful to look at, delightful taste, and it is good for your health as well!
Great Korea.[61]

Kalbi Clip
Hmm, *kalbi*. My mouth waters just thinking about *kalbi*. Heat up the grill with charcoals. Then, grill the fresh meat seasoned with soy sauce, onion,

pear, garlic, and other healthy ingredients. Listen to the sizzling sound. It just sounds delicious!

It tastes beautiful and it is good for your health as well!

Great Korea.[62]

In 2011 the role of *hansik* ambassador was passed on to the pop group Super Junior, which has ten male members. This time, instead of prerecorded clips, the group was engaged for a series of international promotional events during their overseas concert tours. The campaign was labeled "Discover Korea's Delicious Secret" (figs. 16.2 and 16.3). Fragments of different members introducing their favorite dishes are available to view on the Internet (with subtitles in different languages).[63]

In addition to professional performers acting as *hansik* ambassadors, a number of less successful promotional videos about Korean food have been produced within the framework of the Global *Hansik* Campaign. These can be viewed through the "prkorea" and "hansikkorea" channels on YouTube, with *Korean Food, Hansik—The Taste of Korea* as a prime example of how *not* to advertise Korean food to foreigners.[64]

With media attention toward Korean cuisine growing as a result of the efforts made by the South Korean government in the last two years, cooking shows promoting Korean cuisine produced outside of Korea are also emerging. *Kimchi Chronicles*, a 13-episode television series about Korean food and culture that aired on U.S. television in summer 2011, is one such example. Part travelogue and part food fantasy à la *Sikkaek*, the series features Marja Vongerichten, wife of the famed chef Jean-Georges, discovering the delights of Korean cooking. Vongerichten is the daughter of a Korean woman and an African American soldier and was raised by adoptive parents in the United States; thus she has a familial reason to discover Korean food. The setting of this show in itself reflects the fundamentally fragmented and overlapping cultural forms in today's world.

"TOO MANY COOKS SPOIL THE BROTH"

Yesterday I was invited to a launch party at Bann Korean Restaurant (350 West 50th Street) filled with a few high-ranking dignitaries such as Kim Young-Mok (South Korean General Consulate) and journalists including Korean broadcasters, the *Korean Daily Press*, and a few other food bloggers (Rachel from *The Daily Meal*, and Regina from Gastropoda). The star of the event was Korean-born celebrity Kelly Choi of Bravo's Top Chef Masters, who spent a few minutes introducing the food. Our lunch that day was both a celebration of the Korean cuisine and the Lunar New Year.

Figures 16.2 and 16.3. K-pop meets K-food: *Hansik* ambassadors Super Junior promoting Korean food.

Like other Asian cultures, Korea celebrates the Lunar New Year with [its] own auspicious dishes, including the *Tteokguk* or *Dduk Gook*.[65]

The excerpt above comes from Simon Dang's Plate of the Day food blog and describes the Korean New Year's lunch held in New York on February 1, 2011. It is just one of the many activities that the Korean Food Foundation has carried out within the framework of the Global *Hansik* Campaign. Particular efforts seem to have been made toward promoting Korean Food in New York and Los Angeles, cities that already have a well-established network of Korean restaurants.[66] The task appears far more difficult in locations where Korean food is relatively unknown and infrastructure and manpower are insufficient. This complication holds particularly true for Europe. Even London, which is considered one of the most culinary diverse cities in

Europe, has just ten Korean restaurants. "Even though some of them have had good reviews, the overall size is still so small," argues British food journalist Joe Warwick. "Most of the places in London are still catering to Korean tourists and residents only."[67]

According to Sŏng Sŭng-wŏn, local coordinator of the Global *Hansik* Education (*hansik segyehwa kyoyuk*) event organized in Paris in December 2010, believes the old saying "too many cooks spoil the broth."[68] This event was supervised by the Ministry of Agriculture and the Korea Agro-Fisheries Trade Corporation and was managed by the Dongwon Leaders Academy and the Korean Cultural Association in France (Centre Culture Coréen), in cooperation with the Korean Food Culture Association of France and Asiana Airlines. "A policy of manpower with a lack of experience, the conservative people of the restaurant business world, and a continuous 2 percent deficit cannot produce synergy effects," Sŏng argues. "I have had many conversations with involved persons, but their opinions do not differ much. The absence of understanding and interest among the government departments involved in the policy means that the budget is wasted on organizing 'parties' without actual results. There is also no consistency in the instructions of the authorities, and things often come to a standstill due to the fact that the people in charge are continuously shifting from one post to another. . . . In order to succeed, the *hansik segyehwa* policy needs long-term measures, and for this advanced manpower is necessary." One example of how these problems are manifested is that promotional material in English is used for Global *Hansik* activities in Paris, when the French are widely known to be reluctant speakers of English.

It seems highly plausible that a strategy of investment in global food chains serving Korean-style food will be more successful if it is undertaken independently from other activities coordinated through conventional channels such as embassies, tourist organizations, and wholesalers. An example worth noting is the *bibimpap*-specialized restaurant chain Bibigo, managed by Foodville, a leading South Korean food-service company. The first Bibigo outlet was opened in May 2010 in Seoul, and in the autumn of 2010 Foodville officials projected the opening of 15 Bibigo restaurants in the United States, China, Japan, and Southeast Asia by 2011; 38 by 2012; 139 by 2013; and 500 by 2014. By the year 2015, one thousand outlets were scheduled to be up and running around the world.[69] However, this ambitious plan seems to have been slightly delayed. At the time of writing (June 2013), only thirteen Bibigo restaurants were in operation: five in Korea, four in China, two in Japan, three in Singapore, one in Indonesia, and three in the United States.[70]

Bibigo's concept, with its emphasis on health and freshness as well as the restaurant's interior design, resembles the successful U.K.-based noodle-bar chain Wagamama. A creation of Alan Yau, the son of Cantonese immigrants who ran a Chinese takeout restaurant in Norfolk, England, the first Wagamama opened for business in April 1992; the chain now has several dozen outlets throughout Europe, the Middle East, Australia, New Zealand, and the United States. Wagamama features a sleek and minimalist design with an emphasis on branding, offering a style that was quite innovative in the early 1990s. This emphasis on design was widely imitated in the strategies of the posh *kaitenzushi* bars that emerged in London a few years after the opening of the first noodle canteen. The concept has been prized as a role model for the fast-food sector and remains one of the most successful and fashionable restaurant chains in Europe.[71]

The Global *Hansik* Campaign, with strong involvement from the South Korean government, emanates the image of efficiency and control. In reality, however, modernizing Korean cuisine and transforming it into a best-selling global product by 2017 is a complex undertaking. It involves a wide range of players—from business executives and producers' cooperatives to cooks and food writers—who all approach the project from different perspectives and are guided by different motives. Unpicking the relationship between the different parties involved is beyond the scope of this chapter, but it is important to note that for all of them global recognition of Korean cuisine has its benefits. For restaurateurs and cooking instructors who ally themselves with the Global *Hansik* project, the potential for economic gain, along with the fulfillment of professional ambition, is an important motivation. The strong support of organizations such as the Korea Tourism Organization, the Korea Agro-Fisheries Trade Corporation, and agricultural and fisheries cooperatives in the promotional activities of the campaign is directly linked with their business performance. Propagating Korean food abroad boils down to generating profit for Korean produce.

NOTES

1. For media coverage of the "Korean Cuisine to the World Campaign," see Kim Hyun-cheol, "Campaign Starts to Globalize Korean Food," *Korea Times*, October 16, 2008, http://www.koreatimes.co.kr/www/news/biz/2009/10/123_32807.html (accessed March 28, 2011); Do Je-hae, "Korean Food Campaign Launched in Three Austra-lian Cities," *Korea Times*, March 25, 2010, http://www.koreatimes.co.kr/www/news/art/2010/03/146_63013.html (accessed March 28, 2011); Julia Moskin, "Culinary Diplomacy with a Side of Kimchi," *New York Times*, September 22, 2009, http://www.nytimes.com/2009/09/23/dining/23kore.html (accessed March 28, 2011).

2. Chang Tae-pyong, "Korea (14): Korean Food, Infinite Possibilities," *Korea Times*, Feb-

ruary 3, 2009, http://www.koreatimes.co.kr/www/news/include/print.asp?newsIdx =40584 (accessed April 15, 2011).

3. Kim Hyun-cheol, "Hansik Globalization Body Planned," *Korea Times*, October 29, 2009, http://www.koreatimes.co.kr/www/news/include/print.asp?newsIdx=54497 (accessed April 15, 2011).

4. "Promoting Kimchi, Other Korean Food in Costa Rica," *Korea Joongang Daily*, October 13, 2009, http://joongangdaily.joins.com/article/view.asp?aid=2911188 (accessed March 20, 2011); "Win a Trip to Korea and Feast Like a King," *E-Global Travel Media Australia/New Zealand*, http://www.eglobaltravelnews.com.au/tourist-office /win-a-trip-to-korea-and-feast-like-a-king.html (accessed February 20, 2011). For detailed plans concerning the globalization of Korean food see *Han'guk oesik yon'gam* (Seoul: Han'guk oesik chŏngbo, 2009), 458–600.

5. Detailed information about the foundation is available on its Korean-language website at http://www.hansik.org (accessed May 21, 2012). See also "Ministry Launches Specialized Korean Cuisine Foundation," *Korea Herald*, March 29, 2010, http://www.koreaherald.com/business/Detail.jsp?newsMLId=20100317000062 (accessed March 28, 2011); and Kim Hyun-cheol, "Foundation to Promote Food Overseas," *Korea Times*, March 17, 2010, http://www.koreatimes.co.kr/www/news /biz/2010/10/123_62558.html (accessed April 12, 2011).

6. Katarzyna J. Cwiertka, "From Ethnic to Hip: Circuits of Japanese Cuisine in Europe," *Food and Foodways* 13, no. 4 (2005): 241–72.

7. http://www.foodinkorea.org (accessed July 13, 2010). The website is no longer available.

8. "Travel Highlights: Top 10 Korean Dishes and Restaurants," *Korea Be Inspired*, http:// english.visitkorea.or.kr/enu//_3_6.jsp?cid=548164 (accessed March 28, 2011).

9. Sidney W. Mintz, "Eating Communities: The Mixed Appeals of Sodality," in *Eating Culture: The Poetics and Politics of Food Today*, ed. T. Döring, M. Heide, and S. Mühleisen (Heidelberg: Universitätsverlag, 2003), 19–34.

10. Ji-Yeon Yuh, *Beyond the Shadow of Camptown: Korean Military Brides in America* (New York: New York University Press, 2002), 143–51.

11. Anne Murcott, "Food As an Expression of Identity," in *The Future of the Nation State: Essays on Cultural Pluralism and Political Integration*, ed. S. Gustavsson and L. Lewin (London: Routledge, 1996), 21.

12. Ian Cook and Philip Crang, "The World on a Plate: Culinary Culture, Displacement and Geographical Knowledge," *Journal of Material Culture* 1, no. 2 (1996): 140.

13. Raymond Grew, "Food and Global History," in *Food in Global History*, ed. R. Grew (Boulder, Colo.: Westview, 1999), 1–2.

14. Priscilla Parkhurst Ferguson, "Culinary Nationalism," *Gastronomica* 10, no. 1 (2010): 102–9.

15. Okpyo Moon, "Food and Food Consumption as Cultural Practices: Lifestyle Changes in Contemporary Korea?" *Korea Journal* 50, no. 1 (2010): 7.

16. Sea-Ling Cheng, "Back to the Future: Herbal Tea Shops in Hong Kong," in *Hong Kong: The Anthropology of a Chinese Metropolis*, ed. G. Evans and M. Tam (Honolulu: University of Hawai'i Press, 1997), 51–73; Young-Kyun Yang, "*Jajangmyeon* and *Jung-*

gukjip: The Changing Position and Meaning of Chinese Food and Chinese Restaurants in Korean Society," *Korea Journal* 45, no. 2 (2005): 60–88.

17. Grew, "Food and Global History," 11.

18. Laura C. Nelson, *Measured Excess: Status, Gender, and Consumer Nationalism in South Korea* (New York: Columbia University Press, 2000), 70.

19. *Han'guk oesik yon'gam* (Seoul: Han'guk oesik chŏngbo, 2009), 387.

20. Yang, "*Jajangmyeon* and *Junggukjip*," 60–88.

21. Shin Kyŏk-ho (b. 1922) was also known by his Japanese name, Shigemitsu Takeo.

22. Katarzyna J. Cwiertka, *Cuisine, Colonialism, and Cold War: Food in Twentieth-Century Korea* (London: Reaktion, 2012).

23. Sangmee Bak, "McDonald's in Seoul: Food Choices, Identity, and Nationalism," in *Golden Arches East: McDonald's in East Asia*, ed. James L. Watson (Stanford, Calif.: Stanford University Press, 1997), 150, 154.

24. Nelson, *Measured Excess*, 126–30.

25. Laura C. Nelson, "South Korean Consumer Nationalism: Women, Children, Credit, and Other Perils," in *The Ambivalent Consumer: Questioning Consumption in East Asia and the West*, ed. S. Garon and P. L. MacIachlan (Ithaca, NY: Cornell University Press, 2006), 192.

26. Nelson, "South Korean Consumer Nationalism," 205.

27. Sangmee Bak, "Negotiating National and Transnational Identities through Consumption Choices: Hamburgers, Espresso, and Mobile Technologies among Koreans," *Review of Korean Studies* 7, no. 2 (2004): 37–42; Sagmee Bak, "Exoticizing the Familiar, Domesticating the Foreign: Ethnic Food Restaurants in Korea," *Korea Journal* 50, no. 1 (2010): 110–32.

28. *Han'guk oesik yon'gam*, 314.

29. Nelson, *Measured Excess*, 25.

30. For details see the Korea Foundation website: http://www.kf.or.kr (accessed February 2, 2011). Back issues of *Koreana* can be viewed at the Koreana website, www.koreana.or.kr (accessed February 2, 2011).

31. Kim Yea-rim, "Globalization of Korean Food for Good Health of People Across the World," *Korea Times*, December 21, 2010, http://www.koreaittimes.com/story/12323/globalization-korean-food-good-health-people-across-world (accessed August 26, 2011).

32. Katarzyna J. Cwiertka, *Modern Japanese Cuisine: Food, Power and National Identity* (London: Reaktion Books, 2006), 154.

33. Bak, "Negotiating National and Transnational Identities," 35–36.; Robert W. Pemberton, "Wild-Gathered Foods as Countercurrents to Dietary Globalisation in South Korea," in *Asian Food: The Global and the Local*, ed. K. J. Cwiertka with B. C. A. Walraven (Honolulu: University of Hawai'i Press, 2002), 79–80.

34. Helen-Louise Brown, "Conceived in the Past and Raised in Modernity: A Study of the Korean Barbecue Restaurant" (M.A. thesis, University of Adelaide, 2010), 56.

35. Mi Park, "Free Trade Agreements: The Politics of Nationalism in the Anti-Neoliberal Globalization Movement in South Korea," *Globalizations* 6, no. 4 (2009): 457.

36. Renee B. Kim, "Meeting Consumer Concerns for Food Safety in South Korea: The

Importance of Food Safety and Ethics in a Globalizing Market," *Journal of Agricultural and Environmental Ethics* 22, no. 2 (2009): 141–52.

37. Kim, "Globalization of Korean Food."

38. Rumi Sakamoto and Matthew Allen, "There's Something Fishy About That Sushi: How Japan Interprets the Global Sushi Boom," *Japan Forum* 23, no. 1 (2011): 109.

39. Joseph S. Nye, Jr., "Soft Power," *Foreign Policy* 80 (Fall 1990): 153–71.

40. James Farrer, "Eating the West and Beating the Rest: Culinary Occidentalism and Urban Soft Power in Asia's Global Food Cities," in *Globalization, Food and Social Identities in the Asia Pacific Region*, ed. James Farrer (Tokyo: Sophia University Institute of Comparative Culture, 2011). Available as electronic document at http://icc .fla.sophia.ac.jp/global%20food%20papers/pdf/2_3_.pdf (accessed April 12, 2011).

41. E. V. Murray, "Thailand—The Kitchen of the World: Origin and Growth of the Thai Food Industry and Lessons for India," *Cab Calling* (June–April 2007): 21–22; Sunanta Sirijit, "The Globalization of Thai Cuisine," (paper presented at the Canadian Council for Southeast Asian Studies Conference, York University, Toronto, October 14–16, 2005). Available as electronic document at http://www.yorku.ca/ycar /Publications/_Papers_2005/Sunanta.pdf (accessed September 1, 2011), 10–11.

42. Sakamoto and Allen, "There's Something Fishy About That Sushi," 110.

43. "Top 5 Hansik News in 2009," *Korea Times*, December 30, 2009, http://www.korea times.co.kr/www/news/include/print.asp?newsIdx=58236 (accessed July 17, 2010).

44. Cwiertka, *Modern Japanese Cuisine*, 153.

45. Kyung-Koo Han, "The 'Kimchi Wars' in Globalizing East Asia: Consuming Class, Gender, Health, and National Identity," in *Consuming Korean Tradition in Early and Late Modernity: Commodification, Tourism and Performance.* ed. L. Kendall (Honolulu: University of Hawai'i Press, 2010), 164.

46. Cwiertka, *Cuisine, Colonialism, and Cold War.*

47. Han, "The 'Kimchi Wars,'" 140.

48. "Case Studies: Japan Korea Kimchi Dispute," American University, http://www1 .american.edu/ted/kimchi.htm (accessed April 22, 2011).

49. Han, "The 'Kimchi Wars,'" 143.

50. Theodore Jun Yoo, "Shaken or Stirred? Taking Something Plebian to Wash Down All That 'Hansik': Recreating Makgŏlli for the Twenty-first Century," (paper presented at the annual meeting of the Association for Asian Studies, Honolulu, Hawaii, March 31, 2011).

51. Yoo, "Shaken or Stirred?"

52. "State Support for Traditional Korean Liquor," *Korea Joongang Daily*, August 27, 2009, http://joongangdaily.joins.com/article/view.asp?aid=2909296 (accessed May 21, 2012), after Yoo, "Shaken or Stirred?"

53. "What Is the 'Makgeolli Transformer' Exhibition, and Why Is *Makgeolli* Becoming So Popular?" Koreabrand.net, http://www.koreabrand.net/en/know/know_view.do ?_=0012&=321 (accessed May 21, 2012), after Yoo, "Shaken or Stirred?"

54. "Artisanal Makgeolli Movement Underway," *Korea Herald*, March 30, 2010, http:// www.koreaherald.com/national/Detail.jsp?newsMLId=20090930000080 (accessed May 21, 2012), after Yoo, "Shaken or Stirred?"

55. For more information about the activities of the ministry see the official website, http://www.mcst.go.kr/english/index.jsp (accessed April 12, 2011).

56. Dong-cheol Seo, "Korean Cuisine Makes Waves," *Korea: People and Culture* 6, no. 3 (2010): 5.

57. Yu-Shan Lin and Jun-Ying Huang, "Analyzing the Use of Miniseries for Korea Tourism Marketing," *Journal of Travel & Tourism Marketing* 24, no. 2 (2008): 222–27. Available as electronic document at http://dx.doi.org/10.1080/10548400802092858 (accessed May 18, 2011).

58. For details see the park's website, http://www.imbc.com/entertain/mbcticket /mbcplay/2004/daejanggumtheme_eng/ (accessed September 2, 2011).

59. Lin and Huang, "Analyzing the Use of Miniseries," 226.

60. Maria Osetrova, "Our Food Is Our Treasure: Representation of National Food Tradition in Contemporary Korean Popular Culture (Focusing on *Sikkaek* Series)" (paper presented at the Twenty-fifth Biennial Conference of the Association of Korean Studies in Europe, Moscow, June 17–20, 2011), 2.

61. "Korean Food, Bibimbap—Starring Rain / Bi, Korean Pop Star," Youtube, http:// www.youtube.com/watch?v=CBTK2JRrKCs (accessed 20 May 20, 2011).

62. "Korean Dish, Galbi Video—Starring Rain, Korean Pop Star," Youtube, http://www .youtube.com/watch?v=CQDzfgoXcao (accessed May 20, 2011).

63. See, for example, the playlist "Super Junior Promotes *Hansik*," Youtube, http:// www.youtube.com/watch?v=fsqC31GKagQ&feature=results_main&playnext=1& list=PL72A48DA3AE4E5E04 (accessed Sept 2, 2011).

64. "Korean Food, Hansik—The Taste of Korea," Youtube, http://www.youtube.com /watch?v=FywEsje9zAY (accessed May 20, 2011).

65. "Korean Food Foundation Han Sik with Kelly Choi (Top Chef Masters) Spreads the Love of Korean Food with Korean New Year—New York 2011," Plate of the Day Food Blog, http://www.plateoftheday.com/?p=1496 (accessed March 16, 2012).

66. The Korean Food Foundation has set up a separate website, hansikamerica.org (accessed May 21, 2012).

67. Kim Hyun-cheol, "Hansik Does Not Need to Stick to Authenticity," *Korea Times*, October 30, 2009, http://www.koreatimes.co.kr/www/news/art/2011/02/146_54574 .html (accessed April 12, 2011).

68. Personal communication with Sŏng Sŭng-wŏn (March 2011). A former French major, Sŏng Sŭng-wŏn went to Paris in spring 2006 to continue his education in Translation Studies. Sŏng worked part-time in a Korean restaurant in Paris and learned to cook professionally from his aunt, who managed a restaurant in Japan.

69. Cathy Rose A. Garcia, "CJ to Open Global 'Hansik' Franchise," *Korea Times*, October 5, 2010, http://www.koreatimes.co.kr/www/news/include/print.asp?newsIdx=65632 (accessed April 12, 2011).

70. See also the company's website, www.bibigo.com (accessed May 21, 2012).

71. Cwiertka, *Modern Japanese Cuisine*, 197–98.

Seung Woo Back's *Blow Up* (2005–2007)

Touristic Fantasy, Photographic Desire, and Catastrophic North Korea

When an explosive number of South Korean citizens began traveling to North Korea in the late 1990s, these unprecedented physical encounters between the two Koreas were represented through the medium of photography, resulting in a plethora of photographs of North Korea distributed as part of travel journals, photographic albums, and online blogs. Behind this burgeoning visual production—for the first time since the national border along the 38th parallel had hardened sixty some years ago—lay the political context of the Sunshine Policy (*haetpyŏt chŏngch'aek*), the inter-Korean reconciliation policy promoted by the South between 1998 and 2007.[1] Despite the asymmetrical nature of this exchange—the North, unlike the South, refused to send troops of tourists, government officials, and various social actors across the border—the rise of photography as a popular medium of representation offers the possibility of facilitating a new inter-Korean narrative forged from the bottom by the South Korean masses. Breaking away from the ideology-ridden, military-focused inter-Korean relationship that the two governments have dictated as appropriate and thus legitimate, the South Korean people's production of North Korean images marked a paradigm shift in the larger economy of visual images that can travel beyond North Korea's borders.

By 2008, the advent of a conservative government in the South and the reemergence of hostile inter-Korean dynamics put a stop to this brief decade of unique cultural exchange, barring once again Southern citizens from crossing the border. Despite—or perhaps because of—the temporariness of such cultural production, its historical significance in South Korean visual and popular culture is tantamount. South Korean citizens, although provisionally, took on the role of producer, initiator, and visionary in re-shaping the North-South relationship. The travel account and photographs from Seoul-based photographer Seung Woo Back's 2001 visit to Pyongyang illuminates the dynamics of this discontinued phenomenon, once imbued with incommensurable potentiality. By reconstructing the South Korean citizen's desire to cross the Demilitarized Zone (DMZ) before his journey, his confrontation with North Korean censorship in the Northern capital, and his disappointment—and contempt—arising from the thwarted photo-graphic desire, this chapter expands on the photo-taking South Korean sub-ject's negotiation of the North-South relationship. The first section discusses South Koreans' border-crossing and memory production in relation to the oft-problematic notions of touristic desire and truth claims in photography, as they are exemplified in Back's photography series *Blow Up* (2005–2007) (see plate 7). In the second section, Back's confrontation with North Korean censorship drives my analysis about the conflict over these individual photo-graphic productions' proper authorship. As I develop in the third section, Back's photography series not only serves as an example of South Korean citizens' touristic fantasy and photographic desire but also performs a criti-cal play on these very elements. A careful visual analysis of *Blow Up* reveals that the series is a photographic (re-)presentation imbued with the societal desire to see North Korea from outside *and* the accompanying ethical com-mitment to the North Koreans. *Blow Up* therefore signals a rise of new kind of representational tactics with which to reexamine the ideological division and the looming catastrophe that still prevail in the Korean peninsula.

THE JOURNEY IN: NORTH KOREA AS A TOURISTIC AND PHOTOGRAPHIC DESTINATION

The burgeoning photographic representation of North Korea by South Korean citizens can be considered democratic. This phenomenon gives di-versity to and expands the limited spectrum of photographs about North Korea, which had mostly been controlled by the few in power and is now driven by millions of ordinary citizens. But many of the terms with which such representation is discussed and understood are dangerously squared with tourism and perhaps its neoimperialist implications. By exploring the intertwined history of photography and tourism on the post–Cold War Korean peninsula, I seek to shed a critical light on the short-lived popular cultural phenomenon of "touring North Korea." Probing the nature of this cultural phenomenon requires, first and foremost, understanding the onto-logical dependency of photography (as a medium of representation) at the advent of tourism (as a cultural entertainment) in the history of photography. I then consider South Koreans' photographic desire of the North Korea as neocolonial, proposing that Seung Woo Back's border-crossing narrative serves as a case in point.

The genesis of photography as an indexical, reproducible medium of representation shares its roots with tourism; the democratization of travel propelled the invention of the medium. Led by the development of railroads in late eighteenth-century Europe, an unprecedented number of non-elite tourists who desired to arrest the fleeting moments and seize exotic landscapes sought a proper medium with which to express such a desire. It is therefore the *collective desire* and *ethos* rather than the genius of a single individual that gave birth to the photochemical technique—one that coheres images of scenes and people onto a light-sensitive surface such as copper plate, paper, or glass.[2] As revealed by photography historians, multiple individuals invented various forms of photography in separate locales in France and England around 1830, thus confirming the periodic desire for such a medium.[3] Subsequently the possibility of commercial gains, coupled with the sociocultural demands for such a visual form, facilitated a rapid increase in the production and reproduction of photographs. For instance, the nineteenth-century European imperialist desire to capture the unfamiliar landscape and people of North Africa and the Middle East—the then newly developed tourist destinations—was effectively manifested in the creation of *cartes postales*.[4] These mass-produced photographic postcards of tourist sites were bought on site and then were sent to those back in the home country. Where the *sight* (with the dictatorship of the ocular) collapses onto the *site*, photography was born, giving form to the burning desire for the new kind of production of memory, circulation of images, and formation of (inter-)subjectivity.[5]

On the Korean peninsula in the late 1990s, such a collapsing of the sight on to the site took place, as the Northern territory became available for visits en masse for the first time since the end of the Korean War. The influx of South Korean journalists, businessmen, and tourists who participated in the journey was remarkable. For these South Koreans, the significance placed on the historic opening of North Korea corresponds to the desire to capture the exotic life of the "other" Koreans in film negatives. To the Diamond Head tourist district alone, close to two million tourists paid a visit between 1998 and 2007, each of whom produced personal images of North Korea or of themselves posing for the camera in front of majestic mountain gorges.[6] Some also willingly shared their tourist memory with others upon their return, as seen in such photographs that are now readily available on numerous blogs.[7] In addition, South Korean government and corporations' investment in the infrastructure of the North's Kaesong Special Economic Zone enabled repeated border-crossings for those involved in the ambitious economic revitalization project. Business trips to Kaesong were never purely about business; more often, they included sightseeing and photo-taking.[8]

The accessibility to the territory by the masses has therefore resulted in the rise of photography as a medium of representation, communication, and creativity that South Koreans came to possess when facing North Korea. Even though extensive scholarly and media attention has been paid to South Korean filmic representation of North Korea—perhaps owing to the block-buster success of such films as the *Joint Security Area* (2000), *TaeGukGi: Brotherhood of War* (2004), and *Welcome to Dongmakgol* (2005), all made during the Sunshine Policy era—photography was rarely given significance as a popular medium with which to express, articulate, and reimagine the South's relationship with the North.[9] Addressing the problem of this omission, I seek to rearticulate photography as a crucial medium that reflects and propels the formation of new inter-Korean subjectivity in the Sunshine Policy era. Serving as a productive departure point is Seung Woo Back's nar-rativization of his photographic desire prior to his Pyongyang trip, which points to the larger cultural phenomenon, namely, the problematic association of North Korea as a touristic destination or an object to be photographed.

It is important to note that Back was not automatically given the chance to visit Pyongyang; he had to work for it, because even during the Sunshine Policy era a South Korean could not casually enter the Northern capital.[10] A photographer by training, Back discovered in 2001 that a Seoul-based fashion house was planning a show in Pyongyang—and this fashion show required a border-crossing of not only clothes and models but also of a fashion photographer.[11] Back sought out the fashion designer—who was at first unwilling to hire Back, an artist essentially unrecognized as a top fashion photographer—by delivering "small presents," like confectioneries and rice cakes, to the fashion house for three consecutive weeks, the very duration of the trip the designer finally granted to Back. The extreme measures that Back took to cross the border is demonstrative of his desire to seize the rare opportunity to produce creative, unique imprints of the particular locale, the world's last remaining terra incognita. The primary motivation for him to enter North Korea, he revealed, was not to photograph a fashion show but to roam the streets of Pyongyang and arrest the moments of North Korean life, as if he were an invisible flaneur.[12]

This photographic desire for North Korea, which Back incidentally shared

with many other South Korean visitors, is deeply rooted in a particular historical moment of the Sunshine Policy era. When compared with the Cold
War era's outright anti-Communism, the South Korean perception of those
living on the other side of the DMZ in the post–Berlin Wall era entered into a
new phase, where the strong will to demonize and eradicate the "commies"
gave way to the liberal notion of converting and reforming North Korea to
fit in the postmodern world of global capitalism. Doubtlessly this liberal
desire is already reflected in the Sunshine Policy, wherein the economically
superior South Korea sought to exercise "soft power" (that is, the fashion
show) as much as a hardline diplomatic push on the insular, obsolete regime
of little economic power. It is therefore not with a gun (to shoot the enemy)
but with a camera (to shoot the fashion show) that Back was able to obtain
the South Korean government's permission to cross the DMZ. When the
South Korean self, endowed with the power to "shoot," faces the camera-
less North Korean photographed on the streets, the subject/object relationship of photography laid onto the otherized landscape and people ominously
loomed large.[13]

What makes Back's street photography of North Korea decidedly "touristic" can be explained by another side of Back's photographic desire, namely,
a yearning for original, creative photographs that look different from all
other photographic images of Pyongyang to which he had previously been
exposed. On the subject of tourist photography, Carol Crawshaw and John
Urry note the net of inevitable, external influences that affect image-making
at the site. The tourists' photographic memories about a given site are constructed prior to their visit: ". . . people's memories of tourist sites are often
invoked because of particular visual images which they have seen in advance or seen while they are visiting. [M]any of the images that we visually
consume when we are travelling are, in effect, the memories of others."[14] As
Crawshaw and Urry would conjecture, Back's preoccupation with the originality of his photographs is the very attempt to escape from the economy of
memory production. By producing unique photographs of Pyongyang, Back
desired to avoid, moreover critique, the "memories of others." This rhetorical move away from typical tourist photographs that mimic the archetypal
shots of the given sites, however, is *itself* typical of tourist experience, falling
into what Jonathan Culler calls the "semiotic articulation of tourism." For
Culler, all tourists—even the most snobbish and sophisticated ones—enter
into the semiotic exercise of reading tourist markers, because they are constantly compelled to locate the signifiers of the authentic and the inauthentic.[15] Participating in the semiotic interpretation of the North Korean sites,
Back's photographs indeed invoke the tourist obsession and dilemma sur-

rounding the binary of authenticity and inauthenticity, and their desire to locate what they perceive as genuine, candid everyday life. The striking absence of spectacular icons such as the Juche Tower and the Mansudae Monument in *Blow Up* might explain this particular touristic desire to witness the ordinary, the real, and thus the exotic everyday life of Pyongyang residents.[16]

THE JOURNEY OUT: THE STRUGGLE OVER CENSOR, AUTHORITY, AND AUTHORSHIP

Where the epistemologies of tourism and the photographic desire are mutually implicated, the outsiders' gaze laid onto the land and people of North Korea thrives as part of cultural politics during the Sunshine Policy era. Yet all images produced in North Korea are also afflicted with another powerful manifestation of ideology—the North Korean government's imposition of censorship. Exemplified in Back's artistic production, censorship provokes a site of contestation over authorship and authority, wherein the photographic representations of North Korea are unambiguously written in the language of prohibition and control. On the one hand, *Blow Up* embodies a South Korean citizen's fight against such obstacle to freedom of expression. On the other hand, it also points to an exit out of the binary of individual freedom and authoritarian censorship.

The censorship industry in the North, both for its own people and visitors, is well accounted throughout North Korean history and in particular since the year 1967, when Kim Jong-il consolidated the propaganda department under his leadership.[17] Especially for temporary visitors from the South, the North Korean authority's suspicion (of the Southerners as posing a threat to the regime) provides an excuse for the arduous imposition of censorship.[18] Against such restriction of freedom to speak and travel, the visitors respond with an intense eagerness to defy authority. At stake here is the authorship of photographic images, which no longer belongs solely to South Korean visitors-cum-photographers but is controlled by the North Korean authority—therefore further compelling the South Koreans to insert their voice into the frame. As countless accounts narrate North Korean censorship, Back's fight against censors is not unique, serving in this chapter as a vehicle with which to situate such struggle within the larger context of ideological division that dichotomizes the peninsula.

To begin, the artist's testimony is worth quoting at length: "During my visit to North Korea in 2001, I took pictures of Pyongyang, but only within preselected districts. At the time of my visit, I was no different from other tourists. The Communist regime imposed heavy guard and severe control on my visit. All my [exposed] 35mm film had to be thoroughly examined by North Korean officials for security reasons [before my return to South Korea]."[19] The physical presence of a North Korean "minder," combined with the authority's exercise of censorship of Back's negatives, renders all the photographic records of North Korea resembling one another by taking a certain form: a form that keeps the facade of the North Korean regime, whether they are taken by foreign visitors or North Koreans themselves. Because of the double-layered censorship mechanism in practice—first at the moment of taking photographs and second at the inspection process—the highly fabricated nature of his photographs was revealed to the photographer.[20] Perhaps the powerful, immediate presence of the North Korean minders in Pyongyang gave him the conviction that the remaining negatives all together coalesced too well with the Northern regime's narrative about itself. In the end, what Back naively believed to be a subject-forming experience of his picture-taking did not occur, as his individual subjectivity depended, perhaps too profoundly, on the rules of the North Korean authority that have always already been a precondition for his entry.

If Back's photographic activity had stopped at retrieving what is left of his 35 mm film strips, his photographs would have made cliché examples of an individual's fight for artistic freedom in a censorship-ridden Communist regime, while once again highlighting the omnipresence of the meta-border, the DMZ, in every descriptive gesture that South Koreans attempt to make about North Korea. Indeed, the utterly disappointed and discouraged Back left the returned negatives buried in his personal archive for four years. It is only in 2005 that he revisited, for the first time, these archived materials anew. This time, however, he felt lucky to have found a way to counter censorship and photographic memory and reinsert his subjective interpretation into the photographs. With his postproduction process, Back's journey continues as a journey out of the North into the South Korean search for individual freedom against the authoritarian regime.

While reexamining his negatives, Back located intriguing details that he had previously missed. One photograph, for instance, presents two children, a boy and a girl, playing a keyboard to demonstrate their skills in front of the visitors (see fig. 17.1). What seems a perfect theater of good-looking, well-dressed children skilled in a musical instrument shares a striking resemblance with the usual propagandistic reproductions of posters and paintings that visualize one of the phrases that tourists repeatedly hear in North Korea, "We are happy."[21] In this quintessential propagandistic scene, the brand label in white written on the black keyboard—YAMAHA—"pierced" Back.[22] As Yamaha is a Japanese brand, the North Korean inspectors working for a staunchly anti-Japanese regime should have caught this error, thought

Figure 17.1. Seung Woo Back, *BL-05* as part of photography series *Blow Up* (2005–7)
20 x 24 inch. Digital Print. Photo courtesy of the artist.

the artist. It is a flaw in the theater of a regime that profusely professes its self-sufficiency through the rhetoric of Juche ideology (or the ideology of self-reliance). Considering the regime's strict prohibition of the use of the English language or the Roman alphabet, in conjunction with the fact that in "Yamaha" a Japanese brand name has been transliterated to the Roman alphabet, adds to a sense of irony. So Back decided to repossess this detail from a corner of his original negative, by isolating, cropping, and enlarging it to fit in a 20- by-24-inch large frame.

Back also tells of his experience with a mysterious jogging woman in the photograph on the bottom row, second from the left in the installation of *Blow Up* (see plate 7; fig. 17.2). This shot captures two women on opposite sides of the street. The woman on the other side is running toward the right in the picture, while in the foreground a policewoman stands, with her back toward the viewer, looking also to the right. A looming presence of a pedestrian overpass adds urban character to an otherwise empty street. In front of his hotel, Back witnessed this jogging woman in *chosŏnot* (a variation of

Figure 17.2. Seung Woo Back, *BL-11* as part of photography series *Blow Up* (2005–7)
20 x 24 inch. Digital Print. Photo courtesy of the artist.

Korean traditional costume adopted for everyday, contemporary use in the North) passing by his hotel every morning at eight o'clock, as if a character out of *The Truman Show*, the 1998 Hollywood movie about life that is staged, simultaneously live, on air, and in real time.[23] The fact that *chosŏnot* is not usually considered suitable as an exercise outfit for this South Korean witness, coupled with the sense of mystery about such immaculate regularity in the anonymous woman's jogging schedule, amplifies suspicion in Back's mind: that the woman might have been hired by the regime to feign the look of leisurely morning exercise to the audience of foreign tourists who stay at the Koryo Hotel, one of the few lodging choices available to foreigners in Pyongyang.

Back's rereading of his own photographs, not as a photographer but as a viewer, grants him the possibility of refusing the particular ways in which South Korean individuals have to remember North Korea and its people. This refusal, revealing the existence of a room for "play" within the seemingly impenetrable situation of the "reality of division"—or *pundan hyŏnsil* in Korean—opens up a space of imagination where one can disobey and re-interpret the ideology of division. But can this "play," and refusal, be on its own automatically and effectively read as the South Korean citizen's praise-worthy political critique of the Northern regime? Would not this play only reinforce our own perception of freedom, which has its roots in the bour-geois Enlightenment philosophy of Western Europe, applied to the territory that in many ways resists the very notion of neoliberal-capitalist notions of freedom? North Korean censorship does not signify the regime's ban of all photography—both photography and film are the most significant media of propaganda—but the regime's own rules applied to photographic repre-sentation, which scrupulously has to follow the visual interpretation of the Juche ideology.[24] Symptomatic of the clash between different norms of rep-resentation, the censorship in North Korea reveals the ideological conflict embedded at the site of photographic production. If the photographic rep-resentation is inevitably written in the language of division that haunts the peninsula even today, is it then ever enough simply to criticize the difficulty of producing censorship-free photographs in North Korea?

Certainly the unapologetic emphasis on the individual subject and on per-sonal freedom gives rise to the potential of dangerously affirming individual liberalism at the expense of a self-reflexive perception of the self or a forma-tion of collective. By praising Back's assertion of the self who triumphantly discovers and photographically documents the oversights of the regime, one makes the mistake of simply accepting the terms with which South Koreans are compelled to vilify the Northern "others" and elevate the position of the self. The degree to which this discovery is significant to *Blow Up*—this series is essentially made around the unintended details discovered a posteriori the 2001 trip—problematically rhymes with the level of excitement with which South Korean bloggers flaunt the few photographs that they were able to take when the North Korean guards are looking away. These blog narra-tives are essentially written around the cherished moments of individual triumph. The South Korean tourist's search for authentic scenes of North Korean life perilously merges with the detectivelike quest for the "truthful" images, or the moments of "truth" about the regime; these photographs in turn enable the tourists-cum-detectives to criminalize the despotic regime and to make heroes out of individuals. North Korea stands out as a unique site of photographic quest for truth-searching from the daily lives of others, especially in the era of emerging visual and popular culture in photographic terms. Social networking and camera cell phones allow the largest number of individuals in history to take their own photographs and instantly make them available for anyone with Internet access to see. It is, however, simply unthinkable, because of the regime's strict surveillance of its people, that North Korean civilians would capture honest portraits of daily life and self-broadcast them on the web. Bearing in mind the highly fraught nature of photography's truth-searching operation and the aberrant geopolitical status of North Korea that perpetuates it, *Blow Up* can be seen as Back's play on *our* fantasy of asserting the liberal (or neoliberal) self by profiting from the rare chance to photograph "truthful" North Korea. Here, *we* are those who live outside North Korea (including South Koreans) and who endlessly desire to represent the unrepresentable others.

The remarkably complex visuality with which *Blow Up* portrays North Korea, however, defies a singular reading. The South Korean citizen Back visualizes not only the very problematics of this fantasy game but also an alternative to the paradigm in which the act of praising the photographer as an individual genius or a tragic hero against state authority reinscribes the very coordinates with which the binary framework of freedom/censorship, capitalist democracy/authoritarian despotism currently operates. How then does this alternative arise in *Blow Up*, an alternative sensibility that takes into the ethics of representation?

THE MISSION IMPOSSIBLE? REPRESENTING THE UNREPRESENTABLE

Where the act of representing the other in the language of the self is highly contested and when the task of learning the other's language of representation is equally impossible, what kind of intervention can Back as a South Korean citizen envision on the level of both photographic practice and theoretical framework? Back's postproduction process executed back in South Korea actively imagines a possibility to eradicate the Cold War binary. If this chapter, up to this point, has examined the matrix of South Korean production of North Korean landscape (read via *Blow Up*), this section brings the focus to *Blow Up* so as to expound how this photography series as an installation performs a countervisuality to both South Korean visual culture and North Korean politics of photographic production.

Back's postproduction process (that is, editing and enlarging) was first and foremost motivated by his discovery of certain details that had been captured by the camera. Back's photographic production therefore not only involves his struggle against North Korean authority but also the recognition of the third player in such a production—the camera. The very language with which he was able to produce his photographs—not painting or sculpture, nor travel journal—is mechanical and machinelike. Just as important, it was the camera that planted the details that evaded the eyes of the photographer as equally as the censorship board. The camera is more than an extension of the photographer's eye in *Blow Up*: the camera functions *in place of* the photographer's eye, with the camera's desire to see facilitating the nonphysical, nonverbal encounter that Back had with North Korean subjects on Pyongyang's street.[25] Such use of technology and renunciation of authorship—first to the North Korean authority and then later to the camera—acknowledges the multiplicity of players in photography, troubling the binary between the subject/the object, the photographer/the photographed, freedom/censorship that only conveniently accommodates the opposition of South Korea/North Korea. The recognition of multiple agencies collaborating—albeit unwillingly—in the photographic production powerfully alters the logic of opposition, the very operating model of the "reality of division."

Furthermore, locating the camera at the threshold between the two competing authorships opens up the possibility of reconceptualizing these photographs themselves as productive metaphors of in-between space that transcends the opposition between the two nationalistic states. This liminal space is not simply made up of the physical borders of the DMZ. Rather, it is a space of potentiality in which one can reformulate the concept of border itself as a site of constant negotiation. What kind of visual strategies—in both production and exhibition—are then employed to present the photographs as a metaphor of shifting border zone or, in other words, a counter-visuality to the reality of division?

The process of enlarging photographic details in a darkroom produces half-tone effects, or graining surfaces, thereby rendering photographs blurry or seemingly out of focus. In the absence of clarity—resulting from diluted colors and unclear contours—the high-rise apartment buildings, the National Library, the profile of a guard in uniform, and a grove of deciduous trees seem to dissolve into the air. These abstracted, destabilized, or even dismantled sceneries of Pyongyang dexterously function as a critique of the excitement built around the indexical images of North Korea, by refusing to give away a proper set of information or data about the reality that lay before Back's camera. Not unlike Michelangelo Antonioni's 1966 cult film *Blow-Up*, to which Back pays an explicit homage by way of the title, Back's photographs do not deliver forensic evidence for the photographer-cum-detective character. The double meaning of *blow up*—enlargement and destruction—is fully at work in Back's *Blow Up* as well as in Antonioni's; yet in Back's photographs, what is destroyed (or murdered) is the very search for the foreigners' exercise of photographic truth claims in the hermit kingdom.

A composite of photographic details retrieved from corners, edges, and margins of the original negatives, *Blow Up* also usurps the North Korean logic of photographic representation. *Rodong Daily*, North Korea's state-run newspaper, almost always features a group photograph on its front page, featuring the leader Kim standing in the center of a front row of officials, with dozens of party cadres lined up behind him. Here, the individual faces fade into the background, the photograph acting merely as the evidence of the leader's "generosity" to stand with the people. This type of "class photograph" aptly represents the current state of the regime, which upholds only a particular notion of collectivity—one that subsumes everyone into a group that can then be led by the dictator whose body always marks the center of the composition and is never to be photographed at an oblique angle. The close-up shot is highly discouraged by the state's official rules of representation; only the two leaders—the Great Leader Kim Il-sung and the Dear Leader Kim Jong-il—have ever merited a particular kind of close-up: the double-portraits that adorn every public building and private home, even after their death. When Back zoomed in on a schoolgirl and blew up her image as large as Kim Il-sung's head, placing her next to the retaken portrait of the leader from an obtuse angle, Back effectively nullified this photographic logic. Back's disruption of the North Korean photographic norm—and its social norm—continued when he extracted and printed "insignificant" details such as a grove of leafy trees or a partial view of a North Korean guide's head. As a compilation of photographic margins, *Blow Up* imagines a different picture—or indeed multiple close-ups—of a collective that is more heterogeneous, contentious, and agonistic than depicted in the regime's image of national collective.

In terms of display method, Back has chosen a way to defy the "totalizing eye" on North Korea—imposed on the territory by both foreigners and the regime itself—by displaying multiple photographs in 20- by-24-inch frames together rather than singularly.[26] The gridlike composite of multiple photographs in *Blow Up* effectively corresponds to disconnected pieces of memory from disparate times that refuse to form a comprehensive narrative but nonetheless interact with one another. The diversity in the depicted referents does not surmount into a complete picture but rather indicates the incompleteness of the picture, as exemplified by how the individual photographs on display (except for two) do not fit into the uniformly sized frames. With the photographs being surrounded by blank photographic borders, the picture frames in *Blow Up* do not merely demarcate the end of each picture and the beginning of real space. To add another layer to the visual complexity, not all blank spaces are equal in shape and size. The presentation of two children standing by a Yamaha piano is, for example, squeezed by two vertical blank spaces on the left and right sides of the frame. The frame as a grid does not suffocate the image; in contrast, the blank space of emptiness gives breathing room to each image, a room for movement. This room for dynamic movement gains another function: when the viewer connects a blank space in a frame with other blank borders in other frames. The recognition of the frame between two blank strips meets the possibility of crossing it, while the disruptive movement of back and forth between the empty spaces produces a border zone that function as a link between photographs (see plate 8). The participation of the spectator—the act of linking and connecting practiced by the viewer's active looking—is also furthered to include breaking, crossing, and transgressing the frame, another symbol of border.

In viewing *Blow Up*, the spectator is invited to perform the simultaneous act of recognizing and breaking the frame, linking the individual pictures together; by this performance, the spectator remains, however long she may, in the liminal space of perpetual lingering without asserting the material division between each unit. This elimination and refusal of concrete border highly contrasts with the ways in which the inter-Korean relationship has been considered a sum of two distinct units in the rhetoric of South Korean government and academics. Formulating South Korean history under its now democratic regime, South Korean scholars advanced a revolutionary move toward reconceptualizing the North-South relationship as the reality of division, one in which the two Koreas are interlocked.[27] Even when the similarities between the two Koreas are revealed—such as military dictatorship and hypermasculine nationalism—this comparison of two entities within the existing North versus South framework resides within the binarism. South Korean art critic and artist Chan-kyong Park articulates the visuality of such binarism found in the War Memorial's display method. At the South Korean state-run War Memorial in Yongsan, Seoul, the audiovisual material shown at the museum's theater juxtaposes two screens on which similar scenes in North and South Korean histories are projected side by side. For instance, as Park poignantly observes, when the right screen shows a photographic documentation of the U.S. military occupying South Korea, the left screen features a group of Soviet Union soldiers marching into North Korea. This method of double projection, Park believes, demonstrates the opposition between the two countries in the "literal form."[28] The simultaneous presentation of division and linkage between the two Koreas demonstrates the characteristics of self-sufficiency and self-containment of the double framework. Because the visual language confirms and conforms to the framework of identity and difference, the viewer is left to constantly linger within the closed system of self and other. Park also notes that the situations in the South and the North establish a temporal linearity, as if the South and the North exist in different time zones, with the former surpass-

Figure 17.3. Seung Woo Back, *BL-79* as part of photography series *Blow Up*
(2005–7) 20 x 24 inch. Digital Print. Photo courtesy of the artist.

ing the latter. In *Blow Up* it is precisely our inability to identify the North
Korean others and to imprison them in an isolated frame (or a past) that
serves as the starting point for the nonoppositional relationship with North
Koreans and moreover a different picture of collectivity composed of photographic edges and corners.

Such a relationship may be possible only when outsiders (including
South Koreans) come to realize that it is utterly impossible to completely
know, identify, and make judgments about North Koreans. In the epistemological space between the recognizable and the unrecognizable lies the
ethical dilemma of representing the unrepresentable and the possibility of
moving beyond the reality of division. A ghostly photograph in the left center column visualizes this ethical dilemma of representing the unknowable
(see fig. 17.3). Like a proto-photograph on a glass pane, the silhouette of the
North Korean subject fully exerts its presence over there; but this semitrans-
parent, semiopaque glass pane also blocks our view, retaining the detailed
information of the subject such as gender and age we cannot know. What

we do know is that we are brought closer to this abstract representation of a human subject, a North Korean other, with whom we share space. This sense of sharing is not solely spatial; it is also temporal. Back's postproduction and the viewer's activation of photographs reinvigorate the strong sense of refusal to linear temporality that puts North Korea into *our* past, as succinctly captured in such a dictum as "the past is a foreign country."

IN PLACE OF CONCLUSION

It is now the summer of 2011. Though only four years have passed since the end of the Sunshine Policy era, the inter-Korean relationship has drastically changed. The Mt. Diamond resort, for instance, closed its doors in July 2008, when Park Wang-ja, a middle-aged woman from South Korea, was shot multiple times by North Korean security guards. Park had apparently crossed the tourist-designated area and walked along the beach off the hotel resort. Failing to reach a mutual understanding of her unauthorized transgression and the resultant tragedy, the two governments entered a period of hostility. Since then, the sinking of the vessel *Chonan* (May 2010) and the fires on Yonpyong Island (November 2010), along with the South Korea–U.S. joint military drills (2011), have all contributed to the widening communication gap between the two Koreas; and the South Korean government no longer issues permits to its citizens to visit the North. In this time of disconnect, miscommunication, and prohibition, I, as an overseas Korean, had just returned from a six-day trip to Pyongyang.

As always, touristic experience is multisensorial, and to a certain extent so was mine. At the War Memorial Museum in Pyongyang, what I would describe as a certain bureaucratic odor lingered in the moldy and stuffy air around the remnants of crushed tanks and bombshells (allegedly from the Korean War) that are prominently and crudely on display. At another instance, when a summer shower menacingly hit the People's Gymnasium's grounds in the middle of the Arirang performance (the world's largest "mass game," famous for mobilizing an impressive number of 80,000 performers), the shocking image of the innumerable performers who continued without missing a beat remains vivid in my memory, along with the rapid increase of humidity felt on my skin and the sudden aroma of dirt and grass filtering through my nose.

Despite these fragments of memory, my experience in North Korea was above all visual. Most North Koreans whose glimpse I was able to catch were encountered or, more appropriately, viewed from a moving bus. Though my group's minders resembled less the government authority than helpful tour guides and they never deleted any of the photographs stored in my digital camera, they were, before anything, in charge of containing the group of American tourists within the designated parameters. This meant that I was given no chance to stroll along the streets of Pyongyang and talk to the local residents on my own.[29] The limit to which I gained access to the daily life of North Koreans was therefore predetermined, in a way similar to how Back had experienced it. In this aberrant tourist experience, the artificial distance created between the North Koreans and myself precluded other sensorial experiences, forcing me to rely on sight and the camera eye when examining the site.

When seen from a speeding bus, the urban street life of Pyongyang rapidly unfolded before my eyes, evoking an overwhelming sense of nostalgia. All of the neatly lined-up high-rises, the apparent lack of advertisements and marquees, and the humble clothes of the passersby are categorically modern; Pyongyang is undeniably devoid of postmodern paraphilia that decorate other metropolitan cities today. Time might have stopped flowing in North Korea somewhere in the 1970s, when the country's economy was on par with, if not outperforming, that of South Korea. But what is significant here is that for someone who spent her youth in the South during the 1980s and 1990s—and not during the 1970s—this provocative sense of nostalgia is not about the time that I had survived but about somewhere before my time and outside my memory. This imaginary and contested temporality felt in Pyongyang provided me with an entry point to a critical investigation on the rhetoric of linear temporality that dangerously puts the North Korean others in the past of the self. Where and when, then, is North Korea, if not in South Korea's 1970s? Defying a straightforward answer, the question requires a reconsideration of spatiotemporality, on which Back's *Blow Up* seems to hold a tight grip.

On the one hand, the outdated, modern urbanity that I witnessed in Pyongyang and that Back so zealously features in *Blow Up* seems to locate the photographed site in the past, emphasizing the "pastness" of photography that Barthes has designated as the medium's foremost characteristic. On the other hand, *Blow Up*'s spatial play, which I have analyzed in this chapter, is coterminous with its temporal manipulation, thereby rescuing the present-ness out of the photographs. It is with the sense of elongated and ever so deferred temporality of the present-ness that the South Korean citizen's representation of North Korea refuses to comply with the positivist understanding of history as well as North Korean censorship. Indeed, the history of division can or perhaps ought to be written in the "catastrophic time," which Mary Ann Doane theorizes as being defined by the temporality of disruption, deference, and accidentality.[30] Those living on the Korean peninsula for the past sixty years have anxiously been waiting for the final moment—the ultimate catastrophe of either full-on war or the Northern regime's sudden collapse—while experiencing various military, economic, and natural crises. Probing such intervention into temporality, *Blow Up* tackles the two Korean governments' ultimate political pursuit: the often-romanticized national project for reunification. While dangerously assuming the myth of a single nation, the politics of unification (or *tongil*) produces, even more perniciously, a linear temporality within which the march toward the end goal of reunification—and ultimate peace—can take place.

In a sense, the North Korean regime as a whole can be conceptualized as a catastrophe for the rest of the world, if, as the etymology of catastrophe (per Doane) suggests, catastrophe is the "overturning of a given situation" and thus produces "sudden and unexpected effects in a gradually changing situation."[31] In other words, North Korea is a political, economic, and cultural catastrophe in the gradually transforming global village of neoliberalism. What *Blow Up* compellingly alludes to is that the catastrophic North Korea confronts, debilitates, and breaks the ideas of historical progress, refusing to remain in one particular historical moment in the worldwide march toward the neoliberal market economy. In facing such a country, what kind of ethical relationship can we—the outsiders and South Koreans—forge with its twenty million citizens? And what would this relationship look like or feel like?

In my limited conversations with a few privileged North Koreans, including my guides, I felt as if I were walking on eggshells, always failing to predict or to fully recognize their response to my words (that is, the standard South Korean language) as well as the cultural references and socioeconomic status upon which my ideas depended. The temporality that I felt during my short trip to the North resembles a catastrophic one, which attends to "the potential trauma and explosiveness of the present."[32] It is a situation where change is always imminent. Perhaps, even after the achievement of a long-overdue peace treaty or unification, where more people can freely communicate above any ideological differences, it is difficult to imagine that the division on socioeconomic and cultural fronts will suddenly collapse and become irrelevant. If we were to fully respect and attend ethically to these differences, rather than trying to subordinate the economically inferior North Koreans to our decisively firm grip of neoliberalism, we ought to treat them in catastrophic time with self-reflexivity. In other words, we ought to "walk on eggshells" as part of our ethical approach to the same differences that we share with North Koreans. As the catastrophe continues in the peninsula—and so does the need to recognize the catastrophic temporality—the creative representation of North Korea in *Blow Up* reminds the viewer that the unpredictable, uncertain, and catastrophic have always been a part of the everyday and "other" over which we strive yet fail to exercise complete control.

NOTES

1. In South Korea, it was only in the 1990s that the national security law's ban on the production and circulation of North Korea–related documents, especially those with the portraits of the dictators, was lifted.

2. Photography historian Geoffrey Batchen discusses the *collective* desire for photography that was on the rise in Western Europe in the early nineteenth century, during the first revolution in transportation history, hence the difficulty of identifying Louis Daguerre (1787–1851) of France as the sole inventor of photography while denigrating William Henry Fox Talbot (1800–1877) of England to the position of a copier. Geoffrey Batchen, *Burning with Desire* (Cambridge, MA: MIT Press, 1997), 22–53.

3. Carol Crawshaw and John Urry, "Tourism and the Photographic Eye," in *Touring Cultures: Transformations of Travel and Theory* (New York: Routledge, 1997), 180; Dolf Sternberger, "Panorama of the Nineteenth Century" in *October* 4 (autumn 1977): 3–20.

4. The mass tourism emerging in the late eighteenth and early nineteenth centuries was inherently different from the kind of elite travel of the seventeenth and eighteenth centuries, when European elites traveled to the South (that is, Italy) on the Grand Tour.

5. On the Korean peninsula photography was introduced through the Japanese colonizers, who brought with them the tools and techniques of photography; the main function of photography was to visually document the colonized land. See Gyewon Kim's article for visual and cultural analyses on ichthyology and the early use of photography in colonial Korea. Gyewon Kim, "Unpacking the Archive: Ichthyology, Photography, and the Archival Record in Japan and Korea," in *positions: east asia cultures critique* 18, no. 1 (2010): 51–88. About the use of the first video camera in the Korean peninsula, see Soyoung Kim, "Cartography of Catastrophe: Pre-Colonial Surveys, Post-Colonial Vampires, and the Plight of Korean Modernity" in *Journal of Korean Studies* 16, no. 2 (fall 2011): 285–301.

6. Between November 1998, when the first tour embarked, and July 2008, when the South Korean Ministry of Unification put a temporary ban on the tour after the killing of a tourist by North Korean soldiers' gunshots, a total of 1,955,951 civilians visited the Diamond Head tourist district. At first the ferry left the eastern shore from the South to arrive at the mountain resort in the North, but a road that cuts across the DMZ was built to transport the tourists by bus; http://www.mtkumgang .com/ and http://reunion.unikorea.go.kr/ (accessed December 10, 2009).

7. South Korean secondary schools took students on school field trips to Mt. Diamond. Some exemplary blogs are http://blog.naver.com/ghks201/90038845210 (2008) and http://sycho.kr/70097732768 (2002) (accessed April 25, 2011).

8. This comment is regarding a Korean blogger who engages in trade business and was invited to make an investment in the Kaesong Special Economic Zone in 2008, right at a time when the Economic Zone (located off the North Korean side of the DMZ along the Yellow Sea) lost the initial optimistic projection of profit expected from the successful precedence of the Shenzhen Special Economic Zone in Southern China: http://blog.daum.net/toogary2/15801719 (accessed March 28, 2011).

9. *The Joint Security Area* (2000, director Chan-wook Park); *TaeGukGi: Brotherhood of War* (2004, director Je-kyu Kang); and *Welcome to Dongmakgol* (2005, director Kwang-Hyun Park).

10. According to my interviews with South Korean curators and artists who visited Pyongyang during this brief decade, they benefitted from tours that were unrelated to art or the cultural scene and that were sporadically and discreetly available through the South Korean government or peacekeeping nongovernmental organizations (NGOs), whose main purpose was to promote amity in the most general sense. These tours followed a predetermined route and hardly fostered any artistic exchange; yet for South Koreans, being able to set foot in the North was reason enough for joining the tours.

11. Back accompanied the internationally known designer of *hanbok* (traditional Korean costume), Lee Younghee, who now claims the title of the first South Korean designer to hold a fashion show in the North.

12. The artist's interview with the author in Seoul on July 15, 2011.

13. South Korean blockbuster films, wherein North Koreans are depicted as ethnically otherized subjects, cast a neocolonial gaze onto the sanguine brothers. Kyung Hyun Kim, "Mea Culpa: Reading the North Korean as an Ethnic Other," in *Virtual Hallyu: Korean Cinema of the Global Era* (Durham, NC: Duke University Press, 2011), 101–22.

14. Carol Crawshaw and John Urry, "Tourism and the Photographic Eye," in *Touring Cultures: Transformations of Travel and Theory* (New York: Routledge, 1997), 179.

15. Jonathan Culler, "The Semiotics of Tourism," in *Framing the Sign* (Norman: University of Oklahoma Press, 1988), 153–67.

16. Tourist guidebooks to Pyongyang organize their narrative around these monuments and a map that locates them. Chris Springer, *Pyongyang: The Hidden History of the North Korean Capital* (Budapest: Entente Bt., 2003).

17. In 1967, the Central Committee's fifteenth meeting of the fourth term became the infamous site where Kim Jong-il purged several leading figures in the propaganda bureau and took control of North Korean arts of propaganda.

18. South Koreans who visited Pyongyang during the Sunshine Policy era often recall that the control was more severe on South Korean tourists than other non-Korean NGO workers. The level of control differed depending on the nature of the trip too—tourism versus business—but has shifted in recent days. When I, an overseas Korean, visited Pyongyang as part of a group of American tourists in summer 2011, the control exercised by the "minders" over photographing activity was to the minimum. But even in this case, the censorship was exercised through limiting the area of touristic activity: the tourists were not allowed to walk on the streets of Pyongyang, predetermining the range of sights to which I had visual access and also

eliminating any chance to strike up in-depth conversations with average Pyongyang citizens.

19. Artist's statement.

20. The artist tells me that the minder did not allow him to take photographs of, for example, dirty street corners.

21. An exhibition catalogue, *Art Under Control in North Korea*, which accompanies Jane Portal's exhibition on North Korean paintings and posters of the same title (British Museum, London, 2005), features as its first image a painting that depicts a similar scene. This catalogue is the only substantial book on art from North Korea published in English. Jane Portal, *Art Under Control in North Korea* (London: Reaktion, 2005).

22. At first glance, Roland Barthes's conceptualization of the *punctum*, and his understanding that certain photographs emotionally and traumatically "pierce" individual viewers, serve a powerful tool with which the operating model of division on the Korean peninsula can be disrupted. If one follows the earlier Barthesian elegy to the author in "Death of Author," the reader (or the viewer) is born with each reading that opens up diverse interpretative possibilities and thus gives more agency to the reader. Similarly, a shift of power dynamics between the photographer and the viewer is what Barthes attempted to achieve in his reading of photographs in *Camera Lucida* (1980). However, Back's search for the details seem to be motivated by rational and societal rather than psychological and personal reasons.

23. Back makes the reference to *The Truman Show* (1998, director Peter Weir) in his interview with the author.

24. A cultural study of North Korean journalistic photographs published in the *Rodong Daily* (*rodong sinmun*) details the ideological implications of photographic techniques in the North. For example, the preference for full shots since the 1970s has substantially reduced the official appearance of close-ups in all visual media including photography and film. The close-ups are considered "too formalist." These manuals follow the directions noted in Kim Jong-il's articles: *Yŏnghwayesulron* [Theory of filmic arts] of 1973 and *Uri Dang-ŭi Sinmunmaechewo Chulpanmul* [Our party's news media and publications] of 1974. On another point, the leaders' portraits receive utmost attention from North Korean photographers, as both Kims should always be in the center of the picture frame. The Propaganda Bureau's establishment of a manual to formalize details reveals that the photographic language functions to serve the ideological content. See Byŏn Yŏng-wook, *Kim Jŏng-il jaeyipiji imiji-ŭi dokjŏm* [Kim Jong-il.jpg: Monopoly of image] (Seoul: Hanwool, 2008), 42, 75, 119.

25. Clive Scott, *Street Photography: From Atget to Cartier-Bresson* (London: I. B. Tauris, 2007), 57–59.

26. German photographer Andreas Gursky's Pyongyang series, which captures frontal scenes of the mass games of the Arirang Festival, exhibits large, glossy C-prints singularly, effectively formulating a totalizing photographic vision onto the regime.

27. Jo-Han Hye-jeong and Yi Wu-yong, eds. *T'alpuntan sitaerŭl yŏlmyŏ namkwa puk munhwa kongchonŭl wihan mosaek* [Opening an era beyond division: Toward cultural cohabitation between the South and the North] (Seoul: Samin, 2000).

28. Park Chan-kyong, "*Yŏnghwa wa setŭ sai*" (Between cinema and movie set) (unpublished manuscript). This script was written for a presentation given in 2005, and was provided to the author by the artist himself.

29. This also means that most of my photographs are fuzzy, as they are images of people walking I photographed while on a moving bus.

30. Mary Ann Doane, "Information, Crisis, Catastrophe," in *The Historical Film: History and Memory in Media*, ed. Marcia Landy (London: Continuum, 2001), 269–85.

31. Mary Ann Doane, "Information, Crisis, Catastrophe," 275.

32. Mary Ann Doane, "Information, Crisis, Catastrophe," 275.

BIBLIOGRAPHY

Abelmann, Nancy. *The Melodrama of Mobility: Women, Talk, and Class in Contemporary South Korea*. Honolulu: University of Hawai'i Press, 2003.

Abelmann, Nancy, and Kathleen McHugh, eds. *South Korean Golden Age Melodrama: Gender, Genre, and National Cinema*. Detroit: Wayne State University Press, 2005.

Adorno, Theodor W. "On Popular Music" (1992). In *Cultural Theory and Popular Culture: A Reader*, edited by John Storey, 197–209. Upper Saddle River, NJ: Prentice Hall, 1998.

———. *The Stars Down to Earth*. New York: Routledge, 1994.

Adorno, Theodor W., and Max Horkheimer. *Dialectic of Enlightenment*, edited by Gunzelin Schmid Noerr, translated by Edmund Jephcott. Palo Alto, CA: Stanford University Press, 2002.

Ahmed, Sara. "Affective Economies." *Social Text* 22, no. 2 (2004): 117–39.

Ahn, Yongseok, and Misuk Seo. "Ton jal bŏlsurok ap'at'ŭ sanda" [Wealthy Residents Tend to Live in Apartment Blocks]. *Midas*, November 2006. Accessed June 26, 2011. http://past.yonhapmidas.com/06_11/liv/04_001.html.

Allkpop. "SNSD's Trainers Clear Up Their Diet." December 20, 2009. Accessed March 27, 2011. http://www.allkpop.com/2009/12/snsds_trainers_clear_up_their_diet.

Alperstein, Neil M. *Advertising in Everyday Life*. Cresskill, NJ: Hampton Press, 2001.

Althusser, Louis. "Ideology and Ideological State Apparatuses" (Notes Toward an Investigation). In *Lenin and Philosophy and Other Essays*, translated by Ben Brewster. 127–86. New York: Monthly Review Press, 1971.

An, Chŏng-suk, and Kim So-hŭi. "Interview with Sin Sang-ok" in *Cine 21* 8, no. 4 (1998).

An, Jinsoo. "Popular Reasoning of South Korean Melodrama Films (1953–1972)." Ph.D. diss., UCLA, 2005.

Anderson, Benedict R. *Imagined Communities: Reflections on the Origin and Spread of Nationalism*. 2nd ed. London: Verso, 1991.

Andsager, Julie, and Kimberly Roe. "'What's Your Definition of Dirty, Baby?' Sex in Music Video." *Sexuality & Culture* 7, no. 3 (2003): 79–97.

Appadurai, Arjun. *Modernity at Large: Cultural Dimensions of Globalization*. Minneapolis: University of Minnesota Press, 1996.

Appadurai, Arjun, and Carol A. Breckenridge. "Why Public Culture?" *Public Culture Bulletin* 1, no. 1 (1998): 5–9.

Arendt, Hannah. *Love and Saint Augustine*. Chicago: University of Chicago Press, 1996.

Armstrong, Charles. *The North Korean Revolution (1945–1950)*. Ithaca, NY: Cornell University Press, 2004.

"Artisanal Makgeolli Movement Underway," *Korea Herald*, March 30, 2010.

Bak, Sangmee. "Exoticizing the Familiar, Domesticating the Foreign: Ethnic Food Restaurants in Korea." *Korea Journal* 50, no. 1 (2010): 110–32.

———. "McDonald's in Seoul: Food Choices, Identity, and Nationalism." In *Golden Arches East: McDonald's in East Asia*, edited by James L. Watson, 136–60. Palo Alto, CA: Stanford University Press, 1997.

———. "Negotiating National and Transnational Identities through Consumption Choices: Hamburgers, Espresso, and Mobile Technologies among Koreans." *Review of Korean Studies* 7, no. 2 (2004): 33–52.

Balibar, Etienne. "Fichte and the Internal Border: On *Addresses to the German Nation*." In *Classes, Masses, Ideas: Studies on Politics Before and After Marx*. Translated by James Swenson, 61–86. London: Routledge, 1994.

Barthes, Roland. *Camera Lucida: Reflections on Photography*. Translated by Richard Howard. New York: Hill and Wang, 1981.

———. *The Fashion System*. Translated by Matthew Ward and Richard Howard. New York: Hill and Wang, 1983.

———. "The Reality Effect." In *The Rustle of Language*, translated by Richard Howard, 141–48. Berkeley: University of California Press, 1989.

Batchen, Geoffrey. *Burning with Desire*. Cambridge, MA: MIT Press, 1997.

Baudrillard, Jean. *For a Critique of a Political Economy of the Sign*. Translated by Charles Levin. St. Louis: Telos Press, 1981.

Beebee, Thomas O. *Epistolary Fiction in Europe 1500–1850*. London: Cambridge University Press, 1999.

Benjamin, Walter. "The Work of Art in the Age of Its Technological Reproducibility." In *Selected Writings*. Vol. 4, *1938–1940*. Edited by Howard Eiland and Michael W. Jennings. Translated by Edmund Jephcott. Cambridge, MA: Harvard University Press, 2003.

Berlant, Lauren. *The Female Complaint: The Unfinished Business of Sentimentality in American Culture*. Durham, NC: Duke University Press, 2008.

———. *The Queen of America Goes to Washington City: Essays on Sex and Citizenship*. Durham, NC: Duke University Press, 1997.

Bhabha, Homi K. "The Postcolonial and the Postmodern." In *The Location of Culture*. London: Routledge, 1992.

Bordwell, David. "Classical Hollywood Cinema: Narrational Principles and Procedures." In *Narrative, Apparatus, Ideology: A Film Theory Reader*. New York: Columbia University Press, 1986.

Braudy, Leo. *The Frenzy of Renown: Fame and Its History*. New York: Oxford University Press, 1986.

Brooks, Peter. *The Melodramatic Imagination*. New Haven, CT: Yale University Press, 1995.

———. "The Melodramatic Imagination." In *Imitations of Life: A Reader on Film and*

Television Melodrama, edited by Marcia Landy. Detroit: Wayne State University Press, 1991.

Brown, Helen-Louise. "Conceived in the Past and Raised in Modernity: A Study of the Korean Barbecue Restaurant." MA thesis, University of Adelaide, 2010.

Brown, J., and L. Schultz. "The Effect of Race, Gender, and Fandom on Audience Interpretations of Madonna's Music Videos." *Journal of Communication* 40 (1990): 88–102.

Byŏn, Yŏng-wook. *Kim Chŏng-il jpg imiji ŭi dokjŏm* [Kim Jong-il.jpg: Monopoly of Image]. Seoul: Hanwool, 2008.

Cadava, Eduardo. *Words of Light: Theses on the Photography of History*. Princeton, NJ: Princeton University Press, 1997.

Campbell, Jan. *Film and Cinema Spectatorship: Melodrama and Mimesis*. Cambridge: Polity Press, 2005.

Ch'a, U-jin. *"Kŏl kŭrup chŏnsŏnggi."* *Munhwa pipyŏng* 59 (2009): 270–83.

Chan, Dean. "Negotiating Intra-Asian Games Networks: On Cultural Proximity, East Asian Games Design, and Chinese Farmers." *Fibreculture Journal*, March 16, 2006.

Chang, Ha-Joon. *Bad Samaritans: The Myth of Free Trade and the Secret History of Capitalism*. New York: Bloomsbury, 2008.

Chang, Tae-pyong. "Korea IR (14): Korean Food, Infinite Possibilities." *Korea Times*, February 3, 2009.

Chen, Tina Mai. "Internationalism and Cultural Experience: Soviet Films and Popular Chinese Understandings of the Future in the 1950s." *Cultural Critique* 58 (2004): 82–114.

Chen, Xiaomei. *Occidentalism: A Theory of Counter-Discourse in Post-Mao China*. Lanham, MD: Rowman and Littlefield, 2002.

Cheng, Sea-Ling. "Back to the Future: Herbal Tea Shops in Hong Kong." In *Hong Kong: The Anthropology of a Chinese Metropolis*, edited by G. Evans and M. Tam, 51–73. Honolulu: University of Hawai'i Press, 1997.

Cheon, Jung Hwan. *Chosŏn ŭi sanai kŏdŭn p'utppol ŭl ch'ara* [If you are a man of Chosŏn, kick a soccer ball]. Seoul: P'ŭrŭn yŏksa, 2010.

"Chigŭm ilbon e p'iryohan kŏn ton i anin chŏng" [What Japanese people now need is not money but sympathy], JPNews. December 30, 2010.

Ching, Leo T. S. *Becoming "Japanese": Colonial Taiwan and the Politics of Identity Formation*. Berkeley: University of California Press, 2001.

Cho, Chun-hyŏng, et al. *2008 Korean Film History: Oral History Records Series, Sin Films [2008-nyŏn han'guk yŏnghwasa kusul ch'aerok siriju <Chujesa> Sin p'illum]*. Seoul: Korean Film Archive, 2008.

Cho, Jin-seo. "Nintendo Sees Slow Wii Sales in Korea." *Korea Times*, June 2, 2008.

———. "Nintendo Sells 580,000 Mini Game Players." *Korea Times*, October 28, 2007.

———. "Video Game Big 3 Geared for Battle." *Korea Times*, February 14, 2007.

Cho, Kyuil. *"1930nyŏndae Yuhaengga kasa koch'al"* [A study of popular music lyrics of the 1930s]. *Inmun'gwahak* [Journal of the humanities] 31 (2000): 265–75.

Cho, Sunja. Television Interview in *Nanŭn Sesang ŭl Noraehaetta* [I sang about world]. Masan MBC [Munhwa Broadcast Company], February 2, 2003.

Cho, Tongsik. "Sipnyŏnchŏn yŏhaksaeng kwa chikŭm yŏhaksaeng" [Girl students, ten years ago and now]. *Shinyŏsŏng*, January 1925, 15.

Cho, Young-A, Gloria Davies, and M. E. Davies. "Hallyu Ballyhoo and Harisu: Marketing and Representing the Transgendered in South Korea." In *Complicated Currents: Media Flows, Soft Power and East Asia*, edited by D. Black, S. Epstein, and A. Tokita, 09.1–09.12. Monash ePress, 2010. Accessed March 27, 2011. http://www.epress .monash.edu/cc/index.htm.

Ch'oe, Ch'angho. *Minjok sunan'gi ŭi taejung kayosa* [Korean popular music during the colonial period]. Seoul: Ilwol Sŏgak, 2000.

Ch'oe, Ch'ansik. *Anŭisŏng* [The Cry of Wild Geese]. Seoul: Pakmunsŏkwan, 1914.

Ch'oe, Tŏk-gyo. *Han'guk chapji paeknyŏn* [100 years of Korean magazines]. Seoul: Hyŏnamsa, 2004.

Choi, Chansik. *Autumn Moon Shades* [*Ch'uwŏlsaek*]. Seoul: Andongsŏgwan, 1912.

Choi, Jinhee. *The South Korean Film Renaissance: Local Hitmakers, Global Provocateurs*. Middletown, CT: Wesleyan University Press, 2010.

Chŏng, Chaejŏng. "*Kŭndae ŭi Sŏul sari wa taejung munhwa*" [Seoul life and popular culture in the modern period]. In *Popular Art of the Modern Age*, edited by Kwŏn O-Do. Seoul: Seoul Museum of History, 2003.

Chŏng, Chae-sŏk. "*Iryŏksŏ e 'sajin' toech'ukdoelkka.*" *Focus Busan*, June 9, 2010, 6.

"*Chosŏnilbo tae tongailbo sangjaeng sakŏn chinsang kŭp pip'an*" [The conflict between the *Chosŏn Daily* and the *Tonga Daily*: Truth-level criticism]. *Samch'ŏlli*, July 1935.

Chu, Chongyŏn, and Kim Sangtae, eds. *Natohyang chŏnjip*, vols. 1–2. Seoul: Jipmundang, 1988.

Chu, Yu-sin, et al. *Han'gukyŏnghwawa kŭndaesŏng: "Chayu puin"esŏ "Angae"kka'ji [Korean Cinema and Modernity: From "Madame Freedom" to "Mist"]*. Seoul: Sodo, 2001.

———. "*Melodrama genre e taehan yŏsŏngjuŭi jŏk pip'yŏng: yŏsŏng kwan-gaek sŏng nonŭi rŭl chungsimŭro*" [Feminist critique of the melodrama genre: On the discourse of female spectatorship]. *Yŏnghwa yŏn'gu* 15 (2000): 91–114.

Chua, Beng Huat, and Koichi Iwabuchi, eds. *East Asian Pop Culture: Analyzing the Korean Wave*. Hong Kong: Hong Kong University Press, 2008.

Chung, Heejoon. "Sport Star vs. Rock Star in Globalizing Popular Culture: Similarities, Difference and Paradox in Discussion of Celebrities." *International Review for the Sociology of Sport* 38 (2003): 99–108.

Chung, Steven. "The Split Screen: Sin Sang-ok in North Korea." In *North Korea: Toward a Better Understanding*, edited by Sonia Ryang, 85–107. Lanham, MD: Lexington Books, 2009.

comScore. "comScore Publishes the First Comprehensive Review of Asian-Pacific Usage." July 9, 2007. Accessed June 15, 2013. http://www.comscore.com/Press _Events/Press_Releases/2007/07/Asia-Pacific_Internet_Usage.

Cook, Ian, and Philip Crang. "The World on a Plate: Culinary Culture, Displacement, and Geographical Knowledge." *Journal of Material Culture* 1, no. 2 (July 1996): 131–53.

Crawshaw, Carol, and John Urry. "Tourism and the Photographic Eye." In *Touring Cultures: Transformations of Travel and Theory*, edited by Carol Crawshaw and John Urry, 176–95. New York: Routledge, 1997.

Crehan, Kate A. F. *Gramsci, Culture, and Anthropology: Reading Gramsci*. London: Pluto, 2002.

Crosset, Todd W. *Outsiders in the Clubhouse: The World of Women's Professional Golf*. Albany: State University of New York Press, 1995.

Culler, Jonathan. "The Semiotics of Tourism." In *Framing the Sign*, 153–67. Norman: University of Oklahoma Press, 1988.

Culture and Tourism Ministry, Republic of South Korea. *Two-Thousand Years of Korean Fashion* [*Uri ot ichŏn nyŏn*]. Seoul: Misul Munhwa, 2001.

Cumings, Bruce. *Korea's Place in the Sun*. New York: W. W. Norton, 2005.

Curran, James, and Jean Seaton. *Power without Responsibility: The Press, Broadcasting, and New Media in Britain*. 7th ed. New York: Routledge, 2009.

Cwiertka, Katarzyna J. *Cuisine, Colonialism, and Cold War: Food in Twentieth-Century Korea*. London: Reaktion, 2012.

———. "From Ethnic to Hip: Circuits of Japanese Cuisine in Europe." *Food and Foodways* 13, no. 4 (2005): 241–72.

———. *Modern Japanese Cuisine: Food, Power, and National Identity*. London: Reaktion, 2006.

Daum Yŏnye. *"Kara sat'ae hallyu kwoench'anna ajik chikchŏpchŏgin t'agyŏk ŏpta."* [Hallyu has not suffered direct consequence from the Kara incident]. February 22, 2011. Accessed March 27, 2011. http://media.daum.net/entertain/enews/view?newsid =20110222072404743.

David, Paul A. "Clio and the Economics of QWERTY." *American Economics Review* 75, no. 2 (1985): 332–37.

Debord, Guy. *The Society of the Spectacle*. Detroit: Black and Red, 1983.

———. *The Society of the Spectacle*. Translated by Donald Nicholson-Smith. New York: Zone Books, 1995.

De Certeau, Michel. *The Practice of Everyday Life*. Berkeley: University of California Press, 2002.

De Lauretis, Teresa. *Alice Doesn't: Feminism, Semiotics, Cinema*. Bloomington: Indiana University Press, 1984.

Deleuze, Gilles. *Cinema 1: The Movement-image*. Translated by Hugh Tomlinson and Barbara Habberjam. Minneapolis: University of Minnesota Press, [1986] 2006.

———. *Cinema 2: The Time-image*. Translated by Hugh Tomlinson and Robert Galeta. Minneapolis: University of Minnesota Press, 1989.

Deleuze, Gilles, and Félix Guattari. *A Thousand Plateaus*. Translated by Brian Massumi. London: Athlone Press, 1998.

Derrida, Jacques. *Archive Fever: A Freudian Impression*. Translated by Eric Prenowitz. Chicago: University of Chicago Press, 1996.

Do, Je-hae. "Korean Food Campaign Launched in Three Australian Cities." *Korea Times*, March 25, 2010.

Doane, Mary Ann. "Information, Crisis, Catastrophe." In *The Historical Film: History and Memory in Media*, edited by Marcia Landy, 269–85. London: Continuum, 2001.

———. "Scale and the Negotiation of 'Real' and 'Unreal' Space in the Cinema." In *Realism and the Audiovisual Media*, edited by Lúcia Nagib and Cecília Mello, 66–77. New York: Palgrave MacMillan, 2009.

Dobrenko, Evgeny. *Political Economy of Socialist Realism.* Translated by Jesse M. Savage. New Haven, CT: Yale University Press, 2007.

Donald, Stephanie Hemelryk. *Public Secrets, Public Spaces: Cinema and Civility in China.* Lanham, MD: Rowman and Littlefield, 2000.

Du Bois, W. E. B., *The Souls of Black Folk.* Rockville, MD: Ace Minor, 2008.

Ďurovičová, Nataša, and Garrett Stewart. "Amnesias of Murder: *Mother,*" *Film Quarterly* 64, no. 2 (winter 2010): 64–68.

Dyer, Richard. *Heavenly Bodies: Film Stars and Society.* New York: Macmillan, 1986.

——— . *Stars.* London: British Film Institute, 1998.

Eckert, Carter J. "The South Korean Bourgeoisie: A Class in Search of Hegemony." In *State and Society in Contemporary Korea,* edited by Hagen Koo, 95–130. Ithaca, NY: Cornell University Press, 1993.

Elfving-Hwang, Joanna. *Representations of Femininity in Contemporary South Korean Literature.* Folkestone, UK: Global Oriental, 2009.

Elsaesser, Thomas. "Tales of Sound and Fury: Observations on the Family Melodrama." In *Imitations of Life: A Reader on Film and Television Melodrama,* edited by Marcia Landy, 68–91. Detroit: Wayne State University Press, 1991.

Epstein, Stephen. "The Masculinization of (Women in) Korean Cinema?" Paper presented at the annual meeting of the Association of Asian Studies, San Francisco, April 2006.

Fabian, Johannes. *Moments of Freedom: Anthropology and Popular Culture.* Charlottesville: University Press of Virginia, 1998.

Fackler, Martin. "In Korea, Bureaucrats Lead the Technology Charge." *New York Times,* March 16, 2006.

——— . "In Korea, a Boot Camp Cure for Web Obsession." *New York Times,* November 18, 2007.

Farrer, James. "Eating the West and Beating the Rest: Culinary Occidentalism and Urban Soft Power in Asia's Global Food Cities." In *Globalization, Food, and Social Identities in the Asia Pacific Region,* edited by James Farrer. Tokyo: Sophia University Institute of Comparative Culture, 2001.

Feder-Kane, Abigail. "'A Radiant Smile from the Lovely Lady': Overdetermined Femininity in 'Ladies' Figure Skating." In *Reading Sport: Critical Essays on Power and Representation,* edited by Susan Birrell and Mary G. McDonald, 206–33. Boston: Northeastern University Press, 2000.

Fedorenko, Olga. *Tending to the 'Flower of Capitalism': Consuming, Producing and Censoring Advertising in South Korea of the '00s.* Ph.D. diss., University of Toronto, 2012.

Ferguson, Priscilla Parkhurst. "Culinary Nationalism." *Gastronomica: The Journal of Food and Culture* 10, no. 1 (2010): 102–9.

"59th: Hansik Does Not Need to Stick to Authenticity." *Korea Times,* October 30, 2009.

Fiske, John. "The Cultural Economy of Fandom." In *The Adoring Audience: Fan Culture and Popular Media,* edited by Lisa A. Lewis. London: Routledge, 1992.

——— . *Reading the Popular.* London: Routledge, 1989.

Forsberg, Birgitta. "The Future Is South Korea." *San Francisco Chronicle,* March 13, 2005.

Foster, Thomas. *The Souls of Cyberfolk: Posthumanism as Vernacular Theory*. Minneapolis: University of Minnesota Press, 2005.

Foucault, Michel. "What Is an Author?" In *Language, Counter-Memory, Practice: Selected Essays and Interviews*, edited by Donald F. Bouchard and translated by Donald F. Bouchard and Sherry Simon, 113–38. Ithaca, NY: Cornell University Press, 1974.

"Foundation to Promote Food Overseas." *Korea Times*. March 17, 2010.

Fowles, Jib. *Advertising and Popular Culture*. Vol. 5 of Foundations of Popular Culture. Thousand Oaks, CA: Sage Publications, 1996.

Freud, Sigmund. *Group Psychology and the Analysis of the Ego*. Translated and edited by James Strachey. New York: W.W. Norton, 1990.

———. *New Introductory Lectures on Psychoanalysis*. Translated and edited by James Strachey. New York: W. W. Norton, 1990.

Gaisberg, Frederick William. *The Music Goes Round*. New York: Macmillan, 1942.

Garcia, Cathy Rose A. "CJ to Open Global 'Hansik' Franchise." *Korea Times*, May 10, 2010.

Gelézeau, Valérie. *Séoul, Ville Géante, Cités Radieuses*. Paris: CNRS Editions, 2005.

"Girl Bands to Assist in 'Psychological Warfare.'" *Chosŏn Daily*, June 11, 2010. Accessed June 15, 2010. http://english.chosun.com/site/data/html_dir/2010/06/11/2010061100432.html.

girlfriday. "Pop Culture: Piggyback Rides." Dramabeans.com. July 11, 2010. http://www.dramabeans.com/2010/07/pop-culture-piggyback-rides/.

Gledhill, Christine, ed. *Stardom: Industry of Desire*. New York: Routledge, 1991.

Gorky, Maxim. "Soviet Literature." In *Soviet Writers' Congress, 1934: The Debate on Socialist Realism and Modernism; Gorky, Radek, Bukharin, Zhdanov, and Others*, 25–69. London: Lawrence and Wishart, 1977.

Grew, Raymond. "Food and Global History." In *Food in Global History*, edited by R. Grew, 1–29. Boulder, CO: Westview, 1999.

Grewal, Inderpal. *Transnational America*. Durham, NC: Duke University Press, 2005.

Gronow, Pekka. "The Record Industry Comes to the Orient." *Ethnomusicology* 25 (1981): 251–84.

Groys, Boris. *The Total Art of Stalinism: Avant-Garde, Aesthetic, Dictatorship, and Beyond*. Translated by Charles Rougle. London: Verso, 2011.

Gunning, Tom, "What's the Point of an Index? Or, Faking Photographs." In *Still Moving: Between Cinema and Photography*, edited by Karen Beckman and Jean Ma. Durham, NC: Duke University Press, 2008.

Ha Chaebong. *"Nuga Sŏ T'aeji-rŭl turyŏwŏ hanŭn'ga (TV pogi)"* [Who would be scared of Seo Taiji? (TV monitoring)], *Chosŏn ilbo* [Korea daily] November 18, 1995, 16.

Hakuson, Kuriyagawa. *Kindai no renaikan: Renaikanoyobizassan* [The modern view of love: the view of love and other writings]. Tokyo: Kaizosha, 1929.

Hall, Stuart. "Notes on Deconstructing 'the Popular.'" In *Cultural Theory and Popular Culture: A Reader*, edited by John Storey, 442–53. Upper Saddle River, NJ: Pearson/Prentice Hall, 1998.

Ham Ch'ung-pŏm. "A Study on the Process of Forming North Korean Cinema: Focusing on Relations with the Soviet Union" [Pukhan yŏnghwa hyŏngsŏng kwajŏng yŏngu: Soryŏn kwa ŭi kwankye rŭl chungsim ŭro]. *Hyŏndae yŏnghwa yŏngu* 1 (2005): 115–49.

Han, Kyung-Koo. "The 'Kimchi Wars' in Globalizing East Asia: Consuming Class, Gender, Health, and National Identity." In *Consuming Korean Tradition in Early and Late Modernity: Commodification, Tourism, and Performance*, edited by L. Kendall, 149–66. Honolulu: University of Hawai'i Press, 2010.

Han, Suk-Jung. "Those Who Imitated the Colonizers: The Legacy of the Disciplining State from Manchukuo to South Korea." In *Crossed Histories: Manchuria in the Age of Empire*, edited by Mariko Asano Tamanoi. Honolulu: University of Hawai'i Press, 2005.

Han'guk chapji ch'ongnam: Han'guk chapji 70-yŏn sa [Korean magazine survey: 70 years of Korean magazines]. Seoul: Han'guk Chapji Hyŏphoe, 1972.

Han'guk Pangsong 70nyŏnsa [Seventy-year history of Korean broadcasting]. Seoul: Korean Broadcasters Association, 1997.

"Han'guk yŏktae ch'oego hit'ŭ sangp'um: 'Sŏ T'aeji-wa aidŭl ŭmban'" [Korea's biggest product for several generations: "The albums of Seo Taiji and Boys"]. *K'oria wik'ŭlli* [Korea weekly], New Malden, UK, August 8, 1997, 7.

Han'guk yŏsŏng munhak hakhoe. *"Yŏwŏn" yŏn'gu moim eds. Yŏwŏn yŏn'gu: yŏsŏng, kyoyang, maech'e* [Yŏwŏn Studies: Women, Education, Media]. Seoul: Kukhak charyowŏn, 2008.

Hannertz, Ulf. *Transnational Connections*. London: Routledge, 1996.

"Hansik Globalization Body Planned." *Korea Times*, October 29, 2009.

Hardt, Michael, and Antonio Negri. *Empire*. Cambridge, MA: Harvard University Press, 2000.

Harvey, David. *A Brief History of Neo-Liberalism*. New York: Oxford University Press, 2005.

Haug, Wolfgang Fritz. *Critique of Commodity Aesthetics: Appearance, Sexuality, and Advertising in Capitalist Society*. Social and Political Theory Series. Cambridge: Polity Press, 1986.

Hayles, N. Katherine. "Print Is Flat, Code Is Deep: The Importance of Medium-Specific Analysis." *Poetics Today* 25, no. 1 (2004): 67–90.

Hebdige, Dick. *Subculture: The Meaning of Style*. London: Routledge, 1979.

Hegel, G. W. F. *Hegel's Aesthetics: Lectures on Fine Art, vol. 1*. Translated by T. M. Knox. New York: Oxford University Press, 1998.

Herz, J. C. "The Bandwidth Capital of the World." *Wired*, August 2002. http://www.wired.com/wired/archive/10.08/korea.html.

Hills, Matt. "Aca-Fandom and Beyond: Jonathan Gray, Matt Hills, and Alisa Perren (Part 1)." *Confessions of an Aca-Fan: The Official Weblog of Henry Jenkins*. Accessed on August 29, 2011. http://henryjenkins.org/2011/08/aca-fandom_and_beyond _jonathan.html.

———. *Fan Cultures*. London: Routledge, 2002.

"Hip Korea." Discovery Channel. Accessed March 27, 2011. http://www.youtube.com /watch?v=Hr2sOwBGwG8.

Hŏ, Yŏng-suk. *"Palnyŏnkaneilchŏniba'kchang"* [Twelve hundreds in eight years]. *Samchŏlli*, October 1930, 63.

Honig, Bonnie. "Immigrant America? How Foreignness 'Solves' Democracy's Problems." *Social Text* 56, no. 16 (1998): 1–27.

Hosokawa, Shuhei, Hiroshi Matsumura, and Hiroshi Ogawa, eds. *A Guide to Popular Music in Japan.* Tokyo: IASPM-Japan, 1991.

Howard, Keith. "Coming of Age: Korean Pop in the 1990s." In *Korean Pop Music: Riding the Korean Wave,* edited by Keith Howard, 82–98. Folkestone, UK: Global Oriental, 2006.

Hughes, Theodore, *Literature and Film in Cold War South Korea: Freedom's Frontier.* New York: Columbia University Press, 2012.

Hur, Youngman. *Kaksit'al.* Reprint Edition. Seoul: Hanguk Manhwa Chinhŭngwŏn, 2011.

———. *Kaksit'al.* Vol. 7. Seoul: Ŏminsa, 1980. Excerpts reproduced in http://blog .naver.com/PostView.nhn?blogId=rou&logNo=61602005.

———. *Soet'ungso.* Vol. 4. Seoul: Seju Munhwa, 1988.

Hwang, Munp'yŏng. *"Episodŭ ro pon Han'guk kayosa"* [Reading Korean popular song history through episodes] *Ŭmak tonga* 14 (1985): 262–65.

Hwang Chang-yŏp. *National Life Is More Precious Than Individual Life: Peace in the Republic and the Unification of the Nation [Kaein ŭi saengmyŏng poda kwijunghan minjok ŭi saengmyŏng: choguk p'yŏnghwa wa minjok ŭi t'ongil].* Seoul: Tosŏ Ch'ulp'ansa Sidae Chŏngsin, 1999.

Igarashi, Yoshikuni. *Bodies of Memory: Narratives of War in Postwar Japanese Culture, 1945–1970.* Princeton, NJ: Princeton University Press, 2000.

Im, Chŏng-t'aek, et al. *Modernity and Postcoloniality in East Asian Cinema (Tongasia yŏnghwa ŭi kŭndaesŏng'gwa t'alsikminsŏng).* Seoul: Yonsei taehak'kyo ch'ulp'anbu, 2007.

Im, Sanghyŏk. *"Yŏnghwa-wa p'yohyŏn-ŭi chayu: Han'guk yŏnghwa shimŭi chedo-ŭi pyŏnch'ŏn"* [Cinema and the freedom of speech: Korea's changing film censorship]. In *Han'guk yŏnghwa sa: kaehwagi-esŏ kaehwagi-kkaji* [A history of Korean movies: From the enlightenment period to the enlightenment period], edited by Kim Mihyŏn, 101. Seoul: Communication Books, 2006.

Iwabuchi, Kōichi. *Recentering Globalization: Popular Culture and Japanese Transnationalism.* Durham, NC: Duke University Press, 2002.

James, C. L. R. *State Capitalism and World Revolution.* Chicago: Charles H. Kerr, 1986.

Jamieson, Katherine M. "Reading Nancy Lopez: Decoding Representations of Race, Class, and Sexuality." In *Reading Sport: Critical Essays on Power and Representation,* edited by Susan Birrell and Mary G. McDonald, 144–65. Boston: Northeastern University Press, 2000.

Janelli, Roger L., and Dawnhee Yim Janelli. *Making Capitalism: The Social and Cultural Construction of a South Korean Conglomerate.* Palo Alto, CA: Stanford University Press, 1993.

javabeans. "About." Dramabeans.com. Accessed August 20, 2011. http://www .dramabeans.com/about/.

———. "A Day on the Set with Choi Jung-Won." Dramabeans.com. March 6, 2010. http://www.dramabeans.com/2010/03/a-day-on-the-set-with-choi-jung-won/.

———. "Anatomy of a Scene: Tenth Cup." Dramabeans.com. August 1, 2007. http:// www.dramabeans.com/2007/08/anatomy-of-a-scene-tenth-cup/.

———. "Coffee Prince: Seventeenth Cup (Final)." Dramabeans.com. August 27, 2007. http://www.dramabeans.com/2007/08/coffee-prince-seventeenth-cup-final/.

———. "Coffee Prince: Tenth Cup." Dramabeans.com. July 31, 2007. http://www.dramabeans.com/2007/07/coffee-prince-tenth-cup/.

———. "Intel Giveaway." Javabeans. November 24, 2010. http://javabeans.wordpress.com/2010/11/24/intel-giveaway/.

———. "The Moon That Embraces the Sun: Episode 16." Dramabeans.com. February 23, 2012. http://www.dramabeans.com/2012/02/the-moon-that-embraces-the-sun-episode-16/.

———. "The New Monday-Tuesday Lineup: First Impressions." Dramabeans.com. January 4, 2010. http://www.dramabeans.com/2010/01/the-new-monday-tuesday-lineup-first-impressions/.

———. "Sol Pharmacy's Finale Makes It Top-rated Drama of the Year." Dramabeans.com. http://www.dramabeans.com/2009/10/sol-pharmacys-finale-makes-it-top-rated-drama-of-the-year/.

———. "Summary: Dal Ja's Spring, Episode 1." Dramabeans.com. February 25, 2007. http://www.dramabeans.com/2007/02/summary-dal-jas-spring-episode-1/.

———. "Wish Upon a Star: Episode 8." Dramabeans.com. January 29, 2010. http://www.dramabeans.com/2010/01/wish-upon-a-star-episode-8/.

javabeans and girlfriday. "FAQ Frequently Asked Questions." Dramabeans.com. Accessed August 20, 2011. http://www.dramabeans.com/faq/.

Jeong, Deok-hyeon. "Swept Up by Girl Groups." *Korea* 6, no. 3 (2010): 44–48.

Jeong, Kelly Y. *Crisis of Gender and the Nation in Korean Literature and Cinema: Modernity Arrives Again.* Lanham, MD: Lexington Books, 2011.

Jo-Han, Hye-jeong, and Wu-yong Yi, eds. *T'alpuntan sitaerŭl yŏlmyŏ namkwapuk, munhwa kongchonŭl wihan mosaek* [Opening an era beyond division: Toward cultural cohabitation between the South and the North]. Seoul: Samin, 2000.

Jones, Andrew F. *Yellow Music: Media Culture and Colonial Modernity in the Chinese Jazz Age.* Durham, NC: Duke University Press, 2001.

Jung, Eun-Young. "Articulating Korean Youth Culture through Global Popular Music Styles: Seo Taiji's Use of Rap and Metal." In *Korean Pop Music: Riding the Korean Wave,* edited by Keith Howard, 109–22. Folkestone, UK: Global Oriental, 2006.

———. "Playing the Race and Sexuality Cards in the Transnational Pop Game: Korean Music Videos for the U.S. Market." *Journal of Popular Music* 22, no. 2 (2010): 219–36.

———. "Transnational Korea: A Critical Assessment of the Korean Wave in Asia and the United States." *Southeast Review of Asian Studies* 31 (2002): 69–80.

Jung, Sun. *Korean Masculinities and Transcultural Consumption: Yonsama, Rain, Oldboy, K-pop Idols.* Hong Kong: Hong Kong University Press, 2010.

KAA (Korea Advertisers Association [Hanguk Kwang'go Chuhyŏphoe]). *Naega choaha nŭn kwango: sobija ga ppopŭn pesŭt'ŭ kwang'go* [Advertising That I Like: The Best Advertisements Chosen by Consumers]. Seoul: Sodam, 1992.

Kamata, Tadayoshi. *Nisshōki to Marason: Berurin Orinpikku no Son Gijyon* [The flag of the rising sun and marathon: Berlin Olympics and Sohn Kee-chung]. Tokyo: Ushio Shuppansha, 1984.

Kang, Chun-man. *Han'guk hyŏndaesa sanch'aek: 1950 yŏndae p'yŏn* [A stroll through modern Korean history: The 1950s], vol. 1. Seoul: Inmul kwa sasang, 2004.

Kang, Hildi. *Under the Black Umbrella: Voices from Colonial Korea*. Ithaca, NY: Cornell University Press, 2005.

Kang, Kyŏng-nok. *"Han aidol 'Ilyŏldo chŏmryŏng,' ilbon chot'ohwashikida."* [Korean idols invade Japanese archipelago, and knocks out Japan]. *Ashia Kyŏngje* [Asia Economy], August 26, 2010.

Kang, Laura Hyun Yi. *Compositional Subjects: Enfiguring Asian/American Women*. Durham, NC: Duke University Press, 2002.

Kang, Sŏng-ryul. *Ch'inil yŏnghwa* [Pro-Japanese films]. Seoul: Rokŭ Media, 2006.

Kant, Immanuel. *The Critique of Judgment*. Translated by Werner S. Pluhar. Indianapolis: Hackett, 1987.

———. *The Critique of Practical Reason*. Translated by Werner S. Pluhar. Indianapolis: Hackett, 2002.

Khagram, Sanjeev, and Peggy Levitt, eds. *The Transnational Studies Reader: Intersections and Innovations*. London: Routledge, 2008.

Khang, Young-Ho, and Sung-Cheol Yun. "Trends in General and Abdominal Obesity among Korean Adults: Findings from 1998, 2001, 2005, and 2007." *Journal of Korean Medical Science* 25, no. 11 (2010): 1582–88.

Kim, Chin-song. *Sŏul e ttansŭhol ŭl hŏhara* [Grant Dance Halls a Permit in Seoul]. Seoul: Hyŏnsil munhwa yŏn'gu, 1999.

Kim, Chip'yŏng. *Han'guk kayo chŏngshinsa* [A spiritual history of Korean songs]. Seoul: Arŭm ch'ulp'ansa, 2000.

Kim, Chŏnghun, "Ku-ŭmbanpŏp sajŏnshimŭi chohang, hŏnjae wihŏn kyŏljŏng" [Court rules the defunct Music Record Law's aspect of preproduction censorship unconstitutional]. *Tonga ilbo* (Tonga daily), November 1, 1996, 39.

Kim, Do Kyun, and Min-Sun Kim, eds. *Hallyu: Influence of Korean Popular Culture in Asia and Beyond*. Seoul: Seoul National University Press, 2011.

Kim, Gyewon. "Unpacking the Archive: Ichthyology, Photography, and the Archival Record in Japan and Korea." In *positions: east asia cultures critique* 18, no. 1 (2010): 51–88.

Kim, Hong-tack. "Characteristics, History, and Forecasts of Creativity in Korea." In *Korean Advertising: Facts and Insights*, 218–74. Seoul: Korea Broadcast Advertising Corporation (KOBACO), 2007.

Kim, Hoon-Soon. "Korean Music Videos, Postmodernism, and Gender Politics." In *Feminist Cultural Politics in Korea*, edited by Oh jung-hwa, 195–227. Seoul: Prunsasang Publishing, 2005.

Kim, Hoyŏn. *"Chosŏn Kŭndae Akkŭk Yŏn'gu"* [A study of music drama during the modernization period of Chosŏn]. *Tongyanghak* 32 (2002): 55–69.

Kim, Hyegyŏng. *"Noraebang-ŭi shilt'ae-wa yŏga sŏnyong-e kwanhan yŏn'gu"* [A study of the state of noraebang and the use of people's spare time]. *Ŭmak-kwa minjok* [Music and the people] 10 (1995): 286–304.

Kim, Hyŏn-ju. *"1950 nyŏn-dae yŏsŏng chabji <Yŏwŏn> kwa 'chedo rosŏ ŭi chubu ŭi t'ansaeng"* [The women's magazine Yŏwŏn and the birth of the "housewife as institution"]. *Taejung Sŏsa Yŏn'gu*, no. 18 (December 2007): 387–416.

Kim, Hyŏnsŏp. *Sŏ T'aeji tamnon* [Discourses on Seo Taiji]: *Seotaiji Syndrome*. Seoul: Ch'aeg-i innŭn maŭl, 2001.

Kim, Hyun-cheol. "Campaign Starts to Globalize Korean Food." *Korea Times*, October 16, 2008.

Kim, Hyun Mee. "Feminization of the 2002 World Cup and Women's Fandom." In *The Inter-Asia Cultural Studies Reader*, edited by Kuan-Hsing Chen and Huat Chua Beng, 539–49. London: Routledge, 2007.

Kim, Jong Il. *On the Art of the Cinema*. Pyongyang: Foreign Languages Publishing House, 1989.

Kim, Ki-jin. "*Kwannŭngchŏk kwangye ŭi yullijŏk ŭiŭi: yŏnae munje sogo*" [The ethical meaning of sensual relations: A brief treatise on *yŏnae*]. In *Chosŏn munsa ŭi yŏnaegwan* [Perspectives on Love of Chosŏn (Korean) Literary Figures], 16. Seoul: Sŏrhwasŏgwan, 1926.

Kim, Kwangmi Ko. "Advertising in Korea: International Challenges and Politics." In *Advertising in Asia: Communication, Culture, and Consumption*, edited by Katherine Toland Frith, 125–53. Ames: Iowa State University Press, 1996.

Kim, Kyŏng-jae. "*Yangdae chaebŏl-ŭi chep'aejŏn chŏnmo*" [The whole story of the struggle for supremacy between the two corporations]. *Samch'ŏlli*, July 1935.

Kim, Kyu-Cheul. *Sainggak innŭn Kwanggo Iyagi*. Seoul: Epublic Korea, 2006.

Kim, Kyung Hyun. "The Fractured Cinema of North Korea: Discourses on the Nation in *Sea of Blood*." In *In Pursuit of Contemporary East Asian Culture*, edited by Xiaobing Tang and Stephen Snyder. Boulder, CO: Westview Press, 1996.

———. "Mea Culpa: Reading the North Korean as an Ethnic Other." In *Virtual Hallyu: Korean Cinema of the Global Era*, 101–22. Durham, NC: Duke University Press, 2011.

———. *The Remasculinization of Korean Cinema*. Durham, NC: Duke University Press, 2004.

Kim, Minjeong, and Sharron Lennon. "Content Analysis of Diet Advertisements: A Cross-National Comparison of Korean and U.S. Women's Magazines." *Clothing and Textiles Research Journal* 24, no. 4 (2006): 345–62.

Kim, Myoung-Hye. "Woman to Be Seen but Not to Be Heard: Representation of Women in the Contemporary Korean Movie *My Wife Is a Gangster*." Paper presented at the Twenty-third Conference of IAMCR, Gender and Communication Section, Barcelona, Spain, July 21–26, 2002.

Kim, Namchŏn. *Kim Namch'ŏn Chŏnjip* [Kim Namch'ŏn complete works]. Seoul: Pagijŏng, 2000.

Kim, Pong-hyŏn. "'*Sekshihan' sonyŏ shidae choahanŭn ke choeingayo?*" *Pressian*, February 4, 2010. Accessed March 27, 2011. http://www.pressian.com/article/article.asp?article_num=60100203164550&section=04.

Kim, Renee B. "Meeting Consumer Concerns for Food Safety in South Korea: The Importance of Food Safety and Ethics in a Globalizing Market." *Journal of Agricultural and Environmental Ethics* 22, no. 2 (2009): 141–52.

Kim, Ryŏ-sil. *T'usa hanŭn cheguk t'uyŏng hanŭn sigminji* [Projected empire, reflected colony]. Seoul: Samin, 2006.

Kim, Seung-Kuk. "Changing Lifestyles and Consumption Patterns of the South

Korean Middle Class and New Generations." In *Consumption in Asia: Lifestyles and Identities*, edited by Chua Beng Huat, 61–81. New York: Routledge, 2000.

Kim, Si-sŭp. *Novella of Kŭmo [Kŭmoshinhwa]*. Translated by Yi Jae-ho. Seoul: Kwahaksa, 1980.

Kim, So-hŭi, and Yi Ki-rim. "Korean Cinema in Retrospect, Sin Sang-ok" ["Han'guk yŏnghwa hoegorok Sin Sang-ok"]. *Cine 21* (July and August 2003).

Kim, Sŏng-jin. *"Pukhan yesul ŭi sŏsa kujo ilgo: yŏnghwa, hyŏngmyŏng kagŭk, sosŏl 'kkot p'anŭn ch'ŏnyŏ' rŭl chungsim ŭro"* [Reading the Narrative Structure in North Korean Art: Focusing on the Film, Revolutionary Opera, and Novel *The Flower Girl*]." *Hyŏndae munhak iron yŏngu* [Study of Theory of Modern Literature] 25 (2005): 135–59.

Kim, Soo-ah. *"Sonyŏ imiji ŭi polgŏrihwa wa sobi pangshik ŭi kusŏng: sonyŏ kŭrup ŭi samch'on p'aen tamnon kusŏng"* [The visual attraction of girl image and the formation of consumerist pattern: the discourse formation of uncle fandom for girl groups]. *Midiŏ, chendŏ wa munhwa* [Media, Gender and Culture] 15 (2010): 79–119.

Kim, So-yŏn, ed. *Maehok kwa hondon ŭi sidae: 1950-nyŏndae han'guk yŏnghwa* [An age of allures and chaos: Korean cinema of the 1950s]. Seoul: Sodo, 2003.

Kim, Sowol, "Azaleas." In *The Columbia Anthology of Modern Korean Poetry*, translated by David R. McCann. New York: Columbia University Press, 2004.

Kim, Soyoung. "Cartography of Catastrophe: Pre-Colonial Surveys, Post-Colonial Vampires, and the Plight of Korean Modernity." *Journal of Korean Studies* 16, no. 2 (fall 2011): 285–301.

———. "'Cine-Mania' or Cinephilia: Film Festivals and the Identity Question." In *New Korean Cinema*, edited by Chi-Yun Shin and Julian Stringer, 79–94. Edinburgh: Edinburgh University Press, 2005.

———. "Do Not Include Me in Your 'Us': Peppermint Candy and the Politics of Difference." *Korea Journal* 46, no. 1 (2006): 60–83.

Kim, Sunah. *"Yŏnghwa kukka mandŭlgi: 'yŏnghwa yesullon' ŭl t'ong hae pon sahoejuŭi yŏnghwa mihak e taehan koch'al"* [Making the cinematic state: Observations on socialist film, through "On the art of the cinema"]. In *Chuch'e ŭi hwanyŏng: pukhan munye iron e taehan pip'an-jŏk ihae* [The specter of Juche: A critical understanding of North Korean theories of art], edited by Dankook taehakgyo pusŏl hanguk munhwa kisul yŏnguso [Korean Cultural Depiction Research Center of Dankook University], 71–106. Seoul: Tosŏ Ch'ulp'an Kyŏngjin, 2011.

Kim, Su-yong. *Na ŭi sarang ssinema* [Cinema, my love]. Seoul: Cine21, 2005.

Kim, Tae-jong. "Can Nintendo Succeed in Online Heaven?" *Korea Times*, January 9, 2007.

Kim, Tong-in. "Chukŭmki" [Phonogragh]. *Kim Tong-in chŏnjip*, vol. 1, 176. Seoul: Chosŏnilbosa, 1987.

Kim, Wŏnju. "To Avoid Lust" [*Aeyogŭlpiharyŏ*]. *Samch'ŏll,i*, 1932, 4.

Kim, Yea-rim. "Globalization of Korean Food for Good Health of People Across the World." *Korea IT Times*, December 31, 2010.

Kim, Yi-rang. *Hanguk manhwa ŭi mohŏmga-dŭl*. Seoul: Yŏlhwadang, 1996.

Kim, Yŏng-hui. *"Ilchae sidae Ladio ŭi Ch'ulhyŏng wa Ch'ŏngch'ŭijaŏ"* [Radio and radio listeners during the Japanese colony]. *Han'guk ŏnron hakbo* 46, no. 2 (2002): 150–83.

Kim, Yoo-Sun. *Working Korea 2007*. Seoul: Korea Labor and Society Institute, 2008.

Kim, Yun-ji. "Kim Jŏng-il ŭi 'Yonghwa yesullon' kwa pukhan yŏnghwa: 1973nyŏn put'ŏ 1980nyŏn kkaji chejak toen pukhan yŏnghwa rŭl chungsim ŭro" [Kim Jong Il's 'On the Art of Cinema' and North Korean Film: Focusing on North Korean Films from 1973 to 1980]." *Sinema* 2 (2006): 31–65.

Kipnis, Laura. "Towards a Left Popular Culture." In *High Theory/Low Culture*, edited by Colin McCabe, 21. Manchester, UK: Manchester University Press, 1986.

Ko, Kilsŏp. *"386 sedae-ŭi 'kŭnal': chuch'e hyŏngsŏng, sedae chŏngshin, kŭrigo sam-gwa chŏngch'i"* [The days of the 386 generation: the formation of autonomy, the spirit of the generation as well as its lives and politics]. *Munhwa kwahak* [Culture science] 62 (June 2010): 113–35.

Ko, Woo-young. *Kurŭm sogŭi ai*. Seoul: Chaŭm Gwa Moŭm, 2007.

———. *Samgukchi*. 10 vols. Restored edition. Seoul: Aenibuksŭ, 2007.

———. *Taeyamang*. 5 vols. Uncensored and complete edition. Puch'ŏn: Hanguk Yŏngsang Manhwa Chinhŭngwŏn, C & C Revolutions [*Ssi aen ssi rebolusyŏn*], 2010. Koga Masao Music Museum, accessed April 25, 2011. http://www.koga.or.jp/about/index .html.

Korea Advertisers Association, *Naega Choahanŭn Kwanggo: Sobija ga Ppopŭn Pesŭt'ŭ Kwang'go*. Seoul: Sodam, 1992.

KoreaBoo. "Seohyeon's health report reveals she is 9kg underweight." February 6, 2011. Accessed March 27, 2011. http://www.koreaboo.com/index.html/_/general /seohyuns-health-report-reveals-she-is-9kg-r3326.

Korea Food Service Information Co. Ltd. *Han'guk oesik yon'gam*. Seoul: Han'guk oesik chŏngbo, 2009.

Korean Film Art. Pyongyang: Korean Film Export and Import Corporation, 1985.

Korean Motion Picture Promotion Corporation (KMPPC). *Scenario Collection. Vol. 2: 1956–1960 (Han'guk sinario sŏnjip che 2kwŏn: 1956–1960)*. Seoul: Jimmundang, 1982.

"'Kŏri ŭi kkoekkoriŭ'in Siptae kasu rŭl naebonaen chakkok, chaksaja ŭi kosimgi" (Interviews with songwriters who produced top 10 singers, singing-birds on the street). *Samchŏlli*, November 1935.

Kristeva, Julia. *Powers of Horror*. Translated by Leon S. Roudiez. New York: Columbia University Press, 1982.

Ku, Pong-jun. *"Hŏ Yŏng-man 't'ajja' 'sikkaek' wŏngo manhwa pangmulgwan e kijŭng haeyo"* [Hŏ Yŏng-man's original manuscripts, 't'ajja' and 'sikkaek,' are being donated to the Museum of Comics]. *The Hangyore*, April 20, 2011.

"Kŭkchang mandam" [Theater critic]. *Pyŏlgŏn'gŏn*, March 1927.

Kwanggo Yŏngam 2008 [Advertising Yearbook 2008]. Seoul: Cheil kihwek, 2008.

Kwŏn, Podŭrae (Kwon, Boduerae). *Yŏnae ŭi sidae: 1920-yŏndae ch'oban ŭi munhwa wa yuhaeng* [Age of dating: Culture and trends of the early 1920s]. Seoul: Hyŏnsil munhwa yŏngu, 2003.

———. *Après-girl Reads Sasang'gye [Ap'ŭregŏl sasang'gyerŭl iltt'a]*. Seoul: Tong'guk tae-hak'kyo ch'ulp'anbu, 2009.

Lee, Hyangjin. *Contemporary Korean Cinema: Identity, Culture, Politics*. Manchester, UK: Manchester University Press, 2000.

Lee, Hyo-sik. "Downturn Takes Toll on Women Workers." *Korea Times*, July 6, 2009.

Accessed March 27, 2011. http://www.koreatimes.co.kr/www/news/biz/2009/07/123_48021.html.

Lee, Jin-kyung. *Service Economies: Militarism, Sex Work, and Migrant Labor in South Korea*. Minneapolis: University of Minnesota Press, 2010.

Lee, Kee-hyeung. "Looking Back at the Cultural Politics of Youth Culture in South Korea in the 1990s: On the 'New Generation' Phenomenon and the Emergence of Cultural Studies." *Korean Journal of Communication Studies* 15, no. 4 (November 2007): 47–79.

———. "Speak Memory! Morae Sigye and the Politics of Social Melodrama in Contemporary South Korea." *Cultural Studies* ⇔ *Critical Methodologies* 4, no. 4 (2004): 526–39.

Lee, So-hee. "The Concept of Female Sexuality in Korean Popular Culture." In *Under Construction: The Gendering of Modernity, Class, and Consumption in the Republic of Korea*, edited by Laurel Kendall, 141–64. Honolulu: University of Hawai'i Press, 2002.

Leiss, William, Stephen Kline, Sut Jhally, and Jacqueline Botterill. *Social Communication in Advertising: Consumption in the Mediated Marketplace*. 3rd ed. New York: Routledge, 2005.

"Lekodŭ ŭi Yŏlgwang sidae" [Craze over records]. *Pyŏlgŏn'gŏn*, October/November 1933.

Lew, Young Ick. "Dynastic Disarray and National Peril." In *Korean Old and New: A History*, edited by Carter J. Eckert et al., 178–98. Seoul: Ilchokak, 1990.

Lewis, Lisa A. *Gender Politics and MTV: Voicing the Difference*. Philadelphia: Temple University Press, 1990.

Lewis, Peter. "Broadband Wonderland." *Fortune*, September 20, 2004.

Lim, Bomi. "S. Korea Renews Propaganda with Pop Song, Eating Advice." *Bloomberg*, May 24, 2010. Accessed March 27, 2011. http://www.bloomberg.com/news/2010-05-24/south-korean-song-blasted-into-north-as-propaganda-war-revived-on-sinking.html.

Lin, Yu-Shan, and Jun-Ying Huang. "Analyzing the Use of TV Miniseries for Korea Tourism Marketing." *Journal of Travel & Tourism Marketing* 24, no. 2 (2008): 22–27.

Lukács, Gabriella. *Scripted Affects, Branded Selves: Television, Subjectivity, and Capitalism in 1990s Japan*. Durham, NC: Duke University Press, 2010.

Macintyre, Donald. "Wired for Life." *Time*, December 4, 2000. Accessed April 1, 2011. http://www.time.com/time/world/article/0,8599,2040463-1,00.html.

Magnier, Mark. "'PC Bang' Helps Koreans Embrace Net." *Los Angeles Times*, July 21, 2000.

Maliangkay, Roald. "Pop for Progress: South Korea's Propaganda Songs." In *Korean Pop Music: Riding the Korean Wave*, edited by Keith Howard, 48–61. Folkestone, UK: Global Oriental, 2006.

Mankekar, Purnima. "Brides Who Travel: Gender, Transnationalism, and Nationalism in Hindi Film." *positions: east asia cultures critique* 7 (1999): 731–61.

Mann, Michael. *Incoherent Empire*. London: Verso, 2005.

Manuel, Peter. "Popular Music II. World Popular Music." In *The Grove Dictionary of Music and Musicians*. 2nd ed. New York: Macmillan, 2001.

Marshall, P. David. *Celebrity and Power: Fame in Contemporary Culture*. Minneapolis: University of Minnesota Press, 1997.

McCabe, Colin, ed. *High Theory/Low Culture: Analyzing Popular Television and Film*. Manchester, UK: Manchester University Press, 1986.

McGrath, Jason. "Communists Have More Fun! The Dialectics of Fulfillment in Cinema of the People's Republic of China." *World Picture* 3 (2009). Accessed August 20, 2011. http://www.worldpicturejournal.com/WP_3/McGrath.html.

Mha, Joung-Mee (Ma Chŭng-mi). *Kwanggo ro ing'nŭn Hanguk Sahoe munhwa sa* [Korea's Social-Cultural History Read Through Advertising], *Hanguk Sahoe munhwa sa* [Korea's Social-Cultural History]. Seoul: Kaema kowon, 2004.

Miller, Jamie. "Soviet Cinema, 1929–1941: The Development of Industry and Infrastructure." *Europe-Asia Studies* 58, no. 1 (2006): 103–24.

Miller, Laura. "Youth Fashion and Changing Beautification Practices." In *Modern Japanese Culture*, vol. 2, edited by D. P. Martinez, 88–103. London: Routledge, 2007.

Miller, Toby. *Sportsex*. Philadelphia: Temple University Press, 2002.

Min, Kyŏngch'an. *"Sŏyangŭmakŭi Suyonggwa Ŭmakkyoyuk"* [Consumption and Education of the Western Music]. *Ŭmakhak* 9 (2002): 15–36.

Min, Pyŏng-uk. "Research on North Korean Art Films of the Period of Kim Jong Il's Political System" [*Kim Jŏng-il ch'ejegi pukhan yesul yŏnghwa yŏngu*]. *Kongyŏn munhwa yŏngu* 13 (2006): 153–90.

"Ministry Launches Specialized Korean Cuisine Foundation." *Korea Herald*, March 29, 2010.

Ministry of Gender Equality and Family (South Korea). *"Haksupkwŏn poho mihup tung ch'ŏngsonyŏn yŏnyein kibongwŏn ch'imhae shimgak."* Accessed March 27, 2011. http://enews.moge.go.kr/view/board/bbs/view.jsp?topMenuId=NEWS&topMenuName=%B4%BA%BD%BA%B8%B6%B4%E7&subMenuId=1&subMenuName=%C1%A4%C3%A5%B.C.%D3%BA%B8&boardMngNo=1&boardNo=1545.

Mintz, Sidney W. "Eating Communities: The Mixed Appeals of Sodality." In *Eating Culture: The Poetics and Politics of Food Today*, edited by T. Döring, M. Heide, and S. Mühleisen, 19–34. Heidelberg: Universitätsverlag, 2003.

Moksŏng [Pang Chŏng-hwan]. *"Kŭnalpam"* [That night]. Serialized in *Kaebyŏk*, December 1920, 127–39; January 1921, 151–60; February 1921, 133–40.

Moon, Okpyo. "Food and Food Consumption as Cultural Practices: Lifestyle Changes in Contemporary Korea?" *Korea Journal* 50, no. 1 (2010): 5–11.

Morris, Martin. "Interpretability and Social Power, or Why Postmodern Advertising Works." *Media, Culture & Society* 27, no. 5 (2005): 697–718.

Moskin, Julia. "Culinary Diplomacy with a Side of Kimchi." *New York Times*, September 22, 2009.

Mulvey, Laura. *Visual and Other Pleasures*. Bloomington: Indiana University Press, 1989.

Mun, Okpae. *Han'guk kŭmjigog-ŭi sahoe sa* [A social history of censored Korean music]. Seoul: Yesol, 2004.

Murcott, Anne. "Food as an Expression of Identity." In *The Future of the Nation State: Essays on Cultural Pluralism and Political Integration*, edited by S. Gustavsson and L. Lewin, 49–77. London: Routledge, 1996.

Murray, E. V. "Thailand—The Kitchen of the World: Origin and Growth of the Thai Food Industry and Lessons for India." *Cab Calling* (June–April 2007): 16–26.

Myers, Scott M., and Phillip Vannini. "Crazy about You: Reflections on the Meanings of Contemporary Teen Pop Music." *Electronic Journal of Sociology* (2002). Accessed March 27, 2011. http://www.sociology.org/content/vo1006.002/vannini_myers .html.

Nam, Chi-ŭn. "Mommaeman poinŭn kŏl kŭrup 'kwayŏl' shidae." *The Hankyoreh*, August 30, 2010. Accessed March 27, 2011. http://www.hani.co.kr/arti/culture /entertainment/437420.htmlhttp://www.hani.co.kr/arti/culture/entertainment /437420.html.

———. *"Taejungt'ujaeng kwa ch'angjo-jŏk silch'ŏn ŭi munje"* [The debates on popularization and the problem of creative practice]. In *Kim Namch'ŏn Chŏnjip* 1 [Kim Namch'ŏn complete works, vol. 1], 840–51. Seoul: Pagijŏng, 2000.

Negus, Keith. *Popular Music in Theory: An Introduction.* Cambridge: Polity Press, 1996.

Nelson, Laura C. *Measured Excess: Status, Gender, and Consumer Nationalism in South Korea.* New York: Columbia University Press, 2000.

———. "South Korean Consumer Nationalism: Women, Children, Credit, and Other Perils." In *The Ambivalent Consumer: Questioning Consumption in East Asia and the West*, edited by S. Garon and P. L. MacIachlan, 188–207. Ithaca, NY: Cornell University Press, 2006.

Netvalue. "Who's Winning the Asian Online Gaming War?" *ZDNet.* Accessed April 23, 2001. http://www.zdnetasia.com/whos-winning-the-asian-online-gaming-war _p3-21198772.htm.

NTD Television. "Cosmetic Surgery for Young Jobseekers on the Rise in South Korea." Accessed June 30, 2011. http://www.youtube.com/watch?v=QovjzfdDx7c.

Nye, Joseph S., Jr. "Soft Power." *Foreign Policy* 80 (fall 2006): 153–71.

Ong, Aihwa. 1999. *Flexible Citizenship: The Cultural Logics of Transnationality.* Durham, NC: Duke University Press.

———. *Spirits of Resistance and Capitalist Discipline: Factory Women in Malaysia.* Albany: State University of New York Press, 1987.

Osetrova, Maria. "Our Food Is Our Treasure: Representation of National Food Tradition in Contemporary Korean Popular Culture (Focusing on *Sikkaek* Series)." Paper presented at the Twenty-fifth Biennial Conference of the Association of Korean Studies in Europe, Moscow, June 17–20, 2011.

Pae, Yŏnhyŏng. *"K'olumbia Lekodŭ ŭi Han'guk ŭmban Yŏn'gu (1)"* [A study of Korean Columbia Records (1)]. *Han'gukŭmbanhak* 5 (1995): 37–61.

Pak, Ch'anho. *Han'guk kayosa* [History of Korean popular song]. Seoul: Hyŏnamsa, 1992.

Pak, Ch'an-kyŏng. *"Yŏnghwa wa setu sai"* [Between cinema and movie set]. Unpublished manuscript, 2005.

Pak, Chunhŭm. *I ttang-esŏ ŭmag-ŭl handa nŭn kŏs-ŭn* [Saying you play music in this world]. Seoul: Kyobo mun'go, 1999.

Pak, Hye-ran. *"Maŭm ŭl' mujang haeje sik'i nŭn kibun choŭm"* [The one that pleases to the point of completely relaxing the mind]. *Kwanggo Chŏngbo* [Advertisement Information], no. 11 (2005): 10–13.

Pak, In-ha, and Kim Nak-ho. *Hanguk hyŏndae manhwasa* [A History of Modern Korean Manhwa]. Seoul: Doobo, 2009.

Pak, Ki-dang. *Pak Ki-dang sŏnjip: Hanguk manhwa gŏljaksŏn* [Pak Ki-dang Collection: the Best of Korean Comics], vol. 7. Puch'ŏn: Puch'ŏn Manhwa Jŏngbo Sentŏ, 2008.

Pak, Ki-jŏng, *Hanguk manhwa yasa*. Puch'ŏn: Puch'ŏn Manhwa Chŏngbo Sentŏ, 2008.

———. *Tojŏnja*. 5 vols. Restored edition. Seoul: Pada Ch'ulp'ansa, 2005.

Pak, Myŏng-jin. "The Possibility of Film Art Contributing to a Rapprochement Between North and South Korea" [*Nam bukhan chŏpkŭn e issŏsŏ yŏnghwa yesul ŭi kiyŏ kanŭngsŏng*]. *Tonga yŏngu* 19 (1989): 197–209.

Pak, Myŏng-rim. *1950 nyŏndae nambuk'han ŭi sŏnt'aek'kwa kuljŏl* [Choices and distortions of South and North Korea in the 1950s]. Series edited by Yŏksa munje yŏn'guso. Seoul: Yŏksa pip'yŏngsa, 1998.

Pak, Sŏk-hwan. "*Asp'alt'ŭ kŭ sanai nŭn chigŭm ŏdi rŭl talligo itnŭnga.*" [Where is the Asphalt Man running these days?]. In *Hŏ Yŏng-man p'yo manhwa wa hwanho hanŭn kunjung-dŭl* [The Hŏ Yŏng-man-style comics and the enthusiastic masses], edited by Hanguk Manhwa Yŏnguwŏn. Seoul: Kimyŏngsa, 2004.

Palmer, Catherine. "From Theory to Practice: Experiencing the Nation in Everyday Life." *Journal of Material Culture* 3, no. 2 (1998): 175–99.

Park, Aekyŭng. "*Chosŏnhugi Sijowa Chapkaŭi Kyosŏpyangsanggwa Kŭ Yŏnhaengjŏk Kiban*" [The relation of Sijo-Chapka and its basis of performance in the late Chosŏn dynasty]. *Han'gukŏmunhak* 41 (2003): 271–91.

Park, Jin-Kyu. "'English Fever' in South Korea: Its History and Symptoms." *English Today* 97 25, no. 1 (March 2009): 50–57.

Park, Mi. *Democracy and Social Change: A History of South Korean Student Movements, 1980–2000*. Bern: Peter Lang, 2008.

———. "Free Trade Agreements: The Politics of Nationalism in the Anti-Neoliberal Globalization Movement in South Korea." *Globalizations* 6, no. 4 (2009): 451–66.

Park, Sunae, Patricia Campbell Warner, and Thomas K. Fitzgerald. "The Process of Westernization: Adoption of Western-Style Dress by Korean Women, 1945–1962." *Clothing and Textiles Research* 11, no. 39 (1993): 39–47.

Pak, Chi-yŏn. "*Pak Chŏng-hŭi kŭndaehwa ch'eje ŭi yŏnghwa chŏngch'aek: yŏnghwa pŏp kaechŏng kwa kiŏphwa chŏngch'aek chungsimŭro*" [Modernization and film policy under Park Chung-Hee: On the legislation of film law and corporatization]. In *Han'guk yŏnghwa wa kŭndaesŏng* [Korean cinema and modernity], edited by Yu-sin Chu et al., 171–221. Seoul: Sodo, 2000.

Peirce, Charles Sanders. *The Essential Peirce: Selected Philosophical Writings*, vol. 1. Edited by Nathan Houser and Christian Kloesel. Bloomington: Indiana University Press, 1992.

Pemberton, Robert W. "Wild-Gathered Foods as Countercurrents to Dietary Globalisation in South Korea." In *Asian Food: The Global and the Local*, edited by K. J. Cwiertka with B. C. A. Walraven, 76–94. Honolulu: University of Hawai'i Press, 2002.

Poirier, Richard. *The Performing Self: Compositions and Decompositions in the Languages of Contemporary Life*. New York: Oxford University Press, 1971.

Portal, Jane. *Art Under Control in North Korea*. London: Reaktion, 2005.

"Promoting Kimchi, Other Korean Food in Costa Rica." *Korea Joongang Daily*, October 13, 2009.

Puzar, Aljosa. "Asian Dolls and the Western Gaze: Notes on the Female Dollification in South Korea." *Asian Women* 27, no. 2 (2011): 81–111.

Ramachandran, Arjun. "Tech Capitals of the World." *Sydney Morning Herald*, September 13, 2007.

Ramsted, Evan. "YouTube Helps South Korean Band Branch Out." *Wall Street Journal*, January 14, 2011.

Record Industry Association of Korea (RIAK). *Ŭmban shijang kyumo* [Record market size] 1995–2002. Online report, 2003.

Richardson, Jeanita W., and Kim A. Scott. "Rap Music and Its Violent Progeny: America's Culture of Violence in Context." *Journal of Negro Education* 71, no. 3 (summer 2002): 175–92.

Robinson, Michael. "Broadcasting in Korea, 1924–1937: Colonial Modernity and Cultural Hegemony." In *Japan's Competing Modernities*, edited by Sharon A. Minichiello, 358–78. Honolulu: University of Hawai'i Press, 1998.

Roh, Jiseon. "One Out of 2.5 Students Has an Electronic Dictionary." *Asia Economy*, July 20, 2006. Accessed June 15, 2011. http://www.asiaeconomy.co.kr/uhtml/read .php?idxno=2006072014272044158.

Rousso, Henry. *The Vichy Syndrome: History and Memory in France Since 1944*. Cambridge, MA: Harvard University Press, 1994.

Ryang, Sonia. "Biopolitics or the Logic of Sovereign Love—Love's Whereabouts in North Korea." In *North Korea: Toward a Better Understanding*, edited by Sonia Ryang, 57–84. Lanham, MD: Lexington Books, 2009.

Sakamoto, Rumi, and Matthew Allen. "There's Something Fishy about That Sushi: How Japan Interprets the Global Sushi Boom." *Japan Forum* 23, no. 1 (2011): 99–121.

Schiesel, Seth. "The Land of the Video Geek." *New York Times*, October 8, 2006.

Schmitt, Carl. *Theory of the Partisan: Intermediate Commentary on the Concept of the Political*. Translated by G. L. Ulmen. New York: Telos Press, 2007.

Schudson, Michael. *Advertising, the Uneasy Persuasion: Its Dubious Impact on American Society*. New York: Basic Books, 1984.

Scott, Clive. *Street Photography: From Atget to Cartier-Bresson*. London: I. B. Tauris, 2007.

Sen, Amartya. *Development as Freedom*. New York: Anchor Books, 1999.

Seo, Dong-cheol. "Korean Cuisine Makes Waves." *Korea: People and Culture* 6, no. 3 (2010): 4–11.

"Seohyeon's Health Report Reveals She Is 9kg Underweight." *koreaboo*, February 6, 2011. Accessed March 27, 2011. http://www.koreaboo.com/index.html/_/general /seohyuns-health-report-reveals-she-is-9kg-r3326.

Seoul City. "Seoul Population Census." Accessed March 28, 2011. http://www.seoul .go.kr/v2007/publicinfo/statistics/data/4_04_05.html.

Shameen, Assif. "Starting with a Baang: Korea's PC Rooms Have a View on the Future." *Asia Week*, September 1, 2000.

Shih, Shu-mei. *Visuality and Identity: Sinophone Articulations Across the Pacific*. Berkeley: University of California Press, 2007.

Shin, Eui Hang, and Edward Adam Nam. "Culture, Gender Roles, and Sport: The Case of Korean Players on the LPGA Tour." *Journal of Sport and Social Issues* 28, no. 3 (2004): 223–44.

Shin, Gi-wook. *Ethnic Nationalism in Korea: Genealogy, Politics and Legacy.* Palo Alto, CA: Stanford University Press, 2006.

Shin, Gi-wook, and Michael Robinson, eds. *Colonial Modernity in Korea.* Cambridge, MA: Harvard University Asia Center, 1999.

Shin, Hyesŭng. *"1945nyŏn Ijŏn t'ŭrot'ŭ kayo ŭi sŏnyul yŏhyŏng"* [The melody types of Korean popular songs before 1945]. *Inmun'gwahak* [Journal of the humanities] 31 (2001): 293–322.

Shin, Hyun-joon. *"K-pop ŭi munhwajŏngch'ihak."* *ŏllon kwa sahoe* 13, no. 3 (2005): 7–36.

———. "The Success of Hopelessness and Imagined Places: Transformation of the South Korean Indie Music Scene in the 2000s." *Perfect Beat* 12 (2011): 129–46.

Shin, In Sup (Sin In-sŭp). *"Kwangbok ihu."* In *Hanguk Kwanggo 100nŏn.* Seoul: Korea Federation of Advertising Associations, 1996.

———. *"Kwanggo ŭi Ponjil ŭi taehan Pip'ŏn Pang'ŏ."* *Daehong po* 100, no. 9 (1992): 40–43.

Shin, In Sup (Sin In-sŭp), and Sŏ Pŏm-sŏk. *Hanguk Kwanggo sa.* 3rd ed. Seoul: Nanam, 2011.

Shin, Joong Hyun. *Shin Joong Hyun Rock.* Seoul: Tana Kihoek, 1999.

Silverman, Kaja. "Fragments of a Fashionable Discourse." In *On Fashion*, edited by Shari Benstock and Suzanne Ferriss, 183–96. New Brunswick, NJ: Rutgers University Press, 1994.

Simkin, Mark. "Korean Education: An Unhealthy Obsession." Transcript. Australian Broadcasting Company (ABC), Local Radio, "AM." March 29, 2005. http://www.abc .net.au/am/content/2005/s1333165.htm.

Sin, Sang-ok. Interview by Yi Ki-rim. In *Han'guk yŏnghwa hoegorok: Sin Sang-ok 15* [Korean Cinema in Retrospect: Sin Sang-ok, 15], *Cine 21*, September 19, 2003.

Sirijit, Sunanta. "The Globalization of Thai Cuisine." Paper presented at the Canadian Council for Southeast Asian Studies Conference, York University, Toronto, October 14–16, 2010.

Slane, Andrea. *A Not So Foreign Affair: Fascism, Sexuality, and the Cultural Rhetoric.* Durham, NC: Duke University Press, 2001.

Smith, Parker. "Computing in Japan: From Cocoon to Competition." *Computer* 30, no. 3 (1997): 26–33.

Sŏ, Ch'an-hwi. *"Mangaji kkumŭl kkunŭn chakka Manmong Kim San-ho,"* July 31, 2009. http://navercast.naver.com/korean/cartoonist/862.

Son, Min-jung. *Politics of T'ŭrot'ŭ [T'ŭrot'ŭ ŭi chŏngch'ihak].* P'aju, Korea: 2009.

Son, Sang-ik. *Hanguk manhwasa sanch'aek.* P'aju: Sallim Ch'ulp'ansa, 2005.

Sŏn, Sŏngwŏn. *Taejung ŭmag-ŭi ppuri* [The roots of Korean popular music]. Seoul: Tosŏ ch'ulp'an kkun, 1996.

———. *Rog-esŏ indiŭmag-ŭro* [From rock to indie music]. Koyang: Arŭm ch'ulp'ansa, 1999.

Song, Jesook. *South Korea in the Debt Crisis: The Creation of a Neoliberal Welfare Society.* Durham, NC: Duke University Press, 2009.

Sontag, Susan. "Fascinating Fascism," in *Movies and Methods*, vol. 1, edited by Bill Nichols, 31–43. Berkeley: University of California Press, 2009.

"South Korea Drops to 68th in Women's Rights." *The Hankyoreh*, March 10, 2009. Accessed March 27, 2011. http://english.hani.co.kr/arti/english_edition /e_international/343215.html.

Springer, Chris. *Pyongyang: The Hidden History of the North Korean Capital*. Budapest: Entente Bt., 2003.

Squee. "Fanlore." Accessed August 20, 2011. http://fanlore.org/wiki/Squee.

Stacey, Jackie. *Star-gazing: Hollywood Cinema and Female Spectatorship*. New York: Routledge, 1994.

Stavrakakis, Yannis. "Objects of Consumption, Causes of Desire: Consumerism and Advertising in Societies of Commanded Enjoyment." *Gamma* 14 (2006): 83–106.

Sternberger, Dolf. "Panorama of the Nineteenth Century." *October* 4 (autumn 1977), 3–20.

Sullivan, Rachel E. "Rap and Race: It's Got a Nice Beat, but What about the Message?" *Journal of Black Studies* 33, no. 5 (May 2003): 605–22.

Tamanoi, Mariko Asano, ed. *Crossed Histories: Manchuria in the Age of Empire*. Honolulu: University of Hawai'i Press, 2005.

"T-ara Fans Worried about Hyomin's Weight Loss." *Hellokpop*, January 6, 2011. Accessed March 27, 2011. http://www.hellokpop.com/2011/01/06/t-ara-fans-worried -about-hyomins-weight-loss.

"T-ara's Hyomin Has a Terrible Body?" *allkpop*, May 26, 2010. Accessed March 27, 2011. http://www.allkpop.com/2010/05/t-aras-hyomin-has-a-terrible-body.

Television Without Pity website. Accessed May 30, 2010. http://www.television withoutpity.com.

Terada, Rei. *Feeling in Theory: Emotion After the "Death of the Subject."* Cambridge, MA: Harvard University Press, 2001.

Thunderbolt. "Can You Hear My Boss Protect the New Gisaeng's Heart: Episode 1." Dramabeans.com. August 27, 2011. http://www.dramabeans.com/2011/08/can-you -hear-my-boss-protect-the-new-gisaengs-heart-episode-1/.

"T'ok'ŭi Soriwa Ladioŭi Sori" [Sound of talking pictures and sound of radio]). *Donga ilbo*, November 2, 1933.

Tölöyan, Khachig. "The Nation-State and Its Others: In Lieu of a Preface." *Diaspora: A Journal of Transnational Studies* 1, no. 1 (1991): 3–7.

"Top 5 Hansik News in 2009." *Korea Times*, December 30, 2009.

Treat, John Whittier. "Introduction: Japanese Studies into Cultural Studies," in *Contemporary Japan and Popular Culture*. Honolulu: University of Hawai'i Press, 1996.

Tsai, Eva, and Hyunjoon Shin. "Strumming a Place of One's Own: Gender, Independence, and East Asian Pop/Rock Screen." *Popular Music* 32, no. 1 (January 2013): 7–22.

Turoskaya, Maya. "The 1930s and 1940s: Cinema in Context." In *Stalinism and Soviet Cinema*, edited by Richard Taylor and Derek Spring, 34–53. London: Routledge, 1993.

Vertovec, Steve. *Transnationalism*. London: Routledge, 2009.

Warner, Michael. *Publics and Counterpublics*. New York: Zone Books, 2005.

"What Is the 'Makgeolli Transformer' Exhibition, and Why Is *Makgeolli* Becoming So Popular?" Koreabrand.Net. Accessed May 21, 2012. http://www.koreabrand.net/en /know/know_view.do?CATE_CD=0012&SEQ=321.

"What We Believe: Our Vision." Organization for Transformative Works. Accessed May 30, 2010. http://transformativeworks.org/about/believe.

Willoughby, Heather. "Image Is Everything: The Marketing of Femininity in Korean Pop Music." In *Korean Pop Music: Riding the Wave*, edited by Keith Howard, 99–108. Folkestone, UK: Global Oriental, 2006.

Won, Bin. Quoted in "Won Bin's 'Second Life' with *Mother*." *Korea Times*, May 18, 2009.

Wŏn, Hŭiok. Personal interview by author Min-Jung Son. June 30, 2010.

Yamanaka, Chie. *"Doragon bōru to deatta kankoku."* In *Manga no naka no "tasha,"* edited by Itō Kimio. Tokyo: Rinsen Shoten, 2008.

Yan, Yunxiang. "Of Hamburger and Social Space: Consuming McDonald's in Beijing." In *The Cultural Politics of Food and Eating: A Reader*, edited by J. L. Watson and M. L. Caldwell, 80–103. Malden, UK: Blackwell, 2005.

Yanabu, Akira. *Ai* [Love]. Tokyo: Sanseido, 2001.

Yang, Young-Kyun. *"Jajangmyeon* and *Junggukjip*: The Changing Position and Meaning of Chinese Food and Chinese Restaurants in Korean Society." *Korea Journal* 45, no. 2 (2005): 60–88.

Yano, Christine R. "Inventing Selves: Images and Image-Making in a Japanese Popular Music Genre." *Journal of Popular Culture* 31, no. 2 (1997): 115–29.

———. *Tears of Longing: Nostalgia and the Nation in Japanese Popular Song.* Cambridge, MA: Harvard University Press, 2002.

Yi, Hyesuk, and Son Usŏk. *Han'guk taejung ŭmak sa* [A history of Korean popular music]. Seoul: Ries and Book, 2003.

Yi, Hyo-in, et al. *Study of Korean Film History 1960–1979* [*Han'guk yŏnghwasa kongbu 1960–1979*]. Seoul: KOFA, 2004.

Yi, Kil-Sŏng, et al. *Kim Seung Ho: Face of Father, Portrait of Korean Cinema.* Seoul: Korean Film Archive, 2007.

Yi, Kwang-su. "Kaechŏkja" [Precursor]. In *Yi Kwangsu chŏnjip*, vol. 1. Seoul: Samjungtang, 1963.

Yi, Tongyŏn. *Sŏ T'aeji-nŭn uri-ege muŏshiŏnna* [What might Seo Taiji have meant to us?]. Seoul: Munhwa kwahaksa, 1999.

Yi, Yŏng-il. *Han'guk yŏnghwa chŏnsa* [The complete history of Korean film]. Seoul: Sodo, 2004.

Yi, Yŏng-mi. *Han'guk taejung kayosa* [History of Korean popular songs]. Seoul: Sigongsa, 1998.

Yi, Yŏn-ho. *"Sin Sang-ok: Tangsin ŭn nugusimnikka?"* [Sin Sang-ok: Who are you?]. *Kino* 10 (1997): 120–27.

Yoo, Theodore Jun. "Shaken or Stirred? Taking Something Plebian to Wash Down All That 'Hansik': Recreating Makgŏlli for the Twenty-first Century." Paper presented at the annual meeting of the Association for Asian Studies, Honolulu, Hawaii, March 31, 2011.

Yoon, Hee-Seong, and Wee Geun-woo. "[Interview] 2NE1." *Ashia Kyŏngje*, Septem-

ber 9, 2009. Accessed March 27, 2011. http://www.asiae.co.kr/news/view.htm
?sec=ent9&idxno=2009090316583528776.

Yoon, Ja-Young. "YouTube Taking *Hallyu* on International Ride." *Korea Times*, February 8, 2011. http://www.koreatimes.co.kr/www/news/biz/2011/02/123_81039.html.

Yoon, Sunny. "Internet Discourse and the *Habitus* of Korea's New Generation." In *Culture, Technology, Communication: Towards an Intercultural Global Village*, edited by Charles Ess, 241–60. Albany: State University of New York Press, 2001.

Youngblood, Denise J. *Russian War Films: On the Cinema Front, 1914–2005*. Lawrence: University Press of Kansas, 2006.

YStar Media. "Ranking Show High 5." Accessed March 27, 2011. http://ystar.cu-media
.co.kr/news/news_view.php?no=43773.

Yu, Chi-na. *"Han'guk mellodŭrama, wŏnhyŏng kwa ŭimi chakyong yŏn'gu"* [Korean melodrama: On meaning work and the classical form]. In *Yŏnghwa yŏn'gu*, vol. 13, 7–27. Seoul: Seoul Sŭcopŭ, 1997.

Yu, Henry. "How Tiger Woods Lost His Stripes: Post-Nationalist American Studies as a History of Race, Migration, and the Commodification of Culture." In *Post-Nationalist American Studies*, edited by John Carlos Rowe, 223–48. Berkeley: University of California, 2000.

Yu, Hyŏn-mok. *Han'guk yŏnghwa paldalsa* [The Development of Korean Film]. Seoul: Ch'aeknuri, 1997.

Yu, Kyŏng. *"Sahoejuŭi ŭi wigi wa pukhan yŏnghwa: 1980 nyŏndae pukhan yŏnghwa koch'al"* [The Crisis of Socialism and North Korean Film: Concerning 1980s North Korean Film]. *Sinema* 2 (2006): 95–117.

Yuh, Ji-Yeon. *Beyond the Shadow of Camptown: Korean Military Brides in America*. New York: New York University Press. 2002.

Zillmann, Dolf, and Azra Bhatia. "Effects of Associating with Musical Genres on Heterosexual Attraction." *Communication Research* 16 (1989): 263–88.

Zito, Angela, and Tani Barlow, eds. *Body, Subject, and Power in China*. Chicago: University of Chicago Press, 1994.

Žižek, Slavoj. "Fantasy as a Political Category: A Lacanian Approach." In *The Žižek Reader*, edited by Slavoj Žižek, Elizabeth Wright, and Edmond Leo Wright, 87–102. Oxford: Blackwell, 1999.

CONTRIBUTORS

Jung Hwan Cheon teaches Korean literature, novels in particular, and cultural theories at Sungkyunkwan University in South Korea as associate professor. He has conducted research on the history of cultural politics in Korea and engaged contemporary South Korean popular culture as a culture critic. His Korean language publications include *Reading Books in Modern Times* (2003), *The Revolution and Laughs* (2005), and *The Era of Collective Intelligence* (2008). His current research projects include discourses on suicide in early modern times and the history of collective intelligence in Korea.

Michelle Cho is assistant professor of East Asian studies at McGill University. Her research concerns the politics of popular culture and the ways in which film, video, and television express the affect and temporality of compressed modernization in East Asia. She is currently working on a book about the form and function of South Korean genre cinemas in the Sunshine Policy decade, which followed the transition from military to civilian government, and is pursuing a new project on the relationship between popular culture and populism, including the Korean Wave, celebrity labor, and media liberalization.

Steven Chung is assistant professor in the East Asian Studies department at Princeton University. He focuses his research on Korean cinema and is drawn especially to the relationship between politics and aesthetics in the film cultures of the late colonial through the early postwar periods. He has published articles in edited volumes—*North Korea: Toward a Better Understanding* (2009) and *Democracy and Cinema* (Korea)—and in the *Journal of Korean Studies* and *Memory and Vision* (Korea). Chung's first book, *Split Screen Korea: Shin Sang-ok and Postwar Cinema*, will be published in 2014.

Katarzyna J. Cwiertka is professor of Modern Japan Studies at Leiden University (Netherlands). Her research to date has utilized food as a window into the modern history of Japan and Korea. Cwiertka is the author of *Modern Japanese Cuisine: Food, Power, and National Identity* (2006) and *Cuisine, Colonialism and Cold War: Food in Twentieth-Century Korea* (2012) and the editor of *Asian Food: The Global and the Local* (2002) and *Food and War in Mid-Twentieth-Century East Asia* (2013).

Stephen Epstein is associate professor and director of Asian studies at Victoria University of Wellington in New Zealand. He has published widely on contemporary Korean society and translated numerous works of Korean and Indonesian fiction. Recent books include *Complicated Currents: Media Flows, Soft Power and East Asia*, coedited with Daniel Black and Alison Tokita (2010), and translations of the novels *The Long Road* by Kim In-suk (2010) and *Telegram* by Putu Wijaya (2011). He is currently completing a project entitled *Korea and Its Neighbors: Popular Media and National Identity in the Twenty-first Century*.

Olga Fedorenko is assistant professor/faculty fellow in the Department of East Asian Studies at New York University. Her recent research takes an ethnographic approach to discourses and practices of advertising in contemporary South Korea.

Kelly Jeong is associate professor of Korean studies and comparative literature at the University of California–Riverside. She is the author of *Crisis of Gender and the Nation in Korean Literature and Cinema: Modernity Arrives Again* (2011). Her areas of teaching and research include Korean literature, film, and culture, as well as feminist criticism and critical theory.

Rachael Miyung Joo is assistant professor of American studies at Middlebury College. Her work investigates the connections among sport, nation, and gender in transnational Korean contexts. Her new project on the sport of golf brings together cultural studies of sport and environment to explore ideas of nature and nation in Korean and Korean American communities. She is the author of *Transnational Sport: Gender, Media, and Global Korea* (Duke University Press, 2012).

Inkyu Kang is assistant professor at Penn State University, the Behrend College. He teaches communication and media courses, including Media and Society, Applications for Media Writing, and Introduction to Multimedia Production. Before joining Penn State, he taught Korean history and culture at the University of Wisconsin–Madison. Kang's major research interests are cultural studies and new media technologies, particularly with respect to the social shaping of technology in Korea and Japan.

Kyu Hyun Kim is associate professor of Japanese and Korean history at University of California–Davis. He is the author of *The Age of Visions and Arguments: Parliamentarianism and the National Public Sphere in Early Meiji Japan* (2007). He is currently working on a book project tentatively titled *Treasonous Patriots: Colonial Modernity, War Mobilization, and the Problem of Identity in Korea, 1931–1945*. Kim has written articles on modern Japanese history, Korean colonial experience, Japanese popular culture, and Korean cinema and serves as academic adviser and contributing editor for www .koreanfilm.org.

Pil Ho Kim is scholar in residence at the East Asian Studies Program, Lewis & Clark College in Portland, Oregon. Previously he taught at Ewha Womans University in Korea and Ohio State University. As a sociologist, he has been studying East Asian political economy, social policy, and popular culture. His latest publications include "Three Periods of Korean Queer Cinema: Invisible, Camouflage, and Blockbuster" (2011) and *The South Korean Development Experience: Beyond Aid* (2014).

Boduerae Kwon is associate professor in the Department of Korean Language and Literature at Korea University. She is author of *The Age of Romance: Culture and Trends in the Early 1920s Korea* (2003), *Reading the Age of Rumor: Articles and Keywords of the 1910s Maeil-shinbo* (2008), and *The Origin of Modern Korean Fiction* (2012).

Regina Yung Lee is a Ph.D. candidate in comparative literature at the University of California–Riverside. Her research interests include feminist theory, fandom cultures, and transnational popular media.

Sohl Lee is a Ph.D. candidate in the Graduate Program in Visual and Cultural Studies at the University of Rochester. Her dissertation examines works by contemporary artists who practice sociopolitical interventions into national identity, urban development, questions of ethics, and contemporaneity in South Korea. Her interests include contemporary visual cultures in East Asia, discourses of modernities, institutional critique, and curatorial practices. Lee's work has appeared in such publications as *Art Journal, Architecture Paper,* and *Yishu.* In 2009 she coedited a special issue titled *Spectacle East Asia* for the journal *InVisible Culture.* She is the 2012–2013 International Dissertation Research Fellow of the Social Sciences Research Council.

Jessica Likens has concentrated her research on contemporary Korean cinema and popular culture. She juggles a variety of interests, including translating, teaching language, and developing a more intimate relationship with popular culture through her work in the entertainment industry.

Roald Maliangkay is senior lecturer in Korean studies at the Australian National University. His research focuses on folk/popular cultures and cultural policy from the early twentieth century to the present. Recent publications include "The Power of Representation: Korean Movie Narrators and Authority" (2011), "Koreans Performing for Foreign Troops: The Occidentalism of the C.M.C. and K.P.K." (2011), and "A Tradition of Adaptation: Preserving the Korean Ritual for Paebaengi" (2012).

Youngju Ryu teaches in the Department of Asian Languages and Cultures at the University of Michigan.

Hyunjoon Shin is Humanities Korea (HK) professor at the Institute for East Asian Studies (IEAS) at Sungkonghoe University. His research focuses on Korean popular culture and popular music, as well as the inter-Asia cultural studies. He was research fellow at ARI (Asia Research Institute) at the National University of Singapore and taught at Leiden University in the Netherlands as visiting professor. He is currently a member of the International Advisory Editors of *Popular Music* and a member of the Editorial Collective of *Inter-Asia Cultural Studies.*

Min-Jung Son is assistant professor of music and arts at Daejeon University. Her Korean language publications include *World Star Musics* (2009) and *The Politics of T'ŭrot'ŭ (trot)* (2009), in which she examines the multilayered relationships between Korean political history and popular music. Both books were chosen for the Excellence in the Field of Liberal Arts Book Award in 2009 and 2010 by the Korean Ministry of Culture.

James Turnbull is a writer and public speaker on Korean feminism, sexuality, and popular culture who blogs at www.thegrandnarrative.com. He teaches at Dongseo University in Busan, South Korea.

Travis Workman is assistant professor of Korean language, culture, and media at the University of Minnesota–Twin Cities. His research interests include humanism in the Japanese empire, translation studies and minor literature, modern Korean philosophy, and melodramatic film in both South Korea and North Korea.

INDEX

Page numbers in italics refer to illustrations; *plate* refers to the plate number in the color insert.

manse" call for independence, 219; dynasty of, 42, 206, 207, 224n9, 270; film and, 124n23; gender segregation in, 30

Chosŏn chung'ang Daily, 209–12, 223

Chosŏn Daily, 210–12, 220–21, 225n17

Chosŏn Yon'guksa, 273n28, 273nn31,32, 273n36

Cho Yong Pil (Cho Yong-p'il), 282, 294

Chun Doo-hwan, 200, 337

Chung, Steven, 4, 6, 7, 99

Chunghakdong, 216, 219

Chung Woon-chun, 364, 368

cinema and films, 1, 8, 10, 15, 106, 116, 122, 197, 198, 222; American, 196; Beatles', 250; copycat, 252; Deleuze and, 88, 93, 96n41; domestic, 262; fan culture and, 100; celebrities and stars of, 99, 100, 107, 114–15, 129, 131, 168–90; Golden Age of, 7, 99, 100, 126, 127, 129, 130, 138, 141, 141–42n2; home drama in, 132; independent, 168; Japanese, 110; magazines of, 114–16, 119; as mass entertainment, 106, 127; melodramas, 107–8, 120–21, 129–33, 150, 161; New Wave, 3; 1950s fashion culture and, 103–22; North Korean, 9, 99, 100–101, 145–63; nostalgia in, 295n16; postwar, 126–44; realism and, 128, 129; renaissance of, 99, 168; satirical parodies in, 252; South Korean, 99, 103–25, 126–44, 168–93; techniques of, 44. *See also* festival, festivals: film; *sin p'a*; stardom, stars; *and names of individual films and directors*

citizenry, citizens, 148, 205, 245n6; ethnic groups vs., 205; iconic, 177; *inmin* and, 146; middle-class, 49; of soccer, 202, 203; South Korean, 245n6, 369, 371, 385–86, 390, 394, 395, 400, 401; urban, 368; U.S., 231, 239, 245n6, 339

Civil Rights Movement (U.S.), 196

CJ Group, 232, 238

CL, 5, 327. *See also* 2NE1

CNN, 358

Codex Alimentarius Commission (CODAC), 373

Cold War, 146, 234, 295n9; anti-Communism of, 389; binary of, 395; containment in, 103

Coleman, Johannes, 209

colonialism, 16, 196, 221; food and, 338; Japanese, 1, 4, 8, 34, 48, 49, 152, 153, 161, 162, 197, 203, 273n42; colonial period and, 13n11, 28, 35, 38, 43, 45, 51, 106, 108, 110, 113, 114, 122, 144n48, 204–6, 255, 295n12; sports and, 199–200, 205–24

colonial modernity: love letters and, 1–33; sports nationalism and, 199–227; young musical love and, 255–74

comedy, comedians, 270, 271, 277; in advertising, 350, 351; home drama and, 134; romantic, 78, 121; satirical, 273n30; urban, petit-bourgeois, 107

comfort women, 343, 356

comic arts, comic artists, 34, 37, 40–43, 53n13, 54n20; evolution of, 38; *Raipai* and, 39

comics (*manhwa*), 7, 16, 35–54, 45, 46, *plate 1*; adult, 42, 43; "current affairs," 34; evolution of, 37; Japanese manga, 45, 53n13, 252; mass production of, 40, 41; *minam* and, 192–93n33; postwar narrative, 34–52; room for, 57; single-panel, 115

Comics March (Manhwa haengjin), 38

Comics News (Manhwa nyus), 38

Comics World (Manhwa segye), 38

commercialism, 5, 8, 38, 73, 107, 210, 223; commercial films and, 116, 124n23, 130, 171, 191n13, 332; commercial media and, 200, 231, 243, 268, 359; commercial narrative and, 85–86; commercial productions and, 49, 338, 344, 372; commercial sponsorships and endorsements, 238, 315; commercial success or failure, 279, 285, 307, 353, 387; commercial theater and, 258, 273n29, 273n35

commercials, 68–69, 69, 231, 236, 342–43, 347, 352, 355, 358. *See also* advertising, advertisements

Confucian ideals, 11, 16, 58, 170, 192, 198; computers and, 63–65; freeing from, 251, 255

consumption, consumers, 145, 238, 339, 367, 375; advertising and, 11, 243, 245, 338, 342–59; of electronics, 66, 67; entertainment and, 106, 108, 121, 129, 141, 258, 270, 279, 280, 297, 304, 306, 316, 327, 328; fandom and, 80–87, 95n17, 99, 101, 190; fashion and, 103, 106, 114, 117, 238; food and, 363–80; media and, 15, 39–41, 80, 82; patriotism and, 66, 189, 367; patterns of, 106, 113, 243, 245, 248n48, 305, 317; politics and, 8, 148; popular culture and, 6, 8, 17, 83, 85, 190, 279, 308, 316; targets of, 318, 326, 330, 331, 343, 349, 351

correspondence, correspondents, 24, 211; handwritten, 16; love, 24, 30

cosmopolitanism, 5, 180, 243, 360n14, 375

entertainment: advertising and, 338, 344–45, 348, 350, 357, 358; business of, 262, 270, 271, 292, 316; films and, 115, 127, 168, 174, 191n13; image and, 2; media and, 7, 106, 115; music and, 275, 277, 278, 280, 291, 296, 304, 306, 309, 315; popular culture and, 4, 7, 12, 189, 306; scrutiny of, 310n2; sports and, 211, 241; technology and, 57, 73n3; tourism and, 386

Epstein, Stephen, 9, 10, 198, 249, 250

"Era of the Young, The" (*Chŏlmŭniŭisijŏl*), 23

ethnicity, ethnic groups, 205; nationalism and, 35, 37, 47, 50, 224, 245n6; physical defects of, 206; popular culture and, 189; uncertainty of, 197. *See also* race, racism

etiquette, 24, 118, *119*, 241

European imperialism, 387

examinations, 47; culture of, 232–33

Fabian, Johannes, 345

Facebook, 16

family, 235; in cinema, 130–41; fathers and, 247n27; structure of, 21, 32, 129; as golfers' support, 234; values of, 346. *See also* patriarchy

fandom, fans, 173, 188, 190; academic, 94n11; females as, 62, 328, 330, 355; of golf, 238, 241, 242; of *hallyu*, 3, 244; Internet-based communities and, 244; interpellation and, 95n20; of K-dramas, 16, 76–93; of Korean soccer, 201, *201*, 202, 203, 224n1, *plate 4*; of K-pop, 317; magazines of, 114, 118–19; of rock, 287, 294; of Seo, 300–308; of *Taejanggum*, 375

Fans First initiatives, 239, 241

fascism, fascists, 150, 196, 225n15, 252. *See also* Nazis

fashion: actors as models, 111, 117; Americanization of, 104–5; in music videos, 300; 1950s film culture and, 103–22; photographers of, 4, 388; for teenagers, 8

Feder-Kane, Abigail, 242, 245

Fedorenko, Olga, 9, 10–11, 338–39

female athletes, 197, 228, 230, 234, 237; in figure skating, 228, 245; in golf, 232, 234, 236, 239; media and, 229; as national icons, 228, 232, 242, 243; physical abilities and national biology of, 229, 232, 233, 244; as sellers of products, 198, 229, 234; sexualization of, 241; on tour, 238; as translocal symbols of Koreanness, 229

Female Boss (*Yŏsajang*, 1959), 107, *108*

feminism, feminists, 105, 331, 348; film theory and, 100, 120, 121; organizations of, 346; sport and, 241. *See also* Womenlink

festival, festivals, 201, 203, 405n26; cancellation of, 282; *Fest der Völker*, 225n14; film, 126, 127, 135, 138, 139, 172; music and song, 282, 287–91

fiction, 31; classical, 30; New, 22, 25, 26, 27, 28, 33n16; popular, 252

figure skating, 10, 198, 228, 233, 234, 242, 243

film, films. *See* cinema and films

Five Points of Celebrity, 241

Flames of Love (*Sarang ŭi pulkkot*), 16, 24

Flower Girl, The (*Kkotp'anŭn ch'ŏnyŏ*), 152, 153, 154, 156

Fog Grows Thin (*Chisaenŭn angae*), 22, 23

food, 10, 366, 372, 377; aesthetics of, 375, 376; crisis over safety of, 369; "culinary soft power" and, 370; customs of, 21; ethnic restaurants, 367; global export of, 338; global recognition of, 371; *hallyu* and, 374; healthiness of Korean, 368, 373; imported, 369; *kimch'i* standard, 373; Kimchi War, 373, 374; in *Koreana*, 368; Korean royal cuisine, 374; meat, 369; national campaigns for, 338, 339; "slow food" movement and, 375; South Korean vs. North Korean, 371. *See also* cuisine, Korean

Food in Korea (website), 364

Foodville, 379

Forest Is Swaying, A, 158, 160

Foucault, Michel, 16

4Minute, 318, 326–27

Fowles, Jib, 349

France, French, 119, 225n15, 379; fashion of, 111; filmmakers of, 36; Korean culture in, 379; language, 19, 190n4, 368, 384n68; New Wave cinema in, 3; photography and, 387, 403n2; poststructuralists of, 16; Spanish Civil War and, 225n15; Vichy, 36; World Cup in, 201–2

Franco, Francisco, 225n15

freedom, 150, 357, 395, 396; artistic and ideological, 38, 109, 337, 391; censorship and, 115, 396; of choice, 314, 326, 366; of expression, 296, 307, 309, 354, 356, 390; as keyword, 129; moments of, 344–45, 359; perception of, 394; Seo and, 298; sexual, 356, 357

freestyle skiing, 244

f(x), 318, 328–29, 330

melodrama, melodramas: advertising and, 343, 352, 353, 357, 358; emotions and, 100, 146, 150, 156, 159, 181, 353; films and, 101, 107, 120, 121, 128–34, 149–52, 161; moral occult and, 353; realism and, 147, 149, 151, 164n24; theater and, 258, 272n6; Yon-sama, 1

memory: counter-, 8; history and, 186, 188, 204, 206; Japan and, 111; photography and, 389; production of, 386, 387, 389; suppression of, 37; trauma and, 159

Mexico, 201; LPGA and, 238

Mha Joung-Mee, 351

middle class, 131, 132, 138, 338; in *The Bridal Mask*, 49; conformity to, 198; as consumers, 238; men of, 258, 265; purchasing power of, 8; Seo and, 306; upper-, 139; urban, 267

military dictatorship, 7, 349, 353, 398

military occupation, by United States, 2, 113, 124n23, 197, 250, 275–94, 353, 398

Ministry of Culture, Sports, and Tourism, 375

Ministry of Food, Agriculture, Forestry, and Fisheries, 363, 364, 369, 371, 374, 378

Mintz, Sidney, 365

Mi-sŏn and Hyo-sun incident, 201

Miss-A: "Bad Girl, Good Girl," 325–26, *plate 6*; "Can't Nobody," 328

Mississippi Burning, 196

mobilization, voluntary, 203

modernization, 6, 197, 352; of colony, 215; expression of modernity and, 204

Mondale, Walter, 342

Morning Light, 214

mortality rate, 29

Mother (Bong Joon-ho), 10, 101, 102, 168–93, *180, 181, 182, 184, 185, 186*

Motion Picture Law, 110

movies. *See* cinema and films

Mr. Park, 126, 130, 136, 137, 138, 140, 144n38

multiculturalism: in LPGA, 238, 239, 241; U.S. corporate, 229, 239

music, musicians, 1; American pop, 3, 277, 278; cafés for, 279, 280, 294, 309; censorship of, 286–87, 293, 296, 302; classical, 117, 139, 268, 271; college underground, 8; critics of, 259; dance, 297; disco, 287; education and training for, 258, 268, 278; in figure skating, 229; in films, 108, 140, 151, 161; group sound rock, 273–94; identity of Korean, 251–52, 259; industry for, 294, 315;

jazz, 259, 275, 278, 342; live performances of, 269–71, 287, 296; musicology and, 12, 259, 263, 264, 294; of 1930s, 255–72; parody and, 250; popular, 4, 252, 253, 291, 293, 294, 315–17; on radio, 268–69; rap, 301, 302, 311n18; reggae, 301; salons for, 280, 283; of Seo Taiji, 297–309; solemn, 222; in U.S. Military Camp Shows, 277–79; Western, 256, 258–60, 278, 280, 285; *yuhaengga*, 255–56. *See also* girl groups; K-pop; *names of individual musicians and groups*

musicals, musical theater (*akkŭk*), 2, 8, 258, 269, 271, 274n49; troupes of, 261, 269, 270

music videos (M/V), 253, 309, 319, 332; ads and, 358, 362n42; capriciousness in, 250; of girl groups, 10, 314–18; images from, 317; on Internet, 316, 328; as marketing tactic, 317; in rock cafés, 312n38; scholarship on, 316; Seo Taiji's, 304; sexualization of, 315; women in, 322–23, *323*

"My Brother's Secret Letter" (Oppa ŭi bimil p'yŏnchi), 22

Myohu (medicine), 223

naisen ittai policy, 197

Nam, Edward Adam, 232, 233, 235, 236

Nam Sŭng-nyong: in 1936 Olympics, 208, 211, 216, 217, 218, 221; interviewed, 220; used in advertising, 222, 223

Naoto, Tajima, 212

narrative comics, 34–54

narratives, 92, 115, 206, 328, 339, 385, 391; in advertising, 236, 237; of American Dream, 229; anti-Japanese, 34, 48, 49; arc of, 85, 153; of border-crossing, 387; of capitalism, 234; of celebrity, 129; cinematic and film, 128, 130, 131, 134, 138, 139, 141, 151, 189, 317; of *Face Value*, 176; humor in, 135; improbable, 120, 161; of Korean rock history, 294; of LPGA, 234–35; of *Mother*, 181; national, 100, 146, 147, 154, 171; nationalist, 47, 49–50, 232, 236; of New Fiction, 28; of North Korean films, 150–62; *p'ansori*, 259; patriarchal, 234–37; primacy of, 147; race and, 238; realism and, 149, 150; *sinp'a*, 131, 142–43n17; of South Korea's rise, 127; of transnational media, 229, 237, 245; of victimization and redemption, 153; women and, 232, 234

National Agricultural Cooperative Federation (*nonghyŏp chung'anhoe*), 364, 369

National Federation of Fisheries Cooperatives (*susanŏp hyŏptong chohap*), 364

national identity, 8, 10, 35, 37, 228, 229, 237, 365

nationalism, nationalists, 1, 37, 196, 197, 205, 221; advertising and, 343, 349; agenda of, 8, 47; anti-Japanese, 34, 48, 49; culinary, 11, 365, 369; cultural, 206, 222; emotion and, 230, 231; frugality and, 367; hypermasculinity and, 398; *kimchi* as symbol of, 372; of Korean female athletes, 198, 234, 245; patriarchal narrative and, 237; patriotism and, 339; *tongnip yubo ron* and, 221; psychology of, 200; in sports, 199, 200, 203–5, 209, 210, 228; syndrome and, 202, 221, 224; 2002 World Cup and, *201*

National Unification Party Movement (*Minjŏk yuildang undong*), 219

Na To-hyang, 20, 30

Nazis, 36, 197, 203, 209, 225n15, 225n19, 252

neoliberalism, 174–76, 187, 197, 232, 338, 394–95, 402; restructuring by, 354, 357

Netflix, 16

netizenry, netizens, 81, 94n10, 346, 348, 356, 357

New Fiction (*sinsosŏl*), 22, 25, 26, 27–28, 33n16

newspapers, 7, 209; advertising in, 222, 348, 351, 354; competition between, 225n17; Sohn Kee-chun's win in, 225n11. See also *titles of individual newspapers*

New Wave (Nouvelle Vague) cinema, 3

"New Year's Eve" (*Jeya*), 23

New York Times, 16

NHK, 1936 Olympics on, 208, 212, 215–19

Nike, 239

Nintendo, 55, 66–72, *68*

No, Nora, 7, 111, 113

Noh Jayŏng, 24

Nongshim Ramen, 350

Norae-bang (karaoke rooms and clubs), 8, 57, 297

North Korea, North Koreans, 356; in ads, 343; Arirang Festival in, 400, 405n26; art of, 405n21; border crossing and, 386, 387; as catastrophe, 402–3; censorship and propaganda in, 386, 390–92, 394, 401, 404n17, 405n20; daily life in, 401; documentaries on, 152; films of, 145–63; Kaesong Special Economic Zone of, 388, 404n8; "minders" in, 391, 400, 404n18, 405n20; Mt. Dia-

mond resort in, 400, 403n7; opening of, 387; as others, 399, 400; paintings and posters of, 405n21; People's Gymnasium in, 400; photography and, 338, 339, 385–90, 395–97, 405n24; politics of, 395; popular foods of, 371; portraits of dictators in, *9*, 403n2, 405n24; *Rodong Daily* in, 396–97, 405n24; reunification and, 402; in South Korean films, 388, 404n13; South Koreans and, 393–95, 399–401, 403n1, 404n18; Soviet soldiers in, 398; tourist travel to, 385–90, 394, 400–401, 403n6. *See also* Democratic People's Republic of Korea; Sunshine Policy

nostalgia, 141, 343, 373, 401; in ads, 343, 357; of bloggers, 350; for fathers, 132; of filmmakers, 122; in films, 139, 295n16; golf and, 247n29; for Japan, 111; for Korean cuisine, 365; for Manchuria, 47; in *Mother*, 180; in songs, 263, 276

novel, novels, 21, 32, 80, 256; ads vs., 351; characters in, 137; critics of, 31; dime-store, 38; epistolary, 6, *22*; graphic, 7, 15, 34, 38; novelists and, 209, 214; novellas and, 20, 33n20

Non-church Movement, 213

Nuremberg torch marches, 203

Nye, Joseph, 370

Ogamdo (Crow's-Eye View), 214. *See also* Yi Sang

Okeh Records, 222, 262–63, 270

Ok-hui, 215

Olympia, *195*, 196

Olympia Zeitung, 208

Olympics, 196, 222, 232–33; in advertising, 223; bid to host 1940, 197; coverage of, 211; as *Festival of the People*, 225n14; nationalism and, 231; 1928 Amsterdam, 208; 1932 Los Angeles, 208, 214, 217; 1988 Seoul, 357, 366, 367; 2008 Olympics, 246n13; 2010 Winter Olympics, 228; 2018 Pyeongchange, 244; rings, 222. *See also* Berlin Olympics

Ong, Aihwa, 233, 234

Orser, Brian, 244

Orwell, George, 225n15

Osaka Asahi, 212

Osaka Daily, 212

Osamu, Tezuka, 43

other, 30, 141, 395; otherized landscape and, 389; North Koreans as, 387, 389

Owens, Jesse, 196

Sŏngmunsa, 38

Sŏng Nak-hŏn, 210

Sŏngsŏ Chosŏn (Bible Chosŏn), 213

Sŏng Sung-wŏn, 379, 380

Sony, 66, 240

Sŏ Pong-hun, 216

Sŏ Pong-jae, 40

South Korea, South Koreans, 369, 400, 402; as consumers, 238, 366; flag of, 228, plate 4; as golfers of, 231, 234, 240, 241, 246n10; ideologies of, 237; kimch'i and, 372; kimjang ritual in, 372; liberalization of relations between Japan and, 366; makgŏlli industry in, 373, 374; marketing potential of, 239; neocolonial relations of, with United States, 353; North Korea and, 385–89, 403n1; post-democratization in, 358; public culture of, 229; state-sanctioned art in, 338; 2008 financial crisis and, 341; United States military occupation of, 398; visual culture of, 395; War Memorial of, 398. See also Korea, Koreans; Seoul

South Korean National Commission on Human Rights, 168

Soviet Union, 225n15, 398; socialist realism of, 147–48, 152. See also Russia, Russians

Spanish Civil War, 211, 225n15

spectacle, 337; cinema and, 9, 121, 146–51, 161, 172; Han Hyŏng-mo and, 107; music videos and, 318, 326; social spaces and, 106

spying, spies, 43, 162, 342

sports, 197, 204, 234; anxieties in, over perceived lesbianism, 243; controversies surrounding, 246n24; drama in, 197; as entertainment industry, 241; global, 230, 231; modern, 196, 204, 205; nationalism and, 204, 222, 224; star athletes in, 10, 196, 198, 228; state-funded elite, 232; team, 196; transnational, 230, 234. See also female athletes; Ladies Professional Golf Association; Olympics; names of individual sports and athletes

Sports Illustrated, 233

Ssangyong Group, 351

StarCraft, 32, 60, 62, 63, 72, 73

stardom, stars, 7, 8, 48, 68, 100, 117, 126–41, 158, 160, 196, 208, 262, 263, 282, 285, 286, 295n23, 297, 308, 324, 377; American, 251; Campus Song Festival awardees, 291; of cinema, 4, 10, 99, 100, 101, 107, 114, 116, 117, 121, 126, 141, 148, 149, 190n5, 190n7;

as genre, 168–90; global, 249; golfers as, 239; image and, 136, 192n28; K-dramas and, 79; K-pop and, 5, 250, 251, 256, 308, 316; "Okeh Grand Show" and, 271; popular culture and, 5, 8, 198, 278; rise to, 197, "Shin Joong Hyun Jam in the Pacific" and, 285; sports and, 2, 10, 63, 196, 198, 239; television and, 8, 191n21. See also celebrity, celebrities; celebrity culture; names of individual stars

state and government, 337, 338, 349, 369; free-trade agreements and, 368; Japanese-Korean trade relations and, 373; "soft power" and, 370

Stephenson, Jan, 238

stereotypes: of Asian women, 229, 230, 233, 234; of athletes, 234, 240; of Korean golfers, 240; Korean women and, 232, 244; interference in restaurants, 370

Stiles, Maxwell, 209

Sun-jong (King), 219

Sunshine Policy (haetpyŏt chŏngch'aek): cultural politics of, 390; era of, 4, 7, 10, 343, 389, 390, 400, 404n18; films and photography and, 388; identified, 385; origin of name of, 351

Super Bowl, 196

Super Junior, 1, 377, 378

Superstar K (Shusŭk'e), 4

sushi, 364, 370

Sweden, 238

symbolism, symbols: female golfer as, 243; golfer's family as, 237; of ideology, 204; kimchi as, 372; mass, 222; Se Ri Pak as, 230

syndrome, 197, 200–207, 219, 221, 224

Tadao, Yanaihara, 213

Tadashi, Imai, 110

Taech'ang Shoestore, 216, 219

TaeGukGi: Brotherhood of War (2004), 388

Taehan cheguk (1897–1910), 205

Taehanminguk (Republic of Korea), 111, 200, 202, 203, 204, 368

Takayoshi, Yoshioka, 214

T-ara, "Like the First Time," 322

TaylorMade Golf, 232

Tears of Blood (Hyŏl ŭi nu), 25, 27

television, 80, 132, 189, 197, 377; adaptations for, 8; advertising and, 69, 236–37, 237, 349, 357; dramas on, 1, 2, 15, 76, 87, 88, 90, 374, 375, 376; episodic, 76, 78, 377; food

CPSIA information can be obtained
at www.ICGtesting.com
Printed in the USA
LVHW082022181222
735494LV00016B/139